THE ANCIENT NEAR EAST

ROUTLEDGE HISTORY OF THE ANCIENT WORLD

General Editor: Fergus Millar

THE GREEK WORLD 479–323 BC
Simon Hornblower

THE BEGINNINGS OF ROME
753–264 BC
T. J. Cornell

THE MEDITERRANEAN WORLD IN LATE ANTIQUITY
AD 395–600
Averil Cameron

ROMAN WORLD
44 BC–AD 180
Goodman Martin

Forthcoming Title

THE ANCIENT NEAR EAST
c. 3000–330 BC
Volume Two

Amélie Kuhrt

London and New York

First published 1995
by Routledge
11 New Fetter Lane, London EC4P 4EE

Simultaneously published in the USA and Canada
by Routledge
29 West 35th Street, New York, NY 10001

First published in paperback 1997

Typeset in Garamond by
Ponting–Green Publishing Services, Chesham, Bucks
Printed in Great Britain by
T.J. International Ltd, Padstow, Cornwall

British Library Cataloguing in Publication Data
A catalogue record for this book is available from the
British Library

Library of Congress Cataloguing in Publication Data
Kuhrt, Amélie
The Ancient Near East / Amélie Kuhrt.
2 v. cm. — (Routledge history of the ancient world)
Intended audience: Students and scholars working in
history of this region.
Includes bibliographical references and index.
Contents: v. 1. From *c.* 3000 BC to *c.* 1200 BC –
v. 2. From *c.* 1200 BC to 330 BC
1. Middle East–History–To 622.
I. Title. II. Series.
DS62.23.K87   1995
939'.4—dc20   94—41951

ISBN 0–415–01353–4 (Volume 1, hbk)
ISBN 0–415–16763–9 (Volume 1, pbk)
ISBN 0–415–12872–2 (Volume 2, hbk)
ISBN 0–415–16764–7 (Volume 2, pbk)
ISBN 0–415–01352–6 (2 volume set, hbk)
ISBN 0–415–16762–0 (2 volume set, pbk)

CONTENTS

CONTENTS

FIGURES

MAPS

TABLES

ABBREVIATIONS

AA	*Archäologischer Anzeiger*
AAAS	*Annales Archéologiques Arabes de Syrie*
AAASH	*Acta Antiqua Academiae Scientiarium Hungaricae*
AASOR	Annual of the American School of Oriental Research
ABAW	*Abhandlungen der Bayerischen Akademie der Wissenschaften*
ABC	A.K. Grayson *Assyrian and Babylonian Chronicles* (TCS 5) Locust Valley, NY 1975
ABL	R.F. Harper (1892–1914) *Assyrian and Babylonian Letters belonging to the Kouyounjik Collection of the British Museum* (14 vols) London, Chicago
AchHist 1	*Achaemenid History* 1: *Sources, Structures, Synthesis* (H. Sancisi-Weerdenburg ed.) Leiden 1987
AchHist 2	*Achaemenid History* 2: *The Greek Sources* (H. Sancisi-Weerdenburg, A. Kuhrt eds) Leiden 1987
AchHist 3	*Achaemenid History* 3: *Method and Theory* (A. Kuhrt, H. Sancisi-Weerdenburg eds) Leiden 1988
AchHist 4	*Achaemenid History* 4: *Centre and Periphery* (H. Sancisi-Weerdenburg, A. Kuhrt eds) Leiden 1990
AchHist 5	*Achaemenid History* 5: *The Roots of the European Tradition* (H. Sancisi-Weerdenburg, J.-W. Drijvers eds) Leiden 1990
AchHist 6	*Achaemenid History* 6: *Asia Minor and Egypt: Old Cultures in a New Empire* (H. Sancisi-Weerdenburg, A. Kuhrt eds) Leiden 1991
AchHist 7	*Achaemenid History* 7: *Through Travellers' Eyes* (H. Sancisi-Weerdenburg, J.-W. Drijvers eds) Leiden 1991
AchHist 8	*Achaemenid History* 8: *Continuity and Change* (H. Sancisi-Weerdenburg, A. Kuhrt, M.C. Root eds) Leiden 1994
ActSum	*Acta Sumerologica*
ADFU	Ausgrabungen der Deutschen Forschungsgemeinschaft in Uruk-Warka
ADOG	Abhandlungen der Deutschen Orient Gesellschaft
AfO	*Archiv für Orientforschung*
Äg. Abh.	Ägyptologische Abhandlungen

Ägyptische Inschriften	*Ägyptische Inschriften aus den Königlichen Museen zu Berlin* (2 vols) Leipzig 1913–1924
AION	*Annali del'Istituto Universitario Orientale di Napoli*
AJA	*American Journal of Archaeology*
AJAH	*American Journal of Ancient History*
Akk.	Akkadian
AMI	*Archäologische Mitteilungen aus Iran*
ANET	*Ancient Near Eastern Texts relating to the Old Testamant* J.B. Pritchard (ed.) (3rd rev. edn) Princeton, NJ 1969
AnOr	Analecta Orientalia
AnSt	*Anatolian Studies*
AOAT	Alter Orient und Altes Testament
AOF	*Altorientalische Forschungen*
AOS	American Oriental Society
APAW	Abhandlungen der Preussischen Akademie der Wissenchaften
Ar.	Aramaic
ARAB	D.D. Luckenbill *Ancient Records of Assyria and Babylonia* (2 vols) Chicago 1926–7
ARCE	American Research Center in Egypt
ARE	J.H. Breasted *Ancient Records of Egypt* Chicago 1906
ARM	Archives Royales de Mari
ArOr	*Archiv Orientalni*
AS	Assyriological Studies
ASAE	*Annales du Service des Antiquités de l'Égypte*
ASNP	*Annali della Scuola Normale di Pisa*
BaF	*Baghdader Forschungen*
BaM	*Baghdader Mitteilungen*
BAR	British Archaeological Reports
BAR	*Biblical Archaeological Review*
BASOR	*Bulletin of the American Schools of Oriental Research*
BibArch	*Biblical Archaeologist*
BiOr	*Bibliotheca Orientalis*
BMFA	*Bulletin of the Museum of Fine Arts* Boston
Bo.	Symbol for Boghazköy-Texte
BSAG 4 and 5	*Bulletin of Sumerian Agriculture* vols 4 and 5: *Irrigation and Cultivation in Mesopotamia* (parts I and II) Cambridge 1988–90
BSFE	*Bulletin de la Société Française d'Égyptologie*
BSOAS	*Bulletin of the School of Oriental and African Studies*
CAD	*The Assyrian Dictionary of the University of Chicago* Chicago 1956–
Camb.	*Inschriften von Cambyses, König von Babylon (529–521 v. Chr.)* (Babylonische Texte 8–9) J.N. Strassmaier, Leipzig 1890
CBQ	*Catholic Bible Quarterly*

CAH	*Cambridge Ancient History*
CDAFI	*Cahiers de la Délégation Archéologique Française en Iran*
CH	Codex Hammurabi
CHI	*Cambridge History of Iran*
CRAIBL	*Comptes Rendus de l'Académie des Inscriptions et Belles-Lettres*
CT	Cuneiform Texts from Babylonian Tablets in the British Museum
CTH	E. Laroche *Catalogue des textes hittites* (Études et Commentaires 75) Paris 1971
CTN	Cuneiform Texts from Nimrud
DHA	*Dialogues d'histoire ancienne*
D.S.	Diodorus Siculus *The Library of History*
EA	J.A. Knudtzon *Die El-Amarna-Tafeln* (Vorderasiatische Bibliothek 2) Leipzig 1907–15. For completely new translations (with notes, commentary and introduction) see now W. Moran 1987 *Les Lettres d'el Amarna: correspondance diplomatique du pharaon* (LAPO 13) Paris (English version, with some revisions and updating, Baltimore, MD 1992)
EES	Egypt Exploration Society
EI	*Eretz Israel*
El.	Elamite
Encyclopedia	*Encyclopedia of Archaeological Excavations in the Holy Land* (eds M. Avi-Yonah and E. Stern) Oxford 1975–1978
Enclr	*Encyclopaedia Iranica* (ed. E. Yarshater) London, Boston 1985–
EpAn	*Epigraphica Anatolica*
FAOS	Freiburger Altorientalische Studien
FGrH	F. Jacoby *Die Fragmente der Griechische Historiker* Berlin 1923–
GM	*Göttinger Miszellen*
HdO	Handbuch der Orientalistik
Hdt.	Herodotus, *Histories*
HUCA	*Hebrew University College Annual*
IEJ	*Israel Exploration Journal*
IOS	*Israel Oriental Series*
IrAnt	*Iranica Antiqua*
IsMEO	Istituto per il Medio e Estremo Oriente
JA	*Journal Asiatique*
JANES	*Journal of the Ancient Near Eastern Society*
JAOS	*Journal of the American Oriental Society*
JARCE	*Journal of the American Research Center in Egypt*
JCS	*Journal of Cuneiform Studies*
JEA	*Journal of Egyptian Archaeology*
JEOL	*Jaarbericht van het Vooraziatasch-Egyptisch Genootschap 'Ex Oriente Lux'*

JESHO	*Journal of the Economic and Social History of the Orient*
JHS	*Journal of Hellenic Studies*
JNES	*Journal of Near Eastern Studies*
JSOT	*Journal for the Study of the Old Testament*
JTS	*Journal for Theological Studies*
JTVI	*Journal of the Transactions of the Victoria Institute*
K	Symbol for texts from the Kouyunjik Collection in the British Museum
KAH II	O. Schroeder *Keilschrifttexte aus Assur historischen Inhalts, Zweites Heft* (WVDOG 37) Leipzig 1922
KAI	H. Donner, W. Röllig *Kanaanäische und Aramäische Inschriften* (3 vols) Wiesbaden 1973–9
KBo	Keilschriftexte aus Boghazköy
KTU	M. Dietrich, O. Loretz, J. Sanmartin *Die keilalphabetischen Texte aus Ugarit einschliesslich der keilalphabetischen Texte ausserhalb Ugarits* I (AOAT 2, 4) Kevelaer, Neukirchen-Vluyn 1976
KUB	Keilschrifturkunden aus Boghazköy
LAPO	Littératures Anciennes du Proche-Orient
LÄ	*Lexikon der Ägyptologie* Wiesbaden 1975–86
LKA	E. Ebeling, K. Köcher *Literarische Keilschrifttexte aus Assur* Berlin 1953
MAD	Materials for the Assyrian Dictionary
MAOG	*Mitteilungen der Altorientalischen Gesellschaft*
MARI	*Mari: Annales de Recherches Interdisciplinaires*
MCS	*Manchester Cuneiform Studies*
MDAIK	*Mitteilungen des Deutschen Archäologischen Instituts in Kairo*
MDP II	V. Scheil *Textes élamites-sémitiques, première série* (Mémoires de la Délégation en Perse II) Paris 1900
MDP IX	V. Scheil *Textes élamites-anzanites, troisième série* (Mémoire de la Délégation en Perse IX) Paris 1907
MDP XI	V. Scheil *Texts élamites-anzanites, quatrième série* (Mémoire de la Délégation en Perse XI) Paris 1911
MIO	*Mitteilungen des Instituts für Orientforschung*
MVAeG	Mitteilungen der Vorderasiatisch-Aegyptischen Gesellschaft
NABU	*Notes Assyriologiques Brèves et Utiles*
NAPR	*Northern Akkad Project Reports*
NEB	New English Bible
NL	Nimrud Letters
OA	*Oriens Antiquus*
OBO	Orbis Biblicus et Orientalis
OIP	Oriental Institute Publications
OLA	Orientalia Lovaniensia Analecta
OLZ	*Orientalistische Literaturzeitschrift*

OP	Old Persian
Or.	*Orientalia*
PAPhS	*Proceedings of the American Philosophical Society*
PBS 5	A. Poebel *Historical and Grammatical Texts* (University of Pennsylvania Museum, Babylonian Section 5) Philadelphia 1914
PBS 13	L. Legrain *Historical Fragments* (University of Pennsylvania Museum, Babylonian Section 13) Philadelphia 1922
PBS 15	L. Legrain *Royal Inscriptions and Fragments from Nippur and Babylon* (University of Pennsylvania Museum, Babylonian Section 15) Philadelphia 1926
PCPS	*Proceedings of the Cambridge Philological Society*
PEQ	*Palestine Exploration Quarterly*
PRU	Palais Royal d'Ugarit (Paris)
RA	*Revue d'Assyriologie*
REA	*Revue des Études Anciennes*
RIM	Royal Inscriptions of Mesopotamia
RIDA	*Revue international des droits de l'antiquité*
RLA	*Reallexikon der Assyriologie* Berlin 1928–
RSO	*Rivista degli studi orientali*
SAA 1	S. Parpola *The Correspondence of Sargon II* Part I: *Letters from Assyria and the West* (State Archives of Assyria 1) Helsinki 1987
SAA 2	S. Parpola, K. Watanabe *Neo-Assyrian Treaties and Loyalty Oaths* (State Archives of Assyria 2) Helsinki 1988
SAA 3	A. Livingstone *Court Poetry amd Literary Miscellanea* (State Archives of Assyria 3) Helsinki 1989
SAA 4	I. Starr *Queries to the Sungod: divination and politics in Sargonid Assyria* (State Archives of Assyria 4) Helsinki 1990
SAA 5	G.B. Lanfranchi, S. Parpola *The Correspondence of Sargon* Part II: *Letters from the Northern and Northeastern Provinces* (State Archives of Assyria 5) Helsinki 1990
SAA 6	T. Kwasman, S. Parpola *Legal Transactions of the Royal Court of Nineveh* Part I: *Tiglath-pileser III through Esarhaddon* (State Archives of Assyria 6) Helsinki 1991
SAA 7	F.M. Fales, J.N. Postgate *Imperial Administrative Records* Part I: *Palace and Temple Administration* (State Archives of Assyria 7) Helsinki 1992
SAA 8	H. Hunger *Astrological Reports to Assyrian Kings* (State Archives of Assyria 8) Helsinki 1992
SAA 10	S. Parpola *Letters from Assyrian and Babylonian Scholars* (State Archives of Assyria 10) Helsinki 1993
SAAB	*State Archives of Assyria Bulletin*
SAOC	Studies in Ancient Oriental Civilization

SBT	Studies in Biblical Theology
SDB	*Dictionnaire du Bible: supplément*
SCO	*Studi classici e orientali*
SSEA Journal	*Society for the Study of Egyptian Antiquities Journal*
StBoT	Studien zu den Boghazköy Texten
StIr	*Studia Iranica*
StOr	*Studia Orientalia*
Sum.	Sumerian
TAPhA	*Transaction of the American Philosophical Society*
TCL	Textes cunéiformes du Louvre
TCS	Texts from Cuneiform Sources
Theban Tombs	The Theban Tombs Series (London 1915–)
Thuc.	Thucydides *History of the Peloponnesian War*
TIM I	*Old Babylonian Letters, part 1* (Texts from the Iraq Museum) Baghdad 1964
TMO	Travaux de la Maison de l'Orient
TTAED	*Türk Tarih Arkeloji ve Etnografya Dergisi*
TUAT	*Texte aus der Umwelt des Alten Testaments* (O. Kaiser *et al.* Hsg) Gütersloh 1982–
UET 1	C.J. Gadd, L. Legrain, S. Smith *Royal Inscriptions* (Ur Excavation Texts 1) London 1928
UET 3	L. Legrain *Business Documents of the Third Dynasty of Ur* (Ur Excavation Texts 3) London 1947
UET 5	H.H. Figulla *Letters and documents of the Old Babylonian period* (Ur Excavation Texts 5) London 1953
UET 8	E. Sollberger *Royal Texts* part II (Ur Excavation Texts 8) London 1965
UF	*Ugarit Forschungen*
Urk. I	K. Sethe *Urkunden des Alten Reiches* (2nd edn) Leipzig 1933
Urk. III	*Urkunden des ägyptischen Altertums, Abt. III Urkunden der älteren Äthiopenkönige* (H. Schäfer ed.) Leipzig 1905
Urk. IV	*Urkunden des ägyptischen Altertums, Abt. IV: Urkunden der 18. Dynastie* (K. Sethe, W. Helck eds) Leipzig, Berlin 1906–1958
UVB	*Vorläufige Berichte über die von der Notgemeinschaft der Deutschen Wissenschaft in Uruk-Warka unternommenen Ausgrabungen*
VAB	Vorderasiatische Bibliothek
VAT	Vorderasiatische Abteilung Tontafeln, Berlin
WO	*Welt des Orients*
WVDOG	Wissenschaftliche Veröffentlichungen der Deutschen Orient Gesellschaft

WZKM	*Wiener Zeitschrift für die Kunde des Morgenlandes*
Xen.	Xenophon
YNER	Yale Near Eastern Researches
YOS I	Clay A.T. *Miscellaneous Inscriptions in the Yale Babylonian Collection* New Haven 1915
YOS X	Goetze A. *Old Babylonian Omen Texts* New Haven 1947
YOSR	Yale Oriental Series: Researches
ZA	*Zeitschrift für Assyriologie und verwandte Gebiete*
ZÄS	*Zeitschrift für Ägyptische Sprache und Altertumskunde*
ZAW	*Zeitschrift für alttestamentliche Wissenschaft*
ZDPV	*Zeitschrift des Deutschen Palästina-Vereins*
ZSS	*Zeitschrift der Savigny-Stiftung*

Part III

POLITICAL TRANSFORMATION AND THE GREAT EMPIRES (*c.* 1200–330)

8

THE LEVANT *c.* 1200–*c.* 720

Crisis and political change between *c.* 1200 and 900

The political pattern of the Near East *c.* 1200 can be summarised broadly as follows: in the Levant, Cyprus and Mycenaean Greece the basic political unit was the city-state usually controlling a fair stretch of surrounding territory. Between *c.* 1400 and 1200, the small states of the Levant generally formed part of the Hittite or Egyptian sphere of imperial control – Cyprus (or part of it), too, was dominated by the Hittites at the end of the thirteenth century (see chapters 4–6). To the east a contemporary political power was Kassite Babylonia, although it was being eclipsed in the second half of the thirteenth century by the meteoric rise of Assyria to the north (the Middle Assyrian empire), and the establishment of a strong Elamite state to the east (chapter 7).

The western section of this political landscape experienced a breakdown in the period around, and immediately after, 1200; to the east, Assyria, Babylonia and Elam appear to have remained relatively stable until around the mid-eleventh century. Several features suggest that there was a crisis: first, the great Hittite empire, with the exception of one or two of its subject kingdoms (e.g. Carchemish; Hawkins 1988), disappeared completely around (or probably soon after) 1200. Second, several cities in the Levant, most strikingly Ugarit and Emar, were destroyed around this time, and their sites not reoccupied. At roughly the same time the Mycenaean citadels in Greece suffered a decline, and were eventually destroyed and abandoned. On Cyprus, too, there are signs of destruction *c.* 1200, followed by cultural changes. Finally, soon after the middle of the twelfth century, Egypt's control of the southern Levant ended; by the early eleventh century it had withdrawn within its narrowest frontiers, having lost control over Sinai and Nubia (chapter 4d).

What factors were responsible for this situation? The waning of imperial powers or the destruction of a city are not in themselves unusual events, and it would be possible to think of a range of different causes that could have been responsible for individual cases of decline or destruction. In fact, given the fairly elaborate political superstructure of these states, all dependent on maintaining access to limited resources and on unpredictable food-supplies, and mutually linked, the situation is not in itself so remarkable. A series of harvest failures, disastrous floods, natural disasters such as earthquakes, destruction of crops by marauders, interruption of trade routes by herders moving into new grazing grounds, devastating epidemics, enemy action as a result of the chronic internecine strife between the various principalities – any or all of these could provide part of the explanation, especially when we remember the fragility of the economic infrastructure of many of these states.

The remarkable fact about the situation at this time is that it is quite a long time (not until the tenth century) before there is evidence of real recovery. A 'dark age' seems to descend, and when the historical picture clears again a change in the overall political pattern has taken place: there are several new states (e.g. Israel, the Philistine pentapolis) dominated by peoples previously scarcely attested in the Levant. The conclusion must be that the region had undergone a shift in its political configuration, although not all areas had experienced the same degree of change: some appear to have been much more profoundly affected, others only relatively slightly. The sources indicate that within this time-span movements by a number of different peoples were taking place. They include Libyans, Israelites, Aramaeans, Phrygians and the enigmatic 'sea-peoples'. How any, or all, of them may have been connected with the political changes is a much debated and complex question (see, most recently, Ward and Joukowsky 1992).

8a The 'sea-peoples'

Most prominent among the explanations offered for the political collapse of Anatolia and the Levant *c.* 1200 is the idea that the 'sea-peoples' were responsible. The term 'sea-peoples' embraces several movements by various peoples just before and just after 1200. Scholars have argued that, because mention of such groups coincides with the general date of collapse in the eastern Mediterranean, their movements must be causally linked to it. A problem in understanding how the 'sea-peoples' might have been responsible for such widespread devastation revolves around their identity. If it can be established who they were and where they came from, then it might be possible to draw a picture of what kind of movement, or migration, we should envisage.

One point, which cannot be emphasised enough, is that the *only* sources for the role of the 'sea-peoples' in the crisis are the accounts of two Egyptian campaigns. One is the description (inscribed at Karnak) of a war fought by Merneptah in his fifth year (1220 (1209)) against a Libyan coalition attempting to move into the western Delta. Included in the Libyan forces were people who are designated, variously, as 'northerners coming from all lands' and 'of the countries of the sea'. Modern scholars have therefore dubbed them simply 'sea-peoples'. They are listed as being *Šrdn, 3kwš, Trš, Škrwš* and *Rwkw.* A total of the numbers of prisoners taken from the first four groups is preserved: 2200 in all. This needs to be set against the 7000 Libyan prisoners (several different tribes were involved). The impression, then, is that these Libyan allies constituted a proportionally smaller force. The Egyptian account mentions that the 'sea-people' contingents consisted of men only, unlike the Libyans, who were accompanied by their families. This implies that the 'sea-peoples' were mercenary soldiers hired by the Libyan chief, Maryare.

Table 25 The 'sea-peoples'

a) Names of sea-peoples in Egyptian texts

Merneptah (1224/1213–1204)	Ramesses III (1184–1150)
Šrdn	Šrdn
T(w)r(w)š	(Trš?)
Škrwš	Škr(w)š
3kwš	Tjkr
Rwkw	Prst
	Wšš
	Dnyn

b) Possible vocalisation of names

Rwkw	= Lukka
Šrdn	= Sherden
Dnyn	= Denyen/Danuna
Tjkr	= Tjekker/Zakala
Prst	= Peleset/Philistines
Trš	= Teresh
Škrš	= Sheklesh/Shikalayu
Wšš	= Weshshesh
3kwš	= Ekwesh/Akaiwasha

Over forty (or thirty) years later (1176), Ramesses III fought in his eighth year a campaign, which was elaborately commemorated (pictorially and textually) in his great funerary temple at Medinet Habu, against an attack of peoples moving south from Syria by sea and by land. Some of them, such as the *Tjkr, Prst, Wšš* and *Dnn*, had not been mentioned before, while two (*Šrdn, Škrš* [*Trš* – extremely doubtful]) were among the Libyan allies in Merneptah's campaign forty-four (or thirty-three) years earlier (see table 25). The highly wrought literary language employed to celebrate the Egyptian triumph describes the force in these words:

> ... as for the foreign countries, they made a conspiracy in their islands. All at once the lands were on the move, scattered in war. No country could stand before their arms: Hatti, Kode (Cilicia), Carchemish, Arzawa and Alashiya (Cyprus). They were cut off. A camp was set up in one place in Amor (Amurru, i.e. north Syria). They desolated its people, and its land was like that which has never come into being. They

were advancing on Egypt while the flame was prepared before them. Their league was *Prst, Tjkr, Škrš, Dnn* and *Wšš* united lands. They laid their hands upon the lands to the very circuit of the earth, their hearts confident and trusting: 'Our plans will succeed.'

(Edgerton and Wilson 1936; *ANET*: 262–263; *ARE* IV §64)

As Breasted pointed out, years ago, the Egyptian texts 'contain so many epithets of a highly pictorial character as frequently to make even a common word unintelligible ... so much of these Medinet Habu texts is likely to remain unintelligible, without some obliging Egyptian familiar with their style, to explain their overdrawn metaphors and metonymies' (*ARE* IV 13–14). It is an important observation which warns us against taking the exaggerated statements of the inscription at face value. What we *may* deduce with some confidence from the inscriptions and the reliefs is that a land-battle was fought against these people, probably somewhere near the Lebanese coast, and a sea-battle perhaps within the Delta. Another point worth noting is that, in the reliefs of the land-battle, two-wheeled carts, awkwardly drawn by two pairs of oxen and carrying women and children, are shown. The bodies of the carts are of wickerwork, while the wheels are shown as solid wooden discs – so they were nothing like the the fast-moving war chariots with their light spoked wheels regularly used by the fighting forces of the Late Bronze Age. They suggest that, this time around, the people facing the Egyptian army were originally settled agricultural folk forced to move with their stock and families, and perhaps in search of new land to settle.

How far does this rather limited evidence take us? Apart from the fact that all these people were considered to be 'northerners' (sometimes associated with the sea and/or islands) by the Egyptians – an extremely vague designation – the first point is that some were already familiar to the Egyptians. The *Rwkw* (Lukka) can plausibly be equated with inhabitants of the Hittite 'Lukka lands', probably located in or near classical Lycia (see generally Bryce 1986: 1–10). They appear occasionally as pirates in the fourteenth century (EA 38), and some formed part of the Hittite army at the battle of Kadesh (1286 (1275), see chapter 4d). The *Šrdn* (vocalised as 'Sherden' or 'Shardana') are always shown wearing horned helmets, kilts and carrying a type of sword developed in Late Bronze Age Syria. They, too, were already known as mercenary contingents in the Egyptian army from the fourteenth century on; it has even been suggested that the small disc depicted between the horns of their helmets was an Egyptian regimental insignium (Sandars 1978: 106). They are, in fact, shown fighting on both sides in Ramesses III's battles against the 'sea-peoples'. This would tend to indicate that their home was within the eastern Mediterranean, perhaps south Turkey or the Levant. The *Dnn* (Denyen/Danuna) are probably to be associated with the country of that name to the north of Ugarit in the fourteenth century (Hawkins in press); a likely location is Cilicia, specifically the area of Adana.

In terms of dress and equipment the *Dnn* are indistinguishable from the *Prst* ('Peleset') and *Tjkr* (Tjekker/Zakkala). All wear kilts, carry spears, short swords, round shields, and wear a peculiar headdress which has been interpreted variously as consisting of feathers or pleated cloth, or representing a stiffened hairdo. People with this equipment and costume appear as part of Ramesses III's army in a campaign fought in his fifth year, when he had had to fight the Libyans. So it seems that the *Dnn*, *Prst* and *Tjkr* were probably a closely related group, all originally at home in Cilicia and available as mercenaries in the twelfth century. It is impossible to say much about the *Trš* (Teresh) and *Škrš* (Sheklesh/Shikala) – people resembling them in hairstyle (turban and beard) are shown just once as part of the Egyptian army in Ramesses III's Libyan war. The *Wšš* are not distinguished pictorially, and so remain completely obscure. The *3kwsh* ('Ekwesh'/'Akaiwasha'), who only appear in Merneptah's war against the Libyans, have been tentatively identified with the 'Achaeans'; but the interpretation is linked to how we understand the Hittite neighbour 'Ahhiyawa' (chapter 5b), and so remains unfortunately unclear in its implications (Sandars 1978: 110–111).

We must add one further piece of evidence: the Great Papyrus Harris. The document records bequests made by Ramesses III to the temples of Egypt, and was composed, primarily, to illustrate the piety and virtue of the king. It thus includes some passages in which he is depicted as the bringer of peace and conqueror of Egypt's traditional foes. In one of the sections there is an interesting reference to some 'sea-peoples':

> I extended all the boundaries of Egypt. I overthrew those who invaded them from their lands. I slew the *Dnn* [who are] in their isles, the *Tjkr* and the *Prst* were made ashes. The *Šrdn* and the *Wšš* of the sea, they were made as those that exist not, taken captive at one time, brought as captives to Egypt, like the sand of the shore I settled them in strongholds bound in my name. Numerous were their classes like hundred-thousands. I assigned portions for them all with clothing and grain from the store-houses and granaries each year. . . .
>
> I made the infantry and chariotry to dwell [at home] in my time; the *Šrdn* and *Khk* (a Libyan group) were in their towns, lying the length of their backs; they had no fear, for there was no enemy from Kush [nor] foe from Syria. Their bows and their weapons were laid up in their magazines, while they were satisfied and drunk with joy. Their wives were with them, their children at their side [for] I was with them as the defence and protection of their limbs.
>
> (W. Erichsen, *Papyrus Harris I* (1933);
> *ARE* IV §§403–405; *ANET*: 262)

Ramesses III's description confirms what has already been tentatively deduced, that the 'sea-peoples' were used as mercenaries and garrisons. That this did indeed happen is suggested by archaeological and textual evidence, which shows that the *Prst* ('Peleset' = 'Philistines') and *Tjkr* settled in all those areas of Palestine where the Egyptians maintained fortresses with garrisons – places such as Beth Shean, Gaza and Dor (Dothan 1982; Mazar 1990 [0Gd]: 262–283).[1] The current British Museum excavations at Tell es-Saidiyeh (in Jordan) recently found evidence for another garrison town probably staffed by 'sea-peoples' dating to the thirteenth century (Tubb 1988). This is not surprising, in view of the evidence for Egyptian links with several of the 'sea-peoples' before the late thirteenth century. What seems to have happened is that, as Egyptian imperial power in the region crumbled, the soldiers manning the fortresses were thrown on their own resources, reorganised themselves as independent cities, and so emerged as the Philistines of the Old Testament. It is possible that the name 'Philistine' was applied loosely to several different, though related, groups. It has even been suggested (Yadin 1968; Sandars 1978: 163–164) that the Israelite tribe of Dan, which has the peculiar characteristic of being associated with ships in the Old Testament, was originally part of one of the Egyptian garrisons settled by the *Dnn* (Ahlström 1986: 60–63).

The conclusion to be drawn from the Egyptian evidence alone is that some groups of people, perhaps at home in coastal areas of southern Turkey, were affected adversely by a series of economic difficulties in the thirteenth and twelfth centuries and therefore hired themselves out as mercenary soldiers to states such as Egypt, but also to others (e.g. Libyans). A small number were forced by the growing crisis to take their families and farming stock in the hope of finding new lands where they might settle. Others (e.g. the Lukka in EA 38) used boats to raid the coastline, which was probably little more than an extension of their normal piratical activities. The implication is that they were relatively poor people who, perhaps as a result of the gradual decline of central control by major powers, such as the Hittites, moved around in small bands to find further means of survival by plunder, encroaching on land and mercenary activities. Further, although these movements seem to have been on the increase and to have become, in some cases, more aggressive, they were not a new phenomenon, and the Egyptians seem to have had established means for absorbing at least some of the people involved into their service.

This narrow view, which hugs the evidence closely, is not the one normally presented of the 'sea-peoples'. A whole host of destructions and declines in the eastern Mediterranean, which occurred around 1200, are usually associated with them; their movement is, either overtly or implicitly, credited with causing all these disasters. The question then needs to be addressed as to whether there is sufficient evidence to make such a wide-ranging interpretation plausible.

The disintegration of the Hittite empire is widely attributed to the 'sea-peoples', but hard and fast evidence to support this is absent: the dating of the destruction of Hattusa is not certain; evidence for a mass invasion is not established. Were it not for the popularity of the 'sea-peoples' as a general explanation, scholars would most likely have envisaged the Gasga as the group responsible for its destruction and abandonment, as there is evidence in the preceding centuries for the Gasga capturing or destroying Hattusa, and forcing the king to move the court elsewhere (*RLA* 4: 171; see chapter 5d). The only connection between the two events is Ramesses III's reference to 'no country could stand before their arms: Hatti . . . etc.' (see pp. 387–388). But, as emphasised, the text is of a triumphal, rhetorical nature. The impression that Ramesses creates (very effectively) is that a massive federation of sea-peoples plotted destruction of the great empires; they were successful in doing this in the north, devastating everything associated with Egypt's neighbour, the great Hittite realm; but as they rampaged south in their unstoppable flow they were brought up short at the frontiers of Egypt and their ruinous onward stampede was hurled back by the victorious, omni-potent pharaoh. In short, it seems likely that Ramesses deliberately stressed the devastating success of the 'sea-peoples' against the Hittites in order to magnify his own achievement. We should note in this connection that Carchemish, the seat of the Hittite viceroy descended from Suppiluliuma I who administered the Hittite holdings in Syria (see chapter 5d), was not destroyed and its line of kings probably survived, which directly contradicts Ramesses' assertion in this one, checkable instance (Hawkins 1988; in press). There *is* evidence that in the reign of Merneptah the Hittite empire suffered from a serious famine, which the Egyptian king alleviated by sending grain. This could signify that Hittite Anatolia was beset by serious internal problems, which may be symptomatic of a political decline; but there is no evidence that it was caused by the 'sea-peoples'.

The destruction of the magnificent and wealthy city of Ugarit has been universally accepted as due to the advancing 'sea-peoples'. The story of the fall of the city has been beguilingly reconstructed by Astour (1965) in an influential article. He used some of the last letters (written on clay tablets and found in the palace) to create a poignant drama of Ugarit's defences diminished by the military demands of the Hittites and left a prey to the ravening seaborne horde. The references in the letters are in fact quite hard to understand clearly, and their interpretation depends on what kind of picture of the nature and scale of the 'sea-peoples'' attack has already been formed. It is at least as feasible to see the mention in the letters of ships raiding the coast of Ugarit as references to chronically recurring piratical raids as to an unprecedented mass attack. There is evidence now (unknown to Astour at the time he was writing) for one of the sea-people groups, the Shikala (*Škrš*), holding someone in Ugarit hostage and demanding a ransom (Dietrich and Loretz 1978; cf. *TUAT* I: 508 no. 4; p. 314). What we might say, then, is that Ugarit was certainly going through a difficult time: perhaps with the Hittites facing attacks, Ugarit was less protected, because Ugaritic soldiers may have been away helping the Hittite king. This could have created a situation of which pastoralists, bandits and pirates took advantage, pressing into the city's territory, raiding the coast and even kidnapping wealthy individuals for gain.

What is impossible to demonstrate on the basis of the Ugarit letters is who exactly was responsible for the fall of the city of Ugarit and its destruction. It is worth remembering in this context that the main excavator of the site, Claude Schaeffer, was himself convinced that the city was destroyed by an earthquake.

Hatti and Ugarit are the two states whose collapse has been thought to be clearly attributable to the 'sea-peoples', although it is difficult to do so conclusively. Other centres which suffered some kind of breakdown around 1200 are even harder to associate with the 'sea-peoples', because the arguments are based on much debated, and sometimes contradictory, pottery evidence (Mycenaean Greece, Troy VIIA, Cyprus), eked out by a methodologically indefensible use of later Greek legends, which relies to a large extent on speculative onomastic equivalences (see, for example, Strobel 1976; Stager 1991). In not a single instance is it possible to make any definite connection between destruction of a powerful centre and the 'sea-people'. Because the 'homelands' of the 'sea-peoples' remain speculative (as do their sometimes proposed connections with places such as Etruria, Sicily and Sardinia),[2] it becomes even harder to posit any direct connection: i.e. since we cannot pinpoint their place of origin in a manner that commands a significant degree of scholarly agreement, we cannot draw up a clear 'route' for them either. If it is not possible to know who they were, then it is hard to see whence, where, how, when and why they moved. The rather unsatisfactory conclusion must be that all we can use for understanding the 'sea-peoples' is the Egyptian evidence, some archaeological material from Palestine, where there is a reasonable supposition that 'sea-peoples' settled, and hints as to the kinds of activity with which some of the 'sea-peoples' were associated. The wider attribution of destructions to the 'sea-peoples' is very problematic; they may have played a role in the fall of Ugarit, but even that evidence is not as plain as has been thought.

The tendency more recently (beginning with an excellent article by Tritsch 1973; Sandars 1978) has been to see the movement of the 'sea-peoples' (whatever their affiliations and origins might be) as a byproduct of growing economic problems caused by an over-extension of the political superstructures of the Late Bronze Age states. This strained their resources and they could thus be upset only too easily, as they obviously were. One result of the breakdown was that various bands of pirates, brigands, landless farming families and, possibly, some more grandiose aristocratic plunderers (Homer's 'sackers of cities', as suggested stimulatingly by Tritsch) moved in several directions in an attempt to survive in a variety of ways. All the operations were relatively small in scale, independent of each other, and ceased with the decline of the wealthy states on which they preyed and hence depended.

If we accept this way of looking at the question of the 'sea-peoples' (and it is the most satisfactory in the present state of documentation), then the decline of the Late Bronze Age in the eastern Mediterranean must be sought inside the socio-political structures of the Levant and Turkey. The 'sea-peoples' would then be only one of a number of pointers to a complicated series of interlinked problems and changes that had been developing for some considerable time. What they were exactly is not known; but the strong evidence for runaway peasants and outlaws banding together to form marauding groups of bandits (the *'apiru/habiru* of the Amarna letters, see chapter 6d), attested already in the fourteenth century, should be seen as symptomatic of an underlying, long-term, socio-economic malaise in the Levant. A general reduction in urban settlement should perhaps also be linked to this; so, too, should the increasing concentration of resources in the hands of a tiny urban élite, which suggests that the rural communities were being more and more ruthlessly exploited (Liverani 1987). The ultimate failure to resolve these and related problems led to a situation in which, once part of the delicately balanced state superstructure collapsed (for any one of a multiplicity of reasons), the chances of recovery were slight, as the rural population, on whose productivity all states depended, no longer identified their interests with those of the government. Instead, they were tempted to join with other raiders to ravage the formerly wealthy, now tottering, centres (Liverani 1988 [OC]: 629–660; Knapp 1988 [OC]: 212–215). If we insert the 'sea-peoples' into this political scenario, then we can see them as another one of the *signs* of general collapse and disintegration, but not its cause.

8b The Aramaeans

One of the difficulties in accepting the 'sea-peoples' as the chief cause of political collapse in the Near East is that it privileges the evidence for one set of raiders over more scattered evidence for much more widespread problems, involving other peoples (see p. 386). One group, in particular, emerges increasingly in this period creating problems for several centralised states in western Asia – the Aramaeans.

Many problems beset scholarly understanding of the appearance of the Aramaeans. Partly it is connected with the fact that the general designation 'Aramaeans' masks the fact that they are not a unified group, except in terms of their language. Aramaic belongs to the North-West Semitic language-group, and is related to Hebrew and Phoenician. It became the most widely used language of the Near East until its eventual displacement by Arabic in the course of the seventh century AD: Aramaic was the administrative language of the Achaemenid Persian empire, it was the language spoken by Jesus, and an Aramaic dialect was used by the Syriac Christian church (as, indeed, it still is by the modern Assyrian church). By the ninth century, some Aramaean groups had adapted the alphabetic script of the Phoenicians (see chapter 8c(i)) to write Aramaic; because of the widespread presence of Aramaeans, the alphabetic writing system, and Aramaic itself, came to be used increasingly by a number of states; script and language gradually displaced, or at least limited the use of, the previously dominant cuneiform script and the older Akkadian language. One important difference, then, between the elusive 'sea-peoples' and the Aramaeans is that, where the former, with the probable exception of the Philistines, virtually disappear without trace after their two reported raids, the Aramaeans continue to be a major, identifiable, political and cultural factor in the history of the Near East from the ninth century on. That said, accounting for their appearance and 'explaining' their origins remain extremely difficult.

Documentation for Syria and Anatolia virtually ceases some time after 1200. As regards Egypt, the evidence for affairs beyond its frontiers is limited, and becomes very sparse soon after 1100 (chapter 4d). In Babylonia, Assyria and Elam, too, the impression is of a shrinkage in political power and prestige, certainly by 1050, with Assyria losing control of its territories in Upper Mesopotamia (chapter 7). This period of obscurity comes to an end in 934, when the Assyrian state began to recover and its kings produced more detailed accounts of their campaigns. When written evidence becomes available again (primarily in Assyria, but the Old Testament must not be forgotten) from the later tenth century on, one thing is plain. Aramaeans, sporadically attested before c. 1050 as roving, hostile bands of marauders, are now found settled, in a range of political entities, throughout the region from the east Tigris region to the Levant. If we look at the even later evidence of the Assyrian annals from the latter part of the eighth century, when the Neo-Assyrian empire embraced most of the region to some degree, we gain a reasonably full picture of Aramaean settlement. What does it look like?

In Syria and Upper Mesopotamia, the most striking feature is the existence of a number of small states, centred on a capital city, which generally (though not always) deviate from the Late Bronze Age pattern of states (see map 13) – kingdoms such as Damascus, Hamath (modern Hama, on the Orontes), Bit Agusi (capital: Arpad, modern Tell Rifa'at, north of Aleppo), Bit Adini (capital: Til Barsip, modern Tell Ahmar, 20 km downstream from Carchemish), Y'dy/Sam'al (modern Zincirli, at the foot of the eastern flank of the Amanus range), Bit Bahiani (capital: Guzana, modern Tell Halaf, upper Khabur river), Bit Zamani (capital: Amedu, region of Diyarbekr) and Nasibina (modern Nusaybin, on the Syrian–Turkish frontier). Some of the names of the states derive from their main city (e.g. Hamath), others bear a name composed with the word 'house' or 'family' (*bītu/beth*) and a personal name (e.g. Bit Agusi). This shows that some states were literally called 'The House of Adin' or 'The House of Gusi', and suggests that the name of the state was derived from that of an ancestor or prominent member of a dominant family within the kingdom. The Assyrian and Old Testament evidence confirms that the principalities were all in some sense Aramaean by sometimes defining them as such: e.g. 'Aram Damascus'; further, eighth-century inscribed monuments recovered from some of the states are in Aramaic, and the personal names of the rulers are Aramaic. If we look further east, at the region of

Babylonia, especially the territory east of the Tigris, we find a whole multitude of groups located there described as 'Aramaean' by the Assyrian sources. They are characterised in a distinctly tribal fashion as, e.g., 'Gambuleans', 'Puqudians', 'Itu'aeans' and many more. This is the picture in the eighth century; the ninth-century Assyrian evidence allows us to assume that it was also true of that period. This in turn suggests that the crucial changes leading to the political transformation happened within the period between *c.* 1100 and *c.* 900, for which, as has already been said, documentation is exceptionally sparse.

How, then, can we try to explain the appearance of these new population elements? It is in the nature of such questions that they are ultimately unanswerable. In addition to the absence of contemporary material, the bits of scattered evidence that *do* exist inevitably emanate from the older, established states who normally only refer to such people when, and if, they come into conflict with them, which gives a very limited, and ultimately distorted, picture. Perhaps the easiest way to clarify the problem is to look at the different types of evidence in turn.

The Assyrian evidence

From the fourteenth century onwards there are occasional references to a people called *Ahlamû* who, most scholars now agree, were associated with the later Aramaeans. They appear variously as agricultural labourers and marauders from as far afield as Bahrain to Syria. But the earliest *indisputable* evidence for the Aramaeans dates from the reign of Tiglath-pileser I (1114–1076). From his fourth regnal year onwards he undertook at least fourteen annual policing actions against a people called *Ahlamê-Armaya* in the area of the middle and upper Euphrates:

> I have crossed the Euphrates twenty-eight times, twice in one year, in pursuit of the *ahlamû* Aramaeans. I brought about their defeat from the city Tadmar of the land Amurru, Anat of the land Suhu, as far as Rapiqu of Karduniash (Babylonia). I brought their booty (and) possessions to my city Ashur.
> (*ARAB* I §§287; *ANET*: 275; Grayson 1972/1976 §97; 1991 A.0.87.4)

If we add this text to a passage in Tiglath-pileser's annals, it seems that, in the course of his numerous battles against the Aramaeans, the Assyrian king burnt Aramaean settlements in the Jebel Bishri region (north Syrian steppe) and fought to protect routes in the Syrian desert as far as Lebanon and along the Euphrates between Carchemish, Suhu (on the Euphrates, region of modern 'Ana in Iraq) and north-western Babylonia (see map 13). The descriptions of Tiglath-pileser's Aramaean raids make clear that, despite repeated military action, the Assyrian king was unable to make much impression on the situation. It is obvious that Aramaean groups continued to attack or disrupt the caravan routes from Babylonia westwards to the Levant and north as far as south Turkey. It is even possible that, perhaps towards the end of Tiglath-pileser I's reign, Aramaean raiders penetrated right into the heartland of Assyria, as shown by this fragment of an Assyrian chronicle, thought to come from Tiglath-pileser I's library (*ABC* 66–67):

> [In the year x a famine broke out in the land of . . .], the people ate each other's flesh, [. . .]
> [. . .] . . . the houses of the Aramaeans
> [. . .] to render relief, they set out,
> [. . .] conquered Assyria, they took
> [?the Assyrians went up] to the mountains of Kirriuri (to save their) lives
> [?they fled]. They took away their [gold?], silver (and) all their property.
> [Marduk-nadin-ahhe, king of Kar]duniash, passed away; Marduk-[shapik]-zeri,
> [his son,] . . . entered; Marduk-[nadin]-ahhe had reigned 18 years.
>
> ───
>
> [In the year x . . .] the harvest of the land of Ashur, all of it, [was rava]ged
> [. . .] they were numerous, they captured the houses [of the A]ramae[ans],
> [. . .] . . . fortress of Nineveh, Kilizi
> [. . . Tiglath]-pileser, the king of Ashur [went] to Kadmuhi.
> (Tadmor 1958a: 133–134; *ABC* Ass. Chron. Frag. 4)

It is tempting to see this as the final climax of a worsening situation, with Aramaeans encamped around Ashur and Nineveh, while the king is forced to withdraw to the mountains in the north. But that may be too dramatic, and is based on heavy restorations of the very fragmentary text suggested by Tadmor (1958a; not included above). We must also remember that, subsequently, Ashur-bel-kala (1074–1057) was definitely in control of the main Assyrian cities, and fighting vigorously against Aramaeans in his turn (see chapter 7b). Admittedly, Ashur-bel-kala's account makes it quite plain that he was being pressed hard by the Aramaeans in Upper Mesopotamia – around the headwaters of the Khabur, along the upper Balikh, in the mountains and along the Euphrates – and, after his reign, the sources in Assyria are extremely scanty. When they become relatively plentiful again, at the end of the tenth century, the Assyrian evidence shows Aramaean states established just to the west of the Assyrian heartland and stretching right across Upper Mesopotamia. Further, Ashur-dan II (934–912) vividly describes the crisis experienced by the inhabitants of the countryside preceding his reign:

> I brought back the exhausted [people] of Assyria [who] had abandoned [their cities (and) houses in the face of] want, hunger, famine (and) [had gone up] to other lands.
> (E. Weidner *AfO* 3 (1926): 151–161;
> Grayson 1976 §368; 1991 A.0.98.1)

The passage implies that one effect of the Aramaean settlement in the region had been the flight of Assyrians living there (Postgate 1974). With the renewed expansion of Assyria from Ashur-dan II onwards, the Assyrian kings reasserted their claims to Upper Mesopotamia, and the Aramaean states were gradually incorporated into the revitalised Assyrian empire, and some inhabitants were deported to the Assyrian cities. Right from the start of its renaissance, then, the new Assyrian state included Aramaeans within its territorial span. The way in which they were integrated has been startlingly illuminated by the recent find of a statue at the site of Tell Fekheriye (ancient Sikan in the headwaters of the Khabur), part of the Aramaean state of Bit Bahiani with its capital at Guzana (Abou Assaf *et al.* 1982; Millard and Bordreuil 1982). The statue has been plausibly dated to the middle of the ninth century. It represents a governor of the, by then, Assyrian province of Guzana, carved in a style obviously influenced by contemporary Assyrian court-style. The identity of the figure is established by a bilingual text, in Akkadian and Aramaic; it is the earliest long Aramaic inscription so far discovered (Layton 1988):

> To Adad, regulator of the waters of heaven and earth, who rains down abundance, who gives pasture and watering places to the people of all cities, who gives portions and offerings to the gods, his brothers, regulator of rivers, who enriches the regions, the merciful god to whom it is good to pray, who dwells in Guzana, to the great lord, his lord, Adad-it'i, governor of Guzana (*šakin māti (āl)gūzāni*), son of Shamash-nuri, also governor of Guzana, for the life of his soul, for the length of his days, for increasing his years, for the prosperity of his house, of his descendants, of his people, to remove illness from his body, for hearing my prayer, for accepting my words, he devoted and gave. Whoever afterwards shall repair its ruined state, may he put my name (on it). Whoever erases my name, and puts his name, may Adad, the hero, be his adversary.
>
> (Abou Assaf *et al.* 1982: 15 and 17)

This is the Akkadian (Assyrian dialect) version of the main text; the statue also carries another bilingual (Akkadian and Aramaic) text. The important points to notice are the following: first, Adad-it'i is the rendering of an Aramaic name (Hadad-yis'i in the Aramaic text), yet he is functioning as an important Assyrian official in the region (*šakin māti (āl)Gūzāni* = 'governor of Guzana'). The assumption based on this, combined with the Aramaic version of the text, must be that Hadad-yis'i is himself an Aramaean, governing a former Aramaean state, but now an Assyrian province, and dedicating a statue of himself in a local sanctuary to the local god, Hadad (Akkadian Adad). Second, while Hadad-yis'i is called 'governor' (*šaknu*) in the Assyrian text, he is called 'king/ruler' (*mlk*) in the Aramaic version; thus, while being perceived as an official by the Assyrian kings, he was functioning as a 'king' *vis-à-vis* the local population. A third point of some importance is the name of his father, Shamash-nuri, which appears to be an Assyrian name, although not a widely attested one. A man with the same name served as the Assyrian eponymous official (*limmu*, see chapter 7b) in 866 – the position of the name in the cycle of eponyms suggests that he, too, was the governor of Guzana and, therefore, very probably identical with Hadad-yis'i's father, who is said to have held the position of governor/king before him. Whether Shamash-nuri's Assyrian name was his original one, whether he had adopted (or been granted) the name to replace his Aramaic one as a gesture of (or reward for) loyalty, must remain speculative. But everything suggests that already by the middle of the ninth century an extraordinarily close symbiosis had been established between Assyrians and Aramaeans. The evidence implies a practice whereby members of local Aramaean families were appointed to rule their states by the Assyrian kings and, as officially designated Assyrian dignitaries, were fully integrated into the Assyrian system of public honours and office. It is worth remembering that the *limmu*s were formally recorded on stelae set up at Ashur, that the highest officials of state, including the Assyrian king, each held this position in turn and that they formed the ruling élite *par excellence* of Assyria. So while the celebratory form of many Assyrian royal campaign-accounts dictated that Aramaean states were presented as hostile, to be crushed and devastated ruthlessly, and their populations deported, the historical reality is reflected more clearly by the Fekheriye statue. It shows a policy of recruiting distinguished Aramaeans into the highest echelons of Assyrian government, so creating a state where the division between rulers and ruled was not drawn along ethnic lines.

In summary, the Assyrian evidence presents a picture of Aramaeans pressing into Assyrian-held territory in the eleventh century. Their success in seizing and holding stretches of land is reflected in the emergence of a number of Aramaean states in Upper Mesopotamia by the tenth century. As the Asyrians mobilised to reconquer the area from the end of the tenth century on, they gradually absorbed these territories, turning them into Assyrian provinces but, at least in some cases, using members of the local Aramaean population to enforce Assyrian control. Such individuals owed their position to the Assyrian king, and came to form an integral part of the Assyrian imperial machinery at the highest levels. An indication of the fact that this interweaving of Aramaeans and Assyrians happened not only exceptionally at the very highest echelons is the early appearance (eighth century) of 'Aramaisms' in Assyrian, and the use of Aramaic written on parchment in certain contexts and for particular purposes. The conclusion must, therefore, be that despite the aggressive military tone against Aramaeans taken by the royal annals they came to constitute a significant proportion of the Assyrian population at all levels of the socio-political structure (Garelli 1982; Tadmor 1982).

The Babylonian evidence

Babylonian evidence for the Aramaeans is much less full, but one or two hints do exist, which can be combined with our knowledge of the political situation in the ninth and eighth centuries to construct a hypothetical picture. In the eleventh century, Babylonia was probably affected by the Aramaeans reported by Tiglath-pileser I as active around Rapiqu in the north-west of the country. During the reign of Adad-apla-iddina (1069–1048) groups, described as Aramaeans and Suteans, ransacked the shrines of Sippar and Nippur. Although contemporary documentation is practically non-existent in the tenth century, similar disturbances within Babylonia were later attributed to bands of Aramaeans. In the ninth and eighth centuries, the evidence of Babylonian business documents and Assyrian war-accounts indicates the presence of a large number of permanent Aramaean settlements in Babylonian territory, mainly in the east Tigris region, but also in enclaves between cities. They represent various definable groups (cf. p. 395), who led a relatively simple farming life; the main forms of socio-political organisation seem to have been the village and clan or tribe. The extant sources do not allow us to define their structure very clearly, but what there is suggests the presence of local chiefs (*nasīku*), possibly grouped under a tribal head, and a population pursuing a basic subsistence economy (Brinkman 1984). On the whole, the impression is that Babylonian urban society was resilient enough, even under extreme pressure, to repel the Aramaean raids effectively. As a result, the Aramaeans settled in small, tribal groups on the periphery of the dominant political entities, excluded from the richer irrigated fields of the city inhabitants, and were only slowly absorbed into the Babylonian state (Brinkman 1968).

The Aramaean population of Babylonia needs to be distinguished from another group which appears in Babylonia at approximately the same time, namely, the Chaldaeans (inhabitants of *māt Kaldu*). Exactly when and how they penetrated into Babylonia is totally obscure, but when documentation resumes in ninth-century Babylonia they are definitely present. Some scholars (e.g. Dietrich 1970), therefore, associate them with the Aramaeans, but such an identification is not really tenable. Three major Chaldaean tribal groupings are known for Babylonia: Bit Amukani, Bit Dakkuri and Bit Yakin, all centred on fortified towns with royal residences where the 'king' (*šarru*) of each tribe lived. There is no hint of other chiefs operating under these kings, so that each of the Chaldaean groups appears to be subject simply to its one acknowledged king in the royal centre. Another clear difference is that where the names of Chaldaean kings are known they are usually Babylonian – West Semitic names are scarcely ever associated with the Chaldaeans. Finally, the Chaldaeans are distinguished from the Babylonian Aramaeans by their great wealth: the contrast between the booty that Assyrian kings regularly take from the Chaldaeans and Aramaeans is striking. Where they obtain quantities of small cattle (sheep and goats) from the Aramaean villagers, the Chaldaeans are able to supply them with gold, silver, ivory, exotic woods and precious stones. It seems likely that the Chaldaeans, located near the head of the Gulf and along the Euphrates, were the beneficiaries of the luxury trade of the Gulf and the Arabian peninsula in which they seem to have played a crucial mediating role. This also gave them links to the rich states located along the middle Euphrates, Suhu and Hindanu (Brinkman 1977).

Evidence from the Levant

In Syria the situation is similarly obscure for the modern researcher. This is largely due to the scantiness of documentary material. Local royal inscriptions (except for Tell Fekeheriye/Guzana) are not extant before the late ninth century (the dates are only approximate and several are disputed; Layton 1988). The later Old Testament account, naturally, focuses on the kingdom of Israel (later divided into Israel and Judah; see chapters 8d(iv) and (v)), and only incidentally refers to neighbouring Aramaean states, in particular the nearest powerful ones of Damascus and Zobah (in the Lebanese Beqa valley). Zobah was the earliest prominent Aramaean state, according to the account of David's Syrian wars contained in 2 *Samuel* 8, and its formation has been most interestingly analysed, by analogy with David's creation of the strong state of Israel in the tenth century, by Malamat (1963). What Malamat has stressed in his comparison are the similarities in the development of the two regions: both David and Hadadezer (king of Zobah) constructed their initial power-base around a small kernel – Judah in the case of David, Beth Rehob in the case of Hadadezer; both added a larger, more important adjoining region to this small core to create a new, unified state – Israel was added to Judah, Zobah to Beth Rehob; in both cases, the ruler of the new political formation bore the title of the larger group – David was called the 'king of Israel' (not 'of Judah'), Hadadezer 'king of Zobah' (not 'of Rehob'). Finally, Hadadezer of Zobah may have annexed the important and rich oasis of Damascus (cf. Pitard 1987, who is more doubtful) and added some smaller states that owed him allegiance, but were left under their own rulers. Eventually, Damascus established its independence from both Solomon's Israel and the kingdom of Zobah, under its king Rezin (Pitard 1987). Malamat's analysis illustrates brilliantly the kinds of political vicissitude to which all these emergent states (including Israel) were subject.

Conclusions

Malamat's comparison is limited by the nature of the sources to Damascus and Zobah, but it suggests the possibility of assuming that processes analogous to those known for Israel played a role in the formation of other Aramaean states. If we accept this approach, then it is possible to argue that the Aramaean principalities (like Israel) emerged as a result of increased settlement by pastoralists, who took over existing centres and political institutions through both peaceful interaction and conflict. Competition for pre-eminence, between tribal groups and with established cities, resulted eventually in the formation of larger territorial groupings under one leader, who was able to add other units to his power as a result of his increasing political prestige and successful military conquests. An important corollary of this hypothesis is that, while the boundaries of the emergent territorial states differed from the older city-states, and the main language was now that of the new political élite, much of the older local culture and institutions was adapted and integrated into the new Aramaean principalities.

How the Aramaeans emerged as a distinct group is even harder to define. The scattered evidence indicates that they were present in the Near East for well over three hundred years before they emerged as a threat against which the large states had to mount campaigns. This suggests that it was only within the context of political breakdown, beginning in the twelfth century, that the Aramaeans became a definable hostile force, when their numbers were swelled by dissatisfied peasants and outlaws from some of the collapsing city-states (see p. 393). The implications of such a view are that we should probably visualise the Aramaean 'invasions' as a continuous and pervasive movement of pastoralists. Groups of herders (and others) increasingly occupied depopulated zones in hills and semi-arid regions on the fringes of established states, and the resulting intensified settlement changed perforce the pattern of land-use. This, in turn, led to the expansion of the newly inhabited regions and thus brought them inevitably into conflict with existing states and cities. The strength of the forces ranged against them determined their success (or not) in enlarging their territories: i.e. in Mesopotamia, the Assyrian and Babylonian states were not destroyed and preserved their political systems intact, although both suffered setbacks and territorial losses; therefore Aramaean settlement was piecemeal and/or restricted to the periphery. But in the Levant, already so badly affected by the collapse of the imperial superstructures, the small city-states were much more vulnerable, and it was precisely here that the Aramaeans were most successful in settling and seizing political control.

8c The survival of Late Bronze Age centres

Not every shred of the Late Bronze Age city-system was swept away or fundamentally transformed through being included in one of the new states that emerge in the tenth century. Several centres managed to survive the changes with much of their earlier culture and elements of political life intact. One group is the Phoenicians, the other the Neo-Hittites.

(i) The Phoenicians

Even those who know practically nothing of the ancient Near East have some vague impression of the Phoenicians. They are widely famed as traders and navigators, voyaging far afield to explore the west coast of Africa, exploiting bronze-working centres, mining silver in Spain – even perhaps penetrating as far as Brittany and Cornwall in their search for scarce metal deposits – and, of course, they were the inventors of the alphabet from which our own is ultimately derived. The most potent and beautiful image of the far-flung commercial network commanded by the Phoenicians is that of the Jewish prophet Ezekiel's poetic vision of Tyre:

> Tarshish (probably Tarsus, although also a name given to several places that had metal sources) was a source of your commerce, from its abundant resources offering silver and iron, tin and lead, as your staple wares. Yavan (western Turkey), Tubal (central Turkey), and Meshech (Phrygia) dealt with you, offering slaves and vessels of bronze as your imports. Men from Togarmah[3] offered horses, mares, and mules as your staple wares. Rhodians dealt with you, great islands were a source of your commerce, paying what was due to you in ivory and ebony. Edom was a source of your commerce, so many were your under-takings, and offered purple garnets, brocade and fine linen, black coral and red jasper, for your staple wares. Judah and Israel dealt with you offering wheat from Minnith, and meal, syrup, oil, and balsam, as your imports. Damascus was a source of your commerce, so many were your undertakings, from its abundant resources, offering wine of Helbon and wool of Suhar, and casks of wine from Izalla, for your staple wares; wrought iron, cassia, and sweet cane were among your imports. Dedan (north Arabian oasis) dealt with you in coarse woollens for saddle-cloths. Arabia and all the chiefs of Kedar were the source of your commerce in lambs, rams, and he-goats. This was your trade with them. Dealers from Sheba (Yemen) and Raamah dealt with you, offering the choicest spices, every kind of precious stone and gold, as your staple wares. Harran, Kanneh, and Eden (all east of Euphrates), dealers from Ashur and Media, dealt with you; they were your dealers in gorgeous stuffs, violet cloths and brocades, in stores of coloured fabric rolled up and tied with cords; your dealings with them were in these.
> Ships of Tarshish were the caravans for your imports;
> you were deeply laden with full cargoes
> on the high seas.
>
> (*Ezekiel* 27.12–25 (NEB))

Yet defining the Phoenicians and their culture precisely is a very hard task (Salles 1991a); even the origin of their name is problematic. A possible idea is that the term represents a Greek rendering of a word for Canaan (related, perhaps, to the Egyptian term *Fnkhw*, see p. 318); another, that it is derived from the purple dye with which Phoenicians were widely associated. The notion that 'Phoenician' means 'Canaanite' underlines the fact that the Phoenician city-states of Tyre, Sidon, Byblos, Beirut, Arvad and Sarepta represent a direct development of the Late Bronze Age Canaanite coastal cities. That the idea is basically correct is shown by the fact that the Phoenicians called themselves Canaanites; the designation 'Phoenician' is Graeco-Roman. The Phoenician cities were those that appear to have been relatively slightly affected or disrupted by either the Aramaean penetration or the Israelite expansion, and so they were able to maintain what appear to be essentially the earlier Canaanite traditions. A plausible explanation for this continuity is their geographical position: they lay right on the coast, sometimes with offshore island settlements, and were backed by a very narrow plain protected by a steep mountain range crossed by few passes.

One of the reasons for fairly widespread knowledge of the Phoenicians is their extensive commercial activities, especially in the western Mediterranean, where they founded a number of colonies some of which developed into substantial cities (Aubet 1993). The foundations date to the early first millennium, although the precise chronology is disputed. The most famous Phoenician colony was Carthage. Because Carthage seriously threatened Rome's political power and expansion in the third century (and was eventually destroyed by the Romans in the second century), there are several discussions by Roman historians of its political system, religion and culture. But, as Carthage developed to some extent independently of the Phoenician homeland (a feature also true of its language), such descriptions of Carthaginian (Punic – from the Latin for Phoenician) culture, dating from the second century, can not be relied on too heavily for reconstructing Phoenician civilisation in the Levant. For this we must use other sources, which are unfortunately rather unsatisfactory.

Sources and problems

There are references to Phoenicians in the *Iliad* and *Odyssey*, where they appear as highly skilled craftsmen, especially in metalwork, and weavers of elaborate garments. They may also appear as kidnappers and producers of cheap trinkets. The curiously mixed image reflects admiration and fear, the sort of antagonism that is now often felt towards gypsies and tinkers, and the kind of aristocratic contempt for 'trade' which is a hallmark of these heroic poems. Herodotus provides some information on their colonisation, especially in Greece, to which he attributes the origin of the Greek alphabet, and their discovery of the goldmines on Thasos. Thucydides mentions that they formed the earliest foreign settlers in Sicily, predating the Greek presence there. Such depictions remain at the level of stereotypes and generalities, and provide no very coherent picture, especially not of the Phoenician homeland. In the first century AD, Josephus included in his history of the Jewish people some material supposedly drawn from a lost history of Tyre (van Seters 1983 [OK], for discussion); basically it is little more than a list of kings. A little later, in the early second century AD, Philo of Byblos wrote an account of Phoenician religion, which he claimed was a translation into Greek of the work of Sanchuniathon, a priest of Byblos. Philo's work is only preserved in fragments, and there has been considerable doubt as to whether Sanchuniathon's work was ever anything more than a figment of Philo's imagination (Barr 1974; Oden 1978; Baumgarten 1981; Attridge and Oden 1981; van Seters 1983 [OK]). But a more positive tendency (e.g. Moscati 1968: 55) has been to accept the reality of the Phoenician original underlying Philo's account, because some of it seems to correspond to the material now known from Ugarit (see chapter 6b), which has provided important insights into Canaanite mythology and religion. But even if we accept the more positive approach, Philo seems to have 'hellenised' Sanchuniathon substantially, so the question of how we might use his material for reconstructing the Phoenician reality of the early first millennium remains vexed (Clifford 1990).

Texts, in the form of inscriptions, from the Phoenician region itself are very limited, numbering perhaps thirty at most. Moreover, the early ones are mostly very brief, with the longer ones appearing only from the sixth century onwards, when the Phoenician cities were part of the Persian empire, and later (cf. Gibson 1971–82 III; Donner and Röllig 1973–9). They do, however, help to provide the names of some kings, suggesting that some of Josephus' material on Tyre is largely accurate. The earliest inscription dates from *c.* 1000, showing that the Phoenician alphabet had evolved by that time (Naveh 1982 [OH]: 53). The short text is on a decorated sarcophagus and identifies it as belonging to Ahiram, king of Byblos:

> Coffin which Ittobaal, son of Ahiram, king of Byblos, made for Ahiram, his father, when he placed him in 'the house of eternity'.
> Now if a king among kings or a governor among governors or a commander of an army should come up against Byblos and uncovers this coffin, may the sceptre of his rule be torn away, may the throne of his kingdom be overturned, and may peace flee from Byblos! And as for him, if he destroys this inscription, then the . . . !
> (*KAI* no. 1; Gibson 1971–82 III no. 4; *ANET*: 661; *TUAT* II 582–583)

Undoubtedly the reason for the sparsity of written material is that most writing was done on perishable material, such as papyrus, parchment and wood, which has not survived, except for some clay bullae with seal-impressions which were originally attached to them (Culican 1968). Archaeological evidence is also very limited – far more Phoenician material has been found in Sicily, Sardinia, Cyprus, Spain and North Africa than in the Phoenician homeland (Bunnens 1979; Scnyzer 1988). One reason is that many of the cities have had a continuous occupation up to the present day (e.g. Beirut). Another is that most of the surviving earlier remains are of the extensive Roman and Byzantine buildings on the sites. A third factor is that, from the Middle Ages onwards, stone from ancient monuments was removed and used in other structures. As a result, the restricted archaeological investigations have only turned up very meagre Phoenician remains of the Early Iron Age. At Sidon, the earliest levels found so far are those of the Persian period. At Byblos, large parts of the Bronze Age city have been recovered, but the Phoenician settlement area appears to lie under the modern city. At Tyre, where excavation is hampered by later accumulations, Patricia Bikai was able nevertheless to carry out a small excavation in the Bronze Age and Phoenician levels in 1973–4 (Bikai 1978). But it is worth stressing that the excavated area is tiny (150 m²), and constitutes less than 1 per cent of the original island settlement of Tyre. Nevertheless it is important for the new analysis of pottery that it has made possible. Phoenician pottery in the Levant is now much more clearly known as a result of the excavations at a small Phoenician site, Sarepta, just south of Sidon, where excavation on a relatively unencumbered site has been feasible (Pritchard 1978; Anderson 1988; Khalifeh 1988). Among the important finds there was a pottery-manufacturing zone. One archaeological technique that has been applied with particular success to the Phoenicians is the relatively recent one of underwater exploration. This has helped to reveal the impressive old harbour installations of Arvad (Frost 1972), and has been used to recover a number of Levantine shipwrecks – at Motya, off Sicily, Cape Gelidonya and Ulu Burun, off south-west Turkey, and Acre, off Israel, ships with their loads of copper ingots, pottery containers, amulets and figurines have been recovered (Isserlin and du Plat Taylor 1974; Bass 1973; Bass *et al.* 1989). The Sicilian and Israeli wrecks are generally agreed to be Phoenician – the Turkish wrecks date to the thirteenth century, and their identities are less certain.

Phoenician texts from outside their homeland (southern Turkey, Cyprus, Carthage, Sardinia, Malta) are also not enormous in number, and mostly fairly short. Again the majority are relatively late in date, but some of the ones from Turkey, especially Cilicia, date to the eighth and seventh centuries. Phoenician settlement here probably dates to the ninth century, possibly even earlier (Kestemont 1972), and demonstrates the importance and strength of their commercial and political links with other areas. This is most strikingly reflected by one of the longest extant Phoenician inscriptions so far known, the Karatepe bilingual – a long royal inscription commemorating the founding of a new royal city in Cilicia by the Neo-Hittite ruler Azitawada (fig. 27). It is inscribed in parallel texts of Hittite hieroglyphs and Phoenician, probably to be dated to the early seventh century (Bron 1979; *CAH* III ch. 9; Hawkins in press; for part of the text, see pp. 414–415). The intensity of Phoenician trading activities in all these (and other) places, especially Cilicia, Cyprus and the Levant, is also reflected in the material remains found at sites in the areas, such as Phoenician-style buildings, pottery, finely wrought metalwork and carved ivory items and furniture inlays (Helm 1980; Muhly 1985).

Figure 27 Karatepe (courtesy of M.S. Drower)

Much of Phoenician history and Phoenician economic structures has to be reconstructed or inferred from sources that either relate to an earlier period, such as the Ugarit archives (*c.* 1400–1200), or are external to the Phoenician cities, such as the Old Testament. They are among the most important sources, but need to be used with care. In the case of earlier material, it is only too tempting simply to transpose data from four to six hundred years earlier to fill the yawning gap in detailed knowledge, and forget about the important, but unknown, developments that had taken place in the meantime. When relying on evidence from outside Phoenicia, problems are raised by the incomplete nature of many of the references, and by specific biases as a result of political rivalry, religious differences and later ideological requirements (Ahlström 1984). This is particularly true of some of the material in the Old Testament, and emerges most clearly in the extreme hostility with which the Tyrian princess Jezebel is presented, and the vicious caricaturing of Phoenician religion in Elijah's contest with the prophets of Baal on Mount Carmel (1 *Kings* 18, 19.1–2, 21; 2 *Kings* 9.30–37; Ackroyd 1983). Differences between the Late Bronze and Early Iron Ages can be discerned: a dominant role in the Phoenician pantheon was played by the chief gods of the various cities, such as Eshmun of Sidon and Melqart of Tyre. These deities are not attested earlier. A religious practice, for which again no earlier evidence exists, is the notorious ritual of infant sacrifice (*molek*; Edelman 1987). Its (occasional) use is attested for Phoenicians, Carthaginians and Israelites, and may have been linked to a need for population control (Stager and Wolff 1984; Clifford 1990).

The development of the Phoenician cities

With these caveats and restrictions in mind, what can we say about the development of the political and economic structures of the Phoenician cities? The most persuasive and constructive recent approach is that of Frankenstein (1979), and it is her arguments that are summarised here. It is evident, from the extensive material from Ugarit, in particular, and, to a lesser degree, Byblos, that the Canaanite city-states played a central role in the trading and production system of the Near East, and that their commercial activities were stimulated by, and supported, the large centralised states such as Egypt, the Hittite realm, and Babylonia. Because of the demands made on them by these large and complex states, the coastal cities appear to have concentrated their energy and resources on the production of luxury commodities such as ivory inlaid furniture for royal consumption – an industry that certainly continued in the Neo-Assyrian period. At the same time the manufacture of textiles was developed on a large scale to meet demands for tribute payments, as exemplified in the agreements between Ugarit and the Hittite kings (see chapter 6b). Textiles could also be used in exchange for raw materials, that either were used to produce luxury commodities (such as elaborate furniture and metalwork) or could be re-exported. An accompanying and necessary development was the perfecting of ships capable of carrying bulky items, and the refinement of navigational skills – a specialisation that could, and was, exploited by some of the larger states, as shown by the Hittites, who relied on Ugarit to organise some of its grain supply (see chapter 6b). The locally available timber also placed the Phoenicians in an advantageous position with respect to such undertakings: it provided them with the ready raw materials for shipbuilding and furniture production, and was in high demand by the timberless great states of Egypt and Assyria.

There is a certain amount of evidence from such varied sources as the Ugarit archives (1400–1200), the report of the Egyptian official Wenamun (*c.* 1100; see chapter 4a), and a treaty drawn up in the seventh century between the Assyrian king, Esarhaddon, and Baalu, king of Tyre (see below), that trading operations were organised by mercantile companies, independently of the local ruler – although he participated in commercial ventures and was probably one of the most important investors:

> If a ship belonging to Baal or the people of Tyre is wrecked in the land of the Philistines or in the frontier territory of Assyria, then all of what is in the ship belongs to Esarhaddon, king of Assyria; but the people who are aboard the ship shall not be touched(?), they must all be returned to their country.
>
> (Borger 1956: 107–109 §69; *ANET*: 533–534;
> *TUAT* I 158; SAA 2 no. 5)

In this respect, then, we might understand Canaanite commerce as sharing some of the features of the earlier Old Assyrian trading system (see chapter 2c).

An obvious concomitant of this development was that the cities and their politically powerful neighbours were mutually dependent, as the larger states provided the consumer markets on which the economy of the coastal cities had come to depend. A clear illustration of this is the contrast between the reaction of the king of Byblos to Wenamun's request for timber, and the reaction of the Phoenician cities to the triumphal visit of Tiglath-pileser I of Assyria, both datable to around 1100. Wenamun's requirements were only met by the king of Byblos on the basis of a precise equivalence of exchange, and Wenamun had to wait until the requisite supplies (4 jars of gold; 1 gold vessel; 5 silver jars; 10 royal linen garments; 10 special garments of fine linen; 500 special smooth linen mats; 500 oxhides; 500 ropes; 20 sacks of lentils; 30 baskets of fish) were sent from Tanis before the transaction was completed and the timber handed over. By contrast, when Tiglath-pileser I arrived on the Phoenician coast, he was fêted by the inhabitants, who presented him with valuable gifts of decorated linen garments, precious metal objects, ivory and rare woods, as well as laying on a sea-trip for the Assyrian monarch (cf. ch.7b). The difference in response to Egypt and Assyria at this time must, in part at least, be explained by the fact that the Phoenician cities were interested in fostering economic ties with a substantial power, which could provide them with a market for their goods and specialised skills. Egypt had ceased to be such a power, and so they reorientated themselves to the one great surviving state, Assyria.

As a result of the deepening crisis in the Near East, the Middle Assyrian empire collapsed about forty to fifty years later, and Assyria only began to wield extensive political power again from the late tenth century on. There is, fortunately, some evidence illustrating the continuity of typical Phoenician economic activity at this time in the Old Testament. The expansion of Israel under David and its consolidation under Solomon resulted in Israel controlling the main trade routes from the Red Sea to Syria (thence to Anatolia and Mesopotamia) for most of the tenth century (see chapter 8d(iv)). The alliance of the neighbouring city of Tyre with Israel's kings meant that Tyre gained access to these important commercial arteries and, in return, it provided Israel with technology, expert craftsmen, luxury items and materials (best exemplified in Solomon's great building programme). The close relationship between the two states for mutual benefit – a pattern which continued between Tyre and the northern kingdom of Israel in the ninth century – led to intensive trade, attested by finds of Phoenician wares in Israel in tenth- and ninth-century contexts (Bikai 1978; cf. Geva 1982).

The scant literary and archaeological evidence suggests that this profitable co-operation between the two states may have led to an important development in Tyre. Tyre seems to have channelled its wealth into building up its industries (textiles, bronze-working, ivory and wood carving) and trade to an unprecedented degree, with the result that the larger part of the population was drawn into the built-up urban area, becoming traders and artisans rather than farmers. The specialisation was fostered and maintained by the renascent Assyrian empire, which now began to make extensive demands on Phoenician expertise, in the form of skilled craftsmen and luxury finished goods. In fact, the largest collections of carved and inlaid ivory (Strommenger and Hirmer 1965 [OM] pls. 263–268, XLI, XLII) have come from the Assyrian royal centre of Kalhu (modern Nimrud; Winter 1976) – much of it from furniture burnt when the palaces were sacked, and many bearing Phoenician graffiti to indicate fitting. Typical examples of Phoenician metalwork have also been found in Assyria, and several texts refer to the colourful textiles and special embroidered garments of the region. At the same time, the Phoenicians acted as middlemen in organising and facilitating trade between Assyria and Egypt – frit (a substance related to glass-manufacture and popular for its blue pigment; Moorey 1985 [OF]: 134–135), alum (used in dying and treating textiles), and fine linen were certainly imported from Egypt into Assyria, possibly also honey and wines. Another Assyrian requirement met by the Phoenician cities, together with the Syrian principalities, was supplying the growing empire with signficant quantities of iron. It is to these developments that we should probably relate the foundation of the earliest Phoenician colonies in Cyprus, Cilicia and Crete (note the Phoenician harbour at Kommos in southern Crete, functioning by the tenth century; Shaw 1989).

In the late eighth century, Assyrian expansion resulted in the economically important Syrian states losing their independence, and being reorganised as directly governed Assyrian provinces. One effect was that the Phoenicians, who were largely excluded from this development, became the main suppliers of primary raw materials for the empire. It was for this reason, it is argued, that they were compelled to extend their trading network well beyond the traditional circuit of the eastern Mediterranean. The expansion coincides with the generally accepted dates for the foundations of Phoenician settlements in the more westerly Mediterranean, and the Phoenician influence detectable in various categories of objects over an area including former Soviet Armenia, Mesopotamia, central Italy, the central Mediterranean, Spain, Samos and Crete. The conclusion would then be that the Phoenicians, in order to meet the greatly increased demands laid upon them by the new situation, were forced to increase the scale of their production of goods for exchange (such as unguent-jars and glass amulets) with the inhabitants of the localities which they were trying to exploit (especially in Spain, Sicily and Africa), as well as establishing new centres of production. Their highly developed skills in maritime transport were crucial in effecting this; it also enabled them to link previously quite separate trading spheres – an example being Egyptian commodities reaching Greek centres via Phoenician merchants, who themselves profited from the carrying trade.

This elegant and economical hypothesis for understanding the impressive

Phoenician commercial development makes it possible to set it within the context of important political changes in the Near East, and to see Phoenician expansion as directly linked to Neo-Assyrian imperial growth. At the same time it is important to stress two points. First, Phoenician 'colonialism' represented an intensification of earlier commercial activities, stimulated by the recasting of mercantile circuits as a result of Neo-Assyrian political developments (Salles 1991b; 1994) – it was not a total novelty, as some of the early settlements show (tenth-century Kommos). Second, the designation 'Phoenician', in connection with these great manufacturing and trading enterprises, is not limited in any clear cultural sense to the coastal strip of the Levant traditionally called 'Phoenicia'. Phoenician was used at times to write royal texts (including quite long ones) by the dynasts of the small Taurus states, whose personal names (and those of their dynasties) are Anatolian or Aramaic (p. 405). Conversely, some inscriptions found at 'Phoenician' sites abroad may be in Aramaic, not Phoenician (Morris 1992: 126 and n. 104). This suggests that in many contexts where the Greeks used the term 'Phoenicians', they were not making a careful linguistic and cultural statement about the people they came into contact with; rather they attached an ethnic label to a specific kind of activity, in which Phoenicians were certainly prominent, but not the only, players. In many ways, in the Greek perspective, 'Phoenicians' are simply 'eastern merchants'. As a result, our own image of 'Phoenician traders' is generally applicable to the enterprises of all the Levantine states, which developed into important manufacturing and commercial centres in the early Iron Age (Frankenstein 1979: 288; Morris 1992).

(ii) The Neo-Hittite states

Definition and location

'Neo-Hittite' (alternatively 'Late Hittite' or 'Syro-Hittite') is the term applied, after 1200, to a number of small principalities in north Syria, Cilicia and south-central Anatolia. Despite cultural and linguistic similarities, they were not politically united with each other. Scholars use the word 'Hittite' to describe them because, having formed part of the earlier Hittite empire, they retained a number of definable Hittite features. First, they all employ a recognisably Hittite style of sculpture, reflected in details of carving techniques, typical architectural decoration (such as gateway figures), the iconographic repertoire, and the use of relief-carved orthostats, i.e. stone slabs used to decorate walls (Akurgal 1962; Orthmann 1971; Genge 1979). Second, the names of the rulers are often typical of Hittite Anatolia (e.g. Muwatalis of Gurgum); others use the Hurrian names also current in the Hittite empire (e.g. Initeshub of Carchemish, chapter 6b). Third, the script used for public inscriptions in these states is a direct development of the Hittite hieroglyphs used for monumental inscriptions in the late Hittite empire (see chapter 5b), as well as on royal seals. The language rendered by the hieroglyphic script is not Hittite itself, for which cuneiform was always used (see chapter 5b), but Luwian – the language of a substantial part of the population in Hittite Anatolia. But we should not make the mistake of, therefore, assuming that the Neo-Hittite states were inhabited by ethnic Luwians. The names included, as we have noted, Hurrian and Hattian ones, while in some states kings have Aramaean names. We are probably right in assuming that the ethnic mix of the area was as variegated as earlier, including Canaanites, Aramaeans, Hurrians, Hittites and Luwians. The Neo-Hittite states represent a development of some of the Hittite administrative centres which, following the collapse of the Hittite central government, continued to survive as a series of separate petty kingdoms.

There is no evidence from the Neo-Hittite centres that they saw themselves as sharing any particular identity of political interest and culture. But the various references in Assyrian annals, which call the north Syrian region 'Hatti and Aram', seem to reflect an awareness of the distinction in Syria between Hittite-related and Aramaean states. The Assyrian designation can be rather vague: 'Hatti' is at times used to describe the west in a general sense, including Aramaean and Phoenician states in its sweep; while, at other times, it simply implies the northern Levant as opposed to the south (*RLA* 4: 152–159). It is, however, significant that any part of Syria should have been called 'Hatti' at all. It suggests recognition, in some sense, of continuity from the period of Hittite imperial domination. Particularly striking is the fact that Carchemish is occasionally singled out as 'Hatti', which surely reflects the fact that Carchemish had been the main centre of Hittite administration in Syria. It was governed by a line of viceroys, descended from Suppiluliuma I (1370–1330 (1344–1322)), who were regularly called the 'kings of Carchemish' (chapter 5e). Had there been any lingering doubts about the direct link of these small states with the great Hittite realm, they have now been effectively dispelled by the find of a seal of Kuzi-Teshub, 'Great King' of Carchemish, just after the end of the Hittite empire: he was the direct descendant of the imperial Carchemish kings and the Hittite royal family, and predecessor of the later rulers of Carchemish (Hawkins 1988; in press).

Which were the Neo-Hittite states and where were they located (see map 13)? This has been clarified in a series of systematic studies by Hawkins (most recently *CAH* III, ch. 9, and Hawkins in press, where the material is pulled together). The great site of Carchemish, located on the modern Turkish–Syrian border, has been partly excavated, revealing the elaborate carving which decorated the walls and gates, the buildings and defences of the citadel and inner town (fig. 28). Its prominence was partly determined by its strategic position controlling the Euphrates crossing (Hogarth, Woolley, Barnett 1914–52; Mallowan 1972; Hawkins 1980: 426–446; Winter 1983). Hamath, located at modern Hama on the Orontes, has also been excavated (Riis and Buhl 1990). It was the capital city of a kingdom with the same name. Early on, it incorporated Luhuti-Hatarikka as a northern province, and later controlled the northern Phoenician coastal strip from Latakiye to the mouth of the Nahr el-Kebir. It had a number of rulers with Aramaic names and is the source of several Aramaic inscriptions (*RLA* 4: 67–70). Another centre was Unqi-Pattin(a),[4] which covered the Amuq plain and lower Orontes, and dominated the pass to the sea. Its capital was Kinalua/Kullania, possibly identical with the modern site of Tell Tayanat, where a palace and temple have been excavated (Haines 1971). Another site, that was perhaps also part of Pattin(a),

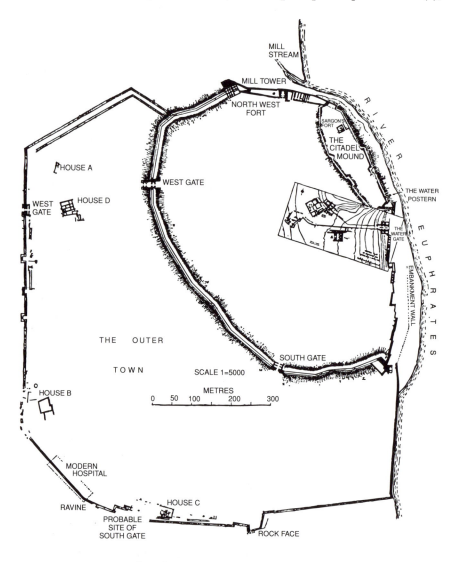

Figure 28 Plan of Carchemish (after Hogarth *et al.* 1914–52)

is modern 'Ain Dara (40 km north-west of Aleppo; Abou Assaf 1985) where a temple with sculpted stonework has been excavated.

Sam'al (modern Zincirli in south Turkey) was capital of a state of the same name; the state was also known as Y'DY (vocalisation uncertain). Although counted as Neo-Hittite, its inscriptions are in fact predominantly Aramaic, yet several of its kings have Anatolian names (and note that the technique of carving the inscriptions with the characters in relief is Neo-Hittite). It was located north of Unqi and south of Gurgum, at the foot of the eastern flank of the Amanus range. The magnificent circular fortified site of Zincirli has been excavated; the smaller site of Yeşemek formed part of the state's territory (Orthmann 1971: 191). The principality Gurgum lay to the north of Sam'al and west of Kummuh, in an angle formed by the Amanus and Taurus ranges. Its capital was Marqas (modern Maraş), which has not as yet been excavated. Kummuh, the later classical Commagene, lay east of Sam'al, north of Carchemish, and south of Melid (modern Malatya), controlling and occupying a significant stretch along the west bank of the Euphrates. Its capital was almost certainly Samsat, which is only now being investigated archaeologically by a Turkish team. Melid (Meliddu), classical Melitene, to the north of Kummuh, lay across the Euphrates from the frontier with Urartu. It controlled the north-eastern passes through the Taurus and the small, poorly known Taurus country of Til-garimmu. Its capital, Melid (at Arslan Tepe, near modern Malatya), has been excavated, revealing a series of (probably early) Neo-Hittite reliefs (Delaporte 1940; Orthmann 1971: 205). Another excavated site in Melid is Karahüyük-Elbistan, the source of a very early Hittite hieroglyphic inscription.

Cilicia was divided into Que (classical Cilicia Campestris) and Hilakku (classical Cilicia Aspera). The political situation here is often difficult to understand. Adana, in the Cilician plain (unexcavated), was obviously an important centre, sometimes dominating the numerous smaller dynasts, such as Azitawada who built, in a wonderful hilltop setting, a city at Karatepe (in the Taurus, above the Ceyhan valley). The founding of Karatepe was commemorated by a long Hittite hieroglyphic inscription with a parallel Phoenician text, accompanied by lively reliefs (see fig. 27 and pp. 414–415; Winter 1979; Hawkins 1979; Hawkins and Mopurgo Davies 1978). Karatepe should probably be identified as part of the small kingdom of Kundu and Sissu; Sissu has now been related by Bing (1991: 165) to classical Issos, site of Alexander's famous battle in 333. 'Tabal' was the general designation of the south-eastern corner of the Anatolian plateau (classical Cappadocia). It was fragmented into a number of small states that were partly united into the principality of Bit Burutash, which covered the area of modern Kayseri and Nevşehir. Its capital may well have been the modern village of Kululu, and it included the principality Tuwana (classical Tyana) centred on modern Niğde. Tuwana, located at the strategic northern end of the Cilician Gates, became independent later.

Sources for political and social conditions

The social and economic structures and the political details of the Neo-Hittite states have to be painstakingly teased out using widely scattered epigraphic material – often spotted by sheer chance, and sometimes inscribed on remote (and weathered) rock faces (cf., for example, Kalaç and Hawkins 1989). Some lead strips inscribed with Hittite hieroglyphs (Meriggi 1966–75, nos. 34–40 (Ashur); Hawkins 1987 (Kululu)) give us a hint of administrative complexity: they include letters, lists of houses with inhabitants and animals, receipts of sheep, and mention a multitude of settlements. The lead documents show that a considerable amount of written material from the Neo-Hittite states may now be lost. More was probably written on wooden writing boards as illustrated by the stele of Bar-rakib of Sam'al (Roaf 1990 [OA]: 178), in which the scribe facing the king holds a hinged diptych, closely resembling a Late Bronze Age writing board found in the shipwreck off Ulu Burun (Payton 1991; Warnock and Pendleton 1991; Symington 1991). Fortunately, the monumental inscriptions are more informative than the contemporary Phoenician ones. Several texts contain hints of political–dynastic problems (as at Carchemish; Hawkins 1979: 157–160), trace earlier history and refer to members of the royal retinue and queens, although scholars are still some way from writing a history of the Neo-Hittite principalities. The ideals of royal responsibility for justice, for the security and prosperity of the country and its inhabitants, as well as the concept of loyalty towards a suzerain, are perhaps most clearly evoked by Azitawada in his long inscription (in Hittite hieroglyphs and accompanying Phoenician text) at Karatepe (see p. 405; p. 413; see also Hawkins 1986):

> I am Azatiwatas, the Sun-blessed(?) man, Tarhunzas' (Baal in the Phoenician version) servant, whom Awarikus, Adana's king, promoted. Tarhunzas made me mother and father to Adana(wa), and I caused Adana(wa) to prosper, and I extended the Adanawa plain on the one hand towards the west and on the other hand towards the east, and in my days there were to Adanawa all good things, plenty and luxury, and I filled the Paharean storehouses, and I added horse upon horse, and I added army upon army, and I added shield upon shield, all by Tarhunzas and the gods. And I broke up the proud(?), and the evils which were in the land I removed out of the land. And I had my lord's house built in good(ness), and I did all good things for my lord's family, and I caused it/them to sit upon its/their father's throne. [Phoenician only preserved: And I established peace with every king,] and every king made me father to himself because of my justice and my wisdom and my goodness. And I built strong fortresses [. . .] on the frontiers wherein were bad men, robbers, who had not served under Muksas' house, and I, Azatiwatas, put them under my feet, and I built fortresses in those places, so that Adanawa might dwell peacefully. And I smote

strong fortresses towards the west, which former kings had not smitten, who were before me. And I, Azatiwatas, smote them, and I brought them down, and I settled them down towards the east on my frontiers, and I settled Adanaweans down [. . .] there. In my days I extended the Adanawean frontiers on the one hand towards the west and on the other hand towards the east, and in those places which were formerly feared(?), where a man feared to walk the road, in my days even women walked with spindles. In my days there was plenty and luxury and good living, and peacefully dwelt Adanawa and the Adanawean plain. I built this fortress, and gave it the name Azatiwataya, and Tarhunzas and Runzas (Phoenician: 'Resheph-of-the-goats') were after me for this fortress to build (it) (Phoenician: 'sent me to build (it)'). [Phoenician only preserved: And I built it by the grace(?) of Baal and by the grace(?) of Resheph-of-the-goats in plenty and in luxury and in good living and in peace of heart, for it to be a protection for the plain of 'DN and for the house of MPSH, since in my days there was plenty and luxury to the land of the plain of 'DN. And there was never in my days night(?) for the DNNYM. And I built this city, and I established its name 'ZTWDY, and I caused to dwell in it Baal KRNTRYSH], (Hittite hieroglyphic text:) and every libation began to honour him, [. . .] the year an ox, and at the reaping a sheep, and at the vintage a sheep. Let him bless Azatiwatas with life and peace, and let him be made highly pre-eminent over all kings. And may Tarhunzas the highly blessed and the gods of this fortress give to him, to Azatiwatas, long days and many years, and (may) a good old age(?) (be to him), and let them give him all strength over all kings. And let this fortress become (one) of plenty and wine, and the nations that dwell in (it), let them become (those) of sheep and oxen, plenty and wine. For us much let them beget, and much let them make great, and much let them be in service to Azatiwatas and to Muksas' home by Tarhunzas and the gods. If anyone from (among) kings – or (if) he (is) a man, and he has a manly name – proclaims this: 'I shall delete Azatiwatas' name from the gate(s?) and I shall incise my name'; or (if) he is covetous towards this fortress, and blocks up(?) these gates, which Azatiwatas made, and proclaims thus: 'I shall make the gates my own, and I shall incise my name for myself;' or (if) from covetousness he shall block them up(?), or from badness or from evil he shall block up(?) these gates, may Tarhunzas of Heaven, the Sun of Heaven, Ea, and all the gods delete that kingdom and that king and that man! Hereafter may Azatiwatas' name continue to stand for all ages, as the Sun's and the Moon's name stands.

(Hawkins and Morpurgo Davies 1978: 114–118)

The late Hittite states were intimately linked to the other states in the Levant and south Anatolia, as evidenced by the mix of languages and names. But the most striking statement of their cosmopolitanism appears in the inscription of Yariris, one of the nobles (later king) of Carchemish, who claims, not only to know a great many languages, but also to be able to read (? and/or write) four different scripts:

> [. . .] in the script of the City (i.e. Carchemish, and therefore Hittite hieroglyphs), the script of Sura (perhaps Urartian or Phoenician), the script of Assyria (Akkadian cuneiform) and the script of Taiman (possibly Aramaic). I knew twelve languages, and to me my lord gathered the son of every country by (means of) travelling for (the sake of) language, and he caused me to know every wisdom.
>
> (Carchemish A15b4; Hawkins 1975: 150–151)

All the Neo-Hittite states lay along major routes, and controlled important river crossings, passes and ports. Much of the later Assyrian evidence points to the fact that they were commercially wealthy, economically developed and artistically and technically sophisticated. They provided one of the important links between Assyria and Urartu to the east, and Phrygia, Lydia and the Mediterranean littoral to the west. Much of their expertise in craftsmanship, as well as their artistic repertoire, was exploited by their larger neighbours (van Loon 1977; Winter 1983). An echo of it is found in the 'orientalising' phase of archaic Greek art, which developed on the fringes of the Near East during the eighth century (Akurgal 1961; 1966; Helm 1980).

Conclusion

The Levant, south Anatolia and Upper Mesopotamia, in the period between 1100 and 900, formed a mosaic of small states: all were heirs, to a considerable extent and in a variety of ways, to the preceding Canaanite culture and the legacy of the great empires which dominated much of the area between 1400 and at least 1200 (c. 1150 in the southern Levant, c. 1050 in Upper Mesopotamia). They shared a degree of surface similarity in terms of political structure, and were closely linked economically. But the resemblance conceals the many cultural differences between them – in language, script, religion and local historical traditions. In the north, several states were strongly marked by the Hittite imperial heritage, although occasionally this was mingled with an Aramaean presence which, in some places, eventually became the dominant element. In Upper Mesopotamia and further south in Syria, Aramaean states predominated. But along the Lebanese coast some Canaanite cities survived as the Phoenician principalities, who also influenced strongly the island of Cyprus (Morris 1992: 127–9). Along the southern part of the coast of Palestine, the Philistines, probably settled originally as Egyptian garrison troops, controlled the major cities, while inland the state of Israel emerged c. 1000, as did the neighbouring countries of Moab, Ammon and Edom. One ethnic group that was probably *not* present in the Levant in significant numbers at this time was the Greeks. Although some Greek pottery of the tenth and ninth century has been found at sites such as Ras el-Basit, Tell Sukas and, most famously, Al Mina (near the mouth of the Orontes), much of it probably came from Cyprus, and it formed only a relatively small proportion of all the pottery found: local pottery forms predominate and all buildings are of local type. Intensive Greek trade, let alone settlement, here earlier than the end of the eighth century is doubtful (Helm 1980; Muhly 1985; Graham 1986; differently, Courbin 1990).

The precise circumstances leading to the formation of any one of the Levantine states, their specific character and sense of identity all remain obscure and must do so in the absence of fuller sources. But there is one striking exception to this rule: the state of Israel produced a detailed and sophisticated literary account, presenting a dramatic and influential narrative of its formation as a state, which was to become our heritage too, for all time. Israel's unique account provides an example of how one of the small states in the region recounted its birth to itself. The Israelite text and the problems it raises need to be examined next.

8d Israel: the formation of a small Levantine state *c.* 1200–900

8d(i) Introduction

The emergence of the state(s) of Israel can be regarded as an example of the general pattern of demographic change and population shifts discernible in the Levant. A link between this broader pattern, shadowy as it is, and the early Israelites is acknowledged, however vaguely, in later Israelite history by the description of the patriarch Jacob as a 'wandering Aramaean' (*Deuteronomy* 26:5). The Israelites were the one group involved in this profound · transformation who preserved an account of how their state(s) had come into being. They thus provide an unrivalled insight into how one of the peoples of the area came to visualise this important formative period. At the same time, the text which contains their narrative – i.e. the Old Testament – is extremely difficult to use as a straightforward historical source. Like many · accounts of the past, it was not intended to provide a critical historical study; rather, it contained stories detailing the interaction of a people, Israel, with their god, Yahweh, who had chosen them to work out his divine plan. It is a complex, ideologically motivated compilation, within which stories were refashioned to drive home particular lessons of the past (Garbini 1986).

Before examining some of the critical approaches to the Old Testament used by scholars, it will be useful to outline briefly the main phases into which Israelite history found in the Old Testament is traditionally divided. These phases represent important markers of what was believed to be the shared historical experience of Yahweh's people. The creation, early humankind and the flood affected everyone 'worldwide'; of particular importance to the Israelites was the succeeding period of the Patriarchs – the wise and pious heads of families, such as Abraham, who moved with their clans around virtually the whole of the Near East and from whom all Israelites later believed they were directly descended. The patriarchal stories associate them with Babylonia, Upper Mesopotamia, Palestine and Egypt. The story of Joseph, Abraham's great-grandson, brought all of Israel into Egypt (known as the 'Sojourn'), where it eventually suffered oppression by Pharaoh, who forced the Israelites to work on building his royal cities of Pithom and Raamses. They were delivered from the oppression by Moses at Yahweh's command, and left Egypt in a body pursued unsuccessfully by Egyptian forces: this is the famous Exodus. Israel's epic escape was followed by forty years (i.e. one generation) during which the Israelites dwelt in the Sinai desert (the 'Wanderings'). During this phase, Moses received the Ten Commandments, which formed part of the Covenant that Yahweh set up with his people. The period of 'Wanderings' was ended by their arrival in, and conquest of, the Promised Land, led now by a new, warrior hero, Joshua. After the conquest, the Israelite tribes settled the land; in the course of that process they came into conflict with neighbours on all sides: Ammonites, Amalekites, Philistines, Canaanites. Their lengthy struggle to survive is the period of the Judges – important leaders raised up by Yahweh to deliver his people when threatened. The time of the Judges was ended by the appointment of Saul as king to face the great threat of the Philistines. For about one hundred years all Israel was ruled by three kings in succession: Saul, David and Solomon, who built the Temple in Jerusalem (the 'United Monarchy'). At the end of that period Israel broke apart (the 'Schism'), and formed henceforth two states: the northern kingdom of Israel, with its capital eventually at Samaria, and the southern kingdom of Judah, with the capital at Jerusalem (the 'Divided Monarchy'). In 721, Samaria fell after a siege to Shalmaneser V of Assyria; this spelt the end of the northern kingdom, with its inhabitants deported and people brought from elsewhere to settle what was now an Assyrian province under an Assyrian governor. Judah continued as an independent state, but fell, after a series of revolts, to the Babylonian king, Nebuchadnezzar II (604–562), who destroyed the Jerusalem temple, took away the cultic vessels, and deported the king of Judah and his entourage to Babylon – the (Babylonian) 'Exile'. This major disaster had its climax in 587, and marks a turning-point in Jewish history. But the time of exile did not last long, since Cyrus the Great of Persia, after his conquest of Babylon in 539, decreed that the Israelite exiles should return and rebuild the Jerusalem temple. This is known as the 'Restoration' and ushers in the time of the 'Second Temple', eventually destroyed by the Roman emperor Titus in AD 70, never to be rebuilt.

The Old Testament canon as it now exists was closed in the second century. But the two latest works, Daniel and Esther, although written in the second century, are set back in the sixth and fifth centuries. The impression therefore given by this great compendium of wisdom, poetry, prophecy, law and history is that it was completed some time in the period of the Persian empire (550–330). This is how the work has been read traditionally, i.e. as a compilation of texts (historical, literary, prophetic) dating from the pre-exilic period and the time of the Restoration when the foundations of Judaism were laid and definitively formed for all time. The powerful manner in which the historical experience of the Israelites has been structured within the Old Testament has imposed a framework from which it is hard for modern historians to free themselves.

The Old Testament

The Old Testament is obviously central to any study of the emergence of Israel, so it is important to consider briefly what it contains and the dominant approaches to the problems of authorship (for a succinct exposition of the classical scholarly position, see Rowley 1967). It consists of · several very different works: first, the Law ('Torah'), more generally now called the Pentateuch, divided (later) into the books of *Genesis, Exodus, Leviticus, Numbers* and *Deuteronomy*, which contains an account of Israel's origins; secondly, the Former Prophets, embracing the narrative books of *Joshua, Judges,* 1 and 2 *Samuel*, and 1 and 2 *Kings*, which continues Israelite history from the Settlement to the destruction of the Jerusalem temple and the Babylonian Exile in 587. Then there are the Latter Prophets, a collection of the visions, prophetic poems and stories of famous Yahweh prophets – traditionally understood as utterances made in their lifetime; and, finally, the Writings, which include the three poetic books of *Psalms, Proverbs* and *Job*, the liturgical and wisdom works ('Five Rolls') of *Canticles, Ruth, Lamentations, Ecclesiastes* and *Esther*, as well as *Daniel, Ezra, Nehemiah* and *Chronicles*. The last three form a more or less coherent work retracing Israel's history from the Patriarchs (in summary fashion) down to the fifth century. It presupposes the existence of some of the narrative books (*Samuel* and *Kings*). Generally speaking, the language of the Old Testament is Hebrew, but there are exceptions in late books such as *Ezra* and *Daniel*, where passages appear in Aramaic. Within this vast body of material, the most crucial for the purposes of this chapter are the first two, the Pentateuch and the historical books.

The Pentateuch begins with the creation of the world and humankind, but rapidly narrows its focus to the story of Jacob's family and their move into Egypt (*Genesis*). *Exodus* contains Moses' birth-story, the Israelite Exodus from Egypt under his leadership and the divine revelation which he received on Mount Sinai ('The Ten Commandments': *Exodus* 20), followed by a corpus of law and description of cultic items such as the ark. It is in this book that Yahweh's initial covenant with Israel is formulated (*Exodus* 19.5–6) – the agreement that in return for Israel's obedience it would come under Yahweh's protection, his power having been already demonstrated by Israel's unscathed escape from Egypt. *Leviticus* continues with regulations governing the religious practices of Israel. Only in *Numbers* is the historical survey resumed and the story of the wanderings through the wilderness and conquest of Transjordan completed. *Deuteronomy* begins with a historical retrospect by Moses at the conclusion of the 'Wanderings' period, followed by a code of laws partly repeating, partly modifying some of the legislative material in earlier books, and then an account of the death of Moses.

The authorship of this great mass of material was traditionally ascribed to Moses, but doubts about this have been expressed for centuries (see generally Rowley 1967; Weitzman 1978). The Pentateuch bristles with anachronisms, duplication (even triplication) of incidents, internal disagreements in stories (there are two different accounts of the creation), and mutually contradictory laws. Even more striking are what seem like fundamental disagreements about when the Israelites first gained knowledge of Yahweh: in *Exodus* 6.2–3, for example, Yahweh tells Moses that the patriarchs 'did not know me as Yahweh' but as 'almighty god', when *Genesis* 4.1 has Eve quite clearly speaking the name of Yahweh. More subtle, but nevertheless marked, is the distinction in the manner in which Yahweh is conceived, which emerges particularly well in the first and second creation stories – in the first he is presented as a being of transcendent dignity and power, in the second as a superior man with human feelings. Finally, there are very clear stylistic differences throughout the Pentateuch. *Deuteronomy* is written in a distinctive rhetorical style not found elsewhere, while scattered throughout *Genesis* and *Numbers* are at least two distinguishable styles: one is rather dry and formal, the other that of the storyteller.

It was noticed a considerable time ago (in the eighteenth century) that the different literary styles provided a key for distinguishing different 'documents' that had been combined to create this, the most important and authoritative, section of the Old Testament. *Deuteronomy* was obviously one such coherent work, but defining the others was harder. However, it has been demonstrated, and on the whole accepted, that the exalted conception of Yahweh, and the use of his name only from Moses on, was associated with the dry, formal literary style, while the simple narrative style called him Yahweh from the beginning of the world and presented him in rather human terms. This basic distinction does not, however, account for all doublets, and yet another, fourth work has been supposed to have existed originally. This, it is generally assumed, also used a storytelling style, but can be differentiated from the previous one by the fact that it, too, only uses the name Yahweh after his revelation to Moses; another feature is that it focuses strongly on dreams and angels. While this all sounds and, indeed, is very complicated, it does help to make sense of the manifold strands of the Pentateuchal narrative; the stylistic differences are much more striking in Hebrew than in translation, although attentive reading can even then bring them out in translation. The analysis must, however, remain hypothetical as long as we have no ancient manuscript of one or other 'source'.

In the absence of named 'authors', has it proved possible to define the hypothetical 'documents' or 'sources' more closely and (very important) to date them? Agreement about the former is rather greater than the latter. The simple narrative style, which refers to Yahweh by name from the creation on, focuses strongly on the south of Israel, i.e. Judah, in several stories; because it uses the name Yahweh throughout (originally vocalised 'Jehovah'), it is known as 'J' = 'the Yahwist'. The other 'storyteller' calls Israel's god 'Elohim' before the revelation to Moses and seems to have a particular interest in the north (Ephraim); it is, therefore, known as 'E' = 'the Elohist'; the E story does not seem to begin before Abraham the patriarch. A shared feature of J and E is that they do not depict priests as necessary to cult; this, and other similarities, can make it problematic to disentangle J and E, so that scholars are forced at times to compromise and talk about 'JE' (this is true, for example, of the so-called 'Book of the Covenant' (*Exodus* 20.22–22.33)). The style of *Deuteronomy*, limited to that book, is simply called 'D'; specific characteristics of the document are that it limits sacrifice to one legitimate sanctuary, gives custody of all ritual to the tribe of Levi, and propounds strongly a fundamental message (also found in *Exodus*): if Israel remains faithful and pure in its adherence to Yahweh and the covenant, then it will prosper; if it turns away from this path, disaster will inevitably ensue. The dry, formal style which presents a very exalted view of Yahweh and does not call him by that name until the Mosaic revelation, is thought to have emanated from a priestly group. It contains the bulk of the regulations for the sacrificial cult, never describes sacrifices before the time of Moses and Aaron, and contains detailed ordering for the priesthood: for example, according to this document only the descendants of Aaron may perform sacrifices, while other Levites are to carry out more menial tasks in relation to the cult. Not surprisingly, therefore, this source is known as 'P' = the 'Priestly Code'. This definition of the sources of the Pentateuch, while not commanding the complete agreement of every scholar with every detail, is widely accepted in its broad outlines. It has dominated Old Testament scholarship for at least the last hundred and fifty years, and is usually known as the 'critical orthodoxy', which neatly describes the scholarly stance of general agreement about critical analysis of the traditional text.

The most important work on the relative dating of the sources was that of Graf (1866) as developed influentially by Wellhausen (1883) – hence it is known as the 'Graf–Wellhausen hypothesis' (alternatively 'documentary hypothesis'). Graf and Wellhausen demonstrated, basically, that D displayed knowledge of historical and legal material contained in J and E, but not in P where P differs. Further, the variety of sacrificial practices and sanctuaries described by J and E, are totally absent in D and P. This resulted in a relative chronological ordering of the sources, as JE, D, P (in contrast to previous views where P had been thought to be the earliest). In order to arrive at some kind of dates for the 'documents', it was argued that, as D seemed to reflect the existence of a code laying down correct ritual practice, 'external' evidence for its compilation should be sought. The one reference to the existence of such a work is 2 *Kings* 22, where it is stated that when Josiah, king of Judah, planned to reform temple worship and associated cult-practices in 621 the priest Hilkiah found a lawbook in the temple during repairs. This 'lawbook' – which is argued to be, in essence, D – formed the cornerstone of Josiah's reforms. The argument continues that the story of 'finding' a hidden lawbook served to make it appear to be an ancient manuscript and hence particularly authoritative, but that the story conceals the fact that it was actually composed precisely to fulfil this function. The result of this hypothesis is to date D to the late seventh century. By implication P is later, and a number of factors make it likely that P was composed in the post-exilic period, perhaps the late fifth or early fourth century. Conversely, because D displays knowledge of both J and E, they must be earlier, and it is possible that they had been combined into one document already at the time of the fall of the northern kingdom of Israel in 721. Dating either J or E more precisely is very difficult: the standard assumption is that, as J is more 'primitive' in literary style than E, it must be older – a date somewhere in the ninth or even the tenth century, is envisaged by some, but remains vague.[5] The arguments concerning the dates of J and E are not very firmly founded. They seemed reasonable in the late nineteenth century when theories of social evolution influenced ideas about literary and religious development. More recently, some scholars picking up on this inadequate explanation, have argued that J was contemporary with D, and the differences in style are related to the function of the texts (Rendtorff 1983). This is very attractive, and exemplifies how unsatisfactory some aspects of the Graf–Wellhausen hypothesis are now felt to be. One scholar has even suggested that J be dated to the post-exilic period (van Seters 1983 [OK]). But we should note that, however uncomfortable contemporary scholars feel with the dating of the documents, or even their order, no alternative analysis has yet been proposed that commands anything like general agreement.

The implications of the 'documentary hypothesis' and its very wide acceptance are immense in terms of how the Old Testament may be used as a historical source, especially with respect to Israel's history before the monarchy and its emergence as a state. It becomes immediately obvious that none of the material, as it now exists, can be dated before the ninth century at best, perhaps even later. This does not, of course, preclude the possibility, even likelihood, that certain sections existed in some form already before then: the Decalogue (i.e. Ten Commandments), for example, is generally agreed to be a very old text; similarly, the 'Song of Deborah' (*Judges* 5) is widely regarded as extremely archaic, and predating the monarchy. But, even if one argues for such kernels of antiquity, the compiling and editing of the material to integrate it into a new work would have resulted in reshaping such early texts to fit specific interests and carry particular messages. It then becomes very hard to know how far anything of what the later compilers presented as past events might actually reflect real historical occurrences. It is this question that has caused deep divisions among scholars, based on different approaches taken to the Old Testament text.

The implications of biblical criticism for Israel's early history

One group of scholars (Albright 1939; Bright 1959; Wright 1962 – with reservations de Vaux 1978, vol. 2 – to name some of the most prominent) argues that archaeological excavations in Palestine and the Near East have revealed, and will continue to reveal, both artefactual and textual evidence that confirms the fundamental historicity of the Old Testament account of Israel's beginnings. The problem with their position is that, while the kind of evidence that has come to light can illuminate, for example, the patterns of pastoral life described in connection with famous Old Testament figures such as Abraham, Isaac and Jacob, they are not chronologically specific, but range in time from *c.* 2000 to *c.* 1400. In other words, this valuable material (particularly the finds at Mari (chapter 2d) and Nuzi (chapter 6a)) does not help to fix the 'time of the patriarchs' in any precise way – it merely provides a broad picture of a mode of existence which, there is every reason to suppose, was present in the Near East in both earlier and later periods. So the historicity of the patriarchal figures remains unconfirmed, while the social and cultural context of the kind of life they are described as leading has been greatly amplified and the picture presented of it in the Old Testament shown to be an accurate reflection of pastoral life *in general*. It goes without saying that, for adherents of the idea that archaeology can confirm the historical truth of the Bible, the destruction of sites in Palestine around 1200 is seen as crucial confirmation of the reality of Israel's conquest and settlement of the Promised Land.

Other scholars have used a radically different approach to the early history of Israel. Although they hold a range of different views and pursue varying analyses, all of them are agreed that the Old Testament is a complex religious, literary work and that it is, therefore, pointless to try to extract a precise course of historical events from it for the period before the time of the monarchy, when Israel becomes a historically definable entity. What it does preserve, they argue, are selected traditions and legends which came to be crucial to how the Israelites themselves viewed their early history and constructed it. All the well-known Old Testament 'higher critics' fall into this category (Wellhausen 1883; Alt 1925/1966; Noth 1958 Eissfeldt 1965; Koch 1969; von Rad 1975; Rendtdorff 1983; Lemche 1985).

An influential and stimulating approach (to select just one) has been that of von Rad. He has argued that the Pentateuch was essentially the literary elaboration of what were originally a series of short, credo-like recitations of early Israelite history, developed in the framework of cult practices of the time of the Judges. Von Rad's idea was supported by Noth, who suggested that it helps to explain the rather limited number of themes prominent in the Pentateuch. They are: Primeval History, the Patriarchs, Exodus, the Sinai Revelation and Wilderness Wanderings. These themes served to drive home the strong, reiterated belief that Yahweh had worked through history to save his people, and so they served to consolidate belief in his future efficacy, provided that his people remained faithful to him. An important divergence between von Rad and Noth is the views they hold on the place of the book of *Joshua* within this scheme: von Rad argued that *Joshua*, too, was in origin a simple statement of belief that Israel had conquered the Promised Land; by implication, then, it forms part and parcel of the Pentateuch, which thus needs to be expanded into a 'hexateuch'. Noth, in contrast, has argued that *Joshua* is a historical book, comparable to *Judges*, and forms a unit with it, 1 and 2 *Samuel*, and 1 and 2 *Kings*. These books have been cast into their present form by the 'Deuteronomistic historian', an editor/compiler (or several? – for the view that it is the historical work of a single creative individual, see van Seters 1983 [OK]) strongly influenced by the theological and moral message of D (see p. 421). Noth would still deny that *Joshua* provides anything approximating to historical 'fact'; but he *would* argue that it is a collection of foundation legends and aetiological sagas closely linked to Israel's formation, and so less remote and ahistorical than the Pentateuch.

This has been of necessity a highly selective and oversimplified presentation of how those parts of the Old Testament most closely linked to the question of Israel's emergence as a state have been analysed by a couple of scholars. But the main implications of the approach used by the 'higher critics' for studying the thorny question of the Israelite settlement should be clear: that the history proper of Israel begins only when the Israelites are already settled in Palestine, the tribes located in their particular regions and the process of state-formation is in progress as a result of their conflict with Ammonites, Moabites, Edomites, Philistines and Canaanites. The story of the Sojourn in Egypt, the Exodus, Wilderness Wanderings, and the Settlement/Conquest itself would, therefore, simply be part of an expression of belief in Yahweh's promise and fulfilment, but in no sense historically recoverable or definable. As such scholars reject the historicity of Exodus and Wanderings, and the Conquest of Israel as described in *Joshua*, the archaeological evidence in Palestine around 1200 (the conventional date of the settlement, see p. 425) is not considered directly relevant, but to be explained by a multiplicity of events.

8d(ii) The problem of the Israelite settlement

Defining the problem

Whatever the virtues or faults of the different schools of thought, the historian is still left with the task of trying to explain a definitely discernible change in

Palestine between c. 1200 and c. 1000. Before 1200, texts and sites show the region divided among a number of fairly developed city-states with kings subject to Egypt, and with a number of Egyptian imperial control-points at Gaza, Jaffa, Beth Shean and Aphek. By c. 1000, this political pattern had changed: most coastal sites were inhabited by Philistines, whose arrival is generally thought to be connected with the Egyptian policy of settling them as garrisons in Egyptian strong-points (see chapter 8a); a new state, Israel, had also come into existence, inhabited by a people who do not appear to have been there earlier. The only information the historian has to explain this change is the Old Testament account of *Joshua*, which states that it is connected with . the Israelite entry into the Promised Land. *Joshua* reports that twelve Israelite tribes, all descended from Jacob, entered the region together, and, by military means, seized the country and settled it. A definite date for this event seems to be given by 1 *Kings* 6.1. Here the exodus from Egypt is said to have happened four hundred and eighty years before the building of the temple in Jerusalem. The temple was constructed in approximately 950, which thus dates the exodus c. 1430. This date is regarded as problematic, because it would coincide with a time when Egypt was very stable, and Egyptian control of the Levant firm (chapter 6e). It seems unlikely, therefore, that a mass exodus of Israelites would have been possible, and their entry into Canaan, in the manner described in *Joshua*, is unlikely to have been successful. Further, in the account of the Sojourn in Egypt, the Israelites are said to have been particularly oppressed when engaged in building two important royal cities, Pithom and Raamses. The latter is certainly to be equated with the new royal centre of Per-Ramesses founded by Ramesses II (chapter 4d), and as he did not come to the throne until 1290 (1279) the Exodus must be dated after that. ·

A way out of the conundrum is to say that, as the date does not fit the historical situation, it needs to be adjusted. Moreover, it is possible to do this, without doing violence to the evidence of 1 *Kings* 6, by assuming that the number 'four hundred and eighty' is based on a generation-count. One generation was conventionally counted as forty years, so the sum reflects twelve generations of forty years each. But, as it is far more realistic to assume that a generation in the pre-modern world could only have been twenty-five years, the number can be reduced to three hundred years (i.e. twelve times twenty-five). The adjustment produces a date of c. 1250 for the exodus, and that fits quite neatly, because in the 'Israel' stele of Merneptah, Ramesses II's successor, there is a reference to 'Israel' (*Y-s-y-r-y-3-r*) as a people (the determinative for 'people' not 'place' is used) present in the area of Palestine. This would allow the Israelites to have fled from Ramesses II, wandered in the wilderness for forty years (or perhaps only twenty-five on the same argument), and to have arrived in Palestine in time to be encountered by Merneptah's troops (see Malamat in Bottéro *et al.* 1966 [OB]: 206).

The 'date of the exodus' illustrates nicely how even something that seems to be a fairly straightforward piece of chronological information actually bristles with problems. The situation, looked at critically, is that there is no clear date in the Old Testament for the entry into Canaan; the date that is given has to be forcibly manipulated to fit 'the facts'. The reference to Israel, contained within the poetic coda ending the triumphant account of Merneptah's Libyan war, is totally vague – it gives no precise information as to where Israel was (except that it was somewhere in Palestine), nor does it connect it with any original residence in Egypt:

> The princes are prostrate saying: 'Shalom!'
> Not one of the Nine Bows lifts his head:
> Tjehenu is vanquished, Hatti at peace,
> Canaan is captive with all woe.
> Ashkelon is conquered, Gezer seized,
> Yanoam made nonexistent;
> Israel is wasted, bare of seed,
> Hor is become a widow for Egypt.
> All who roamed have been subdued
> By the King of Upper and Lower Egypt, Banere-meramun,
> Son of Re, Merneptah, Content with Ma'at,
> Given life like Re every day.
> (K. Kitchen, *Ramesside Inscriptions* (1968–) IV 12–19;
> *ARE* III §§602–617; Erman 1927/1966 [OI]: 274–278;
> *ANET*: 376–378; Lichtheim 1973–1980 [OI] II: 77;
> *TUAT* I: 544–552)

It has been argued that the poem reflects a typical literary 'ring-structure', so that the line mentioning Israel would balance the Canaan line. The implication would be that Israel is a term describing a part of Canaan more closely. The suggestion is that 'Canaan' is being used broadly to describe western Palestine, while 'Israel' describes the eastern hills; i.e., they are supplementary geographical terms defining the sweep of the region within which Merneptah had captured the three cities of Ashkelon, Gezer and Yanoam. This would mean that Israel was merely a term for a part of Palestine, and one that could have been adopted by settlers there to define themselves. Such an argument cancels out the significance traditionally assigned to the Merneptah stele: it does not reflect the arrival of Israelites in Palestine, it simply points to the existence of a place called 'Israel' in the Palestinian hill-country (Ahlström and Edelman 1985; Ahlström 1986: 37–43). It is an interesting interpretation, although controversial (Rainey 1991; Yurco 1991). But whatever view we take of the 'Israel stele', its reference to Israel *is* vague.

Another basic difficulty is that a closer look at the twelve tribes of Israel reveals that in fact there are more (see table 26): the tribe of Joseph is represented by five large subdvisions (Manasseh, Ephraim, Machir, Jair, Nobah); Caleb and Othniel are not part of the twelve tribes at all, although they participated in the settlement; while Levi, definitely considered to be one of the twelve, has no territory. This leaves one with the impression that the notion of twelve tribes, descended from the twelve sons of Jacob, is an artificial creation, which was perhaps constructed at a much later date to bind the various peoples included in the state of Israel together, in order to link them all to the same early history, and derive them all from Abraham and Jacob.

Table 26 The 'twelve tribes' of Israel

Sons of Jacob/Israel:			
a) by Leah	1 Reuben 2 Simeon 3 Levi* 4 Judah 5 Issachar 6 Zebulun	b) by Rachel	7 Joseph (subdivided into 5: Manasseh, Ephraim, Machir, Jair, Nobah)** 8 Benjamin
c) by Leah's handmaid Bilhah	9 Dan 10 Naphtali	d) by Rachel's handmaid Zilpah	11 Gad 12 Asher

* Levi tribe received no tribal territory for itself, but shared in everyone else's.
** Joseph has no tribal territory as such; the territory occupied by its divisions is reconstructed as belonging to the Joseph tribe.

Additional groups

Caleb, the Kenizzite, was allowed to have the area of Hebron for services rendered to the tribes during the 'Wanderings'.

Othniel, Caleb's nephew, was given Kiriath-sepher by Caleb because he captured it.

Apart from the problems raised by such basic information, the detailed account of conquest and settlement presented in *Joshua* and *Judges* 1 raises yet more. *Joshua* 1–12 sets out to show that all the tribes entered Canaan from east of the Jordan as a unified group, and by a series of sieges and set battles victoriously seized the country through their united efforts. On completion they divided the conquered territory among themselves.

Virtually everyone, whatever position they take *vis-à-vis* the biblical text, rejects this version of events and agrees that it is an idealised and over-simplified picture of a complex and long-drawn-out process. But scholars disagree about the extent to which it is unrealistic or simply ahistorical. Given the fundamentally different approaches to the early history of Israel, and the varying attitudes to the reliability of the biblical text, such agreement is striking. But if we look at *Joshua* and *Judges* 1, the inescapable conclusion imposes itself very rapidly that a number of different traditions have been combined which are mutually contradictory and need to be separated out. For example, *Joshua* 1–12 by no means describes the settlement of the whole land, but presents very selective incidents only. Further, of the setting up of an altar on Mount Ebal (*Joshua* 8.30), the territory conquered is geographically limited to the Benjamin tribal area; only at 10.28 does the geographical scope widen. Even then it only recounts the conquest of cities and regions in the southern hill country (e.g. Lachish, Hebron, Debir: 10.28–43), except for one foray into the north (11.1–15), where the capture of Hazor is described. The story, in fact, gives an extremely patchy picture of the settlement, and suggests that a number of localised, albeit dramatic, incidents have been strung together. The fact that this does not account for the conquest is, moreover, shown by the subsequent chapters of *Joshua* (13–22), where the tribes are assigned their territory; but not, it emerges, for settlement but for conquest, which flatly contradicts the earlier description. Finally, *Judges* 1, which depicts the situation following Joshua's death, provides a quite different image of the land-settlement as one achieved piecemeal by individual tribal efforts after the conquest hero's death – not a series of united military attacks under his leadership. It also lists important Canaanite cities (Taanach, Megiddo, Bethel, Gezer) which again had not been conquered as yet. So it is not surprising that even the most fervent advocate of the integrity and essential truthfulness of the biblical text feels that some kind of explanation is necessary.

The reasons suggested to explain the lack of compatibility in the narratives are various; but all emphasise the idea that *Joshua* 1–12 must be the result of a long and complicated transmission history, including a range of different types of story. Some, it is argued, could reflect real historical events. The chief example of such a possibly historical incident is the curious story of Joshua's covenant with the people of Gibeon (*Joshua* 9). The Gibeonites cunningly tricked Joshua into swearing an oath not to harm them by pretending to have come from very far away and being bent on worshipping the Israelite Yahweh. When Joshua discovered the deceit, he laid upon them the duty of chopping wood and drawing water for Yahweh's cult in return for his continued protection. This is followed by a statement that recurs frequently throughout *Joshua*: 'and so it is unto this day'. Why is this anecdote accepted as reflecting a real event? At 2 *Samuel* 21.1–14, the reason for a serious famine in David's reign is attributed to the fact that Saul had broken the covenant and murdered some Gibeonites. But, while *Joshua* 9 and 2 *Samuel* 21 provide one possible explanation, it is by no means the only one, and cannot really prove that the Joshua–Gibeon episode was historical fact. It is also the *only* example of a conquest story surfacing again later. In order to demonstrate a genuine historical kernel for the narrative of *Joshua* 1–12, we would want several such incidents that provide a direct link with later history. Other stories can be argued to have originated in later cult-practices – that is, they were developed to explain the sanctity of certain sites, such as Gilgal, which was identified with the setting up of Joshua's camp after the successful crossing of the Jordan, an event supposedly marked by the setting up of twelve stones.

Yet other tales are thought to be entirely aetiological in their function. The most famous example is the story of the taking of 'Ai (*Joshua* 7–8.30). Two complementary reasons make it unlikely that the story of its capture can be historically true. First, the story reflects the Deuteronomistic preoccupation with the notion that Israel will only be successful if it abides by the word of Yahweh of which the capture of 'Ai is a paradigmatic example. This tends to make one suspicious of its historicity and see it rather as a moralising tale. The suspicion is confirmed by the fact that the site identified by most as 'Ai (modern et-Tell) has been excavated, and the excavation shows clearly that it was a flourishing city in the Early Bronze Age, but was destroyed in the later third millennium, and lay abandoned until a very modest village settlement was established in the Early Bronze Age ruins *c.* 1200, which was again abandoned *c.* 1050 (cf. *Encyclopedia* I 36ff.). So 'Ai, at the presumed time of the conquest in 1200, had been in ruins for perhaps a thousand years. In the face of this incontrovertible archaeological evidence, scholars have adopted different stances. Some suggest that the story of the conquest of 'Ai should be compared to the account of the attack on nearby Gibeah (*Judges* 20), which shows some striking narrative similarities, with the exception that the story concerns an intertribal war. It is then proposed that the Gibeah tale was transposed to 'Ai at a much later date and linked to Joshua in order to explain the name of the site (which literally means a 'ruin') and its abandonment. The utter abandonment of 'Ai is a crucial feature of the 'Ai story:

> and Joshua burnt 'Ai and made it into a ruinheap for ever, even a desolation unto this day.
>
> (*Joshua* 8.28)

This description flies in the face of the archaeological evidence, which shows, first, that there was nothing to be destroyed by Joshua and, secondly, that it is precisely in the Israelite settlement phase that the site was again occupied. Other scholars (Albright 1939; Bright 1959) have dealt with the problem of 'Ai by arguing that the narrative of its destruction really describes the conquest of Bethel by Joshua. Bethel is not far away from 'Ai, there is a destruction level of about the right time at the site, yet the city does not figure in the conquest narratives. The story was then transferred later to 'Ai in order to explain its ruined state and name.

Approaches to the problem

The example of 'Ai gives us a taste of the kind of problems raised by every single bit of information concerning the Israelite settlement. There are no explanations, rationalisations or archaeological discoveries that provide clear answers acceptable to all. In these circumstances three fundamentally different hypotheses about the settlement have been formulated. We should consider them now.

The first hypothesis is associated with the 'biblical archaeology' approach (p. 423). In essence, it is an attempt to harmonise the discrepancies in the archaeological record with relevant sections of *Joshua* and *Judges* 1 (as exemplified above in the case of 'Ai). In the view of the propounders of this theory, Joshua conquered the land as described in the Old Testament, but the tribes delayed in following up his conquest and consolidating their hold. Joshua also conquered certain key cities in the region, but not all. The effect was to weaken the Canaanite city-system, which made the later tribal expansion successful. Archaeological evidence confirms this, showing destruction levels at sites such as Hazor, Lachish, Debir (if it is modern Beit Mirsim), Bethel, Gezer, Beth Shean and others. At all these sites, great Canaanite cities were destroyed *c.* 1200 or soon after, and when they are reoccupied the new occupations display a much poorer material culture; they are fairly small, simple villages which reflect occupation by the incoming, conquering Israelites.

There are serious weaknesses with this approach. First, it ignores the problems raised by the biblical sources, the date of their composition and redaction (none of which may be earlier than the seventh century), the tendentiousness of much of the account, which is designed to affirm aggressively Israel's right to the area, and the aetiological character of certain narratives (cf. the problem of 'Ai above). Second, it arbitrarily associates the end of Late Bronze Age city-sites with the Israelites, who are visualised as attacking and conquering them. It is a tempting explanation and might even be right in some instances, but is too simplistic. The history of each site must be analysed in archaeological terms independently of the Old Testament narrative and evaluated according to its own criteria. If we do that, it becomes obvious that, in the absence of texts, such an analysis of destruction levels is rarely, if ever, going to be specific enough to provide a detailed explanation of who or what destroyed a particular site (Ahlström 1986, ch. 3). Thus, for example, the dating of relevant levels is not always precise, nor consistent with a date around 1200. We must also remember that the end of the Late Bronze Age was a socially and politically disturbed period everywhere in the Levant: Egyptian sources talk of groups of brigands (*'apiru/habiru*) creating problems, of pastoralists, such as the Shasu, raiding Egyptian imperial territory, of revolts within Palestine that had to be quelled by Egyptian kings, and the movement of the 'sea-peoples' (see chapter 8a). Other sources show Aramaeans raiding and threatening the stability of the whole Fertile Crescent (see chapter 8b); yet others indicate that a persistent feature of the Levant city-states was chronic inter-state quarrelling which could end in military conflict. It is also possible that some destruction of cities was caused by earthquakes (Schaeffer on Ugarit, see p. 392), which caused fires and left a burnt layer at a site. In this context it is important for us to note that there were several destructions in other parts of the Levant at approximately this time which are definitely *not* attributable to the Israelites (Ugarit, Alalah, Emar).

Finally, the supporters of the 'biblical archaeology' approach have to contend with a very awkward problem, namely that the archaeological evidence rarely fits comfortably with the Old Testament text. It is precisely those cities where excavation has revealed a destruction datable to *c.* 1200 that do not figure as being destroyed in Joshua's conquest – Gezer, for example, which has a destruction-level datable to this time is never said to have been taken by Joshua (*Joshua* 10.33), and the same is true of Bethel, which was taken only considerably later by the tribe of Joseph (*Judges* 1.22–26) and is not described as having been destroyed. But the most embarrassing problem is the fact that the archaeology of the sites most prominent among Joshua's conquests provide only evidence that contradicts the Old Testament narrative point blank: 'Ai had been in ruins for about a thousand years by the time of its supposed destruction by the Israelites (p. 429); and, Gibeon, with which Joshua is supposed to have made a treaty (p. 428) and which appears as a large, flourishing city in the Bible, seems to have had no occupation at this time at all. Most notorious is the case of Jericho: its fall is a byword for Yahweh's power to bring down great cities, however strongly fortified, and it was the first large Canaanite city to be taken by the invading Israelites. Yet here again evidence for a large Late Bronze Age city is absent. The walls, originally identified as the ones that came tumbling down as the Israelites marched round them (Garstang 1948), have been shown to be those of the substantial town of Early Bronze Age Jericho (Kenyon 1979 [0Gd]). The scale of the difficulty presented by the Jericho evidence can be measured by the level of ingenuity displayed by scholars in arguing the evidence away. This has included trying to shift the Israelite settlement back to the end of the Middle Bronze period (Bimson 1981); while others have maintained (a favourite one, this) that the Late Bronze city destroyed by Joshua has suffered erosion (Bartlett 1982 for conspectus). Redating the Israelite settlement has not found wide acceptance (cf. the sensible discussion of arguments by Stiebing 1989); a careful re-analysis of the Jericho excavations shows that Late Bronze Jericho was a tiny *unwalled* settlement (Bienkowski 1986).

The second hypothesis was first formulated by the great Old Testament scholar Albrecht Alt (1925/1966). It has been followed and adapted by Noth (1958) and largely supported by Weippert in his exhaustive study of the Israelite settlement (1971). Generally speaking, it is the theory most widely accepted by those who approach the Old Testament text critically. The basic thesis is that Palestine was gradually infiltrated by semi-nomadic groups searching for pasture and land. They settled in the thinly populated hill-country, away from the Canaanite cities with whom their contact was very limited – on the whole their settlement was peaceful, although there could be conflicts of interest that led to clashes which are reflected in some of the stories in *Judges*. As the Israelites transformed their way of life into that of settled farmers and drew together into a tribal league, they began to expand from the hill-country into the arable plains dominated by the cities. This process is reflected in the stories about escalating military encounters, particularly with the Philistines, and the development of the monarchy. Evidence for the hypothesis is sought in Egyptian material, such as campaign accounts and the Amarna correspondence (see chapters 4c; 6d), which provides some insight into the location and functioning of the Canaanite cities. The Egyptian texts (and the archaeological evidence confirms them, Weinstein 1981; Gonen 1984; 1992: 217–219) show that they were concentrated in the lower-lying regions of Palestine, scattered or absent in the hill areas, with chains of cities intruding inland at two points, thus dividing the country into three regions (see maps 11 and 12). One such chain runs from Acco (Acre) along the Jezreel valley to Beth Shean, thereby dividing Galilee from the central hill area; the other runs from the coastal plain along the route leading through the hills to Jerusalem, which divided the later Ephraimite (central hill) area from the Judaean hill country to the south. It is these three regions – Galilee, the central hills and Judah – which were especially vulnerable to intruders such as the Israelite tribes, and it is they, as is well known, which formed their central and initial settlement areas.

Alt's approach has many attractions, but its weakness is the central assumption that the Israelites were originally nomadic, came from the desert and were searching for land. That image has been challenged by some scholars for ignoring the fact that the biblical depiction of 'Israel in the desert' is an elaborate metaphor of no historical value (Talmon 1987); by others, more prosaically, on the grounds that it does not fit the kinds of nomadic life possible at this date (van Seters 1975). For example, most of the biblical accounts of Israel in the desert are clearly anachronistic, as the style of existence described would only have been possible if the Israelites had been camel-rearing bedouin of a type not attested until later in the first millennium. If we adjust the picture, and characterise the Israelites as pastoralists, leading a symbiotic existence with the settled states, it is possible to produce a somewhat more convincing scenario, as has been done recently by Fritz (1987). He offers it as a new hypothesis, but it is essentially a modification of Alt's 'nomadic infiltration' theory, arrived at by utilising more recent anthropological research and undertaking a thorough re-analysis of the archaeological evidence. What Fritz defines is a general pattern whereby, at the end of the Late Bronze period, Israelite villages, identifiable by new house-types, appear, yet the material culture of the new settlements (aside from the houses) shows strong Canaanite influence and a clear cultural continuity. He would then argue that, while a new population element was definitely present in Iron I (c. 1200–900), whom we may equate with the 'Israelites', and who settled in the empty territory not occupied by Canaanites and Philistines, their cultural dependence on the Canaanites can only be explained by their earlier, close association with them. Such contact, he suggests, was the result of the fact that they pursued a pattern of 'enclosed nomadism': i.e., although the Israelites were basically transhumant pastoralists, their nomadic life-style

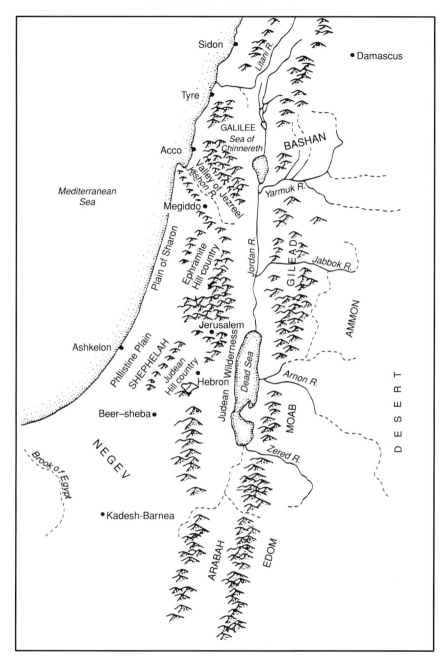

Map 11 Israel: physical features

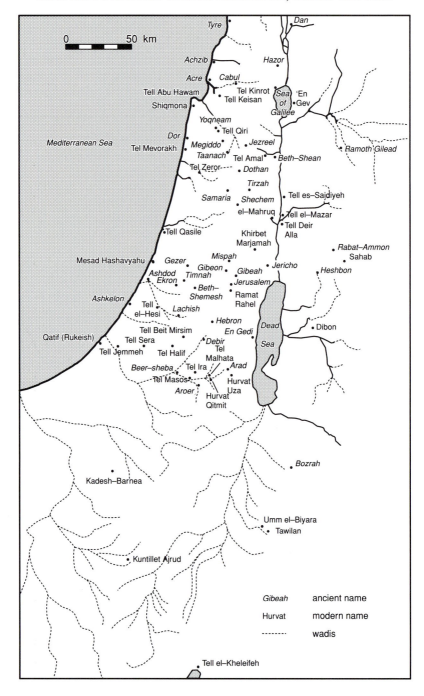

Map 12 Israel: sites

434

was interspersed with stretches of sedentary existence when they interacted closely with the Canaanite cities. As the Canaanite cities collapsed, this 'symbiosis' was shattered and the Israelites gradually abandoned their seasonal transhumant pattern to settle permanently.

Fritz's argument has a number of virtues, but it hinges on an almost desperate attempt to save the theory that the Israelites were nomads. The main flaw, as scholars have hastened to point out, is Fritz's suggestion that the apparently distinctive Israelite house developed from nomadic tents. It has been shown quite incontrovertibly that the 'Israelite houseplan' is not a novelty of this period, that it cannot be derived from (entirely hypothetical) tents (Stager 1985), and that, in any case, no one knows which, if any, of these early villages were Israelite (Ahlström 1986). In fact, everything in the archaeological record points to the fact that the new villages were laid out and settled by peasants familiar with the local culture and conversant with all aspects of farming (Stager 1985; Ahlström 1986; Meyers 1988).

In reaction to the unsatisfactory nature of the nebulous notion of Israel's nomadic origins, a radically different approach to Israel's origins has been developed. Its initial propounder was Mendenhall (1962), who argued that Israel grew out of a social revolutionary movement, which culminated in a 'peasants' revolt'. One of the central arguments of his position is that the name of the 'apiru/habiru, frequently mentioned in the Amarna letters as social outlaws, brigands, runaway slaves, fugitive debtors and landless peasants (see chapter 6d), can be linguistically linked with the Hebrews of the Old Testament, 'ibri. In other words, the Israelites, another name for whom was Hebrews, were in fact political outcasts, who had fled from the city-states and settled in the underused territories of Canaan, where they pursued a small-scale, relatively egalitarian village existence, bringing new land under cultivation by clearing and terracing. As Canaanite city-rulers proved less and less able to protect the peasants on whose labour their political power was based, such revolts and flights multiplied, and seriously weakened the economic base of the city-élites, which eventually crumbled. It is further possible that the chief impetus to more active aggression by the new peasant communities against the city-groups was the result of the peasants being united in their aims and ideology through a small group of people, some of whom may have originally worked in Egypt. They preached a new religion, which rejected the traditional political pattern of a king, but instead provided regulations for a just society with all peoples subject only to a new god, Yahweh, who had communicated these laws to one of their leaders.

There are many strengths in Mendenall's hypothesis. It makes it possible to understand early Israelite society as emerging from the Canaanite background with which it clearly had close links; it solves the difficulties inherent in making them nomadic outsiders and placing them beyond Canaan as a totally new element, and, archaeologically, it creates no problems because it becomes possible to see various destructions and reoccupations as being the result of a multiplicity of causes, happening at different times over a span of several hundred years. The main criticism that the theory has attracted is that some scholars find it unthinkable that a revolutionary movement, as envisaged by Mendenhall, can possibly have existed at this time. This is fairly weak as an argument, and has been effectively countered by Chaney (1983). More to the point is the criticism that the material on the *'apiru/habiru* does not indicate that they were peasant revolutionaries, that the theory discounts the real peasants (*hupšu*) who formed the mass of city inhabitants, and that it might be better to see the new settlers in the hills as a mixed band of people, who escaped the Canaanite states as the economic and political climate worsened (Ahlström 1986). In other words, they do not have to be self-conscious revolutionaries, but could rather be emigrants and pioneers. Other criticisms have centred on the viability of relating *'apiru/habiru* to *'ibri* (e.g. Loretz 1984; Moran 1987). Recently the equation has been rejected in terms of unrivalled vituperativeness by Rainey (1987) in his review of Gottwald's important and influential study of the development of the Israelite state (Gottwald 1979). There are undoubted problems in establishing a linguistic connection between the two words, and, indeed, in the way that the term 'Hebrew' is used in the Old Testament (Cazelles 1973). But what scholars have stressed increasingly in recent years is that the hypothesis does not depend crucially on the linguistic link. Rather, what is important is that the evidence for the existence of groups of social outcasts, such as the *'apiru/habiru*, provides the basis for a more fruitful analysis of the origins of Israel which solves many of the problems raised by the other two approaches, and is more consistent with current sociological analyses. It also makes it possible to set Israel's development within the general context of socio-political change in the wider world of the Near East, especially the Aramaean movements (see chapter 8b).

A final question we need to address is whether the 'social revolt' hypothesis does not do unacceptable violence to the biblical account. How could the Old Testament narrative have been formulated in the way it is, if the Israelites were never nomadic tribes entering the land from outside to settle? Supporters of the 'Mendenhall theory' would reply, first, that the tribes are an artificial later creation, only constructed when Israel was engaged in a process of self-definition in relation to its neighbours, and is derived from the location of different groups, not vice versa. Second, the tribal structure expresses social relationships and does not have to imply a nomadic existence (Fried 1975). Finally, the creation of the story of military conquest and settlement from outside is to be attributed to the seventh century (in response to the fall of the northern kingdom), when it served to differentiate Israel from other peoples in the region, and provide it with an unassailable claim to inhabit the land it held: if the Israelites had conquered the country by military force, then it belonged to them by military right and might and their possession could not be disputed (Lemche 1988).

The sociological approach to the Israelite settlement is now a dominant one embraced by many Old Testament scholars, historians and archaeologists (Gottwald 1979; generally Freedman and Graf 1983; Lemche 1988; Meyers 1988). Some modifications have been proposed by scholars focusing, rightly, on the problem of the origin of Yahweh worship, which upholders of this theory have not explained with total success: Ahlström (1986), for example, has suggested that an important element in the distinctive formation of Israel's ideology came from Edom. But the essence of the theory is accepted by him. This is not true of others. Rainey, for example, has argued for years, and continues to do so, that the origin of the Israelites should be sought among the Shasu bedouin of the eastern Jordan (recently Rainey 1991). The least favourite hypothesis at the moment is that of military conquest – it simply presents too many problems (Finkelstein 1988). But it was still being argued for vigorously as late as 1982 by eminent scholars (Malamat 1982; Yadin 1982) and has informed the account of the early Israelites presented in one of the most popular textbooks on Israelite history (Bright 1959/1972).

Conclusion

In conclusion, all we can say with certainty about Israel's beginnings is that different tales, recounting some of the exploits of individual groups and the heroic deeds of local leaders, were current in later Israel. They were woven together and worked into a complex narrative, perhaps in the seventh century (or later), linking it to a belief in a great religious leader, Moses, who masterminded the escape of a group of people from Egypt and received divine instructions on Mount Sinai. The result of this later literary construct was to place all of Israel outside Canaan, and thus in the position of having to conquer it through a holy war directed by Yahweh, which would lead to the fulfilment of his promise that Israel would settle and prosper in the Promised Land. The powerful nature of the story makes it impossible to say anything definite about the historical 'settlement' – the very process may never have taken place in anything like the way envisaged by the Old Testament. What is definite is, first, that the system of city-states found in Palestine in the Late Bronze Age underwent a fundamental change, and many of the cities formed part of the new state of Israel by about 1000; the change was preceded by a striking increase in village settlement in the period between c. 1200 and 1050 (Stager 1985; Meyers 1988) by people who were obviously familiar with Canaanite culture and were experienced farmers. Second, the later Israelites themselves certainly believed that they had conquered Canaan, entering it from outside, and this belief came to be crucial to the development of Jewish religion and identity. In other words, it is the function of the stories as they stand that came to be important to Israelite self-understanding, and the debatable historical reality is largely irrelevant to that (for an analogy in a different context, see C. Geertz, *Negara*, Princeton, N.J., 1980, especially p. 14).

8d(iii) The emergence of the Israelite state

General overview

For later Israelites the reign of David, his capture of Jerusalem and the acceptance of him as king by all the tribes formed the high point of national achievement. The institution of monarchy in Israel was firmly established by David and he became its classic and ideal representative: he was the perfect ruler in terms of piety and religious fervour; he established Jerusalem as the Israelite capital *par excellence* and began the move to build a temple for Yahweh's cult; he achieved the lasting defeat of the Philistines, as well as other neighbouring states, which laid the foundations of Israel's most prosperous and glorious period ever; and he personally united all the disparate Israelite tribes under his rule. The large, strong Davidic kingdom endured only for the length of the reign of his successor, Solomon, and ended with the accession of Solomon's son, Rehoboam. This rapid decline enhanced David's glory and uniqueness by contrast. It is, therefore, not surprising that well over one third of the biblical material devoted to the monarchic period concerns the reigns of David and Solomon, although in real time their reigns cover only about one tenth (Soggin 1984). At the same time there are no royal inscriptions from the time of the United Monarchy (indeed very little written material altogether; Barkay 1992), and not a single contemporary reference to either David or Solomon in any document outside the Bible. This is not surprising considering how little evidence there exists in this period in the whole of the Near East (see above p. 394) – and, in particular, how little epigraphic material survives from Israel at any period (Smelik 1985; Millard 1990). Against this must be set the evidence for substantial development and growth at several sites, which is plausibly related to the tenth century (Whitelam 1986; Barkay 1992). We should also note that a new Aramaic stele fragment from Tel Dan, probably dating to the mid-ninth century, *may* refer to the kingdom of Judah as the 'House of David' (*BYT DWD*; Biran and Naveh 1993). It is so far unprecedented and shows, perhaps, that David was widely perceived as the founder of the Judaean state (cf. the northern kingdom of Israel, known as the 'House of Omri', chapter 8e).

But how did a situation evolve that led to peasant farmers, scattered through the Canaanite hills, all acknowledging the suzerainty of David? If we are tempted to explain it as the result of their common faith in Yahweh, how was it that this particular religion was accepted by all of them, when, as we saw in trying to understand the process of 'settlement', there is no reason to assume that all the Canaanite hill farmers shared a common historical experience? It is practically impossible to find one, acceptable, substantiable solution to the last question. All that we can say is that, for an unspecifiable time before the emergence of monarchy in Israel with Saul, some groups within central Israel formed distinct socio-political entities, the 'tribes'

(Ahlström 1986: ch. 6). Eventually (although when remains unclear) they came to regard themselves as linked to each other through a common eponymous ancestor, Israel (perhaps no more than the personification of the region they inhabited, Ahlström 1986). At some point, possibly only much later, the ancestor Israel was identified with the patriarch Jacob. With this identification all 'tribes' were linked to Jacob's predecessors, Abraham and Isaac, and to the subsequent 'history' which led from Joseph into Egypt on to Moses, the Exodus, Sinai and finally into the Promised Land. How much, if any, of this was already accepted by all Israelite groups in the period before the monarchy is, and must inevitably remain, unknown.

An influential view for some time (Noth 1930), accepted by several scholars (Meyers 1988), is that the link-up of the tribes in Palestine led to an 'intertribal federation', which met from time to time at certain sanctuaries for worship of deities identified with Yahweh. The coming together of the tribes either resulted in, or proceeded from, a common interest in the face of threats to their independent existence, posed by their neighbours: the states of Moab and Edom, Ammonites and Amalekites, the rulers of some of the surviving Canaanite cities and the Philistines in the coastal plain. In response, a number of tribal heroes emerged – the 'judges' – as deliverers from crises ('charismatic leaders' in Weber's terminology (Weber 1947: 358ff.)). But these famous warriors by no means acted for 'all Israel', since it was not 'all Israel' that was necessarily in danger in each instance. The only time this was the case was when the Philistines pushed successfully into the hill-country and the plain of Jezreel. They inflicted a devastating defeat on the Israelite forces at Aphek, captured the central symbol of Israel's faith, the Ark of the Covenant, and destroyed an important sanctuary of Yahweh at Shiloh. At that point, *all* Israel was seriously threatened and a leader acceptable to all groups who would lead a joint campaign became necessary. Saul, from the tribe of Benjamin, came to the fore in this crisis, appointed by Yahweh acting through his prophet Samuel, and delivered Israel (at least temporarily) from the Philistine yoke. He was also successful against other enemies of Israel and his victory over the Ammonites was followed by his acclamation as king at Gilgal, an old cultic centre.

Saul's new position, unprecedented in Israel, seems to rest entirely on his achievements as a war-leader, and his military success was regarded as reflecting divine favour. The personal, *ad hoc* character of Saul's kingship suffered from the lack of a solid legal–administrative framework. Such a structure was needed in order to extract financial and military contributions from the previously autonomous tribal units on a regular basis – essential for strengthening Saul's embryonic kingship. As Saul's attempts at imposing the necessary administrative requirements became irksome, and his military achievements less spectacular, his position was challenged by the growing power of David, one of his generals, from the southern tribe of Judah. Saul's persecution of his rival forced David to flee to the Philistines, who hired him, along with a band of outlaws, as a mercenary soldier. Saul was eventually disastrously defeated on Mount Gilboa by the Philistines and committed suicide. On Saul's death David, who had already been acclaimed king of Judah in the south, challenged Saul's son and successor, Ishbaal. He was accepted by the northern tribes and, either then or perhaps already earlier, he captured the fortified Canaanite city of Jerusalem with a small band of soldiers. It became, henceforth, not only the capital of Judah, but the personal royal city of the kings of Judah.

Chronology and sources

This, in broad outline, is the conventional view of events leading to Saul's appointment as king and the rise of David. First, we need to consider the chronology, assess the sources and then look at the main problems.

With Saul, David and Solomon, the line of the kings of Israel begins ('United Monarchy'). Following the division of the Davidic–Solomonic state, we have a list of kings of both Israel and Judah, sometimes indicating lengths of reign, in 1 and 2 *Kings*. There are quite a number of chronological problems in the period of the 'Divided Monarchy' (Maxwell Miller 1976: chs 2 and 5), but on the basis of synchronisms, mainly with Assyrian kings, it is possible to work back through this list and establish 930 or 922 as acceptable dates for the end of the reign of Solomon and hence the separation between north and south (the 'Schism'). David and Solomon are given forty years each for their reigns, which is generally regarded as a conventional figure meaning 'a long time' (i.e. a whole generation) rather than reproducing a precise number of regnal years. Nevertheless, in the absence of anything else, these figures are normally accepted, and so the beginning of David's reign dated as starting around (or just before) 1000. Working backwards from this point is very difficult. No one knows how long Saul reigned, nor the exact length of time that elapsed between his death and David's accession, which is itself imprecise. Since the surviving stories concerning Saul do not require him to have a particularly long reign, it is usual to assign him roughly twenty years in power; so his reign begins around 1030/1020. Dating anything before this becomes progressively more difficult and rests on probability and on how one interprets the sources. The disastrous defeat of the Israelites by the Philistine army at Aphek, the capture of the ark, the Philistine occupation of Israelite territory, and the destruction of the Shiloh sanctuary are entirely without chronological indications. Attempts to establish a date rest on the fact that, according to the Old Testament, the prophet Samuel was apparently at Shiloh as a child and young man, whereas he appears as an old man when he anointed Saul as king. The time allowed for Samuel to reach this age is usually about thirty years, so that the beginning of the 'Philistine oppression' is dated to *c.* 1060/1050. Given the tacit agreement that the Israelites were settling in the hill-country by *c.* 1200 (or extending their settlement and increasing in number around that time), a period of almost one hundred and fifty years, at least, remains to be accounted for. This time is filled by the events recounted in *Judges*, which concern mainly intertribal relations and the possible functioning of a tribal confederacy. Although some scholars try to date the exploits of individual judges, there is no general agreement on the chronology of this period nor ever likely to be.

For Solomon and David the biblical sources are quite full, running from 2 *Samuel* 1 to 1 *Kings* 11. Some of the material is thought to derive from a 'court-history', composed possibly not long after Solomon's reign, although this view has been seriously challenged (Rendtorff 1983; Lemche 1988; van Seters 1983 [OK]). Excerpts from administrative lists and census rosters seem also to have been included, making this one of the apparently best-documented periods of Israelite history (see further pp. 447–449). Certainly, the texts concerning it are fuller than for any other area of the contemporary Near East, although the preserved material is not, of course, contemporary. For the period of the Philistine expansion down to the end of Saul's reign, a whole cycle of stories connected with the ark appears to have been used. This provided some details of the Philistine wars, the battle of Aphek and the destruction of the Shiloh sanctuary; it may also have included stories surrounding Samuel, although most of them are usually thought to be derived from prophetic circles. The stories concerning the relationship between Saul and David, with their clear bias in favour of David, probably emanated from the south and were reworked within the Deuteronomistic historian's framework (see p. 421).

The material used for *Judges* (i.e. *Judges* 2ff.) is too complex to be discussed here. But two features are worth noting. First, apart from two bits of material relating to the migration of the tribe of Dan and an intertribal war, the book of *Judges* attempts to show the fortunes of Israel in accordance with the Deuteronomistic thesis that correct religious observance leads to fortune, while turning away from Yahweh results in disaster. The judges that arose are, therefore, represented as specially chosen by Yahweh in response to the penitence of his oppressed people: they appear, deliver Israel from its current oppressor and then 'judge' it for some time (the precise understanding of this term is unclear). Because of the theological message that dictated the organisation of the book, these originally localised and quite separate exploits have been joined together to produce the impression that they all affected the whole of Israel and occurred in chronological sequence. Second, the reason why the various war-leaders are called 'judges' is that a list of seemingly insignificant 'leaders', about whom nothing is known except that they 'judged Israel', was included in *Judges*, and the charismatic deliverer-figures were linked to them. Originally the stories of the deliverers and the list of judges must have been quite separate, and were only tied together at some later point (Martin 1975).

Israel and the judges

In order to try to understand what institutions may have existed in the period of judges, that would allow the disparate groups to unite, Noth developed the extremely influential hypothesis of a tribal amphictyony (Noth 1930). He proposed that since, in spite of certain variations, the number twelve was always retained for the Israelite tribes, and, within that, the six tribes of Leah (supposedly the first to arrive in Canaan) form a constant group, this must have an institutional significance. He then used the structure of Greek and Italic religious amphictyonies as an analogy. One of their characteristics, he argued, was a grouping of either twelve or six cities or peoples around a common central sanctuary, where they gathered periodically for religious feasts and to which they were bound by oath. Each member of such a league retained its political autonomy, but they had league representatives, who ensured that certain rules were observed and initiated joint action against any members in breach of the oath.

Comparing this institution to Israel, Noth suggested that all the essential elements of such a sacred amphictyony were present in the Israel of the time of the judges. He went on to argue that Israel was the name of the league formed by the twelve tribes centred on the sanctuary where the ark was kept. The sanctuary had to be moved for various reasons at times, but there was only ever one: first at Shechem, then Bethel, then Gilgal and finally at Shiloh. According to *Joshua* 24, it was at Shechem that the tribes acknowledged Yahweh and that Yahweh was substituted for all other local gods; it was here that they were united with each other and Yahweh by a covenant; their laws were the regulations contained in *Exodus* 21–23.

Each year they would meet for religious festivals and to renew the covenant at the tribal sanctuary and their affairs were discussed by their tribal representatives, who are listed in *Numbers* 1.5–16. Any transgressions were punished by the amphictyony acting in concert, as exemplified by *Judges* 19–20, where the multiple rape and murder of the concubine belonging to a Levite by men from the tribe of Benjamin at Gibeah was punished by all the tribes uniting to wage an 'amphictyonic' war on Benjamin. The list of the 'minor judges' (see p. 441), Noth interpreted as amphictyonic legal officials.

Several scholars have pointed out problems with Noth's proposal which undermine the validity of his initially attractive hypothesis. First, the repeated appearance of the number twelve (the starting-point for Noth's theory) does not really provide an argument in favour of understanding early Israel as an amphictyony, as the classical amphictyonies have varying numbers of league members. At Shechem the Yahweh message was given only to those northern tribes who had not participated in the Exodus–Sinai episode, so it was not an act of general union among the tribes but a pragmatic act with a specific and limited aim. Although the ark was certainly housed at Shiloh for some time there is no mention of it being a place for regular gatherings of all the Israelite tribes. Further, there is evidence in *Judges* for a host of cult places, such as Beersheba, Mizpah, Ramah, Ophrah, Dan and others, so that the concept of an exclusive, central sanctuary is hard to maintain. Then the tribal representatives of *Numbers* seem to be simply tribal/clan leaders and never appear exercising any administrative function in relation to a tribal league; in addition they are not once mentioned in the book of *Judges* – their activities appear to be confined to the wilderness narrative. When 'all Israel' is said to act, as in the case of the Benjaminite outrage at Gibeah, the text never indicates how they were mobilised or reached the decision to act. Finally, neither the judges nor the 'minor judges' are ever specifically associated with any shrines. It looks as though, despite its attractions, the notion of a tribal amphictyony should be abandoned. De Vaux (1978) concluded, after exhaustive examination, that the hypothesis imposes an artificial structure on premonarchic Israel which is not supported by the Old Testament itself and gives a largely false idea of intertribal relations.

The stories of delivery by great warriors were tales of local heroes, commemorated by different communities, which were linked together by the Deuteronomist to help express his view that sin consists in a turning away from Yahweh which leads to oppression, while repentance means a turning towards Yahweh which leads to him sending a saviour. This narrative structure, in which each deliverer-figure was presented as a charismatic leader appointed by Yahweh to save all Israel, was imposed on the material only later during the Deuteronomistic reworking. It is, therefore, very likely that in origin the deliverers were leaders limited in their regional scope who emerged in the context of crises from various backgrounds. An important implication, then, is that *Judges* does not present a picture of consistently unified tribal action, but rather depicts separate wars fought with people in the regions where the different communities were attempting to consolidate their hold. It also portrays internecine disputes and rivalry for pre-eminence between Israelite groups. If anything, *Judges* serves to emphasise that this was a period of deep division within Israel, as a result of the absence of any effective unifying element and the geographical scatter of the people involved. It could be said that *Judges* presents a period of hopeless anarchy foreshadowing the time when developed political institutions, such as monarchy, would become necessary to resolve conflicts and help Yahweh's people to survive.

Saul, the first king of Israel

Monarchy in Israel emerged very suddenly from this pattern of disunity. Many scholars are, therefore, inclined to see Saul as one of the 'charismatic deliverers' (a result of his victory over the Ammonites), who was then confirmed by the people of the highlands as a king in the face of the Philistine oppression which threatened them all. According to this perception, Saul is a transitional figure in the evolution of the Israelite state – a 'judge' who became a king. The contradictory accounts of his appointment to the kingship suggest that Saul does not represent a fully fledged kingship. According to 1 *Samuel* 9.1–10, 16; 11.1–11 and parts of chs 13 and 14, the initiative for the institution came from Yahweh himself, who chose Saul as a liberator. But according to 1 *Samuel*. 8.1–22; 10.18–25; 12 and 15, it was the people who demanded a king in order to be 'like other nations'. This indicates the ambivalent feelings that Israelites always, supposedly, had about the interpolation of a permanent king between themselves and Yahweh, who had originally made a covenant directly with his people. Resistance to monarchy, it is thought, can be traced elsewhere in the biblical narrative: for example, Saul was not able to found a dynasty because a king was ultimately unacceptable to Yahweh. In this respect Saul is contrasted with two figures. First, with the judge Gideon, who was pressed by the people to become king by founding a dynasty, but, being a pious man, refused to do so. Second, with David who did, of course, found a dynasty, but only because he was the perfect 'servant' (*'ebed*) of Yahweh, submitting to Yahweh's law and remaining faithful to his cult. He was a model king, typifying the future Messiah, who will eventually emerge from his line (de Vaux 1972). In any other context, the dynastic principle, i.e. the routinisation of monarchic power, was not accepted and flew in the face of Israelite ideals about how their state should be run. This interpretation is thought to be confirmed by the history of the later northern kingdom of Israel, where there were constant and rapid changes in rulers, and only very short-lived dynasties. Clearly, the charismatic principle of leadership was retained here, and was in constant tension with attempts by northern kings to consolidate their position. In other words, the way that Israel handled the institution of monarchy was to see a king 'handpicked' by Yahweh as good and acceptable, but an attempt by a king to perpetuate this situation by founding a dynasty of his own volition was to be resisted. Therefore, the principle of monarchy was basically rejected, except in the case of David and his dynasty, which continued to exercise power in the south. The underlying idea is that kingship was not something that the Israelites were prepared to accept, apart from the extraordinary figure of David. Within this framework Saul is seen as little more than a charismatic deliverer, who attempted to perpetuate his power against the general wishes of his subjects.

This conceptualisation of Israelite kingship, which is quite widespread, needs questioning. First, to see the Davidic dynasty as exceptional and, therefore, cultically right is a purely tendentious interpretation. The implication of the successful survival of a single dynasty in Judah must be that the dynastic principle was accepted as an integral and inescapable part of the institution of kingship – it is in the principle of inherited power, after all, that the stability of a monarchic system lies. The fact that there were rapid changes of kings, and short-lived dynasties, in the north does not indicate rejection of monarchy *per se*. There was certainly no return in the northern kingdom to any earlier system of government, nor was any alternative ever envisaged; its political structure remained throughout that of a kingdom, which was never questioned. The reasons for instability in the north reflect other problems. Second, although an aspect of the judge Gideon's virtue was his refusal to perpetuate his leadership by founding a dynasty, the telling element in the story is that the people demanded it. In other words, it was always realised that part of the institution of monarchy was that it is a permanent and hereditary office, and there is no hint in the Gideon story that a king need always be appointed by Yahweh. Finally, it is quite evident that Saul *did* found a dynasty. His son, Ishbaal, succeeded him on the throne after his death. He only ruled briefly, probably because his father's death in a battle, where the Israelites were defeated, made it difficult for him to assert his control. The situation was not helped by the army commander, Abner, who defected to David, the rival ruler (now turning out to be very successful). Abner's betrayal allowed David to extend his power fairly rapidly. The recognised prestige of Saul's rule, and its legitimacy, is further underlined by the fact that David married one of Saul's daughters; the emphasis placed on David's link with Saul's family shows how significant Saul's reign was and how powerful the loyalties he commanded.

If we re-examine Saul's emergence as king in the light of these criticisms, it becomes much harder to fit him into the line of charismatic deliverers. His background is obscured by standard folktale motifs – the obscure peasant youth who becomes a divinely favoured leader. It is much more likely that Saul had established already a quite extensive power-base within the central hill-country and was challenging the authority of the prophet Samuel, who seems to have been trying to build up his own position into one of permanent political dominance for himself and his family. In the context of a critical military situation, when the people demanded a king, it is significant that Samuel felt rejected (1 *Samuel* 8.7). And it seems to have been only as a result of the rejection of Samuel's leadership that Saul, probably already prominent, was anointed by Samuel and presented as the king Israel demanded. Also significant in the story is the fact that the demand was for a king as such, not for a specific individual, nor was there an insistence that someone act as king only after proving himself through a heroic feat. This may have been the result of careful planning and intricate manoeuvres by Saul himself, but what is important is the way in which the episode has been structured: Saul is selected by a prominent political figure (Samuel) in response to an unspecific demand by 'the people' for a king; he is presented as chosen by Yahweh; after this he has to prove his military ability; then he is confirmed as king. With Saul a very different situation and a new mode of arriving at a leader crystallised in Israel. The centuries of anarchy had come to an end and kingship presented a novel and positive political order.

Sadly, Saul's reign is very poorly documented with respect to the development of military and administrative institutions, as much of the Old Testament narrative (which is all there is) focuses on him mainly as a foil for David. Some features do emerge, however, although details remain obscure. One change that we can define is the development of the Israelite army: it became larger as a result of the creation of a permanent central command and the comprehensive programme of attack and defence against all the various threats to Israel's security, which Saul initiated and pushed forward actively. Further, the kernel of a standing army was established, supplemented only as necessary by a general muster, as illustrated by 1 *Samuel* 13.2: 'Saul chose 3000 men ... and sent the rest of the people home.' So a body of young warriors, permanently clustered around the king, was formed. It was probably recruited from the younger sons of farmers, whose opportunities for setting up homes and gaining wealth became harder as the population increased and the availability of new land diminished (Stager 1985). The permanent army corps provided some continuity, as can be deduced from the fact that, after Saul's death (2 *Samuel* 2.12; 4.2), his son, Ishbaal, was able to send out his servants and two companies of soldiers to act on his behalf. The incident implies that there was a military force at the king's disposal, whose allegiance was solely to the royal house; it also shows, incidentally, that Saul's kingdom did not fall apart at his death. A particular office that appears in Saul's reign is that of 'army-commander' responsible to the king. It was held by Saul's cousin, Abner, who seems to have functioned as second-in-command on campaign. The importance of the army-commander's position, and how it could function to defend the kingdom's cohesion at moment's of crisis, is illustrated by Abner's action to protect Ishbaal on Saul's death and ensure his accession to the throne (2 *Samuel* 2.8–9). It is very difficult to reconstruct any more of the nature of Saul's rule: there are references to 'the servants of Saul', who were perhaps rewarded with grants of fields and vineyards (1 *Samuel* 22.7). Are they identical with the hand-picked warriors or are they a separate group of administrators and courtiers? A specific post mentioned is that of 'chief of the shepherds of Saul', who is named as 'Doeg, the Edomite' (1 *Samuel* 21.8; 22.9). He may have had the responsibility of providing supplies for the royal establishment. His name raises the interesting possibility that Saul was beginning to attract people from beyond Israel's borders and integrating them into the Israelite court. Very problematic is the question of where the income came from to support the new permanent superstructure created by monarchy. Booty from successful wars would have provided some resources, and the conquest of some of the remaining Canaanite cities could have swelled the royal coffers further. There is also a reference to gifts (1 *Samuel* 10.27) as an obligation that subjects owe their king. But what did they consist of? Could they have been presented regularly enough and in sufficient quantity to be of real economic significance? Are they not more likely to have been sporadic presentations of symbols of allegiance and items appropriate to royalty? Saul's court is said to have been at Gibeah which, it has been suggested, be identified with Tell el-Ful (Lapp 1981: 1–38; *Encyclopedia* 444–446). If that is correct, then Saul's centre was a small but well-fortified castle whose layout differed markedly from that of the surrounding Israelite villages.

The significant achievements of Saul's reign were his successes against Israel's foes, the incorporation of people beyond the 'tribes' into Israel, and the beginnings, however rudimentary, of an administrative and military machinery. This laid the foundations on which David built his prosperous and spectacularly successful state. Without Saul there could never have been a David.

8d(iv) The triumph of Judah

Introduction and sources

Under David and his son, Solomon, Israel became, for the space of about eighty years, a powerful, strongly centralised state – the fruit of military conquest. The development of a more sophisticated administrative and tax system was closely related to Israel's expansion (Heaton 1974). A gradual, but substantial, social transformation accompanied Israel's growth. Where earlier local family and community links had predominated, a tiered society gradually overlaid the 'tribal' system: king and court in the dominant position, officials dependent on royal favour just below them, people engaged in commerce and industry living in cities, peasants tilling the soil in the countryside (probably always the largest proportion of the population; Meyers 1988), and slaves owned by the more prosperous section of Israelite society.

The story of this most glorious period of Israelite history is contained in 2 *Samuel* and 1 *Kings*. The narrative is part of the Deuteronomistic history (see p. 421), and is therefore structured to present both kings as beginning their reigns very favourably (adhering to Yahweh's law) and ending them badly (falling from divine grace through error). So, despite the apparently rather reliable sources for, and quite full presentations of, David and Solomon's reigns (see p. 441), the arrangement of the material means that all the successes cluster around the earlier time of each reign, all the setbacks around the end. The result is that the chronology of events during the reigns has been distorted to the point where we cannot recover it. There is also a great imbalance in the events covered. David's rise to power has been woven together out of at least three different strands that take up a great deal of the biblical narrative. At the same time they do not hang together very well, so that for all the space that is devoted to it the history of David's rise to power remains very patchy (Soggin in Hayes and Maxwell Miller 1977: 334). Similar reservations apply to the story of the succession to David, with the added problem that much of it belongs more to the category of historical romance (Soggin in Hayes and Maxwell Miller 1977: 337–338) than to historiography as once thought (Meyer 1884–1902 II/2: 284–286). A disproportionately large part of the Solomonic story concerns the Jerusalem temple and its building, which was of central interest for the Deuteronomistic historian (see above p. 421). The famous episode of the visit of the Queen of Sheba to Solomon's court is almost certainly unhistorical (Pritchard 1974), as the archaeological evidence from Yemen shows that the kingdom of Sheba had not developed at this stage. The story circulated later and served to stress Solomon's glory and his legendary wisdom.

The archaeological evidence for this magnificent time is sparse. It is possible to discern a change taking place in some of the small 'Israelite' settlements which developed from around 1000 onwards into fortified larger towns (Whitelam 1986). But there is not a single structure throughout Israel (one of the most intensively investigated parts of the world, archaeologically speaking) that can indisputably and clearly be dated to David and Solomon (Mazar 1990 [0Gd]: 374–397). Jerusalem is, in this respect, particularly disappointing, although that is perhaps not too surprising given the extraordinary, long-lived symbolic significance it holds for three, often mutually hostile, religious groups, including two of the largest in the world (Christianity and Islam). It has, therefore, been fought over ceaselessly for the last fifteen hundred years, and undergone repeated rebuilding especially at particularly sacred spots. Significant traces of Solomon's temple are thus extremely unlikely ever to be recovered, since it lies under the great Dome of the Rock; we can visualise it dominating the city, but little more. Traces of Iron Age city-walls have been found, but dating them precisely is difficult. Excavators have tried to establish a stratigraphical and chronological sequence in the original centre of Jerusalem, and here a layer of fill may well be associated with David's building programme (Kenyon 1987: 89ff.; Shiloh 1984). That is all. Other sites have produced rather more that can be ascribed to the tenth century with some confidence, although there are disagreements about datings (Yadin 1970; 1972; Aharoni 1974; Soggin in Hayes and Maxwell Miller 1977: 340–343; Barkay 1992: 305). But, even if the remains found should in some cases be dated to the ninth rather than the tenth century, there is a strong likelihood that many of the important developments at these centres began earlier, and the Davidic–Solomonic period is the obvious candidate. At several sites, especially those located along Israel's frontiers and on the main routes (the places where the earlier Canaanite cities had flourished), a distinctive new kind of fortification wall and complex gateway are to be associated with the United Monarchy. Particularly striking are those that have been found at Megiddo (see fig. 29), but traces of identical fortifications have now been found at quite a number of places. Generally, it is true to say that they correspond to the list of cities given as the centres of the new administrative districts set up by Solomon. These large towns with their impressive fortifications are a new feature of the tenth century, which reflects the tight grip with which the new rulers of the centralised state of Israel held the country. The cities dominated the countryside and contained the residence of the local governor and his garrison. Each formed the local centre where the taxes levied on the populations were stored. They were a physical expression of the might of the rulers (Whitelam 1986).

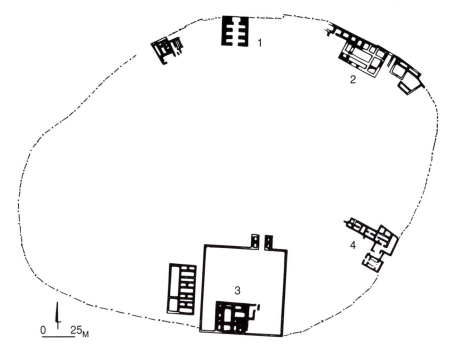

Figure 29 Plan of Megiddo IVB–VA: 1 city gate; 2 palace 6000; 3 palace 1723; 4 dwellings (after Yadin 1972)

David

The story of David contains some obviously romantic elements (e.g. the Goliath incident – almost certainly transferred to him from the original protagonist, Elhanan (2 *Samuel* 21.19; Soggin in Hayes and Maxwell Miller 1977: 334), which can be discounted in a historical reconstruction of his career). Other aspects are more relevant. David is presented as a high officer in Saul's retinue, who excited the king's mortal jealousy and was, therefore, forced to flee to the southern Judaean hills. There he organised a private army made up of a motley crew of fugitives, the disaffected and outlaws (1 *Samuel* 22.2). With his band of followers he carried out a series of desperate raids that can, and have been, characterised as 'protection rackets' (Soggin in Hayes and Maxwell Miller 1977: 345), as in this anecdote:

449

There was a man at Carmel in Maon, who had great influence and owned 3000 sheep and 1000 goats; and he was shearing his flocks in Carmel. His name was Nabal and his wife was Abigail; she was a beautiful and intelligent woman, but her husband, a Calebite, was surly and mean. David heard in the wilderness that Nabal was shearing his flocks, and sent ten of his men, saying to them, 'Go up to Carmel, find Nabal and give him my greetings. You are to say, "All good wishes for the year ahead! Prosperity to yourself, your household, and all that is yours! I hear you are shearing. Your shepherds have been with us lately and we did not molest them; nothing of theirs was missing all the time they were in Carmel. Ask your own people and they will tell you. Receive my men kindly, for this is an auspicious day with us, and give what you can to David your son and your servant."' David's servants came and delivered this message to Nabal in David's name. When they paused, Nabal answered, 'Who is David? Who is this son of Jesse? In these days every slave who breaks away from his master sets himself up as a chief. Am I to take my food and my wine and the meat I have provided for my shearers and give it to men who come from I know not where?' David's men turned and made their way back to him and told him all this. He said to his men, 'Buckle on your swords, all of you.' So they buckled on their swords and followed David, four hundred of them, while two hundred stayed behind with the baggage.

(1 *Samuel* 25.2–13 (NEB))

It seems fairly certain that, whatever the reason, David had been, or certainly was now, attempting to challenge Saul's position as king by building up a power-base in Judah, which may in part have lain outside Saul's territory (Ahlström 1986). Like any ruler threatened by a serious attempt to undermine his authority, Saul hunted David. Possibly to secure his fragile position more firmly, David hired himself out to Israel's enemies, the Philistines, so that at the time of Saul's death in battle with the Philistines he was on their side. At that moment, the Philistines were very powerful: Israel was defeated; its king, three of his sons and many of his closest retainers were dead (2 *Samuel* 3.1); and the increasingly powerful general, David of Judah, was a mercenary captain in their pay. The Philistine dominance seems to have lasted for seven and a half years (2 *Samuel* 2.11; 5.5), although at some point in the confusion following Saul's death his military commander, Abner, was able to ensure the accession of Saul's son, Ishbaal, to his father's throne.

For some time, then, there were effectively two kingdoms in rivalry with each other: Saul's former realm held together with difficulty by his son; David based in Judah. David seems to have been able to take advantage of the chaotic situation following Saul's defeat to attract more followers and, as he grew more powerful, Abner secretly made overtures to David, and helped to convey Saul's daughter and David's wife, Michal, to him. But, because of the deep mistrust between the two areas, he was assassinated by one of David's officers. Ishbaal, now unprotected and in an ever weaker position, was himself killed by the inhabitants of Beeroth, one of the Canaanite cities that had suffered at Saul's hands. From this point on, David's supreme position could not be challenged easily and, after making a formal agreement with Israel, he was crowned king at Hebron.

What did the kingdom forged by David look like? There is no clear account of how and when particular territories, aside from Israel, were added, but that David acquired more, some in the course of exceptionally brutal wars, is plain.

Among David's most important conquests was the capture of Jerusalem, strategically located in terms of routes, but also in a position with clear political advantages as it lies fairly close to the boundary between Israel and Judah. He captured this Canaanite ('Jebusite') city with his personal army, and it became henceforth the royal city of the kings of Judah – it was their personal property and where their palace was located. David, almost certainly building on Saul's initial achievements, eventually integrated all the Canaanite cities in the territory of Israel and Judah, which had not been destroyed earlier, into his kingdom. The tribal hill regions, whose inhabitants had accepted him as king initially, were another constituent element. Here the balance of power differed from area to area – a feature that seems always to have created problems for the kings of the United Monarchy: David started off as king of Judah, where he had been first acclaimed as ruler as a challenge to Israel in the north; some time later, and in conditions of considerable political crisis, he was accepted by the 'elders of Israel' (i.e. the spokesmen for the northern communities). It is quite possible that their acceptance of David was reluctant – forced on them in a situation where two kings had been killed in fairly rapid succession, there was no obvious successor, the victorious Philistines were threatening the territory of Israel, and the Philistine ally, David, militarily and politically greatly superior, was pressurising them to submit.

Against the three states to the immediate east of Israel-Judah, Ammon, Moab and Edom, David fought some bitter wars in which he triumphed, punishing the local population at times very harshly: in Moab, for example, two-thirds of the population was put to the sword (2 Samuel 8.2); in Ammon, the surviving inhabitants were forced to supply Israel with labour for royal projects (2 Samuel 12.31). The Aramaean states further north were led by Aram Zobah (see p. 400). David won an important victory against Zobah, which led to the surrender of its allies and neighbours, and the creation of several tributary states, who owed David political allegiance and had to provide regular material resources. Before his acceptance as king of Israel, David had made a dynastic alliance with the small kingdom of Geshur (east and north of Lake Galilee), by marrying the local ruler's daughter (2 Samuel 3.3), so that this state was friendly to him. Another important possession was the city of Ziklag, which had been presented to David by the Philistines to serve as his base when he joined them (2 Samuel 1.1), and so it constituted his personal property. It is probably to be identified with Tell esh-Sharia (Oren 1982) in the north-western Negev. Although David did not establish a supremacy over the Philistines, his repeated battles with them seem to have led to a clearer defining of boundaries between the two states, and the Philistines as a mortal threat to Israel's survival disappear from the biblical narratives. Whether David entered into alliance with Hiram of Tyre, a relationship so profitably exploited by his son and successor later, is possible but not certain (Soggin in Hayes and Maxwell Miller 1977: 351); it is not unthinkable, as David's kingdom, certainly by the end of his reign, would have made a profitable partner for the Phoenician state.

The political structure of Israel must, as a result, have been quite complex. All these very different peoples and political entities were held together by the person of the king only – a situation usually described, following the great Old Testament historian Albrecht Alt (1930/1966), as a 'personal union'. It is not unusual for states in the process of formation to go through a phase where, for a while, it is solely the power and position of one individual that unites them (Claessen and Skalník 1981). The real difficulties arise in trying to consolidate and routinise such a situation and to integrate all the disparate elements permanently (Weber 1947: 363ff.). The essential tool for achieving this is an administrative system. And with David we can see such a system beginning to take shape, reflected in a number of significant moves. First, army officials of David are named. An important development from Saul's time seems to have taken place in the military sphere: the army command was divided between an officer in charge of the king's personal militia and another responsible for the general call-up of all fighting men. Second, another named administrator is the superintendent of the labour-force who ensured that the king's subjects supplied the manpower required for carrying out essential construction works such as the building of fortresses. Third, there are named officials who reflect the existence of a court hierarchy, for example, the 'superintendent of the palace', a 'secretary' and a 'recorder'. Also closely related to the king were a number of 'priests'. All of this provides a picture of a new and fairly elaborate bureaucracy; the appearance of priests among the royal functionaries emphasises the supreme position of the king in *all* affairs of state.

The all-embracing nature of royal power that appears with David is echoed in the deliberate centralisation of the most important cult in the kingdom, that of Yahweh. The Ark of the Covenant was brought by David to Jerusalem and placed in a position of physical proximity to his official dwelling – at one stroke, the most important cultic symbol of Israel came under direct royal patronage. Whether David planned to build a temple for it, as the Old Testament maintains, is uncertain, but not unlikely, and would fit well with the moving of the ark to Jerusalem. Under David, too, began the attempt to blend Canaanite and Israelite cult practices – not, it would seem, a gradual process evolving as a result of usage, but a syncretism consciously fostered by the king as a matter of policy to help integrate the Canaanite city population and the Israelite tribes. A hint of this is contained in the fact that one of David's chief priests was Zadok, who is thought to have been associated with the pre-Israelite cult of Jerusalem.

In spite of David's reorganisation and centralisation, his new large state was vulnerable, made up, as it was, of a number of disparate groups who did not accept his rule unanimously. Threats to its cohesion came from revolts reported in 2 *Samuel*. Most significantly, the ones recounted had their roots among the northern tribes. The evidence for rebellion by neighbouring conquered kingdoms appears only later, in the reign of Solomon and in the ninth century; in some instances they may have been a response to David's earlier severe treatment. Two serious revolts by the north are mentioned, and both appear to have been attempts by the northern communities to free themselves from David's rule. In one case, the revolt was led by David's son, Absalom (2 *Samuel* 15), who was able to exploit opposition to his father. Another was led by Sheba of the northern tribe of Benjamin (2 *Samuel* 20), and shows that there was a considerable residue of loyalty to Saul's house. Saul's descendants were still seen as a threat to his position by David, as is very clearly shown by David's massacre of practically every surviving member of Saul's family (2 *Samuel* 21.1–14). The excuse put forward for this bloodbath was that Saul had broken an earlier sacred agreement made between the Israelite tribes and the city of Gibeah, which caused a terrible famine. So, in order to cleanse Israel from the sacrilege, all those related to the oath-breaker had to be killed. The only person to survive was Meribaal, Saul's lame grandson, whom David took into his court.

Solomon

The success of David's policies in forging a relatively stable state despite such difficulties is remarkable. A measure of it is that he was able to appoint his younger son, Solomon, as his successor in opposition to general expectations and strong pressures not to do so. Further, at no point do we hear that Solomon had to be acclaimed king publicly – in contrast to Saul, David himself and Solomon's own son and successor, Rehoboam (see p. 457). David's power was obviously so well established that neither divine designation, popular acclaim nor primogeniture needed to be brought into play to legitimise David's successor. Solomon himself, at his accession, acted swiftly to punish those members of the court who had supported his older brother's attempts to succeed to the throne: two were executed, a third banished.

Solomon's accession was underpinned, however, by what is thought to be a piece of Solomonic propaganda contained in 1 *Kings* 3. The tale recounts a visit made by Solomon to a hill shrine and altar near Gibeon. Here Solomon is said to have fallen asleep and had a dream in which Yahweh appeared and guaranteed to grant him one wish, in response to which Solomon asked for wisdom. It is possible that this story was intended to broadcast a message of divine approval for Solomon's kingship and proclaim Solomon as the right successor to David by virtue of his gift of divine wisdom.

In Solomon's reign the close involvement of the king in cult is very plain: the entire cultic programme seems to have been solely in his hands. This is most clearly illustrated by the story of Solomon's temple-building, which is presented as entirely under his control, planned by himself with no request for approval from anyone, human or divine. Phoenician craftsmen were brought in, by royal arrangement, to be the main builders and designers, and provide the sophisticated technology and the raw and precious materials. The tripartite structure of the sanctuary, described in 1 *Kings* 6, was typical of earlier and contemporary Canaanite temples, such as the one excavated at Tell Tayanat (Kenyon 1987: 92–97). The Israelite population only figures as providing the unskilled labour for the enterprise. Other pointers to the king's pre-eminence in cult are passages portraying Solomon engaging in typically priestly acts (1 *Kings* 8.14–66); and the fact that the temple was associated closely with, indeed attached to, the royal palace (*Ezekiel* 43.8; Ussishkin 1973). The Canaanite elements in the cult, dimly visible under David, were fostered further by Solomon who, as part of his accession purge, banished the 'traditional' priest, Abiathar, and elevated (the probably Canaanite) Zadok instead. It has even been argued that it was in Solomon's reign that the king began to be presented as exceptionally close to Yahweh, and thus invested with greater authority. Certainly some of the psalms reflect the resplendent and exalted position that the Israelite kings came to hold:

> My heart is stirred by a noble theme,
> in a king's honour I utter the song I have made,
> and my tongue runs like the pen of an expert scribe.

> You surpass all mankind in beauty,
> your lips are moulded in grace,
> so you are blessed by god for ever.
> With your sword ready at your side, warrior king,
> your limbs resplendent in their royal armour,
> ride on to execute true sentence and just judgement.
> Your right hand shall show you a scene of terror.
> your sharp arrows flying, nations beneath your feet,
> the courage of the king's foes melting away!

> Your throne is like god's throne, eternal,
> your royal sceptre a sceptre of righteousness.
> You have loved right and hated wrong;
> so god, your god, has anointed you
> above all your fellows with oil, the token of joy.
> Your robes are all fragrant with myrrh and powder of aloes,
> and the music of strings greets you

from a palace panelled with ivory.
A princess takes her place among the noblest of your women,
a royal lady at your side in gold of Ophir.

Listen, my daughter, hear my words
and consider them:
forget your own people and your father's house;
and, when the king desires your beauty,
remember that he is your lord.
Do him obeisance, daughter of Tyre,
and the richest in the land will court you with gifts.

In the palace honour awaits her;
she is a king's daughter,
arrayed in cloth-of-gold richly embroidered.
Virgins shall follow her into the presence of the king;
her companions shall be brought to her,
escorted with the noise of revels and rejoicing
as they enter the king's palace.

You shall have sons, O king, in place of your forefathers
and will make them rulers over all the land.
I will declare your fame to all generations;
therefore the nations will praise you for ever and ever.

(*Psalm* 45 (NEB))

Events and institutions, other than the building of the famous temple by Solomon and some, almost certainly ahistorical, anecdotes, are only very sparsely reported in the Old Testament. One fact that emerges with some clarity is that Solomon exploited the commercial potential of Israel, which straddled routes leading up from the Red Sea to Damascus and controlled access to the Mediterranean. In such ventures, he co-operated profitably with the Phoenician city of Tyre by putting up capital, initiating projects, allowing access to crucial routes and ports, and providing a patron with a demand for the products handled or manufactured by the Phoenicians. The state of Tyre contributed the skilled craftsmen and the navigators to realise the opportunities offered by Solomon. Its own economy was stimulated by the demands of Israel, and it became increasingly dependent on commerce and manufacture (pp. 408–409). This development is perhaps mirrored by the disgruntlement of the Tyrians at being presented by Solomon with a strip of land instead of the agreed payment – useless to them, when their resources were most profitably channelled into trade and industry (Frankenstein 1979). Although the visit of the Queen of Sheba belongs to the realm of legend (see p. 448), it is certainly not unthinkable that Solomon used his strategic control of routes to concentrate part of the Arabian incense and spice trade in his hands. He is described in 1 *Kings* 10.28–29 as trading in horses from Cilicia and Egypt, and in chariots from Egypt. Again this shows Solomon acting as an important middle-man in essential military equipment because of Israel's control of a considerable section of the international commercial network.

One important development credited to Solomon is the setting up of tax districts in Israel: on this basis, presumably, the state labour requirements were enforced and met, and through them other essential resources were collected and channelled to the royal purse. At the centre of each district was a 'store-city', heavily fortified, probably equipped with a garrison and housing administrative officials (see pp. 448–449). From the cities listed in this connection, it looks as though the tax districts were only established in the north (Israel), not in the southern region (Judah). If this was the case, it strengthens the impression that the northern tribes were treated as the subjects of privileged Judah.

Israel's wealth depended on maintaining control of the states subjugated by David. But Israel's hold over them began to crumble at some point in Solomon's reign. It is unfortunately impossible to tell when this happened, but certainly by the time of Solomon's death the states of Aram Zobah and Damascus had become independent, and Edom had revolted successfully. This spelt the loss of Israelite control over the important north–south route linking Syria to the gulf of Aqaba. At the same time it reduced Israel's territory and available man-power. As a result, the pressures on Israel's remaining subjects, such as those living in the northern territory, must have become correspondingly heavier, especially if royal enterprises and demands were not scaled down. This, it is argued, led eventually to the successful rebellion by the north against the Davidic dynasty.

8d(v) The separate states of Israel and Judah

The rapid changes, which occurred within the space of a few decades, meant that Israel was, in spite of a spectacular (though shortl-ived) expansion and important institutional developments, a highly volatile state which could easily fragment into its constituent parts. That is precisely what happened immediately after Solomon's death (c. 930/922). At the same time, the entities into which Israel broke down were not the same as they had been when first incorporated into the Davidic state – they, too, had been fundamentally affected and transformed by the political experience of the preceding century. The appearance of developed states in Edom and Damascus at this time bears witness to this; and it is just as true of the northern region, which now emerged as the strong and relatively powerful state of Israel.

The account of the collapse of the Davidic–Solomonic empire in 1 *Kings*, as it stands, has combined a number of sources and shaped them to fit the Deuteronomistic framework. It presents a sequence of events according to which Solomon neglected to maintain purity with respect to the cult of Yahweh, which in turn led to his successor failing to retain control, and

Yahweh raising a rival king in the north. The northern rebellion was sparked off by the prophet Ahijah of Shiloh, who prophesied to Jeroboam, supervisor of the forced labour-gangs, that he would become king of the ten tribes of the north. When Solomon heard of the prophecy he sought to kill Jeroboam, who fled to Egypt. When Solomon's son and successor, Rehoboam, went to the northern town of Shechem to be acclaimed (in itself a hint that relations with the north had reached a critical point), Jeroboam returned and challenged the new king about the forced labour demands imposed by Judah on the north. Only if they were reduced would the region continue to accept rule from Judah (1 *Kings* 12.3–4). Rehoboam proudly and disdainfully refused, at which point the cry for secession went up:

> What share have we in David?
> We have no lot in the son of Jesse.
> Away to your homes, O Israel;
> now see to your own house, David.
>
> (1 *Kings* 12.16 (NEB))

After an abortive attempt to force submission, Rehoboam fled in haste to Jerusalem and, in the words of the Deuteronomist:

> from that day to this the whole of Israel has been in rebellion against the house of David.
>
> (1 *Kings* 12.19 (NEB))

In the perspective of this later writer, the northern kingdom was always considered by Judah to be rebellious – an entity with no legitimate independent existence. It was also presented as consistently irreligious – incapable of proper Yahweh worship since it did not worship regularly at the sole correct sanctuary in Jerusalem. For this it was punished eventually by Yahweh with the Assyrian onslaught and destruction in 721.

This highly biased picture belongs to the debate about the reasons for Israel's destruction, which developed in the seventh century. The underlying message of the narrative, as it now stands, must be remembered when we try to understand the 'schism' between north and south. Some scholars (e.g. Bright 1959) have sought to argue that a major reason for the division was that fundamentally different attitudes to kingship existed between north and south. In the south, David represented an ideal and successful ruler, and the dynastic principle was thus accepted, while the north continued to adhere to the idea of charismatic leadership, and so had a more 'democratic' tendency. This, it is suggested, is borne out by the fact that, for almost a century following secession, there were innumerable changes of kings in the north, few sons succeeded their fathers on the throne, and many kings were violently deposed. Such an interpretation should be rejected. There is no evidence that the institution of monarchy was ever questioned in Israel, and no hint that any other form of government was ever considered (see pp. 444–445). The lack of stability in the north is better understood as linked to the problems faced by a new developing state. A further factor may have been that Israel was larger and richer than its southern neighbour, and much more actively involved with neighbouring states, which led to numerous conflicts and wars that in turn could have had disruptive effects. In considering the question, it is important to realise that the bloody history of the northern kingdom of Israel revolved around the problem of *who* should be its king, not whether there should be a king at all.

The idea that the secession was the culmination of resentment at the privileged position of Judah *vis-à-vis* Israel is more feasible. In support of such a view we can cite the revolts in the north against David, Jeroboam's threatened revolt against Solomon and the protest-demands made by the north of Rehoboam at Shechem. There is further the likelihood that Solomon's tax-districts were only instituted in Israel (1 *Kings* 4.7). Whether this is enough to explain the secession is rather more doubtful, and the biblical account is too limited to allow us a more detailed insight, especially as the events of Solomon's reign and the precise structure of the kingdom under him remain shadowy. Perhaps it is simply erroneous to see the events following Solomon's death as the division of an original whole: Israel and Judah were probably always (Ahlström 1986), and continued to be, two separate political units that were only temporarily united by the astounding successes of David and Solomon. As the kingdom began to suffer losses and defeats, the rulers in Jerusalem proved too weak to hold their conquests together. They had simply not had enough time to forge the links of loyalty and identity of interest that could have held such a large and disparate territory together. The period of David and Solomon is probably best regarded as a fairly short-lived phase along the road leading to the emergence of the two new states of Israel and Judah.

* * *

This is the story of the Jewish states' development as we may reconstruct it on the basis of the biblical text and some correlated archaeological finds. There is virtually no other evidence and it must remain for the moment a moot point whether it is history or historical fiction. Old Testament scholars are divided on the issue, and we shall have to see whether material confirming or denying it is ever found.

8e The states of the Levant and the Assyrian empire in the ninth and eighth centuries

The broad picture

The history of the Levant from the ninth century onwards stands in the shadow of Assyria's expansion, and hence it is dominated by the Assyrian perspective – understandably so, given that it is the Assyrian royal sources which provide the richest and, chronologically and historically, most useful information for the states with which they came into contact. But, admittedly, it makes for a very partial picture only. Is it possible for us to gain an independent insight into the histories of the states in this region, and their developing relations and increasing dependence on their formidable Assyrian neighbour? The answer, unfortunately, must be: only with difficulty and only very patchily.

Some archaeological and inscribed material exists, but excavation of sites has been limited, and the royal inscriptions cannot easily be dated with precision as complete lists of the local rulers are difficult to reconstruct (*CAH* III ch. 9; Hawkins in press; Layton 1988). Yet another impediment is that it is only exceptionally that any of the preserved inscriptions refer in any detail to political events. For example, very little is preserved from Damascus, which was one of the wealthiest and most important of the states in the Levant during the ninth and eighth centuries as is clear from Assyrian records and the Old Testament (Pitard 1987; Lemaire 1991); material from Bit Agusi (North Syria, p. 394), save for the treaty stelae from Sfire (p. 492), is also very sparse; and the same is true of Pattin(a) further west (North Syrian coast, pp. 412–413), although some monumental remains have been found at Tell Tayanat and 'Ain Dara (*CAH* III ch. 9; Abou Assaf 1985). Carchemish on the Euphrates is rather better represented, as the enclosure wall of the great royal acropolis with its relief decoration and inscriptions have been revealed by excavation (Hogarth *et al.* 1914–52; Hawkins 1972). However, apart from providing a king-list (*CAH* III ch. 9; Hawkins in press), the inscriptions are limited almost exclusively to rehearsing the piety of the kings, their building activities, internal dynastic struggles, and generally local concerns (cf. pp. 414–416). Careful analysis of the sculpted remains has allowed a better appreciation of the considerable influence Carchemish exercised over its neighbours, and the gradual limits imposed upon its activities by the expanding Assyrian empire (Winter 1983). There is also an interesting, albeit rather fragmentary and hence hard to understand, letter (in Akkadian) reporting on the difficulties in reorganising Carchemish as an Assyrian province (SAA 1 no. 183). In sum, material exists, but it is not sufficient to allow us to trace the historical experience of the western states from their point of view.

An exception to this rather negative picture is Hamath (modern Hama on the Orontes), where the Aramaic stele of its king, Zakkur (probably to be dated to the early eighth century; Layton 1988), recounts in some detail his conquest of a neighbouring small state, Hadrach (Hatarikka). Zakkur's annexation of Hadrach was challenged by a coalition of states led by the king of Damascus and including Bit Agusi, Que, Pattin(a), Gurgum, Sam'al, Melid and others whose names are lost (for location, see map 13; pp. 411–413). The allies besieged Hadrach but, as Zakkur says:

I lifted my hands to Baal-shamayn, and Baalshamayn answered me, and Baalshamayn spoke to me through prophets and messengers; and Baalshamayn said to me: 'Fear not! It was I who made you king, [and I shall stand] with you, and I shall deliver you from all these kings who have forced a siege upon you.'

Then Baalshamayn said to me: 'Destroyed shall be all these kings who forced this siege upon you. . . and this rampart which they put up shall be cast down.'

(Gibson 1971–82 II no. 5, A.11–17)

The victorious outcome (for Zakkur) was then commemorated by setting up the stele recounting Hamath's divine deliverance and describing Zakkur's building works.

The Zakkur inscription gives us an insight into one of the many wars that raged among the western states. Occasionally, one of the protagonists might call in the Assyrian king to resolve hostilities by, for example, fixing the frontier between the two warring sides. Such an act of Assyrian adjudication is attested for Hamath and Bit Agusi by a stele now in Antakya, and for Gurgum and Kummuh by a stele from Pazarcık (*CAH* III: 400; Hawkins in press; Donbaz 1990). At other times, the western states appealed to the king of Assyria to lend them armed support, either against threatening neighbours or against an internal rival in domestic power struggles. This latter type of Assyrian intervention (by invitation, as it were) is well illustrated by incriptions from Sam'al, the small state north of Pattin(a) on the eastern edge of Cilicia. In *c.* 840–30, the local king, Kilamuwa, had been subjected by the king of Cilicia at Adana. His response was to call in the Assyrian king; with the help of Assyrian arms he was able to regain his independence, establish his power firmly in Sam'al and, as he proudly says (in the Phoenician text inscribed in the vestibule of the palace), put its social and economic inequities to rights:

> I am Kilamuwa, the son of Hayya.
>
> Gabbar became king over Y'DY (Sam'al), but accomplished nothing. There was BMH, but he accomplished nothing. Then there was my father Hayya but he accomplished nothing. Then there was my brother Š'L, but he accomplished nothing. But I Kilamuwa, the son of TM- (probably the name of Kilamuwa's mother), what I accomplished not (even) their predecessors accomplished.
>
> My father's house was in the midst of powerful kings, and each put forth his hand to eat it; but I was in the hand(s) of the kings like a fire that consumes the hand. The king of the Danunians (i.e. Adana) lorded it over me, but I hired against him the king of Assyria. 'He gave a maid for the price of a sheep, and a man for the price of a garment' (i.e. either: a proverb meaning that Kilamuwa got excellent value from the Assyrian king; or: a phrase indicating that Kilamuwa had to pay tribute to Assyria in return for this help).
>
> I Kilamuwa, the son of Hayya, sat upon my father's throne. In face of

the former kings the MŠKBM (a suppressed social group?) used to whimper like dogs. But I – to some I was a father, and to some I was a mother, and to some I was a brother. Him who had never seen the face of a sheep I made owner of a flock; him who had never seen the face of an ox, I made owner of a herd and owner of silver and owner of gold; and him who had never seen linen from his youth, in my days they were covered with byssus (the finest linen textile). I grasped the MŠKBM by the hand and they behaved (towards me) like an orphan towards (his) mother.

Now if any of my sons who shall sit in my place does harm to this inscription, may the MŠKBM not honour the B'RRM (i.e. the ruling elite?), nor the B'RRM honour the MŠKBM! And if anyone smashes this inscription, may Baal-Semed who belongs to Gabbar smash his head, and may Baal-Hammon who belongs to BMH and Rakkabel, lord of the dynasty, smash his head!

(Gibson 1971–82 III no. 13)

About one hundred years later another long inscription from Sam'al records serious dynastic strife: the reigning king, Barsur, was killed in a political coup; his son, Panammu, was able to escape and appealed to Tiglath-pileser III (744–727) of Assyria to come to his aid. With Assyrian help he regained the throne and became henceforth a most loyal Assyrian ally and subject, as movingly described (in Aramaic) on a commemorative statue by his son, Barrakkab:

He (sc. Panammu) ran at the wheel of his lord, Tiglath-pileser, king of Assyria, in campaigns from east to west and . . . over the four quarters of the earth . . . [and added to] his territory did his lord Tiglath-pileser, king of Assyria, from the territory of Gurgum . . .

Then Panammu, my father, died while following his lord Tiglath-pileser, king of Assyria, in the campaigns; even [his lord, Tiglath-pileser, king of Assyria, wept for him] and his brother kings wept for him, and the whole camp of his lord, the king of Assyria, wept for him. His lord, the king of Assyria, took. . . [may] his soul [eat and drink]; and he set up an image for him by the way, and brought my father across from Damascus to Assyria. In my days . . . all his house [wept] for him. Then me Barrakab, son of Panammu, because of my father's righteousness and my own righteousness, did my lord [Tiglath-pileser, king of Assyria] make to sit [upon the throne] of my father Panammu, son of Barsur . . .

(Gibson 1971–82 II no. 14)

The series of texts from Sam'al, more than any others, illustrates beautifully the mutuality of relations that could, and did, exist between Assyria and some of the Levantine states. In a situation where a small state was threatened by a larger, aggressive neighbour it could appeal to Assyria for support (in return for payment or tribute); because of the formal relations of obligation this entailed for both sides, later kings, if ousted by internal opponents, could rely on Assyrian aid to uphold and defend their legitimate claims to the throne. Their loyalty to the Assyrian king was rewarded by their own kingdoms being enlarged through the addition of land detached from adjacent states perhaps less friendly to Assyria. The dynasts, in turn, demonstrated their active support for Assyria by fighting on the Assyrian side during important campaigns at some distance from their homes (Panammu probably accompanied Tiglath-pileser III on his war against Damascus in 734–732). Tribute was paid to their faithful service by public mourning at their death in Assyria and other allied states. In Panammu's case, his loyalty was further marked by the setting up of a commemorative stone by the Assyrian king, perhaps near the spot where he was killed. Another mark of respect was that Panammu's corpse was retrieved and ceremoniously conveyed to Assyria so that it could be properly buried (although the precise place of burial is unclear – perhaps it was eventually brought in state back to Sam'al). A final gesture, signalling how the Assyrian king honoured his obligations to his client, is that he ensured the accession of Panammu's son to his father's throne. The gratitude of the new king to his Assyrian overlord was then expressed by his public erection of the statue proudly recording these mutual services.

The case of Israel and Judah

But full information of this kind is the exception rather than the rule, and it must be admitted that superficial knowledge of the internal politics and structures of the small Levant and Anatolian states is the norm. The one exception is Israel and Judah. Because we have the Hebrew Bible, scholars are in a position to know a bit more about two states in the Levant (and, in part, their neighbours, such as Damascus, Moab and Edom), which both came into direct contact with Assyria, but whose relations with the great empire differed and whose individual fates diverged. It must be stressed that it is above all due to the accounts in the Old Testament that a reconstruction of the history of Israel and Judah is possible – if we did not have it, Israel and Judah would be little more than names in the Assyrian annals,[6] and Hamath, Sam'al, Bit Agusi, even Moab, would be much better known. The reason is that no lengthy monumental inscriptions have been recovered from either Israel or Judah for this period (Smelik 1985; Millard 1990), despite the fact that almost every inch of the 'Holy Land' has, for obvious reasons, been excavated, re-excavated, surveyed and sifted. Apart from one reference to Israel in an inscription from Moab (see pp. 469–470) and the possible mention of Judah in a stele fragment from Tel Dan (Biran and Naveh 1993; cf. p. 438), the only certain extra-biblical mentions of Israel and Judah occur in the Assyrian records.

Sources

The main sources for Israel and Judah are contained in 1 and 2 *Kings*, which cover the history of both states, although the perspective of the compiler(s) is Judah. Israel, from this standpoint, is perceived as really belonging to Judah but rebellious, and hence going astray, which led to its eventual downfall (p. 457). The sources on which the account is based are, first, the 'royal history' of Judah and the 'royal history' of Israel – whether these were official court records or some form of popular (oral) history is disputed (van Seters 1983 [OK]). Second, there was probably a source concerning King Ahab of Israel, perhaps related to a history of the wars between Israel and Damascus; and, finally, another major strand seems to derive from stories told about prophets, such as Elijah and Elishah.

1 and 2 *Chronicles* is a somewhat later reworking of *Kings* (see p. 419), concentrating on the history of Judah and elaborating and explaining a number of historical events. Where the writer(s) of *Kings* presents the history of Israel and Judah as the inevitable tragic outcome of Yahweh's people straying from his commandments, the Chronicler puts forward a harsh, uncompromising view that denies the northern kingdom any validity at all: Davidic rule is the only legitimate option; the northern kingdom is an abomination; the Jerusalem temple is the exclusive place for Yahweh worship. This formulation of Israel's history was shaped decisively by the experience of the restored Jewish community (fifth century) and its struggles to defend and define its identity by recapturing and idealising its past to provide an unmistakable lesson for the present. The amount of primary material and the value of alternative sources that the author of Chronicles used to underpin his message is debated, but not generally thought to be high in terms of historical usefulness (Willi 1972). Given the Chronicler's extreme partisan position it is best, on the whole, to give preference to the books of *Kings*.

Some of the prophetic books of the Old Testament relate to figures active in the eighth century and constitute another important source. The prophecies and biographical material were collected later, and it is difficult to know quite how this was done and to what extent they underwent literary reworking (Rowley 1967). But what must be conceded is that the prophets were historical figures, that some of their activities were remembered later, and that they came to play an influential role in how the Israelites felt their history had been shaped. The prophetic books relevant to this period are, first, Amos, who is thought to have been a sheep-farmer from Judah, living *c.* 760, but prophesying in the kingdom of Israel. His main message was that social inequities and institutional corruption were offences against Yahweh, and that a mechanical performance of the Yahweh cult was useless – only if the moral messages of Yahweh were taken to heart could worship of him be truly effective. Hosea, a northern prophet (*c.* 740), may have been a baker, and the particular focus of his criticism was sexual misconduct, which he saw as incompatible with true Yahweh worship. Best-known of the prophets is proto-Isaiah of Judah, i.e. chapters 1–39 of the book called *Isaiah*, which, in its present form, combines the visions of three prophets widely separated in time. Proto-Isaiah was active between *c.* 740 and 700, and what is particularly interesting is that he was opposed to resistance against Assyria. He prophesied that the north (Israel) would fall, while the south (Judah), despite suffering, would be spared, and that in these ordeals Assyria was actually Yahweh's tool:

> The Assyrian! He is the rod that I (Yahweh) wield in my anger, and the staff of my wrath is in his hand.
> I send him against a godless nation (i.e. Israel),
> I bid him march against a people who rouse my wrath,
>   to spoil and plunder at will
> and trample them down like mud in the streets.
>
> *(Isaiah* 10. 5–6 (NEB))

Virtually nothing is known of Isaiah's professional standing, but, like Hosea and Amos, he was probably not a member of the official cult or court establishment. The prophets reflect some of the discussions taking place in Judah during the later eighth and seventh centuries about the nature of Yahweh's will for his people, and the form the debates took at a time of considerable social change and political upheaval.

Non-biblical sources for Israel and Judah are scanty. There are extensive archaeological remains at the site of Samaria, which was founded as the new and lasting capital of Israel by Omri (*Encyclopedia* IV 1032–1050; Tappy 1992). Like several excavated cities of the Levant and south Turkey (e.g. Sam'al; Amiet 1980 [OM]: 489–490), it consisted of a fortified citadel enclosing the palatial residence and administrative buildings of the king, and dominating from there the houses of the citizens located on the lower slopes (Kenyon 1979 [OGd]: 262ff.). Illuminating for the development of the institution of kingship are some seals, made of precious materials (such as jasper; Vattioni 1969–78: no. 68; *SDB* s.v. 'Sceaux'), and seal-impressions, inscribed with the name of the owner and his position within the royal administration (Smelik 1985: 127–136): a major-domo of the palace, commander of forced labour, city-governor, royal minister, servant, scribe and 'king's son' (responsible, in part, for judicial decisions) are all attested by this material, as is a royal daughter. The material demonstrates how strongly the political systems of both Israel and Judah were centred on king and court. Somewhat different (and considerably later) are the stamped wine-jar handles from el-Jib (possibly second half of seventh century), giving the name of Gibeon and a name which, it has been suggested, represented the name of the vintners from whose vineyards the wine came (Gibson 1971–82 I 54–56). Another group of jar-handles (about a thousand in all) is extremely debated: they are stamped with the word *lmlk* ('of the king'), a scarab or winged disc and one of four place-names; they were in use *c.* 700 in Judah. What they represent (royal administrative districts in Judah? locations of royal vineyards? royal pottery centres? Aharoni 1979 [OGd]: 394–400; Smelik 1985: 124; Na'aman 1991) remains uncertain, but the phrase *lmlk* reflects the great power wielded by the king.

The ostraca found in Samaria offer an important potential insight into the royal court. About a hundred sherds, written in Hebrew, were recovered on the acropolis, and are probably to be dated to the reign of Jeroboam II (787–745). They mostly record receipts for small quantities of luxury articles, mature ('old') wine and purified ('washed') oil, sent from places in the region of the Manasseh tribe to named individuals; e.g.:

> In (regnal) year n(ine)
> from Qouseh to Gadyaw,
> one jar of old wine.
>
> (Lemaire 1977, ostracon no. 5)

As with the *lmlk* stamps, there has been considerable debate about what system the ostraca reflect (Lemaire 1977: 73–77). The most persuasive argument is that they illustrate the economic basis of the court in Israel: i.e. the king's courtiers held land – partly privately owned, partly in gift from the king – in various parts of the kingdom; the produce of their estates, in the form of wine, oil and other fine products, was used by them for consumption at court, which is where they needed to reside in order to maintain their position and carry out their functions; the luxuriousness of the products would relate directly to the high quality of food and dress demanded by court-etiquette and rank. That such refinements were associated with the life of the rich is known from the Old Testament; most familiar is a passage from *Psalm* 23:

> You prepare a table before me in the sight of my enemies;
> you anoint (perfume) my head with oil,
> my cup (of wine) overflows.
>
> (*Psalm* 23.5 (NEB))

Analogous systems for supplying court-personnel are attested for other kingdoms at other times (e.g. Babylonia in the sixth century; Ugarit in the thirteenth century), and are also directly referred to in the Old Testament; *2 Samuel* 9 shows David deciding to take one of the few surviving members of Saul's family, his lame grandson Meribaal, into his court and to let him 'eat at his table':

> Then David summoned Saul's servant to his presence and said: 'I assign to your master's grandson all the property that belonged to Saul and his family. You and your sons and your slaves must cultivate the land and bring in the harvest to provide for your master's household, but Meribaal shall have a place at my table.
>
> (*2 Samuel* 9.9–10)

Historical outline

The political history of Israel and Judah is reconstructed from the biblical material (for a recent account, see *CAH* III chs. 10–11; 29–30). In general, it is true to say that Judah seems to have experienced very little in the way of serious political upheavals throughout the ninth and eighth centuries, as the dynasty of David remained in unchallenged control down to the fall of Jerusalem. There was some intermarriage between the royal houses of Judah and Israel, but the two states always co-existed uneasily, and there were several bloody frontier wars. Judah was by far the smaller political unit, and this, combined with its geographical position, meant that it was drawn into major conflicts less frequently and less disastrously than its larger northern neighbour.

Following the death of Solomon, *c.* 930/922, the new northern state of Israel was politically in flux. It had no generally acknowledged or accepted ruler and no recognised political centre. It is, therefore, not surprising that for some time, until 876, a struggle for its control ensued. In spite of dynastic weakness, Israel remained stable as a political unit, and there was certainly no attempt ever to consider an alternative form of government apart from monarchy (see pp. 457–458). An important development in Israel's history was Omri's successful bid for the throne (876–869). He founded Samaria, which became from then on Israel's political centre. Under Omri's dynasty relations with Judah to the south were placed on a more peaceful footing through a dynastic marriage. A significant indicator of the importance of Omri (about whom very little is known: 1 *Kings* 16.23–28) is that Assyrian records refer to Israel as *Bīt Humri*, i.e 'the house of Omri' – the term 'Israel' appears rarely, the usual alternative being simply 'Samaria'. Israel's wealth in this period is shown by its dynastic alliance with wealthy Tyre, the great contingents which it supplied to oppose Shalmaneser III of Assyria in 853 (see p. 488), and its continued control of territory well to the east of the Jordan and southwards until some point after the middle of the ninth century. Possibly as a result of repeated Assyrian assaults and the loss of Transjordan (recorded by the incription of Mesha of Moab, pp. 469–470), Omri's dynasty was overthrown in a bloody revolt by one of his generals, Jehu (see fig. 30), who wiped out the family of Omri totally, and founded a dynasty that dominated Israel for the next hundred years (see table 27). The main conflict known in this period is that which continued to be waged between Israel and Damascus, primarily concerning control of trade routes and commercial advantages.

The dynasty of Jehu came to an end eventually, probably as a result of renewed Assyrian expansion, beginning under Tiglath-pileser III (744–727; see pp. 496–497; Otzen 1979). It is possible that the rapid succession of usurpations in Israel between 745 and 722 is to be explained by the internal instability within Israel created by conflicting attempts to cope with Assyrian demands. The chronology is extremely problematical (*CAH* III ch. 22/I), but a plausible

Figure 30 King Jehu of Israel doing obeisance before Shalmaneser III of Assyria
(left of kneeling figure of Jehu); black obelisk, Nimrud
(British Museum; drawing by D. Saxon)

reconstruction of events suggests the following sequence of events. In conjunction with Tiglath-pileser III's re-assertion of Assyrian power in the west, and his extension of the policy of incorporating states as Assyrian provinces (see chapter 9c), he established in 738 Assyrian control of some of the important Mediterranean ports, including Gaza. The king of Gaza became an Assyrian subject, and Tiglath-pileser III established an Assyrian commercial centre in its vicinity. At the same time, a local Arab ruler was made answerable to the Assyrian authorities for safeguarding the frontier between Gaza and the routes to Egypt; in other words, he was deputed to operate the area in Assyria's commercial and military interests (Eph'al 1982). Into this period probably falls the payment of tribute to Assyria by Menahem, the new king of Israel; according to 2 *Kings* 15.19–20, Menahem paid it in order to obtain Assyrian support for his seizure of the Israelite throne (cf. Kilamuwa of Sam'al, pp. 460–461). The arrangement seems to have worked only briefly, because Menahem's brutal efforts to raise the payments for Assyria from his subjects, led to his assassination and the eventual triumph of king Pekah. Pekah reversed Menahem's policy of appeasement towards Assyria by allying with Israel's old enemy, Damascus. Both Israel and Damascus had suffered severely from the Assyrian expansion, which had the effect of pushing them to the margins of the international trade network. Their alliance was intended, with the help of Edom, to put pressure on Judah and thus create a bloc of states capable of wresting back control of nodal points in the trade. In this situation Ahaz (Jehoahaz I), the king of Judah, acted like so many other rulers of the small states in the Levant threatened by powerful neighbours: he

Table 27 The kings of Israel and Judah. (There are many alternative chronologies; this follows one proposed by Albright, *BASOR* 100 (1945): 16–22.)

Israel		Judah	
Jeroboam	922–901	Rehoboam	922–915
Nadab	901–900	Abijah	915–913
		Asa	913–873
Baasha	900–887		
Elah	877–876		
Zimri	876		
Omri	876–869	Jehoshaphat	873–849
Ahab	869–850		
Ahaziah	850–849		
Jehoram	849–842	Jehoram	849–842
Jehu	842–815	Ahaziah	842
		Athaliah	842–837
Jehoahaz	815–801	Jehoash	837–800
Joash	801–786	Amaziah	800–783
Jeroboam II	786–746	Azariah/Uzziah	783–742
Zechariah	746–745		
Shallum	745		
Menahem	745–738	Jotham	750–735
Pekahiah	738–737		
Pekah	737–732	Jehoahaz I	735–715
Hoshea	732–722		

Fall of Northern Kingdom
    722/721

		Judah	
		Hezekiah	715–687
		Manasseh	687–642
		Amon	642–640
		Josiah	640–609
		Jehoahaz II	609
		Jehoiachim	609–598
		Jehoiachin	598–597
		Zedekiah	597–587

Fall of Jerusalem to
Nebuchadnezzar II of Babylon

appealed to Tiglath-pileser III to intervene, in return for tribute and alliance, on his behalf against his foes:

> Ahaz sent messengers to Tiglath-pileser, king of Assyria, to say, 'I am your servant and your son. Come and save me from the king of Aram (i.e. Damascus) and from the king of Israel who are attacking me.' Ahaz took silver and gold found in the house of the Lord and in the treasuries of the royal palace and sent them to the king of Assyria as a bribe. The king of Assyria listened to him . . .
>
> (*2 Kings* 16.7–9 (NEB))

Tiglath-pileser responded quickly, besieged Damascus and, at its fall in 732 after a two-year siege, its extensive territory was divided up into Assyrian provinces, some of its people were deported and its king executed. He also detached large parts of Israel's territory, leaving a rump-state centred on Samaria. At the conclusion of the Damascus campaign, Ahaz visited the Assyrian king and formalised his initial appeal for help, probably by swearing an oath of loyalty. Both Israel and Judah were now subject kingdoms of Assyria, and in 722/1, because of Israel's plotting with Egypt, even the rump of the northern kingdom ceased to exist: its king, nobles and crack cavalry corps were deported (Oded 1978; Dalley 1985), and peoples from the Zagros region and Babylonia, as well as Arabs, were eventually settled in Samaria instead (Tadmor 1958b; Becking 1992).

The fall of the prosperous northern kingdom which, despite hostilities and antagonisms, was always regarded as closely linked to the southern area of Judah, seems to have provoked an intensive debate about the historical fortunes of the twelve tribes and Yahweh's plan for them. It is now argued by several scholars (Rendtorff 1983) that it was precisely this disaster that led to the first compilations of Israel's earlier history, and the formulation of all historical experience as a direct reflection of the purity of its adherence to Yahweh's cult (see p. 436).

Conclusion

A direct result of that speculation is that we know so much more about the histories of Israel and Judah than about any of the other Levant states. But it should be remembered that within the context of the ninth to seventh centuries the social, economic, political, and even religious history (in some respects) of these two states was not unique (Millard 1990). The prophetic books and the prophets that figure in the *Kings* narrative illuminate valuably details of social problems, political divisions and religious beliefs; but the few surviving inscriptions from other states hint at comparable concerns and practices: the Zakkur inscription from Hamath refers to the help and support the king of Hamath received in obtaining divine messages through prophets and seers in a time of crisis (see pp. 459–460); the Sam'al texts illustrate the political pressures which small states experienced at the hands of more powerful neighbours, and the fact that social injustices were problems that concerned (or could be exploited by) the local kings (see pp. 460–461; also Karatepe, pp. 414–415). The celebrated (Moabite) inscription of King Mesha of Moab[7] shows how the concept of a war inspired by the local god, Khemosh, was used to explain victories and justify massacres:

> I am Mesha, son of Khemosh-yat, king of Moab, the Dibonite. My father was king over Moab for thirty years, and I became king after my father. I built this high place for Khemosh in *qarho* (probably part of

the city of Dibon where Mesha had his citadel), a high place of salvation, because he delivered me from all assaults, and because he let me see my desire upon my adversaries.

Omri, king of Israel, had oppressed Moab many days, for Khemosh was angry with his land. His son succeeded him, and he too said, I will oppress Moab. In my days he said it; but I saw my desire upon him and his house, and Israel perished utterly for ever. Omri had taken possession of the land of Medeba, and dwelt there his days and much of his son's days, forty years; but Khemosh dwelt in it in my days. I rebuilt Baal-meon, and I made a reservoir in it; and I rebuilt Kiriathaim. Then the men of Gad had settled in the land of Ataroth from of old, and the king of Israel had fortified Ataroth for himself; but I fought against the town and took it; and I slew all the inhabitants of the town, a spectacle for Khemosh and Moab. I brought back from there 'the lion figure of David'(?), and dragged it before Khemosh at Kerioth; and I settled in it the men of Sharon (unidentified town) and the men of Mharit (unidentified town).

Next Khemosh said to me, Go take Nebo from Israel. So I went by night, and fought against it from break of dawn till noon; and I took it and slew all in it, seven thousand men and women, both natives and aliens, and female slaves; for I had devoted it to Ashtar-Khemosh. I took from thence the vessels of Yahweh and dragged them before Khemosh. Then the king of Israel had fortified Jahaz, and he occupied it while warring against me; but Khemosh drove him out before me. I took from Moab two hundred men, his whole division, and I led it up against Jahaz and captured it, annexing it to Dibon.

I carried out repairs at *qarho*, on the parkland walls as well as the walls of the acropolis; and I repaired its gates and repaired its towers; and I repaired the king's residence, and I made banks for the reservoir at the spring inside the town. But there was no cistern inside the town at *qarho*; so I said to all the people, Each of you make for yourselves a cistern in his house. I had the ditches dug for *qarho* with Israelite prisoners. I carried out repairs at Aroer, and I mended the highway at the Arnon. I rebuilt Beth-bamoth, for it had been destroyed; and I rebuilt Bezer, for it was in ruins, with fifty men of Dibon, because all Dibon had become subject (to me).

So did I become king (over) hundreds in the towns which I annexed to the land.

Then I rebuilt Medeba also, and Beth-diblathaim. And as for Beth Baal-meon, I led (my shepherds) up there (in order to tend the) sheep of the district. (Remainder fragmentary)

(Gibson 1971–82 I no. 16; *ANET*: 320–321; *TUAT* I 646–650; Smelik 1985: 33–35)

The spoils of war were used to enrich the victor's temples, cities, land and subjects; deportees were used to labour on the building projects of the conqueror for the greater glory of his gods – just as David had done earlier. The thoughtworld that produced the Mesha stone is identical to the one which presented Jehu's blood-soaked revolt against his king in 841 as an act willed, initiated and blessed by Yahweh (*2 Kings* 9–10).

A fairly recent find at the site of Kuntillet Ajrud in the south of Judah suggests that Yahweh was sometimes conceived to have a divine consort (Emerton 1982; Smelik 1985: 141–143). This evidence, combined with the texts from Khirbet el-Kom (Dever 1969–70), now makes it likely that at least some sections of Israelite society associated Yahweh with a female deity, Asherah (Ackroyd 1983; Hestrin 1991), as shown by this tomb inscription:

'Uriyahu, the prosperous one (? or: 'the chief'; or: 'the singer'), wrote this: A blessed man is 'Uriyahu because of Yahweh – from his troubles he saved him through his Asherah.

(Mittman 1981; Smelik 1985: 138–141)

The inscriptions raise the possibility that many of the 'foreign' divinities reviled in the Old Testament for contaminating the cult of Yahweh, were not intrusive, non-Israelite religious elements introduced by outsiders, but formed, at least for some Israelites, a regular part of their religious beliefs. Exclusive, pure monotheism – the hallmark of later Jewish faith – was perhaps not as yet fully established, but still in the process of crystallisation (Ahlström 1984).

The most striking find illustrating how closely interwoven the Israelites and their neighbours were is an Aramaic text, written in ink on plaster and preserved on the wall of a sanctuary at Deir Alla, located in the territory of Israel's neighbour, Ammon. It contains a tale about Balaam, the seer, a figure familiar from a story in *Numbers* 22–24, beginning as follows:

[This is the in]scription of [Bilea]m, [the son of Beo]r, the man, (who) is the seer of gods. He (it is)! And the gods came to him in the night, [and they spoke to hi]m in accordance with the word of El, and they spoke to [Bilea]m, son of Beor, thus: 'He will make . . .'

Then Bileam arose the following morning . . . while he wept, yea wept.

Then there came to him Eliqa . . .: 'Why do you weep?'

Then he spoke to them: 'Be seated! I will tell you what Shag[ar (deity) will do]. And come, see the doings of the go[d]s!

[The gods] gathered, and the Shadday-deities gathered together, and they spoke to Sha[gar]: "You can break the bolts of heaven, in your cloud (may be) darkness and no gleam of light, dark(?) and not your . . . You can create fear [with the] dark [clo]ud, but do not be angry for ever!"'

(Hooftijzer and van der Kooij 1976; *TUAT* II 139–141;
Smelik 1985: 79–80)

The text is very fragmentary and only partly reconstructable, but the main outline is clear: Bileam has a divine vision in his sleep, warning the people against a coming catastrophe about to be unleashed by the goddess Shagar. The style is closely comparable to some of the prophetic stories in the Hebrew Bible, yet the deities involved are non-Israelite ones, while the prophet is a character known from the Old Testament. More clearly than almost anything else the Deir Alla text shows how intimately Israel and Judah were linked to their neighbours: they shared a similar political and cultural texture. While it happens that we know more about the Israelite states than their contemporaries, their history, social and cultic institutions were in many respects not unique in this pre-exilic period, but, in several important aspects, typical of the region of which they formed an integral part.

Notes

1 The origin of the Philistines from Egyptian garrison soldiers in the Levant has recently been challenged (Wood 1991). It is, admittedly, an inference, not a fact, and Wood's arguments against it present a feasible alternative hypothesis, although not one so far generally accepted.

2 For a recent rebuttal of the idea, based on Herodotus, that the Etruscans came from Asia Minor, see Drews 1992.

3 Lipiński (*Studia Phoenicia* III: 218 and n. 20) suggests amending Togarmah to *Twgdmh* and translating 'from the homeland of Tugdamme', i.e. Lygdamis, leader of an invading horde (possibly Cimmerian) which ravaged Anatolia in the seventh century; *RLA* 7: 186–189. (The Ezekiel passage has been discussed recently by I.M. Diakonoff, 'The naval power and trade of Tyre', *IEJ* 42/3–4 (1992): 168–193.)

4 Until fairly recently the name was read 'Hattin(a)'. Scholarly opinion now holds that 'Pattin(a)' is the more correct rendering.

5 For a provocative and stimulating argument that J was written by a woman in the tenth century, see D. Rosenberg and H. Bloom, *The Book of J* (New York 1990); cf. the sympathetic, though critical, review by J. Barton, 'It's a Girl!', *New York Review of Books* 37/18 (22.11.1990): 3–4.

6 The earliest Assyrian mention of Israel occurs in the context of Shalmaneser III's battle against a coalition of Levant states at the Battle of Qarqar on the Orontes in 853 (see chapter 9b).

7 The text was found inscribed on a large black basalt stele (115 x 60–68 cm) in 1868 at Dhiban (ancient Dibon) in Jordan, *c.* 21 km east of the Dead Sea. It was subsequently broken up by local people. With the help of a squeeze of the complete text, two large fragments and about eighteen smaller ones, it has been possible to reconstruct most of the text (now in the Louvre, Paris).

9

THE NEO-ASSYRIAN EMPIRE
(934–610)

The history of the Near East in the period from the ninth to the seventh centuries – well over two and a half centuries – is dominated by first the recovery, and then the rapid expansion, of the Assyrian state. In accordance with modern linguistic terminology this phase of Assyrian history is called the Neo-Assyrian period (934–610). By the seventh century Assyria dominated, either directly or indirectly, the entire area of the Fertile Crescent (including Egypt for a while). It controlled the terminal points of the great caravan routes in the Syrian desert, the rulers of several oases were subject allies, and the powerful kingdoms of Urartu and Phrygia (and later Lydia) maintained diplomatic relations with Assyria. So, too, did Elam at times – although its increasing political instability, occasionally exploited by the Assyrian régime, created serious problems along the empire's southern and eastern flank. A result of Assyria's political dominance is that, in order to reconstruct the history of any region of the Near East at this time, we have to examine the development of the Assyrian empire, and to rely, to a significant extent, on Assyrian evidence.

The formation of the empire is usually divided into two main phases of development. The first is the period from 934 to 745, when the Assyrians re-established their claims to territories in Upper Mesopotamia held in the Middle Assyrian period (c. 1300–c. 1100, see chapter 7b) and tightened their grip on these and adjacent regions. Smaller neighbouring states came to accept Assyria's pre-eminence at this time, and entered into political and commercial alliance with it. But what has given the Assyrians their great reputation is the second phase from 745 to c. 610. In that period the Assyrian empire expanded enormously, incorporating and reorganising, as directly governed provinces, territory stretching from the Arab-Persian Gulf to Commagene in Turkey. The new shape of the empire was fixed by 705, and only minor changes on its fringes occurred between then and the collapse of the Assyrian régime in the 610s.

9a The Assyrian annals and other historiographical sources

A very large proportion of the sources for this period emanate from the Assyrian court; they provide the backbone for reconstructing the history of

473

Assyria and adjacent territories, many of which eventually became provinces of the empire. The main type of evidence, preserved in considerable quantity for most of this period, is the 'royal annals' (see chapter 7b). They come primarily from the main Assyrian sites, such as Ashur, Kalhu (modern Nimrud), Nineveh and Dur Sharrukin (modern Khorsabad), and are written in Akkadian. They are not chronicles, but personal memorials of individual kings. They cover almost the entire span of time from the late tenth century on and provide accounts of royal achievements, especially military campaigns, arranged year by year. There are, however, problems with using them.

One problem, which received attention early this century (Olmstead 1916), is the fact that different versions of the annals are preserved for a number of kings. They are normally called 'editions', because the datings (where preserved) make it clear that campaign accounts were composed at various stages in a particular reign. Each updating could involve not merely adding the most recent events to an existing account, but refashioning the whole narrative of the king's exploits, by rearranging material, omitting some events, magnifying certain achievements, or stressing particular political aspects (Fales 1981a; Liverani 1981). The complexity of literary production implied by this is quite extraordinary (cf. Tadmor 1981; Gerardi 1987, for the most recent discussion). It has now been recognised that the occasions for which new editions of the annals were produced were highly significant (Tadmor 1983). Knowledge of Assyrian history is, however, not exact enought to allow us to pinpoint in all instances what the circumstances were which dictated a revision of the annals; yet the historical occasion surely influenced the form and content of the text. Perhaps the point most immediately relevant for historians is still Olmstead's rule of thumb that the earliest edition of any king's annals is always likely to be more reliable than the latest and most complete one. Unfortunately, we are not always in a position to have various editions available for comparison and Olmstead's dictum cannot be applied mechanically: there is, in fact, enormous variation in the composition of the annals of different kings, and so the pattern of distortion is not always as consistent as Olmstead's analysis might suggest.

Another difficulty with the annals is that they are primarily royal commemorative texts, often inscribed on specially prepared objects, such as prisms and cylinders, which were deposited in the foundations or walls of the building whose construction was being memorialised. Some scholars have, therefore, suggested that the accounts were primarily addressed to the gods, and that this explains why particular aspects of a king's achievements were stressed, e.g. his piety, his protection of subjects, his care for the country's well-being, and the fact that he undertook campaigns as a religious duty. The view has something to recommend it, but a further feature, namely the address to future kings (including blessings and curses), suggests that another (or additional) function was self-presentation to posterity, particularly subsequent rulers. The text recalled the achievements of the king on all fronts, domestic and military; and the particular place where the text was deposited, as well as the verbal description, showed him to be a responsible monarch governing in harmony with the divine sphere by virtue of the kind of building he had constructed (temples, palaces, armouries, city walls). It was, therefore, likely to be a later king who would read the text, as only someone of royal rank would be in a position to dig up foundations, or pull down walls in order to repair them. Examples of the finding of earlier texts in the course of rebuilding are known. Perhaps one of the most interesting is the finding of one of Ashurbanipal's (668–631?) building texts by Cyrus the Great of Persia (559–530) in Babylon (Berger 1975). This dialogue between past and future kings, together with context and occasion, shaped the message of the text: considerations such as factual truthfulness, balanced assessments, historical precision and objectivity were bound to play a less important role in inscriptions of this nature than an emphasis on spectacular exploits, success rather than failure, and the king's personal role in these achievements: the king as centre of all action. What was presented was the truth according to Assyrian ideology, and that might, on occasion, be very different from a modern historian's description.

At the same time there is no need to reject the factual content of the annals totally because of such difficulties. The annals seem to have used material such as booty-lists, counts of enemy dead, and calendrical data (Tadmor 1977; 1981; Gerardi 1987). Their descriptions of unfamiliar territory, although tinged with the exotic and full of dramatic hyperbole, can be amazingly vivid and exact, as in this example, where Ashurnasirpal II (883–859) provides a thumbnail sketch of campaigning in the mountains:

> The troops (sc. of the enemy) were frightened (and) took to a rugged mountain. Since the mountain was exceptionally rugged I did not pursue them. The mountain was as jagged(?) as the blade of a dagger and therein no winged bird of the sky flew. Like the nest of the *udīnu*-bird their fortress was situated within the mountain which none of the kings my fathers had penetrated. For three days the hero (i.e. Ashurnasirpal II) explored the mountain. His bold heart yearned for battle. He ascended on foot (and) overwhelmed the mountain. He smashed their nest (and) scattered their flock. I (Ashurnasirpal II) felled 200 of their fighting men with the sword (and) carried off a multitude of captives like a flock of sheep. With their blood I dyed the mountains red like wool, (and) the rest of them the ravines (and) torrents of the mountain swallowed.
>
> (L.W. King, *Annals of the Kings of Assyria* (London 1902): 254ff.; *ARAB* I §440; Grayson 1976 CI 1; 1991 A.0.101.1)

Here, in a few words, the precipitous mountain terrain is evoked, its desolate nature, and the difficulties faced by an army trying to force the surrender of people gathered in fortified towns on high crags, separated from each other by deep ravines and dangerous streams. The high drama of the scenery serves to make the king's victory all the more impressive – to have overcome these physical obstacles, to have set foot where (acording to him) no earlier Assyrian king had trod enhances his achievement. Total falsehoods in the annals are rare – omission of failures and emphasis on successes are used to tilt the picture in a positive direction. Note, for example, in the passage quoted how Ashurnasirpal does not deny that he could not pursue these people immediately, and admits that it was only with great effort ('on foot') that he was finally able to dislodge them. Reading the text carefully, we begin to see the wearisomeness of this war and its perhaps only limited success. But the language creates a picture of extremes – totally hostile territory vanquished rapidly by the absolute ability of the king. With such devices the annals can make at times very exciting, even gripping, reading.

Clay tablets containing annals or annalistic-type accounts indicate that archive copies of the texts were kept for consultation (Gerardi 1987; Porter 1987). This suggests that the images of Assyrian kingship and power propagated by the annals were not simply hidden from sight, but played an integral role in hammering home their message to a wider public. A process of 'repeated self-indoctrination' (Liverani 1979) by the scribes engaged in producing the annals took place, as they studied and selected material to weave into a suitable laudatory account. More vexed is the question of public declamation of some of this material. Oppenheim (1960), in a stimulating article, suggested that certain types of text, which contain the account of one campaign only in considerable detail (and could thus have been another source on which the annals were based), were read aloud to the citizens of Ashur. The basis for his argument is the form of the single campaign texts, which is that of a letter addressed to the gods, buildings and peoples of Ashur. Modern scholars, therefore, generally call them 'letters to the god'. At present they are attested for Sargon (Thureau-Dangin 1912 – the most famous), Sennacherib (Na'aman 1974 – very fragmentary), Esarhaddon (Borger 1956 §68) and Ashurbanipal (Weippert 1973–4) – although putting all of them into one category implies a greater uniformity than they display. The occasion for public reading of such a 'letter', Oppenheim argued, could have been a ceremony commemorating Assyrians killed on campaign, as, at the end of two of the 'letters to the god', several war dead are named. It is an attractive idea, but the problem is that the language of the 'letters' is the highly literary dialect commonly used for royal inscriptions, which would have been virtually incomprehensible to most Assyrians. Nevertheless, the possibility that there was some formal occasion, during which a form of what is preserved now as a purely literary account was publicly proclaimed, seems very likely and should not be discounted (Porter 1987: 197ff.; for the complex interplay between written texts and oral recitation, see generally Thomas 1992).[1]

There are also other texts, aside from the annals, on which historical reconstruction is based. Inscriptions, composed specifically for 'display' and often forming part of the architectural features of palaces, usually cover the same ground as the annals, but tend to be briefer and are not arranged chronologically but geographically (*Orientalia* 49/2: 152–155 [OK]). They provide a survey of royal achievements according to the four compass-points, as it were, and bunch material together in keeping with that principle. Inscribed stelae, obelisks and rock inscriptions are another analogous category, although differing in that they were specifically intended to proclaim royal achievements far and wide by being set up along roads, in or near conquered cities, and at the furthest point a king had reached (Börker-Klähn 1982).

A means of checking the chronology of events is available from the middle of the ninth to the end of the eighth century in the form of the '*limmu*-chronicle' – a list of Assyrian eponyms (officials who gave their name to each year of the Assyrian calendar; cf. Athenian dating by archons and Roman dating by consuls), accompanied by a short notice of a particular event that happened in that year. A problem with the *limmu*-chronicle, however, is the brevity of the entries and the fact that, in some instances, it has selected, for example, the dedication of a temple as the significant event of the year, when the annals describe a campaign. It is, nevertheless, a most useful and important corrective to the triumphal rhetoric of the royal inscriptions: defeats, internal revolts, famines and diseases are mentioned which the function of the royal texts precludes (Ungnad 1938: 428–435).[2]

From 744 to 668, the *Babylonian Chronicle* (*ABC* no. 1) – a dispassionate, usually year-by-year account (in Akkadian) of political events as they affected the region of Babylonia – provides a sober version of events. It is extant (on clay tablets) in three different copies; the best-preserved version dating from 500/499. What the sources for it and other Babylonian chronicle-compositions was remains a puzzle (Brinkman 1990), but the value of the chronicle in helping to pinpoint some of the events recounted in the Assyrian texts, and in giving us information on what was happening in one region outside, yet profoundly affected by, Assyria is immense. The only other source that occasionally does this is the Old Testament, providing valuable glimpses of how the Assyrian empire was perceived by a small state (Judah), which eventually became one of Assyria's satellites. Most interesting are the occasions (unfortunately, few) when we can compare the account of the same event through the eyes of the Judaean historian and the writers of the Assyrian annals. The best example is Sennacherib's invasion of Judah in 701. According to the Deuteronomist (2 *Kings* 18.13–19.36), Sennacherib devastated a great part of Judah and took considerable booty, climaxing in the siege of Jerusalem which he raised without taking the city: this was the result of Yahweh's direct intervention on behalf of Judah, since he sent an angel to slay the Assyrian army with a deadly plague, forcing it to leave Jerusalem intact – in other words, the Assyrian withdrawal was a divinely wrought miracle. Sennacherib himself (Luckenbill 1924: 32–34 iii 18–4) dwells on the misery Jerusalem went through during the siege, attributes his withdrawal to the fact that Hezekiah, the king of Judah, sent him valuable treasures, and celebrates his destruction of other cities within Judah; of a fatal plague breaking out among his forces not a word is mentioned. Both accounts are probably 'true'; but the differing emphases in the two – the deliberate omission of a setback in Sennacherib's account; placing the abortive Jerusalem siege at the culmination of the campaign in the account of 2 *Kings* – provide exactly the effect each side wanted to create: the merciful raising of the siege in response to humble submission by an already defeated king who had suffered much territorial loss in Sennacherib's case; a divine delivery, which saves the sacred city with its temple at the last moment and frustrates the conqueror's ambitions in the perspective of the Deuteronomist (cf. Millard 1990).

9b From territorial state to imperial power (934–745)

An important point to remember in studying the development of the Neo-Assyrian empire is that imperial power was not something new to the Assyrians. The great Assyrian rulers had a tradition of earlier conquest and control to look back to and on which they could build. The continuities with the Middle Assyrian state (chapter 7b) were marked: the Assyrian kings were presented as part of a centuries-old monarchic institution, and as direct continuators of an unbroken line of kings, supposedly from the same family, since about 1500; the structure of the annual eponym system, the backbone of Assyrian calendrical reckoning, which rotated among the members of Assyrian noble families and in which the king participated, remained in force right through the period of decline (*c.* 1050–934) separating the Middle from the New Assyrian period; the centrality of the city of Ashur, its environs (called simply 'the land') and its god Ashur remained unchanged; royal ceremonial, such as the coronation ritual and elements of court hierarchy and procedure, were preserved; the literary form of royal inscriptions and campaign reports developed in the Middle Assyrian period continued into the Neo-Assyrian phase; and, finally, the creation by the Middle Assyrian rulers of a territorial state spanning the region of north Iraq and including the great cities and plains of Ashur, Nineveh, Arbela, Kalhu and Kilizi remained intact as the heartland of Assyria right through the period of waning power.

The development of Assyrian strategy: 934–884

The earliest Neo-Assyrian kings (Ashur-dan II to Tukulti-Ninurta II (934–884), see table 28) sometimes refer in their inscriptions to the fact that they were campaigning in areas which had already been conquered by their predecessors in the Middle Assyrian period. This suggests that one of the justifications for Assyrian expansion in the tenth to ninth century was that the conquerors were following precedents set by the Middle Assyrian kings; in other words, they presented themselves as simply re-asserting and consolidating control in the region up to, and beyond, the Khabur which was by right theirs. By means of this ideology, local rulers in the region could legitimately be regarded as 'in revolt' against Assyrian authority. This helps to explain why, at least initially, there appears to have been very little difference in the pattern of conquest and control from the earlier period. So the campaigns of individual kings were not necessarily always great wars of conquest, but warlike marches intended to reconfirm their dominance over areas regarded as legitimately Assyrian. As territory was added to the Assyrian sphere it was often left under its existing ruler, now regarded as an Assyrian governor (Millard and Bordreuil 1982; chapter 8b); the reorganisation of newly incorporated regions and the imposition of tribute seems to have been of an *ad hoc* nature. Such action is typical of the formative stages of an empire (Claessen and Skalník 1981). At the same time some new organisational features gradually develop as the density of the Assyrian network of control intensified (Liverani 1988), and they foreshadow the shape of the mature Assyrian empire in the second half of the eighth and seventh centuries.

Table 28 Kings of the Neo-Assyrian period

Ashur-dan II	934–912
Adad-nirari II	911–891
Tukulti-Ninurta II	890–884
Ashurnasirpal II	883–859
Shalmaneser III	858–824
Shamshi-Adad V	823–811
Adad-nirari III	810–783
Shalmaneser IV	782–773
Ashur-dan III	772–755
Ashur-nirari V	754–745
Tiglath-pileser III	744–727
Shalmaneser V	726–722
Sargon II	721–705
Sennacherib	704–681
Esarhaddon	680–669
Ashurbanipal	668–631? (or 627?)
Ashur-etel-ilani	630? (or 626?)–623?
Sin-shar-ishkun	622?–612
Ashur-uballit II	611–609

Already with Ashur-dan II (934–912), whose annals are only preserved in fragments, certain characteristic aspects of Assyrian military activity can be observed. An area in which Ashur-dan II fought extensively was the frontier directly to the north, a region in which the Assyrians campaigned almost more than anywhere else. The explanation, in part, must be the mountainous terrain, which made control particularly problematical. At the same time it lay close to the Assyrian heartland and so securing borders here was vital. Finally, several important routes ran through this region leading into Anatolia, which was a source of crucial metals. The king of the northern state of Kadmuhu (close to Assyrian territory) was captured, flayed, and his skin displayed publicly on the walls of Arbela, while his place as ruler was taken by someone loyal to the Assyrian king. A valuable booty of bronze, tin and precious stones was taken from Kadmuhu, instead of the flocks of sheep more usually mentioned as war-loot.

In the west, the king waged war against 'Aramaeans' (sometimes, but not always, more closely specified). Here the Assyrians were claiming to be retaking what they felt to be rightfully theirs. This is implied by Ashur-dan in his fragmentary annals:

[In my accession year (and) in] my first regnal year, after [I nobly ascended] the royal throne, [. . .] the troops of the Yausa (an Aramaean group) came up(stream), [. . .] they trusted in their own strength, they brought(?) their [. . .]. With the support of Ashur, my lord, [I] mustered [. . . my chariots and troops]. I plundered their depots from the city Ekal-pi-nari [. . .] (and) inflicted [upon them a major defeat]. Those that survived I slaughtered. [I carried off] their [herds?] (and) flocks without number. [I] burnt their [cities?] (with) their inhabitants. I brought up from the Aramaeans [valuable booty?]. [. . . which] from the time of Shalmaneser, king of [Assyria, my forefather], had destroyed [people of Assyria(?) by . . .] and murder, had sold all(?) their [sons and daughters?]; by the command [of Ashur] my lord I took prisoners, I inflicted [upon them] a major [defeat], I carried off their booty, possessions, [property, herds, (and)] flocks (and) [brought (them)] to my city [Ashur . . .]
(E.F. Weidner, *AfO* 3 (1926): 151–161; Grayson 1976 XCVIII 1; 1991 A.0.98.1)

The impression conveyed here is that the territories had been seized from Assyria, and that the Assyrian inhabitants had been either slaughtered or sold into slavery.

In the east, the Zagros foothills down to the lower Zab were strategically crucial both for Assyrian security and to safeguard access to the limited routes through the mountains (Levine 1974). Again, this was a region where later Assyrian kings frequently campaigned, motivated by the need to defend Assyria's frontiers, and to ensure that Assyrians shared in the profits of commerce: horses, in particular, were received from, and via, this area, as well as the highly prized lapis lazuli mined in north-east Afghanistan.

After re-establishing the Assyrian boundaries, Ashur-dan embarked on a resettlement and land-reclamation programme:

I brought back the exhausted [people] of Assyria [who] had abandoned [their cities (and) houses in the face of] want, hunger, (and) famine (and) [had gone up] to other lands. [I settled[] them in cities (and) houses [which were suitable] (and) they dwelt in peace. I constructed [palaces in] the (various) districts of my land. [I hitched up] ploughs in the (various) districts of my land (and thereby) [piled up] more grain than ever before. I hitched up [numerous teams of horses [for the forces of?] Assyria.

(E.F. Weidner, *AfO* 3 (1926): 151–161;
Grayson 1976 XCVIII 1; 1991 A.0.98.1)

The Assyrian conquest is here presented as the welcome return of peace and prosperity after an awful period of disruption: those who had been forced out of their homes by want were rehoused in towns, and new fortified centres were built equipped with ploughs, stores of grain and horses. A recurring (and central) concern of the Assyrian rulers emerges: namely, the construction of new towns and increasing the arable base of the Assyrian state, linked, naturally, to the perennial need for security.

Ashur-dan followed the description of his military exploits, like Tiglath-pileser I (1114–1076; see chapter 7b) before him, with a count of the wild animals (lions, wild bulls, and elephants) that he had hunted and killed, which served to underline the heroic and protective character of the king. The account concludes with his building activities, stressing that, as the king was divinely chosen and blessed, he did not use the spoils of his campaigns to enrich himself but to honour and exalt the gods.

Ashur-dan sets the basic pattern in terms of strategy and ideology which was elaborated by succeeding Assyrian kings. Adad-nirari II (911–891) campaigned repeatedly in all the same areas that his father had already attacked, extending and consolidating his predecessor's successes. He campaigned west of the Khabur river and captured Husirina (modern Sultan Tepe, near Urfa) and Guzana (modern Tell Halaf). Nasibina (modern Nusaybin), physically much closer to Assyria, was only taken by an elaborate siege after six attacks, as recounted in his annals:

In the eponymate of Adad-dan, with the rage of my strong weapons I marched a sixth time to the land of Hanigalbat (region to the west of Assyria, earlier the Assyrian term for Mitanni). I confined Nur-Adad, the Temannite (an Aramaean group), in the city Nasibina (and) established seven redoubts around it. I stationed therein Ashur-dini-amur, the commander-in-chief. He (Nur-Adad) had dug a moat, which had not previously existed, in bedrock all around it (sc. the city). He had made (it) nine cubits wide (i.e. nearly 5m) and had dug it down to water-level. The wall was next to the moat. I encircled his moat with my warriors like a flame (and) they shouted to him:

'The roar of the king is as strong as the destructive flood.' [I laid] traps for him [and] deprived him of grain.
(*KAH* II 84; *ARAB* I §355–377; Grayson 1976 XCIX 2; 1991 A.0.99.2)

Adad-nirari also campaigned in the north and north-east, in one instance to assist a city friendly to Assyria, more usually to extract by force tribute which had been withheld.

A new direction for Adad-nirari's wars was the Babylonian frontier. In the east Tigris region and on the Euphrates, frontier posts were established and an alliance was made with the states of Hindanu and Laqe lying along the Euphrates, north-west of Babylonia. But the forays into Babylonian territory did not damage Babylonia substantially: Nabu-shuma-ukin I (*c.* 895) of Babylon was able to redraw the frontier again east of the Tigris, and territory had to be ceded back to Babylon. The situation was stabilised in 891, when a peace treaty was drawn up between Assyria and Babylonia and cemented by a dynastic marriage, with the neighbouring monarchs marrying each other's daughters. This resulted in a relatively peaceful co-existence between the two states for the next seventy to eighty years.

Very striking in Adad-nirari II's reign are the amazingly rapid and repeated military movements, for which he was able to mobilise troops and resources year after year. This can only have been achieved by developing an efficient system of supply-points, probably begun by Ashur-dan II, on which he could rely. The tribute imposed on conquered regions served to provision the army *en route*, and the king is described as stopping along the way to demand chariots, horses, oxen, precious items and food supplies so that Assyria's triumphal progress might continue. The basis for Assyria's awesomely efficient military machine was clearly laid down in this period.

The reign of Tukulti-Ninurta II (890–884) is usually regarded, with some justification, as rounding off this stage of Assyrian recovery. An important event of his short reign was the victory over the ruler of Bit Zamani (Diyarbekr region), opening the major route north-west into Anatolia. He gives quite a bit of detail about how the defeated state was formally attached to Assyria, showing that the procedure was, in most essentials, identical to that attested later. First, grain, straw, iron, bronze, tin, silver, horses, mules and men were taken to replenish the Assyrian army. Amme-baal, the defeated king, had to swear that he would not provide any other state with horses, aside from the Assyrians. Then he was allowed to continue ruling over a reduced territory, while some of the land that had been part of his realm was put under the control of Assyrian officers.

Most interesting is the account of a march by Tukulti-Ninurta II around the southern and western frontiers of Assyrian-controlled territory in 885. Setting off from Ashur, he moved down the Wadi Tharthar and then over to the Tigris around the region of Samarra, where he raided the Itu'a pastoralists. Continuing south, he reached Dur Kurigalzu and Sippar in northern Babylonia. Here he turned north and west towards the rich states and their cities lying on the Euphrates: at Ana in Suhu and at Hindanu, he received tribute and costly gifts from the local governors; some of this was undoubtedly to feed and re-equip the Assyrian forces (camels, oxen, donkeys, ducks, sheep, bread, beer and fodder), some to swell the Assyrian king's disposable wealth of precious and rare materials (silver, gold, tin bars, myrrh, bronze, antimony (processed and raw)), while many of the items presented to Tukulti-Ninurta by the governor of Suhu were finely crafted luxury articles celebrating his royal visit (furniture legs of *meskannu*-wood, a bed and dishes of the same wood, a bronze bath, linen garments, garments with multi-coloured trim, purple wool). The triumphal march continued to Laqe on the Khabur, turned north to Shadikannu and Nasibina and then struck west towards Husirina, whence a punitive raid was mounted against the Mushki (normally associated with the Phrygians, see chapter 10b). The itinerary is very detailed, and the march remarkable for the lack of opposition encountered, aside from the raids mounted against peoples living outside the settled communities. The impression is of a formal military procession displaying Assyria's power, inspecting subject states, visiting an allied state (Babylonia) and collecting supplies for king and army from established points along the route: if we tot up the figures of the number of horses collected, the total comes to 2720. While the precise boundaries in the north and east remain hazy, Assyria's frontiers in the west and south emerge very clearly from this account, and the effectiveness of its control in the west is borne out by two inscriptions of Tukulti-Ninurta II: one at Kahat (Tell Barri) on the upper Khabur, where the Assyrian king built a palace; the other a stele (almost illegible) from Terqa (Tell 'Ashara) on the Euphrates, in which Tukulti-Ninurta II commemorated his father, Adad-nirari II.

Ashurnasirpal II and Shalmaneser III (883–824)

These three kings laid the solid foundations that allowed Ashurnasirpal II (883–859) to mount his far-reaching campaigns, which brought Assyria quite spectacular wealth and established it as one of the largest international powers in the Near East. There is a marked increase in documentation from Ashurnasirpal's reign, and this is not solely explicable by the chance of discovery and preservation. It reflects the energetic campaigns (fourteen recorded) and the huge effort involved in his extensive building at the city of Kalhu (biblical Calah; modern Nimrud).

Several of Ashurnasirpal II's campaigns were directed northwards, where his most crucial success was the 'pacification' of this difficult region. The strategically placed state of Bit Zamani was ravaged following two revolts: the first involved the murder of Assyria's treaty-partner, Amme-baal, which gave Ashurnasirpal the excuse to intervene in pursuit of his assassins. The Assyrian grip was consolidated by settling Assyrian colonists at Tushhan, directly on the route to Amedi (centre of Bit Zamani, near modern Diyarbekir) and beyond to central Anatolia. Ashurnasirpal established a string of fortresses and proclaimed Assyria's presence by building a palace in Tushhan, placing in the city a stone statue of the king, inscribed with his achievements in the north, and setting a royal stele in the city-wall. In Habhu, directly north of Assyria, a mountain town was renamed 'Ashurnasirpal City' (Al-Ashur-nasir-apli) to drive home to all Assyria's control. The impact of these intensive military efforts was enormous: many of the small, but wealthy, adjacent states of south Anatolia, Upper Mesopotamia and north Syria expressed their goodwill by sending rich gifts to congratulate the royal warrior, while material supplies and manpower flowed from the north into Assyria for the remainder of Ashurnasirpal's reign. Eastwards, too, repeated military expeditions, setting out from the Assyrian city of Kilizi, brought large sections of the foothills of the Zagros under firm Assyrian control, and a local headquarters and supply-point, Dur Ashur ('Ashur Fortress'), was founded. Babylonia in the south and Bit Adini on the mid-Euphrates stirred the states of Suhu and Laqe between them to revolt. Profitable commercial interests linked all these neighbours. Ashurnasirpal dealt ruthlessly with the Laqean and Suhean turmoils, but avoided any direct move against Assyria's larger ally, Babylonia, concentrating his attacks instead on Bit Adini.

Partly in response to his successes in this quarter and his striking triumphs in the north and east, Ashurnasirpal was festively welcomed when he crossed the Euphrates, and received gifts of homage and friendship. The extraordinary wealth in raw materials, finished luxury articles and exotic goods commanded by the north Syrian states is well illustrated by the lists of royal presents; they are contained in Ashurnasirpal's long annals, found in the Ninurta temple at his new city of Kalhu:

I received tribute from Sangara, king of the land of Hatti (Carchemish),

20 talents of silver,
a gold ring,
a gold bracelet,
gold daggers,
100 talents of bronze,
250 talents of iron,
bronze (tubs),
bronze pails,
bronze bathtubs,
a bronze oven,

many ornaments from his palace the weight of which could not be determined,

beds of boxwood,
thrones of boxwood,

dishes of boxwood decorated with ivory,
200 adolescent girls,
linen garments with multi-coloured trim,
purple wool,
red-purple wool,
gišnugallu-alabaster,
elephants' tusks,
a chariot of polished (gold),
a gold couch with inlay,
(objects) befitting his royalty.

(L.W. King, *Annals of the Kings of Assyria* (London 1902): 254–387;
ARAB I §476; Grayson 1976 CI 1; 1991 101 A.0.1; *TUAT* I 358–360)

Similar lists of gifts were received from the coastal state of Pattina (lower Orontes, see chapter 8c(ii)). Here and elsewhere Ashurnasirpal says that he took troops from the states with him, which shows a readiness to accede to the Assyrian demand for military aid. In Pattina, the town of Aribua was actually taken over by Ashurnasirpal as a store-centre for Assyrian army supplies, and settled with Assyrian colonists (Tadmor 1975). A further interesting feature, mentioned both here and in the context of the northern campaigns, is the gift of a daughter of the local ruler complete with dowry, suggesting that the relationship between Assyria and the smaller states may have been cemented by a series of marriages. If so, exactly what position such princesses would have occupied among the royal wives and concubines at the Assyrian court is unknown. But the significant point in all the transactions is that the relations between Assyria and its smaller neighbours were not always marked by aggression, destruction and plunder – careful decoding of the rhetoric of the royal inscriptions reveals that several states were anxious to establish mutually profitable relations, and so share in Assyria's growing glory and power by linking themselves to the Assyrian court via precious gifts, military aid and perhaps marriage. This is very much the tone of Ashurnasirpal's progress south from Pattina along the Orontes and into the Lebanon. There he ceremonially washed his weapons in the Mediterranean and offered sacrifices, graciously received welcoming presents from the Phoenician cities (including two types of monkey, exotic sea-creatures (*nāhiru*) and ebony (from equatorial Africa)). He then felled timber for his temple-building projects and erected a commemorative stele on Mount Amanus before returning home. The relationship between the Levantine states and Assyria was, nevertheless, always an unequal one: Assyria'a military might and brutal tactics were an ever present threat, which Ashurnasirpal was prepared to employ to devastating effect if co-operation was denied.

The close links established by Ashurnasirpal II with the northern Levant had direct repercussions on Assyrian artistic production. Before the time of Ashurnasirpal, Assyrian sculpted items were small in number and limited in scope. In his reign, virtually overnight, there appear the magnificently accomplished, highly developed and beautifully finished relief sculptures which covered practically every inch of the walls of Ashurnasirpal's new palace at Kalhu (modern Nimrud). From his time onwards, reliefs depicting royal campaigns, hunts, and rituals became a standard part of palatial decoration in Assyria. In Ashurnasirpal's palace they extended to head-height and were painted, while the palace doorways were decorated with huge, winged, human-headed bulls and lions. If we compare the quality of this carving with the stele of Tukulti-Ninurta II (Moortgat 1984 [OM] 2 pls. 50–51), made only a few years earlier, the change is breathtaking. Many aspects of the origins of this celebrated Assyrian art-form remain enigmatic, but several scholars have argued that some of the iconography, the repertoire of motifs and the concept of combining inscription with pictorial illustration were heavily influenced by the powerful state of Carchemish, from where Ashurnasirpal had received lavish gifts earlier (pp. 484–485; Hawkins 1972; Winter 1983).

Much of Ashurnasirpal II's newly acquired wealth was ploughed into his building of Kalhu (Nimrud); the 'banquet stele', found in the courtyard of his palace there in 1951, presents a fairly full account of the work (Wiseman 1952; Mallowan 1966: 57–73). Kalhu was not an entirely new foundation (see chapter 7b), but it had been neglected, and was probably only thinly inhabited: Ashurnasirpal mentions that he had to prepare the ground by levelling the rubble from older buildings, and that he settled people brought from areas where he had campaigned or which he had visited. This suggests that an important aim in building Kalhu was to increase the city population. It is not necessary to assume that all the people settled in the refurbished city were deportees, groaning under forced labour conditions and deprived of all rights: people from Carchemish and Pattina are mentioned among the new citizens – they could have been some of the soldiers that the rulers of these states had supplied to the Assyrian army; others may have been sent at the behest of local rulers as craftsmen and traders. The fact that '16,000 people of Kalhu' are mentioned at the end of the text being feasted by the king, alongside his palace staff, his dignitaries, invited ambassadors and '47,074 men and women from the whole of my land', implies that they were treated at least like the Assyrians settled in royal centres such as Tushhan. The 'banquet stele' dwells in detail on the construction and decoration of the magnificent palace and temples, the formation of herds of wild and exotic animals, the making of a figure of the king with a face of red gold and inlaid with shining stones, and, most important, the digging of a canal to supply the city, its orchards and the beautiful palace garden filled with fragrant plants and fruit-bearing trees:

> The canal cascades from above into the gardens. Fragrance pervades the walkways. Streams of water (as numerous) as the stars of heaven flow in the pleasure garden. Pomegranates, which like vines are covered with

grapes ... in the garden ... [I?], Ashur-nasir-apli, in the delightful
garden pick fruit continuously like a mouse (meaning uncertain) ...
(Wiseman 1952; *ANET*: 558–560; Grayson 1976 CI 17;
1991 A.0.101.30; cf. Glassner 1991: 13)

But the most remarkable feature of the text, which has given it its name, is
the enormous feast that was held to celebrate completion of the building and
inaugurate the king's new city. The text ends with an immense, detailed list
of the varied and luxurious foods consumed by the invited guests. The
participants included men and women, the inhabitants of the king's realm,
the population of Kalhu and ambassadors from the neighbouring states with
whom Ashurnasirpal had established friendly relations – Pattina, Carchemish,
Tyre and Sidon in the Levant; Gurgum, Meliddu and Kummuh in Anatolia;
Hubushkia, Gilzanu and Musasir on the north-east frontier; Suhu and
Hindanu on the Euphrates:

> Altogether 69,574 (including) those summoned from all lands and the
> people of Kalhu – for ten days I gave them food, I gave them drink, I
> had them bathed, I had them anointed. (Thus) did I honour them (and)
> send them back to their lands in peace and joy.

(Wiseman 1952; *ANET*: 558–560; Grayson 1976 CI 17; 1991 A.0.101.30)

Ashurnasirpal's son and successor, Shalmaneser III (858–824), had the hard
task of following up and consolidating his father's remarkable achievements.
It is not, therefore, surprising that the course of his reign was a chequered
one, and that he had to expend considerable military effort to force the
political balance to remain favourable for Assyria. He encountered particular
difficulties with the states to the west, who were beginning to find themselves
hemmed in by Assyria's control of routes, especially in the north (Winter
1983). Almost immediately on his accession Shalmaneser was faced by a
coalition of Carchemish, Pattina, Sam'al, Que and Hilakku (in north Syria,
the eastern Taurus and Cilicia), all closely linked in their commercial interests
and, hence, interdependent. At the same time, inter-state rivalries in this area
are revealed by the fact that Gurgum, Kummuh and Bit Agusi did not join
the group of states challenging Assyria, but offered it support instead. The
ringleader of the hostile group was Bit Adini, lying closest to Assyrian
territory (on and to the east of the Euphrates) and already diminished in its
territory and wealth by Ashurnasirpal II (p. 484). Shalmaneser III succeeded
in defeating the coalition, and annexed Bit Adini, which was turned into an
Assyrian province, its chief city, Til Barsip, on the Euphrates crossing and a
bare 21 km distant from Carchemish, was renamed 'The Harbour of
Shalmaneser' (Kar-Shulman-asharedu), and another town, Pitru, further
west, became the starting point for Shalmaneser's many campaigns in the west
(Tadmor 1975).

In 853, Shalmaneser collected supplies and tribute from the states he had defeated earlier at Pitru, and proceeded via Aleppo into the territory of Hamath, where, at Qarqar on the Orontes, he was faced by the combined forces of a number of southern states. The fullest (and earliest) text is inscribed on a slab found at Kurkh, near Diyarbekir, and hence known as the 'Kurkh monolith'. It is widely quoted and translated as it contains the earliest mention of the northern kingdom of Israel and its king, Ahab:

> 1,200 chariots, 1,200 cavalry and 20,000 men of Hadadezer [from] 'the Land of the Ass' (i.e. Damascus), 700 chariots, 700 cavalry and 10,000 men of Irhuleni of Hamath, 2,000 chariots and 10,000 men of Ahab of Israel, 500 men of Byblos, 1,000 men of Egypt, 10 chariots and 10,000 men of Irqata (north-east of Tripoli), 200 men of Matinubali of Arvad (Phoenician city), 200 men from Usanat (coastal city, north of Arvad), 30 chariots and 10,000 men of Adunubali of Shianu (territory on coast, north of Arvad), 1000 camels of Gindibu' the Arab and [. . .]000 men of Baesa of Beth-Rehob, the Ammonite – these 12 kings he (Irhuleni of Hamath) took to help him.
>
> (G.Smith (H.C. Rawlinson), *Cuneiform Inscriptions of Western Asia* III (London 1870), pls. 7–8; *ANET*: 278–279; *TUAT* I/4, 360–362)

The allies shared economic interests and were attempting to maintain the *status quo* as it had existed – the coastal Phoenician cities provided the crucial seaports into which the trade in incense and spices debouched from the Arab caravan centres; both in turn were dependent on the routes controlled by states such as Israel, Hamath and Damascus, and all were linked to Egypt's demands on their markets and resources.

Shalmaneser had to fight against this formidable force four times in all and was not successful against it until after 845. The seriousness of the Assyrian setback is made plain by the fact that it stiffened opposition from some of the more northerly states, which Shalmaneser had either dealt with successfully earlier (Carchemish) or which had formerly been friendly (Bit Agusi). But by 841 the coalition had finally disintegrated – partly perhaps the result of the repeated Assyrian campaigns, and partly perhaps the result of changes of ruler in two of the most powerful states involved, Damascus and Israel. Only after 841 was Shalmaneser III able to claim the receipt of tribute from Jehu of Israel, depicted on his black obelisk from Kalhu (see fig. 30), where Jehu's surrender serves as a symbol of the southernmost extent of his victories (Marcus 1987). Only when the southern states had been defeated was Shalmaneser able to consolidate the Assyrian presence in Anatolia (Que, Meliddu and Tabal). His strategy was probably linked to the several campaigns he mounted against the newly emerging powerful state of Urartu, centred on Lake Van, which was threatening to become a serious rival to Assyria (see chapter 10a).

Shalmaneser honoured the treaty with Babylonia by aiding the Babylonian king, Marduk-zakir-shumi (*c.* 854–819), when the latter's tenure of the throne was challenged by his brother. Shalmaneser hastened to help his ally and put down the revolt; following the re-establishment of peace, he paid ceremonial visits to major shrines in northern Babylonia – Babylon, Borsippa and Cutha – where he was formally welcomed and feasted by the citizens. He further displayed his concern and reverence for Babylonia's cities by plundering some of the tribal Chaldaean and Aramaean groups of the region. Rounding off this publicly advertised act of co-operation, the two kings reaffirmed their pact (*ABC* no. 21 iii 2'–5'; Grayson 1970: 165), an event commemorated in a fine relief carved around the socle of Shalmaneser's throne-base: the two kings, shown equal in size, each with his train of dignitaries, stand under a canopy and clasp each other firmly by the hand (Mallowan 1966: 447).

The throne-base comes not from the acropolis of Kalhu, but from the great 'review palace' (*ekal māšarti*) built on the edge of the lower city by Shalmaneser (Mallowan 1966, vol. 2). It is a very large building, not decorated with reliefs, but with painted friezes, and, on the wall behind the throne base, a panel of coloured glazed brick, depicting two images of the king set facing each other on either side of a formalised tree (the so-called 'sacred tree'; Stearns 1961). The same scene, but in relief (and again placed behind the throne), has been found in the palace of Ashurnasirpal at Kalhu (see fig. 31). The review palace, excavated by the British in the 1950s and dubbed 'Fort Shalmaneser', was the place where military equipment was kept, treasure stored and where the whole court, including the queen's household, could be accommodated. Each of the great Assyrian cities had a similar great store-house (Turner 1970), but only the one at Kalhu has been fully excavated, providing a large amount of material in the form of texts (Dalley and Postgate

Figure 31 North-west Palace, Kalhu (Nimrud), relief behind throne-base: two kings facing each other either side of 'a sacred tree'; winged disc (god Ashur?) hovering above; flanking protective spirits (British Museum; drawing by D. Saxon)

1984) and artefacts, such as the remains of ivory inlays from fine furniture (Mallowan and Herrmann 1974; Herrmann 1986; 1992).

Problems in Assyria: 823–745

In spite of Shalmaneser III's hardwon successes, his reign ended in revolts within Assyria, according to the valuable *limmu*-chronicle (see p. 477). The revolt was widespread, affecting Ashur, Nineveh, Arbela and twenty-four smaller Assyrian cities. The reasons for it are unknown,[3] but, in a general way, we should perhaps connect them with the problems that inevitably arise at the centre of a state which has acquired a large territory and enormous wealth in a relatively short time. How are the new resources and positions of power and influence to be shared out? How can the king ensure that his officials, who now enjoy greater prestige and power through commanding armies and governing new provinces, remain loyal? Who are the new people that the king is promoting to high position, and are older families being elbowed out? Unfortunately, none of the details are known and so the precise nature of the difficulties besetting Assyria remains obscure.

What is certain is that one outcome of the revolt in the last years of Shalmaneser III was that the accession of his son, Shamshi-Adad V (823–811), was contested. He had to fight for the throne for four years, and was only finally successful by receiving help from Babylonia. On the basis of an extremely fragmentary treaty-text (*SAA* 2, no.1), it has been argued that, following Shamshi-Adad's final victory, the Babylonian king demanded his pound of flesh for helping him by redrawing the terms of the Assyro-Babylonian agreement in favour of Babylonia, and placing the Assyrian king in a humiliating position. The nub of the argument is the fact that Shamshi-Adad V is not called 'king' in the very lacunose text; but, as Parpola has argued cogently (*SAA* 2: xxvi–xxvii), this could simply show that the treaty was drawn up *before* Shamshi-Adad's successful accession, i.e. during the time of the years of revolt and fighting at the end of Shalmaneser III's life. If we accept this view, then it is more plausible to interpret the text as showing Marduk-zakir-shumi honouring the earlier agreement made with Shalmaneser, and returning the favour Shalmaneser had done him in beating down the threat from his brother (pp. 488–489). In his turn, then, Marduk-zakir-shumi was now helping Shamshi-Adad, as the righful successor, to accede to the throne.

Much less clear is the reason for Shamshi-Adad V's intervention in Babylonia a few years later (see chapter 11b). It is possible (though no more) that it was connected with some irregularity in the Babylonian royal succession, so that he may have been avenging the son and successor of his old ally. What is certain is that Shamshi-Adad's action at that time was brutal and ruthless: he removed the Babylonian king (or pretender) and ravaged the country, with the result that there was no recognised ruler in Babylonia for the next twelve years or so. The rather obscure Babylonian campaign by

Shamshi-Adad is one of the few attested for this king; other references to 'campaigns' in the north and north-east sound like relatively small-scale raids.

It was assumed at one time that Shamshi-Adad V's son, Adad-nirari III (810–783), acceded to the Assyrian throne under-age, and that for the first five years of his reign his mother, Shammuramat (the historical personage on whom the legendary Semiramis was based), acted as his regent. The suggestion that Semiramis was regent was based on misunderstanding of a text, and now has to be rejected, nor is there any particular reason for assuming that Adad-nirari was a child on his accession (Schramm 1972). But his mother did occupy an unusual position, being named with her son in a stele and included in a dedication set up by an Assyrian governor. The reasons for her prominence are unknown, but they may be connected with the fact that she had played a crucial role in defending dynastic stability on her husband's death in ensuring her son's succession.

There is not a great deal of documentary material for Adad-nirari III's reign (although more than for his father), and several military expeditions seem to have been organised by his governors rather than by the king himself. Despite this, Assyria's presence west of the Euphrates continued to be felt (Tadmor and Millard 1973), and inscriptions of governors together with the eponym-lists suggest that the frontiers remained much what they had been under Shalmaneser III. The curious chronicle known as the *Synchronistic History* (*ABC* no. 21), which traces Assyrian–Babylonian relations from an avowedly Assyrian perspective, provides a little more information on Adad-nirari III's activity in this region. Adad-nirari is here presented as trying to restore some measure of normality to devastated Babylonia, by returning deportees from Assyria. At the same time he seems to have been treated as king of Babylonia himself: he received the 'remnants' of the divine meals offered to the gods at Babylon, Borsippa and Cutha, and imposed regular Assyrian taxes (straw, grain and labour) on the local population (see chapter 11b).

Although the impression from this scanty material is that Assyria's power was waning, at least in some areas, a number of factors indicate that Assyria still played an important role internationally. A stele from Antakya, for example (Hawkins in press; Donbaz 1990), records a boundary agreement between Bit Agusi and Hamath mediated by Shamshi-ilu, the Assyrian commander-in-chief (*turtānu*), whose provincial residence was at nearby Til Barsip. Similarly, the Assyrian king was called in to resolve a boundary dispute between Gurgum and Kummuh (Pazarcık stele: Hawkins in press; Donbaz 1990). The evidence suggests that, while Assyrian military exploits were not perhaps as impressive as they had been, Assyria was still the major power that could intervene in inter-state conflicts and was indeed asked to do so; and it could, of course, exploit such quarrels to regulate them in its own interests.

The surviving evidence on administration and the provincial structure for the ninth and early eighth centuries gives the impression that Assyrian governors were installed (or local persons raised to this position) and then left to their own devices. They passed the office from father to son as a hereditary right, acquired more positions and thus built up their power-bases to the point where they could operate virtually independently of central control – a situation that emerges most clearly and dangerously at times of weakness or problems at the centre. This is usually perceived as a fatal flaw in the system of Assyrian administration as it developed throughout the ninth century – a flaw that threatened to break the empire into fragments from late in Shalmaneser III's reign onwards, and weakened it progressively as the kings on Assyria's throne were not strong enough to counteract the growing power of the provincial governors. As a result, the period from Shamshi-Adad V to the accession of Tiglath-pileser III is generally described as one of 'decline'.

The picture can, however, be slanted differently. It is just as possible to argue that, although very powerful, the governors essentially maintained the Assyrian empire, by ensuring its survival in the areas which it had conquered in the course of the ninth century, and defending its frontiers. Significantly, the governors never pose as kings, they never take royal titles and they define their positions always within the framework of the Assyrian court hierarchy. Also, despite the severe problems that Assyria experienced, especially after Adad-nirari III's reign, when it was plagued by epidemics, famines, revolts and succession problems for almost forty years, it never lost control of the great gains it had made in the tenth and earlier ninth century. The territory remained ultimately intact – when Tiglath-pileser III came to the throne in 745, he was able immediately to campaign in the mountains to the east, in Babylonia to the south, fight a battle beyond the Euphrates in Kummuh and put Arpad (in Bit Agusi) under siege for two years. Further, Ashur-nirari V (754–745) is definitely known to have been able to impose a loyalty treaty on Mati'ilu, the ruler of Bit Agusi, centred on Arpad (*SAA* 2, no. 2). Attractive arguments, put forward recently (Lemaire and Durand 1984), raise the possibility that the Assyria–Bit Agusi treaty had been imposed, and regularly re-affirmed, in the time of Ashur-nirari's predecessors by Shamshi-ilu, the Assyrian governor of Til Barsip and *turtānu*. If this interpretation is right, then Bit Agusi remained under Assyria's control right through the forty years of Assyrian weakness. The argument centres on the 'Sfire treaties' – stelae bearing almost (but not quite) identical Aramaic texts, found in the region of Aleppo, which lay within Bit Agusi (KAI Nr. 222–4). The Sfire treaties were imposed on the same Mati'ilu who swore a loyalty oath to Ashur-nirari V (see above) by a mysterious personage called Bargayah of *KTK*, whose identity has defied every attempt at explanation, as has that of his home-state. That he was more powerful than Mati'ilu is obvious from the wording of the treaties. Lemaire and Durand's proposal is that, in the Aramaic context of the treaties, Shamshi-ilu of Bit-Adini used his alternative Aramaic name and title which was Bargayah, king of *KTK*. As a result, a text that has been adduced to show how weak the Assyrian state had become, how easily another power could seduce its satellites, could now be inter-preted in precisely the opposite manner, i.e. illustrating its continued hold. It would also demonstrate the importance of the Assyrian governors in actively supporting the interests of the central power – maintaining a close watch on the politics of states along its frontiers.

The suggestion (despite some problems) is not quite as unthinkable as it may appear at first sight, given the evidence of the Tell Fekheriye statue (see chapter 8b), which calls the person represented 'governor' in the Assyrian text, but 'ruler/king' in the Aramaic version. What Lemaire and Durand propose is that Shamshi-ilu was descended from the ruler of a small territory (*KTK*) which had been absorbed by Bit Adini; on Shalmaneser III's conquest, this family, which had suffered at the hands of Bit Adini's kings, was elevated to the position of local governors – a position they owed, of course, to the Assyrian king. Shamshi-ilu himself may have been brought up at the Assyrian court (a practice attested later), and thus been groomed to take over the position of governor of Bit Adini, as well as gaining the important state and military office of *turtānu*. In the Assyrian perspective, he and his predecessors were provincial governors, servants of the Assyrian king; but within their area of authority and in relation to neighbours they could present themselves, with some justification, as local dynasts (see also the evidence for the 'governors of Suhu and Mari' in the ninth and early eighth century who were members of a long-established local dynasty there (reaching back to Hammurabi), cf. Ismail *et al.* 1983). This attractive argument, if right, re-emphasises how closely intertwined Assyrians and Aramaeans were already within the ninth century. It is quite impossible to separate them out into ethnic Assyrians dominating subjugated ethnic Aramaeans – the ruling group of Assyria from early in the Neo-Assyrian period became an Assyro-Aramaean amalgam, governing a similarly mixed group of subjects who were called 'Assyrians', but were not necessarily 'natives' of the Assyrian heartland.

9c Imperial expansion and consolidation (744–c. 630)

The Assyrian empire acquired its definitive shape and structure between 745 and 705. Then it stabilised and dominated the larger part of the Near East continuously and with little perceptible change for the next eighty years (see Postgate 1979: 194). During the preceding forty years the essentials of imperial administration were worked out and refined, although many institu-tions of the ninth and earlier eighth centuries continued to exist. But they become a palimpsest, as it were, overlaid by the many developments in provincial structure and administration, the evolution of imperial policy and the emergence of the empire in its classic form. All these changes had repercussions on the role and position of the king, the hub around which the Assyrian empire revolved. The documentation, in terms of annals and other

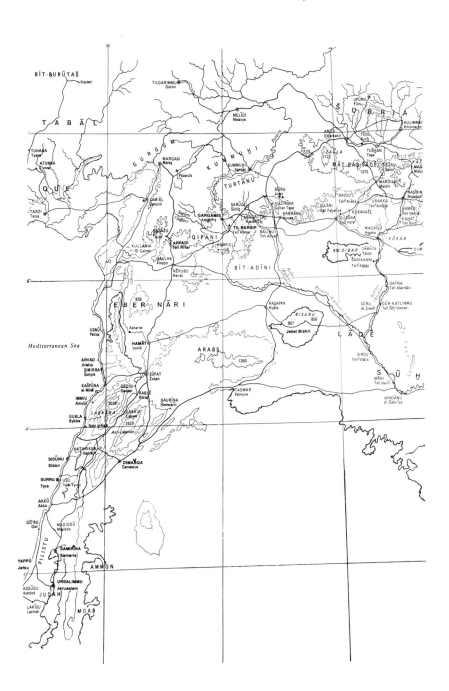

Map 13 The Assyrian empire

494

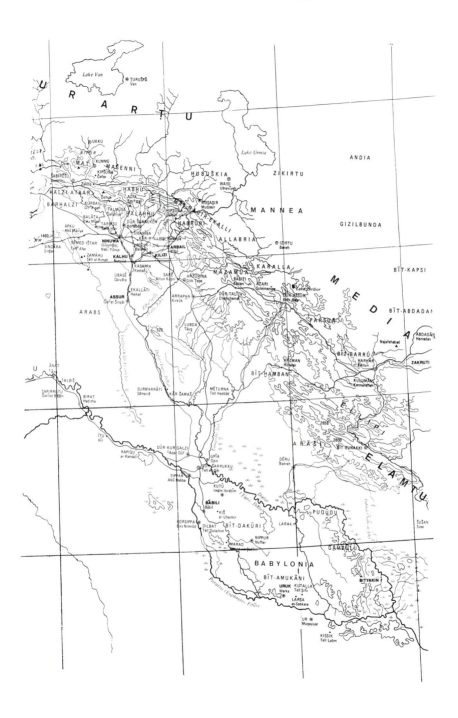

495

royal inscriptions, chronicles, biblical material, administrative and legal texts, and archives of royal correspondence is extraordinarily full for this period, and allows a quite detailed reconstruction of the wars of conquest and the consolidation of frontiers (for a detailed discussion, see *CAH* III/2, chs. 22–24).

Tiglath-pileser III and Shalmaneser V

Tiglath-pileser III (744–727) acceded to the throne following three fairly weak reigns (see p. 492). But, as already stressed, there had been no real loss of the areas incorporated into the empire in the reigns of Ashurnasirpal II and Shalmaneser III, and the eponym-lists give a good idea of what lay inside the boundaries of Assyria in 745: the area east of the Euphrates bend, the whole of the north Mesopotamian plain and the mountainous foothills to the north, as well as the entire Assyrian heartland (Ashur, Nineveh, Kalhu, Arbela and Kilizi) and the foothills of the Zagros mountains immediately adjoining to the east. This is not to deny that there had been losses. First of all, Assyrian prestige in the client states in north Syria seems to have diminished considerably; subsequent evidence suggests that many of the states, here and in Anatolia, had shifted their focus towards the northern power of Urartu (see chapter 10a), which had increased its influence at the expense of Assyria. Second, Urartu had also expanded enormously, both territorially and in terms of political influence, into the Mannaean area of the Zagros; the strong Urartian presence here probably reached right down to the area of the important Diyala–Kermanshah–Khorasan route – the main artery leading up from the Babylonian plain through the Zagros to Ecbatana and the Iranian plateau (Levine 1974: 99ff.). Third, Babylonia had reversed the situation that obtained in Adad-nirari III's reign (see p. 491) and was independent under its own king, with the dynasty friendly to Assyria (cf. chapter 11b). A new feature in Babylonian politics, from this time on, is that various Chaldaean groups made occasional attempts to seize the throne of Babylon with Elamite help, and so formed a recurrent destabilising factor locally, which allowed Assyria to intervene in defence of its southern frontier. The struggles in Babylonia reflect competition between Chaldaean, Elamite and Assyrian forces for control of its strategic and potentially rich territory (see chapters 11b and 11c).

All these factors determined Tiglath-pileser III's military actions, and, by the end of his reign (727), the Assyrian provincial system had been extended to embrace some of the north Syrian states (Agusi/Arpad; Pattina/Kinalua), and parts of southern Syria (Damascus). Client states, tightly controlled, stretched from south Turkey (Kummuh, Sam'al) to the frontiers of Egypt (Gaza, Israel, Judah). In the east, the main route from the Mesopotamian plain up to the Iranian plateau was under a reasonable degree of Assyrian control. Urartu's role, both here and along the western frontier, had been considerably reduced by definitive Assyrian victories in battle and by Tiglath-pileser's invasion of Urartu, in which he penetrated the high mountain terrain right up to the Urartian royal city of Tushpa on Lake Van. Finally, Babylonia was ruled directly by Assyria in the guise of the Assyrian king assuming the ceremonial role of king of Babylon, while parts of north-eastern Babylonia were detached and incorporated into existing Assyrian provinces. A brief takeover of the Babylonian kingship by a Chaldaean chieftain had provided an opportunity for the Assyrians to invade Babylonia; under the pretext of re-establishing peace, Tiglath-pileser had been able to seize control of the country.

The events of the reign of Tiglath-pileser III's son, Shalmaneser V (726–722), are virtually unknown: there are no royal inscriptions, the *limmu-*chronicle is broken for his reign, and the *Babylonian Chronicle* records nothing of his activities, save (probably) the taking of Samaria (also reported in 2 *Kings* 17.1–6; Becking 1992). The fall of Samaria marked the end of the northern kingdom of Israel and turned it, too, into a directly governed Assyrian province. The arrangement, whereby Shalmaneser V's father had governed simultaneously as king of Babylonia and Assyria, is known to have continued in force.

By 722, then, Assyria governed Babylonia directly; its control had been extended in the eastern mountains; a block of provinces extended to the Mediterranean; and the commercially important states of Israel and Damascus also formed Assyrian provinces. The coastal cities, smaller inland states and some of the Arab groups involved in trade with them were linked to Assyria by oaths of loyalty and obligations to supply forces and pay tribute, while the frontier with Egypt was policed on Assyria's behalf by a local Arab sheikh. Urartu's influence had been substantially curtailed, but by no means extinguished, as the events of Sargon II's reign show.

Sargon II

Sargon II (721–705) acceded to the throne in an irregular way: this is clear from several hints and veiled references. The reasons for the disruption in the kingship are obscure. Sargon was another son of Tiglath-pileser III (Thomas 1993), who probably seized the throne from Shalmaneser V in a violent coup. As a result, Sargon's most immediate concerns were domestic problems caused by the resistance unleashed inside Assyria by his usurpation (or leading to it). This instability at the centre seems to have been exploited by Yaubidi, ruler of Hamath, who was almost entirely encircled by Assyrian provinces and had possibly lost some territory. He was able to gather a coalition of neighbouring states and lead them in revolt against the new king, who was still struggling to establish himself. The defeat of Yaubidi of Hamath, in the midst of serious problems at home, was one of Sargon's great triumphs, and probably helped to firm up his tenure of the throne. The flaying of Yaubidi was portrayed in detail later on the walls of Sargon's palace in his newly founded city of Dur Sharrukin (modern Khorsabad). But in the south Sargon had to concede defeat: on the death of Shalmaneser V, another Chaldaean, from the most southerly tribe of Bit Yakin, Marduk-apla-iddina II (the biblical Merodach-baladan: 721–710), placed himself on the throne of Babylonia. Sargon was resoundingly beaten at Der (720) by an Elamite army supporting the Babylonians, when he tried to reverse this situation. So here the Assyrians lost an important region – a loss not made good for another ten years. Despite Tiglath-pileser III's successes, Urartian influence in some areas was still very strong and Urartu could, and did, exploit the unsettled situation in Assyria by extending its power again in Mannaean territory and in central Anatolia. Another problem faced by Sargon was the increased activity in the central area of modern Turkey by Mita of Mushki, generally identified as the famous king of Phrygia, Midas. Sargon mentions him several times making common cause with Urartu to pressurise some of the small states lying in the zone between Phrygia and Assyrian territories (see chapter 10b).

These complex problems determined Sargon's policy, and it is not surprising that he scarcely stopped fighting throughout his reign. Basically, he was in the situation of having to complete and bring to its logical conclusion the programme of new conquests and expansion initiated by Tiglath-pileser III. In this effort, he was remarkably successful. By the end of his reign, the western area from central Anatolia (southern Cappadocia = Tabal) as far as Judah and Philistia formed a virtually solid block of Assyrian provinces, ringed by dependent subject-states under local rulers. The strength of Assyrian success is reflected in the friendly overtures made by the Phrygian king in 709 (see pp. 565–566), which led to ambassadors from the two countries residing at the royal courts in Gordion and Kalhu (*CAH* III/1, ch. 9).

In the north and north-east Sargon re-affirmed Tiglath-pileser's strategy of maintaining very close control over the areas between the lower Zab, the Diyala and Elamite border and along the Kermanshah route. At the same time, substantial efforts were made to ensure that Mannaea (northern Zagros) and associated areas remained pro-Assyrian, and to frustrate Urartian counter-moves in order to enjoy the benefits of the rich trade of these regions (Levine 1977). In this process some towns along the main route were garrisoned and renamed. Eventually, Sargon led a campaign into Urartian terrritory in 714, during which he defeated the Urartian ruler and his Mannaean allies in battle, and sacked the small frontier state of Musasir, which had wavered between allegiance to Assyria and Urartu (Levine 1977; Lanfranchi and Parpola 1990).

Between 710 and 707 Sargon was finally able to re-impose the dual kingship on Babylonia after defeating Marduk-apla-iddina II in battle and driving him into exile in Elam. This was the acme of his achievements – shown by the fact that friendly embassies from states on the edges of the empire hastened to congratulate Sargon while in Babylon: from Phrygia, from the king of Dilmun in the Gulf, where maritime trade was reviving in this period (Potts 1990 [0Gf] I ch. 9), and from the petty dynasts of Cyprus. This great triumph was followed by the celebrations inaugurating the new royal foundation of Dur Sharrukin ('Fortress of Sargon'), north of Nineveh. But in 705 a military emergency arose, associated by most modern authorities with the Cimmerians, and located by them in Anatolia (Tadmor 1958; *CAH* III ch. 9; Lanfranchi 1990). It was obviously serious enough to require the king's personal participation. Sargon led his forces in the fight and, in the terse words of the *limmu*-chronicle for 705 (one of its latest fully preserved entries):

> The king was killed; the camp of the king of Assyria [was captured].
> (C^{b}6, rev. 10; Ungnad 1938: 435)

Sennacherib, Esarhaddon and Ashurbanipal

The campaigns and conquests of the successors of Tiglath-pileser and Sargon aimed at consolidating and maintaining the enormous and rapid gains made in the period between 744 and 705. Their basic success can be measured by the fact that their wars were waged in territories either very recently conquered, or in areas along and just beyond the frontiers – always the most difficult to control securely. So, for example, the major preoccupation of Sennacherib's reign (704–681) was trying to sort out the political situation in Babylonia, which had only recently been conquered after twelve years of independence and three years of fierce fighting (chapter 11c). His other campaigns (southern Levant, Anatolia and in the Syrian desert against Arabs) can be regarded as frontier wars. Esarhaddon (680–669) reaped the fruits of Sennacherib's hard-won successes in Babylonia (Porter 1987; chapter 11c), and practically all his campaigning was related to safeguarding frontier security. In one case, this led to a temporary Assyrian expansion: following Sargon II's aggression in southern Palestine, Egypt had moved from a stance of friendliness to hostility and fomented revolts among some of the Assyrian subject kingdoms in Palestine. Sennacherib had to face an Egyptian army supporting rebels against Assyria in 701. Egypt's repeated meddling in Palestine eventually provoked Esarhaddon to extend Assyrian activity into Egypt itself, and in 671 the Assyrian armies captured Memphis. Establishing Assyrian control over Egypt, with its basically fragmented political system (chapter 12a), required more than just the defeat of Egypt's Napatan rulers (dynasty XXV), and in 669 Esarhaddon mounted another campaign to Egypt to cement Assyrian suzerainty but died *en route*.

A predictable result was that Esarhaddon's successor, Ashurbanipal (668–c. 630), had to complete his father's Egyptian conquest, which he did by capturing Thebes and driving the Napatans right out of Egypt. The Assyrians tied some of the Delta kinglets to themselves as subject rulers, and it was on the basis of this (poorly understood) arrangement that Psammetichus I (dynasty XXVI) was able to make his ultimately successful bid to unite Egypt under his kingship by 656 (chapter 12b). Although this looks like a reversal for the Assyrians, it seems that Assyria and Egypt nevertheless maintained relatively friendly relations (Kitchen 1986). Assyria's enduring international prestige is reflected by the fact that, when Gyges of Lydia (western Turkey) was threatened by an attack of Cimmerian raiders who had destroyed the Phrygian kingdom, he sent an embassy to Ashurbanipal requesting an alliance with the Assyrian king (chapter 10b).

One region where Ashurbanipal extended Assyrian control was in Elam, which was itself torn by political rivalries and broken into a number of separate, practically independent, political units. Some of the Elamite kings aided a serious attempt at revolt in Babylonia (652–648) led by Ashurbanipal's brother, Shamash-shum-ukin, who was acting as Babylonian ruler under the overlordship of his brother (chapter 11c). After ruthlessly crushing his brother's revolt, Ashurbanipal moved into Elam itself and devastated its most important city, Susa, and environs (646), described in terrifying terms in the latest version of Ashurbanipal's annals:

> I tore out the raging wild bull(-figures), the attachments of the gates; the temples of Elam I destroyed so that they ceased to exist. I counted their gods and goddesses as powerless ghosts. Into their hidden groves, into which no stranger goes, whose bounds he does not enter, my battle troops penetrated, beheld its hidden (place), burnt it with fire. The burial places of their early (and) later kings, who had not feared Ashur and Ishtar, my lords, (and) who had made my royal predecessors tremble, I devastated, I destroyed (and) let them see the sun; their bones I removed to Assyria. I laid restlessness on their spirits. Food-offerings (to the dead) and water-libations I denied them. For the distance of one month (and) 25 days, I devastated the region of Elam. Salt and cress I sowed over them.
>
> (Streck 1916: 54–57)

Although the destruction was probably not as total as described by Ashurbanipal (Miroschedji 1985), Elam as a major political factor ceased to present a problem (Carter and Stolper 1984; Gerardi 1987). Indicative of Assyria's success is that regions beyond Susa now made overtures to the Assyrian court. Most notable was Kurash of Anshan (thought by many to be the grandfather of Cyrus (II) the Great of Persia), who sent an embassy, together with a son as hostage, some time before 640. It is possible that the evolving state of Media (Sancisi-Weerdenburg 1988) came to fill the gap left by the destruction of Elam, and took over the role of supporting Babylonian groups in fighting against Assyria, which was eventually successful (chapter 9e).

It is important to note that in spite of problems of control, particularly in frontier areas (and what imperial power does not experience these?), the

Assyrian kings in the period between *c.* 700 and *c.* 630 exercised control over a very large territory with singular success and relative ease: it is not totally inappropriate to describe this period as the *pax Assyriaca* (Hallo in Hallo and Simpson 1971 [OC]: 138).

9d The structure of the Assyrian empire

The sources

On what is our knowledge of the Neo-Assyrian empire as a functioning whole, an overall successful system, based? From the second half of the eighth century on there is a plethora of documentation, which is particularly dense for the reigns of Sargon II (721–705), Esarhaddon (680–669) and Ashur-banipal (668–*c.* 630).

The main, hugely important, sources (in Akkadian) are the letters – *c.* 2,300 – written between king and governors, members of the court, royal advisers, cities, cult personnel and military commanders. They provide an unrivalled insight into the workings of the central Assyrian administration. The majority were found in the ruins of the great Assyrian palaces at Nineveh (Kuyunjik), and a large proportion – 1,471 – were published in cuneiform copy at the turn of the century by Harper (1892–1914), and edited with transliterations, translations and indices by his pupil Waterman (1930–36). They are now in need of drastic revision and updating, a task being undertaken (together with producing modern editions of all other Neo-Assyrian documents) by a team of scholars as part of the *State Archives of Assyria* project, of which nine volumes have so far appeared (1987–93; abbreviated SAA). A selection of the letters exchanged between the Assyrian kings and the learned scholars they consulted regularly has also been produced in a modern edition (Parpola 1970/1983; now SAA 10). To the Kuyunjik collection we must now add the Nimrud Letters, found in the ancient city of Kalhu in the course of the British excavations conducted in the 1950s. They date mainly to the reigns of Tiglath-pileser III and Sargon II, and a selection was published in a series of articles by Saggs (1955a and b; 1956; 1958; 1959; 1963; 1965; 1966). As the *State Archives of Assyria* project progresses, the Nimrud Letters are being integrated with the earlier material from Kuyunjik and appearing in new editions in the SAA series. There are also quite extensive groups of legal texts, mainly, but not exclusively, from Nineveh, Ashur and Kalhu (Johns 1898–1923; Kohler and Ungnad 1913; Postgate 1976; Kwasman 1988; Kwasman and Parpola 1991; Fales and Jakob-Rost 1991), and administrative documents (Kinnier Wilson 1972; Postgate 1973; Dalley and Postgate 1984; Fales and Postgate 1992; Pedersen 1985). A collection of relevant documents was also recovered at the provincial capital, Guzana (Weidner 1940).

Other types of text are literary and cultic ones from Ashur, Kalhu (the Nabu temple), Nineveh and, interestingly, a small provincial temple library from Husirina (modern Sultan Tepe; Gurney 1956; Gurney and Finkelstein 1957; Gurney and Hulin 1964). Examples of what might be described as 'court poetry' have been edited in the *State Archives of Assyria* series (Livingstone 1989). One category of texts, which gives some insight into the workings of the court and reveals one of the facets of the royal decision-making process, is the so-called 'oracles'. They are, in fact, requests made to the sun-god (Shamash) to grant yes/no answers, by marking the liver of (usually) a sheep slaughtered for the purpose, in response to carefully formulated questions of somtimes considerable political importance. The matters on which the sun-god's responses were solicited range from deciding on the royal successor, or the possibilities of military attack or revolt, to appointing relatively low-ranking officials and the health and safety of the king or crown-prince. For example:

(Beginning missing)
[Should Ashurbanipal, the crown prince of the] Succession Palace, [drink this drug which] is placed [before] your great [div]inity, [and in drinking this drug will he] be rescued and spared?
[Will he live and get well? Will he . . ., be s]aved and escape? [Will the illness of] his [body] be released? Will it leave (him)? Does your great divinity know it?
[Is the res]cue, survival [of Ashurbanipal, crown prince of the Suc]ces[ssion Palace], by drinking this drug, [decreed and confirmed in a favourable case, by the command of your great divinity], Shamash, great lord? [Will he who can see, see it? Will he who can hear], hear it?
(There follows a section of standard formulae intended to protect the procedure against possible human error and pollution, which is worth quoting:)
[Disregard that . . . an oa]th by the god (may be) upon [him].
[Disregard the (formulation) of today's case, be it good, be it] faulty.
[Disregard that a clean or an unclean person has touched the sacrificial sheep, or] blocked the way of the sacrificial sheep.
[Disregard that an unclean man or woman has come near the place of the extispicy and] made it unclean.
[Disregard that an unclean person] has performed extispicy [in this place].
[Disregard that the ram (offered) to your great divinity for the perform-ance of the extispicy] is deficient or faulty.
[Disregard that he who touches the forehead of the sheep] is dressed [in his ordinary soiled garments], (or) has eaten anything unclean.
[Disregard that I, the haruspex your servant], have jumbled [the oracle query in] my [mouth, or changed or altered the proceedings.
Let them be] taken out and put aside!
(End of standard protective prayer)

[I ask you, Shamash, great lord, whether this drug] which [is] now [placed before your great divinity, and which Ashurbanip]al, crown prince of the Succession House (is to) drink –
[(whether) by drinking this drug he will . . .] be saved, [and escape]. Be present [in this ram, place (in it) a firm positive answer . . .]
(End lost)

(SAA 4 no. 187)

The 'oracle' texts, which were known for a long time in two old editions (Knudtzon 1893; Klauber 1913), are now available in a new edition, including a substantial number of previously unpublished texts (Starr 1990). They must be carefully separated from court prophecies, which, like the well-known Old Testament prophecies, were divine utterances directly revealed to individuals, who had few or no professional cultic links (more often than not they were women). They were spontaneous divine revelations, and did not require technical knowledge (such as astronomical observation and interpretation; Hunger 1992) or procedures. They were formally reported to the king, and kept in the royal archives; they are occasionally quoted in royal inscriptions, together with the circumstances in which they were given (Weippert 1981). An example will make the fundamental difference from 'oracles' clear:

Esarhaddon, king of lands,

fear not!

What wind has there been, that has rushed against you, whose wings I have not broken?

Your enemies roll about before your feet like ripe apples.

I am the great lady!

I am Ishtar of Arbela, who throws your enemies down before your feet!

What are these words of mine, that I have spoken to you, on which you have not been able to rely?

I am Ishtar of Arbela!

I flay your enemies, give them to you.

I am Ishtar of Arbela!

Before you, behind you I go.

Fear not!

You lie in agony –

I am in pain.

I arise –

seat myself (at your side)!

From the lips of the woman Ishtar-la-tashiat of Arbela
(T.G. Pinches, *The Cuneiform Inscriptions of Western Asia* (London 1891) IV, pl. 61; *ARAB* II §§617–638; *ANET*: 605; Weippert 1981; Weippert in Veenhof 1983 [OH]: 285; *TUAT* II 56–57)

There are also examples of treaties, in the form both of 'loyalty oaths', which were a vital element in linking subject to king, and of agreements defining obligations between the small states at the edges of the empire and the Assyrian king. The most famous preserved examples are the so-called 'Esarhaddon vassal treaties' found at Nimrud in the 1950s. They are multiple copies of one text (all fragmentary, although one preserves the seal impressions), establishing, and defining precisely, the relations of subject and overlord between Esarhaddon and a number of petty local rulers in the Zagros (Wiseman 1958; *ANET*: 534ff.; *TUAT* I 160–176; Watanabe 1987; Parpola and Watanabe 1988, no. 6).

An invaluable source for studying the Assyrian empire, which should not be forgotten, is the magnificent narrative reliefs with which the Assyrian kings, from Ashurnasirpal II's reign onwards (see pp. 485–486), decorated their palaces (see generally Madhloom 1970; Reade 1979; 1983). In Ashurnasirpal's palace, the amount of wall space devoted to depictions of the king's battles, court-scenes and hunts is relatively restricted (Stearns 1961; Paley 1976): the façade and interior of the throneroom only contained such scenes – the remaining rooms and corridors were adorned with reliefs showing figures of genies and 'sacred trees', which almost certainly had an apotropaic function (Stearns 1961).[4] Until the reign of Tiglath-pileser III, no new major palaces were built, with the exception of Shalmaneser's armoury (see p. 489). So we have few sculptures illustrating royal campaigns from the 850s to the 740s, save for the finely carved base of Shalmaneser III's throne (see p. 489). But Shalmaneser, like his father, equipped the temple at the small site of Balawat (ancient Imgur-Enlil), near Nimrud (Kalhu), with a gigantic pair of doors. They had bronze bands fitted to them, worked in repoussé, showing miniature, detailed scenes of his wars (King 1915). They are well preserved, and now on view in the British Museum. Tiglath-pileser III built a new royal residence in Kalhu, and several reliefs from it have been found (Barnett and Falkner 1962). Sargon II's new foundation of Dur-Sharrukin contained a superb large palace with very fine reliefs (now mostly in the Louvre, Paris Place 1867–70; Albenda 1986). Most of the recorded slabs recount Sargon's military achievements, with the novel addition of scenes depicting the transport of timber for the royal building project. When Sennacherib renovated the old city of Nineveh (see p. 536) he, too, built a new grand 'Palace Without a Rival' (Russell 1991). The king gave it this name because of its enormous size; every inch was decorated with detailed narrative scenes. One courtyard was almost entirely decorated with scenes showing the cutting of a colossal winged bull (to be placed in the palace doorways) in a quarry and its laborious transport to Nineveh. Esarhaddon's palace at Kalhu has not survived well, but his son Ashurbanipal added some fine reliefs to his grandfather's building at Nineveh and built a new one there. Ashurbanipal's palace reliefs are among the finest examples of Assyrian sculpture, and include the justly celebrated lion-hunt (Barnett 1976).

The Assyrian reliefs echo the ideological message of the royal inscriptions; their repertoire, too, is identical: war, victory, building – in short, the mastery and triumph of the king in all, and over all, aspects of life with the aid of the gods. But they add much more than that. They depict army life and warfare, royal and court dress, non-Assyrian buildings, cities and peoples (Hrouda 1965; Reade 1972; Wäfler 1975). The scenes are detailed and realistic: they take us right into the Assyrian camps and into beleaguered cities (e.g. the siege of Lachish); they allow us to witness horrific scenes of execution (e.g. the flaying of Yaubidi of Hamath), marvel at the Assyrian exploration of the sources of the Tigris, and become spectators, along with the Assyrian populace, of the king's hunting feats. We can observe the weary lines of deportees, moving with their few possessions on carts, the women carrying their children (Albenda 1983). One exquisitely carved scene shows some Chaldaeans hiding from Sennacherib's soldiers among the tall reeds of Iraq's southern marshes (see fig. 38, page 584). An Assyrian rural idyll forms the background for Sennacherib's quarrying reliefs: a man is fishing with a net perched on an inflated skin floating on the river; houses are set among trees on the riverbank; two men operate a shaduf to lift river water for their fields, while in the thicket on the banks a sow suckles her brood of piglets. Without the reliefs, our knowledge of the Assyrian empire would be immeasurably poorer.

Another feature of Assyrian relief art is worth noting. Its styles and motifs are mirrored in other objects, such as seals, metal vessels, jewellery and furniture. All that remains of the latter are the ivory inlays which originally decorated chairs, beds and footstools (Barnett 1957); ivory was also used for boxes, mirrors and handles (e.g. of fans). Some of the same artistic motifs decorated royal garments, perhaps in the form of appliquéed metal plaques (Canby 1971). Assyrian art formed a distinctive, influential court-style, which proclaimed its message, repeatedly and unmistakably, in monumental and miniature form.

Kingship, war and imperial ideology

The lord of life and death

The king was the fulcrum of the empire, the hub around which the whole system was organised. Like all autocratic rulers, his power was absolute and unchallengeable. Absolute royal power was part of the gradual development of the institution of kingship in Assyria, directly linked to the acquisition of empire and hence of the evolution of a system to govern it. In the Old Assyrian period (nineteenth century), the king played the role of *primus inter pares* (see chapter 2b). In spite of the great increase in his power in the Middle Assyrian and earlier Neo-Assyrian periods, there are strong hints that his power was in some measure counterbalanced by a powerful traditional élite.

There is, first, the evidence of the system of eponymous officials (*limmu*s), always held in prescribed sequence by very important individuals, headed by the cupbearer, the palace-herald, the *turtānu* (chief army commander), the chief steward, the governor of Ashur and the king himself. Second, there is the fact that the *limmu*s were formally commemorated by stelae set up facing those of the kings in Ashur (see chapter 7b). Finally, a recent discovery shows that the king, at least at times, took his chief queen from this group of dignitaries (Fadhil 1990b). All of this suggests that in the ninth and eighth centuries the Assyrian king was closely related to, and interlinked with, a privileged and powerful aristocratic group of families – a group whose standing was not solely dependent on royal favour, but who had claims to rank and privilege based on tradition and family-descent (van Driel 1970). In the course of the second half of the eighth century this situation changed. With the enormous expansion of the empire by Tiglath-pileser III and Sargon II, and hence the greatly increased need for military commanders, provincial governors and administrative personnel, the Assyrian kings began to create new positions of authority that rivalled those of the hereditary aristocrats. As a result, the older family-based nobles were compelled to compete for privilege and rewards with a new, royally created aristocracy. This, in turn, undermined their inherited, *ex officio* status and prestige. The change was probably gradual, related to the circumstances created by renewed imperial expansion – not part of some kind of blueprint for reform introduced by Tiglath-pileser III, as often assumed (cf. the pertinent criticisms of Garelli in Garelli and Nikiprowetzky 1974 [OC]: 231–234). There is no evidence for any 'reforms of Tiglath-pileser III': all that we can say is that, over time, new powerful men, who rivalled and eventually submerged the traditional powers claimed by the older Assyrian aristocracy, emerged. The process probably began with Tiglath-pileser III and was only completed by the reign of Sennacherib.

The absolute power of the king is emphasised in several ways. All nomination to office and the accompanying benefits were in the end totally dependent on royal favour, just as the king held the power of life or death over all his subjects. The fundamental principle was that all owed total loyalty to the king, as shown in this passage from Esarhaddon's 'vassal treaties':

> On the day that Esarhaddon, king of Assyria, your lord, passes away, (on that day) Ashurbanipal, the great crown prince desi[gnate], son of Esarhaddon, your lord, shall be your king and your lord; he shall abase the mighty, raise up the lowly, put to death him who is worthy of death, and pardon him who deserves to be pardoned. You shall hearken to whatever he says and do whatever he commands, and you shall not seek any other king or any other lord against him.
>
> (SAA 2 no. 6 ll.188–197)

At the same time, the ideal was that all could appeal to the king in order to lay their case before him and receive justice from him (Postgate 1974b). The term for this was 'to speak the word of the king', and a small, but growing, number of texts show that the right of appeal was not just an empty formula, but had real legal force. So the administrator of the Esagila temple in Babylon (*šatammu*) writes to Esarhaddon:

> Because (these people) 'spoke the word of the king' I have sent them to the king's presence, so that the king may hear what they have to say.
>
> (Landsberger 1965 ll. 26–32)

So the king, ideally, encompassed all his subjects equally from the highest to the lowest. How this actually worked in practice is, of course, much less clear.

One of the titles regularly borne by the Assyrian king was '*šangû* of Ashur', a term whose cultic overtones have led to it being frequently translated 'priest of Ashur', although 'administrator' is also a possibility (van Driel 1969: 170–175; Seux 1980–3: 169–170). The Middle Assyrian coronation ritual implies that in some sense the king was perceived only as the executive of Ashur, while the god himself was considered the ultimate ruler. Although the coronation ceremony is only known from this earlier period (see chapter 7b), it is clear that the essentials of the ritual were the same in the Neo-Assyrian period. The Ashurbanipal 'coronation hymn' from Ashur makes this plain; it also illustrates how the country's physical well-being and social harmony were thought to be inextricably bound up with the personal virtues of the ruler:

> May Shamash, king of heaven and earth, elevate you to shepherdship over the four [region]s!
>
> May Ashur, who ga[ve y]ou [the sceptre], lengthen your days and years! Spread your land wide at your feet!
>
> May Sherua extol [your name] to your god!
>
> Just as grain and silver, oil, [the catt]le of Shakkan and the salt of Bariku are good, so may Ashurbanipal, king of Assyria, be agreeable to the gods [of his] land!
>
> May eloquence, understanding, truth and justice be given to him as a gift!
>
> May [the people] of Ashur buy 30 kor of grain for one shekel of silver! May [the peopl]e of Ashur buy 3 seah of oil for one shekel of silver! May [the peop]le of Ashur buy 30 minas of wool for one shekel of silver!
>
> May the lesser speak, and the [greater] listen! May the greater speak, and the [lesser] listen! May concord and peace be established [in Assyri]a!
>
> Ashur is king – indeed Ashur is king! Ashurbanipal is the [representative] of Ashur, the creation of his hands.
>
> May the great gods make firm his reign, may they protect the life [of Ashurba]nipal, king of Assyria!

May they give him a straight sceptre to extend the land and his peoples!

May his reign be renewed, and may they consolidate his royal throne for ever!

May they bless him (by) day, month, and year, and guard his reign!

In his years may there cons[tantly?] be rain from the heavens and flood from the (underground) source!

Give our lord Ashurbanipal long [days], copious years, strong [we]apons, a long reign, y[ear]s of abundance, a good name, [fame], happiness and joy, auspicious oracles, and leadership over (all other) kings!

After he has pronounced the blessing he turns and pronounces the (following) blessing at the opening of the censer (placed) before Shamash:

Anu gave his crown, Illil gave his throne; Ninurta gave his weapon; Nergal gave his luminous splendour. Nusku sent and placed advisers before him.

He who speaks with the king disloyally or treasonably – if he is notable, he will die a violent death; if he is a rich man, he will become poor. He who in his heart plots evil against the king – Erra will call him to account in a bout of plague.

He who in his heart utters improprieties against the king – his foundation is (but) wind, the hem of his garment is (but) litter. Gather, all the gods of heaven and earth, bless king Ashurbanipal, the circumspect man!

Place in his hand the weapon of war and battle, give him the blackheaded people, that he may rule as their shepherd!

(LKA 31; SAA 3 no. 11)

The defender of the Assyrian order

The coronation hymn shows, strikingly, the way in which the concept of the king as caring protector is intimately linked with the stress on the king as warrior: he is ordered to 'enlarge his land' (as earlier in the coronation ceremony) – in other words, one of his duties as king was to fight wars. Yet wars were not undertaken lightly: a ritual published recently (Mayer 1988) concerns the actions to be taken by the king and his people when threatened by an enemy. It prescribes an extremely lengthy series of ritual activities, including penitential prayers offered by the king, purification rites by king and people, and public prayer by all before the arming. Only after this were sheep slaughtered and the livers examined for the omens, and if all portents were favourable, then the diviner said:

Expand your land! Your heroic deeds are guaranteed!

If the omens were bad, the message given to the king was:

Empty your land; tear out . . . (end broken)
(BM 98583, Mayer 1988: 147–149)

The stress is on the fact that only in harmony with the divine will and in a pure state, free from all evil, can the war succeed, as the king acts as defender of the god-given order against chaos.

The justification for going to war seems to have been carefully worked out: either it was provoked by direct threats (as above), or a cumulative list of acts interpreted as hostile and damaging to Assyria was drawn up that made war inevitable, including the rejection of attempts at peaceful settlement (Oppenheim 1960: 143–144; Gerardi 1987; Oded 1992). A series of exchanges by messenger preceding a war are partially preserved in Esarhaddon's 'letter to the god' (p. 476). The text contains a detailed account of Esarhaddon's campaign against mountainous Shupria, which formed a buffer between Assyria's northern frontier and the powerful state of Urartu, and seems to have been a place for political fugitives from both countries:

> . . . who did not pay attention to the word of Ashur, king of the gods, did not respect my lordship . . . robbers, thieves or whoever had committed a crime and shed blood . . . officers, governors, inspectors, leaders, commanders had fled to Shupria. . . . I wrote to him (sc. ruler of Shupria) thus:
> 'Have a herald call out these people in your land . . . gather them, let not a single one escape . . . have them go to the temple before the great lady Pirrigal . . . a pardon (or: amnesty?) for them . . . together with my messenger they shall take the road to Assyria . . .'
> The good . . . concerning saving his life he forgot . . . the Assyrians, my subjects. . . . he before him . . . together with a standard(?) by means of the messenger . . . . [The messenger] reported to me everything he had replied. [Then my heart grew angry and] I became enraged . . .
> (Eventually the menaced Shupria ruler offered to surrender and implored mercy from the king, but it was too late; Esarhaddon responded:)
> 'Have you ever heard the word of a mighty king twice? And I, an outstandingly powerful king, even wrote to you three times, but you did not obey the word of my lips, . . . you were not afraid to defame me and did not pay attention to my letter. You began fighting and battle against me and disturbed the grim weapons of Ashur from their resting-place.' I did not listen to his pleas, I did not accept his imploring, I did not allow his pleading. I did not turn my averted face towards him, my enraged senses were not calmed against him. My turbulent heart did not find rest, I felt no pity for him and did not speak 'Mercy (*ahulap*)!' to him.
>
> (Borger 1956 §68 col. I; col. II: 29–35)

The situation, as presented by the Assyrian king, is that of a powerful head of state making a reasonable request from the ruler of a small neighbouring country, for political fugitives and traitors to be gathered up and extradited. The Shuprian king's refusal to accede to the politely phrased, repeated demand becomes the *casus belli* – his rejection reveals him to be Assyria's enemy: it stirs the weapons of war from their resting place and leaves the Assyrian king no option but to go to war.

The king as warrior is one of the most prominent aspects of Assyrian kingship: it is the royal role most emphasised in the splendid narrative reliefs decorating the palaces and celebrated by the annals and other royal inscriptions. All the Assyrian kings personally planned and led campaigns, marching with the divine standards before them (Dalley and Postgate 1984: 40), which were set up on high poles in the royal camp (Pongratz-Leisten *et al.* 1992). This is plain for all the kings down to Sargon II, who was killed in battle (see p. 499), and there is no reason to assume that the later seventh-century rulers were not also actively involved in campaigning: Sennacherib participated in all the major campaigns in Babylonia, the Elamite frontier and Palestine; Esarhaddon led the three campaigns to Egypt, and died in the course of the third one. In the case of Ashurbanipal the situation is less clear, as there were certainly instances where he was not present in person (e.g. the Egyptian campaigns); but there is no reason to assume that he was not personally involved in the fall of rebellious Babylon in 648 and the destruction of Susa in 646. The last Assyrian kings, Ashur-etel-ilani, Sin-shar-ishkun and Ashur-uballit II, all fought personally.

In campaigns where Ashurbanipal was not himself a participant, the annalistic accounts depict him as the central co-ordinator, sending his commanders out with the armies, and gathering forces from subject states to swell their number. The way his annals describe one incident, when the king did not go to war himself (probably because the situation was not serious enough to warrant it; Gerardi 1987), while still making him central to its conduct, is revealing. The scene is set, with Ashurbanipal in Arbela for a festival of Ishtar, the city's patron-deity; there he receives a report that the Elamite king, Teumman, is preparing for battle. Ashurbanipal enters Ishtar's festival of Ishtar, the city's patrondeity; there he receives a report that the shrine, and beseeches her, with tears in his eyes, to destroy the Elamite foe. Then:

> The goddess Ishtar heard my anxious sighs and said 'Fear not!' and gave me confidence, (saying) 'Since you have lifted your hands in prayer and your eyes have filled with tears, I have had mercy.' During the night in which I appeared before her, a *šabrû* (cultic attendant) lay down and had a dream. He awoke with a start and reported to me as follows:
>
> 'Ishtar, who dwells in Arbela, entered. Quivers hung to the right and left of her, she held a bow in her hand (and) held her sharp sword unsheathed, ready to do battle. You (sc. Ashurbanipal) stood before her,

while she spoke with you like a real mother. Ishtar, the highest of the
gods, addressed you, by giving you instruction:

"You are set on fighting. Wheresoever I wish to go, there I am on my
way."

You said to her:

"Wheresoever you may go, there I will go with you."

The mistress of mistresses, however, answered you:

"Stay here where you belong! Eat bread, drink sesame-beer, prepare
joyful music, praise my divinity, while I go, carry out this work (and)
let you gain your goal! Your face shall not become pale, your feet shall
not falter, your strength not yield(?) in battle!"

She took you in her lovely babysling (*kurimmu*) and thus protected
your entire figure. In her face fire flamed, with raging anger she marched
forth; against Teumman, the king of Elam, with whom she is very angry,
she set out.'

(Piepkorn 1933 Cyl. B v. 46–76; *ARAB* II §861; *ANET*: 606)

Some elements of the story seem to fit the procedure described by the war
ritual: the king hears of the enemy's approach, he abases himself with tears
before the gods and prays for help and deliverance; in response, a promise of
divine help, together with a strict command not to go into battle himself, is
vouchsafed – the warlike Ishtar will personally fight on behalf of the king she
loves like a mother.

Naturally only the king celebrated the rituals and triumphs concluding a
war, making offerings to deities to mark the close of hostilities and parading
around the Assyrian cities, with prominent prisoners-of-war led in chains,
and the severed heads of leading dead enemies held aloft for all to see:

I (am) Ashurbanipal, king of Assyria: after I had made an offering for
the goddess Shatri (and) celebrated the festival of the *akītu*-house, had
seized the reins of Ishtar, surrounded by Dunanu, Samgunu, Aplaya,
and (with) the severed head of Teumman, king of Elam, whom Ishtar,
my lady, had given into my hands, I made my entry into Arbela with
jubilation.

(Weidner 1932–3 no. 34)

War was presented as a divine commandment, never as an act of pure military
aggression: it served to defend the Assyrian political order and extend it –
enemies, inside and out, constantly endangered it and the king's duty was to
eliminate that threat through constant vigilance and action; hence the stress on
the king as warrior even when the empire was stable and relatively peaceful.

The Assyrian king and the divinities of subject peoples

The political order consisted in the acknowledgement of Assyria and its gods
as superior to the gods of defeated peoples, and, along with that, the
acceptance of obedience to Ashur and his representative, the Assyrian king:

You shall guard [this treaty tablet which] is sealed with the seal of Ashur, king of the gods, and set it up in your presence, like your own god.

(SAA 2 no. 6 ll. 407–409)

The implication is that the duties of loyalty to the Assyrian imperial order overarch all others, not that the worship of Ashur was imposed on subjects. There is no evidence of the Assyrians ever demanding worship of Assyrian gods by conquered peoples (Cogan 1974; McKay 1973). It is perfectly clear that the Assyrians acknowledged the power of foreign gods and, indeed, respected them. The clearest example appears in the story of the siege of Jerusalem (701), where the Assyrian commander addressed the Judaean king's courtiers, while the citizens of Jerusalem listened in:

> Tell Hezekiah that this is the message of the Great King, the king of Assyria: 'What ground have you for this confidence of yours? Do you think fine words can take the place of skill and numbers? On whom then do you rely for support in your rebellion against me? On Egypt? Egypt is a splintered cane that will run into a man's hand and pierce it if he leans on it. That is what Pharaoh king of Egypt proves to all who rely on him. And if you tell me that you are relying on the Lord your God, is he not the god whose hill-shrines and altars Hezekiah has suppressed, telling Judah and Jerusalem that they must prostrate themselves before his altar in Jerusalem?'
>   Now, make a bargain with my master the king of Assyria: I will give you two thousand horses if you can find riders for them. Will you reject the authority of even the least of my master's servants and rely on Egypt for chariots and horsemen? Do you think that I have come to attack this place and destroy it without the consent of the Lord? No; the Lord himself said to me, 'Attack this land and destroy it.'
>
> (2 Kings 18.19–25 (NEB))

The tenor of the speech is that Yahweh has been offended by Hezekiah's cultic reforms and has, therefore, consented to Judah's destruction. He is on the side of the Assyrians and is using them to wreak vengeance on Judah – a view that the people of Judah were familiar with to explain the fall of the kingdom of Israel, which probably gave rise to the Old Testament idea of the Assyrians as raised up by Yahweh to scourge his people (Isaiah 10. 5–6; p. 464).

It is important to realise that the different belief-systems of this area and time, however much they diverged in detail, connected at crucial points, and one of these was the deeply held conviction that the local gods controlled directly what happened to their communities, and without their consent there could be no victories or defeats. So, when a city or state was defeated, the local god(s) was thought to have already abandoned it because it had offended the deity. The best-preserved example of this construction of reality is

Esarhaddon's description of the sack of Babylon by his father Sennacherib in 689: the disaster was brought down upon themselves by the Babylonians through their appalling behaviour, which caused the Babylonian gods to flee in despair, thus handing the city over to destructive forces (Borger 1956 §11). Sennacherib's defeat of an Arab tribe is presented in very similar vein:

> To the goddess x x [, beloved of(?) Telhunu, 'priest]ess' (*kumirtu*) of the [land of Arabia], who, angered at Haza'el, king of Arabia, [. . .] handed him over to Sennacherib, my own grandfather, and caused his defeat. She (i.e. the goddess) determined not to remain with the people of Arabia and set out for Assyria.
>
> (K3405; Cogan 1974: 29ff.)

Divine abandonment was paralleled by the actual seizure of divine statues: Musasir (in the northern Zagros), which had reneged on its agreement with Assyria, had its god, Haldi, and his divine consort seized by Sargon in 714; the god Marduk of Babylon was supposedly destroyed by the Assyrian soldiers when they sacked the city in 689, but was probably simply removed to Assyria (Landsberger 1965); and the gods of an Arab tribe were seized by Sennacherib – an act ideologically reshaped to make it seem that at least one of them had preferred residence in Assyria to staying with her faithless community (cf. passage quoted above).

Conversely, the return of divine images to their homes symbolised the now friendly relations obtaining between Assyria and formerly rebellious states. The return always had to be sanctioned by the deities involved: the gods themselves had to acquiesce in their homeward journey – an agreement established through the elaborate system of omen enquiry:

> [Shamash, great lord, give m]e a firm [positive answ]er [to what I am asking you!]
> [Should Shamash-shumu-ukin, son of Esarhad]don, king of [Assyria, within this year] seize the [han]d of the great lord [Marduk i]n the Inner City (i.e. Ashur), and should he lead [Bel(-Marduk)] to Babylon? Is it pleasing to your [great] divinity and to the great lord Marduk?
>
> (SAA 4 no. 262 ll. 1–6)

When a divine statue was sent home, the staff for its cult were also sometimes returned with it or appointed by the kings. The image was, at times, also inscribed with a message and the name of the Assyrian king who was bringing it back. The restored divinity thus only flourished back in its local shrine by the grace of the Assyrian monarch; it owed its renewed life to him, so in future it would help and bless him:

> As to Adummutu, the fortress of Arabia which Sennacherib, king of Assyria, my own father, had conquered and whose goods, possessions and gods, together with Abkallatu, the queen of Arabia, he had carried

off to Assyria, Haza'el, the king of Arabia, came with costly gifts to Nineveh, my lordly city, kissed my feet and implored me to give (him) his gods. I had mercy upon him, repaired the damages (suffered by) these gods, had written upon them (an inscription in praise of) the might of Ashur, my lord, and my own name, and returned (them) to him. I made the woman Tabua, who was reared in my palace, their queen (probably a cultic function) and sent her back together with her gods.

(A. Heidel, *Sumer* 12 (1956): 18ff.)

Care for the cult and shrines of subjected places could also be manifested by Assyrian kings. This is documented in considerable detail in the case of Esarhaddon's rebuilding of Esagila (the main temple in Babylon) and Ashurbanipal's restoration of its cult of Marduk. If Babylonian gods were the only example of such Assyrian concern, it would be simple to argue that, since Assyria and Babylonia were so closely intertwined linguistically, culturally and cultically (it is well known that many Babylonian gods, such as Marduk and Nabu, had long been revered in Assyria), the 'special relationship' between the two places determined Assyrian royal reverence to Babylonia's gods. But there is some significant evidence that shows Assyrian kings could also display such generosity towards other foreign gods – as in this instance where Esarhaddon made a dedication to an Arabian deity:

As for Tabua, he (i.e. Esarhaddon) inquired of the Shamash oracle: She [. . .] Then he gave him (sc. Haza'el) back [Tabua] together with his goddess.

He had a star of red gold made, which was studded with precious stones, [. . . and presented it] for a healthy life and long days, the prosperity of his descendants, the constancy of his rule, and the overthrow of his enemies. [He showed] kindness towards the captured gods of all lands, whose sanctuaries had been trampled, (so that the gods) might grant him the blessing of long life and [permit] his offspring [to rule] over mankind.

(K3405; Cogan 1974: 29ff.)

Active belief in the power of non-Assyrian gods, a strong desire to obtain their blessings and the wish to procure this by caring for, and embellishing, their cult centres and statues is evoked here. It is worth noting that in the Old Testament, too, the restoration of a form of the Yahweh cult in Samaria (unorthodox from Judah's point of view), together with a Yahweh priest sent back from among the deported Israelites, is attributed to the Assyrian ruler (12 *Kings* 17. 25–28) in response to a petition from Samaria's newly settled inhabitants.

Loyalty, terror, mercy and vengeance

The conviction that the gods participated directly in all human events is most strikingly reflected in the loyalty oaths. They were normally sworn to the person of the king and his successors, although at times they could be sworn to a governor acting on behalf of the king (Lemaire and Durand 1984). The oaths were imposed upon everyone: the court and royal family, palace staff, soldiers together with their wives, cultic personnel, and 'Assyrians great and small' (i.e. all subjects). They were also sworn by adjacent states seeking Assyrian protection and hence adopting the stance of subjects, although then it would be their rulers who took the oaths. This is how we should understand the series of agreements (seven in all) sworn between Esarhaddon and the city-governors in the Zagros (misleadingly termed 'vassal-treaties'; Parpola 1987; Parpola and Watanabe 1988: xv); it was also, almost certainly, the type of agreement made between Ahaz of Judah and Tiglath-pileser III in the 730s (2 *Kings* 16. 7–9; see p. 469). The oaths were administered in a formal ceremony on divinely determined favourable days and in the presence of divine statues. The gods of *all* parties were called upon to witness the solemnity of the occasion, and the divine punishments and curses for oathbreakers were described in blood-curdling detail. There is one instance where Ashurbanipal refers, with grim satisfaction, to the fact that an Arab tribe who broke their sworn agreement with Assyria suffered the appropriate curses invoked in the treaties:

> The rest of Arabia which had fled in front of my weapons, Erra the strong overcame them. Disaster broke out among them so that they ate the flesh of their children to keep from starving. All the curses which are written in the oath in the naming of my name and those of the gods, you (sc. the god) decreed for them exactly as their terrible destiny: a camel-foal, a donkey-foal, a calf, a lamb might suck at seven milk-giving animals yet could still not satisfy their bellies with milk. The people in Arabia asked each other: 'Why has such a dis[aster] fallen on [Arabia]?' – 'Because we [did not abide by the great] o[aths] of Ashur, [sin]ned against the kindness of A[shurbani]pal, [the king] who pleases the heart of Enlil!' [Iauta'] (tribal chieftain) suffered misfortune, so that he fled [alone] into the land Nabayati.
>
> (VAT 5600+, Weippert 1973–4: 74ff. Ep. 2)

Compare with this the curses of the (Aramaic) Sfire treaty (see p. 492):

> and seven wetnurses shall anoint their breasts and suckle a child and it shall not be satisfied, and seven mares shall suckle a foal and it shall not be satisfied, and seven cows shall suckle a calf and it shall not be satisfied, and seven sheep shall suckle a lamb and it shall not be satisfied . . .
>
> (Sfire IA, 21–24; Gibson 1971–82 II no. 7; *TUAT* I: 180)

The duties laid upon those swearing the oaths can be summed up simply as total loyalty to Assyria and its kings, to defending the political *status quo*. The Esarhaddon treaties spell this out in detail (SAA 2 no. 6) and cover every conceivable aspect of loyalty: being prepared to die for the king; to avert all conspiracies, revolts, assassination attempts, incitements to revolt; the obligation to report anything that might affect the king's safety or the country; to obey royal orders, shun the king's enemies, and to assist in military expeditions. These were virtues that could be, and were, compared to the bonds between a faithful servant and his master:

> A man who loves his master's house promptly brings to the attention of his master what he sees and what he hears.
>
> (*ABL* 288)

Constant reaffirmation of the sworn relationship was expected, expressed by regular enquiries after the king's well-being, sending gifts to congratulate him, assisting him in war and paying any taxes and tribute due.

The morally binding character of the oaths, sworn in the presence of the gods of the Assyrian king *and* the gods of the contracting party, is very clear from the royal inscriptions. Individuals who have broken their oaths are described as people who have lost their minds, literally gone mad, by 'trusting in their own strength' or 'in themselves', i.e. they have abandoned the divine framework, without which no secure, fulfilled life was possible, and which they had sworn to uphold. Not only did this action endanger the transgressor himself, it also undermined the Assyrian-structured harmony. So oath-breakers became embodiments of a godless evil, allies of chaos, which was a threat to the ordered existence created by the gods themselves. It was, therefore, the Assyrian king's inescapable duty to pursue them relentlessly, seize them and execute or punish them publicly in a variety of horrible, but appropriate, ways. As here:

> [Mannu-ki-ahhe] (and) [Nabu-usalli], who had spoken insolently against Ashur, the god who created me, their tongues I ripped out, I flayed them.
>
> (Weidner 1932–3 no. 28)

The king of the small state of Kundu and Sissu (north Cilicia), and his fellow conspirator, the ruler of Sidon, who rebelled against Esarhaddon, were beheaded. Their courtiers were forced to march in Esarhaddon's triumphal procession through the streets of Nineveh, wearing the heads of their former masters around their necks, to the accompaniment of singing and harp-playing (Borger 1956 §27: Nin A III: 32–38). The date of the arrival of the severed heads of the reckless kings in Nineveh is noted in the *Babylonian Chronicle* (*ABC* 1 iv 7–8), which shows that the news of the beheading and humiliation was broadcast through the empire. In several instances, oath-breaking enemies were shut up in cages with wild animals set up at the city-gates, where their slow, horrible death could be witnessed by all entering and leaving. The remains of rebel ringleaders who had been killed in battle were recovered as far as possible and brought to Assyria so that all would be convinced of their death:

> I, Ashurbanipal, king of Assyria, publicly set up the head of Teumman, king of Elam, opposite the towers of the city-centre. What had been announced in distant days by extispicy, thus: 'The heads of your enemies you shall cut off, wine you shall libate over them . . .' In my days, now, Shamash and Adad have fulfilled(?) (this). The heads of my enemies I cut off, I libated wine [. . .]
>
> (Weidner 1932–3 no. 14)

A relief from Ashurbanipal's palace shows the king reclining on an elaborately carved and inlaid couch in a pleasant bower of vines, surrounded by trees and flowers, drinking with his queen while attendants wait on them. Birds twitter in the trees, emphasising the tranquillity of the scene. The king's quiver dangles from the headrest; and from a tree, suspended by his nose, hangs the severed head of Teumman, the defeated Elamite king: the battle is over and peace has been visibly restored (Strommenger and Hirmer 1965 [OM] pl. 241).

These brutal acts, so abhorrent to modern sensibilities, worked to demonstrate that the Assyrian king embodied a moral force. He knew what was right and what was wrong, he was able to distinguish between good and evil and, therefore, he was not afraid to act against that which was wrong and bad: he represented the good by punishing the evil remorselessly, and publicly proclaimed this as a positive achievement. The king was awe-inspiring: the fear that filled his enemies was the terror of those knowing that they will be ruthlessly, but justly, punished. The royal power to inspire fear was visualised as a shining radiance (*melammu*; Cassin 1968), a kind of halo, that flashed forth from the royal face and figure in awesome splendour, making him both beautiful and terrifying: it made him fearsome to behold and it could strike his enemies down, so that they fell to their knees before him, dazzled by the fearful glow. This is described in Sargon's account of his eighth campaign in the Zagros:

> Zizi of Appatar, Zalayya of Kitpattia, city-lords from Gizilbundi, a district, which lies in far distant mountains in a distant place, and places itself crosswise like a bolt in the region of the land of the Mannaeans and the Medes, and (where) the people, the inhabitants of those cities, trust in their own strength and know no lordship, whose dwelling-places none of the kings, my predecessors, had seen nor heard their name or received their tribute – through the mighty word of Ashur, my lord, who bestowed on me as a present the subjection of the highland rulers and the receipt of gifts, they heard of [the approach] of my army; the fear of my terrible radiance (*melammu*), panic came upon them in the midst of their country. Their tribute – horses, yoke-teams without number, cattle, small cattle – from Appatar and Kitpat(ia) they brought

and they brought it before me in Zirdiakka in the land of the Mannaeans. For the protection of their lives they besought me and, so that I might not destroy their walls, they kissed my feet.

(*TCL* 3, ll. 64–72)

The possibility of royal mercy also existed, and kings present themselves as persuaded by true penitence and heartfelt submission. Further, in a situation where a city or state had revolted, not all the inhabitants were punished regardless of individual guilt. One of the acts perpetrated by the Palestinian rebels in 701 was to remove Padi, the king of the Philistine city of Ekron, who was loyal to Assyria, and hand him over in chains to Hezekiah of Judah to guard (Luckenbill 1924: 31 ll. 73–76). Sennacherib, as the defender of his treaty-partner, attacked and captured the rebellious city which had mistreated his loyal subject, and:

The governors and nobles who had sinned, I executed, I hung their corpses on the towers of the whole city. The citizens, who had committed offence and sacrilege, I counted as booty. Their remainder, who were not burdened with sin and sacrilege, who showed themselves to be guiltless, I ordered them to be released. Padi, their king, I brought out from Jerusalem and set him on the throne of lordship over them. Tribute for my lordship I laid upon him.

(Luckenbill 1924 III 7–17)

Here, the ringleaders of the revolt, who had broken the oaths that bound them to the Assyrian king ('who had sinned'), were publicly executed, and their bodies hung from the city-walls and towers; those who had supported them were taken prisoner and probably deported ('I counted as spoil/booty'), while those who had remained loyal to Padi and avoided involvement in the revolt were released. The passage shows that care was taken to establish guilt and identify those responsible for revolt. It also illustrates the divisions of loyalty and fierce competition for political control, endemic in Assyria's client-states: any violent changes of ruler risked vengeance from the Assyrian king who, through the mechanism of the loyalty-treaties, was himself sworn to safeguard his subjects' position.

The fruits of war

The many wars of conquest and punitive campaigns beyond the immediate frontiers of the empire enriched the Assyrian state enormously: exotic materials for palace building, novel styles of architecture, strange animals and plants tended in palace gardens underscored the greatness of the king's conquests. More mundanely, they provided the king with much-needed manpower, particularly for agriculture, the army and royal construction works (see p. 533). But wars not only enriched the king personally and the

Assyrian state and temples: the king was a provider for his country and people, pouring war-generated income into Assyria and thus boosting his subjects' prosperity. Royal texts mention this as one of the direct benefits of Assyria's wars: Sargon, for example, says that his conquest of states in Anatolia led to his discovery of, and Assyrian access to, tremendous mineral deposits, and that the impact of this in Assyria was to make silver as plentiful as copper had been for all Assyrians (Lie 1929 ll. 222–234; *ARAB* II §28). Similarly, one of the results of Ashurbanipal's Arab campaigns was, as he proudly records:

> [Pe]ople of both sexes, donkeys, camels, [cattle and small [cattle] without number I brought to Assyria. [The area] of my whole land, [in] its [entir]ety], they filled as far as it stretches. [Ca]me[l]s I shared out like small cattle [t]o the people of Assyria. Within my land one bought a camel at the market gate for a few pence (lit. '1 sheqel). The ale-wife obtained for one portion, the brewer for one jar, the gardener for a bundle of cress(?), camels and people.
>
> (VAT 5600+, Weippert 1973–4: 74ff. Ep. 2)

The king flooded the market with the spoils of war, so that even the humblest could afford previously expensive commodities, which was one of the many benefits his wars bestowed on Assyrians. Individual soldiers were almost certainly rewarded for the number of enemies slain, as suggested by reliefs showing Assyrian soldiers carrying cut-off heads to the army-scribes recording the war-dead and booty (not an unusual practice, cf. the Paeonians, Plutarch, *Alexander* 39; see fig. 32). A system of reward for individual war-exploits is also implied by one of Ashurbanipal's epigraphs:

> Urtak, the in-law of Teumman, who was wounded by an arrow, but did not die; to sever his own head, he called to an Assyrian thus: 'Come, cut off my head. Bring (it) before the king, your lord, and make a good name (for yourself).'
>
> (Weidner 1932–3: no. 15; cf. Gerardi 1987: 274–275, slab 2)

Undoubtedly, the killing of an illustrious and noble enemy would earn a soldier high rewards and perhaps preferment.

The royal succession, the royal family and the court

The selection and education of the crown-prince

The central position of the king in the system meant that safeguarding the succession to the kingship was crucial, and that the established order was particularly vulnerable during the time of transition from one king to the next. The selection of the royal heir was confirmed by divine approval obtained through an elaborate process of divination. One request for divine decision

Figure 32 Assyrian soldiers with heads of enemy dead (North-West Palace, Kalhu (Nimrud), British Museum; drawing by D. Saxon)

about a proposed successor is preserved among the collection of queries to the sun-god (see pp. 502–503):

> Shamash, great lord, give me a firm positive answer to what I am asking you!
>
> Should Esarhaddon, king of Assyria, strive and plan? Should he enter his son, Sin-nadin-apli, whose name is written in this papyrus and placed before your great divinity, into the Succession Palace? Is it pleasing to your great divinity? Is it acceptable to your great divinity? Does your great divinity know it?
>
> Is the entering of Sin-nadin-apli, son of Esarhaddon, king of Assyria, whose name is written in this papyrus, into the Succession Palace, decreed and confirmed in a favourable case, by the command of your great divinity, Shamash, great lord? Will he who can see, see it? Will he who can hear, hear it?
>
> (SAA 4 no. 149)

This particular candidate for the succession seems to have failed, for he did not become king. Another possibility is that Sin-nadin-apli was the original name of the next king, renamed Ashurbanipal when he became the official successor (Parpola 1970/1983 part 2: 106). Renaming the designated successor is attested in at least one instance. When Sennacherib presented Esarhaddon, as crown-prince, with precious gifts, he said that he was giving them:

to Esarhaddon, my son, who will henceforth be called, Ashur-etel-(ilani)-mukin-apli ('Ashur, sovereign of the gods, who guarantees a successor')

(*ABL* 1452 rev. 2–4; cf. *ABL* 308 rev. 3)

However, Esarhaddon rarely used his new name (Seux 1980–3: 149–150), either as crown-prince or king, and the practice of renaming is not certain for other Assyrian kings. So the question of formal assumption of a new name by the designated successor remains unclear (for the special, exclusive nature of Assyrian royal names, see Katja 1987). Another question that is uncertain is which royal sons were considered eligible for the succession. In as far as the procedure can be reconstructed, it seems likely that, as a general rule, the king selected his eldest son to succeed him – although who exactly counted as a 'son' for this purpose and what the ranking of the offspring from different royal wives might have been is unknown.

Once the gods had confirmed the king's choice (through affirmative signs and omens), the selected son was presented to the court during a public ceremony as the crown-prince. It was on this occasion that he would be robed in the formal crown-prince's gear (an attenuated form of the royal dress; Reade 1972) and inducted into a part of the royal palace specifically reserved, at least in the seventh century, for the crown-prince, the *bīt redûti* ('succession palace'). He would now have received his own advisers, doctors, and learned men, one of whom was perhaps specifically appointed as his personal tutor (Parpola 1970/1983 part 2: 39). It has also been suggested that he may have married at this point (Parpola 1970/1983: no. 129 r. 24). Probably on the same occasion oaths were sworn by all subjects, binding them to support the king's decision and pledging themselves to ensure that the divinely and royally selected successor would become the new king.

As in many other states ruled by absolute kings (e.g. Egypt, Achaemenid Persia, the Seleucid empire), the Assyrian monarch was not in any sense subject to a constitutional law, whereby the eldest son succeeded him automatically. At least one, possibly two, instances are known where the Assyrian king selected a younger son to succeed him (Seux 1980–3: 155–157; for the successive different candidates put forward by Sennacherib, see Kwasman and Parpola 1991: xxix–xxxiv). The political considerations motivating such a decision are not known. What is plain is that, as in the case of David's choice of his younger son, Solomon, as successor in Israel (see p. 453), such an unexpected choice could provoke political problems and infighting at court. When Sennacherib selected his younger son, Esarhaddon, for the future kingship, opposition from Esarhaddon's older brothers threatened the safety of the new crown-prince. Esarhaddon seems to have fled, perhaps with the connivance of his parents, to safety on the north-western frontier of the empire and stayed there until Sennacherib's death. Significantly, Sennacherib did not die peacefully in his sleep, but was murdered by his son, Ardi-mulissi, who had been selected as successor earlier (Kwasman and Parpola 1991: xxix–xxxiv), then been displaced by Esarhaddon and expected, through his parricide, to seize the throne for himself (Parpola 1980). The complex sequence of events is still not entirely clear. What is certain is that Esarhaddon successfully challenged his murderous brother and his supporters and defeated them in a battle, after which some of the most prominent fled, probably to Shupria (see pp. 509–510). In his account of his successful bid for the throne, Esarhaddon makes an interesting reference to the potency of the oaths that had been sworn in support of Sennacherib's choice:

> I marched rapidly along the road to Nineveh despite difficulties, but in the land of Hanigalbat (Upper Mesopotamia) all their experienced troops barred my way, sharpening their weapons. But fear of the great gods cast them down; when they saw my tremendous attack, they lost their senses. Ishtar, the lady of battle and war, who loves my priesthood, moved to my side, broke their bows, and dissolved their battle-order. Then there sounded in their army the cry:
> 'This is our king!'
> At their (sc. the gods') lofty command they all came over to my side and stood behind me, crowding around like lambs and imploring my lordship. The Assyrians, who had sworn loyalty to me by the great gods, approached me and kissed my feet.
>
> (Borger 1956 §27: 44, ll. 69–81)

Undoubtedly, part of Esarhaddon's success was his swift attack and the military advantage he seems to have gained; but a part in consolidating that advantage, and watering down the support of the regicides, was that the soldiers were prepared very quickly to recognise that Esarhaddon had a superior, divinely sanctioned, claim to the throne.

Once the successor had moved into the 'succession palace' with his entourage and mentors, he was increasingly given responsibilities in running the empire as part of his grooming for future royal duties. The activities of Sennacherib, particularly but not only in co-ordinating intelligence reports and ensuring the security of the northern frontier, as crown-prince are amply reflected in the many letters he wrote to his father (SAA 1 nos. 29–40; SAA 5 no. 281). The impression from some of the letters is that he was entrusted with considerable responsibility in overseeing all royal interests. Senna-cherib's first crown-prince, Ashur-nadin-shumi, was installed by his father on the throne of Babylon (700–694), in order to rule that country on behalf of Assyria (Brinkman 1984: 60–61; CAH III/2: 35–36). The arrangement seems to have worked quite well, until he was surrendered to the invading Elamites by some treacherous Babylonian citizens (Parpola 1972; Brinkman 1984: 61); he probably died miserably in Elamite captivity. It is possible that yet another crown-prince of Sennacherib played a role in relation to Baby-lonia (Kwasman and Parpola 1991: xxxi). Ashurbanipal, as crown-prince, is shown in one letter (*ABL* 434) acting like Sennacherib: he orders garrisons stationed along the northern and north-eastern frontiers to despatch fugitives immediately for interrogation by himself.

The successor's education also involved learning royal etiquette, military skills – riding, hunting, shooting with the bow – and a training in the traditional learning and wisdom of Mesopotamia, in which he was instructed by the scholars assigned to him on moving into the 'succession palace'. Ashurbanipal, who repaired the palace apartments where he had dwelt as crown-prince, several times refers to his proficiency in this learned education:

> I am versed in the craft of the sage Adapa (i.e. exorcism); I studied the secret lore of the entire scribal craft, I know the celestial and terrestrial portents (i.e. omen-science). I discuss with competence in the circle of the masters; I argue about (the work) '(If) the liver is a correspondence of the sky' (i.e. haruspicy) with expert diviners. I can solve the most complicated divisions and multiplications which do not have a solution (i.e. mathematics). I have read intricate tablets inscribed with obscure Sumerian or Akkadian, difficult to unravel, and examined sealed, obscure and confused inscriptions on stone from before the Flood.
>
> (Streck 1916 II 252–253, ll. 13–18)

Obviously we should make some allowance for royal hyperbole; but there is no reason to assume that the kings were uneducated and illiterate. As clearly shown by this passage, and also by the much earlier royal hymns of the Ur III and Isin period (see chapters 1d; 2a), part of the royal virtues in Mesopotamia resided in a profound intimacy with scribal lore. This is further reflected by Ashurbanipal's attempt to gather all written knowledge to himself in Nineveh through the creation of a great library of literary and learned texts (Livingstone 1989: xviiii).

The king and his learned advisers

Another testimony to the king's active involvement with the great corpus of recorded wisdom is that he was in constant correspondence with a variety of scholars. They reported omens of all kind and advised him on their implications for him, and hence the country, and the appropriate action that needed to be taken. The king was the central actor in innumerable rituals, since the well-being and stability of Assyria was inextricably linked with his own: the well-attested purification rituals were constructed for his protection, and the hemerologies, listing lucky and unlucky days, were written as a guide for the king (Parpola 1971). A ritual which illustrates concern for the king's safety particularly well is that of the 'substitute king' (*šar pūhi*), activated when a lunar eclipse (considered to be particularly life-threatening to the king) was forecast (Parpola 1970/1983 part 2: xxii–xxxii). The importance of the king's participation in a multitude of rituals is strikingly demonstrated by a letter

(*ABL* 667), in which the king was asked to send his robe as a substitute for himself for the celebration of the New Year feast, since he could not himself be present.

The prominence of scholars at the Assyrian court is amply attested by the many letters in which they communicated their findings and advice to the king (Parpola 1970/1983; 1971; cf. SAA 10). It is probable that their written reports were supplemented by personal discussion and explication of interpretations (Parpola 1970/1983: no. 60; Starr 1990: xxxi). It is argued that sixteen scholars formed a kind of inner circle of learned advisers. They included a chief interpreter of celestial and terrestrial omens (who was the closest to the king), a chief liver diviner, or haruspex, a chief exorcist, a personal exorcist whom the king consulted about the health of the royal children, and several more exorcists, two doctors, a chief chanter and at least two astrologers (Parpola 1970/1983 part 2: xiv–xvi). Several of these wise men were succeeded, in turn, by their sons, trained in the same expertise as their fathers. Testimony to the great respect in which the scholars were held is that one Assyrian king-list (Weidner 1926; Grayson 1980–3: 116–121) records the names of several 'royal scholars' next to the names of the kings they served. The tradition of associating a famous wise man with a particular king is found even later in Hellenistic Babylonia: a text from Uruk lists a number of kings, from the earliest times right down to the Assyrian period, together with their 'sages' (*ummānu*; van Dijk 1962 t. 27). The suspicion here is that famous figures of legend and folklore have been systematised into a list, especially as the Hellenistic text names the *ummānu* of Esarhaddon as 'Aba'enlildari, whom the Aramaeans call Ahuqar' (van Dijk 1962: 44–45, ll. 19–20). Aba'enlildari/Ahuqar does not figure among the many known scholars of Esarhaddon, but is none other than the legendary sage Ahiqar. The folk-story of his career at the courts of Sennacherib and Esarhaddon, together with his wise sayings, is known to have been in circulation in the Near East already in the fifth century (Grelot 1972: 427–452), and continued to be widely read into the twelfth century AD. The popular tradition was that behind every great king there stood a celebrated wise man.

It would be false to think of the king as a mere puppet in the hands of some kind of sinister group constituted by these learned specialists. He himself, it is clear from the correspondence, had sufficient knowledge to be in a position to estimate the likely accuracy of statements, and, moreover, checked reports against each other. Even more obvious from the letters is the fact that the scholars did not form a unified group working together for some end of their own, but individuals locked in fierce competition with each other in their bid for royal favour. There are several instances in the scholarly correspondence of scholars denouncing each other to the king and challenging interpretations proffered by their colleagues. For example:

> He who wrote to the king, my lord: 'Venus is visible [in the month of Add]aru', is despicable, a fool and a liar! [And he who] wrote to the

king my lord: 'Venus [. . .] is rising in the constellation A[ries]', [does] not [speak] the truth (either). Venus is [not] yet visible! Why does he so [deceitf]ully send such (a report) to the ki[ng, my lord]? 'Venus is stable in the mor[ning]': (this) signifies 'morningtime'. If [. . .], it signif[ies. . . .]. (But) [Venus is not] vi[sible at p]resent.

Who is this person [that] so deceit[fully] se[nds] such reports to the king, my lord? [Tom]orrow they should let me glance over th[em], every single one of them.

What the king, my lord, wrote to me: 'What month do you have now', the month we have at present is Addaru, (and) the present [day] is the 27th; the coming [month] is Nisannu.

Why does someone tell lies (and) boast ab[out] (these matters)? [I]f he does not know, [he should] keep his mouth shut!

(*ABL* 1132+; Parpola 1970/1983 no. 65; SAA 10 no. 72)

Or take another one:

What the king, my lord, wrote to me: 'One of your colleagues wrote to me: the planet Mercury will be visible in the month Nisannu. What month do you have now?' The month we have (is) Addaru, the day we have (is) the 25th.

(Break in which, from what follows, the writer expressed irritation about his colleague's incompetence and then quotes an appropriate proverb:)

'The inept can frustrate a judge, the ignorant can trouble even the mighty.'

(*ABL* 37; Parpola 1970/1983 no. 12; SAA 10 no. 23)

It served the purpose of the Assyrian scholars to distinguish themselves before the king by showing their knowledge was better than that of their colleagues (cf. the Old Testament story of Daniel). The rewards were great: favour at court, income, social prestige, possibly procuring a lucrative position for their sons, and a hand in educating the future occupant of the Assyrian throne.

The royal funeral

The first activity of the crown-prince on the death of the king, his father, was to bury his predecessor. This is certainly the implication of the socalled 'Sin of Sargon' text, which portrays Sennacherib's anxiety about the situation that had arisen when Sargon II was killed in battle and his body not recovered for burial (SAA 3 no. 33; Landsberger *et al.* 1989). The reconstruction of the royal funeral is based on texts relating to the burial of Esarhaddon's queen (Parpola 1970/1983 part 2 nos. 195; 197), but is likely to be applicable to that of the king. The body was publicly displayed for some days after death (*taklimtu*) and was elaborately mourned by his family, with perhaps female family-members playing a specially prominent role. It seems probable that there was public mourning as well. The corpse was repeatedly washed, anointed and kissed before being conducted for formal burial in the great stone sarcophagi set in an underground chamber in the 'Old Palace' in Ashur (Haller 1953). Some of the queens were also buried here, although recent finds at Nimrud (Kalhu, see below) show that several Assyrian queens were buried under the floor of the palace there. The burial would probably have been accompanied by lavish funerary gifts, although the sarcophagi themselves were unadorned. In honour of the dead king a great fire was lit (*šurruptu*; cf. *2 Chronicles* 16.14) when he was buried. The new king stayed for some time after in 'the house of mourning', wearing dirty garments and abstaining from eating; probably following a ritual purification in the river, he emerged dressed in white clothes ready to prepare himself for taking up the reins of office.

Queens and royal women

One important aspect relating to the Assyrian king and court that we still know very little about is the royal matrimonial practices, i.e. whom did the kings marry? There is a tendency in scholarship today (e.g. *CAH* III/2: 197–198) to elide the lack of clarity about this, and about the way women associated with the king were organised, by casual references to the 'harem' as though it explains everything. While it is the case that, as far as the evidence goes, the kings had several wives, it is quite uncertain what considerations determined their relative ranking, if they were ranked, and what status their children might have dependent on this. With rare exceptions, queens and Assyrian women are not portrayed in the palace reliefs or referred to in royal texts (Reade 1979; 1987; Seux 1980–3: 161–162; Albenda 1983). The identity of the women married to the kings is also obscure: the text found with the magnificent treasures accompanying a ninth-century Assyrian queen's burial in the palace at Kalhu (George 1990; Fadhil 1990b) shows that the king could, and did, marry daughters of the Assyrian nobility (p. 506). No such evidence is available in the eighth and seventh centuries: we know the names of several royal wives (relatively well attested are those of Sennacherib, Esarhaddon and Ashurbanipal); the names of two wives of Sargon II and one of Tiglath-pileser III were revealed in the surprise finds, by Iraqi archaelogists in the palace at Kalhu, of their graves with inscriptions and accompanying treasures (George 1990; Fadhil 1990a). But the family background of these women is unknown.

One thing that is now considerably more certain than it was until recently is the title of the Neo-Assyrian queen. The term is written logographically MÍ.É.GAL (or MÍ.KUR), which could be rendered literally as having the meaning '(woman) of the palace' (*ša ekalli*), i.e. queen; it is now argued, persuasively, that the Assyrian word indicated by this writing is '*sēg/kallu(i)*' (Parpola 1988). There is a suggestion, but again it is not absolutely firm (Dalley and Postgate 1984: 11), that the title may have been borne by that wife of the king whose son was selected to be the future ruler, i.e. the crown-prince's mother, whose position at court would have become much more respected and eminent in parallel with that of her son. The esteem in which the queen was held, and the active share she was deemed to play in her son's life is mentioned in one instance; it comes in a passage where the crown-prince says, with reference to his now dead mother:

> 'Ashur and Shamash chose me as crown prince of Assyria because of her (i.e. my mother's) righteousness.' And her ghost blesses him just as he had revered the ghost: 'May his descendants rule over Assyria.'
> (Parpola 1970/1983 part 1 no. 132 r. 3ff.; SAA 10 no. 188)

The names of the queens revealed by the new finds at Kalhu (apart from Ashurnasirpal II's wife) are all West Semitic in type, but the significance of this is slight. It is very possible that some queens had more than one name – a practice clearly attested for Esarhaddon's mother, who bore both an Akkadian name, Zakûtu, and the West Semitic name Naqi'a. This may simply reflect the linguistic diversity of the empire, in which Akkadian and Aramaic were both current (Millard 1983).

Several legal texts refer to the queens' estates and large households, and their residences in all the main palaces of Assyria (SAA 6). At Fort Shalmaneser (see p. 489) an area of the palace, which could be closed off from the main complex, has been identified, by text-finds, as the queen's residence (Dalley and Postgate 1984: 9ff.). The queen's household was administered by a female official, the *šakintu*. She was a woman of high status, who commanded considerable wealth, as texts relating to her legal transactions (lending silver, buying slaves (SAA 6), arranging a marriage with large dowry for her daughter (Postgate 1976 no. 14)) reveal. Also included in the household was a deputy *šakintu*, a 'female scribe of the queen's household', the queen's cook, and her male and female confectioner (Dalley and Postgate 1984: 11ff. and no.87). There are also references to females defined as *sekretu* (MUNUS.ERIM.É.GAL), which literally means an enclosed woman. Are they royal concubines – perhaps including some of the daughers of local dynasts subject to Assyria, whose presentation to the Assyrian king together with large dowries are mentioned in the official royal texts from the ninth to seventh centuries? Or are they female palace servants, perhaps associated with the queen? So far they do not figure in texts of the queen's household, so perhaps the assumption that they are concubines is the more likely. Or were they simply the pool of royal wives from among whom might emerge the mother of the eventual royal heir? Or is the term altogether more general? It is as well to emphasise the real problems in understanding that beset this question, to avoid importing possibly inappropriate notions associated in our minds with the term 'harem' (for a discussion of confused European notions about the Middle Eastern harem, see J. Mabro, *Veiled Half-truths*, London, 1991).

In time, of course, if she survived, the mother of the crown-prince became the mother of the reigning king, and as 'queen-mother' (*ummi šarri*) she occupied an honoured position. She owned extensive tracts of land, fully staffed with estate managers, secretaries, guards and household troops and worked for her by agricultural workers. They provided her with an income, and also the possibility of increasing it by commercial ventures (Seux 1980–3: 161; SAA 6 nos. 253; 254; 255; 256). Some of her staff were carefully selected for her by her son, the king, himself (SAA 4 no. 151).

While obviously important in terms of their position and rank at court, the queen and queen-mother did not exercise any official power. However, in situations of political uncertainty occasioned by the sudden death of the king or the accession of a very young ruler, they could function to defend and protect the existing régime, and ensure that arrangements for the succession worked smoothly (Goody 1966: 11). This is perhaps how we should read the role played by Shammuramat/Semiramis early in the reign of Adad-nirari III (see p. 491; Schramm 1972). It may also explain the action taken by Naqi'a-Zakûtu, mother of Esarhaddon and grandmother of Ashurbanipal, who, on Esarhaddon's death *en route* to campaign in Egypt, stepped into the temporary (and potentially dangerous) power vacuum in Assyria. A text shows her dealing with the delicate situation by organising the Assyrian population, the members of the court and the royal family, particularly Shamash-shum-ukin (probably the older brother of the crown-prince), to renew their oaths of loyalty to uphold Ashurbanipal's right to accede to the Assyrian throne (SAA 2 no. 8).

Royal children

The fate of the royal children, apart from the crown-prince, is very hard to trace. The number of royal offspring is rarely known: Sennacherib seems to have had six or seven, Esarhaddon had about nineteen, of whom nine are known by name (Parpola 1970/1983 part 2: 117–118), while only two are known for Ashurbanipal. The anxiety with which the royal father watched over his children is beautifully illustrated by a series of letters exchanged daily (or even more frequently) between king and doctors about the health of a royal baby (Parpola 1970/1983 nos. 126; 136; 152; 154–156). Some sons received important governmental positions, such as Shamash-shum-ukin, who was installed as king of Babylonia (668–648) subject to his brother, Ashurbanipal. Others were appointed to important posts in temples, like another of Ashurbanipal's brothers, who was appointed chief functionary of the temple of the god Sin of Harran after it had been extensively restored by the king (Streck 1916: 250–251, ll. 17f.). They could also hold court posts with accompanying military commands, such as Sargon II's brother, Sin-aha-usur; a special residence was even built for him at Sargon's new city of Dur Sharrukin (*CAH* III/2: 101). A daughter of Sargon II is known to have been married to the ruler of the buffer state of Tabal, lying between the Assyrian imperial frontier and Phrygia; she brought the territory of a small nearby state to her husband as dowry, and may have continued to administer Tabal following her husband's revolt and execution (*CAH* III/1: 419). Esarhaddon contemplated the possibility of marrying one of his daughters to Bartatua, the Scythian chieftain (perhaps to be identified with the Protothyes of Herodotus 1.103), in the hope that it might keep these unpredictable raiders under control; the information comes from a formal enquiry to the sun-god, Shamash:

> Bartatua, king of the Scythians, who has now sent his message to Esarhaddon, king of Assyria, concerning a royal daughter in marriage – if Esarhaddon, king of [Assyria], gives him a royal daughter in marriage, will Bartatua, king of the Scythians, speak with [Esarhaddon, king of Assyria], in good faith, true and honest words of peace? Will he keep the treaty of [Esarhaddon, king of Assyria]? Will he do [whatever i]s pleasing to Esarhaddon, king of Assyria?
>
> (SAA 4 no. 20)

But not all princesses were married off to help keep Assyria secure: a sister of Esarhaddon appears buying a garden, house, land and associated workers for silver (SAA 6 no. 251), which suggests that, as one would expect, each royal child was well equipped with property, and that some perhaps married within the Assyrian nobility. One letter seems to refer to the order of precedence at court, and the superior position held by the daughters of the king over their sisters-in-law:

> Message of the daughter of the king to Libbi-ali-sharrat:
> Why do you not write me a letter or send me a communication? Or shall people say: Perhaps this one (i.e. the sender of such a letter) is superior to Sherua-etirat, the oldest daughter of the Succession Palace, of Ashur-etel-ilani-mukinni (Esarhaddon), the great king, the mighty king, king of the world, king of Assyria, while you are (only) the daughter-in-law, the lady of the house of Ashurbanipal, the great crown-prince of the king of the Succession Palace of Esarhaddon, king of Assyria.
>
> (*ABL* 308)

The royal entourage

Some of the divisions of rank within the royal family appear in texts which seem to list the entire royal entourage, and then continue down to palace servants and soldiers. The texts are enquiries made to Shamash asking whether anyone is likely to prove disloyal within a stated period of time:

> [Will any of the] 'eunuchs' (and) the bearded (officials), the king's entourage, or (any) of his brothers or uncles,

[his kin], his fa[ther's line], or junior members of the royal line, or the 'third men', chariot drivers (and) chariot fighters,
[or the recruitment officers, or] the prefects of the exempt military, or the prefects of the cavalry, or the royal bodyguard, or his personal guard,
[or the keepers] of the inner gates, or the keepers of the outer gate, or the . . . 'eunuchs',
[or . . .], or the palace superintendents, the staff-bearers (and) the wa[tch]men, or the mounted(?) scouts (and) the trackers,
[or the lackeys, tailor]s, cup-bearers, cooks, confectioners, the entire body of craftsmen,
or the Itu'eans and the Elamites, the mounted bowmen(?), the Hittites, [or] the Gurreans, or the Aramaeans, [or the Cimmerians, o]r the Philistines, or the Nubians (and) the Egyptians or the Shabuqeans, [or the 'eunuchs' who b]ear [arms], or the bearded (officials) who bear arms and stand guard for the king
(the text continues listing the relatives, friends and guests of any of these and then moves on to enemies and concludes:)
will any human being make an uprising and rebellion against Ashurbanipal . . . . ?

(SAA 4 no. 142)

The people closest to the king seem to have been those most intimately involved with him, i.e. those who drove with him in his chariot, held spare quivers for him and so forth. They and the royal bodyguard probably formed the core of the standing army. They also provided the king with a group of men personally devoted to him and, hence, used by him as special messengers and for conducting delicate enquiries (Postgate 1974a; 1979; Parpola 1987: xiv). Several scholars argue that a substantial proportion of this group were eunuchs, *ša rēši*. There are a number of factors, such as their distinction from 'the bearded' (*ša ziqni*), which suggest that eunuchs played an important part in the Assyrian court (Parpola 1983: 20–21). However, it must be noted that the number of scholars that argue in favour of equating *ša rēši* with 'eunuch' is balanced by the number who do not (for a list of discussions and positions, see Elat 1982: 24). It is possible that the term reflects a rank at court, which included eunuchs (for a discussion of the problem in the Achaemenid empire, see Briant in press). So there is no final agreement as yet on this important question. The debate so far has centred solely on whether the disputed term means that eunuchs were, or were not, a feature of Assyrian court-life. What remains to be considered, when the question is finally settled, is how they were perceived socially, when and why the practice was introduced – in short, how exactly the system of eunuchs might have worked in this, as in so many other, empires (for a helpful discussion, see K. Hopkins, *Conquerors and Slaves* (Cambridge, 1978): 172–196).

The high personages surrounding the king were extremely wealthy: they could be granted extensive estates by him, free of taxes, although whether they gained outright ownership of the land grants, held them as emoluments related to their office, or received the revenues for life as royal rewards for loyal service remains debated (Postgate 1969; van Driel 1970). Their wealth is also shown by the purchases of tracts of land, dotted throughout the empire, by high-ranking courtiers (Kwasman and Parpola 1991: xx–xxi). One of the best-attested is Remanni-Adad, 'the chief reinholder of Ashurbanipal' who, between 671 and 660, acquired landed property for silver in Arrapha, the Harran region, Sinjar, around the Khabur, in Rasappa and possibly Izalla (van Driel 1970: 170; SAA 6 nos. 296–350).

The organisation of the empire

The provinces

Beyond the royal court, the whole of the Assyrian empire was divided into provinces, including the core area of Assyria itself. Each province was usually called after the name of its chief city, so that there were provinces of Kalhu, Nineveh, Dur Sharrukin, Arbela – as well as Samaria, Damascus, Arpad (the earlier Bit Agusi), Kinalua (earlier Pattin(a)), Marqasi (earlier Gurgum) and many more; one exception was the province of Ashur, which was called 'the land' (Pečírková 1977). Each provincial centre had a governor's residence. Some have been identified, such as the residence of the eighth-century army-commander (*turtānu*) Shamshi-ilu, at Til Barsip, splendidly decorated with painted frescoes comparable in their motifs to the royal palace reliefs (Thureau-Dangin and Dunand 1936; also Moortgat 1984 [0M]: 112–118). Three other governors' residences have been excavated: one at Kalhu (Postgate 1973), the others at Megiddo and Dor in Israel (Barkay 1992: 351–352). The king would have stayed in these provincial palaces during visits, or *en route* to campaigns; taxes were collected here, some to be used within the provinces, some to be forwarded to the central authorities. So the empire presented a uniform image, with each province governed in fundamentally the same way – at least that is the impression. In practice, there was probably far more variation, although the details are not known. The evidence for small dynasts in Cilicia (Que), which certainly also had an Assyrian governor by the late reign of Sargon II, suggests that in this area the Assyrian governor's authority embraced local rulers and their small kingdoms within his province (*CAH* III ch. 9; Hawkins in press). The later pattern of Achaemenid satrapal control, where local autonomous structures continued to function inside the Persian provinces (see chapter 13e), may be comparable, in some respects, to the Assyrian system.

The duties of the provincial governors (*šaknu*, *bēl pīhāti*) were the obvious ones: to keep order in the provinces with the troops stationed in local garrisons at their disposal; to maintain roads; to arrange safe-conduct for groups of merchants and the transport of tribute; to organise the feeding of deportees *en route*; finally, to supply the king, his entourage and army when they passed through the province, as a passage in Sargon's eighth campaign shows:

> Ullusunu, together with the population of his country, loyally awaited my army to do service in Sirdakka, his fortress.
> As if they were my 'eunuchs' or governors of the land Ashur, he poured out flour and wine for the supply of my troops in a heap.
>
> (*TCL* 3 ll. 52–3)

They also supplied the king with forces for campaigns, levied locally from people owing service to the king; in precisely the same way demands for building, or other royal labour needs, were met. The provincial obligation to supply labour-gangs is most clearly illustrated by a letter (from Nineveh) from an official overseeing the building of the wall of Sargon's new city of Dur Sharrukin:

> To the king, my lord: your servant Tab-shar-Ashur. Good health to the king, my lord!
> As to the work assignment of the governor of Kalhu about which the king, my lord, wrote to me: 'Why has the governor of Arrapha left half of the gate to him?'
> On the 3rd, when they started on the city wall, they came to me, saying: 'Come and settle our work allocation between us!' I went and settled it between them. Perhaps the king, my lord, now says: 'Why [. . . .]'
> (Break)
> [Out of the . . .] work assignment (units) of the governor of Kalhu, that of the wall reached as far as the edge of the gate of the Tower of People, and out of the 850 work assignment (units) of the governor of Arrapha, the wall (assignment) extended as far as the edge of the gate of the Tower of People.
> I deducted this (stretch of) wall from the gate (assignment), calculated the bricks for the balance of the gate, and gave three fourths to the governor of Arrapha and . . . one fourth to the governor of Kalhu even before the king's sealed message had come to me.
> The governor of Kalhu [did] not know that his wall assignment extended [only as far as the edge] of the gate, and that is why he said: 'I have too large an assignment.' I have now arbitrated between them and they are both doing their work.
>
> (SAA 1 no. 64)

Manpower, conscription and taxation

The basis on which the labour-gangs and military forces were raised was, in essence, land: individuals were assigned land, which might be held in addition to other plots; the landgrant obliged the holder and his descendants to supply a man for building or fighting purposes as and when required. This seems to be the underlying principle of the system, which existed in basically similar forms in other areas and periods (Egypt, the Old Babylonian period, the Achaemenid empire). The great numbers of subjects acquired by the Assyrians through wars of conquest, and the carefully planned policy of deportation (which meant that people were moved great distances and resettled in new areas), meant that much of the manpower in labour-gangs and the army originated from deportees. Most deported peoples were kept in family groups and settled together as small communities, mainly in the countryside, in order to work the land, which increased the crucial agricultural base, and to provide manpower for the Assyrian government (Oded 1979). An oft-repeated phrase (with variants) found in the Assyrian inscriptions refers to this process and its profitability: 'x (i.e. number) I carried off, I settled them, as Assyrians I counted them; the yoke of Ashur, my lord, like the Assyrians, I laid on them; tribute and tax like the Assyrians I laid on them' (Oded 1979: 81–84). This reflects the integrative effort of the Assyrian rulers: deportees were not treated differently, in either juridical or social terms, because they were defeated foreigners; indeed, the evidence shows deported peoples incorporated at all levels into the Assyrian army (Malbran-Labat 1982), formed into special crack regiments (see, e.g., Dalley 1985 for a striking example), or added to the corps of artisans and scribes working for the palace (Oded 1979: 54–59; Tadmor 1975). Former deportees tending their small-holdings are listed in a group of texts, called by their first editor the 'Assyrian Doomsday Book' (Johns 1901). The precise function of this 'census' is still debated (van Driel 1970; Zablocka 1971; Fales 1973; Postgate 1974a), but it is our main source for the size and pattern of families in the Neo-Assyrian period (Roth 1987), and shows that many deportees lived in small rural communities.

From the reign of Sennacherib onwards, the phrase for taking prisoners of war and the removal of people from defeated countries changed: the reference is no longer to mingling them with Assyrians with the same duties, but to 'reckoning them as booty'. What exactly the change in terminology signifies is hard to tell: were the vanquished treated more contemptuously (Oded 1979: 84ff.)? Or were there simply not as many, as the number of campaigns of conquest decreased? Esarhaddon's account of his Shupria campaign refers in some detail to the fate of prisoners-of-war (Borger 1956 §68 col. III: 8–34). According to this, some were presented to the temples, some were selected as special fighters for the relevant army regiments, and some were used as farmers, gardeners and shepherds. After the needs of the state had been met, the rest were shared out among the royal palaces, the 'nobles', and the inhabitants of Assyrian cities. Assyrian refugees found in Shupria were mutilated and returned to their former masters; the fugitive Urartians sheltering in Shupria were returned to the Urartian ruler after questioning by the Assyrian king. This text does not suggest a fundamental change in Assyrian practice with respect to war captives, although it is possible that more prisoners-of-war were used to swell the number of slaves available on the market than earlier (see p. 519). In that case, perhaps the main profit now lay in turning the human booty of wars into liquid assets through sale; and/or strengthening political support by presenting them to courtiers and officers as a reward for loyal service.

A vexed question is to what extent. and how large a proportion of, the population was made up of 'semi-free' persons, or 'helots' as Diakonoff (1974) has proposed they should be called. What is clear is that there is no specific terminology for such a group, and no indication of a distinct juridical status that might imply such clearcut social divisions (Postgate 1987). One group that did exist were chattel-slaves, including privately owned ones. How much of the labour force was made up of slaves is not known, but it is a reasonable assumption that they lived as servants with their owners and may have been used in privately run and owned workshops (Postgate 1987: 265; 266). Slaves were presumably acquired in wars – people given as personal pledges seem to have been used only to work off debts, and did not become permanent slaves (although occasionally a more formal redemption of pledged persons was necessary (Postgate 1987: 262–263)). One aspect of Assyrian society that has emerged more clearly is the existence of free persons working for hire:

> To the king, my lord,
> your servant Samnuha-bel-usur:
> Health to the king, my lord.
> The king my lord knows
> that the people of village X
> are hired workers.
> In the lands of the king
> they work for hire.
> They are not fugitives,
> (but) perform *ilku* service (i.e. carry out obligations to the state);
> from among them they
> supply 'king's men' (i.e. people who perform work required by the king).
> (CT 53: 87; Postgate 1987: 261)

The central authority met many of its requirements for manufactured goods by giving out raw materials to its employees and requiring a return in specified finished items. This was the *iškaru* system, which used groups of artisans organised into work-groups called *kiṣru* (Postgate 1974a; 1979; 1987), a term which also described military cohorts. By employing weavers, victuallers, leatherworkers, oil-pressers, ironsmiths, shepherds, farmers and gardeners most of the basic supplies needed by the state appear to have been produced fairly successfully. The system operated not only in the central area of Assyria but also in the provinces (Postgate 1987: 260). An interesting change in the *iškaru* system has been observed in the seventh century, when the government's needs became less pressing as the empire stabilised. In consequence, the groups of artisans seem to have been exploited more as a commercial concern by the government (Postgate 1974a: 100–110; cf. 1987: 268).

When personal service was not required by the state, either because a standing army developed or because campaigning became more limited as the empire firmed up within set boundaries, the obligation to supply a person for state needs (*ilku*) could be, and frequently was, commuted to payments in silver (Postgate 1974a; 1979). The authorities also benefited from tolls levied on crossing-points and bridges, which particularly affected commercial caravans. In addition, tax was payable on grain, straw and cattle; a good proportion of the taxes paid in kind were probably stored in the different provinces to feed and supply garrisons and provide resources for the king and army when on campaign. Other taxes consisted of providing supplies earmarked for the Assyrian temples and cults, for which the king bore responsibility.

Communications, commerce and prosperity

The size and complexity of the empire made it essential that communications should be swift and reliable, and there is now some evidence that a large and efficient road-system was established by the Assyrian kings, linking the major centres of the empire; their upkeep was another duty of the provincial governors (SAA I no. 29). The roads were probably equipped with way-stations, where provisions for royal messengers and officials on state business were stored and mule teams kept, so that the messengers could obtain fresh animals for their long journeys. The highly organised system of communications crisscrossing the empire foreshadows the well-known, later Achaemenid 'royal roads' (SAA I: xiii–xiv). Use of the facilities required royal authorisation. Such royal documents (which could be written either in Akkadian on clay tablets or in Aramaic on papyrus or parchment) were easily recognisable, as they bore the king's seal. This was a stamp seal impression of the king mastering a lion (Sachs 1953; Millard 1965; *RLA* 6: 136; fig. 33) – the most widely diffused royal image with which the majority of people would have been familiar: very few penetrated into the inner rooms of the great palaces and saw the detailed depictions of royal battles and victories (Reade 1979).

It has been a general assumption that the Assyrian kings simply creamed off the profits from subject territories and failed to reinvest in provincial development, so that formerly wealthy areas declined and stagnated economically (see most recently, *CAH* III/2: 216). It is not hard to see how this impression has been created when we read the royal annals, where the literary genre demands that each place attacked by the king is razed to the ground,

Figure 33 Assyrian royal seal (courtesy of British Museum)

emptied of people and goods, and a smoking ruin left in the army's wake. Sustained perusal of royal inscriptions and the royal correspondence, however, shows that the picture is more positive: there was extensive settlement of peoples in newly conquered areas (e.g. Hamath, Samaria); deportation was selective, limited to those needed for specific purposes; great efforts were made to expand the amount of land being worked (see p. 481); mass-deportations of people seem often to have been, in effect, 'exchanges' of populations (e.g. people from Media settled in the Levant and vice versa; Oded 1979: 65). All around the empire, denuded centres were rebuilt (on the same spot or nearby), sometimes larger than before (Luckenbill 1924: 27 I 80– II 1), repopulated either with defeated people from other regions or by Assyrians, and sometimes given a new Assyrian name. An important aim was security, but the effect was also to keep land under cultivation and trade routes open.

A widespread royal concern for prosperity in Assyria itself is shown by several texts. Some describe the 'new cities', such as Kalhu and Dur Sharrukin, built at royal command; others depict Nineveh's revitalisation as a result of Sennacherib's massive refurbishment of the old city; the provision of water for the population is stressed in all three cases – most striking is Sennacherib's construction of an impressive aqueduct to supply the garden-plots of the citizens of Nineveh (Jacobsen and Lloyd 1935). An interest in stimulating new activities is reflected by Sennacherib's attempt to grow Indian cotton in the palace gardens (Luckenbill 1924: 111, l.56; Potts 1990 [OGf] II 133–135), less clearly by the text of the governor, Shamash-resha-usur, in which he says that he introduced bee-keeping from Syria to Suhu (F.H. Weissbach, *Babylonische Miscellen* (1903) no. IV).

The activity of merchants is relatively sparsely documented, which is probably due in large measure to the fact that the source of much of the evidence is royal palaces and so reflects the king's concerns. Another factor that may explain the dearth of documentation is that a good many mercantile transactions will have been written in Aramaic on perishable materials. But there are references to merchants. and their role and activities have become clearer recently (Elat 1987; Deller 1987); it is plain that they were not simply crown agents. The evidence for royally granted exemptions on harbour and crossing tolls also implies the existence of private trade, normally taxed by the state (Postgate 1969: 9–16). Other evidence, both archaeological (Mazar 1990 [0Gd]: 534–535; 547) and textual, shows that strings of new centres were established at several points in the empire, especially along its margins (north-west, east, south-west). They were by no means merely military stations, but also specifically intended to promote trade. Sargon II, for example, says that he opened the 'sealed harbour' of Egypt, located in the vicinity of the Wadi el-Arish, in order 'to make Egyptians and Assyrians trade with each other' (Tadmor 1958: 34). So it was intended to function as a mercantile colony, settled with Assyrian merchants, and act as an intermediate station for Palestinian–Egyptian trade (Eph'al 1982: 101–115). Sargon II also reopened links with the Arab-Persian Gulf (Salles 1989; Potts 1990 [0Gf] I 333–338), and his new friendly relations with Phrygia probably resulted in extending Assyria's commercial interests. Centres such as Damascus, Samaria and Hamath which had been important commercial centres were not left in ruins but resettled (Hamath with Assyrians) and continued to function as import-ant provincial centres and crucial points for organising and tapping the extraordinarily rich Arabian spice and incense trade. Along the Medi-terranean coast, two Assyrian harbours are attested: Kar-Ashur-ahu-iddina ('Harbour of Esarhaddon') faced the city of Sidon, and a 'harbour of the king' (*kāru ša šarri*) was maintained in the territory of Arvad (*ABL* 992; Helm 1980: 196). There is no particular reason to disbelieve Esarhaddon when he says that one of his projects in rebuilding Babylon was to:

> open up its roads so that the (resettled) inhabitants would set their minds to trading and communicating with all the lands in their entirety.
> (Borger 1956: 25–26 Ep. 37)

An agreement between Esarhaddon and the king of Tyre, perhaps a locally autonomous enclave in the empire, clearly reveals the Assyrian involvement in regulating, monitoring and exploiting commerce (SAA 2 no. 5). *Ezekiel* (27.23; see p. 402) mentions Assyria as a source of carpets and embroidered textiles exported to Tyre, while Herodotus 1.1 says that among the earliest items brought to Greece by Phoenician traders were Assyrian goods (*phor-tia*). Nahum's dictum (3.16) that Assyria's merchants are 'more numerous than the stars of heaven' may have a good deal of truth in it.

Cities and kings

Within the provinces were the cities. Exactly how many there were and whether the number declined significantly after their absorption by the empire (Postgate 1979) is not known. There is, as suggested already, no particular reason to assume such a decline, although the cities were surely transformed – a process hard to analyse in detail and probably differing from place to place. Relations between cities and king could be, and certainly were in some instances, conducted independently of the provincial governor. Civic authorities and groups of citizens could appeal directly to the king and be in correspondence with him. The king, in turn, prided himself on treating the inhabitants of some cities circumspectly and granting them occasional privileges, such as exemptions from certain taxes and labour obligations (for Ashur, see Saggs 1975: 16–17, ll. 36–40). The clearest information comes from Babylonia (see pp. 612–617), but it is likely that other cities, too, enjoyed similar opportunities of direct approach to (perhaps even privileges granted by) the king. The possibility of petitioning the king lies behind the situation portrayed by the story in 2 Kings 17.25–28. According to this, the new inhabitants of Samaria were saved from a plague of lions by the Assyrian king sending them a Yahweh priest, when 'the king was told of it'. Harran, in north-western Mesopotamia outside the Assyrian heartland, is known to have been honoured with a royally guaranteed 'freedom' (H. Winckler, Die Keilschrifttexte Sargons (1889), pl. 40 v 10; ARAB II §78). King and city inhabitants, then, could conduct a dialogue on the basis of rights acknowledged by both sides to exist and demanding consideration from the king. It worked because the cities were recognised to be crucial centres for political support. Thus cities could expect to obtain protection by threatening the Assyrians that they would side with the enemy if no action was taken to help them (ABL 327; Oppenheim 1967 [OI]: no. 121), or by appealing to a set of warnings of the bad end likely to befall a king who disregarded their special status (see p. 614). So protecting and privileging cities can be seen to be not just a one-way benefit extended by a king to a city, but a framework within which cities could exert pressure on the Assyrian king as well.

These privileges and agreements existed in writing, sometimes perhaps inscribed and set up in public (see pp. 614–616). But they probably took a number of different forms depending on circumstances. When Sargon II wished to build the new city of Dur Sharrukin in northern Assyria, he found a group of people (perhaps a village) already living there, who had been granted the land together with special exemptions by Adad-nirari III, in return for providing supplies for the cult of Ashur. A tablet (fragmentary in places) records the action taken by him:

> ... who love his lordship, of his own accord(?) ... to have the waste land settled he turned his mind ... all the people(?) of the god Nanna, the true king (Sargon) ... whose lordship the goddess Ninmenanna has magnified, that he may not oppress the weak, and may cause the feeble to prosper.
> The town of Magganuba, a ... city, which lies like a fortress in the district of Nineveh, ... its woods(?), in its irrigated fields ... the plough

was left idle, in its meadow land . . . the lives of the people of Nineveh(?), which former princes who had exercised the kingship of Assyria before me and governed the subjects of Enlil . . . . no one among them . . . had known how to have the land settled . . .

With a plan conceived in my wide understanding . . . I decreed the building of a city and a temple of Ea . . . that city I built anew . . . I placed . . . in it, and I called its name Dur-Sharrukin . . . the fields surrounding it, in accordance with tablets of purchase . . . to its owners . . . and so that no injustice should be caused I . . .

The 'town of the bakers' which Adad-nirari, son of Shamshi-Adad, a king who preceded me, had exempted (from taxation) and given to Qanuni, Ahu-lamur and Mannu-ki-abi, and imposed on them ten *imēru* (*c.* 2000 l) of (a special type of) corn for offerings to Ashur and Bau, and sealed them a tablet.

That town had reverted to fields, and the people who had lived in it had been evicted from it by the spade. I paid great respect to the command of Ashur, my lord, who named me, who makes my kingship flourish and magnifies my arms, and I cleared ninety-five *imēru* of land in the irrigated fields of the town of the *ērib bīti* (cult personnel) in the district of Nineveh, one field to one field, and gave them to Shulmu-sharri, Parshiddu and Ishid-ishtar, the sons of Ahu-lamur, to Risisu, the son of Qanuni, and to Mannu-ki-abi, and their sons. The previous ten *imēru* of (special) corn, which Adad-nirari had offered as offerings to Ashur, I reaffirmed . . . in famine and need . . . they shall not default all the year round.

The corn taxes of that land shall not be collected, the straw taxes shall not be gathered, it is exempt for all time in order to provide (special) corn for Ashur.

So that the offerings of Ashur should not cease, and to respect the command of an earlier king, I sealed the tablet with my royal seal and gave it to them.

In the fear of god, which Ashur, my lord, had given me, and to give the temple its full due, to strengthen the offerings, to guide the world, and to exalt my head, I received ninety-five *imēru* of land of the 'town of the bakers', in return for the land of the town of the *ērib-bīti*, as an exchange from their hands.

That land I allotted and assigned to the province of Dur-Sharrukin, and himself . . . possessions, ten *imēru* of (special) corn . . . I exempted. A future prince whom Ashur . . . and his shining countenance and joyful heart . . . like me, Sargon, mighty prince . . . and exercises lordship of land and people . . . let him add to the land (which supplies) the offerings of Ashur . . . from the hands of these men and their sons let him not take it away.

(Postgate 1969 no. 32)

This text, and a more summary account contained in a cylinder inscription from Khorsabad (Lyon 1883 no. 1; *ARAB* II §§119–120), tells us that, when Sargon started planning his new city, he asked the local inhabitants and landowners to present their title-deeds. In some cases he offered them fields in exchange or offered to buy them out; in the case of the 'town of the bakers', whose inhabitants had been given their land with special conditions and privileges, he examined the royally sealed document containing the earlier grant, which they presented to him, measured land for them in another location and gave them, in his turn, a new sealed tablet guaranteeing their rights subject to the same conditions.

So, while the Assyrian king was technically omnipotent and not constrained by any laws, in practice he and his subjects engaged in much more dialogue than is sometimes thought. Upholding, restoring and honouring traditionally sanctioned rights, caring for the oppressed and ensuring that justice was done were crucial in defending the divine order. The king's fair dealing in such matters was considered a royal virtue, one that made his reign into a 'golden age' of peace and plenty, beautifully evoked in the introduction to a letter written to Ashurbanipal:

> Good health to the king, my lord! May the gods Nabû and Marduk very much bless the king, my lord. Ashur, the king of the gods, (himself) called by name the king, my lord, to the kingship of Assyria, (and) the gods Shamash and Adad, through their reliable extispicy, established the king, my lord, for the kingship of the world. The reign is good, (its) days are righteous (and) the years justice; there are copious rains, abundant floods (and) a fine rate of exchange; the gods are appeased, there is much reverence to god (and) the temples abound in riches; the great gods of heaven and earth have become revered again in the time of the king, my lord. The old men dance, the young men sing, the women and girls are happy and joyful; women are married, adorned with earrings, boys and girls are brought forth, the births thrive. The king, my lord, has revived the one who was guilty (and) condemned to death; you have released the one who was imprisoned for many years. Those who were sick for many days have got well, the hungry have been sated, the parched (or: 'the dirty') have been anointed with oil, the needy have been covered with garments.
>
> (*ABL* 2; Parpola 1970/1983 no. 121; SAA 10 no. 226)

9e The fall of Assyria

The sudden disappearance of the Assyrian empire, which seemed impregnable and solid, especially in the period of the seventh century, is a phenomenon as yet poorly understood. In 630 everything appeared to be as it had always been, yet by 612 Ashur, Nimrud and Nineveh were in ashes, destroyed by allied Babylonian and Median forces. By 605 the larger part of the Assyrian empire was in the hands of a new Babylonian dynasty with its political centre in southern Mesopotamia, while the eastern fringes and, eventually, the territory to the north, formed part of a new confederation controlled by the Medes, centred on Ecbatana (modern Hamadan) in western Iran. The impression is that the Assyrian heartland had lost any real political significance by the end of the seventh century. The change is sudden and abrupt; the process and circumstances, and possible underlying causes, all remain obscure.

Problems of evidence

One reason for the difficulties in understanding Assyria's collapse is that the sources are very problematical. First, we have Babylonian chronicles for the period 626–623, and then again continuously for 616–608, 608–605, 605–594. So, from 616 on, at least the thread of events survives. But in the crucial preceding fifteen-year period, 631–616 – the time during which Assyria lost control of Babylonia after several defeats – only three years, 626–623, are preserved in a brief historical account (*ABC* no. 2). But the text is fragmentary, so the names of the protagonists in the Assyro-Babylonian conflict are missing at important points, i.e. we frequently do not who was fighting against whom or the identity of kings. Moreover, the Babylonian chronicles are generally interested only in activities either in Babylonia itself or, if they report events occurring beyond its frontiers, then only if they involve the Babylonian king. As a result, the chronicles do not provide any direct information on the situation within Assyria or in the rest of the empire.

Second, Assyrian royal inscriptions and archival material are very sparse for this period. This must partly be due to succession problems in Assyria: the evidence shows that the hold on the throne of Ashurbanipal's heir, Ashur-etel-ilani, was contested; he was eventually succeeded by his brother, Sin-shar-ishkun. At one point, even one of his officials (or eunuchs), Sin-shum-lishir, briefly claimed the throne. Where we should date these struggles in the period 630–620 is debated. All that is certain is that Ashur-etel-ilani succeeded Ashurbanipal on the throne; that his brother, Sin-shar-ishkun, ruled until 612; that the official, Sin-shum-lishir, claimed the kingship at some point before Sin-shar-ishkun's accession; finally, that the Babylonian general, Nabopolassar, claimed the Babylonian throne in 626 and was in undisputed control there by 616.

The surviving evidence in both Assyria and Babylonia gives the impression that Sin-shar-ishkun wielded less direct control over Babylonia than his brother, Ashur-etel-ilani; i.e. that the Babylonian supporters of the local leader, Nabopolassar, had made significant gains by the time of Sin-shar-ishkun's accession (whenever that was exactly). Perhaps Sin-shar-ishkun deliberately lessened Assyria's grip on Babylonia, in return for its support in his struggle against his brother. On the other hand, the situation in Babylonia probably remained in a state of flux for some time during Sin-shar-ishkun's reign; this is implied by a loyalty treaty and several letters, which suggest that the Assyrian king had considerable support in Babylonia until quite late in his reign (SAA 2 no. 11).

Third, a reasonable number of contemporary dated documents from Babylonia exist which can provide information, from their date-formulae, as to who was recognised as king in what Babylonian city at any one point. By drawing up tables of these dates, shifts of political control, civil war, struggles for power, and the existence of several different claimants to the throne can be charted. But fixing exact dates is by no means easy to do, as the texts date by regnal years, but we are not certain from what point a particular ruler's regnal years are to be counted. As a result, the reconstruction of events in the 620s is so speculative that there are at least three different hypotheses in existence, all of which have arguments in their favour (as well as against), and not one of which is wholly satisfactory (Borger 1965; Oates 1965; Reade 1970; Na'aman 1991a). A further problem is created by some texts from Nippur, dated while the city was under siege (Oppenheim 1955) – it looks as though different factions (pro- and anti-Assyrian) dominated the city at various times, which created such confusion that the citizens were unable to date documents according to a specific king and instead simply dated by 'siege years'. Again, there is no precise indication as to when to date the siege. Later Babylonian king-lists (and other material) only add to the confusion: in their attempt to present an orderly roster of kings for this period of chaos, they plump for certain rulers and ignore others, and they fill chronological gaps in a variety of ways which cannot reflect contemporary reality. There is absolutely no way of harmonising all the available evidence, and the chronological problems remain at present insuperable.

Another contentious issue is the identity of Kandalanu. He appears as king of Babylonia after the death of Ashurbanipal's brother, Shamash-shum-ukin, in 648, and he definitely continued to rule in Babylonia until 627 (see chapter 11c). The obvious assumption is that Kandalanu was a subject-ruler installed there by the Assyrians. But some scholars have argued that Kandalanu is an alternative name for Ashurbanipal (most recently, Zawadski 1988: 57–62), on the model occasionally used by Assyrian kings in Babylonia earlier (e.g. Tiglath-pileser III; see p. 580). If this is right, then Ashurbanipal's reign ended in 627, and we have to try to accommodate four different claimants to power in Babylonia in as many years (627–623). This is by no means impossible, as the chronicle and documentary evidence all indicate that the situation bordered on anarchy. But if Kandalanu is not another name for Ashurbanipal, as has been strongly, and convincingly, argued by Brinkman (*RLA* 5: 368–369; Frame 1992: 193ff.), then we can assume that Ashurbanipal died *c.* 630 (no documents are dated by him after 631), and that Ashur-etel-ilani acceded to the throne in Assyria in 631/630, while Kandalanu was able to protect Assyrian interests in Babylonia for another three years (until 627).

The new Assyrian king then only had to try to deal with problems in Babylonia from 627 on, possibly using his brother, Sin-shar-ishkun, to act as regent, a policy which misfired badly (Reade 1970). In the ensuing battle for control of the Babylonian cities, Ashur-etel-ilani quickly lost out, and was perhaps killed there in 623. None of these questions can be resolved conclusively at present. An added difficulty is that we only know about select events inside Babylonia, and hardly anything about what was happening elsewhere in the empire.

Information for the end of Assyria from other regions and from later periods is either unclear or sparse. The Old Testament, apart from later stories such as Jonah, has little solid information. There is a somewhat ambiguous reference to Josiah of Judah clashing with Necho II of Egypt (610–595), who was marching north to help the Assyrians in 609 (2 *Kings* 23.29), which ended in Josiah's death. The usual interpretation is that Josiah challenged the Egyptian king in order to hasten the fall of his hated Assyrian overlord and was killed in battle. More recently it has been argued, rather persuasively, that he was in fact executed for disloyalty to his Egyptian overlord, i.e. Egypt dominated Palestine in 609. If this interpretation is correct, then the Assyrians were so hard-pressed by the Babylonians and Medes in the 610s that they may have formally relinquished control over the Levant to Egypt in return for Egyptian military help (Na'aman 1991b).

The evidence of Berossus, who wrote a history of Babylonia in Greek (in the early third century) using Babylonian sources, has unfortunately been rather garbled by his later excerptors (see Kuhrt 1987). But we can glean two bits of information from him: first, he seems to say that Sin-shar-ishkun appointed Nabopolassar as a general in Babylonia; secondly, that the Median and Babylonian kings sealed their mutual aid pact with a dynastic marriage.

The evidence of classical writers, such as Herodotus and Ctesias, is less helpful than it seems at first sight (see generally Kuhrt 1982). Herodotus' brief account of the fall of the great Assyrian city of Nineveh (1.106) forms part of his Median history, and serves to highlight the military success of the Median king, Cyaxares. It does not add any useful details in terms of evidence, but it is important in showing what a historical watershed the fall of the Assyrian empire was felt to be. The same is true of Ctesias (*ap.* Diodorus 1.24–28), who shows valuably how important it became for the Persians to link the origins of their own empire to the Median defeat of Assyria. Its dramatic collapse reverberated around the Near Eastern and Aegean world, and became for some Greeks an object lesson that 'small is beautiful', as shown by the epigram of Phocylides of Miletus (mid-sixth century):

> A city which is small but on a lofty promontory and well-ordered is stronger than foolish Nineveh.
>
> (E. Diehl, *Anthologia Lyrica Graeca* (Leipzig 1924–5),
> Phocylides no. 4; J.M. Edmonds, *Greek Elegy and Iambus*
> (Loeb, London, 1931) I, Phocylides no. 5)

Reconstructing Assyria's demise

What are we to make of this jumble of information? The only things that can be said with certainty are, first, that Ashurbanipal was definitely ruling in 631, but the date of his death is unknown. Second, Kandalanu certainly ruled in Babylonia until 627; the year following his death is referred to in contemporary dated documents as 'after Kandalanu', implying that no other king was generally recognised in Babylonia in 627–626. Somewhere into the period immediately after Ashurbanipal's death (whenever that was), three holders/claimants to the throne must be fitted: Ashur-etel-ilani, who was certainly Ashurbanipal's son and immediate successor (Postgate 1969 nos. 13 and 14); Sin-shum-lishir, an Assyrian official and general, originally a supporter of Ashur-etel-ilani (*ibid.*), who seems to have revolted later and then seized the kingship briefly; Sin-shar-ishkun, the brother of Ashur-etel-ilani, who eventually gained undisputed control of the Assyrian throne, and ruled until 612. All three were recognised at various times as kings in the 620s in different Babylonian cities. Third, there is Nabopolassar, whose rise to prominence also has to be placed in the 620s. It is usually assumed that he was a Chaldaean from marshy Bit Yakin in South Iraq (the 'Sealand', see chapters. 7a; 11a). Bit Yakin had been governed, in the later part of Ashurbanipal's reign, by a Babylonian appointed by the Assyrian authorities. It has been argued, on the basis of late and slight evidence (including Berossus, cited p. 543), that Nabopolassar may have held a similar position, and used this tribal territory to build up a power-base. From there, he was able to make a bid for the throne in 626 during the turmoil following Kandalanu's death. But we should note that there is no firm evidence to support this view (von Voigtlander 1963). Nabopolassar's accession to the Babylonian throne did not go unchallenged, as shown by the chronicle (*ABC* no. 2) and dated documents. The Babylonian evidence shows that it took Nabopolassar at least until 621/620 before all of Babylonia was under his control; some would date it even later to 616 (cf. *CAH* III ch. 25 for a judicious survey of the evidence and arguments). What is indisputable is that, by 616 at the latest, he was in a strong enough position to mount attacks on Assyria beyond Babylonia's frontiers.

Nabopolassar's first move was against the Assyrian provinces of Suhu and Hindanu, which rendered him tribute. But only three months later he had to reimpose his hold on the region by fighting a battle there against the Assyrians, who were assisted by Mannaean contingents. Only after that was he able to move further up the Euphrates to the area of the confluence with the Balikh river. The Babylonian advance was accompanied by plundering, sacking, removal of religious images and deportations of peoples. A combined force of Egyptians and Assyrians attempted to push the Babylonian troops back, but was not successful. Early in 615, Nabopolassar penetrated into Assyrian territory east of the Tigris (Arrapha), drove the Assyrians back as far as the Zab river, and captured large numbers of prisoners, horses and chariots. But only two months later he experienced a check when he attempted to fight the Assyrians at Ashur itself, but was defeated and briefly put under siege in Takrit.

It was at this moment, when the very heart of Assyria was threatened, and it had lost its grip on a crucial section of the strategic east–west route, that the Median army appeared on the scene for the first time. They entered the area around Arrapha (east of the Tigris), but their further actions are not known as the chronicle is broken. The archaeological evidence in Media suggests that the development of the Median state was closely tied to, and dependent upon, the economic stimuli exercised on the Zagros region by the growth of Assyrian provincial control and increasing tribute demands (Brown 1986). If this interpretation of the evidence is accepted, then it seems likely that the Medes were inevitably drawn into the Assyrian–Babylonian conflict as Assyria's declining power threatened the very basis of their political *status quo* (Sancisi-Weerdenburg 1988).

In the height of summer 614, the Medes returned, attacked Nineveh unsuccessfully, captured nearby Tarbisu, and laid siege to Ashur, which was captured, plundered and sacked. The Babylonian army under Nabopolassar arrived too late on the scene to participate, but the Babylonian king and Cyaxares, the Median ruler, established a treaty of mutual aid and support. However, no immediate action could be taken against the other great Assyrian cities because Nabopolassar had to face a serious revolt by Suhu (mid-Euphrates) in the spring of 613, involving laying siege to two cities and fighting off an Assyrian attack. But in 612 the Babylonian and Median forces met in northern Babylonia and marched together up to Nineveh. After a three-month siege the city fell, and the booty from its sanctuaries and palaces was removed. Recent excavations have uncovered the corpses of Assyrian soldiers who fell defending their city (Stronach 1989; Stronach and Lumsden 1992). It is possible that Sin-shar-ishkun was forced to beseech Nabopolassar for his life; but we do not know his subsequent fate, and he is not heard of again.

The fall of Nineveh and disappearance of Ashurbanipal's son did not spell the total extinction of the Assyrian regime. With Egyptian support, another Assyrian, Ashur-uballit (II), set himself up as king at Harran in north-western Mesopotamia. A series of attacks and counterattacks ensued before the Assyrian hold there was finally crushed by the combined forces of Babylonians and Medes, accompanied by a massive destruction of the city of Harran and its temple. Only from 608 onwards do all traces of the Assyrians disappear from the record.

What is striking, and needs emphasising, is the enormous amount of fighting that was needed to defeat the Assyrians: their tenacity and apparent ability to put armies in the field after repeated, and seemingly devastating, defeats is remarkable. We should also note that they received considerable support from their allies and subjects – at no point is there a hint that Nabopolassar was welcomed as a liberator, nor any suggestion of other people rising spontaneously to throw of the Assyrian yoke. If anything, the evidence points in the opposite direction: there was repeated rebellion by the Euphrates states, and a possible revolt even within Babylonia at Uruk in 613 (Zawadski 1988). The only people who definitely aided the Babylonians were the Medes – the possible, often asserted, role played by the Scythians in the fall of the empire remains very uncertain (Zawadski 1988). One important result of the ultimate Babylonian victory was the changed landscape of Mesopotamia: the great Assyrian royal cities of northern Iraq were almost all wiped out – Nineveh, Kalhu and Ashur only recovered their urban identity centuries later; just one important Assyrian site, Arbela, continued to flourish. The totality of the physical destruction of the Assyrian cities has probably been exaggerated, but the political importance of the region was profoundly diminished. The extraordinary impact of Assyria's fall is echoed in the awed words of the Babylonian chronicle, which ends its accounts of the fall of Ashur and Nineveh each time with the words:

> They (sc. Babylonians and Medes) inflicted a terrible defeat upon a great people . . .
>
> (*ABC* no. 3 l. 27 (cf. l. 43))

Notes

1 The Babylonian 'Epic of Creation' would have been even less intelligible, yet it was read publicly at festivals (see chapter 7a; 7d).
2 All the eponym-lists are now available in a new edition by A.R. Millard: *The Eponyms of the Assyrian Empire 910–612BC* (SAA Studies 2), Helsinki, 1994.
3 It is possible that Shalmaneser III was either very old or ill towards the end of his reign, as his later campaigns were conducted by his generals and not himself.
4 A substantial number of the reliefs from Ashurnasirpal II's palace, excavated by Henry Austen Layard at Nimrud in the 1840s, are displayed in the British Museum, together with those of Tiglath-pileser III, Sennacherib and Ashurbanipal.

10

ANATOLIA *c.* 900–*c.* 550

In Anatolia, closely bordering the Assyrian empire, several important states (Urartu, Phrygia, Lydia) developed in the first half of the first millennium. Apart from the small Neo-Hittite principalities (see chapter 8c(ii)), they remained politically independent of Assyria and its successor state, the Neo-Babylonian empire (see chapter 11d) – although all, like the rest of the Near East, were eventually incorporated into the Achaemenid Persian empire (see chapter 13). As near neighbours of the great Mesopotamian empires, the Anatolian states interacted with them, culturally, economically, politically. But reconstructing their history is not an easy task. The Urartian state is perhaps the best-known: the territory of ancient Urartu has been quite intensively explored, Urartian inscriptions have been recovered, and, as the kingdom closest to the Assyrian heartland, it often figures in Assyrian documents (both formal and informal). Phrygia and Lydia present much greater problems, as there is little inscribed material from this period. That textual sparsity is balanced to some degree, in the case of Phrygia, by substantial archaeological finds (particularly at Gordion), and, in the case of Lydia, by Herodotus' history of Lydia in the seventh and sixth centuries and his story of its conquest by Cyrus of Persia (Herodotus 1. 6–95).

All the Anatolian kingdoms were affected in the eighth and seventh centuries by the destructive raids of horse-borne warriors, known from Greek sources as Cimmerians and Scythians. The exact nature, organisation and movements of these nomadic groups (especially the Cimmerians) are still not very clearly understood (cf. Lanfranchi 1990 for detailed analysis).[1] Some groups made agreements with the Assyrian kings, and supplied forces to the Assyrian army (*RLA* 7: 186–189). The culture of the Scythians in their 'homelands' of the Ukraine and central Asia has become known through a series of spectacular finds (Rolle 1989), which add considerably to the long, though problematical, 'Scythian ethnography' of Herodotus 4. 1–82 (Hartog 1988). Along the western and northern coast of Anatolia were the Ionian Greek cities and their colonies in the Black Sea. Groups called 'Yaman/Yawan' figure occasionally in Mesopotamian sources, and it is usually assumed that they must be 'Ionians', i.e. Greeks. Examination of the personal names associated with this group has shown, however, that the names are Anatolian in type, so that such a clear identification is by no means certain (Brinkman 1989). Two other politico-cultural entities should be noted: the Carians and Lycians in south-west Turkey. Neither is very well known, nor very fully attested, before the sixth century (*CAH* III/2: 655–665; 671–676; *RLA* 5: 423–425; 7: 189–191; Bryce 1986), but we must remember their presence as a force in the history of Anatolia in the first half of the first millennium.

10a The kingdom of Urartu

Location, exploration, origins and sources

The area covered by the Urartian kingdom is roughly coextensive with Armenia, i.e. it is centred in eastern Turkey (Lake Van), extending to former Soviet Armenia in the north and including parts of Azerbaijan (north-west Iran) and a strip of north-east Iraq. The name comes from Assyrian documents (Urartu/Uruatri), and mirrors that of Biblical Ararat – the mountain where Noah's ark was thought to have come to rest. This extremely high, twin-peaked mountain lies at the heart of the precipitous region.

Until the Assyrian annals and similar texts revealed the existence of a large and powerful kingdom here between the ninth and seventh centuries, the very existence of Urartu had scarcely been suspected. Some archaeological work was done sporadically in the region of Lake Van in the nineteenth century, and the existence of a distinctive culture was recognised. But scholars did not pay much attention to the material, and a lot has been scattered throughout many different museum collections. Early this century, the main epigraphical studies began. They were carried out particularly by Russians, who, together with Armenian scholars, have become the main exponents of the Urartian language (Melikishvili 1971). The most spectacular discoveries were made in the course of excavations conducted in Soviet Armenia after 1945 by the Russian archaeologist Piotrovsky. They have advanced Urartian studies considerably, particularly the finds at the large site of Karmir Blur. Here the great fortified citadel had been burnt, and an enormous wealth of material, including great quantities of foodstuffs, was recovered and analysed (Piotrovsky 1967). These dramatic finds are now supplemented by other sites in the vicinity (Arinberd, Armavir Blur), extensive excavation by Turkish and other scholars in Turkey (Toprakkale, Patnos, Adilşevaz, Altintepe, Kayalidere), and major American, German and British expeditions to north-west Iran (Hasanlu, Bastam, Haftavan Tepe; for general discussion see Burney 1977 [OA]: ch. 6). Unfortunately, much of this work has not yet been published, so that the results cannot be exploited fully. Apart from excavations, many more sites have been identified as Urartian on the basis of building remains and pottery (Kroll 1976).

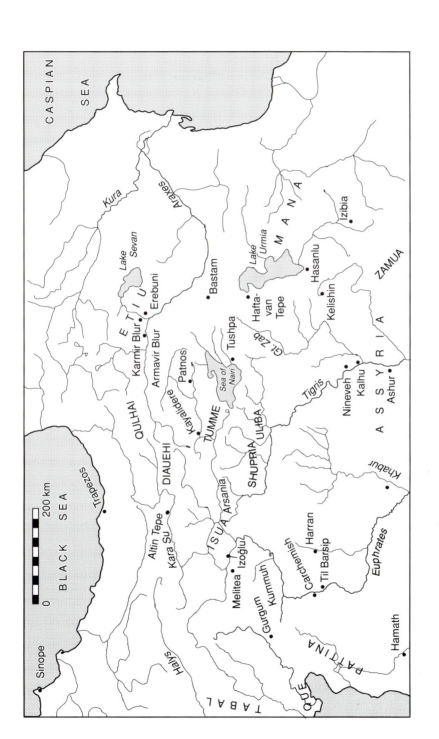

Map 14 Urartu

Tracing the evolution of the Urartian state and its culture is problematical. When Urartu appears in the ninth century, it is already fully developed, but, archaeologically, the second millennium of the region is something of a blank at present.[2] Trying to define Urartu's roots is therefore very difficult. Some information from Hittite imperial documents shows that several places with which the Hittite rulers maintained treaty-relations and alliances (e.g. Azzi-Hayasa) were located here. Preserved Hittite treaties make it clear that, at least in some instances, these small polities were ruled by local dynasts and that agreements were made not only with 'rulers', but also with the peoples and elders (see chapter 5e). This suggests that the area was politically splintered into innumerable different entities with no uniform political structure (Haas 1986a). The accounts of the Middle Assyrian kings who campaigned here (in particular Shalmaneser I (1274–1245/1263–1234) and Tiglath-pileser I (1114–1076), see chapter 7b) largely bear out this picture. They regularly refer to campaigning in the 'region of Nairi' (around Lake Van) against a plurality of 'kings'. In one instance they use the name 'Uruatri' – a form of 'Urartu', regularly used by the Assyrians for their powerful northern neighbour in the first millennium.

A possible way of understanding Urartu's development is that a pattern of small-scale, scattered, transhumant societies was gradually transformed into a state, with much of the population concentrated in and around fortified urban centres and a centralised political structure. An important stimulus in this may have been repeated Assyrian aggression. As the Urartian state evolved, expanded and defined itself, it adopted (and, in the process, adapted) a number of key elements from its culturally more advanced neighbours. Most striking among such influences was the Assyrian cuneiform system, which was first used along with the Assyrian language for Urartian royal inscriptions, then quickly adapted to render the Urartian language itself. A result is that Urartian can be read, although problems in understanding particular terms and usages remain to be clarified.

One factor that is rather less helpful in understanding early Urartian history than it appears at first is that Urartian has linguistic affinities with Hurrian. It has, therefore, been thought that Urartian represents a direct chronological development of Hurrian (chapter 6a). Because Urartu lies near the earlier Hurrian kingdom of Mitanni, some scholars have suggested that there were close cultural and structural links between the two. But more recently it has been argued, persuasively, that Urartian and Hurrian had branched off from basic Proto-Urarto-Hurrian already by the third millennium, and developed quite independently of each other from then on (Wilhelm 1982). All we can say, in the most general way, is that Caucasian and Indo-European languages co-existed in the zone between the Zagros and central Anatolia, but there is probably no particular significance in the language link between Urartian and Hurrian.

The preserved epigraphic corpus in Urartian is not immense. Much of it commemorates royal constructions – interesting and important in itself, of course, but not generally useful for reconstructing details of political history. Only two texts have been identified so far which describe military exploits and which can, in a general sense, be compared to the Assyrian annals in that they recount campaigns arranged year by year: one dates to the reign of Argishti I (early eighth century; König 1965–7: no. 80), and one to his son, Sarduri II (mid-eighth century (see table 29); König 1965–7: no. 104). Day-to-day documents, so richly available in the later Assyrian empire, are very sparse. So far only twenty-one tablets (mostly letters, but including at least one royal decree) have been recovered from three sites (Karmir Blur, Toprakkale, Bastam; Diakonoff 1963; Zimansky 1985: 80–83; recently also, Armavir Blur). Several are very fragmentary, so understanding their content is quite hard, but the majority seem to be administrative directives. A very important source is the clay bullae that have been found at Bastam in their hundreds (well over a thousand; Salvini 1979; Seidl 1979). They carry royal seal impressions, and show that the main political centres and economic resources were under tight state control. A form of hieroglyphic writing also used in Urartu is still rather puzzling. So far only a small number of signs have been found, incised on containers and storage jars, where they seem to indicate capacity. They are not identical with Hittite hieroglyphs (although their form may be influenced by them), except for the hieroglyphs found at the western site of Altintepe, which do reflect a strong Neo-Hittite influence (*RLA* 4: 400–401). Were the signs simply used as a kind of 'commercial shorthand' for purposes of labelling? Or do they represent the existence of an alternative script that could have been used for writing on perishable materials (cf. the Hittite empire, chapter 5b)? At present the evidence is too sparse to allow any conclusions, except that the hieroglyphic script was apparently not used to render a different language.

In the absence of historically informative texts from Urartu itself, historians have to rely on Assyrian documents for tracing Urartu's history. The Assyrian references, usually in the context of wars between the two states, provide the basis (through synchronisms) for the list of Urartian kings and their approximate chronology (table 29). They also allow us to define something of Urartu's expansion westwards and eastwards at times. Most interesting and important is Sargon II's detailed account of his battle in 714 with the Urartian king in the northern Zagros, his march around part of the kingdom in the vicinity of Lake Urmia (north-west Iran), and his capture and sack of the strategically and cultically important Urartian frontier state, Musasir (Thureau-Dangin 1912). Sargon's description, despite its military focus and inflated rhetoric, is a prime source for gaining a picture of the Urartian landscape. Several letters from his reign, written by Assyrian governors and the crown-prince, Sennacherib, retail reports and rumours received from refugees and spies reporting on internal Urartian affairs. They give us glimpses of serious events such as a defeat inflicted on Urartu by the

Cimmerians, followed by an internal revolt (Lanfranchi 1983; Lanfranchi and Parpola 1990).

Table 29 Chronology of Urartian kings

	Urartu	Assyria
–c. 840	Aramu	Shalmaneser III
–c. 825	Sarduri I (son of Lutipri)	Shalmaneser III
–c. 810	Ishpuini (son of Sarduri I)	Shamshi-Adad V
–c. 785	Menua (son of Ishpuini)	Adad-nirari III
–c. 763	Argishti I (son of Menua)	Adad-nirari III
		Shalmaneser IV
		Ashur-dan III
– c. 734	Sarduri II (son of Argishti I)	Ashur-nirari V
		Tiglath-pileser III
– c. 714	Rusa I (son of Sarduri II)	Tiglath-pileser III
		Shalmaneser V
		Sargon II
– c. 685	Argishti II (son of Rusa I)	Sargon II
		Sennacherib
– c. 645	Rusa II (son of Argishti II)	Sennacherib
		Esarhaddon
		Ashurbanipal
?–c. 635	Sarduri III (son of Rusa II)	Ashurbanipal
(?–c. 629	Erimena)	
?-c. 601	Rusa III (son of Erimena)	chronology very doubtful
?-c. 585	Sarduri IV (son of Sarduri)	

The physical environment

A crucial feature of Urartu, which explains some of the specific structures it developed and which made it resilient to Assyrian military attack, is its geography (Zimansky 1985). The territory of ancient Urartu was very extensive – Zimansky (1985) has estimated it to be about 200,000 km². It is uncertain whether all of it was directly controlled by the Urartian kings at any one time – fluctuations in control may well have to be reckoned with. Three large lakes – Van, Urmia and Sevan – are located in Urartu: the two largest, Van and Urmia, are limited in their economic usefulness, as Lake Van has a high soda content, while Lake Urmia is very salty. Fishing is, therefore, their only real economic value – the lake waters cannot be used for irrigation. But against this we must set the fact that the region is drained by a multitude of rivers from different sources, which makes the water supply for agriculture relatively secure: any attempt by an enemy to block some of the water-sources could never result in cutting off essential water totally.

Because of the high, mountainous character of the country, the number of major routes through it is limited, and many of them become virtually impassable in winter because of the deep snow. This is strikingly illustrated by the fact that, although Van is only about 130 km north of Nineveh as the crow flies (less than half the distance that separates Nineveh from Babylon), movement directly north to Van from Nineveh rarely occurred because of the great physical obstacles: i.e. for a large part of the year what routes there were would have been covered by snow, and even when they were free the steep mountain terrain made it virtually impossible for the Assyrians to move wheeled vehicles, carrying siege-equipment, along them. As a result Assyrian attacks on Urartu tended inevitably to be mounted from either the west or the east – a circuitous way to penetrate into its heartland at Van, and a rare achievement.

Arable land is concentrated in three main areas. First, to the east and north-east of Lake Van stretches a high-lying, potentially very fertile, plain. Slow-ripening plants require irrigation, but this is not a problem as there are plenty of mountain springs that can be diverted for this purpose, and the Urartian kings are known to have constructed a magnificent canal to carry water to the plain. An added advantage for farmers here is that, because access for hostile armies is difficult, the plain is fairly safe from the ravages of war. In the Lake Urmia region, which is much lower-lying, settlement and land use close to the lakeshore are impossible because of the shifting water-line, and the eastern bank is very swampy. The major area for agriculture lay to the west and south of the lake. Sargon, in the account of his eighth campaign (714), paints a lively picture of the dense settlements here, the great quantities of grain stored in the many Urartian centres, the extensive herds of cattle and the development of viticulture and orchards, made possible by the irrigation schemes of the Urartian rulers. The third region lies north of the Araxes river, extending toward Lake Sevan. This is a very dry, low-lying plain which escapes the heavy snowfalls typical elsewhere. It is also by far the largest plain within Urartian territory. But irrigation is not a problem as there are plenty of streams and water sources to provide it.

The pattern of herding in Urartu was one of seasonal transhumance with animals sheltered in houses during the harsh, icy winters. It was probably very similar to the system described by Xenophon soon after 400; his *Anabasis* contains wonderfully graphic descriptions of the physical and climatic hardships of the area and provides useful additional evidence:

> The houses were built underground; the entrances were like wells, but they broadened out lower down. There were tunnels dug in the ground for the animals, while the men went down by ladder. Inside the houses there were goats, sheep, cows and poultry with their young. All these animals were fed on food that was kept inside the houses.
>
> (Xenophon *Anabasis* 4.5)

In the summer the herders would fan out and disperse over the upland pastures. This would again have worked to their advantage in the face of war, which was normally fought in the summer months.

These environmental constraints helped to shape Urartu which, in spite of its centralised superstructure, retained a decentralised system of production and distribution. In the face of continuous Assyrian military attacks, the initially separate polities seem to have drawn together to form the Urartian state. A network of fortified centres was set up, which protected its diffused economic base and guarded its strategic routes (Forbes 1983). This effectively limited the damage that the Assyrians could inflict.

Historical outline

It is hard to get beyond a skeleton outline of Urartian history, given the available sources, and the events we can reconstruct are inevitably dominated by Assyrian–Urartian relations. The reign of Shalmaneser III (858–824) provides the first insight. He fought several times in Urartu; first, against Aramu, described as having royal centres at Arzashkun and Sugunia, later against Sarduri, the son of Lutipri, whose main centre was the rock-fortress of Tushpa on Lake Van. This suggests that some kind of political shift took place in this period: first, Tushpa seems to have become an important ceremonial and royal centre only now; secondly, the reign of Sarduri (not a descendant of Aramu) marked the beginning of a new dynasty, which dominated Urartu, without major disruption, for the next two hundred years (Salvini 1986). The key elements of the Urartian state and economy are depicted on the great bronze temple gates of Shalmaneser III at the site of Balawat (near Nimrud, p. 504): fortresses set on mountain peaks are shown being burnt by the Assyrian army; Assyrian soldiers cut down fruit trees and wheel away gigantic storage jars. At the same time the horrendous physical obstacles that the soldiers had to overcome are illustrated, with Assyrian soldiers heaving their horses up and down the sheer mountains.

By the late ninth century, Urartu was in firm control of its southern frontier against Assyria and consolidating its hold by conquering and building up the local Mannaean centres in the Urmia basin.[3] Evidence comes from archaeological sites: at Hasanlu (Dyson and Muscarella 1989) and Haftavan Tepe (Burney 1969–70/1972–6; *RLA* 4: 39), where the local Mannaean cities were transformed into typical Urartian fortresses; the large Urartian citadel of Bastam was also founded around now (Kroll 1972). A bilingual (Urartian and Akkadian) inscription, set up on the modern boundary between Iran and Iraq and declaring Urartu's firm control of Musasir (*c.* 80 km north-east of Nineveh), shows Urartu's hold in the east even more clearly:

> When Ishpuini, son of Sarduri, mighty king, king of the Shura, king of the Biaina, lord of Tushpa-city, and Menua, son of Ishpuini, came before (the god) Haldi to the city of Ardini (Musasir), they built a sanctuary for Haldi on the highway(?). Ishpuini, son of Sarduri, placed an inscription before the sanctuary. He brought fine arms, fine goods,

he brought standards of copper, he brought a basin of copper, he brought x x, he brought many goods (and) established them at the gates of Haldi. He gave them to Haldi the lord for his life. He brought 1,112 cattle, 9,020 free-running goats and sheep and 12,480 rams for offerings. When Ishpuini, son of Sarduri, mighty king, king of Shura, king of the Biaina, lord of Tushpa-city, came before Haldi to the city of Ardini, at the command of Haldi he made this citadel(?). The words of this command were placed on the road at the gates of Haldi.

As a warning for him who removes from Ardini from the gates of Haldi the goods, they have taken the following measures:

When Ishpuini, son of Sarduri, (and) Menua, son of Ishpuini, came before Haldi to the city of Ardini, they dedicated goods to Haldi and said: 'Whoever takes the goods from the gates of Haldi . . ., whoever causes someone else to take (them) and does nothing(?), whoever hides it from the rulers, . . . whoever hears (that) someone has taken the goods from the gates of Haldi for himself or has caused someone to do so, may Haldi wipe out his seed on earth! Whoever removes this inscription from its place, whoever breaks (it), whoever causes another (to do) these things, whoever says to someone: 'go, destroy it!', may Haldi, Teisheba, Shiwini, (and) the gods of the city Ardini wipe out (his) seed on earth.

> (Benedict 1961; van Loon in Veenhof 1983 [OI]: 34–36)

Other texts show that Haldi was the principal deity of the Urartian pantheon, always named first in the trinity with Teisheba (storm-god) and

Figure 34 Relief from Kef Kalesi, Lake Van (after Bilgiç, *Anatolia* 8 (1964), figure 2)

Shiwini (sun-god), who together headed the many gods of the region (for depiction of Urartian deities see fig. 34). The later text of Sargon (see p. 551), describing his sack of Musasir and removal of immense quantities of precious goods from the Haldi sanctuary, also indicates that this small frontier state was a major cult centre of this most important Urartian deity, who is often presented as directly granting the Urartian kings victory in war. The inscription quoted above contains hints of how the incorporation of cultur- ally linked states could be, and was, managed by the Urartian rulers (*RLA* 5: 568–569): the Urartian king cast himself in the role of official patron and provider of the local cults – he became their chief benefactor and guardian; the cities were thus dependent on Urartu's goodwill and obliged to reciproc- ate with political support.

Following Urartu's successful expansion into the Urmia basin, the kings turned to the west. Urartian western conquests may have begun under Menua (*c.* 810–785), but they are most clearly documented for Argishti I and Sarduri II (between *c.* 785 and *c.* 734), both of whom have left annals-style accounts describing battles in that region. Argishti I even refers to fighting against Ashur-nirari V of Assyria (754–745); both kings describe their victories in Malatya and Kummuh beyond the Euphrates. The text recounting Sarduri's war of his second regnal year (752?) was found inscribed in the side of a cliff overlooking the Euphrates, at the foot of a Urartian fortress (perhaps Tumeshki, mentioned in the text):

Haldi went forth, his weapon smote Hilaruada, son of Shahu, the king of the Meliteans' country (Malatya/Melid), subjected him before Sar- duri, son of Argishti. Haldi is mighty, Haldi's weapon is mighty.

Sarduri, son of Argishti went forth. That which Sarduri (speaks):

'The Euphrates was a clean place, there was not any king who from there had crossed over. I prayed to Haldi the lord, to Teisheba, to Shiwini, to the gods of Urartu for that which from the princes' greatness I desired. The gods listened to me, they made a way (for) me. I crossed over among the soldiers in front of Tumeshki. On this same day I went forth to the country. South of Qalawa I kept, I reached as far as (the) Karnishi mountain range north of Melitea. I reached as far as Mushani beyond Zabsha. Fourteen castles and seventy towns I conquered in one day. The castles I pulled down, the towns I burned. I took fifty battle chariots. From the battle I returned, I surrounded Sasi, a royal city of Hilaruada, which was fortified, in battle I took. Goods, men, women from there I brought home.'

That which Sarduri (speaks):

'I went in, I ordered: Let Melitea be besieged! Hilaruada came, before me he prostrated himself, he took hold of (my) feet. I showed myself merciful. I carried off gold, silver, goods as booty to Urartu I brought. Himself I kept under tribute. Nine castles (from) there I removed (and) added to my country: Hazani, Yaurahi, Tumeshki, Wasini, Maninui,

Arushi, Qulbitarrini, Tashe (namely) Quera's Tashe, Meluiani. Through Haldi's greatness, Sarduri, son of Argishti, is the mighty king, the great king, king of Urartu, prince of Tushpa city.'

That which Sarduri (speaks):

'He who should wipe out this writing, who should destroy it, who should hide it, who should make anyone do these things, who should say: "go, wipe out!" – let Haldi, Teisheba, Shiwini (and) the gods wipe himself (and) his family out from under the sun. They shall not afford him shelter(?), neither divine nor human being shall let him go anywhere.'

(König 1965–7 no. 104; van Loon 1974; van Loon in Veenhof 1983 [OI]: 42–45)

The campaigns in the west established a strong Urartian presence for over fifty years. It was only diminished eventually by Tiglath-pileser III (744–727), who defeated Sarduri II and his north Syrian and Anatolian subjects and allies in a great battle fought in Kummuh (Commagene) in 742. The kind of control the Urartian kings established is illustrated by the passage cited above: first, several strategic places were attacked, which led to the surrender of the local ruler; he was re-installed on his throne, but was obliged henceforth to support the Urartian king with materials and manpower as needed; then, some centres along the frontier were detached from the subject territory and incorporated into the Urartian state, thus reducing the subject ruler's power base; further, the defeated king's treasures were removed to Urartian centres; and, finally, his human resources were permanently depleted by deportation of part of the population, which was settled within Urartu in order to swell its peasantry, armed forces and garrisons. Direct Urartian rule stretched to the Euphrates as shown by the extensive finds of Urartian pottery and the remnants of a Urartian fortress commanding the Euphrates crossing at Izoğlu.

Into this period must also be dated Urartian expansion into the northern area where the huge, fertile Yerevan plain (around Lake Sevan) was incorporated. The integration of this region was marked by the construction of enormous fortresses (one with a royal name) to control and administer the region: Argishtihinili (Armavir Blur) on the Araxes and Erebuni on the edge of modern Yerevan. Both were foundations of Sarduri II, and the texts reveal that Erebuni was settled by deportees from North Syria and Sophene (*RLA* 5: 158–161). Sarduri II also reached the north-westerly region of Qulha (classical Colchis), although the relevant account gives the impression that the main achievement (and perhaps aim) was a frontier raid rather than the imposition of Urartian control.

Urartu's sudden growth seems to have profited from Assyria's relative weakness and lack of campaigning in the late ninth and first half of the eighth centuries. Assyrian inactivity allowed Urartu to build up its political and commercial network to Assyria's disadvantage – an understandable reaction to Assyria's ninth-century expansion, which had hemmed in Urartu. With renewed Assyrian aggression in the second half of the eighth century, the two states came into violent conflict in North Syria and central Anatolia, on the one hand, and in the northern Zagros, on the other. Urartian power was particularly dangerous for Assyria in the area west of the Euphrates: the Phrygian kingdom and Urartu seem to have made common cause over several decades, which threatened to squeeze out Assyria from access to mineral deposits and important trade routes. Similar factors probably operated in the Zagros area: here Urartian interests crept ever southwards and, together with Elam and Babylonia, they threatened to cut Assyria off from access to the main routes linking the Mesopotamian valley to the Iranian plateau. These considerations ultimately determined Assyrian strategy over the next forty years or so (see chapter 9c), with the Assyrians whittling away at the western and eastern edges of Urartian power in an attempt to limit its spheres of activity. The high point of this strategy is represented by Sargon II's eighth campaign in 714, which climaxed in his sacking of the frontier state of Musasir (see p. 498).

A factor that helped the Assyrians to defeat Urartu was that, in the late eighth century, Urartu suffered from attacks by the Cimmerians. The precise identity of the Cimmerians and their movements are still extremely hard to pin down, but they were probably mounted nomad warriors, akin to the Scythians (Rolle 1989; Lanfranchi 1990). The Cimmerians were able at one point to inflict a devastating defeat on the Urartian army, resulting in considerable internal and dynastic chaos (Lanfranchi 1983; Lanfranchi and Parpola 1990: xix–xx). Although Urartu obviously experienced setbacks on several fronts (Argishtihinili in the north seems to have been destroyed around this time too), the effects were not long-lasting and seem to have been limited in their effect. The important western Urartian site of Altintepe was founded in the seventh century, perhaps as a counterweight to Assyria's control of Malatya and Kummuh further south (Özgüç 1967). There was extensive building, too, in the seventh century at Bastam in the east; it expanded greatly in the reign of Rusa II (c. 685–c. 645), and epigraphic finds confirm that Urartu's hold in the east did not slacken. Although Argishtihinili was destroyed around the end of the eighth century and not rebuilt, it was replaced by the massive citadel of Teishebaina (Karmir Blur) close to Erebuni. Any losses in the Yerevan region were therefore clearly temporary in nature. To the south, Urartu and Assyria seem to have arrived at a firmer agreement about boundaries, and a policy of friendly diplomatic relations (cf. Esarhaddon's Shupria campaign, above pp. 533–534) replaced the earlier pattern of military hostilities between the two powerful neighbours: an Urartian embassy is mentioned in 643 visiting Ashurbanipal's court.

This is the last certain mention of the Urartian state – its subsequent history is shrouded in obscurity. In 609, the Babylonian king Nabopolassar (626–605; see chapter 9e; 11d) undertook military operations along the Urartian frontier, presumably as part of his strategy to consolidate Babylonian control over the old Assyrian empire. By 585, as we know from Herodotus (1.74), the Medes dominated territory up to the Halys river, which implies that the Urartian state no longer existed. No kings or local leaders of Urartu figure in Darius I of Persia's account of the great revolts against him in 522–521 (the Behistun inscription; chapter 13c), although many battles had to be fought in the territory now called 'Armenia' by the Persians. But how and when Urartu declined or disintegrated is completely unknown and cannot be reconstructed from this scanty material. Some names of kings following Rusa II are known from inscriptions, but it is possible that several were contemporaries and that the unity of the country had fragmented (Kessler 1986). The history of the region from 643 until it reappears as the Achaemenid satrapy of Armenia is at present a blank.

The Urartian state

The structure of the Urartian state is difficult to pinpoint, because of the limited sources. We know very little about its administrative organisation, although sites, particularly Karmir Blur and Bastam, have revealed the existence of massive centres capable of storing vast quantities of foodstuffs. They were clearly constructed as part of the central authority's attempt to supply and control economically productive and strategic areas (Forbes 1983). At the same time they served the function of royal capitals and military establishments. We know only a few titles of officials from Urartian texts, and personal names are rarely attested. The Assyrian intelligence reports about the northern frontier are rather more helpful than the sparse Urartian documents; as, for example, here:

> To the king, my lord: your servant Ashur-resuwa (Assyrian official located in Kurdistan). Good health to the king, my lord!
>
> As regards Naragê, the chief tailor, about whom I wrote to the king, my lord: 'He and 20 of his fellow "eunuchs" (see discussion p. 530) who conspired against the king have been arrested' – the king of Urartu has now entered Turushpa (i.e. Tushpa) and questioned them. They have dragged forth and killed the rest of the people involved in the plot – 100 men, including the 'eunuchs' and the 'bearded courtiers'. Ursenê, the deputy general, brother of Abliuqnu, was likewise arrested in Turushpa.
>
> (SAA 5 no. 91)

The report gives the impression that the king's entourage consisted of body servants and courtiers, seemingly organised along similar lines to the Assyrian court. There were also high military officials, such as a general and a deputy general. Another, fragmentary Assyrian letter (SAA 5 no. 93) shows that there was further a 'general of the right (wing)', who is described as a member of the royal family. That suggests that (as one would expect) the top posts were held by people closely related to the king himself. The courtly and military nobility associated with the king probably formed the élite whose elegant houses and elaborate burials have been located in the Van area and at Altıntepe. It is they, presumably, who provided a demand for some of the fine metalwork for which Urartu is famous (van Loon 1966; Wartke 1990; Merhav 1991). Another Assyrian letter (SAA 5 no. 90) reflects the existence of regional governors, indicating that Urartu was divided into a series of districts under local governors, whose main task will have been to levy and lead local forces in wars. Along the edges of the state, beyond the provincial districts, lay the small, but strategically and commercially important, states under independent local rulers tied by a complex of political obligations to the Urartian king.

The monumental inscriptions present the king as the sole wielder of power, inspired and helped by the god Haldi. Sometimes he is described as the 'king of kings', ruler of all the inhabitants of Bia (a local term for Urartu), governor and lord of the city of Tushpa. Tushpa seems, from early on, to have been considered the royal centre *par excellence*: some of the longest, surviving royal inscriptions were carved in the great rock walls there; it was the centre of important cults; elaborate rock chambers (whose function is unclear) were constructed at Tushpa (Salvini 1986). It was also here that the investigations into the revolt against Rusa II and the execution of the conspirators took place (see text cited p. 559). Royal residences were located probably throughout the kingdom, and the remnants of elaborate wall-paintings suggest the manner in which they may have been decorated (Özgüç 1966). The finely carved furniture with bronze and ivory inlays known from Urartu was also presumably part of the regular palace equipment.

The king was normally the direct descendant of his predecessor, a link often stressed in the inscriptions. There may have been occasional deviation from this ideal pattern: Rusa I is said by Sargon II to have dedicated a statue in the temple of Musasir bearing the inscription 'with two horses and one chariot-eer, he (Rusa) took into his hands the kingship of Urartu' (TCL 3 l. 404). This hints at a struggle for the throne, and the apparently smooth succession stressed in royal inscriptions probably glosses over considerable internal dissension and competition. The crown prince played an important role, as shown by the inscription of Ishpuini (pp. 554–5), accompanying the king in ceremonial and political activities. When, in the confusion following the Cimmerian defeat, it was thought that the king had been killed, the crown prince, Melartua, was raised to the kingship by the soldiers in the royal camp (SAA 5 no. 90) – showing that he would normally participate in his father's campaigns and that his official position made him the automatic choice in the case of the king's sudden death. It is possible that the Urartian king was invested with symbols of kingship on his accession at several different important cultic centres of the kingdom. But this is pure guesswork, based on a broken reference in Sargon II's report of 714, where he *seems* to describe the frontier state of Musasir as a place where the Urartian kings were 'crowned' in some sense (Zimansky 1985). But the passage is obscure and capable of alternative interpretations (Kristensen 1988).

Frontiers and routes were always of major importance, and hence were marked by royal stelae, as well as by the royally built and heavily garrisoned fortresses set on summits dominating the surrounding terrain. From such high points the approach of hostile forces could be watched for and then signalled with torches to other look-out posts, as graphically described by Sargon II. The forts provided almost impregnable refuges for the population from the lower-lying towns located in the arable plains, although they, too, were often (according to Sargon's description) heavily walled, with gates and towers, and encircled by deep moats. A good deal of land was made available through royal canal-projects, which diverted perennial rivers into the plains where large-scale farming, viticulture and fruitgrowing were feasible. It seems that such land was often retained by the king himself, or given to members of his family and entourage. Sargon's campaign account of 714 contains an evocative description of one royal irrigation enterprise near the city of Ulhu. It is worth quoting in full:

> A canal which brought flowing water he dug, . . . he caused water to flow abundantly like the Euphrates. He diverted ditches without number from its bed, . . . and so caused the fields to be irrigated . . . fruit-trees and vines he caused them to water like rain; planes and other trees . . . like a forest he caused to grow over its environs like a protective roof. And on its fallow plain, he caused the *arahhu*-song [to sound] – like a god he had given his people the lovely *alalu*-cry (these are idyllic, rustic songs). 300 donkey-loads of seed-corn he caused to germinate on the grain-field in the furrows. The area of its deserted plain he made into meadows . . . He made it into a stall for horses and herds, and he let the whole of this inaccessible land learn camel breeding . . .
>
> A palace, a royal dwelling place, he built for his pleasure on the canal-bank, roofed it with cypress-beams and made it smell sweet. The fortress of Sardihurda he laid out for its protection on the mountain and soldiery(?) for the protection of his land he stationed therein.
>
> (TCL 3 ll. 203ff.)

After Sargon's capture of Ulhu and its royal palace, he was impressed by the great wine-cellars he found:

> I entered his hidden wine-cellar, and the whole body of the troops of Ashur ladled out the good wine like river-water with hoses and leatherbuckets.
>
> (TCL 3 l. 226)

The image of an idyllic landscape, its prosperity created and protected by the king, is striking in these passages.

* * *

In spite of a considerable amount of archaeological material, it remains very hard to be precise about Urartu's history and organisation. But its size, the length of time it lasted, its raw materials (copper, silver, iron), its fertility and extensive pasturage, and its great material wealth serve as a salutary reminder that Assyria had a very serious, at times threatening, rival in the scramble for resources, commercial control and political domination.

10b Phrygia and Lydia

If the history of Urartu is woefully hazy, that of Phrygia and Lydia is even harder to trace in any detail. There is practically no local documentation which we can understand. Instead we have to rely on sporadic and incidental mentions in Assyrian sources and a certain amount in Greek accounts (especially Herodotus on Lydia, see p. 567ff.). The archaeological material, by contrast, is impressive (particularly for Phrygia) and provides tantalising glimpses of these powerful, but poorly understood, kingdoms.

Phrygia

The Phrygian state seems to have developed at some point in the dark period following the collapse of the Hittite empire (*c.* mid-twelfth century). It is thought to have included groups that moved into the region from the west (Thrace) and eastern Anatolia. Its chief political centre was Gordion (in the Ankara region) in Greater Phrygia. But by the eighth century its control extended eastwards beyond the Halys to embrace the heartland of the earlier Hittite state (Boğazköy). This may have been the region settled by the people called 'Mushki' in Assyrian texts (Sevin 1991). Because the Assyrians first came into contact with the eastern end of the Phrygian state, they used the name Mushki for the whole kingdom. Greek legend preserves dim echoes of the fabled wealth of the kingdom in the story of 'the golden touch of King Midas', and a Midas was said to have made a dedication at Delphi (Herodotus 1.14); but little more of any substance, save the additional royal names, Gordias and Adrastus, are preserved in the classical sources. The Midas of Greek stories clearly corresponds to 'King Mita of Mushki' of the Assyrian texts from the later eighth century (*RLA* 8: 271–273).

Quite how far Phrygian control stretched is uncertain. Finds of pottery and inscriptions suggest that it reached from the region of the salt lakes into Cappadocia. Most spectacular are the finds from Gordion itself and the magnificent sculpted rock façades at several Phrygian centres, such as 'Midas City'. A specifically Phrygian cultural trait is the great tumuli used for royal and aristocratic burials, which recall the burial mounds of south Russia dating to the second millennium. The largest ones date to the late eighth century when Phrygia was at the acme of its power. They were elaborately constructed with timber beams and furnished with substantial, but not lavish, grave-goods – the items were fine bronze utensils, rather than precious metal ones (Young 1981). One large excavated tumulus contained the complete

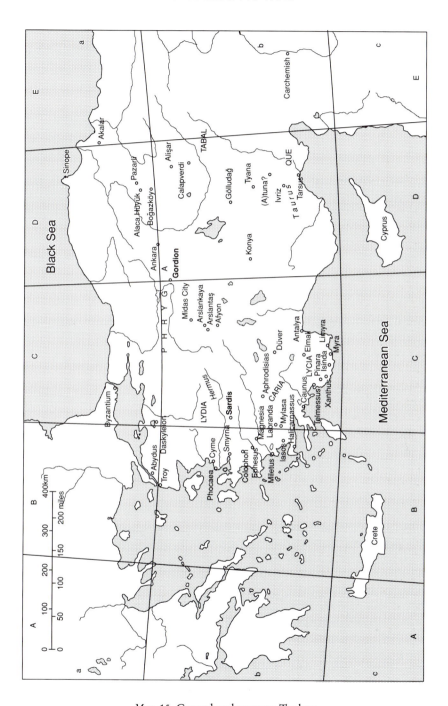

Map 15 Central and western Turkey

skeleton of a man. The grave furniture, size and location of the burial suggested that this was a Phrygian king, probably Midas himself. Using the well-preserved skull, a forensic specialist has been able plausibly to reconstruct the original head, so that the features of this great ruler can now be viewed (Prag 1989).

The small states in southern Cappadocia had close relations with Phrygia, as shown by inscriptions, Assyrian references and finds of Phrygian pottery. Particularly close seem to have been the links between Phrygia and Tyana (Tuhana). It is possible that the so-called 'Black Stone of Tyana' represents a Phrygian version of the local king's proclamation inscribed on a stele in Neo-Hittite hieroglyphs (*CAH* III/2: 625–626). If that is right, it is important evidence of Phrygia's power. This same ruler, Warpalawas of Tyana, also accompanied King Midas' emissary to the Assyrian governor in Cilicia (SAA 1 no. 1, see below), when the Phrygian king made overtures for peace with Sargon II, which, again, points to particularly close links between this small

Figure 35 King Warpalawas of Tyana (right) praying to a god of fertility; near Ivriz
(drawing by D. Saxon)

564

state and Phrygia. It is also likely that a rock monument shows Warpalawas wearing a Phrygian garment (Boehmer 1973; see fig. 35). Phrygian links with Neo-Hittite Carchemish are reflected in the development of the iconography of the Phrygian goddess Matar Kybele and the strong Neo-Hittite influence in sculpted decoration found near Ankara and at Gordion (*CAH* III/2: 642). Phrygian interest in southern Cappadocia, and even further south and east, was perceived as a political threat by the Assyrians, who repeatedly accused small states of making common cause with the Phrygian king, Midas. Assyria's fears were probably not without foundation, particularly when we realise that Carchemish also had for a while links with Urartu – the eastern neighbour and natural partner for Phrygia.[4] A Phrygian–Urartian coalition was a real threat to Assyria's dominance. It was one of Sargon II's greatest achievements to have succeeded in breaking up the close linkage between these two powerful northern states, vividly illustrated by a remarkable letter from Nimrud:

> The king's word to Ashur-sharru-u[sur] (governor of Que/Cilicia): I am well, Assyria is well: you can be glad.
>
> As to what you wrote to me: 'A messenger [of] Midas, the Phrygian, has come to me, bringing me 14 men of Que whom Urik (a local dynast) had sent to Urartu as an embassy' – this is extremely good! My gods, Ashur, Shamash, Bel and Nabû have now taken action, and without a battle [or any]thing, the Phrygian has given us his word and become our ally! As to what you wrote: 'I shall not send my messenger to the Phrygian without the permission of the king, my lord!' – I am now writing to (tell) you that you should not cut off your messenger from the Phrygian's presence. Write to him in friendly terms and constantly listen to news about him, until I have more time.
>
> As to what you wrote: 'Should I send his subjects to him just as he sent me the subjects of the king my lord?' – send them to him that he will be favourably disposed towards us. Whether 100 of his men or 10, write to him like this: 'I wrote to the king my lord about the men of Que whom you sent me, and he was extremely pleased; and in return he wrote to me [as follows]: "Do not hold back even a single one of the Phrygians at your court, but send them to Midas [immediately?]" Thus at the king my lord's behest I am (now) sending you th[ese] men.'
>
> As to what you wrote: 'A messenger of Urpala'a (Warpalawas, king of Tuhana/Tyana, Cappadocia) came to me for an audience with the Phrygian messenger' – let him come, and let Ashur, Shamash, Bel and Nabû command that all these kings should polish your sandals with their beards (i.e. by prostrating themselves for the formal obeisance)!
>
> As to what you wrote: 'Kilar (local dynast in Que) [has request]ed from me four districts, saying: "Let them give them to me"' – should you give them to Kilar, would he not become your equal, and what would you yourself be ruling over as governor then? Tell him as

follows: 'Earlier, you were afraid of the Phrygian, but now the Phrygian has made peace with us, so what are you afraid of? Now eat your bread and drink your water under the protection of the king, my lord, and be happy. Do not worry about the Phrygian.'

As to what you wrote: 'Urpala'a [may slip away?] from the king, my lord, on account of the fact that the people of Atunna (Tynna, Cappadocia) and Istuanda (in Cappadocia) came and took the cities of Bit-Paruta away from him' – now that the Phrygian has made peace with us and . . ., what can all the kings of Tabal (Cappadocia) do henceforth? You will press them from this side and the Phrygian from that side so that (in no time) you will 'snap your belt' on them. Thanks to my gods Ashur, Shamash, Bel and Nabû, this land has now been trodden under your feet! Move about as you please, do whatever you have to do, cut the long and lengthen the short(?) until I come and give you work.

(The end of the letter concerns other matters.)

(*SAA* 1 no. 1)

It is probable that, as a result of this concordat between Assyria and Phrygia, commercial and cultural links intensified between the two states. Eastern imports found in Gordion may reflect this: among them is an ivory horse-bridle attachment closely comparable to the Nimrud ivories in style and technique (although it is not impossible that it was imported from north Syria at an earlier date).

Phrygian inscriptions are not as yet very well understood (Brische and Lejeune 1984; *CAH* III/2: 666–669). They are usually divided into two groups, 'Old Phrygian' and 'Neo-Phrygian'. The older group can be assigned to the period between the eighth and third centuries, while the later ones date to the Roman period, after a gap of several centuries. The script used is an alphabetic one with affinities to some of the early Greek alphabets. What is debated is from where the Phrygians adopted their alphabet: a north Syrian source is not impossible, given the links of the Phrygians with some of the Neo-Hittite principalities, and the attested strong Phoenician and Aramaic influences in Cilicia, which included inscriptions (see chapters 8b; 8c). But it is more usually assumed that the script was derived from the Greeks, although the late and gradual evidence for 'hellenisation' in Phrygian material culture – not until after *c.* 680/670 (*CAH* III/2: 630–631) – needs to be noted. The classification of the Phrygian language also bristles with problems, and it is still not certain whether it belongs to the Indo-European family or not. The one thing that seems to be undisputed is that it has no close links with the earlier Hittite or Luwian languages (*CAH* III/2: 668–669).

Some time early in the seventh century the Phrygian centres suffered a destruction, associated by later Greek writers with the Cimmerians. There is no reason to question this, especially as there is evidence that Urartu, a little earlier (p. 558), and Lydia, a little later, also suffered from raids by these people. Phrygian sites were rebuilt in an entirely Phrygian style after the destructions. This implies that a kingdom of sorts, probably greatly weakened and reduced, survived – a suggestion borne out by the mention in Herodotus (1.35) of the continued existence of a Phrygian royal house down to the sixth century. Following the Cimmerian ravaging of Phrygia, Lydia, much further west and centred on Sardis, developed its power and, eventually, came to dominate Phrygia too. The Lydian domination is reflected in the very gradual appearance of west Anatolian and Greek pottery and other Greek elements on Phrygian sites (*CAH* III/2: 630–631; Schaus 1992).

Lydia

The history of Lydia, with its capital at Sardis, is known to us from the stories contained in Book I of Herodotus' *Histories* (Herodotus 1.6–94). His aim was to set out how the small Greek city-states came into conflict with the great Achaemenid Persian empire in the later sixth and fifth centuries, so he began by examining the Greeks' nearest powerful neighbour who preceded the Persians. This was the Lydian kingdom, which represented for the Greeks a large and fabulously wealthy, as well as menacing, state. A lot of local Greek stories and exploits are woven into Herodotus' tale, and the factual historical content of his Lydian *logos* is actually quite slight. There is a long novella about the rise of the Mermnad kings (beginning with Gyges, see table 30), and an extended, partly moralising, description of the reign and fall of Lydia's last king, Croesus; the other kings are treated sparsely. Herodotus' prime focus was the experience of Greek cities *vis-à-vis* the Lydian rulers – not a balanced assessment of the history and organisation of Lydia.

According to Herodotus, there had been a long-lived dynasty ruling in Lydia, the Heraclids, whose last king, Candaules, was deposed by one of his courtiers, Gyges, who thus founded the new Mermnad line of Lydian rulers. The precise lengths of reign that Herodotus gives for the Mermnads make it possible to date Gyges' seizure of power into the early seventh century. Although only a very little of the grandeur of pre-Achaemenid Sardis, Lydia's capital, can as yet be glimpsed, the long-standing American excavations there (Hanfman 1983b) do suggest that the settlement became a much more impressive site around this time and houses roughly contemporary with Gyges' reign have been found. So it was in the early seventh century, following the demise of Phrygia, that Lydia began to extend its territories and control. Greek cities on the Aegean coast were attacked, suzerainty over some was established and links with Greek sanctuaries, such as Delphi, were created through lavish royal dedications that astonished the Greeks. One source of Lydia's wealth was the gold extracted from deposits washed down by the

Table 30 Anatolia *c.* 740–*c.* 540: Chronology

Assyria/Babylonia	Lydia	Phrygia	Iran
Sargon II (721–705)		Midas (738–696/5?)	
Sennacherib (704–681)	Heraclid dynasty		
Esarhaddon (680–669)	Gyges (*c.* 680–*c.* 652)		
Ashurbanipal (668–*c.* 631)	Ardys (*c.* 652–*c.* 630)		
Ashur-etel-ilani (*c.* 630–623?)	Sadyattes (*c.* 630–*c.* 610)		
Sin-shar-ishkun (622?-612)			Cyaxares (625–585)
Asshur-uballit II (611–609)	Alyattes (*c.* 610–*c.* 560)		
Nabopolassar (626–605)			Astyages (585–550)
Nebuchadnezzar II (604–562)			
Amel-Marduk (561–560)	Croesus		
Neriglissar (559–556)	(*c.* 560–540s)		Cyrus (II) the Great (559–539)
Nabonidus (559–539)			

Pactolus river, on whose banks Sardis lay. They began to be exploited at this time to underpin the state's expansionist policies.

But Gyges himself and his son, Ardys, had to face continuous threats from the Cimmerians over a period of time (about twenty years); at one point they even succeeded in burning Sardis. In this critical situation, the Lydian king appealed to Ashurbanipal of Assyria (668–*c.* 630) for Assyrian help against this menace. The Assyrian monarch granted him aid and, for a while at least, friendly relations obtained between the two states, confirmed by Gyges sending Cimmerian prisoners-of-war in iron fetters to Ashurbanipal, after a Lydian victory over them. When the Lydians first approached the Assyrians, the latter were astonished by the strangeness and distance of their kingdom:

> . . . his (sc. Gyges') rider [set out] to enquire after my well-being. He reached the border of my country. My men spotted him, and asked him: 'Who are you stranger, you, whose (country's) rider never travelled the road to the frontier?' They brought him [. . .] to Nineveh, my royal city, into my presence. (But of) all the languages of east and west, over which the god Ashur has given me control, there was no

interpreter of his tongue. His language was foreign, so that his words were not understood.

(Cogan and Tadmor 1977: 68)

Gyges also set up links with the newly emerging independent power of Egypt under Psammetichus I (664–610; see ch.12b). He seems to have supplied him with additional soldiers, including probably Greeks and Carians. What the relations between Caria and Lydia were at this point is not clearly known, although a late source (Plutarch *Quaestiones Graecae* 45) says that one of the local Carian dynasts, Arselis of Mylasa, helped Gyges in his usurpation of the throne. The reference points in the direction of political alliances between the Lydian court and the local élites of adjoining states. Such a conclusion is strengthened by the fact that Ardys' successor, Alyattes, is supposed to have been married to a Carian woman (the mother of the last Lydian king, Croesus, cf. Herodotus 1.92) and an Ionian.

Herodotus' picture of Alyattes is that of an energetic consolidator of the kingdom and an aggressive expansionist. His siege and capture of the Greek city of Smyrna (Herodotus 1.16) has been confirmed archaeologically (*CAH* III/2: 647–648). It was also he who seems to have expanded Lydian power definitively over Phrygia, where a massive fortress was constructed at Gordion (Hanfman 1983a: 71). This brought him into conflict with a new power, the Medes (see chapters 9e; 13b), who were laying claim to the territory of Cappadocia. The war between the two powers dragged on for six years, and only ended in May 585 on the occasion of a solar eclipse, which was taken as a bad omen by the combatants (Herodotus 1.74). Peace between the two sides was negotiated by the ruler of Cilicia and the Babylonian king, and sealed by the marriage of Alyattes' daughter, Aryenis, to the son of the Median ruler, Astyages.

It was Croesus, Alyattes' successor, who reaped the rewards of his predecessors' wars. Under him all of Anatolia west of the Halys, except Caria and Lycia, were either directly or indirectly subject to Lydia. To the south-east the kingdom fronted on western Cilicia, which had come under Babylonian control in 556 (*ABC* no. 6). Westwards, friendly relations were established with the Ionian islanders. According to Herodotus, Croesus built up an alliance against the growing power of Persia (whose king, Cyrus, had conquered the Medes in 550 (*ABC* no. 7, ii.1–4)), including Babylonia, Egypt and Sparta, and he was, of course, dynastically linked through his sister to the defeated Median king. Lydia was at the acme of its power. Greeks flocked to Croesus' court; according to Herodotus (1.29), they were mainly sophists, including the famous Athenian lawgiver, poet and sage, Solon. It is very likely that craftsmen would also have been attracted by such a wealthy patron. Certainly Croesus' spectacular dedications to Delphi (Herodotus 1.50–51) included a gigantic silver bowl, said to have been made by Theodorus of Samos (cf. the silver bowl with a welded iron stand dedicated by Alyattes, and said to have been made by Glaucus of Chios, Herodotus 1.25). But cultural influences probably moved not just in one direction. Croesus contributed substantially to the rebuilding of the Artemis temple at Ephesus, providing a number of magnificent columns (Herodotus 1.92) – the ethnicity of the stone-cutters is not known.[5] Several small ivories from Ephesus (*CAH* III plates vol.: 286–287) are thought to represent a 'Lydian' art-style, although defining such a style and separating it from 'Greek' is problematic (*CAH* III/2: 654–655): some early sixth-century pictorial tomb-paintings in the Phrygo-Lydian area and fine Lydian-style pottery with animal friezes (*CAH* III/2: 650) provide tantalising hints of the sophistication of Anatolian art-production. At the Carian-Greek site of Ephesus, where an important Hellenic cult, incorporating Anatolian and Greek features, was located, there is a definite suggestion that artistic styles and craft traditions mingled.

It is unfortunate that more traces of this grand period of Lydian history have not been recovered, although we can dimly discern its magnificence in the American excavations at Sardis (Ramage 1987). There is some cultural similarity to Phrygia in the use of tumuli (at Bintepe) for burials, including royal ones (e.g. the great tumulus of Alyattes and the possible 'Gyges tomb'), although there are formal differences too. But, unlike the Phrygian tombs, all the Lydian ones opened so far have been robbed, so that the undoubtedly wonderful grave-gifts they once held have vanished. Sardis consisted of an acropolis with a palace, located on the north slopes of the Tmolus (Boz Dağ), which dominated the lower walled town and Hermos plain. It was a nodal point for east–west routes, and the extensive plains were agriculturally rich. Tumbling down the Tmolus mountain was the tributary of the Hermos, the Pactolus river, which washed down and deposited electrum, a mixture of gold and silver, first exploited by the Mermnad kings, to obtain gold. It was used to produce the first coined money, although the exact date is still disputed. The gold-refinery has been located at Sardis near the main north–south road. Here, too, lay the great Artemis temple, probably representing a form of the Lydian Kubaba, linked to the Phrygian Matar Kubele. The market was also in this area. From Herodotus' description (5.101), it appears that many Sardian houses used reeds in their construction and had thatched roofs. The archaeological evidence, by contrast, shows that early in the sixth century spacious houses, inhabited by the wealthier segment of the population, roofed with tiles and decorated with terracotta friezes, formed part of the townscape (Hanfman 1983a: 69–72). This mirrors the increasing wealth commanded by the Lydian rulers following the great upsurge in their power.

Little is known of Lydia's political structure. King Herod's court-historian and philosopher, Nicolaus of Damascus, who used a number of earlier local histories, said that the Lydian crown-prince was governor of the Adramyttion area, in the Troad (*FGrH* 90 F65). It is possible that Phrygia was ruled by local kings subject to Lydia, while the Greek cities certainly retained their own local governments despite subjection to Lydian power. Socio-cultural aspects of Lydia are also poorly known. There are hints that the lion was associated symbolically with the kingship, which would explain the use of a lion's forefront on Lydian coins and possibly also the inscription 'walwi', which, it has been suggested, means 'lion' in Lydian (Wallace 1988). It is also possible that a specific royal artistic imagery was evolving (*CAH* III/2: 650). The Lydian language is more fully attested than Phrygian in inscriptions from the sixth to fourth centuries; it used an analogous alphabet (although local variants existed). Lydian is clearly related to the earlier Hittite–Luwian language group (see chapter 5b), but the number of texts is not yet sufficient to allow for a full understanding (*RLA* 7: 186).

Figure 36 Set of pottery, knife-blade and puppy skeleton, remains of a 'ritual dinner'; from Sardis (drawing by D. Saxon)

An intriguing discovery was made at Sardis in the years between 1961 and 1970: about thirty caches of artefacts were found in the residential and commercial districts of the city. Each cache contained four pottery vessels – a single-handled jug, a small pitcher, a deep cup and a shallow dish (see fig. 36) – and an iron knife; each jug contained the skeletal remains of a puppy. In a careful study of these finds (Greenewalt 1976), it was argued convincingly that these were the residue of ritual meals offered to a Lydian god or hero, to whom dogs were especially important. The identity of the god is not certain, but may perhaps have been Kandaulas, whose name was associated by classical writers with the meaning 'puppy-choker'. Even more mysterious is the possible occasion on which the ritual meals were eaten. If they happened regularly, why were there not more remains and why are they not spread over a longer period? In the view of the excavator of Sardis, Hanfman, the ritual must have been performed on the occasion of a specific crisis, which he thought could have been the Persian siege of Sardis in the 540s (Hanfman 1983a: 96).

The Persian defeat of Croesus spelt the end of Lydian independence and its dynasty, but Sardis became the capital of the most important north-western Achaemenid province and Lydian culture and language continued to flourish. Sardis remained one of the great cities of the ancient world for many centuries to come.

Notes

1 A new book has just been published on the Cimmerians, which I have not yet seen: A.I. Ivantchik 1993 *Les Cimmériens au Proche-Orient* (Orbis Biblicus et Orientalis 127) Freiburg. For an offbeat interpretation of the Cimmerians, see Kristensen 1988.

2 A joint American–Armenian archaeological team is now investigating the site of Horom, north-west Armenia, which may well produce material to fill some of the gaps in Urartu's prehistory. It indicates the existence of a highly developed site in the Early Iron Age (late second to first millennium); see Badaljan *et al.* 1992; 1993.

3 'Mannaea' was the general term used by the Assyrians for the small kingdoms of the northern Zagros. The site of Hasanlu IV (south of Lake Urmia) has provided the most important evidence of the development and rich culture of a Mannaean city (Dyson 1964; 1965; Porada 1965, ch. IX).

4 Işik 1987 has argued for substantial Urartian influence on Phrygian rock monuments.

5 Some of Croesus' column-bases can be seen in the British Museum.

11

BABYLONIA c. 900–539

11a Introduction

We can subdivide the period from c. 900 to 539 in southern Mesopotamia
into several phases: most of the ninth century is a time of recovery and relative
stability (as far as we can tell); the late ninth century and most of the eighth
is marked by severe political disturbances, ending in Assyrian invasion and
conquest; for most of the seventh century, Babylonia was firmly under
Assyrian domination, until Nabopolassar (626–605) liberated it (see chapter
9e) and founded the Neo-Babylonian empire; finally, from 605–539 Babylonia controlled an empire comparable to the Assyrian realm until its last
king, Nabonidus, was defeated by Cyrus the Great of Persia. Before sketching
the historical events, we need to consider the sources and the broad political
landscape.

The sources

Sources illuminating the fluctuating fortunes of Babylonia between c. 900 and
539 are unevenly distributed in the period. The convention of Babylonian
royal inscriptions, unlike the Assyrian ones, is to stress almost exclusively the
pious building-work of kings, not to describe in any detail their military
achievements. This is true even of the numerous lengthy texts of the great
warrior kings of the Neo-Babylonian empire, which succeeded the Neo-
Assyrian at the end of the seventh century (c. 610–539): Nabopolassar,
Nebuchadnezzar II, Neriglissar and Nabonidus (Langdon 1912; see also
Berger 1973). One result is that much of Babylonian history is reconstructed
on the basis of Assyrian accounts, which give only a very partial picture.
Fortunately, the great *Babylonian Chronicle* series (see p. 477), beginning
around 744, provides an invaluable outline of events, although the series is
by no means completely preserved (*ABC* nos. 1–7) and its information is
often very terse.

Contemporary documents relating to social and economic affairs are,
generally speaking, small in number in the period from the ninth to the

seventh centuries (Brinkman 1968; 1984a; Brinkman and Kennedy 1983; 1986), but copious from then on right through the Persian conquest of Babylon in 539 and down to the early fifth century (Dandamaev 1984; 1990; *CAH* IV ch. 3a). A considerable number are private texts from Babylon, including the archive of a prominent 'banking' family, the Egibi, who operated in Babylonia and beyond from the late seventh century to the end of the sixth century (Weingort 1939; Ungnad 1941–4; also Shiff 1987; Wunsch 1993). But the bulk of texts comes from the archives of two Babylonian temples: that of Eanna, the great shrine of Ishtar in Uruk, is the biggest and best-studied; the other comes from the important Shamash temple in Sippar, and has been rather less intensively analysed (San Nicoló 1941; MacGinnis 1991). The chronological span of the archives is roughly the sixth century. One facet of the Babylonian state scarcely represented by documents is the central authority: nothing like the rich collection of royal correspondence that illuminates the working of the Assyrian empire exists for Babylonia. One exception is a few texts relating to the issue of rations at the Babylonian court in the early sixth century (Weidner 1939). But there are letters written by Babylonian communities, individuals, temple administrators and Assyrian officials stationed in Babylonia to the Assyrian king (or vice versa) in the Kuyunjik and Nimrud archives (eighth and seventh centuries, see p. 501). They shed light on the Babylonian response to Assyrian political intervention and then domination.

Another important source is the *Synchronistic History* (*ABC* no. 21; see p. 491), which provides a generally hostile picture of Babylonia *vis-à-vis* Assyria. But, in the absence of other evidence for the ninth and early eighth century, it does tell us about some important events. A further source, which supplements our material, is the Old Testament, especially the circumstances leading to the destruction of the Jerusalem temple and the extinction of the kingdom of Judah by Nebuchadnezzar II in 587. It contains insights into Neo-Babylonian imperial policy, which is otherwise only very scantily attested.

Archaeological remains of the time before the Neo-Babylonian empire (610–539) are slight, because many Babylonian cities were extensively rebuilt by the Neo-Babylonian rulers, in particular by Nebuchadnezzar II (604–562). Babylon is the most striking example of this: the massive Ishtar gate (now in Berlin) and beautifully paved processional way, decorated with brilliant blue- and gold-glazed bricks and brick reliefs, must rank as one of the most stunning archaeological finds ever made (Strommenger and Hirmer 1965 [OM] pl. XLIV). Settlement surveys have suggested that, in the ninth to seventh centuries, Babylonia saw a decrease in the number of large centres, an increase of village settlements in some areas, and a general decline in population density (Adams 1981). But full analysis of the findings is still needed and some criticisms have been levelled at the methods employed in arriving at the results (Brinkman 1984b).

To sum up: Babylonia's history between c. 900 and 745 is very thinly documented. Between 744 and the 620s, the Babylonian chronicles and Assyrian documents give us a much better picture of conditions in the country. Finally, the time from c. 610 to 539, when Babylonia had a large empire before falling to the Persians, is the best-documented – long royal inscriptions, several chronicles, a wealth of business texts and many impressive building remains.

The population of Babylonia

A feature of basic importance for understanding the history of Babylonia in this period is the fact that several distinct groups and patterns of political organisation co-existed. First, there were the Chaldaean tribes: three major ones held extensive stretches of tribal territory, including centres described in Assyrian texts as 'royal cities'. They were fortified with walls, and their palaces were filled with substantial quantities of commercially acquired wealth, such as ivory, gold and exotic timber. Incense, from South Arabia, was probably another item which was traded through Chaldaean territory. The name and location of the main Chaldaean tribes was: a) Bit Dakkuri, in the region south of Babylon; b) Bit Amukani, on the lower Euphrates above Uruk; c) Bit Yakin, by far the most powerful, located roughly in the region of the 'Sealand', i.e. the territory around the old city of Ur and the marshy region to the east (RLA VIII 6–10). Besides the Chaldaean tribes (but almost certainly ethnically unrelated to them, see above, chapter 8b), there was an immense number of small tribal groups of Aramaeans (about forty tribal names are attested) living in tiny settlements. They were not united politically and seem to have engaged in little more than subsistence farming. The main concentrations of Aramaeans were in the south, near the Elamite border and east of the Tigris – well away from the main Babylonian cities, although Aramaeans sometimes made hostile encroachments on the rich fields of Babylonian city-dwellers, perhaps pushed to do so by famine. These unassimilated Chaldaean and Aramaean groups lived cheek by jowl with the old, traditional urban communities – centred on their great sanctuaries, with their own civic administration, but subject to the king in Babylon.

The main arena for conflict between Babylonia and Assyria was the region around the Diyala river, where the important route leading from the Iranian plateau debouched. Another spot where the interests of the two countries could clash was the north-west where, just beyond Rapiqu (downstream from modern Hit), lay the wealthy state of Suhu. Links between Suhu and Babylonia seem to have been close: Babylonians gave military aid to Suhu from time to time; Suhu's considerable wealth (see p. 483) implies that it had commercial ties with Babylonia through which the main routes ran; possibly also significant is the fact that the local rulers of Suhu had Akkadian names (Ismail, et al. 1983; Cavigneaux and Ismail 1990).

11b *c.* 900–705

Co-operation and conflict: Babylonia and Assyria *c.* 900–747

The ninth century in Babylonia was marked by a reasonable recovery after the terrible problems of the preceding hundred and fifty or so years (see pp. 378–379). The dynasty was comparatively stable, and a peace-treaty with Assyria was concluded (see p. 482), which was reaffirmed after Shalmaneser III's campaign to help the Babylonian king retain his throne (851). A beautiful foundation text commemorates the refashioning of the divine image of Shamash by Nabu-apla-iddina (*c.* 870 (table 31); King 1912 no.XXXVI),

Table 31 Babylonian chronology: *c.* 900–605

Babylonia		Assyria	
Nabu-shuma-ukin I	*c.* 895	Adad-nirari II	911–891
		Tukulti-Ninurta II	890–884
Nabu-apla-iddina	*c.* 870	Ashur-nasir-pal II	883–859
Marduk-zakir-shumi I	*c.* 854–819	Shalmaneser III	858–824
		Shamshi-Adad V	823–811
Marduk-balassu-iqbi	*c.* 818–813		
Baba-aha-iddina	812		
(5 unknown kings)		Adad-nirari III	810–783
Ninurta-apla-x			
Marduk-bel-zeri		Shalmaneser IV	782–773
Marduk-apla-usur			
Eriba-Marduk	*c.* 770	Ashur-dan III	772–755
Nabu-shuma-ishkun	*c.* 760–748	Ashur-nirari V	754–745
Nabu-nasir	747–734	Tiglath-pileser III	744–727
Nabu-nadin-zeri	733–732		
Nabu-shuma-ukin II	732		
Nabu-mukin-zeri	731–729		
←	[728–7]	(= 'Pulu)	
←	Shalmaneser V	726–722 (= 'Ululayu') ——→	
Marduk-apla-iddina II	721–710	Sargon II	721–705
←	[709–705]		
		Sennacherib	704–681
←	[704–703]		
6 kings: Assyrian appointees and Babylonian rebels	703–689		
←— [official Babylonian sources: 'no king'		688–681]	
←	Esarhaddon	680–669 ——————→	
←	668–667	—— Ashurbanipal	668–631(?)
Shamash-shum-ukin (Ashurbanipal's brother)	667–648		
Kandalanu (Ashurbanipal's appointee)	647–627		
One year without king	627–626	[political and dynastic confusion	
Nabopolassar	626–605	in Assyria; defeated; falls *c.* 609/608]	

which accompanied new temple endowments at Sippar – a sure sign of a return to political normality. Because of the alliance between Babylonia and Assyria, the Babylonians helped Shamshi-Adad V to accede to the Assyrian throne in succession to Shalmaneser III (823; see p. 490). A few years later (814?), however, political problems arose in Babylonia, and Shamshi-Adad V, honouring the treaty in his turn, moved into Babylonia. The situation must have been very serious, because the Assyrian intervention failed to bring about an acceptable solution. Shamshi-Adad V, therefore, treated Babylonia as a hostile country: he captured Dur Papsukkal and Der (east of the Tigris), the gods of the latter were removed, and the Babylonian king, Baba-aha-iddina, was taken prisoner (812). It is clear that the Assyrian king wrought havoc in the always contentious north-eastern area. But he went even further and assumed for a time the title 'king of Sumer and Akkad', which suggests that he laid claim to some kind of suzerainty; he also appears to have levied tax on some Babylonian cities.

The details of the period following Shamshi-Adad V's intrusion are very confused and obscure. Babylonian politics was in such chaos that even the sequence of Babylonian kings is unknown for some time, and one document is dated to 'year 5, no king'. Adad-nirari III of Assyria (810–783), heir to the anarchy created by Shamshi-Adad V, tried to normalise the situation by reconstructing the country politically. This took the form of some cultic rebuilding and the return of deported peoples. Yet it seems that the northern Babylonian cities continued *de facto* to be under direct Assyrian control, shown by this entry in the *Synchronistic History*:

> He brought [back] the abducted peoples [and?] laid upon them an income, a regular contribution (and) barley rations. The peoples of Assyria (and) Karduniash (i.e. Babylon) were joined together.
>
> (*ABC* no. 21 iv 19–21)

Further evidence for Assyrian sovereignty is that the inhabitants of Babylon, Borsippa and Cutha sent the Assyrian king 'the remnants' of divine meals, normally offered to the Babylonian ruler only. Moreover, Adad-nirari III sent offerings to Babylonian shrines as the local ruler might do, rather than going in person to worship, as a pious outsider would normally have done. This situation of effective Assyrian rule over northern Babylonia is presented in the Assyrian-centred *Synchronistic History*, which ends at this point, as right and just for Babylonia:

> Let a later prince, who wishes to achieve fame in Akkad (i.e. Babylonia), write about the prowess of [his] victories. [Let him] continually [turn?] to this [very] stele (and) [look at it?] that it may not be forgotten. Let the . . . vizier heed all that is [engraved? (thereon)]. May the praises of Assyria be lauded for[ever]. May the crime of Sumer and Akkad be bruited abroad through every quarter (i.e. of the world).
>
> (*ABC* no. 21 iv 23–30)

One result of Assyrian domination in the north of the country was that the fulcrum of political activity within Babylonia shifted from the north to the south, and that the Chaldaean leaders gradually entered more directly into Babylonian politics. When Adad-nirari III died and Assyria entered on a period of relative impotence, a Chaldaean from Bit Yakin, Eriba-Marduk (c. 770), made a successful bid for the Babylonian throne. He was able to establish reasonable control over the country, re-asserting Babylonian authority over the Diyala area and preventing Aramaean encroachments on city-owned land. A time of relative calm seems to have followed, although Eriba-Marduk was not able to make the Chaldaean hold on the throne a permanent feature of Babylonian politics.

The Assyrian conquest of Babylonia: 747–705

With the reign of Nabu-nasir (747–734), we can glean rather more information with the help of the *Babylonian Chronicle* (*ABC* no. 1). Early in his reign, Tiglath-pileser III of Assyria (744–727) seized control of the disputed east Tigris–Diyala region, and consolidated his gain by moving further into Babylonia to levy tribute from the Chaldaean tribes and worship reverently in one of the great Babylonian shrines at Hursagkalamma (near Kish). Although he claimed the title 'king of Sumer and Akkad', this seems to have expressed a purely formal, though potentially significant, claim to guarantee the political *status quo* in Babylonia. Despite an appearance of tranquillity and central governmental control, there are hints that communications between different parts of the country were difficult. Repairs to the New Year festival shrine at Uruk, for example, had to be undertaken by the local authorities because the king had neither the resources, nor perhaps sufficient control, to carry out such building-work, which was normally one of the most important royal duties:

> To Usur-amassu (goddess connected with Uruk), the exalted lady, who gives (oracular) judgments for the land, who makes decisions for the heavens and netherworld, daughter of Adad, beloved of Marduk, whose word is unalterable.
> The *akītu*-temple (New Year festival temple) – which long ago had grown old, whose name had been forgotten, and which stood in ruins – its walls had collapsed and their foundations crumbled; its outlines had been forgotten and their shape changed. Neither king nor commissioner (*qīpu*) nor dignitary (*rubû*) nor city ruler (*bēl āli*) had turned his attention to perform this task and to renew the *akītu*-temple. Finally, Bel-ibni and Nabu-zera-ushabshi, sons of Bullutu of Uruk, turned their attention to perform this task and to renew the *akītu*-temple; and they wholeheartedly took up hoe and basket and built a chamber of pure abundance for the goddess. Wherefore, when Usur-ammassu, the

exalted lady, enters joyfully into her *akītu*-temple and when she sits on high in the dwelling of her great divinity, may she steadily turn her shining countenance upon Bel-ibni and Nabu-zera-ushabshi; and may she lengthen their days. They have built anew the *akītu*-temple to prolong their days, to sustain their lives, to ensure the wellbeing of their offspring, to ward off illness (from themselves).

(Date) Year 5, Nabu-nasir, king of Babylon (i.e.743). In the presence of Nabu-mukin-zeri, son of Nabu-apkal-ili, 'viceroy' (*šakkanakku*) of KUR.UG.UD.KI (unidentifiable place-name). (Document) which Arad-Nana, son of Annamua(?), *šangû* of Uruk, . . .

(Brinkman 1969)

The absence of the king's role in this document is emphasised: no king nor any other member of the central government was prepared to undertake the desperately needed repairs; two prosperous local inhabitants shouldered the burden instead. They did not carry out the work as a display of loyalty to the king (which is how it could have been presented; A. Falkenstein, *Topographie von Uruk* (Leipzig 1941): 4–8), but called down divine blessings on themselves alone as the sole benefactors of the city. Yet the dating formula of the text shows that Nabu-nasir's rule was acknowledged in Uruk.

An indicator of Nabu-nasir's relative (if limited) success as king is that he was succeeded by his son, Nabu-nadin-zeri (733–732). But the underlying anarchy is reflected by the fact that the latter was assassinated, less than two years later, by one of his provincial governors, Nabu-shuma-ukin II (732). He, in turn, was rapidly eliminated by the ruler of the Chaldaean tribe of Amukanu, Nabu-mukin-zeri (731–729), who was obviously able to exploit this unstable situation. This Chaldaean seizure of the throne allowed the Assyrians to intensify their involvement in internal Babylonian affairs. Assyrian intervention is now illuminated by some of the Nimrud letters (Saggs 1955). The Assyrians were able to set up a military control- and marshalling-point in northern Babylonia from which they launched their offensives, beginning in 731. The course of events is hard to disentangle completely, but some areas and cities, including Aramaean groups, seem to have been friendly to the Assyrian forces, and one letter (NL 1; quoted p. 616) suggests that Nabu-mukin-zeri's hold of the city of Babylon was rather shaky. Tiglath-pileser III eventually triumphed: he detached yet further Aramaean groups east of the Tigris, incorporating them into the Assyrian province of Arrapha, and forced the submission of the Chaldaeans. The ruler of the southernmost tribe, Bit Yakin, a descendant of Eriba-Marduk, Marduk-apla-iddina (the biblical Merodach-baladan, 2 *Kings* 20.12), formally acknowledged Tiglath-pileser's lordship, and proffered royal gifts (Leemans 1944–8: 441–443).

Following the Assyrian victory over Nabu-mukin-zeri, Tiglath-pileser III proclaimed himself formally king of Babylonia, and for the next two years (729–727) celebrated the symbolically important New Year festival in Babylon (Black 1981; Kuhrt 1987). In combining the position of king of Assyria with the Babylonian kingship, he was followed by his son and successor, Shalmaneser V (726–722). Very little is known about precisely how this 'dual monarchy' was organised, but the available documentation shows that both Assyrian kings were definitely counted as rulers of Babylonia. In the Babylonian king-lists and chronicles, they are called by rather curious names: 'Pul(u)' (see also 2 *Kings* 15.19; 1 *Chronicles* 5.26) and 'Ululayu'; the reasons for this remain obscure (Brinkman 1968).[1]

With the usurpation of the Assyrian throne by Sargon II (721–705), the Assyrian arrangement of Babylonian affairs came to grief. Marduk-apla-iddina of Bit Yakin seized the opportunity together with his ally, the Elamite king, to detach Babylonia from Assyrian control. A great battle was fought in 720 at Der, in which the Assyrian army was defeated. Although Marduk-apla-iddina claims to have carried off the victory, the sober *Babylonian Chronicle* makes it clear that he arrived too late on the scene and that the victors were actually the Elamite forces (*ABC* no. 1 i 33–37). The Assyrian setback was sufficient for Sargon II to resign himself to the loss of Babylonia for the next ten years and accept Marduk-apla-iddina as the Babylonian sovereign: there were even trade contacts between Bit Yakin and Assyria (Durand 1979; Dalley and Postgate 1984 nos. 79–81 and p. 16).

The new Chaldaean ruler of Babylon took considerable pains to make himself acceptable to the inhabitants of the old cities by protecting (or restoring) their traditional privileges, returning (or granting) fields to urban communities and beautifying temples. He also presented himself as personally chosen by Marduk for the kingship from the entire world, after Marduk had abandoned Babylonia in anger (Leemans 1944–8: 444–448). This presumably refers to Assyrian rule of Babylonia which Marduk-apla-iddina had quashed, and served as a justification for his own seizure of the throne, to which he, after all, had no real claim. Marduk-apla-iddina's legitimising self-presentation forms the introduction to a land-gift (inscribed on a finely carved *kudurru* (boundary stone)), which Marduk-apla-iddina presented to the district governor (*šakin ṭēmi*) of Babylon (see fig. 37). The witnesses to the sealing of the grant listed near the end of the text show something of the administrative system in Babylonia at this time: members of the royal court, such as the crown-prince, palace herald and chief scribe appear; so do a provincial governor, the district governors of Kutha and Borsippa, the mayor (*hazannu*) of Babylon, and the chief administrator (*šatammu*) of Esagila, the main sanctuary of Marduk in Babylon. The presence of these officials suggests that the basic structure of urban institutions, as well as that of the central government, had survived the periods of chaos and anarchy.

There is no evidence of opposition to Marduk-apla-iddina II's reign among the urban population of Babylonia. But we must remember that the sources are not of a type to allow glimpses of dissension and resistance. When Sargon II reconquered Babylonia after 710 and drove Marduk-apla-iddina II into

Figure 37 Kudurru of Marduk-apla-iddina II
(Vorderasiatisches Museum, Berlin)

exile in Elam, he, too, presented himself as a legitimate and divinely chosen ruler, invited to become king by the Babylonian populace. Yet we know that Sargon, in fact, had to fight hard and persistently to dislodge Marduk-apla-iddina, including besieging him in his tribal centre of Dur-Yakin, and damaging substantially the economy of the region by cutting down date-palm groves. Sargon adopted the policy of his predecessors, becoming formally king of Babylonia and participating personally several times in the new year festival to strengthen (perhaps grudging) support among the leading groups of the urban inhabitants.[2] In keeping with his policy of conciliation, Sargon also confirmed their traditional privileges, as his defeated enemy had done just a few years earlier.

With the reconquest of Babylonia the Assyrians gained access to a region of great agricultural and commercial wealth. Its potential for high agricultural yields was enormous (Powell 1985), although it required careful organisation and control of the irrigation system to succeed. With respect to trade, Babylonia was central. One of the main caravan roads running across the desert from south Arabia had its terminus in southern Babylonia. In order to reap the full benefit of the important route linking the Iranian plateau to the Mesopotamian lowlands, it was essential to control northern Babylonia so that goods could be moved across from the Tigris to the Euphrates for transport westwards. Babylonia also provided the crucial link for the whole of western Asia with the Gulf and its rich resources and commerce (Potts 1990 [OGf]; Salles 1987). It is at present not clear what Babylonia's connections with the Gulf area had been since the Kassite period (see p. 340). The fact that Sargon received an embassy from Uperi, king of Dilmun (central Gulf), once his victory over Marduk-apla-iddina was assured, suggests that the ruler of Dilmun maintained close enough links with Babylonia to be anxious to negotiate new arrangements with the conqueror, and ensure that the market for goods traded through the Gulf would continue to function smoothly. Another result of Sargon's conquest of Babylonia was to marginalise Elam. He had already restricted its access to the Diyala route, and an important part of his activities during the long campaign in Babylonia was to tighten Assyrian control over the larger part of Elam's western frontier. Although this did not eliminate Elamite support for Babylonians prepared to resist Assyrian control, it created the framework for penning Elam in. It may have contributed to the gradual political disintegration of the Elamite state, which began to fragment more and more during the seventh century – a kind of Balkanisation (Carter and Stolper 1984; Brinkman 1986; Gerardi 1987).

11c Babylonia under Assyrian rule: 705–627

Sennacherib and Babylon

The legacy which Sargon II left his successor, Sennacherib (704–681), was the consolidation of this last, and perhaps greatest, conquest. Assyria was now absolutely committed to keeping Babylonia subject, which was no easy task given its size, its diverse population, and its long frontier with Elam, constantly ready to take advantage of any political problems. It is not surprising therefore that, with one exception, all Sennacherib's major campaigns were directed against Babylonia or its ally Elam.[3] An element of Sargon's policy abandoned by Sennacherib was the 'dual monarchy'; instead, he tried to control the country through Assyrian nominees to the Babylonian throne. Why he turned his back on his father's system is unknown. One influential idea is that Sennacherib reacted against what was seen as Sargon's 'pro-Babylonian' policy, resented by a party at the Assyrian court. Its members used the opportunity offered by Sargon's ill-omened death (p. 525) to persuade the king that he should not pay undue respect to the Babylonian gods (Landsberger and Bauer 1927; Tadmor 1958). The argument is based on a text difficult to understand (Landsberger, Parpola, Tadmor 1989; SAA 3 no. 33), and it requires considerable special pleading to wrest such a precise meaning from it (Garelli n.d.; Frame 1992: 70 and n. 34). It is at least as feasible to assume that it simply proved impracticable to maintain the joint monarchy arrangement, given the internal dissensions and divided loyalties in Babylonia. But that does not explain why the Assyrian king did not simply install a provincial governor; so the reasons for Sennacherib's policy-change remain speculative.

It took Sennacherib about fifteen years to settle the Babylonian situation, and it was finally achieved only with great brutality. His task was extraordinarily difficult. Very soon after he came to the throne, in 703, Babylonia made a bid for independence under a new king. He was almost immediately displaced by Marduk-apla-iddina, who returned from exile with Elamite support, re-established himself in Bit Yakin and received armed troops from the cities of Ur and Uruk in the south (Brinkman 1965). Sennacherib was able to defeat him in a battle at Kish and force his renewed flight. Sennacherib then made the decision to appoint as king a Babylonian, Bel-ibni – a man who had been brought up at the Assyrian court 'like a puppy'. This arrangement came to grief with the revolt of Bel-ibni in 700. Simultaneously, a ruler of Bit Dakkuri rebelled and Marduk-apla-iddina returned yet again and gained control of part of the south, including Ur. Sennacherib's campaign in response to this crisis must have been fairly successful, as the seemingly irrepressible ruler of Bit Yakin removed a number of objects associated symbolically with his royal power (his gods and the bones of his ancestors) to his new refuge in a swampy region of the Elamite frontier. Having successfully dislodged him and put down the other two revolts, Sennacherib appointed his crown-prince, Ashur-nadin-shumi, as king of Babylonia – an arrangement that lasted with no signs of disturbances for six years (Brinkman and Dalley 1988).

In 694 Sennacherib mounted a large, partly seaborne, campaign, intended to winkle out his old enemy, Marduk-apla-iddina, from his marshland refuge (at the head of the Gulf; see fig. 38). But while the Assyrian army was engaged

Figure 38 Chaldaeans hiding in marshes from Assyrian soldiers (Palace of Sennacherib, Nineveh, British Museum; drawing by D. Saxon)

in the south of Babylonia, the Elamite king took the opportunity to enter
northern Babylonia, take Sippar and capture Ashur-nadin-shumi, surrendered to him by some Babylonian citizens (Parpola 1972). The unfortunate
Assyrian prince was deported to Elam and probably died there. An Elamite
candidate replaced him on the throne of Babylon, and the Assyrians, who
had been penned into the south during these events (Levine 1982), were
defeated in battle by the Elamites. The situation was critical, with the Elamite
appointee gaining ground; but it was reversed in another battle, in which the
Assyrians were victorious and able to take the Elamite stooge captive.
Sennacherib followed up his success by campaigning deep into Elam in order
to strengthen and reassert Assyria's grip on the east Tigris region which the
Elamites had penetrated. Meantime (693), the vacancy on the Babylonian
throne had been filled by another ruler of Bit Dakkuri, Mushezib-Marduk,
and Assyria appears to have been unable to take any action against this for
the moment. In 691 (or 690) there was a confrontation of the massed forces
of Elam, with an enormous number of allies (from Babylonia, the east Tigris
area and possibly further east), and the Assyrians at Halule (near Samarra).
Despite Sennacherib's vaunted victory, the outcome seems not to have been
so positive. On the other hand, it was not quite the serious Assyrian defeat
that some have thought it (Levine 1982), as the Assyrians were not pushed
back and the city of Babylon was under Assyrian siege shortly afterwards. In

689, Babylon fell and, according to the inscription carved on the rockface at Bavian, close to the head of Sennacherib's great canal constructed to supply the ancient city of Nineveh with water:

> like the oncoming of a storm I broke loose, and I overwhelmed it (Babylon) like a hurricane. I invested that city, with breaches and engines my hand[s seized], plunder . . . his powerful . . . small and great, I left none. With their corpses I filled the city squares. Shuzubu (Mushezib-Marduk), king of Babylon, together with his family [and] his [nobles] I carried off alive into my land. The wealth of that city: silver, gold, precious stones, property and goods, I counted into the hands of my [peop]le and they made it their own. The gods living in its midst the hands of my people took them and smashed them. Their [property] and goods they seized.
>
> Adad and Shala, the gods of Ekallate, whom Marduk-nadin-ahhe, king of Babylon, in the reign of Tiglath-pileser (I), king of Assyria, had seized and carried off to Babylon [see chapter 7b], after 418 years I brought them out of Babylon and returned them to Ekallate, their place.
>
> The city and houses, from their foundations to crenellations, I destroyed, I devastated, I burned with fire. The wall and outer wall, temples, gods, the ziggurat of brick and earth, as much as there was, I razed and dumped them into the Arahtu canal. Through the middle of that city I dug canals, I flooded its ground with water, the structure of its foundation I destroyed. I made its destruction more complete than that by a flood. That in days to come, the site of that city, and its temples and gods might not be remembered, I completely wiped it out with water and made it like a meadow.
>
> (Luckenbill 1924: 83–84, ll. 44–54)

The completeness of the devastation, painted so dramatically here, has been doubted (Landsberger 1965; Galter 1984). It is not easily confirmed by the sparse archaeological finds (Frame 1992: 55–56), although that could be read either way – absence of evidence may point to the effectiveness of destruction wrought on simple wooden houses, for example (Porter 1987). What is certain is that this overwhelming catastrophe is not mentioned by the *Babylonian Chronicle*, which states soberly:

> On the first day of the month Kislev (November/December) the city (i.e. Babylon) was captured. Mushezib-Marduk was taken prisoner and transported to Assyria. For four years Mushezib-Marduk ruled Babylon.
>
> (*ABC* no. 1 iii 22–24)

The one reference to this event by a later Babylonian ruler (Langdon 1912 Nab. 8) reviles Sennacherib for letting Babylonian temples fall into disrepair, discontinuing temple rituals and removing the statue of Marduk to Assyria, but makes no mention of a total devastation. But, however we read the texts, what is not in doubt is that Babylon, particularly its temples, suffered considerably – it was plundered, the image of its patron deity and chief god of the Babylonian pantheon was removed, and its sanctuaries were left in disrepair. The great festivals and regular daily cult acts, which involved so many of the citizens and around which so much civic activity revolved, ceased and the city presented a sad spectacle. Later, the remaining period of Sennacherib's reign (689–681) was officially considered 'kingless', so tightly intertwined was the concept of king and appropriate care for the gods. If the number of economic documents is an accurate mirror of the economic health of a country, then Babylonia went through a very difficult time (Brinkman 1984a: 69–70). But there are signs that towards the end of his reign Sennacherib attempted to re-organise southern Babylonia, and to foster pro-Assyrian feelings there. He returned cult-statues to Uruk, presented the Uruk temple with slaves, and perhaps appointed locally prominent individuals as governors in Ur and the troublesome Sealand (Brinkman 1984a: 70; Frame 1992: 59–62).

Babylon restored

This dark picture of a depressed Babylonia is generally thought to lighten substantially with the reign of Esarhaddon (680–669), although the changes in Assyrian policy were very gradual. The new Assyrian king encountered several difficulties, including problems with Chaldaean rebels (twice involving Babylonian city-officials), and a renewed Elamite invasion, climaxing in a massacre of the population of Sippar. Resentment at Assyrian control was rife, as shown by letters reporting on eminent citizens intriguing with Elam (e.g. Parpola 1972). It was even expressed at a popular level:

> To the king, my lord, (from) your servant Mar-Ishtar: Good health to the king, my lord! May the gods Nabû and Marduk bless the king my lord! May the great gods bestow long days, well-being and joy upon the king, my lord.
>
> (There follows a report on the safe receipt of jewellery sent by the king and queen mother to be used for the divine tiara of the statue of Nabû.)
>
> The commandant (*šakin ṭēmi*) of Babylon will, perhaps, write to the king, my lord, 'The citizens of Babylon have thrown lumps of clay at me', (but) that is a lie. As the commandants were told to prepare their chariots, they imposed heavy silver (dues) on the citizens of Babylon, Borsippa and Kutha, (and) collected (them). The citizens of Babylon, poor wretches who have got nothing, set up a wail (and) protested. (Whereupon) the commandant imprisoned (some) men from amongst them (with the accusation): 'You threw lumps of clay at my messengers.'

He has also written to the wife of the judge (named) Tabi:
'Let your husband be in your custody – he may not go outdoors!' I
have heard that (this) judge Tabi incited the men who protested.
    This was the story; the king, my lord, should know (it).
                    (*ABL* 340; Parpola 1970/1983 no. 276; SAA 10 no. 348)

But, if there had ever been a united front against Assyria, it was beginning to
break down. Protest about excessive Assyrian demands for money was as far
as it went, and it was sufficient to place local Babylonian dignitaries suspected
of colluding with hostile mobs under house-arrest. Some Assyrian officials
(as Mar-Ishtar here) saw that, if Assyrian control of the country was to work,
then fair dealing and an appreciation of economic realities were in order.
More and more the impression is of the inhabitants of Babylonia divided
among themselves, shopping each other to the Assyrian king and thus
ingratiating themselves with the wielders of power. Elam's responses to
Babylonian appeals for refuge became so reluctant that a son of Marduk-apla-
iddina II, who fled there, was murdered; as a result, his brother sought asylum
at the Assyrian court and was rewarded by being installed as the Assyrian-
appointed ruler of Bit Yakin.

A number of carefully calculated, conciliatory moves were made by
Esarhaddon: first, he planned, and probably proclaimed publicly (Porter
1987), the rebuilding of Babylon and the restoration of its temple. He must
indeed have done some work, since, on his death in 669, his successor,
Ashurbanipal, was poised and ready to set in train the rapid return of the
Marduk statue to its shrine. Secondly, the deities of Der, Larsa and Sippar
(and more from Uruk) were brought back to their shrines, and temple repairs
(notably Borsippa) were undertaken. Thirdly, some of the booty from the
campaign in Shupria (673) was presented by Esarhaddon to the temples of
Uruk. Whether Esarhaddon's announcement in 672 that his son, Shamash-
shum-ukin, would be the future king of Babylonia, ruling it subject to his
brother, formed part of this policy is less certain. It is more likely that it was
intended to round off Esarhaddon's final pacification of this particularly
difficult region by ensuring firm Assyrian control.

Civil war and economic recovery

The transition to rule by Shamash-shum-ukin, brother of Ashurbanipal,
seems to have gone fairly smoothly, although the new Babylonian king's
power appears to have been substantially curtailed. Some parts of Babylonia
were directly answerable to Ashurbanipal, and local governors reported on
the political situation to the Assyrian king, rather than to Shamash-shum-
ukin (Brinkman 1979). Ashurbanipal also participated personally in com-
pleting and continuing Esarhaddon's programme of restoration, so there can
have been little doubt within Babylonia about who held effective power.
Evidence for uprisings within Babylonia between 668 and 652 is limited, save

for the always problematical east Tigris region, where some of the rival Elamite dynasts allied at various times with the Aramaean tribes along their frontier (Gerardi 1987).

But the potential for revolt in Babylonia was strong, and it was exploited eventually by Shamash-shum-ukin. He led a rebellion against his brother, lasting from 652 to 648, for which he managed to recruit Chaldaean, Aramaean, Arab and Elamite support, as well as pressurising a number of Babylonian cities to join his side. The seriousness of the situation for Ashurbanipal may be reflected in the fact that, about a year after the start of the revolt, there was a revolt within Assyria itself, possibly instigated by supporters of Ashurbanipal's rebellious brother. But hard and continuous fighting by the Assyrians and their king led to step-by-step gains, and in 650 Babylon was put under siege. Dated economic documents from this period show that the city inhabitants experienced great hardship, with famine so severe that some were forced to sell their children into slavery. Not surprisingly, the New Year festival could not be performed in these tense and difficult times. Finally, probably late in 648, Babylon fell to the Assyrian forces and Shamash-shum-ukin perished in the flames of his burning palace. The war between the brothers, and Shamash-shum-ukin's ignominious death, made a huge impression on the contemporary world: a popular story (in Aramaic) about these dramatic and tragic events has recently been identified among a collection of papyri from Elephantine in Egypt dating to the early fourth century (Vleeming and Weselius 1985: 31–37).

What the situation was in Babylonia after the collapse of the revolt is disputed, and must remain obscure for the present. According to one of the late editions of Ashurbanipal's annals (Cylinder A; see Streck 1916) there was, from around 643 on, a regular Assyrian governor of Babylonia (Frame 1992: 196, 301–302). At the same time a Babylonian is attested as Assyrian-installed military commander of the Sealand, obviously to preserve Assyrian dominance of this always problematical area, and prominent locals continued to govern Ur and Uruk. Yet another figure appears in Babylonian dated documents after 648: Kandalanu, king of Babylonia. A lengthy and inconclusive debate has raged (and continues to rage) about the identity of this individual (for the most recent full discussion, see Frame 1992: 296–306; see chapter 9e). Some argue that this is simply another name for Ashurbanipal, and shows that the Assyrian king reverted to the policy of his eighth-century predecessors for governing Babylonia, i.e. the 'dual monarchy' (see pp. 579–582). The name 'Kandalanu' would then have to be understood as an alternative for 'Ashurbanipal', on the pattern of Tiglath-pileser III and Shalmaneser V, who were referred to in some contexts in Babylonia as 'Pul(u)' and 'Ululayu' (see p. 579). Unfortunately, the analogy does not work completely. First, we find Babylonian documents in some places which are consistently dated by Ashurbanipal. This is the case, for example, at Nippur which seems to have had a strong Assyrian garrison stationed in it. Secondly, at the time of the earlier dual monarchy, *contemporary* Babylonian texts never use the alternative names for the Assyrian kings, but only their standard throne-names. The alternative names *only* appear in chronographic texts and a later (mid-seventh century) Aramaic letter (Ashur ostracon; Gibson 1971–82, II no. 20). These considerations make it more likely that Kandalanu was a separate personage installed by Ashurbanipal to rule Babylonia on the pattern of his rebellious brother (*RLA* 5: 368–369; Brinkman 1984a: 105–106). But the situation is obscure, and many continue to believe that Kandalanu is identical with Ashurbanipal in view of the existence of an Assyrian governor of Babylonia contemporary with Kandalanu's reign (*CAH* III ch. 25; Zawadski 1988).

One thing that can be stated unequivocally about the span of twenty-one years following the civil war, when Babylonia was under Kandalanu's rule (648–627), is that Babylonia was relatively tranquil and peaceful. There are no very informative annals or chronicles that relate to this time, but there are many more business texts from this period than there had been for about six hundred years previously (Brinkman 1984a: 107–8), which implies an upturn in the Babylonian economy. The shrines of northern Babylonia were repaired and kept intact by the Assyrian king, and Babylon does not appear to have suffered permanent damage after its two-year siege. Ashurbanipal returned the divine image of the goddess Nanaya to Uruk after his capture and devastation of Susa (see p. 500) – a statue that, according to his annals, had been robbed by Elam 1,635 years earlier (Gerardi 1987) – so that at least one city in Babylonia benefited directly from his final Elamite campaign. Apart from the evidence for the rapid recovery of Babylonian agriculture in this period, there is also some evidence for long-distance trade in iron with Cilicia (Brinkman 1984a: 108), suggesting that Babylonian commerce, too, was in a healthy state. The general impression from this kind of material is of Babylonia enjoying a greater prosperity than it had known for several centuries.

11d The Neo-Babylonian dynasty (626–539)

Nabopolassar and the 'War of Liberation'

Although the impression in Babylonia during the last twenty years or so of Ashurbanipal's reign is one of peace, the crisis which arose on Kandalanu's death in 627 suggests that the situation was far more problematic, and that Babylonia was still riven by deepseated political rivalries and factions. The course of events between 627 and 616 is unfortunately almost impossible to reconstruct, as the fragmentary evidence is ambiguous at crucial points about the identity of the protagonists in the military struggles for control of Babylonia (Zawadski 1988; *CAH* III ch. 25). The points that are clear are, first, that immediately following Kandalanu's death no king was recognised in Babylonia, which suggests that maintaining Assyrian control was difficult

– perhaps exacerbated by, or linked to, political problems in Assyria itself. Second, in 626, Nabopolassar, acceded to the throne in Babylon; his background is unknown, except for a much later statement by Berossus (*FGrH* 680 F7) that he was a general appointed by the Assyrian prince Sin-shar-ishkun (see chapter 9e).[4] Nabopolassar's accession was not welcomed by everyone, and he met with both Babylonian and Assyrian resistance. Fighting for control of Babylonia was protracted and violent for the next six to ten years, with some cities, such as Uruk and Nippur, subjected to long sieges and suffering such severe hardship that some families were forced to sell their children into slavery (Oppenheim 1955). The various sides in this war cannot always be identified with certainty, although it is possible that at times two Assyrian-led armies as well as Babylonian forces were involved. Third, by 616 Nabopolassar held Babylonia securely enough to move beyond its frontiers and launch attacks on Assyrian-held territories and even the Assyrian heartland (see chapter 9e). With assistance from Median forces (formalised by a treaty perhaps cemented by a dynastic marriage), the Babylonians were able, over the next eight years, to capture and destroy some of the most important cities of the Assyrian empire: Ashur, Nineveh, Tarbisu, Kalhu, Harran. How this sustained Babylonian military effort was possible remains obscure, although the military role of the Medes was crucial for Nabopolassar's ability to launch continuous, devastating and victorious attacks on the Assyrians and their Egyptian and Mannaean allies.

The main outcome of the long war against Assyria was that the Babylonians effectively inherited the Assyrian empire, but not without hard, repeated fighting. Between 609 and 607 Nabopolassar's main efforts were directed to securing the northern mountain frontier for Babylonia. The most serious challenge to Babylonia's takeover came from Egypt, which tried to take advantage of its ally Assyria's collapse by seizing control of the Levant (see chapter 12b). In 605, Nebuchadnezzar, Nabopolassar's son and heir, fought a difficult battle against the Egyptians, who had established themselves at Carchemish. Nebuchadnezzar's hard-won victory at Carchemish was followed up successfully by another battle against the fleeing Egyptian forces in the region of Hamath. The double victory allowed Nebuchadnezzar to extend Babylonian control over the important area of Hamath, and it probably helped him to accede smoothly to the Babylonian throne on his father's death, which occurred during the campaign.

The reign of Nebuchadnezzar II (604–562)

Immediately after his coronation, Nebuchadnezzar marched back to northern Syria and campaigned there for another five months – right through the winter. Nebuchadnezzar's unusual action demonstrates how important it was for the Babylonians to maintain a constant military presence in order not to lose the region to Egypt. It explains why the Babylonian ruler directed eight, out of the nine, campaigns fought in the next ten years at imposing his control on this area. In 601, he marched right down to the Egyptian frontier; in the ensuing battle both sides suffered serious losses. After one year's respite spent refitting his army, Nebuchadnezzar marched again to the Levant, tightening Babylonia's grip along the desert frontiers and driving out Egyptian-supported opposition. In the course of this struggle between the two sides, Jerusalem was taken, its king, Jehoiachin, was deported to Babylon and Nebuchadnezzar's nominee installed instead:

> The seventh year (598/7): In the month Kislev (November/December) the king of Akkad mustered his army and marched to Hattu (Syria). He encamped against the city of Judah and on the second day of the month Adar (16 March 597) he captured the city (and) seized (its) king. A king of his own choice he appointed in the city (and) taking the vast tribute he brought it into Babylon.
>
> (*ABC* no. 5 11–13)

Nebuchadnezzar's legendary thirteen-year siege of Tyre should probably be linked to this continuous and drawn-out effort (Josephus *Contra Apionem* 1.21; von Voigtlander 1963). It is not mentioned in the preserved portion of the Babylonian chronicles, and the chronology is extremely confused (Wiseman 1985: 25). A document dated to Nebuchadnezzar's reign from Tyre, and other references, has generally been taken to suggest that it, too, was incorporated into the Babylonian imperial system at some point after its fall (Wilhelm 1973; but cf. Joannès 1982). A glimpse of the critical position of the small states, caught between Egyptian and Babylonian military ambitions, is provided by an Aramaic letter (unfortunately fragmentary) found at Saqqara in Egypt:

> To lord of kings, Pharaoh, your servant Adon, king of [. . . The welfare of lord of kings, Pharaoh, may . . . and all the gods] of heaven and earth and Baalshamayn, the [great] god, [seek at all times; and may they make the throne of lord of kings,] Pharaoh, enduring like the days of heaven. What . . . [the forces] of the king of Babylon have come; they have reached Aphek and (encamped) . . . they have taken . . . For lord of kings, Pharaoh, knows that your servant . . . to send an army to deliver me. Let him not abandon me . . . and your servant has kept in mind his kindness. But his territory . . . a governor in the land, and as a border they have replaced it with the border . . .
>
> (Dupont-Sommer 1948; KAI no.266; Gibson 1971–82 II no. 21; Porten
> *BibArch* 44 (1981): 36–52)

Not enough survives to identify the dynast who sent out this cry for help. But the terror of a ruler faced by the inexorable advance of the Babylonian forces, whose only hope lay in appealing to Egypt's self-interest, is plain.

Only one campaign (in 596) was directed towards Babylonia's eastern border. The reference in the chronicle is very fragmentary, but indicates that the Babylonian king had to take action against an Elamite ruler in the east Tigris area. What exactly the political situation in Elam was at this period is not very clear. A small archive from Susa shows that it had a palace-centred administration at least by the early sixth century (Miroschedji 1985; 1990); inscribed bricks, bearing Nebuchadnezzar's name, hint at a probably brief period of Babylonian suzerainty (Carter and Stolper 1984). Two great fortified structures extending from east of the Tigris to the Euphrates (one to the region of Sippar, the other to Babylon) have been partially traced (Killick 1984; Gasche *et al.* 1987; 1989). They have been identified as the 'defences' later known as Nebuchadnezzar's 'Median Wall' (Xenophon *Anabasis* 1.7); but whom they were intended to keep out (if indeed anyone) is unknown.

The Babylonian chronicle is not preserved for the years following 594, but the Old Testament and a fragment of a Babylonian historical text (Edel 1978) show that Nebuchadnezzar's involvement with southern Palestine and Egypt continued: in 587 Zedekiah, the Babylonian-appointed king of Judah (2 *Kings*

Table 32 Chronology of Neo-Babylonian rulers

Babylonia	Judah	Lydia	Medes	Persians
		Gyges (d. 652) Ardys Sadyattes		
Nabopolassar (626–605)	Josiah (640–09)	Alyattes	Cyaxares (625–585)	Cyrus I
	Jehoahaz (609) Jehoiachim (609–598)			
Nebuchadnezzar II (604–562)				Cambyses I
	Jehoiachin (598) Zedekiah (597–87) (Gedaliah: governor)			
Amel-Marduk (561–560) Neriglissar (559–556) Labashi-Marduk (556) Nabonidus (555–539)		Croesus (–540s)	Astyages (585–550)	Cyrus (II) the Great (559–530)
				Cambyses (II) (530–522)

24.17), rebelled, was blinded and deported; Gedaliah, a governor of local origin, was installed in Judah – now a Babylonian province (2 *Kings* 25.22). When the Egyptian ruler Apries (589–570) was deposed in a military coup in 570, he managed to escape, appealed to Nebuchadnezzar for help and, in 567, the Babylonian king embarked on a war against Egypt to try to reinstall him. The Babylonian army was beaten back in a dramatic battle and the Egyptian pretender killed (see chapter 12b). It is possible that this led eventually to a more peaceful co-existence between the two rivals, although that impression may simply be due to the absence of sources.

The most spectacular evidence of Nebuchadnezzar's extraordinary military successes can be found in the remains of his building-works in Babylonia. All the great old cities were extensively rebuilt, their shrines repaired and beautified. Most notable in this massive effort at reconstruction is the development of Babylon into the immense and beautiful city of legend. Its size was enormous for the time at 850 ha (over 3 square miles). It was ringed by huge double walls and moated; the river flowed through the middle of the city and was crossed by a finely built stone bridge (see fig. 39). At the centre rose the gigantic ziggurat, Etemenanki ('House of the frontier between heaven and earth'), next to the great Marduk sanctuary (Esagila), with its many chapels and large courtyard. From there the handsomely paved processional way led to the monumental Ishtar gate. The walls lining the splendid ceremonial street and the great gate were decorated with bricks glazed in deep blue and with moulded reliefs of bulls and *mušhuššu* – the dragons sacred to Marduk (see fig. 40). At the northern end of the city, built out from the wall, was a great fortified palace, some of it, too, decorated with glazed coloured bricks. These are just some of the fabulous remains revealed by the German excavations early this century (Koldewey 1913; see also fig. 41). There were several other city-gates, smaller temples dotted around the city and dwelling houses. It has been possible to locate and label some of these buildings, as well as the city-gates, precisely on the basis of Babylonian texts which describe the city at this time (Unger 1931/1970; cf. George 1992; 1993 for corrections and improvements). The many lengthy, royal inscriptions and stamped bricks show that most of this building was the work of Nebuchadnezzar during his long reign of forty-three years (605–562; Berger 1973; Wiseman 1985).

As the Babylonian convention in royal inscriptions was the long and elaborate building text, this particular genre of texts does not help with tracing military events in the way that the Assyrian annals do. For reconstructing the history, scholars depend on the chronicles, which are a valuable source where preserved. As already said, they are sadly lost for the remainder of Nebuchadnezzar's reign after 594. So the impression, based entirely on the texts celebrating in fine literary language Nebuchadnezzar's many buildings and provisions for cults, is one of peace and tranquillity. This picture is almost certainly false: the chronicle entry for 595 mentions a serious

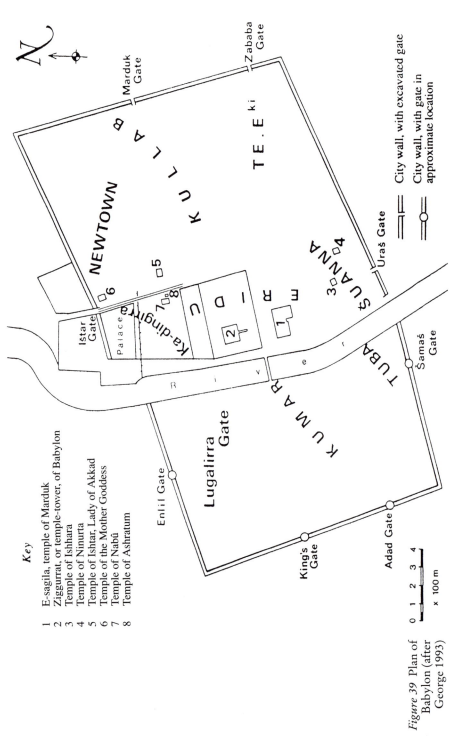

Figure 39 Plan of Babylon (after George 1993)

Key

1 E-sagila, temple of Marduk
2 Ziggurat, or temple-tower, of Babylon
3 Temple of Ishhara
4 Temple of Ninurta
5 Temple of Ishtar, Lady of Akkad
6 Temple of the Mother Goddess
7 Temple of Nabû
8 Temple of Ashratum

City wall, with excavated gate

City wall, with gate in approximate location

0 1 2 3 4
x 100 m

NEWTOWN

KULLAB

TE.E ki

ŠUANNA

KUMAR

TUBA

Ka-dingirra

Palace

Marduk Gate

Zababa Gate

Uraš Gate

Šamaš Gate

Adad Gate

King's Gate

Enlil Gate

Lugalirra Gate

Istar Gate

Figure 40 mušhuššu-dragon of Marduk; glazed brick relief from Processional Street, Babylon (Vorderasiatisches Museum, Berlin)

internal rebellion, probably involving the army. In the following year, a legal text reports the public condemnation by the king of an eminent Babylonian found guilty of breaking his oath of loyalty to Nebuchadnezzar:

Baba-aha-iddina, son of Nabu-ahhe-bullit, descendant of . . .-limmir, caused sin and crime and planned evil. The oaths of the king, his lord, he did not keep, but planned treason. In those days Nebuchadnezzar, king of Babylon, the judicious prince, shepherd of the widespread people, who like the sun-god oversees the totality of the lands, who determines right and justice, who destroys evildoers and criminals, examined the evil deeds of Baba-aha-iddina and brought his conspiracy to naught. He established that he had committed the despicable deed in the assembly of the people; angrily he looked upon him. 'No life' he spoke for him and his throat was cut.

And the land of Nabu-ahhe-bullit, his father, which Nabopolassar, the king of Babylon, the father, his (sc. Nebuchadnezzar's) begetter, had made into property of Ezida (temple of Nabû in Borsippa), (but which) Nabu-ahhe-bullit [by] treason and . . . had left . . . Baba-aha-

595

Figure 41 Reconstruction of Babylon and Ishtar gate (Unger 1931/1970)

iddina ... Nebuchadnezzar, the king of Babylon, the prince .... who by his just decision, which like the great gods ... the remainder of the land of Nabu-ahhe-bullit in city and country, as much as there is, determined as property [of Nabu] and sold the people (on it).

(Weidner 1954–6: 1–3)

It is a revealing text, showing that one of the ways in which officials were tied to the central authority was, as in the Assyrian empire, the oath of loyalty sworn to the king personally. Any breach of the solemn obligations this entailed was punished by the king with the death sentence and public execution in his presence. The traitor's property (at least, in this case) was confiscated and part of it granted (or 'returned') to the Nabu temple in Borsippa. It is possible that Baba-aha-iddina was implicated in the revolt reported in the chronicle for 595; but it is likely that such political problems were in any case more widespread than the scant historiographical sources allow us to see. Consolidating Nabopolassar's achievements inside and outside Babylonia cannot have been an easy task.

Nebuchadnezzar II's successors

Another hint that the new Babylonian kingship faced a number of difficulties is provided by the history of Nebuchadnezzar's successors. Amel-Marduk (biblical Evil-Merodach), Nebuchadnezzar's son, reigned barely two years (561–560; Sack 1972) before being assassinated by his brother-in-law, Neriglissar, which could suggest that the central authorities were beset by problems. We can trace a little of Neriglissar's background and family-relationships (cf. von Voigtlander 1963; Weisberg 1974; Joannès 1980), but his short three-year reign (559–556) is scantily known, save for some building-work and a campaign in the north-west part of Cilicia along the Lydian frontier (*ABC* no. 6). His son, Labashi-Marduk, probably a mere child on his father's death, stood little chance of surviving the murderous intrigues of the Babylonian court: he was accepted as king by only a limited number of cities, and for little more than a month, before being ousted by a conspiracy of Babylonian nobles who probably murdered him. The new king brought to the throne by this bloody route was Nabonidus (555–539). He had no direct family connection with the Babylonian royal family, but was old enough to have a mature son (Bel-shar-usur, the biblical Belshezzar) and was almost certainly an experienced soldier. The effects of these problems in the royal succession should not be exaggerated: there is no evidence that the Babylonian grasp on its provinces was seriously shaken by the struggles for the throne. The empire seems, on the whole, to have weathered the abrupt changes of ruler fairly well – a tribute to Nabopolassar's and Nebu-chadnezzar's achievements.

Nabonidus and Cyrus of Persia

For Nabonidus we have quite full sources in the form of fine literary royal inscriptions with echoes of political events, a chronicle covering (with gaps) the whole of his reign and continuing into the early period of Persian rule (*ABC* no. 7), and some literary compositions from later periods. This makes it possible to reconstruct his reign more fully than the previous ones, which is particularly valuable as Nabonidus' reign ended with his defeat by the Persian king, Cyrus (II) the Great (559–530), and the absorption of all Babylonian-controlled territory into the new world empire of the Achaemenids (chapter 13c). At the same time we must be careful not to be misled by texts composed after Cyrus' victory over the Babylonian king – some of them exploit Nabonidus' defeat for propaganda purposes in order to present him, in retrospect, as a godless ruler. Such *post eventum* effusions do not necessarily reflect the realities of Nabonidus' rule.

A number of Nabonidus' inscriptions include historical retrospects intended to show that his irregular accession to the throne had the blessing of the gods and of earlier Babylonian kings, such as the great Nebuchadnezzar.[5] They are therefore 'apologetic', and reflect his struggle to rally support for his kingship. Linked to this concern are the recurring references to Nabonidus' search for the traces of earlier buildings in the course of his own construction work. Typically, the texts report that the vanished outlines of the ground plans of temples were revealed to the king; he found the inscriptions of previous kings who had erected sanctuaries on exactly the spot where Nabonidus planned to build; on one occasion he found a statue of Sargon of Agade (2340–2284) with its head broken – he had it repaired and set up with offerings in the repaired temple (Lambert 1968–9). He also revived the ancient practice of installing a royal daughter as *ēntu* of the moongod at Ur, and for the details of the induction ceremony he again claimed to have been instructed by an earlier royal text miraculously found:

> When Nannar (the moongod) requested a high priestess (*ēntu*)
> the Son of the Prince showed his sign to the inhabited world;
> the Bright Light manifested his reliable decision.
> To Nabonidus, king of Babylon, provider for Esagila and Ezida,
> the reverent shepherd, who shows concern for the sanctuaries of the
>   great gods
> Nannar, the lord of the crown, who bears the signal for all peoples,
>   revealed a sign concerning his request for a high priestess (*ēntu*).
> On the thirteenth of Ululu, the month of the work of goddesses,
> the Fruit (i.e. moon) became eclipsed and set while eclipsed.
> 'Sin (moongod) requests a high priestess' – such was his sign and
>   decision.
> As for me, Nabonidus, the shepherd who reveres his divine majesty, I
>   reverently heeded his reliable order,
> so that I became concerned about his request for a high priestess.

I sought out the sanctuaries of Shamash and Adad, the patrons of
  extispicy,
and Shamash and Adad, as usual, answered me a reliable yes,
wrote a favourable omen in my extispicy,
the omen pertaining to the request for priestesses, the request of the
  gods to man.
I repeated the extispicy for confirmation and they answered me with an
  even more favourable omen.
I made an extispicy inquiring about a daughter born to one of my
  relatives, but they answered me no.
A third time I made an extispicy inquiring about my own daughter and
  they answered me with a favourable omen.
I heeded the word of Sin, the supreme lord, the god my creator,
and the verdict of Shamash and Adad, the patrons of extispicy;
I installed my own daughter as high priestess
and gave her the name En-nigaldi-Nanna.
Because for a very long time the office of the high priestess had been
  forgotten
and her characteristic features were nowhere indicated, I bethought
  myself day after day.
The appointed time having arrived, the doors were opened for me;
Indeed I set eyes on an ancient stele of Nebuchadnezzar [I],
son of Ninurta-nadin-shumi, an early king of the past,
on which was depicted the image of the high priestess;
moreover, they had listed and deposited in the Egipar (part of temple
  in which *ēntu*s lived)
her appurtenances, her clothing and her jewellery.
I carefully looked into the old clay and wooden tablets
and did exactly as in the olden days.
A stele, her appurtenances, and her household equipment
I fashioned anew, respectively inscribed on it,
and deposited before my lord and lady Sin and Ningal.

At that time Egipar, the holy precinct, wherein the rites of the high
  priestesses used to be carried out,
was an abandoned place, and had become a heap of ruins,
palm trees and orchard fruit were growing in its midst.
I cut down the trees, removed the rubble of its ruins,
I set eyes on the temple and its foundation terrace became visible.
Inside it I set eyes on inscriptions of old earlier kings,
I also set eyes on an old inscription of En-ane-du, high priestess of Ur,
  daughter of Kudur-Mabuk, sister of Rim-Sin (1822–1763), king of Ur,
  who renovated Egipar and restored it,
and surrounded with a wall the resting place of the old high priestesses

adjoining Egipar,
so that I made Egipar (too) anew as in the old days. . .
(*YOS* I: 45; Böhl 1937–8; Reiner 1985 [OJ]: 2–5)

Here, as in many of his other inscriptions, there is an emphasis on the absolute rightness of Nabonidus' rule, confirmed again and again by the harmony of his actions with ancient precedent. The king's interest is not that of an antiquarian, but that of someone piously seeking, and finding, benediction for all his plans, so that his rule will be seen to form a link in a continuum of bountiful and blessed kingship – not the disruptive, violent seizure of power that in fact it was.

A particularly interesting set of inscriptions comes from Harran, a city destroyed, together with its great temple of the moon-god, by the Babylonians and Medes in their final onslaught on the remnants of the Assyrian forces (609, see chapter 9e). The statue of the moon-god, Sin, of Harran had been removed to Babylon together with temple treasures. This famous temple (and presumably the city) was rebuilt by Nabonidus. The work was commemorated in two long texts: one presents the autobiography of his mother and celebrates her long life (she lived to the age of 102) and reverence for Sin. The other describes Nabonidus' accession to the throne (here attributed to the will of Sin), the dissension within Babylonia immediately following it, and Nabonidus' military triumphs in Arabia over a period of about ten years. Nabonidus established a Babylonian base at the oasis of Teima, a nodal point along the Arabian caravan routes, from which he launched a series of campaigns against several other rich oases, and apparently secured their surrender and allegiance. The tactical difficulties of war in such terrain are reflected by the length of time Nabonidus was absent (ten years), and by the fact that he made careful arrangements to have Babylonia administered by his son, the crown-prince Bel-shar-usur (the Belshazzar of the book of *Daniel*, see *Daniel* 5).

On the basis of Nabonidus' Harran texts (and some others) and the later texts celebrating the Persian triumph, scholars have argued that Nabonidus attempted to change Babylonia's traditional religion by promoting the cult of Sin at the expense of the god Marduk; his long stay in Arabia is argued to be connected with problems raised by this. Some scholars go further, and argue that Nabonidus' 'religious reform' led to massive popular disaffection within Babylonia. This unrest was exploited by the Persians and allowed Cyrus practically to walk into Babylon, invited in by the Babylonians themselves. But there are problems with such a view: most of the evidence for Nabonidus' devotion to Sin appears in his Harran inscriptions because Sin was the local god; it is very difficult to define what else Nabonidus may have done in relation to the Babylonian cult; his absence in Arabia, seen as flight from the Babylonians furious with the king's religious attitudes, may be explained by strategic considerations. It is entirely possible that the extent to which Nabonidus promoted the cult of Sin and the discontent it unleashed has been exaggerated by modern scholars. The relevant evidence is highly ambiguous and chronologically unclear (Beaulieu 1987; Kuhrt 1990b), and popular opposition to Nabonidus is attested solely by texts proclaiming the Persian conqueror's right to rule, which must be treated cautiously. One example is the famous Cyrus Cylinder from Babylon, written in Akkadian:

> An imitation of Esagila he (sc. Nabonidus) made [. . . .] to Ur and the other cult centres
>
> A cult order that was unsuitable [. . .] he spoke daily, and, an evil thing,
>
> he stopped the regular offerings [. . .] he placed in the cult centres. The worship of Marduk, king of the gods, he removed from his mind.
>
> He repeatedly did that which was bad for his city. Daily [. . .] he destroyed all his [subjects] with an unending yoke.
>
> In response to their lament the Enlil of the gods (Marduk) grew very angry [. . .] their territory. The gods who lived in them left their dwelling-places,
>
> despite his anger(?) he brought them into Babylon. Marduk [. . . .], to all the places, whose dwelling-places were in ruins,
>
> and to the inhabitants of Sumer and Akkad, who had become like corpses, he turned his mind, he became merciful. He searched through all the countries, examined (them),
>
> he sought a just ruler to suit his heart, he took him by the hand: Cyrus, king of Anshan (in Fars), he called, for the dominion over the totality he named his name.
>
> Gutium and all the Ummanmanda (probably a reference to the Medes) he made subject to him. The black-headed people, whom he (Marduk) allowed his (Cyrus') hands to overcome,
>
> he protected in justice and righteousness. Marduk, the great lord, who cares for his people, looked with pleasure at his (Cyrus') good deeds and his righteous heart.
>
> He (Marduk) ordered him (Cyrus) to go to Babylon, and let him take the road to Babylon. Like a friend and companion he went by his side.
>
> His massive troops, whose number was immeasurable like the water of a river, marched with their arms at their side.
>
> Without battle and fighting he let him enter his city Babylon. He saved Babylon from its oppression. Nabonidus, the king who did not honour him, he handed over to him.
>
> All the inhabitants of Babylon, the whole of the land of Sumer and Akkad, princes and governors knelt before him, kissed his feet, rejoiced at his kingship; their faces shone.
>
> 'The lord, who through his help has brought the dead to life, who in (a time of) disaster and oppression has benefited all' – thus they joyfully celebrated him, honoured his name.

I, Cyrus, king of the universe, mighty king, king of Babylon, king of Sumer and Akkad, king of the four quarters,

son of Cambyses, great king, king of Anshan, grandson of Cyrus, great king, king of Anshan, descendant of Teispes, great king, king of Anshan,

eternal seed of kingship, whose reign was loved by Bel and Nabu and whose kingship they wanted to please their hearts – when I had entered Babylon peacefully,

I set up, with acclamation and rejoicing, the seat of lordship in the palace of the ruler. Marduk, the great lord, [. . .] me the great heart, [. . .] of Babylon, daily I cared for his worship.

My numerous troops marched peacefully through Babylon. I did not allow any troublemaker to arise in the whole land of Sumer and Akkad.

The city of Babylon and all its cult-centres I maintained in well-being. The inhabitants of Babylon, [who] against the will [of the gods . . .] a yoke unsuitable for them,

I allowed them to find rest from their exhaustion, their servitude I loosened. Marduk, the great lord, rejoiced at my [good] deeds.

(the text continues to describe Cyrus' cult-offerings, his restoration of cult-centres and the return of deportees to them; it ends with his building in Babylon, and his find of an inscription of Ashurbanipal)

(Berger 1975; *TUAT* I: 407–410)

If we compare this text, which uses the typical cylindrical form of a Babylonian foundation-document (see fig. 42), with some earlier texts written at the command of usurpers and conquerors,[6] we find a very similar range of motifs, which served to vilify the defeated, legitimate ruler and enhance the claims of the new holder of the throne to rule in harmony with, and with the direct assistance of, the gods (Kuhrt 1987). The reference to Ashurbanipal at the end of the text is interesting – it suggests that Cyrus was picking out this Assyrian king as a former benefactor of Babylonia and so a suitable role-model; in another text, Nebuchadnezzar II was selected as the king whose work Cyrus continued and completed. These features must throw considerable doubt on the smoothness of Cyrus' conquest. Such doubts are confirmed by the relevant Babylonian chronicle (*ABC* no. 7), which says that the Babylonian and Persian armies fought a fierce battle at Opis east of the Tigris. After the Babylonian defeat, Cyrus followed up his victory by looting Opis and massacring its inhabitants. He then moved to Sippar on the Euphrates, and waited for Nabonidus to be taken prisoner and the city of Babylon to surrender to his general, Gobryas. Only *then*, when Babylon was invested with Persian troops to ensure that all went well and the Babylonian king a captive, did Cyrus stage a triumphant entry and promise the city peace (Kuhrt 1988; 1990a). The widespread idea that Nabonidus was hated by his

Figure 42 The Cyrus Cylinder (British Museum)

subjects reflects the success of Cyrus' legitimising propaganda, but leaves the real reasons for Babylonia's defeat and the precise nature and problems of Nabonidus' reign obscure.

11e The Neo-Babylonian empire

The socio-political structure of Babylonia and its empire is illuminated by a variety of material. There is an enormous number of legal and economic texts, which becomes dense from the reign of Nebuchadnezzar II (604–562) onwards and does not thin out (quantitatively) until the end of the reign of the Persian king Darius I (522–486). An important insight provided by this wealth of material is a basic institutional continuity within Babylonia: there was no obvious or immediate change in the Babylonian cities that can be easily associated with Cyrus' conquest and Babylonia's transformation into a province of the immense Persian empire. By far the largest number of texts come from Uruk a somewhat smaller, but still sizable, group from Sippar. One drawback of the Uruk and Sippar texts is that they emanate from the main sanctuaries in these cities, and, thus, primarily illustrate the day-to-day activities of temples, their estates and staffs. This is valuable, but it raises difficult questions as to how temple and city interacted. The problem is exacerbated by the fact that documents from the central administration, such as exist in profusion for the Neo-Assyrian empire, are almost totally absent (see p. 574). The Babylonian fiscal system, provincial government, court and military organisation are therefore very poorly known indeed. In other words, the day-by-day functioning of two important temples can be reconstructed in astonishing detail, but the political landscape within which they operated remains fairly obscure.

Many features of Babylonian kingship and royal ideology have to be inferred, rather than being directly illuminated, by the surviving evidence. The one aspect that stands out clearly is the kings' close involvement in the cultic foundations of Babylonia and their frequent personal participation in the New Year festival in Babylon. The splendid public processions associated with the festival provided an opportunity for the rulers to display their troops and war-trophies (Berger 1970; Kuhrt 1987). A later, fragmentary epic poem, which celebrated Nabopolassar's victory over the Assyrians, gives us a glimpse of the Babylonian coronation ceremony; it also stresses the importance of the king's role as warrior:

> The princes of the land being assembled, Nab[opolassar they bless?],
> Opening their fists [they . . .] the sovereignty.
> Bel (Marduk), in the assembly of the gods, [gave?] the ruling power to
>   [Nabopolassar?].
> The king, the reliable command [. . .]
> 'With the standard I shall constantly conquer [your] enemies,
> I shall place [your?] throne in Babylon.'
> The chair-bearer, taking his hand, . . . [. . .]
> They kept placing the standard on his head.
> They had him sit on the royal throne [. . .]
> They took the royal seal [. . .]
> The 'eunuchs', the staff-bearers [. . .]
> The great ones of Akkad approached the cella.
> When they had drawn near, they sat down before hi[m]
> The great ones in their joy [exclaimed?]:
> 'O lord, O king, may you live forever! [May you conquer] the land of
>   [your] enemies!
> May the king of the gods, Marduk, rejoice in you . . . [. . .]!
> May Nabu, the scribe of E[sagil], make your days long!
> May Erra, your sword, Nergal [. . .]!
> [May you av]enge Akkad . . . [. . .]'

(Grayson 1975: 84–5)

There are some general similarities here to aspects of Assyrian kingship: the king is blessed by the gods, invested with power by the supreme god of the pantheon; his courtiers and officials congratulate him formally on his coronation, wish him long life and victory on all fronts, and ask him to avenge past Babylonian humiliations and defeats. It looks, too, as though part of the ceremonial consisted of the king being formally handed the royal seal. In the absence of central archives, this seal has not so far been identified, but its significance must have been similar to that of the Assyrian royal seal, i.e. authenticating royal orders and giving them the force of law. The king in his role of protector of the realm from rebellion and sedition is illustrated by the document recording his public condemnation of a traitor (see pp. 595–596) – a text which also shows that loyalty oaths were as important in Babylonia as they had been in Assyria. In cult, the king was central in all respects: he was the chief builder and provider of essential resources; he participated in rituals and authorised the offerings to be made. Intercalations in the calendar were made at the command of the king, probably acting in consultation with his learned advisers.[7]

The organisation of the Babylonian court is obscure, and our knowledge of the royal family remains opaque. It is possible that Nebuchadnezzar was married to a Median princess, the daughter of Cyaxares (Berossus, *FGrH* 680 F7), as part of the political deal his father and the Median ruler made in 614. Whether she was his only wife, or at least his chief spouse, is unknown. His own eldest daughter was married to Neriglissar, one of his generals, who was a man locally powerful on the eastern fringes of the empire (and later seized the throne, p. 597). Perhaps there was felt to be a need to strengthen support for Nabopolassar's family by drawing provincial Babylonian nobles into the royal family network (Weisberg 1974). The succession system seems to have been rather similar to the Assyrian one, from the little evidence we have: the crown prince was groomed for the kingship, taking on some of the functions of his father when necessary. This is true of Nebuchadnezzar, who fought major campaigns in the last years of his father's life, and of Belshazzar, who administered and defended Babylonia in the 540s during his father's long-drawn-out war in Arabia (Beaulieu 1987).

An inscription of Nebuchadnezzar II gives us a rough guide to the Babylonian court and the imperial structure. The text is usually called Nebuchadnezzar's 'court calendar', although it is in fact a building text:

Mašennu (i.e. functionaries in the royal household):
Nabu-zer-iddina, chief baker,
Nabu-zer-ibni, chief of the *kāṣiru* (meaning uncertain),
Erib- . . ., superintendent of the palace,
Sin-shar- . . ., major-domo,
Atkal-ana-Mar-Esagila
[. . .]
Ina-qibit-Bel, [the . . .],
Bel-erish, the chief [. . .],
Ardia, *mašennu* of the House of the Palace Women,
Bel-uballit, scribe of the House of the Palace Women,
Silla, master of ceremonies(?) (or: chief of police?),
Nabu-ah-usur, chief barber (or: chief engineer? chief of couriers?),
Mushallim-Marduk, Nabu-ushibshi, Erib-shu, overseer of slave-women,
Nabu-bel-usur, overseer of slave-women,

Nabu-zer-ibni, cupbearer,
Nergal-resua, chief singer,
Ardi-Nabu, secretary of the crown-prince,
Ea-idanni, chief of cattle,
Rimutu, chief of cattle,
Nabu-mar-sharri-usur, chief of boatmen,
Hanunu, chief of the king's merchants.

The great ones of Akkad:
Ea-dayan, governor (*šaknu*) of the sea(land),
Nergal-sharri-usur, the *sinmagir*,
Emuqahi of Tupliash,
Bel-shum-ishkun of Puqudu,
Bibiea, the Dakkurean,
Nadin-ahi, 'official' ((lú)É.m a š) of Der,
Marduk-shar-usur of Gambulu,
Marduk-sharrani, governor (*bēl pīhāti*) of Sumandar,
Belidarum, the Amukanite,
Rimutu, 'lawful' governor (*šaknu kēnu*) of Zame,
Nabu-etir-napshate, governor (*šaknu*) of Yaptiru,
. . ., 'offici[al' . . .]
Mushezib-bel, 'off[icial' [. . .]

The 'officials' ((lú)É.m a š(meš)):
Shumkenum, 'official' of Dur-[Yakin]
Bania, 'official' of Limet[um],
Marduk-zer-ibni, 'official' of Matkall[u],
Shula, 'official' of Ninid-Laguda,
Shuma, 'official' of Kullab,
Nergal-zer-ibni, 'official' of Udannum,
Marduk-erish, 'official' of Larsa,
Nabu-kin-apli, 'official' of Kissik,
Bel-uppahir, 'official' of Bakushu

qīpi ālāni (i.e. royal city officials):
Iba, governor of the town Dur . . . .
Shalambi, governor of . . .
Ziria, governor of . . .
Zabina, *qēpu* of . . .
Shuma, *qēpu* of . . .
Adad-aha-iddina, governor of the to[wn . . .]
Nabu-zer-ukin of the province?/land? . . .
Animepush, *qēpu* of . . .
Bel-shum-ishkun, *qēpu* of the town N[i . . .]

(and:) the king of Tyre,
the king of Gaza,
the king of Sidon,
the king of Arvad,
the king of Ashdod,
the king of Mir- . . .
the king of . . .

(Unger 1931/1970: no. 26; ANET: 307–308)

Not everything is clear here, and the list does not include all officials by any means. The survey lists, first, the top members of the court hierarchy. Among the most important is the chief baker, Nabu-zer-iddina, known from 2 *Kings* 25.8 to be identical with the chief commander of the Babylonian armed forces, Nebu-zar-adan. This implies that, as at other periods and in other regions, a literal translation of these court-titles is no guide to the functions performed by the holder. As the list shows, several of the old tribal Chaldaean and Aramaean districts remained under local leaders; the various governors of the Babylonian districts are followed by the obscure (to us) 'town/city-officials'. Right at the end, and not fully preserved, some of the client-kings of the empire appear. We should perhaps add to them the local ruler of Cilicia (Herodotus 1. 74). There must have been more provincial governors than named here and, indeed, we know a governor of Kadesh (Milki-etiri, cf. Pinches 1917: 128ff.; McEwan 1982: 5, n. 2) and one of Judah (Gedaliah, see p. 593) from other sources.[8] Recent evidence (Potts 1990 [0Gf] I: 348–350) shows that Nebuchadnezzar exercised some kind of control over the island of Failaka at the head of the Gulf, while in Nabonidus' reign a 'governor of Dilmun' (central Gulf) is attested. This reflects Babylonia's close involvement in the Gulf trade. The strong commercial interests of the monarchy are also shown by the relatively high position accorded to the 'chief of the boatmen/sailors' and the 'chief of the king's merchants' at court (see also Oppenheim 1967). It is conceivable that the 'governor of the sealand' had responsibility for promoting Babylonian trade in the Gulf. It is tempting to associate with this attested Neo-Babylonian activity in the Gulf region the later statement by Alexander the Great's admiral, Nearchus, that 'it was here [sc. Ras Musandam] that the Assyrians imported cinnamon and other spices' (Arrian *Indica* 32.7). But the reference is chronologically unspecific.

The system of provinces and the duties of governors were probably organised along lines analogous to the earlier Assyrian ones: a broken chronicle reference (*ABC* no. 5: 23–24) may imply that governors (along with client-kings) were responsible for gathering taxes and tribute for the king. A reference at the end of Nabonidus' 'epitaph' for his mother (the chief evidence for royal burials in this period) implies that governors were required to attend the public funerals of members of the royal family:

She died a natural death in the 9th year of Nabonidus, king of Babylon.

Nabonidus, king of Babylon, the son whom she bore, laid her body to rest [wrapped in] fine [wool garments and] shining white linen. He deposited her body in a hidden tomb with splendid [ornaments] of gold [set with] beautiful stones, [. . .] stones, expensive stone beads, [containers with] scented oil, and [. . .]. He slaughtered fat rams and assembled into his presence [the inhabitants] of Babylon and Borsippa together with [people] from far off provinces, he [summoned kings, princes] and governors from the [borders] of Egypt on the Upper Sea (Mediterranean), to the Lower Sea (Arab-Persian Gulf), for the mourning and [. . .] and they made a great lament, scattered [dust] on their heads. For seven days and seven nights they walked about, heads hung low, [dust strewn], stripped of their attire. On the seventh day [. . .] all the people of the country shaved and cleaned themselves, [threw off?] their (mourning) dress [. . . . I had] chests with (new) clothes [brought] for them to their living quarters, [treated them] with food [and drink], provided them lavishly with fine oil, poured scented oil over their heads, made them glad and looking presentable. I provided them well for their [long] journey and they returned to their homes.

(Gadd 1958: H₁ B; *ANET*: 561–562)

A small number of ration texts have been found in the great palace in Babylon which name some of the people who received provisions from the royal purse. Among them appears Jehoiachin, the former king of Judah, and his family; they are listed several times as recipients of substantial quantities of oil, which shows that some of the 'royal prisoners' lived at the Babylonian court and ate at the royal table (Weidner 1939; *ANET*: 308). Also featured in these texts are people from western Turkey (Lydians, 'Ionians' (see pp. 547–548)), Iran and Egypt, as well as some of the coastal cities (Tyre, Byblos), which shows that the kings relied on different ethnic groups, inside and outside the empire, to swell the Babylonian workforce and army. Excavation has revealed a possible settlement of Greek soldiers in Judah, who may well have been subject eventually to the Babylonian king (Mesad Hashyavehu, Helm 1980; Eph'al 1983). The glittering prizes that Babylonia held out to poor Greeks, who hired themselves for mercenary service in its armies and eventually returned home greatly enriched, are nicely caught by Alkaios (early sixth century) in a well-known poem welcoming his brother home:

You have come from the ends of the earth, dear Antimenidas, with the gold-bound haft of the sword with which, fighting for the Babylonians who dwell in houses of bricks four hands long, you performed a mighty deed and saved them all from grievous troubles by slaying a warrior who wanted but a palm's breadth of five royal cubits of stature.
(Diehl, *Anthologia Lyrica Graeca* (1924–5): Alkaios no. 50; Edmonds
Lyra Graeca (Loeb 1928) 1: Alkaios no. 133)

Some of the splendour and wealth of Babylon and its court is echoed by the legendary anecdotes and romantic stories (particularly in the Old Testament) which have the Babylon of this period as their setting. The stories in the late (second century) book of *Daniel* are the best-known, but there are many more: the fabled hanging gardens (attributed to Nebuchadnezzar II) were counted among the seven wonders of the world,[9] and Babylon became a byword for luxury and cosmopolitan life (e.g. *Genesis*; *Revelation*). Nebuchadnezzar himself later counted as a world conqueror, reaching the frontiers of the known world (Megasthenes (*FGrH* 715; Sack 1992)) like the legendary Assyrian queen, Semiramis, and the Egyptian Sesostris. The immense wealth commanded by the Babylonian kings is reflected in their large-scale building projects, especially at Ur, Sippar, Borsippa and Babylon itself, which presented glorious spectacles, with their magnificent temples and towering ziggurats, now lying in sad ruins. The royal inscriptions describe in loving detail many more impressive royal constructions of which nothing has survived. The colourful embellishments and decorations in precious metals, too, have vanished. Some evidence for the manufacture of perfume (En-gedi), oil and purple dye for textiles (Mizpah) and fine wines on royal estates in Judah (Mizpah, Mozah and Gibeon) has been teased out (Graham 1984). Such production of luxury items for court consumption was probably replicated in other areas of the empire, where the Babylonians took over and developed earlier crown estates and local industries.

Cuneiform documents (mainly from Babylon), including family archives, illustrate private economic life. Their number is substantial, despite the fact that Aramaic was becoming the dominant language of Babylonia from the late seventh century onwards. They reflect a wide range of activities, such as investment in land (Joannès 1989), advantageous marriages made between members of propertied families (Roth 1989), their credit-transactions and trading enterprises (Shiff 1987; Wunsch 1993). The best-known and largest archive is that of the great Egibi family, often described as a 'banking house', given their immensely diversified and complex commercial and credit business. They seem to have built up their profitable enterprise in the seventh century, and were probably one of the most prominent business families in Babylonia in the sixth century; members of the family were involved in deals well beyond the borders of the empire in Iran (Weingort 1939; Ungnad 1941; Zadok 1976).

The documentary material is rich enough to allow us to study Babylonian family structure and households (Roth 1987); one scholar has even estimated the numbers of privately owned slaves (Dandamaev 1984). In one case we can observe a wealthy Babylonian family using its daughters to create and maintain a profitable social alliance. Despite their acknowledged legal rights, women were effectively constrained by the larger interests of their families (Joannès 1987). The texts inform us mainly about the marriages of the more prosperous Babylonians, because the large dowries, over which the wife and her family retained control, needed to be carefully itemised:

> Nadin, son of Lusi-an-nur-Marduk, descendant of Ili-bani, promises to marry Kabta, the daughter of Nabu-shum-ishkun, descendant of Ili-bani. Nabu-shum-ishkun voluntarily has promised to Nadin: a 3-*panû* orchard, including the fallow area, in the territory of Sur-amilatu, adjacent to the 1-*kurru* ... field (which is) the previously (promised) dowry and) which (extends) from the irrigation dike of the estate of Bit-Shamu (the 1-*kurru* field being that) which Nabu-shum-ishkun had promised to Nadin as the dowry with his previously (promised) daughter – for an outstanding (total) of a 1-*kurru*, 3-*panû* field.
>
> (In addition, the woman) Inba, the *mulūgu*-slave, a bed, two chairs, a table, three bronze goblets, a bronze bowl, one copper cooking vessel, and one lamp – in total, ten household objects (for) the later and earlier (dowries), Nabu-shum-ishkun has promised Nadin.
>
> (As for) Ishtar-shiminni and Diditi, the slave(-women promised) earlier with the earlier dowry, which Nabu-shum-ishkun recorded on a document and gave to Nadin – instead of Diditi, Nabu-shum-ishkun has now given Banitu-sharrat to Nadin.
>
> By the end of month IV Nabu-shum-ishkun will release and give Ishtar-shiminni to Nadin.
>
> (Witnesses and date)
>
> (Roth 1989 no. 9)

The humbler inhabitants of Babylonia shared to some degree in the increased wealth generated by the Neo-Babylonian empire. The kings were active in revitalising agriculture, and settled deportees and foreign soldiers, which helped to bring more land under production. This also served to increase the government's profits through taxation. The many texts from this period show that the economic upswing, which began in Babylonia in Ashurbanipal's reign (see p. 589), continued apace. A more direct result of participation in campaigns was the acquisition by relatively low-ranking soldiers of slaves. They could sell them to more prosperous Babylonians, who might use them to generate income by renting them out as prostitutes or having them apprenticed to various trades, such as cobbling or beer-brewing (Dandamaev 1984). The profitable and wide-ranging activities of the Egibi family (pp. 574; 609) in slave-dealing are well documented in this period (Weingort 1939).

11f The cities of Babylonia in the Late Babylonian period

How did the great ancient cities of Babylonia function in this period? Babylonia experienced much political turmoil from the late ninth right down to the second century:[10] from being subject to the Assyrians it became the heartland of a new empire; then it was conquered by the Persians (539), two hundred years later by Alexander the Great (331), and, finally, it was incorporated into the Seleucid empire (from 312). But in spite of all these upheavals the basic form of the Babylonian city appears to have remained fairly constant. The civic institutions tended to survive and be reasserted, often with direct royal support, particularly on the occasion of military conquest. Certainly there were modifications and changes within this long period, but they were introduced gradually and piecemeal: there were no abrupt or total revolutions (van der Spek 1987).

The evidence for understanding the Babylonian cities is complex and not limited to the period of the Neo-Babylonian empire – some of the most illuminating material comes from the time of Assyrian domination. The specific factors which affect our understanding of the structure of civic life are the difficulties inherent in the corpus of surviving evidence: it comes from a limited number of centres only, often from temple complexes (see p. 603). This leaves certain areas of city-structure blank and we can only guess at them. For example, to what extent may we assume that the situation reconstructed for one city is true of another? Their historical roots differed, after all, and so did their local institutions and the terminology used for certain administrative officials. Yet the cities of Babylonia had also been bound together within a territorial state for several hundred years, and subjected to an overarching royal control which reached into the fabric of local life and led to some convergence in function if not name. So each city in the first millennium represented a kind of institutional palimpsest. The fact that the size of the agricultural hinterland of different cities remains unclear, as does the population of individual cities, presents further insuperable problems – especially as most urban sites have been only partially excavated, although the area of the walled portions of some is fairly precisely known (e.g. Babylon and Uruk). Additionally, there is always a danger in combining material spread over about three to four centuries, as it tends to obscure major historical shifts – outward continuity of form may conceal profound dislocations.

Some of the fundamental questions that have exercised scholars, and on which a wide range of very different opinions are held, are: Was there a concept of something we might render by the term 'citizenship'; i.e. some way in which people defined themselves as belonging to this or that urban community? If so, who claimed to belong to it? How did such a body of citizens function? How did it interact with the great temples and priests? How did the king, controlling the larger territorial state within which the cities were located, relate to them?

By the first millennium all the cities were embraced within the kingdom of Babylonia, but a consciousness of their distinct identity remained. In other words, although it becomes usual to call the area of south Iraq 'Babylonia' from c. 1500 on (see chapter 7a), and to speak of Babylon from then on as 'the capital' of the country, it seems that individuals often defined themselves as belonging to a particular city. The comic tale of the *Poor Man of Nippur* (preserved in Akkadian on a tablet from Sultantepe (seventh century)), for example, begins:

> (There was once) a man, a son of Nippur, poor and humble,
> Gimil-Ninurta was his name, a miserable man.
> In his city Nippur wearily he sat.
> He had no silver, as befits people,
> he possessed no gold, as befits mankind.
> His storeroom thirsted for the pure grain.
> With craving for bread his liver was oppressed(?)
> with craving for meat and beer his face was disfigured.
> Daily for lack of food he used to lie hungry.
> He was clad in garments for which he had no change.
> With his weary heart he took counsel:
> 'I will take off my garments, for which I have no change,
> in the city-square of my city, Nippur, I will buy a sheep.'
> (O. Gurney, *AnSt* 6 (1956): 150/151, ll. 1–13)

The story goes on to describe the eventual triumph of the poor man over the greedy and obsequious mayor of Nippur. Nippur is the setting of the story, and it gives us a vivid and amusing slice of Babylonian city-life. The term 'son of city X' to identify the member of an urban community (as in this story) is also used, revealingly, in another document, known as the 'Babylonian *Fürstenspiegel*' ('Mirror of Princes'). The text (in Akkadian) is known from exemplars found at seventh-century Nineveh and Neo-Babylonian Nippur:

> If a king does not heed justice, his people will be thrown into chaos, and his land will be devastated.
> If he does not heed the justice of his land, Ea, king of destinies, will alter his destiny and will not cease from hostilely pursuing him.
> If he does not heed his nobles, his life will be cut short.
> If he does not heed his adviser, his land will rebel against him.
> If he heeds a rogue, the *status quo* in his land will change.
> If he heeds a trick of Ea, the great gods in unison and in their just ways will not cease from prosecuting him.
> If he improperly convicts a son of Sippar, but acquits a foreigner, Shamash, judge of heaven and earth, will set up a foreign justice in his land, where the princes and judges will not heed justice.
> If the sons of Nippur are brought to him for judgement, but he accepts a present and improperly convicts them, Enlil, lord of the lands, will bring a foreign army against him to slaughter his army, whose prince and chief officers will roam (his) streets like fighting cocks.
> If he takes the silver of the sons of Babylon and adds it to his own coffers, or if he hears a lawsuit involving men of Babylon but treats it

frivolously, Marduk, lord of heaven and earth, will set his foes upon him, and he will give his property and wealth to his enemy.

If he imposes a fine on the sons of Nippur, Sippar, or Babylon, or if he puts them in prison, the city where the fine was imposed will be completely overturned and a foreign enemy will make his way into the prison in which they were put.

If he mobilised the whole of Sippar, Nippur, and Babylon, and imposed forced labour on the people, exacting from them corvée at the herald's proclamation, Marduk, prince of the gods, the prince, the councillor, will turn his land over to his enemy so that the troops of his land will do forced labour for his enemy, for Anu, Enlil, and Ea, the great gods, who dwell in heaven and earth, in their assembly affirmed the freedom of those people from those obligations.

If he gives the fodder of the sons of Sippar, Nippur, and Babylon to (his own) steeds, the steeds who eat the fodder will be led away to the enemy's yoke, and those men will be mobilised with the king's men when the national army is conscripted.

Mighty Erra, [who goes] before his army, will shatter his front line and go at his enemy's side.

If he loosens the yokes of [their] oxen and puts them in other fields or gives them to a foreigner, [. . .] will be devastated [. . .] of Addu.

If he seizes [their . . .] stock of sheep, Addu, canal supervisor of heaven and earth, will extirpate his pasturing animals by hunger and will amass offerings for Shamash.

If the adviser or 'chief officer' (?) of the royal entourage denounces them (i.e. the sons of Sippar, Nippur, and Babylon) and so obtains bribes from them, at the command of Ea, king of the Apsu (watery underground home of Ea), the adviser and 'chief officer' will die by the sword, their place will be covered over as a ruin, the wind will carry away their remains, and their achievements will be given over to the storm wind.

If he declares their treaties void, or alters their inscribed stelae, sends them on a campaign, or [press-gangs] them into hard labour, Nabu, scribe of Esagila, who organises the whole of heaven and earth, who directs everything, who ordains kingship, will declare the treaties of his land void, and will decree hostility.

If either a shepherd, or temple overseer, or a chief officer of the king, who serves as temple overseer of Sippar, Nippur, or Babylon, imposes forced labour on them (i.e. the men of these cities) in connection with the temples of the great gods, the great gods will quit their dwellings in their fury and will not enter their shrines.

(Lambert 1960: 110–115)

According to this text, the inhabitants of three cities – always described as 'the sons of Sippar/Babylon/Nippur' – claimed specified privileges *vis-à-vis* the monarch: if the king infringes them, disaster will befall his reign. They, in effect, dispute the king's right to exercise absolute sovereignty, and even deny his authority in some aspects of jurisdiction: taxes of all kinds, labour service, army service and the right to exact fines are repeatedly singled out as demands that the king may not make without divine punishment descending on him. Further, the king is warned against passing corrupt and biased sentences, suggesting that the authors of this tract perhaps reserved the right to judge themselves in some sense. The reference (near the end) to a king rescinding the 'treaties' of the cities and changing the 'inscribed stelae' is noteworthy. The implication seems to be that the rights claimed by the cities, which the king is urged to respect, were enshrined in writing.

We do not know the date of composition of this text and so we cannot narrow down the historical context of its genesis. Was it, therefore, just a literary exercise, or did it reflect an unrealistic yearning for an earlier, long-gone ideal existence? It has become evident recently that the document circulated and was well known in the seventh century. A letter addressed to the Assyrian king Esarhaddon (680–669), probably from Nippur, mentions exemptions traditionally claimed by Sippar, Babylon and Nippur. The writer then stresses that this means that the city of Nippur is as privileged as Babylon. At this point he says, significantly:

> May the lord of kings look; that tablet (called) 'If the king does not heed justice' (i.e. the opening lines of this text) says as follows:. . .
>
> (CT 54: 202)

He then quotes the last five lines of the *Fürstenspiegel*, with only a few paraphrases, emphasises that the text is reliable (i.e. correct and authentic) and advises that the king have it read out to him (Reiner 1982). This shows us that Babylonians definitely used the tract as a framework for conducting a dialogue with kings (including powerful conquerors like the Assyrian monarchs) and to exert pressure on them. It is, in fact, likely that all the major cities of the region laid claim to a similar privileged status (Landsberger 1965). So we may visualise all the ancient cities of Babylonia as having a strong tradition of civic rights, which a king could not easily override.

From Assyrian royal grants of similar special conditions to the inhabitants of Ashur and Harran (see p. 538), we learn that the term for such civic privileges was *kidinnu/kidinnūtu*. This means, literally, 'divine protection': i.e. the entire area of the city was deemed to come under the protection of its patron-deity. The people living in it were thus the *ṣābe kidinni*, the 'people of the *kidinnu*', which implies a basic meaning of 'the protected people' (Leemans 1946). It is likely that this protection was, or could be, physically represented by divine symbols erected at the city-gate. The term *kidinnu/kidinnūtu* appears in several contexts relating to Babylonian cities, notably in the context of Esarhaddon's rebuilding of Babylon (680–669) and the return of its deported inhabitants. An integral part of that restoration was:

> The 'freedom' (?debt-remission: *andurāru*) of the oppressed Babylonians, the protected people (*ṣābe kidinni*), those 'entitled to release' by Anu and Enlil I established anew. Those people who had been sold into slavery and whose lot had been fetters and chains, I gathered together and made them again into Babylonians; their pillaged property I returned to them. I clothed the naked. Then I caused them to take the road to Babylon. I encouraged them to settle in the city, build houses, lay out orchards, and dig canals. Their *kidinnūtu* which had ended and been lost, I set up anew . . . I reaffirmed by writing (it) down their tax-exemption (*zakûtu*). I opened their roads to the four points of the compass, so that they might direct their minds to traffic with all the world.
>
> (Borger 1956 §11 Bab. A Ep. 37)

In his summing up, Esarhaddon utters curses on anyone who might destroy his work in Babylon – especially the removal (or dissolving) of the *kidinnūtu* of Babylon. We receive a strong impression here of the king priding himself on restoring privileges and exemptions to the restored city, replacing it effectively under divine protection. *Kidinnūtu* appears to represent a whole package of city-rights, a kind of 'charter of autonomy', which marks their renaissance as 'Babylonians'.

A letter (*ABL* 878: still not very well understood) addressed by the inhabitants of Babylon to the Assyrian king (in the seventh century) may bear this out. It looks as though a royal official had executed someone in Babylon. The Babylonians refer to their *kidinnūtu* and seem to say that anyone entering Babylon comes automatically under the divine protection of the city and enjoys a sort of right to asylum. The letter even claims that anyone entering Babylon (including foreigners and dogs) was protected and could not be killed. This smacks of rhetorical exaggeration and the precise meaning is perhaps somewhat different. The point of the letter seems to be that the inhabitants of Babylon alone have the right of initial jurisdiction over anyone within the limits of the city. No one can be executed without a decision by the city authorities; even people claiming to act for the king have no right to infringe the city's rules – such behaviour would be an offence affecting the whole urban community. In the words of the mayor, in the story of the *Poor Man of Nippur*, when he is being thrashed to within an inch of his life by the poor man in disguise:

> My lord, do not kill a 'son of Nippur', do not stain your hands with the blood of a *kidinnu*-person; (it is) an abomination of Enlil (i.e. chief god of Nippur).
>
> (O. Gurney *AnSt* 6 (1956): 154/155, ll. 105–6)

There are definite indications in *ABL* 878 of a claimed autonomy in civic matters, enshrined in the term *kidinnūtu*. On that basis, the Babylonians were able to complain, in this instance, about the high-handed execution of one of their number by a royal official.

The reference by Esarhaddon (p. 615) to the fact that he had affirmed the tax-exemption in writing, also deserves notice. The *Fürstenspiegel* mentions stelae on which the agreements (presumably between king and city-dwellers about rights) had been inscribed; the letter to Esarhaddon quoting some of the text (p. 614) implies the circulation of the document in written form and the existence of multiple copies. To this evidence for the existence of 'city-charters', we can add the report of an Assyrian siege of Babylon in 731 sent to Tiglath-pileser III (744–727). It recounts the following events:

> On the 28th we came to Babylon. We took our stand before the Marduk-gate (and) argued with the Babylonian ... the servant of Mukin-zeri (the rebel ruler, see above p. 579) was present at his side. When they came out they were standing before the gate with the Babylonians. We spoke to the Babylonians thus: 'Why are you opposing us for the sake of them? Their place is among the Chaldaeans ... Babylon indeed favours a Chaldaean! Your *kidinnūtu* has been set down (in writing).'
>
> (Saggs 1955: NL 1)

The commanders of the besieging Assyrian force here address the people of Babylon directly asking them to surrender – they were watched by an official of the usurping Chaldaean ruler with whom the Assyrians were at war, but he did not intervene at any point and the Assyrian appeals were not directed at him.[11] In trying to persuade the Babylonians to surrender the Assyrians pointed out to the inhabitants that they had nothing to lose by doing so, as their protected status (*kidinnūtu*) existed in written form and would therefore be respected. In this critical situation (it was unclear, after all, who would win the war) the Babylonians were understandably wary of committing themselves, especially to an Assyrian official who had no direct royal authority. A later passage of the letter implies that the city might be prepared to negotiate a surrender, but only with the Assyrian king himself, as only he would be in a position to guarantee fully their protection and affirm their rights. It was clearly important that, before handing the city over to the guardianship of a new ruler, its rights be clearly understood and agreed.

In connection with this, we should remember that an important ritual during the New Year festival in Babylon consisted of the king being stripped of his royal insignia, struck in the face, forced to his knees before Marduk by having his ears pulled, and then making this solemn avowal:

> I have not sinned, lord of the lands,
> I have not neglected your godhead,
> I have not destroyed Babylon,
> I have not ordered her to be dispersed,

I have not made Esagila (main temple in Babylon) tremble
I have not struck the people of the *kidinnu* in the face
I have not humiliated them.
I have paid attention to Babylon,
I have not destroyed her walls.
(Thureau-Dangin, *Rituels accadiens*, 1921: 144, ll. 423–428; *ANET*: 334;
TUAT II: 222)

This shows that the king was crucial as the defender of the rights of citizens, because he himself, through such formal and ritual protestations, was tied into the system of civic religion and belief.

The cumulative evidence indicates that there was a strong sense of corporate identity among city-dwellers in Babylonia. It was expressed through a package of rights and privileges, including a wide range of tax- and service-exemptions and a measure of autonomy in civic affairs. The king's personal involvement in, and guarantees of, these was vital, and they were probably recorded in written form – perhaps even publicly displayed. City-inhabitants knew the contents of their charters and they formed the basis for negotiation between city and king. Finally, these rights seem to have been conceived as relating to the divine order of things (which included the concept of city-life as the basis of ordered existence; Berossus *FGrH* 680 F1), and so placed the city and its people under divine protection.

The further, and even more tricky, question is who precisely enjoyed these privileges and the attendant status? Certainly not everyone: privately owned chattel-slaves, temple-slaves, royal slaves, certain dependent groups (whose exact position is obscure), holders of military land grants and foreigners settled either in small village communities or in a Babylonian city were almost certainly not included. Some of them could change their status in time – a slave, for example, could be freed; but on the whole they were distinguished carefully from 'citizens': they are listed separately in documents, and foreign settlers appear to have had their own administrative organs, implied by references to the 'elders of the Jews' (*Ezekiel* 8.1) and 'elders of the Egyptians' (*Camb.* 85, cf. Dandamaev 1982: 38). So the citizen-body was exclusive and gaining membership of the body of privileged inhabitants was neither automatic nor easy. One designation in Late Babylonian documents probably renders the concept 'citizen', more or less in our sense: *mār banî* (lit. 'free/noble man'; Frame 1992: 230–231). Despite some recent doubts (Roth 1988), most scholars think that the term indicates that they were 'free' persons, and that membership of this group was probably not determined purely by property or rank: it was primarily a juridical definition (Oelsner 1976). It is from the group of *mār banî* that those administering the city came (although by what procedure is not clear), and the city administration seems to have been in large part co-extensive with the temple organisation.

* * *

What do we know about city-structure? Uruk is the chief Babylonian site providing dense, fairly continuous and reasonably well studied documentation for the Late Babylonian period; the texts come in large part from its sanctuary. The more patchy and scattered material from other Baylonian centres, however, suggests that, while cities varied in the details of their arrangements, the general pattern of administration was broadly similar. The Uruk material shows us a small body of high-up administrators more or less fully engaged in directing temple affairs: seeing that rents and produce due on the extensive temple-lands were collected, ensuring that fields, flocks, orchards, slaves produced profits, that the calendar was kept in order through intercalation, regular rituals performed and royal orders transmitted. Some of the agricultural work was done by temple-slaves and (perhaps) dependent groups, but a considerable extent of temple-land and income was in the hands of people who performed specialised duties relating to the cult, ranging from diviners and singers to butchers, bakers, shepherds, launderers, goldsmiths etc. All of them participated in the cult and their duties (however mundane they seem to us) required some knowledge of cult practice and associated learning. This is clear from some of the ritual instructions for daily offerings to be made to the gods at Uruk, where the butcher, for example, is enjoined to recite a special prayer as he slaughters the necessary animals; during the New Year festival at Babylon, too, the craftsmen who prepared the golden canopy for Marduk's enthronement were obliged to utter an incantation on completion of their task.

Most cult-participants did not carry out their tasks on a full-time basis, but leased or sold shares of the offices to other people. Since the offices could also be divided through inheritance, a situation developed whereby any one cult-officiant may only have performed his duties for a few days per year. But what is important in this is the fact that, given the cultic and ritual importance of the tasks and the expertise they demanded, such posts could only be obtained or bought by someone either able to carry them out or to provide a substitute acceptable to the temple authorities (Doty 1977; Oelsner 1981). So while the numbers involved in the cult overall were probably quite large, because of the divisions of office and accompanying income, holding and performing such duties was restricted to a specific group, and the likelihood is that this group was the *mār banî* – the legally definable citizen-body. They derived some of their status from their recognised entitlement to hold the temple posts, but, in fact, spent most of the year transacting their own familybusiness – such as slave-dealing, credit-facilitating or real-estate investments. In no sense can these people be classed as 'priests' in our understanding of the word, and indeed, as has been repeatedly pointed out (Kümmel 1979: 147 n. 1; Brinkman *JCS* 35 (1983): 232), the term 'priest' as such does not seem to exist in Akkadian. How extensively poorer people may have been involved in temple work is unknown: since temple posts could be sold and we have evidence (attested in Hellenistic Uruk; Doty 1977) for extensive investment by propertied families in them, we should perhaps assume that they were, in practice, excluded from participation, although, theoretically, their right of access remained.

Poorer people would also have been effectively debarred from active participation in the assembly (*puhru* or *kiništu*), made up of *mār banî* and presided over by the city-governor or the head of the temple administration. This assembly (its size and constitution are uncertain) is documented as acting both to resolve matters relating to temple property, such as thefts, and in the collection of outstanding rents due on temple lands; in one instance, it decided to take over the house of an insolvent debtor and add it to the property of the temple. But its jurisdiction does not seem to have been limited always to matters directly affecting temple affairs: quarrels between citizens about unpaid debts, goods paid for but not delivered, and theft from private houses are also documented. Two examples illustrate how the king and the city assembly might interact. The text (quoted pp. 595–596) in which Nebuchadnezzar II condemned to death a prominent Babylonian found guilty of transgressing his loyalty oath provides a hint: the death sentence and the reason for it were pronounced in the presence of 'the assembly of the people'. This shows that the body was called together to witness the accusation and sentence of death passed by the king in a case of high treason. Also illuminating is the case of the man who made a murderous assault on a royal commissioner at Uruk (TCL 12: 17): the assembly of Uruk heard the case, 'tied up and sealed the iron dagger which he had pulled from his belt' and, as no final decision is given, almost certainly passed the case on to the king for sentence, as the attack had been made on one of his officials. In both cases, we see the assembly acting in conjunction with royal interests, with their own right to be informed formally, witness royal decisions or make preliminary investigations about the culpability of one of their number apparently acknowledged by the king.

For the Babylonian cities monarchic rule was part of the traditional structure, and continued to be central to their institutions even when they were incorporated within a larger territorial state, with the centre of royal power located elsewhere. While it is impossible to define any one of the citizens acting out his particular bit of temple ritual as a 'priest', in our contemporary sense of the word, i.e. as someone particularly holy and more in touch with the divine sphere than others, the position of king did carry with it such sacred overtones. A whole range of politically significant rituals, particularly the New Year festival, ideally required the participation of the king; and, if his personal presence was impossible, some symbol of his presence, such as his robe, might be requested. It was first and foremost the king who partook of the divine meals – the remains from which, after the gods had finished, were sent to him. The daily offerings to divine statues, the expenses incurred by festivals and, above all, temple and other public city building (e.g. walls), all required royal authorisation, royal funding and, in the case of temple-building, royal participation for at least the ceremonial of foundation-laying. Exceptions to this latter rule are rare. When they do occur, it is normally stated that the building has been carried out 'for the life of the king', which implies his support and blessing for the undertaking (for a significant exception, see pp. 578–579).

Each city's deity both protected the city and depended on the citizens to supply its day-to-day needs, but it also related to the king with whom it communicated both through direct revelation to individual citizens (prophecy) and through omens interpreted by relevant experts. Divine revelations were reported to the king, as all such messages affected him directly and personally and through him, ultimately, the cities of his realm. The interdependence of king and cities was finely balanced: the Babylonian city depended economically, cultically and politically on the king and his guarantees to respect their autonomy and exemptions, so that in turn their care of the gods could continue uninterrupted, thus benefiting and protecting the king himself who in turn needed the assurance of this divine support. The critical moment, when this balance, and hence the civilised order itself, was threatened, emerged starkly on the occasion of military conquest with its potential for socio-political disruption. Where evidence survives, the sources illuminate clearly the delicate situation in which a city such as Babylon found itself: in 709, after Sargon's decisive defeat of the Babylonian king Marduk-apla-iddina II, in 539 after Cyrus' resounding triumph over Nabonidus, and in 331 after Alexander's victory at Gaugamela and Darius III's flight, the inhabitants decided, only after negotiation with the new conqueror, to welcome the victor as their new king (Kuhrt 1990a). While it was un-doubtedly politic for them to do so, the negotiations, the formal ceremony of reception of the conqueror by the whole body of citizens and the new ruler's acts in authorising continued divine offerings, and initiating, com-pleting or refurbishing sacred and other buildings, all help to illuminate the real strength and vitality of the Babylonian city and its institutions.

As far as it is possible to judge (and the patchiness and difficulty of the evidence must always be remembered), the cities of Babylonia from the late eighth to second centuries were important and wealthy centres. The focus of the walled city was formed by the sanctuary of the chief deity, located in the middle of the town, with important streets for processions leading from it and others marking different city quarters, in some of which groups of foreigners were settled (see also Herodotus I 178–183). The body of 'citizens' were involved part-time in all aspects of the local cult and its administration, and derived an income related to it from the temple properties. This income augmented their existing property, which mainly consisted of land located in the city's hinterland, but also of houses, flocks, orchards and slaves. It is likely, and the surviving evidence generally supports the hypothesis, that the various cultic offices were in practice restricted to a relatively limited number of extended families who formed the urban élite (Brinkman 1979; 1984a; Kümmel 1979; Frame 1984; 1992); much of the training essential for performance of these duties may have been done within families (Charpin 1986). A clear separation of civic and religious offices is virtually impossible to establish, as one and the same individual could be, for example, both a city-governor and hold a cultic post at the same time (Frame 1984). Similarly, either city-governor or chief temple-administrator could preside over the assembly, whatever business it was conducting, and it is significant that the assembly's competence was not limited to temple matters. The temple and its deity was the fulcrum of city life: *not* a distinct category of life, but an institution serving to integrate the citizens, from which they derived their protected status and on which they based their claim to privileges *vis-à-vis* the king.

The question of the structure of Babylonian cities, and hence Babylonian society, bristles with problems, as this discussion makes evident: the terminology and functions of offices are poorly understood, and many aspects remain hazy and hotly debated.[12] The foregoing can be no more than one approach at trying to interpret some of the material and to suggest a possible picture. But there can be little doubt that, however frustratingly elusive it is for us, the cities of Babylonia had a clearly defined, traditional form and some of their inhabitants formed an identifiable community that merits being called a citizen body.

Notes

1 Pul may be a hypocoristic of Tiglath-pileser; Ululayu ('born in (month) Elul') could be the king's personal name.

2 Alan Millard has gone through Sargon's dated documents, several of which show that Sargon numbered his years as king of Babylon even in Assyria; e.g.: 'eponymate *x*, year *Y* king of Assyria, year *Z* king of Babylon' (personal communication). It underlines the political importance of Sargon's conquest of Babylonia.

3 By 'major campaigns' I mean those involving the king in person and extensively commemorated in his inscriptions. Sennacherib fought eight campaigns in Babylonia and along the Elamite frontier, and one (701) in Phoenicia, Palestine and Judah, which may be considered to fall into this category. His generals fought campaigns in southern Anatolia and there was Assyrian campaigning against Arab tribes, in which royal participation is not clear.

4 A text from the Hellenistic period refers to Nabopolassar as the 'king of the Sealand' (Thureau-Dangin *Rituels accadiens* Paris 1921: 80 and 86). It is *possible* that this means that Nabopolassar was the Assyrian-installed Babylonian commander of the southern marshes (see p. 588), or even that he was a Chaldaean from Bit Yakin. But the evidence is late and not very clear (cf. von Voigtlander 1963).

5 It is usually assumed that the king Nebuchadnezzar mentioned by Nabonidus is Nebuchadnezzar II (604–562), but another suggestion is that it is the much earlier Nebuchadnezzar I (1124–1103: Berger 1973: 63).

6 Many of the themes that appear in the Cyrus Cylinder were used by Marduk-apla-iddina II in his *kudurru* inscription, cf. the discussion on p. 580.

7   There is no evidence for 'sages' at the Neo-Babylonian court, but we are probably right to assume their existence. They appear in the later story of Daniel, and are likely to have been present at most courts.

8   A governor of Arpad (in Nebuchadnezzar II's nineteenth regnal year) is now attested, see F. Joannès *NABU* 1994, note 20.

9   Stephanie Dalley has argued recently that the 'hanging gardens of Babylon' were created at Nineveh by Sennacherib; their association with Babylon and Nebuchadnezzar II is due to a series of misunderstandings (*Iraq* 56 (1994): 45–58).

10 Several Babylonian cities continued in existence, of course, well beyond the second century (Oelsner 1986). The marked decrease in the number of cuneiform documents (due, in part, to the increasing use of Aramaic) does not allow us to follow their later existence in any detail.

11 The scene is very reminiscent of the address by the *rab šāqê* (cupbearer) to the citizens of Jerusalem in 701 (2 *Kings* 18; cf. p. 512).

12 Herodotus' famous description of the city of Babylon and the customs of the Babylonians has exercised many scholars since excavations were undertaken at the city and the cuneiform texts began to be read. It is by no means easy to arrive at full agreement between his account and the reality reconstructed by archaeologists and philologists. Whether he actually visited the country and described his personal observation remains subject to debate (see most recently Rollinger 1993).

12

EGYPT *c.* 1000–525

12a The Third Intermediate Period: dynasties XXI–XXV (1069–664)

Chronology and sources

The end of the New Kingdom is followed by an extremely complex period, lasting over four hundred years, during which Egypt was nominally ruled by a single king (or several co-rulers). But effectively it consisted of an ever more complicated network of small states linked to each other by lines of obligation and fealty that are hard to understand clearly (see table 33).

The situation established at the end of dynasty XX, with Egypt run by the king in Tanis and the high priest of Amun in Thebes, the two dividing the country between them, prevailed for about a hundred and twenty years (see pp. 209–210; table 17). In this time, the Libyan infiltrations, attacks and raids, which had begun early in dynasty XIX, continued to be a problem that had to be faced. It seems that not only were Libyans taken in as soldiers and given land grants, but also that a number of marriage alliances were made by the Theban rulers with various Libyan chiefs, so that, increasingly, some Libyan groups were integrated into the Egyptian state (Kitchen 1986: 252). The main change came when Libyans successfully claimed the Egyptian throne. Dynasties XXII and XXIII were from fairly closely related Libyan tribes, and dynasty XXIV (based at Sais) was also Libyan, although with different cultural and political links. All these dynasties were replaced in about 715, following Egypt's annexation by the Nubian rulers (Napatans). In Egyptian eyes, the Nubian dynasty, which had come into being much earlier and lasted much longer than its political presence in Egypt, formed the twenty-fifth dynasty. The period ends with the Assyrians' invasion of Egypt, in the course of which they eventually managed to expel the Nubian rulers from Egypt. At the same time, one of the Assyrian client-kings in Egypt, Psammetichus, managed, in the wake of the expulsion of the Nubians, to establish himself comparatively swiftly as the new sole ruler over the whole of Egypt. This marked the beginning of dynasty XXVI, which will be examined in the next section.

The main sources that provide a guide through this complex web are, first,

Table 33 Egypt: chronology of the Third Intermediate Period

Dynasty XXI					
Smendes I	1069–1043				
Amenemnisu	1043–1039				
Psusennes I	1039–991				
Amenemope	993–984				
Osochor	984–978				
Siamun	978–959				
Psusennes II	959–945				
Dynasty XXII					
Sheshonq I	945–924				
Osorkon I	924–889				
Sheshonq II	c. 890				
Takelot I	889–874				
Osorkon II	874–850				
Takelot II	850–825	*Dynasty XXIII*			
Sheshonq III	825–773	Pedubast I	818–793		
		Iuput I	804–783		
		Sheshonq IV	783–777		
Pimay	773–767	Osorkon III	777–749		
Sheshonq V	767–730	Takelot III	754–734		
		Rudamun	734–731	*Dynasty XXIV*	
Osorkon IV	730–715	Iuput II	731–720	Tefnakht	727–720
		Sheshonq VI	720–715	Bakenrenef	720–715
		Dynasty XXV (Napatans)			
		Alara	c. 780–760		
		Kashta	c. 760–747		
		Piye	747–716		
		Shabako	716–702		
		Shebitku	702–690		
		Taharqa	690–664		
		Tantamani	664–656		

Manetho, whose list of kings provides a beginning, although it needs considerable rearranging and checking against contemporary finds. Manetho is certainly not reliable at all times, and many of his kings actually reigned contemporaneously with each other. The chronological picture is complicated further by the fact that the members of dynasties XXII and XXIII used the same limited range of names (including Horus and *nbty*-names), so that they are not easily distinguishable. As if this were not enough to cause confusion, the two dynasties were intimately related, held virtually all important priestly offices in the country, and their offspring all had the same names as well: 'Osorkon', 'Iuput', 'Takelot' recur again and again, and it can be very hard to work out where they belong. The known women also used a restricted range of names, e.g. Shepenwepet and Karomama (six of the latter are known).

An important historiographic text is the great stele of Piye (or: Piankhy) from Gebel Barkal in Nubia. This records the great campaign mounted by the Napatan ruler against the petty dynasts of Egypt perhaps before 727 (the dating is very uncertain). It is a wonderfully lively text, and presents a vivid picture of Egypt's political structure at the time. The so-called 'chronicle of Prince Osorkon' (Caminos 1958) sheds more light. Osorkon was a member of the royal family of dynasty XXII, who was appointed to the position of high priest of Amun. The text is not, in fact, a chronicle in the usual sense that the term is used by historians; rather, it is more in the nature of an autobiography inscribed on the walls of the temple at Karnak. It provides an insight into the political situation in the Theban area, particularly with its description of a civil war in the reign of Takelot II (*c.* 850–825), in the wake of an attempt by Thebes to secede.

This very sparse material has to be supplemented by a variety of other inscriptions. Most important perhaps are several, not many, Theban tomb-biographies. They show us sometimes how the ruling kings tried to manipulate and control the 'Theban state', by installing members of the royal family in positions of power or by creating marriage alliances with local nobles (e.g. Djed-khons-ef-ankh, early dynasty XXII; Lichtheim 1973–80 [OI] III: 13–18). Shifts in the effective power wielded by members of the Theban hierarchy emerge from this: the different grades of 'prophet of Amun' can be seen to have eclipsed eventually the position of 'high priest', for example. One office that becomes increasingly important in the period is that of 'god's wife of Amun'. It is best-documented for the time of the Napatan rulers (dynasty XXV) and dynasty XXVI (i.e. 715–525), but it must already have developed its main features before that time. Unlike in the New Kingdom, when the office was often held by the queen, it seems now to have been held always by a daughter of the Egyptian king, who was not married. She controlled enormous estates, run for her by a steward at Thebes. Her successor was always formally adopted by her. It seems that this powerful office, with its direct links to the reigning king, effectively helped to contain the power of the Theban state, and was deliberately developed for this purpose. There are also several votive inscriptions from sites such as Abydos, Memphis, Denderah and Herakleopolis. Inscriptions recording quarrying (Gebel es-Silsileh), and a number of donation stelae, which are an important source for the size of landholdings of high officials, are further valuable sources.

To this we must add material from beyond Egypt's boundaries: the Piye stele has already been mentioned, but there are other important texts, royal tombs at Kurru and other buildings in Nubia that throw important light on the nature of the Napatan state. There is material from the Levant, particularly a stele from Megiddo of Shoshenq I and some inscribed objects from Samaria. Egypt also figures a number of times in the Old Testament and Mesopotamian texts (especially Assyrian annals), which show Egypt dabbling in the politics of Palestine in pursuance of political advantages. For dynasty XXVI in particular, a valuable source, although one not always easy to use, is Herodotus book II, where a wealth of historical anecdotes about some of the kings of that dynasty is preserved (Lloyd 1975–88).

Historical outline

It is quite impossible to write a narrative history, as there are so many gaps. What we can define is a rough sequence of the main developments. First, the phase from Sheshonq I (945–924) to Osorkon II (874–850), when dynasty XXII was centred on Tanis. Tanis had been the main royal city of the dynasty XXI rulers, which the new Libyan kings must have taken over, although their own original power-base was Bubastis in the eastern delta. The family was descended from a 'Sheshonq, great chief of Meshwesh (a Libyan group)', who had held an important priesthood in Bubastis. The Libyans had settled large parts of northern Egypt, from Herackeopolis into the delta, during dynasties XX and XXI. These Libyan groups seem to have acculturated to a considerable extent. First, there is the priesthood held by Sheshonq I's grandfather ('the great chief'). Secondly, a stele recalls the petition sent by the same man to the Amun oracle at Thebes asking that misappropriations of funds for the mortuary cult of his son at Abydos be rectified and recording the divine decision in his favour:

'... great chief of chiefs, Sheshonq, triumphant, his son in the glorious place by his father, Osiris, that he might lay his beauty to rest in the city of Abydos, over against ... You will let him survive to attain old age, while his heart ... You will let him join the feasts of his majesty, receiving full victory.' This great god saluted exceedingly (i.e. the statue of the god swayed strongly in agreement).

Then his majesty spoke again before this great god: 'O my good lord, you shall slay the (some kind of military official), the administrator, the scribe, the inspector, everyone who was sent on any commission to the field, of those who stole his things from the offering table of Osiris, the great chief of Me(shwesh), Namart, triumphant, son of Mehetnusekhet (wife of Sheshonq), who is in Abydos; all the people who plundered from his divine offerings, his people, his cattle, his garden, his every oblation and all his excellent things. You will act according to your great spirit throughout; show your great anger to their women and their children.' The great god saluted exceedingly. His majesty smelled the earth before him; his majesty said: 'Make to triumph, Sheshonq, triumphant, the great chief of Me(shwesh), chief of chiefs, the great ..., and all who are [before you], all the troops ...' [Said to] him, Amun-Re, king of gods: '... I will do ... for you, you shall attain old age, abiding on earth; your heir shall be upon your throne forever.'
(Mariette *Abydos* II: 36f.; *ARE* IV §§675–677; *Tanis* 1987: 106)

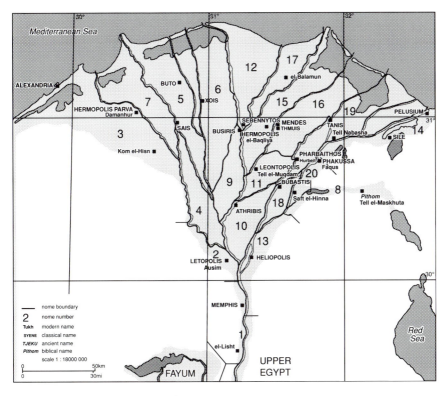

Map 16 Lower Egypt

This suggests that the Libyan groups enjoyed a considerable measure of political autonomy within Egypt before the foundation of dynasty XXII: the great chief had set up a regular Egyptian funerary cult for his son; he was able to call on the Amun oracle at Thebes to redress misuse of its funds and the powerful oracle responded positively.

How the takeover by the Libyan, Sheshonq I, was managed is unknown; there is no hint of chaos or opposition, except that Thebes may have delayed recognising him as king for a couple of years. What is clear is that the Libyan chiefs at Bubastis had developed links with the ruling élites of Egypt, such as the high priests of Ptah in Memphis and even the kings at Tanis, including marriage into the royal family. Possibly, therefore, dynasty XXII came to power through such connections (Kitchen 1986 §239). Once Sheshonq I was installed, he acted to constrict the power of Thebes by appointing his son as high priest of Amun and strengthening his military powers. At the same time, the boundary of the Theban administrative area was shifted south to Asyut, while the region between Asyut and Memphis was placed under the control of another king's son, called the 'general of Herakleopolis'. For the next almost one hundred years, the new dynasty seems to have been fairly successful and stable. It maintained good relations with Byblos, and shifted from a stance of military aggression towards Palestine (Sheshonq I) to one of friendly co-operation (cf. the thousand Egyptian soldiers who fought at the battle of Qarqar in 853, p. 488) and diplomatic relations (cf. alabaster vase from Samaria inscribed with the name of Osorkon II, Reisner *et al. Harvard Excavations at Samaria* (1924) II pl. 56g).

But then this stable picture begins to break up, as the civil war, recorded in the 'chronicle of Prince Osorkon', broke out during the reign of Takelot II (850–825). Immediately after this, and perhaps connected, the principle of control by a single ruler came to an end. In 818, during the reign of Shoshenq III (825–773), a man called Pedubast claimed the kingship. He seems at first sight to be no more than a co-regent, a practice employed a couple of times already by rulers of dynasty XXII. But, when we look more closely, the signs are that he was actually the founder of a new royal line, counting by his own regnal years, adopting a separate residence in the delta at Leontopolis and, in his fifteenth regnal year, appointing his son, Iuput I, as co-regent. As a result, from 804 onwards, there were three Pharaohs in Egypt. It is probable that the members of dynasty XXIII were related to dynasty XXII, but the kings of the new dynasty certainly seem to be the stronger politically: it is they who now organise the appointments to key posts in Thebes and Herakleopolis; it is their sisters and daughters who become the 'god's wives of Amun'.

Yet further political fragmentation took place from about 770 onwards in the western delta, with the emergence of a family at Sais, called the 'great chiefs of Libu'. Although this group had been there already much earlier (*c.* 870), a definite line of chiefs only emerges at this point. In 727 this family also claimed the traditional titles of Egyptian kingship, and it is they who constitute Manetho's dynasty XXIV. Although their claim to kingship was ended, as was that of the other 'Pharaohs', by the Nubian dynasty XXV in 715, a line of rulers (probably from the same family) continued to govern the western delta, until they finally re-emerged as the great Saite dynasty (XXVI) of a united Egypt (see chapter 12b). It seems to have been the growing power of the Saite chiefs, especially the advance by Tefnakht on Memphis, that led to the Napatan king Piye's famous campaign northward through Egypt. This laid the foundations for forty years of Nubian control of Egypt.

There is no certain date for Piye's invasion, and the chronology of many of the Napatan rulers, save for what can be gleaned from the accounts of the Assyrian invasion of Egypt, is uncertain (Kitchen 1986). But the situation in Egypt, as presented in the account of Piye's campaign, is fairly clear (Yoyotte 1961). King Piye set up his stele in the Amun temple at Napata, which had been considerably enlarged by Piye himself. A relief decorates the top: on the left is the goddess Mut, standing behind Amun, who is seated on a throne;

facing him is Piye; behind him is Namart, the dynast of Hermopolis, with his horse and wife, her hand raised in prayer. Below this scene are depicted Osorkon IV, Iuput II and Peftuaubast, the ruler of Herakleopolis, all prostrating themselves; behind them, kissing the ground, are Pediese and four chiefs of the Meshwesh. If we put this together with other information in the text, we obtain a political silhouette of Egypt c. 730. In the western delta, the main power-centre was at Sais, ruled by Tefnakht, with local Libyan tribal leaders probably owing him allegiance. In the central delta, there were dynasts at Sebennytos, Busiris and, further south, Athribis. In the eastern delta, Tanis and Bubastis were the seats of 'dynasty XXII' claiming kingship over all of Egypt, but long overshadowed by dynasty XXIII at Leontopolis. Probably allied to the 'kings' were the local rulers of some of the cities in the eastern delta. To the south, Memphis was under a tribal chief and had been absorbed by the expanding power of Tefnakht of Sais. The local ruler of the important area of Herakleopolis was being threatened by a pincer movement, engineered by Tefnakht and his ally, Namart, ruler of Hermopolis, immediately to the south of Herakleopolis. The area between Aswan and Asyut (just to the south of Hermopolis) continued to be controlled by the Theban temple hierarchy. But Thebes itself was under the overlordship of the Napatan rulers, who had expanded into Egypt some time around 750. Relations of suzerainty had also been imposed by the Napatans on some of the dynasts further north, in particular Namart of Hermopolis. Namart had broken his allegiance to the Napatan king by joining Tefnakht in the attack on Herakleopolis. This was the immediate reason for Napatan military intervention beyond the Theban area.

Piye's first action, on hearing of the betrayal, was to send an army to fight Tefnakht and his allies. The army was successful, defeated the coalition, and the various leaders fled into the delta. But Namart, whose home lay in a much more exposed position, was besieged by part of the Napatan army, while other detachments captured several neighbouring centres in the course of which one of Tefnakht's sons was killed. But, obviously, until Hermopolis had been taken, it would be impossible for the Napatans to claim a definitive victory. Piye, therefore, decided to intervene personally after celebrating new year ceremonies in Napata and then the great Opet festival at Thebes. The description of the siege and fall of Hermopolis, as recounted by Piye in his victory stele, is one of the most vivid pieces of Egyptian historical writing and deserves to be quoted:

> First month of the first season, day 9, his majesty went north to Thebes. He performed the feast of Amun at the feast of Opet. His majesty sailed north to the harbour of the Hare nome (Hermopolis). His majesty came out of the cabin of the ship. The horses were yoked, the chariot was mounted, while the grandeur of his majesty attained the Asiatics and every heart trembled before him.

His majesty burst out to revile his troops, raging at them like a panther: 'Are you continuing to fight while delaying my orders? It is the year for making an end, for putting fear of me in Lower Egypt, and inflicting on them a great and severe beating!'

He set up camp on the south-west of Khmun (part of Hermopolis). He pressed against it every day. An embankment was made to enclose the wall. A siege tower was set up to elevate the archers as they shot, and the slingers as they hurled stones and killed people there each day. Days passed, and Un (the other part of Hermopolis) was a stench to the nose, for lack of air to breathe. Then Un threw itself on its belly, to plead before the king. Messengers came and went with all kinds of things beautiful to behold: gold, precious stones, clothes in a chest, the diadem from his (sc. Namart's) head, the uraeus that cast his power, without ceasing for many days to implore his (sc. Piye's) crown.

Then they sent his (sc. Namart's) wife, the royal wife and royal daughter, Nestent, to implore the royal wives, the royal concubines, the royal daughters, and the royal sisters. She threw herself on her belly in the women's house before the royal women: 'Come to me, royal wives, royal daughters, royal sisters, that you may appease Horus, lord of the palace, great of power, great of triumph! Grant . . .

(fifteen lines destroyed: they covered the intercession of Piye's women-folk, Piye's acceptance of Hermoplis' surrender, and Namart's appearance before him. Then Piye chided him and Namart responded with protestations of loyalty:)

He threw himself on his belly before his majesty, [saying: 'Be appeased], Horus, lord of the palace! It is your power that has done it to me. I am one of the king's servants who pays taxes into the treasury. . . . I have done for you more than they.' Then he presented silver, gold, lapis lazuli, turquoise, copper, and all kinds of precious stones. The treasury was filled with this tribute. He brought a horse with his right hand, and in his left hand a sistrum of gold and lapis-lazuli. (This is how Namart is shown at the top of the stele.)

His majesty arose in splendour from his palace and proceeded to the temple of Thoth, lord of Khmun. He sacrificed oxen, shorthorns, and fowl to his father Thoth, lord of Khmun, and the Ogdoad in the temple of the Ogdoad (eight primeval gods whose cult-centre was Hermopolis). And the troops of the Hare nome shouted and sang, saying:

'How good is Horus at peace in his town,
The Son of Re, Piye!
You make for us a jubilee,
As you protect the Hare nome!'

His majesty proceeded to the house of King Namart. He went through all the rooms of the palace, his treasury and his storehouse. He (sc. Namart) presented the royal wives and royal daughters to him. They saluted his majesty in the manner of women, while his majesty did not direct his gaze at them (i.e. in order not to embarrass them).

His majesty proceeded to the stable of the horses and the quarters of the foals. When he saw they had been [left] to hunger he said: 'I swear as Re loves me, as my nose is refreshed by life: that my horses were made to hunger pains me more than any other crime you committed in your recklessness!' (Remainder of Piye's speech is obscure.)

Then his goods were assigned to the treasury, and his granary to the endowment of Amun in Ipet-sut (Thebes).

(*Urk.* III, 1–56; *ARE* IV §§796ff.; Lichtheim 1973–80 [OI] III: 71–73)

The fall of Hermopolis was followed by Herakleopolis publicly ranging itself on the side of Piye. Piye fought his way north successfully, until he was halted at Memphis which had been well prepared for a siege by Tefnakht, although Tefnakht himself had fled in the face of Piye's advance. A typical literary device is used to evoke Piye's bravery outside Memphis: everyone is floored by the strength of its defences and makes various elaborate suggestions for how they might be breached. Piye becomes irritated and orders it to be attacked in the simplest, most obvious manner. His straightforward plan succeeds and Memphis falls, thus vindicating the king's courageous simplicity. After investing the city and performing rituals in the great temple of Ptah, all the chieftains in the delta, including Tefnakht, and the nominal Pharaohs surrendered.

The situation in Egypt after Piye's victory is obscure. It looks as though Piye returned to Napata to celebrate, and there is no evidence that he ever returned to Egypt. It is generally thought that Tefnakht and his successor both briefly claimed the Egyptian throne after the Napatan campaign (dynasty XXIV; Kitchen 1986 §§332; 337). But with Piye's successors (Shabako, Shebitku, Taharqa and Tantamani) such claims were definitively extinguished. Between 715 and 671, the Napatan kings imposed quite a firm control on Egypt, including one of the major oases in the western desert (Kharga). Their monuments have been found in most of the important Egyptian centres; they controlled the Theban hierarchy tightly through their own appointees, particularly the god's wife of Amun (see p. 625); they cast themselves in the role of legitimate Pharaohs, with their performance of rituals in Thebes. Most interesting is that king Shabako ordered a 'copy' to be made (from worm-eaten scrolls) of the antique Memphite theology, which extols the god Ptah as the creator of all and king of a single Egypt (cf. pp. 145–146). The accounts of the Assyrian conquest of Egypt make it clear that most of the local rulers retained their positions – although now they were subjects of the Napatan king, obliged to supply labour, tribute and taxes to the Nubian state. Their attempts to lay claim to the Egyptian throne had been firmly nipped in the bud.

The Napatan kingdom

What do we know of the great Napatan kingdom, which developed in the south of Nubia, so often invaded and dominated by Egypt in the past? Excavation has recovered quite a bit of material, but many uncertainties remain (Adams 1975 [0Gg]; Trigger 1976; Priese 1978). Nubia was lost to Egypt at the end of dynasty XX, and there is no Nubian material datable to the period between c. 1050 and c. 900. After 900, a state developed which eventually stretched from the first cataract to Khartoum and lasted about twelve hundred years. The Egyptians called this state Kush, using traditional terminology; the name was eventually adopted by the kings in Nubia themselves. For convenience, the history of the Kushite kingdom is divided into two separate phases: the period from 750 down to 270 is called the 'Napatan' phase; the subsequent period, down to AD 320, is called the 'Meroitic' phase. The division is related to structural changes in the state, signalled, first, by the the transfer of the royal cemetery from Napata to Meroe; second, by the appearance of a new written language, Meroitic (alongside the earlier exclusively used Egyptian), which was used by the politically dominant group; third, by the gradual evolution of a new iconography.

The nucleus of the kingdom was probably the area between the third and sixth cataract. The population seems to have included Nubians in the third to fourth cataract region, 'Meroitic' people further south, and pastoral groups to the west and east of the Nile, who were organised under local leaders. Millet, barley, spelt, sheep and goats, and sesame formed tha base of the agrarian economy. The region, known as the 'Island of Meroe' (because the Nile surrounds it on three sides), has mineral resources in the form of gold, precious stones, copper and iron, although the last was very little used in this period. According to later tradition, a king called Alara founded the kingdom. He is generally dated between 780 and 760. Finds in the cemetery at Kurru date back to around 900, but a line of kings cannot really be reconstructed much beyond Alara. His successor, Kashta, certainly controlled the area up to the first cataract, and had begun moving further north into Upper Egypt, probably up to and including Thebes.

The kingdom's main centres were, first, Napata, which seems to have been an important dynastic centre throughout the first ('Napatan') period, and it was close to here that the kings were buried. Second, there is Meroe, about which not much is known at the time of the Napatan domination of Egypt, and it was thought that it did not really develop as an important centre until later. But it now looks as though Meroe played a significant role from quite early on. This is indicated by the fact that, from Piye's reign (747–716) onward, many members of the royal family and courtiers were buried at Meroe, with only the kings themselves, the royal wives and royal mothers buried at Napata. There is also a hint in a text of Tantamani (*ARE* IV §924) that, when he went up to Egypt, he set out from somewhere far to the south, only calling in at Napata on his way. Excavations have confirmed that there was a settlement on the edge of Meroe at the latest by the early seventh century.

As the state developed, the neighbouring culture of Egypt with its highly developed script, sophisticated art-forms and complex political structure exerted considerable influence on the formulation of Kushite power. The Egyptian script and language were used to express the Kushite kings' achievements; a pyramidal style of tomb was developed for royal burials; and the cult of Amun at Gebel Barkal was linked to the kingship and used to justify expansion into Egypt. Taharqa is known to have deported Egyptians from Memphis to help build his great temple at Kawa, and personnel for conducting the cult was also imported from Egypt. The kings expanded the economy by introducing vine-cultivation and date-palms from the north. The concern that Piye displayed for the fate of the horses in Hermopolis during the siege provides a charming vignette in the Piye stele (see p. 631), but is not in itself very significant. But finds in the Napatan royal tombs show that horses were very closely associated with the ruler, as the royal mounts were killed on his death and formally buried in the royal cemetery.

The Kushite king was titled *qore*, a Meroitic term. He is depicted wearing a tight-fitting cap with two snakes ('uraei') attached and encircled by a diadem with dangling ends. This is quite different from the Egyptian regalia, where only one snake reared up on the king's forehead. How the succession worked is not known precisely, although it has been assumed that kingship was traced through the maternal line and normally went from older to younger brother. This hypothesis is based on rather slender evidence, and needs to be tested further.[1] In one instance (Tantamani), the king's succession is presented as an oracular decision by Amun of Napata – this could indicate an irregularity in the usual succession, or simply be additional confirmation of the regular process.

An elaborate ritual seems to have surrounded the installation of the new king. At the death of the king, the army went to the palace to lament the absence of a leader to the courtiers; then, apparently in a formalised response, the successor was named and the wish expressed that he be placed on the throne. The accession of the new king was formally broadcast by a ceremonial coronation journey, taking in Napata, Kawa and Tabo (see map 17), receiving regalia from the gods in each location in return for his promise to continue to support the cult. This was done by confirming the temples' rights to property, and creating new cult-offices. The royal procession route was cleared of sand before the royal cortège, and must surely have been an occasion when local groups could present petitions to the new king and affirm their loyalty to the throne. This probably explains why the coronation journey was entitled 'the creation of order in all provinces'.

The king was the chief military leader, and his victories filled the treasuries of the palaces, the granaries of the cities and the storehouses of the great temples. Piye's stele shows that the entire income (treasure and granary) of every captured Egyptian city was made over to the Amun temple in Thebes. How officials were rewarded is not clear, but a later story in Herodotus (2.30–31) suggests that soldiers, at least, were given land-plots for themselves and their families, as they were in Egypt (cf. p. 643). Certainly the wealth of the Kushite kings was legendary (Herodotus 3.23; 114), and their ability to mount impressive military campaigns far to the north (e.g. southern Palestine, eastern delta, Memphis) is testimony to the state's strength and efficiency.

The Assyrian invasions of Egypt (674–664)

The Assyrian conquest of Egypt was the logical development of Assyria's attempts to consolidate its frontiers in southern Palestine (see chapter 9; p. 499). It took a considerable amount of time and effort and was not achieved without setbacks. The first, failed, attempt was made by Esarhaddon in 674. Only in 671 was he successful, conquering the territory from the edge of the eastern delta to Memphis, which was taken by siege. His celebratory commemoration of his Egyptian victory, preserved primarily on a stele from Sam'al (south Turkey), says that he took the whole court, royal family and heir-apparent prisoner, and 'rooted out' the Nubian presence; a tiny Taharqa is shown on the stele being humiliatingly led by a ring through the nose. Esarhaddon also mentions the installation of governors, administrators, port controllers, inspectors and military commanders (Borger 1956 Mnmt. A). But how intensive Assyrian administrative and military control really was remains a moot point. Ashurbanipal's only slightly later texts refer vaguely to this Assyrian presence and twenty local dynasts in northern Egypt. Certainly, the initial defeat of Egypt needed to be consolidated, and Esarhaddon was engaged on an essential follow-up campaign when he died in 669. This allowed the Kushite ruler, Taharqa, to retake Memphis and encourage some of the delta kinglets to revolt against Assyria. In 667, Ashurbanipal defeated Taharqa, regained control of Memphis, Taharqa fled to Thebes, and the rebellion in the delta was crushed. One of the dynasts, Necho of Sais, was shown mercy by the Assyrian king and formally reinstalled with substantial Assyrian support. He is the Niku referred to in Ashurbanipal's annals from Nineveh:

> Towards Niku amongst them I was merciful and made him live. A treaty firmer than earlier I made with him; I clothed him in coloured garments and a gold necklace, the symbol of his kingship, I made for him; golden rings I placed on his fingers; on an iron dagger, with gold decoration, I wrote my name and gave it to him. Chariots, horses, mules for riding (appropriate to) his lordship I bestowed on him. My (soldiers of some

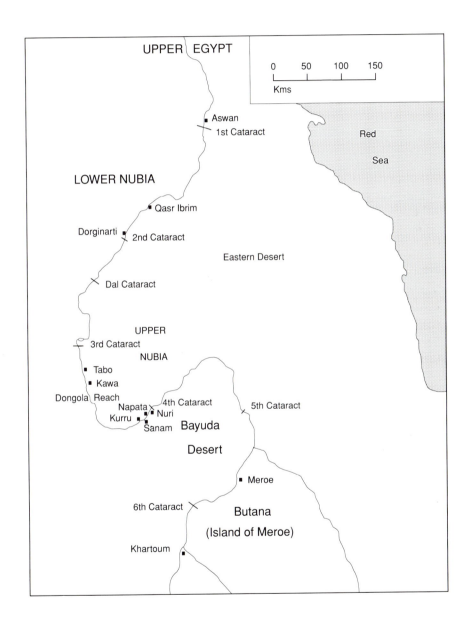

UPPER EGYPT

0   50   100   150

Kms

Aswan
1st Cataract

Red

Sea

LOWER NUBIA

Qasr Ibrim

Dorginarti
2nd Cataract

Eastern Desert

Dal Cataract

UPPER

3rd Cataract

NUBIA

Tabo

Kawa

Dongola Reach
Napata 4th Cataract   5th Cataract

Kurru   Nuri

Sanam   Bayuda

Desert

Meroe

6th Cataract

Butana

(Island of Meroe)

Khartoum

Map 17 Nubia

635

kind?) I sent as governors for his support with him. To Sais, where my father, who begat me, had placed him in kingship, I brought him back to his place, and Nabu-shezibanni (i.e. Psammetichus), his son, I set over Hathariba (Athribis). More splendidly than his father I bestowed on him benefaction and favour.

(Streck 1916: II 14–15, ll. 8–19)

Taharqa seems to have died soon after this. But his nephew and successor Tantamani rallied his forces against the Assyrian regime, and tried to reconquer Egypt (*ARE* IV §§919–934). In 664, Ashurbanipal had to send another army to drive him back and assert Assyria's control. This time, the Assyrian army pursued the Napatan king right down to Thebes, which fell after a siege and was sacked. This spelled the end of Kushite control in Egypt, and marked the beginning of the Saite dynasty (XXVI). It is possible that Necho was killed or died in 664, because his son, Psammetichus, the first king of dynasty XXVI, counted his first regnal year from 664.

12b The Saite period (dynasty XXVI: 664–525)

General observations

Linguistically and culturally the Saite period is usually thought of as the start of the 'late period' in Egypt, with certain social, legal and artistic conventions continuing right through into the Persian period, and beyond to about AD 100. Obviously there were quite a number of profound changes in the political sphere which must not be forgotten, but, just as in Mesopotamia, certain developments can be seen to start now and are not swept aside by them. At the same time, the Saite period itself does not mark an entirely new start – changes were gradual, and some can be traced back to the twenty-fifth dynasty (Bothmer 1960). Perhaps the most striking development is the emergence of the demotic script, a development of the Egyptian cursive script, hieratic, used to render the Egyptian vernacular (see, recently, Tait 1992). So the divergence between formal inscriptions (statues, tombs, buildings) using classical Egyptian, for which traditional Middle Egyptian in hieroglyphs continued to be used (a development beginning in the New Kingdom), and legal documents, letters and folktales using the demotic script and dialect became even more marked. Although the bulk of demotic texts date from the Hellenistic and Roman periods, the earliest-known ones date from the Napatan and Saite periods, and reflect a series of gradual changes in society (Menu 1988).

The hundred-and-forty-year period down to the conquest of Egypt by the Persian king Cambyses seems to have been been relatively stable within Egypt. There was one crisis in the kingship, when Amasis deposed king

Apries in 570. This event generated a number of stories, as shown by the fact that it is narrated at length by Herodotus (2.161–172). Apart from this one incident, reconstructing the course of political events is difficult: there is some incidental information in the Old Testament (2 *Kings* 23.32–35; 2 *Chronicles* 35.20–23; *Jeremiah* 44.30) and in Babylonian chronicles and Assyrian annals, which provide some information on Egypt's wars in the Levant. Herodotus (book 2) and Diodorus (book 1), especially the former, contain quite detailed narratives on conditions inside Egypt, as well as Egyptian relations with some of the Greek states and Greek soldiers serving in the Egyptian army. Most interesting is the picture of contemporary Egyptian ideas about early history that are preserved here. But the material, not surprisingly, is selective and has, of course, been shaped by Greek writers to serve a number of quite specific interests (Lloyd 1975–88; Murray 1970). But, despite the need to exercise due caution, Egypt's political, social and cultural history is in very large part reconstructed on the basis of Herodotus' extraordinary, detailed description of the country. Without his vivid picture, we would know little more about Egypt at this time than in the preceding Third Intermediate Period.

Material from Egypt, both inscriptions and archaeological remains, is, however, more plentiful than in the preceding period. One particular type of evidence is worth mentioning specially here. This is the Serapaeum at Saqqara near Memphis, where stelae and inscribed sarcophagi record royal initiatives in selecting the cultic Apis bull and organising his mummification and burial at death (Mariette 1882). The Apis bull was the animal sacred to Ptah, kept in a special enclosure and worshipped as a physical manifestation of the god. Because of the importance of Ptah, as creator-god and god of Memphis, the Apis bull cult was also particularly associated with kingship. The cult existed very early on in Egypt, as did the cult of all sorts of animals sacred to particular deities, but they only become prominent (proliferating to a quite startling degree) in the late period. The catacombs where some of the cult animals were buried (ibises, cats, cows ('mothers of the Apis'), Apis bulls) have been quite extensively excavated (Smith 1974). Written material, particularly from the Hellenistic period, has made it possible to reconstruct the elaborate ceremonies connected with the funeral of the Apis bull (Vercoutter 1962; Thompson 1988; for the obsequies for the mothers of the Apis, see Smith 1992). Otherwise, Memphis in this period remains underexplored, except for parts of the Ptah temple and a palace belonging to Apries (Petrie and Walker 1909a; 1909b; Kemp 1977).

The foundation of dynasty XXVI

Psammetichus I began his reign as a client-king of the Assyrians (see p. 636). Not all details are clear, but it seems that he followed his father Necho in the rule of Sais in 664. Necho is counted conventionally as the first king of the dynasty ('Necho I'), although his area of control was very circumscribed and he never ruled independently of Assyria. It was his son, Psammetichus I, who achieved independence both from Assyria and Kush and was able to unite Egypt under one supreme ruler. How exactly this was achieved is not known. He obtained access to soldiers from Lydia, Greek cities, Caria and the Syro-Palestinian area, which must have helped him achieve and retain military supremacy over rival dynasts in the delta. These local rulers, as well as Psammetichus himself, had highly skilled and experienced warriors in their armies (Herodotus' *machimoi*), who held land in exchange for military service. But it looks as though only Psammetichus was able to lay his hands on additional military forces. Why he, rather than any of the other rulers, was able to do this is unknown. It is possible that the strong Assyrian support given to Sais (pp. 635–636), meant that the kingdom in the western delta was a much stronger and wealthier entity. Perhaps it was deliberately built up by the Assyrians to protect the always vulnerable western frontier. Whatever the reason, in the 650s Psammetichus I received support from Gyges of Lydia (see chapter 10b), as texts of Ashurbanipal report. In these the action of Gyges is presented as hostile to Assyria, yet it seems that Assyria took no action against Egypt, and that relations between the two powers were not particularly hostile (cf. Egypt's military help for Assyria later, see pp. 544–545). About the tricky ins and outs of how the changed situation was regularised scholars are in the dark.

Table 34 The Saite (dynasty XXVI) kings

Psammetichus I	664–610
Necho II	610–595
Psammetichus II	595–589
Apries	589–570
Amasis	570–526
Psammetichus III	526–525

Egypt united

By 656, Psammetichus had extended his control to Upper Egypt. This is established by the 'Adoption stele of Nitocris' (Caminos 1964). The text from Thebes records the festive journey of Psammetichus' daughter to Thebes with a large retinue in order to be adopted into the future office of 'god's wife of Amun' by Amenirdis, current 'god's wife' and sister of the late king Taharqa. The stele recording this is the prime source for the functioning and incomes of the 'god's wife' and her establishment, and it shows one of the means used by Psammetichus to tighten his grip on the country, and restrict the power of the Theban administration. A later demotic text, called the 'Petition of Petiese' (reign of Darius I, 522–486), provides more information (Griffith 1909; Wessetzky 1963). It is a long account rehearsing the ups and downs of the family history of Petiese from the reign of Psammetichus I down to his own day in an effort to obtain official confirmation that he had the right to a number of offices. The text shows that the family held considerable administrative powers in the important area of the Fayum, Herakleopolis, and stretches of the Nile up to Memphis. They were supporters of Psammetichus, yet their power seems later to have been limited quite substantially. This provides a hint of Psammetichus' approach to trying to break down the centrifugal pattern, which had dominated Egyptian history for about a hundred and fifty years. Hand in hand with this went long-term plans to reorganise the administration of temples and restructure their incomes. Several texts, throughout the period, reflect this activity, and show land being removed from local potentates and assigned instead to nearby temples (Abydos; Heliopolis; Memphis). In one such instance the newly generated income was to be used to pay for the burials of the town's inhabitants:

I provisioned the temple of Khentamenti (i.e. Osiris),
Enlarged its income,
Established with daily supplies
Its storehouse furnished with male and female slaves.
I gave it a donation of a thousand arouras,
In the countryside of Tawer (nome of Abydos),
Provided with people and herds of all kinds,
Its name being made 'Osiris-town',
So as to make a divine endowment of it for all time.
I renewed its divine endowment of bread, beer, oxen and fowl,
Exceeding what it had been before.
I made for it an orchard,
Planted with all fruit trees,
Its gardeners being foreigners,
Brought in as prisoners.
Thirty pints of wine were given from it daily
To the altar of Khentamenti,
As an offering from it for all time.

I renewed the House of Life (temple-school) after its ruin,
I established the sustenance of Osiris,
I put all its procedures in order.
I built the god's boat of pine wood,
Having found (it) made of acacia wood.
I suppressed crime in Tawer,
I guarded Tawer for its lord,
I protected all its people.
I gave income from Tawer's desert to the temple,
Having found it in the hands of the count,

So that Abydenes would have burials.
I gave the ferryboat (probably: the revenue from it) of Tawer to the
    temple,
Having taken it away from the count,
. . .
His majesty praised me for what I had done.

> (Peftuaneith: *ARE* IV §§1015ff.; Otto 1954: 164–166;
> Lichtheim 1973–80 [OI] III: 35)

This text, which dates from as late as the reign of Amasis, shows how slow
was the process of divesting local powerholders of their great incomes, and
making them accessible to the kings. The process was obviously a delicate
one if the Saite kings were not to alienate supporters and find themselves
deprived of power. One city crucial to Psammetichus' power and certainly
tightly controlled by him was Memphis, always central to anyone claiming
to control Egypt. At the same time, Sais was turned into an important dynastic
centre. It contained the temple of the goddess Neith, closely associated with
the Saite kings, which was extensively repaired and embellished; and it was
here, now, that the kings were buried.

The army must have been reorganised to accommodate the contingents of
foreign soldiers that flocked to service with the Saite rulers from the Aegean
and Syria-Palestine (see p. 638). Quite a number of these, such as the Jewish
contingent at Elephantine (Porten 1968) were given land-parcels, and they
cannot be considered 'mercenaries' in the contemporary meaning of the word
(Austin 1970). Others only hired out their services for a period of time on
the assumption that they would make enough out of war-booty and bounty-
payments to be able to return and buy land at home eventually (Wallinga
1991). An interesting hint of how the army was structured is contained in the
famous Greek graffito carved on the leg of a colossal statue of Ramesses II
at Abu Simbel in the course of a campaign against Kush in 593:

> When King Psammetichus came to Elephantine, this was written by
> those who sailed with Psammetichus, son of Theocles; and they came
> beyond Kerkis as far as the river permits. Those who spoke foreign
> tongues (i.e. the foreign army contingents) were led by Potasimto, the
> Egyptians by Amasis.
>
> > R. Meiggs and D.M. Lewis, *Greek Historical Inscriptions*,
> > Oxford, 1969, no. 7)

This shows clearly that the foreign and Egyptian soldiers were in separate
contingents, but both had Egyptian commanders. It is possible that the
Egyptian name of the Greek who wrote the graffito shows that some of the
Greek soldiers were becoming acculturated, a process certainly illustrated for
the Carians in Egypt later (Masson 1978).[2] Another important development
at this time was the development of a navy by Necho II, operating both in

the Mediterranean and the Red Sea (Wallinga 1987). It is possible that the Phoenicians provided important knowhow and assistance with the technicalities of construction and navigation. Egyptian royal interests in this were obviously twofold, both strategic and commercial. This is shown by Necho's building of a canal linking the Nile to the Red Sea, although it was apparently only completed by Darius I (Herodotus 2.158), and (more obscurely) by the story in Herodotus of the circumnavigation of Africa by the Phoenicians at Necho's command (Herodotus 4.42; Rougé 1988).

The commercial interests of the dynasty are particularly clearly reflected in their active encouragement of the activities of foreign merchants, among which Greek trading is best-known because of the prominence of the surviving Greek sources (Austin 1970; Boardman 1980). According to Diodorus (1.66; 67), it was Psammetichus I who opened the country to Greek and Phoenician traders, and became immensely rich as a result. Certainly by about 625 (at the latest) Naucratis and other Greek trading stations were established in northern Egypt (Coulson and Leonard 1981; Petrie 1886). How many such emporia existed is uncertain, but it is plain that the Egyptian rulers charged custom-dues and taxes on imports and exports. It was probably in order to ensure that the royal profit on this trade should be as large as possible that, soon after 570, Amasis concentrated all Greek trading at the Egyptian town of Naucratis, only 16 km from Sais (Herodotus 2.97; 178).

Frontiers and defence

Egyptian defence and foreign policy was determined by traditional concerns and interests: strong policing of frontiers against invasion, with attempts at territoral expansion where possible, in the north-east. To the west, the oases of Bahriya, Dakhla, Kharga and Siwa all contain buildings of the twenty-sixth dynasty, which implies a firm system of control of these important centres and their routes. Herodotus (2.30) indicates that the western delta was strongly garrisoned. It is possible that there may have been treaty-relationships maintained by Egypt with some of the tribal groups in the western desert, because Apries at one point supported such a group in their conflict with the Greek colony of Cyrene. In the south, the frontier lay at Aswan, and Egyptian control effectively never stretched beyond it. This frontier was heavily garrisoned, given the size and power of the Napatan kingdom and their earlier control of Egypt (see pp. 628–634). Although it looks as though direct confrontations with Kush were generally avoided, there were occasional conflicts. A major one took place in the reign of Psammetichus II (595–589) when, in 593, his army fought a battle in the area of the third cataract, which was commemorated on stelae. (It is from this war that the Greek graffito (p. 640) at Abu Simbel dates):

(date and Psammetichus II's names and titles)
His majesty was roaming the marshes at lake Neferibre (near Aswan),
circling its inundated land, traversing its two islands, viewing the
sycamores of god's land on its mud bank, his heart eager to see the
beauty, like the Great God traversing the primeval water. Then one
came to tell his majesty:
'The troops your majesty sent to Nubia have reached the hill-country
of Pnubs (third cataract). It is a land lacking a battlefield, a place lacking
horses (i.e. it is mountainous). The Nubians of every hill-country rose
up against him (Psammetichus II), their hearts full of rage against him.
His attack took place (i.e. the Egyptian army's attack), and it was misery
for the rebels. His majesty has done a fighter's work. When the battle
was joined the rebels turned their backs. The arrows did not stray from
piercing them. The hand did not let loose. One waded in their blood as
in water. Not one bound pair escaped of the 4,200 captives. A successful
deed has been done!'
Then the heart of his majesty was happy beyond anything. His majesty
presented a great sacrifice of oxen and shorthorns to all the gods of
Upper and Lower Egypt, and an offering to the gods of the palace in
the palace chapel. May he be given life, stability, dominion, all health
and happiness like Re forever.
    (H. Bakry, *OA* 6 (1967): 225–244; Lichtheim 1973–80 [OI] III: 84–86)

The importance of this victory, illustrating how serious the Napatan threat
still was, is emphasised by the fact that the account of the battle was set up
both at Karnak and at Aswan. A rather different kind of problem, perhaps a
persistent one, that the Egyptians faced on their southern border is recorded
in the reign of Apries (589–570). A stele of an army-commander, Nesuhor,
at Aswan recounts that a number of garrison troops tried to defect to Nubia,
but he was successful in stopping them from doing so:

(After his name, prayer, account of good works for the gods etc. he
says:)
For you (the god) rescued me from an evil plight, from the mercenaries,
Libyans, Greeks, Asiatics and foreigners, who had it in their hearts to
. . ., and who had it in their hearts to go to Shas-heret (i.e. southern
Nubia). His majesty feared because of the evil which they did. I re-
established their heart in reason by advice, not permitting them to go
to Nubia, but bringing them to the place where his majesty was; and his
majesty executed their punishment.
    (Maspero *ZÄS* 26 (1884): 88f.; *ARE* IV §§989–994)

The episode in the Nesuhor stele is mirrored by a story in Herodotus:

They (i.e. the 'deserters') were a body of men two hundred and forty
thousand strong, of the Egyptian warrior class, who went over to the

Ethiopians (i.e. Nubians) during the reign of Psammetichus. The Egyptians had guardposts in various parts of the country: one at Elephantine against the Ethiopians, another in Daphnae at Pelusium against the Arabians and Assyrians, and a third at Marea to keep a watch on Libya. . . . Now it happened in Psammetichus' time that the Egyptians were kept on garrison duty for three years without being relieved, and this was the cause of their desertion. They discussed their grievances, came to a unanimous resolution, and went off in a body to Ethiopia. The king, on hearing the news, gave chase and overtook them; and the story goes that when he besought them to return and used every argument to dissuade them from abandoning their wives and children and the gods of their country, one of their number pointed, in reply, to his private parts and said that wherever those were there would be no lack of wives and children. So they continued their journey to Ethiopia and put themselves at the disposal of the Ethiopian king, by whom they were well rewarded, for he gave them permission to expel certain Ethiopians with whom he was on bad terms, and to settle on their land.

(Herodotus 2.30–31)

Obviously, then, there was continuous tension between Egypt and Kush, with the Nubian king trying to seduce members of Egyptian army contingents to his side. Important to note is the very mixed nature of the garrison at Aswan as recorded by Nesuhor. It included Libyans, Greeks, 'Asiatics' (almost certainly people from the Levant), and further unspecified 'foreigners'. The later evidence from the Achaemenid period shows that a Jewish garrison was established at Elephantine from the reign of Psammetichus I onwards. They were probably included in Nesuhor's 'Asiatics'. This evidence shows very clearly that the Saites drew their manpower resources from all over the Near East, and were not particularly (certainly not exclusively) dependent on Greek soldiers, as the primarily Greek narrative sources (in particular, Herodotus) naturally suggest.

In the Levant, Egypt attempted with only occasional and limited success to seize control with the decline of Assyrian power. From the 620s on it briefly established itself as the new dominant power in Palestine, including Judah as a client kingdom (Yoyotte 1960; Na'aman 1991). A fragmentary inscription of Necho II (610–595) from Sidon shows that Egyptian influence was also strong along the Phoenician coast. Egypt tried to extend this northwards by aiding Assyria against Babylonia, and ensconcing itself at Carchemish, from which it was only dislodged after being defeated in battle by Nebuchadnezzar II in 605 (see chapter 11d). This was followed by a period of almost continuous fighting between Babylonia and Egypt until 601, when a battle was fought at the Egyptian frontier. It is possible that some kind of agreement was reached following this, conceding the area up to the 'brook of Egypt' (Wadi el-Arish) to Babylonia. Certainly it is significant that when

643

Nebuchadnezzar II besieged Jehoiachin in 598/597 there was no Egyptian intervention, although earlier Judah had been subject to them. This brief period of peace between the two powers is confirmed by the pious pilgrimage made by Psammetichus II to Byblos in 591. But it was a very uneasy and superficial tranquillity, with the Egyptians constantly ready to take advantage of any problems that Babylonia encountered. In 588/587, for example, Apries attacked Tyre and Sidon, subject-states of Babylonia, while Nebuchadnezzar was occupied with the second siege of Jerusalem. On this occasion the Egyptians did intervene on the side of Judah, which suggests that the Babylonians were struggling to retain control. The success of the destabilisation engineered by Egypt is shown by the fact that, as soon as Jerusalem had fallen, the Babylonians were forced to besiege rebellious Tyre, supposedly for thirteen years. One success that the Saite kings did have was that Cyprus became tributary to them in the reign of Amasis, which provided a naval base for them close to the Syrian coast.

Amasis

One event that it is possible to reconstruct in considerable detail, and that shows most strikingly the tremendous political tensions between Egypt and Babylonia, is the usurpation of the throne by Amasis. Amasis was an important general; both he and his mother were close to the king and obviously occupied high positions at Apries' court (de Meulenaere 1968). According to Herodotus (2.161–3), Apries, perhaps as part of a plan of expansion, sent a force to support a Libyan tribal group against the Greek kingdom of Cyrene. The campaign seems to have been rather poorly organised and the Egyptians suffered heavy losses. This led to a revolt among the survivors in the army, in the course of which Amasis seized the opportunity to take the throne. Apries, as has been shown by Edel (1978), went into exile and made two separate attempts to regain his throne with support from outside. In the first (570/69) he had support from the cities of Cyprus, who supplied him with ships, and an army of Ionians and Carians. He was not successful; but it is fairly clear now that, contrary to Herodotus' image where he appears as a very unpopular figure, Apries enjoyed considerable support throughout Egypt (Leahy 1988), and his attempted comeback posed a serious threat to Amasis. It is possible that Egypt at this time entered a period of civil strife. Apries had, on his defeat, taken refuge at the Babylonian court, and persuaded Nebuchadnezzar II to take advantage of Egypt's internal crisis by mounting a campaign to reinstate Apries. If successful, this would have augmented Babylonia's power enormously. The situation for Egypt was critical. From a rather fragmentary Babylonian text, it emerges that, at this crisis-point, Amasis approached the ruler of Cyrene and received military support from him to face the Babylonian forces (an alliance probably cemented by a dynastic marriage; Herodotus 2.181). The battle between the two armies was bitter. As Amasis presents it, in the fragmentary stele commemorating his ultimate victory (Edel 1978), the gods were on his side by creating terrible weather conditions and, in the course of the fighting, Apries was killed. In a brilliant propaganda move, Amasis gave the body a well-publicised, full royal funeral in the dynastic centre of Sais, which must have helped to divide the opposition.

Herodotus provides some splendidly lively anecdotes about Amasis: his ironic sense of humour, his apparent popularity, and his friendship with Polycrates, tyrant of Samos, who grew fabulously rich from supplying the Egyptian king with soldiers. A fragmentary demotic story about Amasis (from the third century) echoes the tone of some of these Herodotean stories. It also gives a flavour of the humour typical of some Egyptian popular stories about kings and is worth quoting:

> It happened one day in the time of Pharaoh Amasis that the Pharaoh said to his people: 'I wish to drink Egyptian *kolobi*-wine!'
>
> They replied: 'Oh, our great lord, it is difficult to drink Egyptian *kolobi*-wine!'
>
> He said to them: 'Do not obstruct my orders!'
>
> They said: 'Oh, our great lord, if it is the desire of Pharaoh, then may it be so.'
>
> The Pharaoh spoke: 'Let us go to the lake!'
>
> All was done in accordance with the command of Pharaoh.
>
> The Pharaoh ate with his women and there was no wine before him save Egyptian *kolobi*-wine. The face of Pharaoh was happy with his women, and he drank a lot of wine, because Pharaoh had a great desire for Egyptian *kolobi*-wine.
>
> Pharaoh slept that night by the lake, and he lay down under a vine on the north side (of the garden-house).
>
> It happened in the morning that, because of the serious headache he had, Pharaoh could not get up. When the time for getting up arrived, he could not raise himself (from the bed). The courtiers raised a lament and said: 'Is it possible to imagine such a thing? That the Pharaoh should have a headache? No one on earth is allowed to go to speak to Pharaoh.'
>
> The courtiers went to the place where Pharaoh was, and said: 'Oh, great lord, in what a pitiful state does Pharaoh find himself?'
>
> Pharaoh replied: 'I have a headache. It is impossible for me to carry out any business whatsoever. But see whether you can find someone among you who can tell me a story which may entertain me.'
>
> (Spiegelberg 1914: 26)

* * *

Eventually Babylonia and Egypt drew closer together in the face of the growing power of Persia. Egypt's allies, Lydia and Babylonia, were both conquered by Cyrus several years before Egypt was absorbed. There is no evidence of Egypt offering them any help against the Persians. Cambyses attacked Egypt soon after Amasis' death, when his son, Psammetichus III, was still trying to consolidate his position. Some of the stories in Herodotus about Cambyses' invasion (3.1–3; Lloyd 1988) hint that the Persians may have manipulated lingering resentment against Amasis and attempted to cast the Persian invader in the role of Apries' avenger. It certainly looks as though the northern part of the country surrendered fairly swiftly, and a number of the Egyptian king's former officials moved over with apparent ease to serve the Persian kings (Lloyd 1982). The Persian kings adopted the formal Egyptian titles and names, and were presented in Egyptian contexts in the guise of legitimate Egyptian Pharaohs performing the necessary rituals required by the gods, well illustrated by Darius I's temple at Hibis in Kharga oasis (Cruz-Urribe 1988). From now on, with a long break in the fourth century (401–343), Egypt was a Persian province; its subsequent history must be considered in the context of the Achaemenid empire (chapter 13).

Notes

1 Similar assumptions about matrilineal rules of succession elsewhere have been shown not to stand up to rigorous analysis, see chapter 4b (dynasty XVIII); chapter 7c (Elam).)

2 For the suggestion that the name indicates that Theocles was a *xenos* of Psammetichus I, see G. Herman, *Ritualised Friendship in the Greek City* (Cambridge 1987): 102.

13

THE ACHAEMENID EMPIRE
(c. 550–330)

The Achaemenid empire was the earliest and biggest Persian empire. It precedes those of the later Parthians (c. 140–AD 224) and Sassanians (AD 224–651), which were contemporary, and in frequent conflict, with the Roman empire, and had important states as neighbours to the east (India, China). By contrast, in the Achaemenid period no country could rival its power. 'Achaemenid' derives from the eponymous founder of the ruling dynasty, 'Achaemenes'; it was the name of the Persian royal family, members of which ruled the empire for nearly two hundred years. Its formation began c. 550, with the great conquests of Cyrus (II) the Great (559–530) and Cambyses (II, 530–522); it was brought to an end by Alexander's conquest between 334 and 323. It was the largest empire the world had seen, spanning the territory from the Hellespont to north India, including Egypt (most of the time) and extending into central Asia up to the frontiers of modern Kazakhstan.

13a The sources

The sources for studying the Persian empire present particular difficulties, not so much because they are sparse but because they are extremely disparate and exist in a number of different languages and forms. Before excavation and the subsequent decipherment of ancient Near Eastern scripts in the last century, the Achaemenid empire was primarily known through classical writers, especially Herodotus writing in the fifth century. His aim was to celebrate the victories won by the mainland Greeks over the Persians between 490 and 478, so his valuable information is limited chronologically to the early period of the empire. Although he is unrivalled in his coverage of many areas and aspects of the empire, his greatest interest, and the focus for his most detailed discussion, was its north-western frontier (Drews 1973: 45–96; Briant 1990). Later classical writers, aside from the Alexander historians, such as Ctesias and Xenophon (early fourth century), have similar geo-political limitations – although in the case of Ctesias this could also reflect the taste of his later excerptors rather than Ctesias' original work, which is now lost. An exception is the curious semi-philosophical work of Xenophon called *The Education of Cyrus* (*Cyropaedia*). But its moralising tone, its novelistic style and its aim – to present the founder of the Persian empire as the ideal ruler whose legacy was corrupted by later descendants – mean that historical realities have been subordinated to this larger purpose, so that it is difficult to know how the historian might use it (cf. *EncIr* vol. 6: 512–514). All the Greek writers were fascinated by the wealth and power of the Persian rulers, so they often recount stories of court intrigue and the moral decadence that comes from indulging in unlimited luxury. In such anecdotes, the Persian king appears as an essentially weak figure, a prey to the machinations of powerful women and sinister eunuchs. This is an inversion of Greek social and political norms, with which we, as Europeans, have usually identified: the image of the cowardly, effeminate Persian monarch has exercised a strong influence through the centuries, making the Persian empire into a powerful 'other' in European Orientalism, contrasted with 'western' bravery and masculinity (Said 1978; Sancisi-Weerdenburg 1983a; 1987b; Hall 1989; 1993). We must remember this in studying the Persian empire: the popular and wide-spread impression of its political system is fundamentally flawed (Sancisi-Weerdenburg 1987a).

Table 35 Kings of Persia

Teispes (of Anshan)	*c.* 650–620
Cyrus I (son)	*c.* 620–590
Cambyses I (son)	*c.* 590–559
Cyrus II the Great (son)	559–530
Cambyses II (son)	530–522
Bardiya (Smerdis) (brother)	522
Darius I (son of Hystaspes, grandson of Arsames, descendant of Achaemenes)	522–486
Xerxes (son)	486–465
Artaxerxes I (son)	465–424/423
Darius II (son)	423–405
Artaxerxes II (son)	405–359
Artaxerxes III (son)	359–338
Artaxerxes IV (Arses, son)	338–336
Darius III (second cousin)	336–330
Alexander of Macedon	330–323

The Old Testament has bequeathed to us two divergent pictures of the Persian kings. In *Ezra* and *Nehemiah* they appear as restorers of the Jerusalem temple and active supporters of the Yahweh cult, although the historical problems of these texts loom large (Grabbe 1992). The image is positive because the Persian kings ushered in the period of the 'Second Temple' and ordered the return of the Jewish deportees from Babylonia (cf. chapter 8d(i)).

But in the book of *Esther*, which was almost certainly written in the Hellenistic period (second century; Bickerman 1967), the picture of Persian court life is similar to that found in Greek writers (Momigliano 1977).

The Persians of the Achaemenid period spoke an early form of modern Persian called 'Old Persian', a member of the Indo-European language family. Texts in Old Persian were written using a cuneiform-shaped script, quite different from Akkadian cuneiform. It began to be deciphered in the early nineteenth century. The greatest advance was made by Henry Rawlinson, who was able, with great difficulty, to make squeezes of the longest Old Persian inscription known, the long text (with accompanying relief) of Darius I (522–486), carved high on the rockface dominating the main road leading to Ecbatana (modern Hamadan) at Behistun (fig. 43). Darius' inscription gives us a detailed account of the circumstances surrounding his accession to the throne. But the Behistun text is an exception: material written in Old Persian is largely limited to monumental inscriptions, intended to reflect the unchanging majesty of Persian imperial power, and so they provide rather less insight into the Achaemenid empire than scholars originally hoped; political events, historical changes and administrative structures are not (with the exception of Behistun) recorded in them (for the texts, see Kent 1953; Gharib 1968; *CDAFI* 4). This limitation of the Old Persian texts is linked to the fact that the Old Persian script was probably an artificial royal creation (Herrenschmidt 1990): it was intended to make a visual impression, it provided a script unique to the Persians and stamped the empire as Persian, but it was not used outside the formal public sphere. All inscriptions appear on buildings and rockfaces in Iran (the one exception is an inscription of

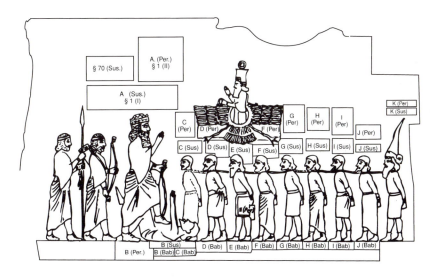

Figure 43 Behistun relief (Per.: Old Persian; Bab.: Akkadian; Sus.: Susian or Elamite)

Xerxes above Lake Van in eastern Turkey), or on smaller portable objects probably emanating from the court (stone vases, metal vessels, seals). One other interesting aspect of the Old Persian inscriptions is that they are virtually always accompanied by versions in other languages – normally Elamite and Babylonian Akkadian (occasionally Egyptian hieroglyphs).

To illuminate the essential socio-economic aspects, we have to use other sources – Babylonian, Egyptian, Aramaic and Elamite documents. The Aramaic texts are especially important. Aramaic was widely used already in the Near East before the Persian conquest (see chapter 8b), and it was perhaps for this reason that it was adopted by the new conquerors as the most widely used administrative imperial language. We have evidence for its use in Persepolis, Babylonia, Egypt, the Levant and Asia Minor (*CHI* II ch. 15). The fact that Aramaic was used in the former eastern provinces of the Achaemenid empire in the Hellenistic period (Schlumberger *et al.* 1958), and that the later Parthians used an Aramaic script to write contemporary Middle Iranian languages, shows that the Achaemenid bureaucracy used Aramaic the length and breadth of the imperial territories (Naveh 1982 [OH]).

The most important texts, central to gaining an insight into the workings of the empire, are, first, two groups of Elamite texts from Persepolis. One set, dating between 492 and 458, i.e. from late in the reign of Darius I (522–486) into the early years of Artaxerxes I (465–424/423), are records of silver payments made to workers instead of their regular rations; they number just over a hundred (Cameron 1948). They were found in a building on the palace terrace identified as the treasury; hence they are known as the 'Treasury Texts'. A much larger group is formed by the tablets found dumped near the north-west fortifications at Persepolis. These 'Fortification Texts' record authorisations for all kinds of food rations to workers (women, men and children), cultic functionaries (for sacrifices), high-ranking Persian nobles – even one of Darius' queens, Artystone, has been identified. They date to the period 509–494. This material is extraordinarily rich in its potential for understanding the labour system, agricultural production, landholding, demography, diet, settlement in the Fars region, and the organisation and provisioning of travel through the empire (Hallock 1971 (also *CHI* II ch. 11); Hinz 1971; Lewis 1977; 1990). So far, just under 2,200 texts of this valuable corpus have been published (Hallock 1969; 1978); transcriptions of approximately another two thousand exist, and a very large number of texts and fragments (housed in the Oriental Institute in Chicago) have yet to be studied and published. The 'Treasury' and 'Fortification' texts reflect part of the court's accounting and administrative system. Why they do not cover later periods of the empire is uncertain – possibly the chancellery switched to using Aramaic, written on perishable material, at some point and so the later records have not been preserved.

Another important archive of material (written in Akkadian) comes from Nippur in Babylonia and dates to the second half of the fifth century. It reflects the transactions of a great Babylonian business firm, the Murashu family. They engaged in leasing and managing military land grants to soldiers and landed estates belonging to members of the royal family and high court personnel, and carrying out associated commercial transactions. This allows important insights into some of the most basic and crucial aspects of imperial functioning, which was replicated, in its essentials, elsewhere in the empire (Cardascia 1952; Stolper 1985; van Driel 1989). Almost contemporary with the Murashu documents are the Aramaic texts from Egypt (Grelot 1972). They come from three distinct locations: one is an enormous and disparate collection of papyri and ostraca (now scattered across the museums of the world) generated by a small community of Jewish soldiers and their families, who served as part of the Achaemenid frontier garrison on Elephantine island (Aswan). Some individual family histories emerge with great clarity, as well as the religious life of the Jewish soldiers and their relations with the Persian authorities (Porten 1968). Another, much smaller, group comes from Hermopolis; they are letters written by soldiers to their families further south (Bresciani and Kamil 1966). Fragments of an archive from the Persian bureaucracy have been found at Saqqara, near Memphis: some 202 are in Aramaic (published by Segal 1983); many more are in demotic Egyptian and still await publication. The texts are unfortunately very damaged, but they provide some important information on administration in Egypt. Most important is a pouch containing a collection of sealed letters written on leather; unfortunately, they were acquired on the antiquities market and their exact find-spot is not known. The preserved documents (now in the Bodleian Library, Oxford) contain the correspondence between the Persian satrap of Egypt, Arsames, and his estate-manager(s), and provide detailed insight into the structure of great landed estates (Driver 1957/1965). These are merely the largest and most important concentrations of documents – smaller collections (such as the Aramaic papyri from Samaria, Cross 1963; Gropp 1986; the bullae from Daskyleion, Kaptan-Bayburtluoğlu 1990) and more scattered finds help to amplify the material.

Archaeologists have explored the area of the empire only partially. The chief sites to have been excavated and studied, for their Achaemenid-period remains, are the great royal centres in Iran: Pasargadae (Stronach 1978), Persepolis (Schmidt 1953–7; Tilia 1972–8), Susa (Boucharlat 1990) and the associated rock-cut tombs (at Naqsh-i Rustam and Persepolis). But recently more attention has been paid to the Achaemenid levels of long-occupied sites such as Sardis in Lydia (Mierse 1983) and Achaemenid settlements in the Levant (Moorey 1975; 1980; Stern 1982; *Transeuphratène* vols I ff.) and central Asia (*CAH* IV ch. 3c; Briant 1984a). One problem is that several sites, known to have been very important in the period, are covered by extensive modern towns, which makes excavation difficult. This is true of Arbela (modern Erbil) in northern Iraq, Damascus and Hamadan (ancient Ecbatana). A number of monuments with Iranian motifs have been recovered in western

Turkey, reflecting the presence of Persians or local dignitaries influenced by Persian court practices (see, in general, *CAH* IV ch. 3e; also Jacobs 1987; Calmeyer 1992; Nollé 1992). Material from western Asia Minor and Phoenicia, in particular, illustrates the enormously rich cultural interaction that took place within the empire – especially striking is the strong influence of Greek-style art which begins in the time of the Persian empire (Root 1991).

In sum: there is quite a lot of material for understanding the Persian empire, but it is not always easy to use. For reconstructing political history, we are largely dependent (after the first decades) on Greek historians, whose interest is normally limited to the north-west, and who, as often hostile outsiders, present a somewhat skewed picture. Administrative material is available in quantity from Fars, Babylonia and Egypt, but it is largely restricted chronologically to the fifth century; the fourth century, the time preceding Alexander's victories, is poorly documented. The eastern imperial regions are very scantily known; archaeological material is the only source here, and its interpretation is much disputed (Briant 1984a).

13b Persians and Medes

Who were the Persians? The Persian homeland is Persia, which in origin coincides approximately with the modern Iranian province of Fars, at the south-eastern end of the Zagros mountain range. The Persians are part of a larger group of peoples, identified via their language as Iranians. People speaking related languages are found not only in modern Iran, but also in Afghanistan and parts of central Asia. Iranian also has affinities with Sanskrit, the old classical language of India. Iranian is divided into several 'dialects': the archaic language of the Avesta, the sacred book of the Zoroastrians (the pre-Islamic religious community of Iran; Boyce 1975–; 1984), for example, represents an eastern form of Iranian, called 'Avestan'. Persian is a western Iranian dialect: the language of Persia, heartland of the empire. The earliest form of Persian we know (from Achaemenid royal inscriptions) is Old Persian.

The background to the Persian empire bristles with problems and warring hypotheses. Most scholars now accept the argument of Cuyler Young (*CAH* IV ch. 1) that the Iranians were originally cattle-herders who moved, over a very long period, from central Asia into Iran. Some groups eventually coalesced with the small principalities and local communities of the Zagros (the Medes) and Fars (the Persians). It is here that the Assyrian records of the ninth to seventh centuries place Medes and Persians. The Medes, located in the Kermanshah-Hamadan (ancient Ecbatana) region, are much the more prominent group in the Assyrian texts, because of repeated Assyrian military contacts with the Zagros area (see chapters 9b; 9c).

The Persians, as a distinguishable population, are not attested in the Near East before the first millennium, and we hear nothing certain about them or the development of their state in modern Fars (OP *Parsa*; Greek *Persis*) before the seventh century. Fars had, at an earlier period, formed part of the kingdom of Elam; it was here that the important Elamite city of Anshan was (see chapter 7c). Anshan declined in the twelfth century, and there seems to have been a virtual absence of settlement centres between c. 1000 and the seventh century. In the course of the seventh century, however, there is a marked change and several settlements develop. How are we to understand this? A recent approach (Miroschedji 1985; Carter 1994) has been to argue that, in the course of the eleventh and tenth centuries, when Elam was politically at a very low point, Iranian pastoralists moved into Fars and intermingled with the local Elamites. This was not a unified mass movement, but a gradual process by scattered groups, facilitated by Elam's political impotence. The region continued to be under whatever control the Elamite kings were able to wield; certainly, the Elamites claimed it as part of their kingdom from c. 800 possibly right down to 646, when Ashurbanipal's violent attack on Elam and Susa (see chapter 9c) fundamentally dislocated the Elamite polity. At this point (if not earlier), Elam lost control of Fars. Perhaps partly in response to the Assyrian threat, this detached territory now formed itself into an independent political unit ruled by a Persian family. The distinct movement towards sedentarisation, reflected in the archaeological record, would then be directly linked to the emergence of Persia (Fars) as a state in the late seventh century. Interestingly, another, perhaps the more regular, name for the early Persian state is 'Anshan': the earliest surviving evidence for the titles of the Persian kings, the Cyrus Cylinder from Babylon (539; see chapter 11d), calls Cyrus the Great and all his predecessors – Cambyses I, Cyrus I, Teispes – 'kings of Anshan'. Further, a seal impressed on several Persepolis tablets is labelled as belonging to 'Cyrus, the Anshanite, son of Teispes', i.e. Cyrus' grandfather (seal 93; Hallock 1977: 127). This suggests that the early Persian kings saw themselves as reviving and/or continuing a local Elamite kingdom, although they were themselves Iranian. As they had been living for several hundred years in close symbiosis with the Elamites of Fars, it is possible that they no longer considered themselves as markedly distinct (Amiet 1992).

The Medes, closely related to the Persians, were located further north around the area of modern Hamadan (ancient Ecbatana). They appear more prominently than the Persians in Mesopotamian records of the eighth to early sixth centuries. Assyrian accounts of campaigns directed to the Zagros region mention them frequently. The region was inhabited by innumerable peoples, not all of whom were poor, nomadic groups; some prosperous cities (e.g. Hasanlu), with elaborate public buildings and a material culture reflecting their contact with Assyria, also flourished and played an important role in the larger trade-pattern (Dyson 1965). The Assyrians list Medes as just one of many population groups – others were Mannaeans, Allabrians, Ellipeans. The region was clearly an ethnic hotch-potch, a conclusion borne out by the surviving personal names. In all cases, the Assyrians mention that contact with the various groups was mediated through a multitude of rulers of individual towns. By the second half of the eighth century, Assyrian activity in this area intensified, in response to Urartu's eastward expansion (see chapter 10a). The Assyrian kings began to penetrate the great mountain range much more deeply than they had earlier. In particular, they moved further along the Great Khorasan route, which leads directly from the Mesopotamian lowlands to the Iranian plateau. In a controlling position along it in western Iran lies Ecbatana. In the context of their expansionist effort, the Assyrian kings name the Medes: some were close enough to the Assyrian sphere to be placed under direct Assyrian rule; others were fought against as far as the area of Mount Alvand, west of Ecbatana, to force recognition of Assyria's suzerainty, but they were not formally added to the Assyrian empire. The Assyrian kings distinguish the two groups of Medes (inside and outside the empire), by describing the latter as 'distant Medes'; but *all* Medes were ruled by numerous petty kings. Links with some of the 'distant Medes' were set up by the Assyrians, and *nothing* in their accounts from the seventh century testifies to the development of a large, unified Median state. Yet at the end of the seventh century (see chapter 9e) a Median king, Cyaxares, was able to mobilise considerable forces and use them to sack, both singly and together with the Babylonians, some of the great Assyrian cities (Ashur, Nineveh, Harran, cf. chapter 9e). By 585, the same Median king had expanded his power over eastern Anatolia, and came into conflict with Croesus of Lydia on the banks of the Halys river (Herodotus 1.79), which then became the frontier between the two areas (see chapter 10b). In 550, Cyrus of Persia fought off an attack by Cyaxares' son, Astyages. He was victorious, took over Astyages' 'royal city', Ecbatana, and removed its rich booty to Persia.

Many historians, brought up on Herodotus, who tells us (1.95–106) that the Medes developed a large empire beginning some time around 700, tend to accept that a powerful Median state developed in west Iran. They feel that, as the two last Median kings named by him (Cyaxares and Astyages) have been confirmed as historical by Babylonian chronicles (*ABC* nos. 3 and 7), we should trust his earlier history, too. They explain the Assyrian silence on the Median state by the fact that it evolved somewhere beyond their frontier, i.e. in the land of 'the distant Medes' (Brown 1988). It is a possible solution, but it presents problems too. The most significant one is how to marry the view of an evolving, centralised Median state coalescing ever more until its defeat by the Persian Cyrus with the archaeological picture. Three sites of the seventh century have been excavated, on and to the south of the Khorasan route, in Median territory: Godin Tepe, Tepe Nush-i Jan, Baba Jan. All exhibit similar, though not identical, features, especially in their organisation of public space, which reflects an important change in their socio-political structure. One of the sites has impressive fortifications; all have important buildings with multi-columned halls (see fig. 44). All seem to have been

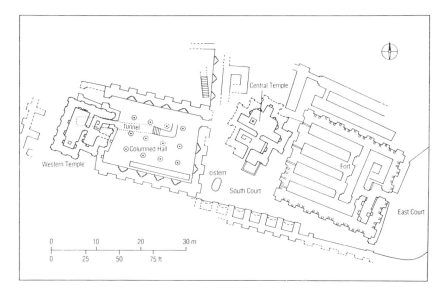

Figure 44 Plan of Tepe Nush-i Jan (after Roaf 1990 [OA])

centres under local rulers, as no settlement hierarchy is detectable; none is particularly large or luxurious in its appointments. Most important is that all seem to have been reduced to poor squatter sites by the sixth century – hardly the pattern we would expect in a flourishing, strong state.

In the absence of any Median evidence from the capital Ecbatana, the three sites have been hailed as giving us finally some clue to Median history. But what exactly do they tell us? If we take all the evidence together (Babylonian chronicles and Herodotus), we see that, by the time of the last Median ruler, Ecbatana had become a royal centre with substantial amounts of goods stored there. The Medes appear to exercise some sort of hegemony, or claim to do so, from the Halys to the Iranian plateau, but its precise nature and extent is nebulous. The Medes are able to mobilise sizeable forces, to mount attacks on neighbours (Assyria, Persia, Lydia), although the success of their ventures is limited: the war against the Assyrians is fought together with the Babylonians, and it is the Babylonians who benefit territorially by Assyria's defeat (see chapters 9e; 11d); the war against Lydia ends in a draw, and the Persian conflict in the elimination of Media. At the very point when Herodotus' story would suggest that the Medes are at the peak of their power (early sixth century), the development of several centres in the Median heartland comes to a halt, and they decline dramatically. One way of dealing with this internally contradictory picture is that advanced by Sancisi-Weerdenburg (1988; 1994). She stresses the absence of any real evidence for the Median state, apart from Herodotus' later story, and turns to an evaluation of the

655

archaeology and the significance of the *absence* of material from the Median realm (Genito 1986; Muscarella 1987). She suggests that there were certainly developments towards state-formation in seventh-century Media, to which Nush-i Jan, Godin and Baba Jan testify: this was the result of Assyrian tribute and trade demands which stimulated the growth of local centres (Brown 1986). However, precisely because this development depended on Assyrian demands, it ground to a halt when the Assyrian empire collapsed in the late seventh century. From this point on the Medes never moved beyond a loose, tribal confederacy, because they lacked the sustained stimulus and the organised tapping of resources generated by a large empire. Such an approach would certainly explain the curious gaps in material and the retro-development of the Median sites. But it makes it difficult to say anything about the possible influence exercised by the Medes on later Persian institutions (strongly argued for by some, e.g. Cook 1983; Dandamaev and Lukonin 1989): the Persian kingdom was a close neighbour (it may even have been in some sense subject to the Medes for a while); the languages of the two people were closely related, as were elements of their culture; Media was always regarded as one of the core regions of the Persian empire. But whether this is to be explained as the result of the formative influence exercised by a developed state on a fledgling one, or whether it simply reflects general geographical proximity and a cultural *koine*, must remain a moot point at present.

13c The formation of the empire

Cyrus the Great

The founder of the Persian empire was Cyrus of Persia/Anshan. We know from the Cyrus Cylinder (see pp. 601–602) that he was descended from a line of local kings, who had governed the small kingdom of Persia for three generations, beginning with king Teispes. According to later Greek writers (Herodotus and Ctesias), Persia was a client-state of the Medes, but there is no earlier evidence to corroborate this. Herodotus gives us very precise regnal years for Cyrus (29), which suggests he had access to a reliable (written?) source (Sancisi-Weerdenburg, in press). Babylonian documents, which date by Cyrus after his conquest of Babylonia (539), give us a fairly precise date of August 530 for his death. We may therefore date Cyrus' accession to the Persian throne with some confidence in 559.

The precise boundaries of Persia at this time are not certain. There is evidence that a small principality may have existed in Fars at Gisat in the late seventh–early sixth century, which perhaps Cyrus II's predecessors had to incorporate (Carter and Stolper 1984: 55). Another small kingdom, centred on Susa, is attested around the same time by an archive of some three hundred administrative Elamite texts, found beneath Darius I's buildings

(MDP 9; 11: 301–307, 309). Neo-Babylonian rulers from Nebuchadnezzar II (604–562) to Nerglissar (559–556) claimed control over Susa (see chapter 11e), but what form this took, how tight it was, is debated. Individuals with Persian names and ethnic labels appear in the Susa texts, showing that some Persians were in close contact with this Elamite centre; perhaps their presence is to be explained by a small Persian settlement (Briant 1984b). In the Cyrus Cylinder (see pp. 601–602), composed after the Persian conquest of Babylon (539), Cyrus says that he restored sanctuaries in the region of Susa and Der (east of the Tigris). This suggests that he had conquered Susa before the Babylonian war. As we have no evidence for Babylonian rule of Susa in the reign of Nabonidus (555–539), we should probably date the Persian takeover to Cyrus II's reign, and before 539. More precision is, unfortunately, impossible. It is not impossible that the fall of Susa predates Cyrus' war against the Medes (550) and that it led to hostility between Babylonia and Persia.

Much better attested is Cyrus' defeat of Astyages of Media (550). A Babylonian chronicle gives us the following details:

> (Astyages) mustered (his army) and marched against Cyrus, king of Anshan, for conquest [. . .] The army rebelled against Astyages (Akk. *Ishtumegu*) and he was taken prisoner. Th[ey handed him over?] to Cyrus. Cyrus marched to Ecbatana (Akk. *Agamtanu*), the royal city. Silver, gold, goods, treasures [. . .], which he carried off as booty (from) Ecbatana, he took to Anshan. The goods (and) treasures of the army of [. . .]
>
> (*ABC* no. 7 ii. 1–4)

The reason for Astyages' attack on Cyrus could have been Persian growth, as a result of its absorption of Susiana; but that is speculation. Herodotus (1. 123–8), for example, links it to a planned revolt by Cyrus against his Median overlord, although we should note that there is no clear evidence that the Persians were ever subjects of the Medes. Common to both the Babylonian chronicle and Herodotus' account is the revolt of the Median army, and the imprisonment of Astyages, with no hint of an execution. The shift of power (political, economic) from Ecbatana to the Persian centre is very clear in the Babylonian text, and there is no hint that either Cyrus or his son, Cambyses, built there. Later evidence, however, shows that Ecbatana became – predictably, given its strategic location – a crucially important centre of Persian control: capital of the Median satrapy (valued particularly for its horses and grazing). Inscriptions of several Persian kings and precious metal items have been found here, royal building is recorded (Kent 1953), and it was regularly used as a royal residence. The second-century Greek historian Polybius paints a glowing picture of its splendours:

> It had always been the royal residence of the Medes and is said to have greatly exceeded all the other cities in wealth and the magnificence of

its buildings. It lies on the skirts of Mount Orontes and has no wall, but possesses an artifical citadel the fortifications of which are of wonderful strength. Beneath this stands the palace ... (it) is about seven stades (well over 1 km) in circumference, and by the magnificence of the separate structures in it conveys a high idea of the wealth of its original founders. For the woodwork was all of cedar and cypress, but no part of it was left exposed, and the rafters, the compartments of the ceiling, and the columns in the porticoes and colonnades were plated with either silver or gold, and all the tiles were silver.

(Polybius 10.27.5–10)

We can only guess at the results of Cyrus' Median victory: greatly increased resources, material and manpower, are obvious. Both Herodotus and Ctesias (*FGrH* 688 F9) present him as the heir to Median hegemony, thus gaining control of territory from eastern Iran to the Halys river.

The precarious balance of power in the Near East was affected by the Persian victory, as we see from the Lydian king Croesus' reaction (Herodotus 1.53–55, 71). He seems to have seized the opportunity, now that the accord between Lydia and Media no longer prevailed (see chapter 10b), to realise Lydia's territorial ambitions. He crossed the frontier into Cappadocia and met the Persian army at Pteria (Boğazköy?). The battle ended in a draw and the two armies withdrew for the winter. Croesus disbanded his army, the soldiers of his subjects returned home, and the Lydian king prepared to call for aid from his allies: Egypt, Babylonia, Sparta. Whether Cyrus was quite as lacking in expansionist aims as Herodotus' account implies may be doubted: it is signficant that he is said to have encouraged the Greek cities of the Ionian coast to revolt against Croesus by joining the Persian side on generous terms – they refused (Herodotus 1.76; Walser 1987). Cyrus, unlike Croesus, did not leave Cappadocia, but pursued the Lydian army to their capital, Sardis. After another battle, the Lydians were forced to retreat into Sardis, which the Persians besieged for two weeks, before it fell (Herodotus 1.79–81). The several traditions about Croesus' fate are contradictory; according to Herodotus, he became a valued and honoured adviser at the Persian king's court.

With the fall of Lydia, the whole of western Anatolia lay open to the Persian conqueror. Cyrus' immediate action was to appoint a local official, Pactyas, to act as treasurer under the command of the Persian Tabalos, who was left in Sardis with a garrison (Herodotus 1.153), while Cyrus returned to Ecbatana with Croesus as his prisoner. The precariousness of the situation is illustrated by Pactyas absconding with the funds and raising a revolt, for which he had some support from the Ionian cities. The Persian response was swift and brutal: Cyrus sent his general Mazares to pursue Pactyas, who was surrendered by Chios; Mazares sacked Priene, sold the inhabitants into slavery and ravaged the plain of Maeander. On his death, Harpagus took over the Persian command and brought the Greek cities Caria, Caunia and Lycia to heel. Some places resisted and had to be besieged, some surrendered, while half the population of Phocaea abandoned their city and fled to their colony of Alalia in Corsica (Herodotus 1.154–176). The precise date of the Lydian conquest is not known. It is thought that a Babylonian chronicle (*ABC* no. 7 ii.15–17) refers to Cyrus' march to Lydia in 547/6; but the text is broken, and Cyrus' destination is *not* preserved (Cargill 1977). General considerations, however, make it likely that we should place the Lydian campaign somewhere in the 540s, although the hypothetical nature of the chronology must be remembered.

Babylonia, too, was affected by Cyrus' defeat of the neighbouring Medes, and the fall of Lydia, with whom the Babylonians were allied, brought Cyrus and the Babylonian king, Nabonidus, face to face. As stated above, Babylonia may already have suffered a setback through Cyrus' conquest of Susa; his subsequent victories can hardly have lessened the tension between the two sides. Unfortunately, there is no information which allows us to trace the history of Babylonian–Persian relations preceding the final confrontation, although there are hints that there was some fighting between the two in the years before 539 (von Voigtlander 1963; *CAH* IV ch. 3a). It is also possible that Cyrus exploited hostility to the Babylonian king felt among some members of the population (e.g. Jewish deportees), although the evidence is not always easy to interpret (Kuhrt 1990b; but see Machinist and Tadmor 1993). Despite uncertainties, it is probably right to see Cyrus' invasion of Babylonia as the culmination of long-term hostilities. The Persian and Babylonian armies met at Opis, east of the Tigris, near the traditional point of entry for Elamite armies. As a Babylonian chronicle tells us:

In the month Tishri (September–October 539), when Cyrus did battle at Opis on the [bank of?] the Tigris against the army of Akkad (Babylonia), the people of Akkad retreated. He carried off the plunder (and) slaughtered the people.

(*ABC* no. 7 iii. 12–14)

The Persian victor followed up his massacre at Opis by receiving the surrender of Sippar and sending his general Gobryas to invest Babylon, where the defeated Babylonian king, Nabonidus, was taken prisoner. In the calm following battle and defeat, the Babylonian populace received Cyrus formally into the great capital as their new king. Cyrus accepted the surrender, cast himself in the role of divinely blessed ruler of Babylon and expressed it through sanctioning civic and sacred building-works, authorising offerings to the gods and proclaiming formally the restoration of destroyed sanctuaries and the return of their peoples (see Cyrus Cylinder, pp. 601–602; Kuhrt 1983). Such public proclamations were part of the traditional rhetoric of Babylonian conquerors after triumph (see chapters 11d; 11f): they guaranteed continuity to the defeated and provided a way for the local élite to collaborate with the new rulers (Kuhrt 1990a). It was thus a politically potent tool, which made it possible for the Persians to strengthen their support: it does not imply a radical reversal of existing policies, nor a liberation.

The Neo-Babylonian empire had embraced territories from the frontier of Egypt to the Zagros foothills, so Cyrus' victory gave him access to an immense region. That the conquest of Babylon was particularly significant for the Persian king is shown by the fact that he installed his son, Cambyses, as co-ruler with the duty to act formally as king of Babylon (Petschow 1988). The arrangement lasted for only one year (538/7), and we do not know why it was abandoned. From then until the reign of Darius I, Gobryas (not identical with the general during Babylon's conquest) held the governorship of the gigantic province. Below the highest echelons, local Babylonian officials continued in post – a sensible arrangement, which appears to have worked successfully: there are no hints of local unrest, certainly no open revolt of the type attested for Lydia. The fate of Nabonidus, like that of his defeated fellow-kings, was to become a prisoner of Cyrus, probably with an estate in Carmania (Grayson 1975: 32–33; *FGrH* 680 F9; Briant 1985). The situation outside Babylonia proper, i.e. in its former provinces, is much less clear. The rebuilding of Jerusalem's temple and its repopulation by Jews from Babylonia is tradition-ally attributed to Cyrus (*Ezra* 1). But the many vicissitudes encountered by the Jerusalem community make it difficult to know how soon a real 'restoration' was effected (Grabbe 1992). It is not impossible that part of the effort to occupy and control the large territory that fell to the Persians as a consequence of the Babylonian defeat was the resettlement and strengthening of provincial centres. The reconstruction of Jerusalem could have been part of such a policy. Unfortunately, there is no other evidence for Cyrus' strategy, and nothing throws light on how rapidly the Persians imposed their control. It is possible that a chain of defensive positions along the Levant coast were constructed or repaired around this time, but the chronology of this work is not (and cannot be) precise (Wallinga 1987: 65 and n. 60).

At some point, possibly after the fall of Babylon, Cyrus turned his attention to eastern Iran and central Asia. Both Herodotus and Ctesias place campaigns by him in the 'Far East' at the end of his life; both assert that he was killed while campaigning in the east. This aspect of the great conqueror's achieve-ments is the least well documented. Since we do not know how far Median claims to control might have extended here, it is difficult to judge what Cyrus actually did. He is associated with the submission of Bactria (*FGrH* 688 F9), and with trying to push Persian power beyond Sogdiana to the further side of the Jaxartes river (Syr Darya; Herodotus 1.205–214) – perhaps no more than an attempt to consolidate frontiers by a punitive raid against the steppe nomads here. A string of Achaemenid forts on the Jaxartes river included Cyreschata, the foundation of which was certainly later linked to Cyrus. Although the progress of the Persian conquest in this region remains uncertain, we should accept that Cyrus brought the larger part of Afghanistan and south central Asia (modern Turkmenistan, Uzbekistan and Tadjikistan) under Persian control.

Darius I, when describing his realm at the beginning of his reign (Kent 1953, DB I 12–17) in 522, includes all this region in the list of countries subject to him. We know of no action by Cambyses in the east, so the stories of Cyrus' conquest of the east have a foundation in historical reality.

One direct result of Cyrus' many conquests was the development of the Persian homeland. Cyrus founded a new royal centre, about 75 km northwest of the old Elamite city of Anshan, named, after his tribe, Pasargadae. Several palaces were laid out on a spacious plan, set among irrigated gardens (Stronach 1978; 1994). Their columned halls hark back to the Zagros architectural tradition (see pp. 654–655), but the iconography and techniques of the conquered peoples with their sophisticated knowhow in working stone and creating a royal environment was also tapped: the fragmentary remains of reliefs show the use made of Assyrian palatial sculptural prototypes; the chisel-marks show Ionian stonemasons at work; the gabled tomb of Cyrus set on a stepped platform follows western Anatolian models (Nylander 1970; Root 1979). The new city, which drew craftsmen from the ends of the young empire, acted as a stimulus to development of the central area. The population of Persia was swelled by newcomers, prisoners-of-war, servants attached to the court which led to an attendant change.

Cyrus' achievements can only be described as spectacular: in less than thirty years, he brought a vast territory under the control of a kingdom which, at the beginning of his reign, had been tiny. He was a brilliant tactician and strategist, able to move rapidly across enormous distances, take his opponents by surprise, and make calculated use of brutal and placatory gestures. The Persians celebrated his fame in song and story (Xenophon, *Cyropaedia* 1.2.1). His astonishing success led rapidly to the creation of innumerable popular stories, which obscured his true background: he was presented variously as the grandson of the Median king, Astyages, exposed by his jealous grandfather, brought up by humble herding folk, ultimately identified and eventually returned to his parents (Herodotus 1.107–108), and as the son of poverty-stricken parents who worked his way up at the Median court and eventually overthrew the Medes (*FGrH* 688 F9). Other stories abounded, according to Herodotus. They are typical of the tales told about culture-heroes and founders of great empires (e.g. Sargon of Agade (see chapter 1c), Moses, Romulus and Remus). They illustrate the cultural and political importance of the protagonist, but cannot be relied on as a guide to historical reality. In the case of Cyrus, we have his own testimony, which flatly contradicts the later romances created by his countrymen; we know that he was preceded as king of Persia by his father, grandfather and great-grandfather.

The conquest of Egypt

One power, and former ally of the defeated kingdoms, left unconquered by Cyrus' lightning campaigns was Egypt. It is probable that the Egyptian king,

Amasis (570–526), responded to the Persians picking off his partners by trying to strengthen his own position. It is possible that he moved to support the Greek tyrant, Polycrates of Samos, after the fall of Lydia in order to create difficulties for the Persians in the Aegean, and that his conquest of Cyprus was an attempt to counter Persia's seizure of the Levant (Wallinga 1987; 1993). The increased naval power of Egypt perhaps forced Cyrus' son and successor, Cambyses (530–522), to make preparations to act against this formidable foe. The first essential was to create a Persian navy, which Cambyses did by investing enormously in the building of triremes and harbours; the crew for the warships were the inhabitants of Persia's maritime subjects, although the chief naval commanders were invariably Persians. The enormous effort involved took a considerable time. The invasion force against Egypt was not ready until 526/5. It was preceded by Persian moves to strengthen their control in the eastern Mediterranean by detaching Cyprus from Egypt (Herodotus 3.19), and by negotiations with the Arabs of the Sinai peninsula, whose help was essential for crossing the desert with an army (Herodotus 3.7–9).

The Egyptians met the Persians in battle on the easternmost branch of the Nile, but were routed and fled to the fortress of Memphis. When they massacred the Persian herald (and the crew of his boat), who asked them to surrender, the fort was besieged and fell after ten days; the Egyptian king, Psammetichus III, was taken prisoner. The fall of Egypt's age-old capital persuaded the neighbouring peoples in the west (Libya, Barca, Cyrene) to offer submission to the Persian conquerors. Cambyses further tried to establish a rapport with the Napatan kings, ruling well to the south of Aswan (see chapter 12a). Although Herodotus presents this as a foiled attempt at conquest by the Persians, it is likely that the real aim was to consolidate Egypt's southern frontier and, if so, it was successful (Morkot 1991). Persian concern to take full control of Egypt's possessions is also reflected by Cambyses' attempt to reach the Kharga oasis, which was certainly in Persian hands in the reign of Darius I.

The evidence for Cambyses' conquest of Egypt falls into two main categories: first, contemporary documents from Egypt; second, Herodotus' later description. The latter becomes extremely hostile to Cambyses very rapidly, describing him as a ruthless despot with growing delusions of grandeur and suffering from a bad case of paranoia. Although the outline of events in Herodotus is probably correct, it has been deformed by later anti-Persian Egyptian stories and by shaping incidents to satisfy Greek narrative conventions (Lloyd 1988). Cambyses' image in Herodotus is of a brutal foreign invader with no interest in, or sensitivity to, Egyptian social and religious attitudes. The contemporary Egyptian texts do not bear out this picture. Most important is the autobiographical, hieroglyphic inscription of the statue of Udjahorresnet (now in the Vatican), a high officer and naval commander under the Egyptian kings. He reports events as follows:

The Great King of all Foreign Lands, Cambyses, came to Egypt, the foreigners of all foreign lands being with him. He gained mastery over the entire land. They set themselves down therein, since he was the great ruler of Egypt, the Great King of all foreign lands. His majesty handed over to me the office of chief physician. He caused me to be beside him as a 'friend' and 'controller of the palace', while I made his royal titulary in his name of the King of Upper and Lower Egypt Mesuti-re. I caused his majesty to recognise the importance of Sais (dynastic centre of Saite kings, see chapter 12b); it is the seat of Neith the great, the mother who bore Re, who began birth when no birth yet existed; and (I caused him to recognise) the nature of the greatness of the Neith temple . . .

I asked the majesty of the King of Upper and Lower Egypt Cambyses on account of all the foreigners who had set themselves down in the temple of Neith that they should be expelled therefrom in order to cause that the temple of Neith should be once more in all its splendour as it had been earlier. Then his majesty commanded to expel all the foreigners who dwelt in the temple of Neith, to tear down their houses and their entire refuse which was in this temple. Then they brought (all their things) themselves outside the wall of this temple. His majesty commanded to purify the temple of Neith and to restore to it all its people . . . and the hourly-priests of the temple. His majesty commanded that offerings should be given to Neith, the Great One, the Mother of God, and to the great gods who are in Sais as it was earlier in it. . . .

The King of Upper and Lower Egypt came to Sais. His majesty betook himself to the temple of Neith. He touched the ground before her very great majesty as every king had done. He organised a great feast of all good things for Neith, the Great One, the Mother of God, and the great gods who are in Sais, as every excellent king has done. This his majesty did because I had caused him to know the importance of her majesty; for she is the mother of Re himself.

(Posener 1936: 1–26; Lichtheim 1973–80 [OI] III: 36–41; Lloyd 1982)

Udjahorresnet shows that Cambyses' policy in Egypt closely followed that of Cyrus in Babylonia: forging links with the local élites, installing them in honoured (though not politically powerful) positions, exploiting their familiarity with local conditions in order to make acceptance of his rule as palatable as possible and moulding himself to fit the role an Egyptian king was traditionally expected to fill – honouring the gods, authorising continued offerings, maintaining their sanctuaries in purity, adopting ceremonial Egyptian titles and names.

Other Egyptian evidence does not contradict this. We have the epitaph of a sacred Apis bull (closely associated with Egyptian kingship, see chapter 12b), who was buried with elaborate funeral equipment by Cambyses in 524; the sarcophagus for the same Apis bull also survives. Another Apis epitaph, from

Darius I's fourth year, records the death of the new bull who had been formally installed by Cambyses in 524. So here again is clear evidence for Cambyses' deporting himself in accordance with the sacred dictates of Egyptian kingship. Herodotus got it wrong. Why? This is not easy to answer. On the back of a demotic Egyptian document (Spiegelberg 1914), a decree of Cambyses is partially preserved. It concerns the incomes of Egyptian temples, and may indicate that, apart from the Ptah temple in Memphis, they were curtailed. That is a possible understanding of the text, but it is very hard to read (many signs are faint or rubbed off), so we need to be careful before seeking the explanation for the adverse picture of Cambyses harboured in Egypt later in this text. It may be that by the time Herodotus gathered his information Cambyses' memory had been damned by the harsh reality of Persian control in the intervening years: the burden of Persian taxation, the two Egyptian revolts (486/485; 460–454) brutally crushed, the loss of status and property suffered by those who had refused to rally to the Persian flag. But whatever the explanation is we cannot gainsay the contemporary Egyptian evidence, which shows that Cambyses manipulated local ideology and cast himself as much as possible in the mould of a legitimate Egyptian Pharaoh.

The crisis of empire

The end of Cambyses' reign is obscure and we have no monuments from Persia that can with any confidence be attributed to him. The story of his last days, as Darius I (Kent 1953 DB) and Herodotus (3.30; 61–67) retail it, shows that serious problems beset the new empire while Cambyses was in Egypt and they assign Cambyses a sinister role in them. The two authors, in their very different ways (although Herodotus' version ultimately depends on Darius' account; Balcer 1987), say that Cambyses secretly murdered his full brother, Bardiya ('Smerdis' in Herodotus) – before he left for Egypt according to Darius, while he was there through a trusted agent according to Herodotus. But the dark deed had a nightmare ending for Cambyses: a magus (Persian learned man) called Gaumata took advantage of the cover-up, said he was Bardiya and proclaimed himself king; many Persians went over to his side and Cambyses was isolated in Egypt. Herodotus tells us that Cambyses immediately set out to return to Persia and challenge the impostor, but died along the way in Syria. At the last moment he confessed the fratricide to his courtiers to warn them not to accept Bardiya as Cyrus' son and so a legitmate king; they were uncertain as to whether to believe him or not. This is followed by a thriller-like story of the discovery of the impostor by a group of seven Persian nobles, who formed a conspiracy and killed the magus. One of their number, Darius, was selected by an omen to become king and ascended the throne. Darius only says that Cambyses died, and that he himself, aware of the imposture, killed Gaumata and became king. There are so many oddities in the story, particularly Gaumata's supposedly startling physical resemblance to Bardiya, that a majority of scholars have long suspected that the individual murdered by Darius was none other than Cambyses' brother and Cyrus' son, Bardiya himself (Dandamaev 1976; Bickerman and Tadmor 1978; although see Wiesehöfer 1978; Sancisi-Weerdenburg 1980, ch.3).

If that is so, then Darius was in effect a regicide and usurper, and the story of Bardiya's secret murder by Cambyses and Gaumata's imposture is a fiction created by Darius to hide the fact he had assassinated Cyrus' son, who, albeit in revolt against his brother, had a reasonable claim to the Persian throne. Several features point to Darius' lack of any prior right to become ruler of the Persians. In his genealogy, given at the beginning of the Behistun inscription, he insists on his claim by birth to accede to the throne: he ties his family tree to that of Cyrus and presents his own forefathers and those of the great conqueror as descended from his familial ancestor, Achaemenes. This was almost certainly a device by Darius, designed to legitimise his seizure of the throne and link him (tortuously) to the family of the great conqueror. Several scholars have noted the artificial nature of Darius' lineage (Sancisi-Weerdenburg 1982; Miroschedji 1985; Briant in press, ch. 3). Herodotus' story, too, emphasises Darius' marginality in his rights to the kingship. Further, we know from Darius' own inscriptions that his grandfather and father were both alive at the time of his accession. If the family of Darius really were closely related to Cyrus, so that its members were the next in line to the throne, then one of them would have been the more likely candidate for the throne, not the young Darius. Moreover, a public sense of outrage at Darius' bloody seizure of the throne is reflected in the numerous revolts which broke out on Darius' accession, and seriously threatened the fundamental cohesion of the young empire: some of the revolts were undoubtedly fed by a feeling that the crisis in the kingship might provide the opportunity for subjugated peoples to make a bid for independence (Elam, Babylonia, Media); but others (such as the one in Persia itself, by a leader declaring himself to be Bardiya) show the deep dismay felt by the populace at the murder of the legitimate Persian ruler, son of the empire's founder.

It took Darius just over a year (522–521) to cope with the massive uprisings against him, which shook all of Iran, Mesopotamia, Armenia, Afghanistan and parts of Central Asia, and probably had repercussions in Egypt and Lydia (although we know very little about that). His achievement in putting them down in a series of set battles, followed up by brutal and public execution of the ringleaders and their supporters, is astonishing. It is clear from Darius' Behistun inscription that he was able to rely for support on several Persian nobles, who, together with the sizable armies they commanded, were staunchly loyal to him throughout. So what we see at this moment in the empire's history is deep political divisions in Persian society, which point up the grave problems caused by territorial growth: there was clearly dissatisfaction among some groups with Cambyses, as shown by the considerable support enjoyed by his brother, Bardiya, in his bid for the throne; there was another group among the Persian nobility, resentful at the way in which the empire had developed, which had probably diminished their status – they, too, had more widespread support and were not a tiny disgruntled group operating in isolation. We can only speculate about what the precise reasons might have been for this major crisis, which almost destroyed the fledgeling empire less than a decade after its foundation (Dandamaev 1976; Briant in press, chs. 2 and 3). What we can say is that the rapid expansion of territory had brought great changes to Persia, which unleashed competition and rivalries for position and power. Darius' success in dealing with them, by reuniting the imperial lands and, above all, the Persian nobility around himself and his tenure of the throne must be counted one of his greatest triumphs. It is with him that the Achaemenid family becomes the royal clan of Persia, a position it never relinquished until Alexander's conquest; and it is only with Darius that we can really speak of the Achaemenid dynasty and the Achaemenid empire.

The magnitude of Darius' achievement can be measured by his commemoration of it: Darius ordered a relief of himself triumphing over the rebels to be carved on a high rock-face at Behistun (alternatively: Bisitun, Bagistan), dominating the main road leading from Mesopotamia to Ecbatana at a spot which had sacred associations (Wiesehöfer 1978). The picture (see fig. 43) shows him with his foot set on the prostrate body of Gaumata, who stretches his hands pleadingly upwards; the other rebel leaders, hands behind their backs and chained together at the neck, face the king; behind him stand two Persian officers. The relief is accompanied by inscriptions in Old Persian, Akkadian and Elamite, which recount in detail Darius' accession and wars, and commend his loyal and noble helpers to posterity. It is now well established that the earliest version of the text was the Elamite one (Trümpelmann 1967), because no way of writing Old Persian existed at the time. Darius himself seems to refer to the fact that he ordered a script for rendering the Persian language to be created, which underlines the watershed his reign marks: he consolidated the empire's territories and strengthened its Persian character by having a unique form devised for writing its language (Dandamaev 1976). The message of Persian control over all subject countries was driven home by disseminating versions of the text far and wide in the different languages of the empire:

> Says Darius the King: By the favour of Ahuramazda (chief Iranian god) this is the inscription which I made. Besides it was in Aryan (Iranian), and on clay tablets and parchment it was composed. Besides, a sculptured figure of myself I made. Besides, I made my lineage. And it was inscribed and was read off before me. Afterwards this inscription I sent off everywhere among the provinces. The people unitedly worked upon it.
>
> (Kent 1953 DB IV 88–92)

This is not empty rhetoric. A Babylonian version, inscribed on a stele, together with a form of the Behistun relief (Seidl 1976), was set up in Babylon (von Voigtlander 1978); another, in Aramaic, was found among the Elephantine papyri (see p. 651), where it was still being copied at the end of the fifth century (Greenfield and Porten 1982).

13d Achaemenid history and its problems

Although our evidence for Persian history is never complete, the sources we have for the first thirty years of the empire do allow us to trace the course of the main events in broad outline and deduce something of imperial policy. After Darius' successful suppression of the revolts against him, he describes, briefly, two more campaigns in his second and third regnal years, against Elam and the Scythians of Central Asia. But then the text breaks off. From now on we have no more Persian texts which tell us about military history. In Babylonia very few chronicles between 538 and 321 are preserved. So far, only one from the fourteenth year of Artaxerxes III's reign (345/4) has survived (*ABC* no. 9); a fragment probably relates to Alexander's conquest (Glassner 1993 [OK] no. 29; cf. *ABC* no. 8). The Babylonian astronomical diaries (Sachs and Hunger 1988) also provide only unconnected pieces of information for this period, not easy to understand (van der Spek 1993). Our main, often sole, guide to events is, therefore, Greek historiography and the Old Testament. But these sources give us a very partial insight because of their generally circumscribed perspectives (see pp. 647–649): the history of Greek–Persian relations in the Aegean and western Asia Minor predominates; we can piece together a little on Persian policy in the Levant and Egypt; the rest is a virtual blank.

The reign of Darius I

We know that Darius I added north-west India to the Achaemenid realm, because it appears in the list of subject countries in his later inscriptions and Herodotus (3.94) lists Indians among Persia's subjects. But the exact date of the conquest is not known. Darius certainly pursued the consolidation of Persia's westernmost frontiers: in the Aegean, several islands, notably Samos, were conquered and Persian power was extended across the Hellespont into Thrace (*c.* 513); the story of Darius' abortive campaign against the Black Sea Scythians (Herodotus 4.83–142) may mirror his (and Cyrus') strategy in central Asia against nomadic groups living along the imperial frontier; an alliance was also struck with the Macedonian royal house and Athens (Kuhrt 1988). But it was not a simple victorious progress: in 598 the Ionian cities led by Miletus, Caria and parts of Cyprus revolted, with limited support from Eretria and Athens. The rebels even succeeded in burning the Persian stronghold of Sardis. The Persian response was swift, but the struggle was protracted and it took four years of hard fighting on sea and land to put down the revolt. The final act of 'pacification' – a punitive attack on Eretria and Athens – ended in defeat for the Persians at Marathon in 490, although they lost no territory at this point. Persian punishment of the rebellious cities was harsh, but some political factions in Ionia benefited by gaining control in their cities in place of the earlier city-tyrants (Graf 1985). City-land was measured for tribute-assessment and to enable the Persian governors at Sardis to resolve and control the endemic inter-city wars about territorial claims (Briant 1987).

Action by Darius in recently conquered Egypt was crucial. Its situation during the great crisis of 522–521 is not certain, but there are hints that its satrap's loyalty was suspect and he was removed. Darius followed up Cambyses' attempt to gain control of the important western oases, and was able to build a great temple in Kharga oasis; the reliefs depict Darius in typical Egyptian style worshipping, and nourished by, the Egyptian gods. A statue of Darius set up at Heliopolis proclaimed a rather different message: it was carved in Persian style, with a short inscription in Old Persian, Elamite and Akkadian on the folds of the garment. The front of the base was carved with the age-old Pharaonic scene of the Nile-gods uniting the 'two lands' of Egypt; the sides were decorated with figures representing all the peoples subject to Persia. Its Egyptian hieroglyphic text on the surface of the base (also covering one foot, one side of the garment-folds, and the belt-tassels) declared Darius to be both a pious Egyptian warrior-monarch *and* a foreign conqueror:

> The strong Upper Egyptian king, great in his powers, lord of strength like Khenti-Khem (Falcon of Letopolis), lord of (his own) hand, who conquers the Nine Bows (Egypt's traditional enemies), excellent in council, outstanding in his plans, lord of the curved sword, when he penetrates the mass (of the enemy), shooting at the target without his arrow missing (it), whose strength is like that of Mont (Egyptian god of war), the king of Upper and Lower Egypt, lord of the two lands [Dariu]s, may he live for ever! The exalted, the greatest of the great, the chief of [the whole . . .] land, [son of the god's] father, Hystaspes, the Achaemenid, who has appeared as king of Upper and Lower Egypt on the Horus throne like Re, the first of the gods, for ever.
>
> (*CDAFI* 4: 235–266; *TUAT* I 609–611)

The statue we have was one of a pair and actually found at Susa, but the text makes it clear that either it (they), or a copy, was originally set up at Heliopolis, a centre of the Re cult, in Egypt. What the occasion was is unclear, but it shows Darius in control of Egypt in no uncertain terms. Further evidence for Persia's grip is the completion by Darius of the canal linking the Mediterranean to the Red Sea begun by Necho II (cf. chapter 12b). Four fragmentary stelae with Egyptian iconographic decorations, cuneiform and hieroglyphic text, which were set up along the banks of the canal, have survived (Posener 1936: 48–87). There is a reference in the texts to sending ships (with tribute?) from Egypt to Persia, and it has been thought that Darius' aim was to open a maritime trade route from the eastern Mediterranean to the Persian Gulf. But there are problems with this view, because of the difficulties of the route for regular use (Salles 1988). It seems more likely that it was linked to setting Darius into the line of Egyptian pharaonic endeavour (Tuplin 1991), and amounted to a public declaration of the Persian grasp of imperial territory. The exploratory sea expedition sent by Darius from the mouth of the Indus to the Persian gulf and beyond, in which Scylax of Caryanda participated (Herodotus 4.44), also fits this ideological aim, although the commercial link between India and Mesopotamia was an old one, which was now taken over for their own benefit by the Achaemenids (Salles 1990).

Under Darius I, two great royal building projects were initiated: palatial structures were founded in the ancient city of Susa (Khuzistan), and the building of the new dynastic capital of Persepolis (Fars, perhaps near the site of Darius' defeat of the second false Bardiya (Sumner 1986)) was begun and continued by his successors. Not far from Persepolis, at Naqsh-i Rustam, the king's tomb was cut in the rock-face – a markedly different funerary monument from that of Cyrus (see p. 661). The new royal sites expressed, in their iconographic decoration, techniques, materials and the craftsmen who worked there, the cultural diversity and massive resources of the empire and how the Persian king could mobilise them. The varied elements, on all levels, were used to create a novel iconography of kingship. It showed the Persian king supported by, and at the apex of, an empire made up of many peoples whose individual character was emphasised, yet who were all drawn together in a harmonious union to serve their Persian ruler (Root 1979). A fine verbal expression of this is Darius' 'foundation charter' from Susa:

> This palace which I built at Susa from afar its ornamentation was brought. Downward the earth was dug, until I reached rock in the earth. When the excavation had been made, then rubble was packed down, some 40 cubits (*c.* 20 m) in depth, another (part) 20 cubits in depth. On that rubble the palace was constructed.
>
> And that earth was dug downward, and that the rubble was packed down, and that the sun-dried brick was moulded, the Babylonian people – it did (these tasks).
>
> The cedar timber, this – a mountain by name Lebanon – from there was brought. The Assyrian people, it brought it to Babylon; from Babylon the Carians and the Ionians brought it to Susa. The *yaka*-timber (type of wood) was brought from Gandara (Kabul region) and from Carmania (Kirman). The gold was brought from Sardis and from Bactria, which here was worked. The precious stone lapis-lazuli and carnelian which was worked here, this was brought from Sogdiana (Uzbekistan/Tadjikistan). The precious stone turquoise, this was brought from Chorasmia (lower Oxus), which was worked here.

The silver and the ebony were brought from Egypt. The ornamentation with which the wall was adorned, that from Ionia was brought. The ivory which was worked here, was brought from Kush (Nubia), and from India and from Arachosia (Kandahar region).

The stone columns which were worked here, a village by name Abiradu, in Elam – from there were brought. The stone-cutters who worked the stone, those were Ionians and Sardians.

The goldsmiths who worked the gold, those were Medes and Egyptians. The men who worked the wood, those were Sardians and Egyptians. The men who worked the baked brick, those were Babylonians. The men who adorned the wall, those were Medes and Egyptians.

Says Darius the King: At Susa a very excellent (work) was ordered, a very excellent (work) was (brought to completion). Me may Ahuramazda protect, and Hystaspes my father, and my country.

(Kent 1953 DSf 22–58)

The reality of the multinational enterprise in the royal construction projects is amply confirmed by the thousands of administrative texts from Persepolis (see p. 650), which are preserved from Darius' reign. They show an enormous range of peoples engaged in building, processing materials, and involved in the official bureaucracy. Persia was the teeming centre of a vast empire, its agricultural potential harnessed to feed the greatly increased population.

The western front, 486–431

Firm action to contain revolts and maintain cohesion, consolidation of conquests, tightening the Persian hold of subject territories are our impressions of Darius' reign. His son and heir, Xerxes (486–465), can be seen to continue, in all essentials, his father's policies: again our knowledge is almost totally confined to the western periphery. His first task was coping with a rebellion in Egypt (Cruz-Urribe 1980), which had begun just before Darius' death and took another year to put down (Herodotus 7.1; 7.7). In Babylonia, another revolt had to be scotched in 481 (Briant 1992b). At some point in his reign (possibly quite early), Xerxes worked to make Persian provincial administration more efficient by subdividing the gigantic Babylonian province (see p. 690) into two: 'Babylonia', embracing all of modern Iraq and Syria to the banks of the Euphrates, near Carchemish, and 'Beyond the River' (Akk. *ebir nāri*), including Syria–Palestine west of the Euphrates (Stolper 1989). A similar modification and tightening of control may have been effected in the west, with the separation of Hellespontine Phrygia from the large province of Lydia (Petit 1990: 181–186).

One aim, in which Xerxes ultimately failed, was to force the mainland Greeks to acknowledge Persian power: some Greeks did bind themselves to Persia (Thebes, Thessaly), but others refused (Sparta, Athens). From the perspective of Persia's long-term Aegean policy, extending a measure of control to European Greece was logical. The importance of this Persian tactic is signalled by the fact that the Persian king himself led the expedition, by sea and land, to try to bring the Greeks to heel. After initial Persian victories, the Greeks won an important victory against the Persian navy in the straits of Salamis in 480. It is probable that we should date a second revolt in Babylonia to 479 (Briant 1992b), which suggests that the action to deal with this important region two years earlier had not been completely successful. This was serious: control of Babylonia was crucial for holding the empire together, given its strategic location on north–south and east–west routes; renewed unrest here would explain Xerxes' rapid departure from the Greek front after Salamis, but before the situation had been resolved. Xerxes' rapid intervention in Babylonia was successful, and as far as we know the province did not revolt again. One continuing misapprehension about Xerxes' action in Babylonia should be cleared up: he did not destroy Babylon's temples, nor did he remove the cult-statue of Marduk. Undoubtedly, Babylonia was not treated with kid gloves after two revolts, but exactly what form Xerxes' punishment took we do not know; certainly, its sanctuaries and cults suffered no noticeable decline (Kuhrt and Sherwin-White 1987).

The substantial Persian army left behind in Greece was ultimately defeated in a hard-fought land battle at Plataea in 479. The Greek victories were followed by the revolt of several Aegean islands, and Ionian cities begged for support, first from Sparta, then Athens, to help them escape Persian rule. The Athenians formed the Delian League to supply regular financial and military resources for pursuing the war against the Persians in the Aegean and along the Thracian and Asia Minor coast. In this the Athens-led confederacy, which enforced adherence, was very successful in the 470s and 460s: despite heroic resistance offered by several local Persian commanders, most Achaemenid strategic positions were lost. In 466, the Athenian general Cimon crowned the league's triumphs by winning a battle, on sea and land, against Persian forces at the mouth of the Eurymedon river in Pamphylia (Thucydides 1. 100).

In August 465, Xerxes and his crown-prince, Darius, were murdered in a court-plot. The events are obscure: it may have been in the interests of the next king, Artaxerxes I (465–424/423), to obfuscate them in order to hide his own complicity and pose as the avenger of his father and brother (D.S.11.69; 71) by executing the supposed assassins publicly. For a while the problems on the western frontier grew, with the Athenians widening their involvement to threaten the Levant coast and supporting the revolt of the local Egyptian leader, Inaros (460–454, Thucydides 1.104). But Artaxerxes moved fast to counteract them: an Achaemenid general, Megabazos, was sent to crush the Egyptian revolt, which he did brutally, annihilating the Egyptian rebels and the Athenian contingent (Thucydides 1.110). Archaeological evidence from several sites in the Levant suggests that new fortified garrison-points were set up to strengthen Persia's defences. The missions of the Achaemenid Jewish courtiers, Ezra and Nehemiah, to Jerusalem (perhaps to be dated to 458 and 445 respectively) may well be linked to this vigorous Persian effort to beat back the Greek threat (Hoglund 1992; but cf. now Grabbe 1994). Despite the tragedy in Egypt, the Athenians continued the war against the Persians and extended their attacks to Cyprus. But the Cypriot campaign was not successful, and, according to several ancient writers, the decision was taken to conclude a peace with Persia, whereby the Persians relinquished control over the western coast of Asia Minor. It is known, after the main Athenian negotiator, as the 'Peace of Callias' (D.S. 12.4.4–6). By this, the *status quo* on Persia's north-western frontier was formalised, while Athens abandoned attempts to intervene further east. But there is a problem: the treaty is only mentioned by writers who compiled their accounts several centuries later. The contemporary Athenian historian Thucydides, whose *History of the Peloponnesian War* gives a valuable outline of Greek political history between 479 and 431, passes over it in silence. The historical reality of the 'Peace of Callias' has, therefore, and continues to be, debated by scholars and there is as yet no consensus (Badian 1987; Briant in press, ch. 14/4). Moreover, if such an agreement was reached, the Persians certainly did not abide by it for long: Pissouthnes, Persian governor of Lydia, gave military aid to Samian exiles when they tried to take control of the island (*c.* 440). The outbreak of the Peloponnesian war between Sparta and Athens (431) meant that the two most powerful mainland Greek states were locked in mortal combat with each other for the next twenty-seven years. Persia was able to exploit the situation over the years to its own advantage.

Darius II and Artaxerxes II

When Artaxerxes I died (together with his wife) in Babylonia in winter 424/423 (Stolper 1983), he was succeeded by a bastard son, Ochus, who took the name Darius (II). But his tenure of the throne was disputed by two other brothers, Xerxes, Artaxerxes' legitimate son and probably the designated successor (Ctesias, *FGrH* 688 F15), and another bastard called Secundianus (or Sogdianus). The struggle for the throne lasted several months, ending with the death of both rivals. The support mobilised among the partisans of the royal candidates can be charted in Babylonian business documents, which show a massive rise in mortgaged land-grants as the military holders were forced to equip themselves for fighting (Stolper 1985: 104–124). With Darius, a new arena of conflict surfaces in the Greek writers: from now into the reign of Artaxerxes III (D.S. 17.6.1), the Persians had to fight again and again against the Cadusians, a tribal group living south-west of the Caspian Sea in northern Media (Xenophon *Hellenica* 2.1.13). The wars were serious enough to involve the king personally at times (*ibid.*; Plutarch *Artaxerxes* 24–5). We know very little about these wars, or about the nature of the Cadusians, hence it is impossible to assess the seriousness of the chronic conflict and the impact it may have had. But they serve as an important reminder of how one-sided and patchy our knowledge of Achaemenid political and military history is. In Asia Minor, Darius used the opportunity offered by an Athens seriously weakened by the disastrous expedition to Sicily (414/413) to order his governors (Tissaphernes, Pharnabazus) to begin levying tribute again from the Ionian Greeks, and to support Sparta in order to hasten Athens' ultimate defeat (404). But rivalry between the two Persians eventually led Darius to send his younger son, Cyrus, with special powers to the western front to take command of the situation (Xenophon *Hellenica* 1.4.3).

The succession in 405/404 from Darius II to his eldest son, Arses, who assumed the throne-name Artaxerxes (II), seems to have been smooth. But Artaxerxes' younger brother, Cyrus, nursed ambitions for the throne and gathered a group of Persian supporters, aided by troops from his area of command in Asia Minor and a force of Greek mercenaries. Among the latter was the Athenian soldier Xenophon, who has left us a valuable description of Cyrus' ill-fated revolt (*Anabasis*). The rebellious army managed to make its way with some difficulty into northern Babylonia, where it was met by Artaxerxes' troops at Cunaxa in 401. The insurgents were rapidly defeated, and their leader left dead on the battle-ground together with most of his Persian friends. His bid for the kingship had failed to gain more widespread support among the Persian nobility and Artaxerxes' tenure of the throne remained unshaken.

Cyrus had probably calculated on taking advantage of the problems the Persian king was facing at this moment from Egypt, where a revolt led between 401 and 399 to the expulsion of the Persian rulers. This was a serious loss, and Achaemenid history for the next fifty-six years is dominated by the continuous efforts to regain control. At the same time, the Persians struggled to limit the damage by ensuring that Syria–Palestine and Asia Minor remained under firm control. On the whole, their efforts at containment were successful: in 387/386, Artaxerxes was able to impose a settlement on the Greeks (the 'King's Peace'), whereby they had to accept that, henceforth, the cities of Asia Minor were under Persian control – the victories of Salamis and Plataea had been definitively reversed. Although Artaxerxes had to contend with some rebellious Persian governors in Anatolia in the 360s, Persia's hold of the region remained firm from now until Alexander of Macedon's invasion (Weisskopf 1989).

Artaxerxes II was the longest reigning of all the Persian kings (405–359) and it is a pity that, apart from some internal problems about the succession, we know so little about him – although the Greek moralist of the Roman empire, Plutarch, provides us with a largely sympathetic sketch in his *Life of Artaxerxes*: he portrays him as a generous ruler, anxious to make himself accessible to his subjects, a loving husband and a courageous warrior prepared to share the hardships of his soldiers. The royal inscriptions preserved from

his reign show an interesting new development: the usual formula, acknowledging the help of the god Ahuramazda, was expanded to include the Iranian
gods Mithra and Anahita. The exact significance of this is hard to gauge, but
suggests a development in Achaemenid concepts of kingship and cult. The
Hellenistic Babylonian historian Berossus (*FGrH* 680 F11) mentions that
Artaxerxes introduced a statue-cult of Anahita in the imperial centres, Sardis,
Babylon, Damascus, Susa and Ecbatana, as well as in Persia and Bactria. The
most likely interpretation is to see this as a way of strengthening the ties of
the Persian communities of the imperial diaspora to the political heartland;
some link between this and the novel element in the royal inscriptions is likely
(Briant 1986). We also have evidence of extensive building by Artaxerxes at
Ecbatana (Kent 1953 A²Ha-c); the construction of a Persian-style palace in
Babylon should probably also be attributed to him (Vallat 1989).

Artaxerxes III and the reconquest of Egypt

Long reigns often create problems when it comes to the question of
succession, with several mature and experienced sons ready to jockey for
position. Three of Artaxerxes II's sons, including his crown-prince Darius,
died violent deaths, and another son, Ochus, who eventually succeeded as
Artaxerxes III (359), is credited with engineering the fatalities, directly or
indirectly (Plutarch, *Artaxerxes* 30). The major achievement of his reign was
the reconquest of Egypt in 343, after long and hard campaigning. His success
here was preceded by the crushing of a revolt of the Phoenician cities, headed
by the Sidonian ruler, Tennes, who had a substantial Greek mercenary force
sent to him from Egypt to help. After an initial victory over Persian forces,
he is said to have betrayed the city when Artaxerxes advanced against it. The
(alleged) treachery saved neither him nor his city: he was executed, some of
the city was probably burnt (D.S. 16.41–45) and part of its population
deported, as shown by a short Babylonian chronicle:

> The fourteenth [year] (i.e. 345) of Umasu, who is called Artaxerxes: in
> the month Tishri (September/October) the prisoners which the king
> took [from] Sidon [were brought] to Babylon and Susa. On the
> thirteenth day of the same month a few of these troops entered Babylon.
> On the sixteenth day the ... women prisoners from Sidon, which the
> king sent to Babylon – on that day they entered the palace of the king.
> (*ABC* no. 9)

The Phoenician rebellion was clearly linked to Egypt's attempts to consolidate its position against the Persians, which helps to explain Artaxerxes'
ruthless treatment of Sidon and his personal role in dealing with it. The way
to Egypt now lay open, and with its recapture Artaxerxes' reputation for
harshness and cruelty was confirmed. It is hard to determine how justified

this is: some of the horror-stories told about Cambyses' earlier conquest were told also about Artaxerxes, which must make one hesitate a little before accepting them; the evidence of an autobiographical stele (Somtutefnakht; Lichtheim 1973–80 [OI] III: 41–44) suggests that individual prominent Egyptians were as ready to collaborate now as they had been earlier.

The fall of the Persian empire

Artaxerxes and most of his family died in a veritable bloodbath (338), instigated and masterminded by a eunuch, Bagoas, if our late Greek sources are to be believed. Bagoas then raised the sole surviving young son of Artaxerxes, Arses, to the throne; he again took the name Artaxerxes (IV). But after only two years he was murdered by his former patron, who now supported the claims of a member of a collateral branch of the Achaemenid family, Artashata, to the kingship. He had a reputation for exceptional physical bravery. Once Artashata was firmly established on the throne, having adopted the royal name Darius (III), he had Bagoas eliminated.

Darius III's reputation has suffered badly: fated to be the opponent of Alexander of Macedon, whose brilliant military victories, comparable to those of Cyrus the Great in their breathtaking sweep and speed, spelt the end of the Achaemenid dynasty, he has gone down in history as a weak-kneed coward. Careful analysis of Alexander's campaign shows that Darius followed a perfectly reasonable and well-planned strategy, husbanding his resources as far as possible and trying to raise revolts against Alexander in his rear. Alexander's total victory was by no means a foregone conclusion: he encountered considerable resistance from some cities on the coast of Asia Minor, Tyre and Gaza in the Levant, and had to fight three major set battles before the western section of the empire fell into his hands (334–331). His treatment of those who resisted was harsh, and the Persian nobility was slow to rally to his side, as were the Greek mercenaries in Persian service. His real breakthrough came when, after the fall of the Persian homeland and the capture of Ecbatana, Darius was murdered by one of his generals, Bessus. From this point on, Alexander was able to cast himself in the role of avenger of the legitimate Persian king and his rightful heir (330). But he still had to fight every inch of the way, taking province after province in the east by force, before he could claim the Persian empire as his. It was a remarkable achievement, and the difficulties Alexander encountered in twelve years of continuous fighting bear witness to the remarkable solidity of the Achaemenid realm. Contrary to widespread perceptions, the Persian empire was not in a state of decay; it had weathered its many problems (and we only know about some of them) extraordinarily well. One of the great, still unsolved, historical questions, therefore, is why Alexander was able to defeat the Persians (Briant 1994a; in press, ch. 18).

13e The structure of the Achaemenid empire

The Achaemenid empire covered an enormous and extremely diverse territory, which held together for nearly two hundred years, despite internal revolts, recurring problems along frontiers, attempts at secession (including the loss of Egypt for nearly sixty years), problems with the succession and a history of regicide. The question, then, is how was it able to be so successful? Two points are fundamental: first, after the serious crisis of 522–521, when Darius I violently usurped the throne, the Achaemenid family never lost its exclusive hold on the kingship (see p. 666); secondly, in the reigns of Darius I and Xerxes the empire matured and stabilised. From then on, 'nationalist revolts' occur rarely (Egypt is the exception, although their number and nature has been exaggerated; Briant 1988) – the aims of rebels centred on who should wield power in the empire (e.g. Cyrus the Younger, see p. 673), not setting up separatist states. Also, from Xerxes on there was no further territorial expansion; efforts were directed to tightening and consolidating the administration: rationalising of the provincial system (see p. 670) and greater uniformity in taxation and accounting are evidence of this (Descat 1985; 1989).

The ideology of kingship

At the centre of the imperial system was the Persian king. The great god Ahuramazda had set him over the varied lands and peoples of the earth and given Persia supremacy over them; without his divine support no king ruled in Persia. The king was Ahuramazda's creature, part of his bountiful creation that ensured happiness for all mankind. All therefore owed reverence, obedience and 'tribute' (OP *baji-*; Sancisi-Weerdenburg 1989) to the Persian king: it strengthened Ahuramazda's plan for maintaining perfect order from which all would benefit – king and god were complementary in the universal scheme of things and worked for the same ends. The inscription carved to the left of the royal figure on the façade of Darius I's tomb at Naqsh-i Rustam illustrates the symbiosis of the two:

> A great god is Ahuramazda, who created this earth (*bumi-*), who created yonder sky, who created man, who created happiness for man, who made Darius king, one king over many, one lord of many.
>
> I am Darius the great king, king of kings, king of countries containing all kinds of men, king on this great earth far and wide, son of Hystaspes, an Achaemenid, a Persian, son of a Persian, an Aryan, having Aryan lineage.
>
> Says Darius the king: By the favour of Ahuramazda these are the countries which I seized outside Persia; I ruled over them; they bore me 'tribute'; what was said to them by me, that they did; my law (*data-*) - that held them firm; Media, Elam, Parthia, Aria, Bactria, Sogdiana, Chorasmia, Drangiana, Arachosia, Sattagydia, Gandara, India, Scyth-

ians who drink *hauma* (an intoxicating ritual drink), Scythians with pointed caps, Babylonia, Assyria, Arabia, Egypt, Armenia, Cappadocia, Sardis, Ionia, Scythians who are across the sea, Thrace, *petasos*-wearing Ionians (a type of hat worn by Greeks), Libyans, Ethiopians, men of Maka, Carians.

Says Darius the king: Ahuramazda when he saw this earth in commotion, thereafter bestowed it upon me, made me king; I am king. By the favour of Ahuramazda I put it down in its place; what I said to them, that they did, as was my desire. If now you should think: 'How many are the countries which King Darius held?' look at the sculptures (of those) who bear the throne, then shall you know, then shall it become known to you: the spear of a Persian man has gone forth far; then shall it become known to you: a Persian man has delivered battle far indeed from Persia.

Says Darius the king: This which has been done, all that by the will of Ahuramazda I did. Ahuramazda bore me aid, until I did the work. Me may Ahuramazda protect from harm, and my royal house, and this land: this I pray of Ahuramazda, this may Ahuramazda give to me!

O man, that which is the command of Ahuramazda, let this not seem repugnant to you; do not leave the right path; do not rise in rebellion!

(Kent 1953 DNa 1–38)

The message of the text is mirrored in the reliefs carved on the royal tomb façades from Darius I on (Root 1979). The king stands on a stepped podium with a bow resting on the tip of his foot; opposite him is a fire altar; he raises his hand, in a gesture of salutation, to a divine figure, which hovers above in a winged disc. The god in the winged disc faces the king and raises one hand in an identical gesture of greeting; with his other hand he holds out a ring, an old symbol of kingly power. It is not certain that the figure in the disc is Ahuramazda, but its intimate relationship to the king echoes the text so perfectly that many scholars believe that we see here the king and his god (Root 1979; Sancisi-Weerdenburg 1993; for a different view, see Calmeyer 1979; Shahbazi 1980).

Other important motifs of Persian kingship emerge from Darius I's tomb inscription and relief. The podium and the fire-altar are set on a kind of throne; its struts are supported by representatives of the different subject-people, all carefully differentiated by their clothing and labelled; the viewer is exhorted to look at them in order to be awed by the Persian achievement. Wars have been fought by Persians at the distant boundaries of the earth, and, with Ahuramazda's help, have delivered the people here depicted into the Persian king's hand. Although they retain their individual character, they are now united in service to the king, whose mastery they uphold and whose law they obey. It is a recurrent theme of the royal inscriptions to dwell on the variegated nature of the king's subjects (see the inscription from Susa, pp. 669–670): the Persian king dominates the divine creation in all its colourful variety; he combines their various skills and resources to serve his and Persia's ends. The motif is echoed at the dynastic centre of Persepolis: the sides of the platform and great staircases leading up to the columned *apadana* (palace) are decorated with reliefs showing deputations from Persia's subject-lands waiting to present the king with precious and valuable gifts acknowledging his power and their subservence. In return for their acceptance of Persia's divinely backed order, god-given peace and tranquillity will prevail.

The Persian character of the king and his realm is another feature of the royal inscriptions, stressed again and again. The king himself is a Persian, descended from Persians; he has conquered lands outside Persia; the 'Persian man' has had to fight far from home to create the present perfect state. The continued well-being of Persia – 'a good country, possessed of good horses, possessed of good men' (Kent 1963 DPd) – is one of the king's prime concerns. If Persia and its people are kept safe, by the continued adherence of its subjects to the Persian imperial order, then happiness will reign supreme (Kent 1953 DPe). The Persians are clearly distinguished from the subject-peoples on the *apadana*-staircases, too:[1] they are the courtiers, officials, soldiers; they hold back the gift-bearing ambassadors until the moment comes to usher them into the king's presence; some bear items of food, perhaps for the royal table; in every respect, their relationship to royal authority is markedly different from that of the conquered. Herodotus may be echoing the Persian-centred nature of the Achaemenid empire, when he says:

> They honour most of all those who live nearest to them, then those who are next farthest, and so going ever on they give honour in this way; those who live farthest they give the least honour; because they consider themselves to be the best of men by far, the rest to have a claim to virtue in proportion, those living at the greatest distance from them being the worst.
>
> (Herodotus 1.134)

In the text quoted above (p. 677), Darius says that one reason Ahuramazda gave him the kingship was because the earth 'was in commotion (*yaudatim*)', and Darius 'put it down'. The theme of the king as a defence against disorder recurs in several of Darius' inscriptions, most notably the great Behistun inscription (see p. 666). There the motif of rebellion, which causes unrest, is linked to the growth of the 'lie/falsehood (*drauga*)': as things start to go wrong for Persia, with Cambyses' secret fratricide, Darius describes the situation as the lie taking hold in the land:

> Afterwards, Cambyses slew that Bardiya. When Cambyses slew Bardiya, it did not become known to the people that Bardiya had been slain.

Figure 45 Royal hero stabbing lion, from a doorway at Persepolis (photograph courtesy of Margaret Root)

Afterwards, Cambyses went to Egypt. When Cambyses had gone off to Egypt, after that the people became evil. After that the lie waxed great in the country, both in Persia and in Media and in the other provinces.

(Kent 1953 DB I 30–35)

As the pretenders start their revolts, Darius invariably describes them as arising and 'lying' to the people. The concept of falsehood is thus linked to revolt against the divine and royal order: to misrepresent oneself is to mislead people so that they stray from the path of righteousness, which is obedience to the Persian king and Ahuramazda. It is possible, though not certain (Sancisi-Weerdenburg 1993), that the Old Persian word encapsulating the concept of correct behaviour, and hence acceptance of the imperial order, is the opposite of falsehood, i.e. 'truth' (*arta*). One way of understanding Herodotus' famous statement that Persian boys were taught three things only, namely 'to ride, to shoot with the bow, and to tell the truth' (1. 136), is that part of the education of young Persians consisted in learning the duty of total devotion to king and country (Briant 1982b: 449). One problem with this view is that, while *drauga* figures prominently in Darius' texts, *arta* never appears. The only king who mentions it is Xerxes in a foundation text from Persepolis:

> Says Xerxes the king: When that I became king, there is among these countries which are inscribed above (one which) was in commotion. Afterwards Ahuramazda bore me aid; by the favour of Ahuramazda I smote that country and put it down in its place.
>
> And among these countries there was (a place) where previously false gods were worshipped. Afterwards, by the favour of Ahuramazda, I destroyed that sanctuary of the demons (*daivadana-*) and I made proclamation, 'The demons shall not be worshipped!' Where previously the demons were worshipped, there I worshipped Ahuramazda and *arta* with reverence. And there was other (business) that had been done ill; that I made good. That which I did, all I did by the favour of Ahuramazda. Ahuramazda bore me aid, until I completed the work.
>
> You who (shall be) hereafter, if you shall think, 'Happy may I be when living, and when dead may I be blessed,' have respect for that law which Ahuramazda has established; worship Ahuramazda and *arta* with reverence. The man who has respect for that law which Ahuramazda has established, and worships Ahuramazda and *arta* with reverence, he both becomes happy while living, and blessed when dead.
>
> (Kent 1953 XPh 28–56)

The message of this text is that rebellion against the Persian king is equivalent to the worship of false gods and hence a denial of the king's god, Ahuramazda (Sancisi-Weerdenburg 1980, ch. 1). Xerxes' restoration of order is expressed through his worship of Ahuramazda and *arta*. It is possible, then, that here the king is specifically equating the elimination of moral–political disorder with due reverence for *arta* in the sense of 'order/truth'. But the precise meaning of *arta* is not unequivocal, and we must remember that this is the *only* place where the celebrated Persian idea of 'truth' appears in the entire Old Persian text corpus. It may be an implicit concept, around which Persian royal ideology was organised – but, if so, it is conspicuous by its absence.[2]

The king was an absolute monarch: all were subject to his power and his law. But that does not mean that he exercised power in an arbitary manner. As guardian of Ahuramazda's creation, ruling over 'this earth' with his aid, he himself was bound to uphold the moral–political fabric and his actions were determined by the demands of appropriate high principles. He presented himself as an embodiment of positive virtues, which fitted him to rule. Two identical royal inscriptions, one in Darius' name, one in Xerxes', are the best expression of these royal ideals. The fact that both kings had the same text inscribed *verbatim* shows that the sentiments expressed central and eternal tenets of Persian kingship – not the character traits of an individual monarch:

> A great god is Ahuramazda who created this excellent work which one sees; who created happiness for man; who bestowed wisdom and energy upon Darius (Xerxes) the king. Says Darius (Xerxes) the king: by the favour of Ahuramazda I am of such a kind that I am a friend to what is right, I am no friend to what is wrong. It is not my wish that to the weak is done wrong because of the mighty, it is not my wish that the weak is hurt because of the mighty, that the mighty is hurt because of the weak. What is right, that is my wish. I am no friend of the man who is a follower of the lie. I am not hot-tempered. When I feel anger rising, I keep that under control by my thinking power. I control firmly my impulses. The man who co-operates, him do I reward according to his co-operation. He who does harm, him I punish according to the damage. It is not my wish that a man does harm, it is certainly not my wish that a man if he causes damage be not punished. What a man says against a man, that does not convince me, until I have heard testimony(?) from both parties. What a man does or performs according to his powers, satisfies me, therewith I am satisfied and it gives me great pleasure and I am very satisfied and I give much to faithful men.
>
> I am trained with both hands and feet. As a horseman I am a good horseman. As a bowman I am a good bowman, both afoot and on horseback. As a spearman I am a good spearman, both afoot and on horseback. And the skills which Ahuramazda has bestowed upon me and I have had the strength to use them, by the favour of Ahuramazda, what has been done by me, I have done with these skills which Ahuramazda has bestowed upon me.
>
> (Kent 1953 DNb; Gharib 1968 XNb)

Here the king's qualities as a just ruler are the central motif: Ahuramazda has equipped the ruler with the insight and ability to distinguish right from wrong, which makes him a guarantor of justice and maintainer of social order; he can do this because he does not react unthinkingly and is able to control his temper; as a result, the king metes out reward and punishment absolutely fairly, and only after due consideration of a case; he judges services rendered according to the potential of the individual, and is ready to reward loyalty. At the same time, not only the moral, but also the physical abilities of the king are stressed – he is a supremely able rider, and can wield the bow and spear both on foot and on horseback with consummate skill.

It is interesting to see that we have the same text preserved for two different kings. It implies that this package of royal virtues encapsulated best what it meant to be a Persian king, and was an important part of the broadcast ideals of kingship. The end of the text exhorts subjects to spread abroad the superiority of the Persian king. Part of the text, in Aramaic translation, is preserved on papyrus at Elephantine (late fifth century; Sims-Williams 1981)). We find very similar qualities ascribed to Cyrus the Younger by Xenophon (*Anabasis* 1.9), who significantly precedes his encomium by saying that Cyrus was the most kingly of men and the most fitted to exercise power. The conclusion must be that this image of kingship circulated widely in the empire.

Royal rituals

The king was a person set apart, unlike other people, as the texts reiterate. How did the transformation from ordinary mortal to king happen? How was the heir to the throne selected? What happened on the king's death? How was the king's unique standing marked?

An element of prime importance in the king's legitimacy was his descent. From Darius I on, the Persian kings trace their genealogy, and stress that they are descended through their father, ideally in a direct line, from Achaemenes. The future king was, thus, normally selected from a tight-knit family-group. The reigning king was acknowledged to have total power over choosing his successor, as shown in an inscription of Xerxes from Persepolis:

> Says Xerxes the king: other sons of Darius there were, (but) – thus unto Ahuramazda was the desire – Darius my father made me the greatest after himself. When my father Darius went away from the throne (i.e. died), by the will of Ahuramazda I became king on my father's throne.
> (Kent 1953 XPf 27–36)

In an absolute monarchy the king was not subject to constitutional laws which dictated that the eldest son should succeed. Political considerations might lead him to pick a younger son. In the case of Darius I and Xerxes (above), Darius' choice may well have been dictated by the fact that the mother of his eldest son, Artobazanes, was the daughter of the Persian noble Gobryas. Had Darius promoted him, his maternal family could have gained considerable influence on the kingship, which might ultimately have undermined the Achaemenid hold on the throne. By choosing Xerxes, the son of Atossa and so a grandson of Cyrus, from whose family no male offspring survived, Darius circumvented the danger. This anxiety to keep power inside the inner Achaemenid royal group explains several later instances of apparently arbitrary murders of royal wives (e.g. Parysatis' poisoning of Artaxerxes II's wife, Stateira; *FGrH* 688 F27) and the recurrent practice of the king marrying his very close female relatives (Sancisi-Weerdenburg 1983a).[3]

Several of the Persian kings had more than one wife; for Darius I, we hear of six, Artaxerxes II three, and Darius III two. Although we do not know how many wives the other rulers had, polygamy was probably the norm. One aspect, which remains unclear, is how the king's wives were ranked: when Greek writers refer to princes as bastards (*nothoi*; Herodotus 3.2), they imply the existence of different grades among the king's spouses. Ctesias (*FGrH* 688 F15) names three Babylonian women who, he says, bore Artaxerxes I bastard offspring. As the crucial factor in establishing legitimacy of claim to the throne was solely paternal descent, it is hard to understand what the criteria for dubbing some children 'bastards' and others 'legitimate' were. The impression we get is that the first-ranking royal wives were Persian; but how correct is such an impression, when our evidence is so random? Two things seem certain: first, that the position of royal wives was dependent on the status of their sons (Sancisi-Weerdenburg 1983a); second, that there was a group of royal sons among whom the king expected normally to select his successor – only if there were no male offspring in this preferred circle, did it become possible for other royal sons to become eligible.[4]

We know relatively little about the ceremony of choosing the crown prince. There are hints that it was a public occasion, marked by the future successor being allowed to wear the 'tiara [Persian headdress] upright'. This was a privilege reserved for the king; in anyone else it was tantamount to rebellion (Arrian *Anabasis* 6.29.3). Once raised to his new position, the crown-prince formally requested his father to grant him a favour, which the king was obliged to grant if it lay within his power (Plutarch *Artaxerxes* 26.5). The new future king was further honoured by being allowed to drink the special water, which only the king was permitted to use (Heraclides of Cumae, *ap.* Athen. 12.51A; Briant 1994b).

The young princes were educated, along with the children of the nobility, from an early age (five years) to adulthood by the 'wisest men' (Strabo 15.3.18). These were almost certainly the magi, who were associated with divine worship and were the guardians of Persian lore – stories of gods, of heroes, of past noble deeds. They instilled this Persian oral tradition into their young charges, along with training in military skills, hunting and survival techniques. The duties of, and to, a king formed part of the teaching (Sancisi-Weerdenburg 1993). The royal princes will have formed friendships in this environment, from among whom the crown-prince may have selected his later close intimates.

When the king died, the sacred fire (associated with him in a way we do not understand very well) was extinguished throughout the land (D.S. 17.94.4.–5). A period of public mourning followed: the Persians shaved their hair and put on mourning garb; the manes of horses were clipped. Exactly how long the mourning lasted is not certain. As in many societies, the heir designate was responsible for the funeral of his father. This could be a major operation, because the body had to be transported to Persia for burial in the royal tombs: Naqsh-i Rustam in the fifth century; identically decorated rock-tombs at Persepolis in the fourth. Several Persian kings are known to have died away from Persia (Cyrus, Cambyses, Artaxerxes I, Darius III): a mule-drawn hearse conveyed the royal corpse back to the Persian homeland, which gave the ruler-to-be the opportunity to display his filial piety and stress his legitimacy as the official successor. When Alexander arranged for Darius III's body to be sent to Persia for burial, he declared himself publicly to be the official heir to the Achaemenid throne. We have no descriptions of Achae-menid hearses, but possibly the one prepared for Alexander gives us some idea of their sumptuousness (DS 18.16–18.28.1; see generally Briant 1991). There is no evidence, unfortunately, of what items may have been placed in the tomb together with the body; nor is there anything attesting a cult at the royal tombs. The one exception is Cyrus the Great, the design and location of whose tomb differed from the later Achaemenid ones (see p. 661). Arrian has preserved a valuable description of its setting and contents:

The tomb of the famous Cyrus was in Pasargadae in the royal park (*paradeisos*); a grove had been planted round it with all sorts of trees and irrigated, and deep grass had grown in the meadow; the tomb itself in the lower parts was built of stones cut square and was rectangular in form. Above, there was a stone chamber with a stone roof and a door leading into it so narrow that it was hard and caused much distress for a single man of low stature to get through. In the chamber lay a golden sarcophagus, in which Cyrus' body had been buried; a couch stood by its side with feet of wrought gold; a Babylonian tapestry served as a coverlet and purple rugs as a carpet. There was placed on it a sleeved coat (*kandys*) and other garments of Babylonian workmanship. According to Aristobulus, Median trousers and robes dyed blue lay there, some dark, some of other varying shades, with necklaces, daggers (*akinakes*) and earrings of stones set in gold, and a table stood there. It was between the table and the couch that the sarcophagus containing Cyrus' body was placed. Within the enclosure and by the ascent to the tomb itself there was a small building put up for the magi who used to guard Cyrus' tomb, from as long ago as Cambyses, son of Cyrus, an office transmitted from father to son. The king used to give them a sheep a day, a fixed amount of flour and wine, and a horse each month to sacrifice to Cyrus.

(Arrian *Anabasis* 6.29.4–7)

So Cyrus was buried very elaborately, with fine furniture, textiles, typical Persian garments and precious accessories. Protection of the tomb was entrusted to hereditary guardians, who belonged to the learned group of magi; they were fed at royal expense and carried out sacrifices (ordered and supplied by the king) in Cyrus' honour. But Cyrus, as founder of the empire, was a special case; there is no hint that any other Persian king was treated like this after death.

Our main source for the accession-ceremonial of the new king is Plutarch's *Life of Artaxerxes* (probably using Ctesias). Unfortunately, he only describes part of it:

> Soon after the death of Darius (II), the king (sc. Artaxerxes II) went to Pasargadae to take part in a ceremony of royal initiation, performed by the priests in Persia. It takes place in the sanctuary of a warrior goddess, rather like Athena: the person who is to be initiated has to go here, take off his own dress, put on that which Cyrus wore before he became king, eat a cake of figs, chew terebinth and drink a bowl of sour milk to the last drop. It is possible that there were other rituals as well, but they are unknown to outsiders.

> (Plutarch *Life of Artaxerxes* 3)

Plutarch is describing here a 'rite de passage', which paved the way for the king's son to be transformed into a king. Unfortunately, he does not give us any more details of the coronation ceremonial. But, despite its incompleteness, the passage contains some very significant points. First, the king goes to Pasargadae, the city of Cyrus, heroic founder of the empire. Part of the ceremony involves the king-to-be linking himself even more explicitly with Cyrus: he takes off his old identity, symbolised by his personal garments, and puts on Cyrus' dress 'before he became king', i.e. he becomes in some sense Cyrus the man, whose rise to power and great conquests are still to be accomplished. Perhaps his consumption of fig-cake, terebinth and sour milk encapsulated in ritual form the training undergone by young Persians, including the future king, which fitted them to exercise power.

The ritual also had a military aura by its location in the sanctuary of a warrior-goddess. We should probably understand this to be the Persian goddess, Anahita, who appears as martial and a patron of warriors (Malandra 1983: 117–119) – very appropriate for the Achaemenid soldier-kings. There is a question as to whether the royal initiation ritual always took place in the Anahita sanctuary or whether Plutarch is describing a development new in Artaxerxes II's reign. Artaxerxes II's predecessors name no gods other than Ahuramazda (see pp. 676–677); only with Artaxerxes II do we find Anahita and Mithra named in the royal inscriptions, and other evidence shows that this king particularly promoted the cult of Anahita (see pp. 673–674). Perhaps previously the royal initiation ritual had been linked exclusively to Ahuramazda, as suggested by the repeated fomula: 'Ahuramazda gave me the kingdom' (Herrenschmidt 1977: 24).

At some point, following the initiation, the king was presumably robed and crowned in the special royal coat (*kandys*) and head-covering (*tiara*; *kidaris*); perhaps he also received on this occasion the shield, spear and bow with which he is often shown on coins, seals and tomb-reliefs. It is possible that the royal insignia may have been stored in tower-like structures at Pasargadae and Persepolis (Zendan; Ka'bah). There is evidence that originally a staircase led down from a great door about half-way up the towers (Stronach 1978: 117ff.), and one scholar has suggested that the newly crowned king made a formal appearance in all his royal glory at the top of the steps here (Sancisi-Weerdenburg 1983b). It is possible that, as in the Assyrian state (see chapter 7b), the king's governors formally surrendered their office to the king – an acknowledgement that they owed their position to him, and an opportunity for him to express his trust by reinstating them or, conversely, dismissing them (D.S. 11.71.1; Briant 1991). Another act of the new reign may have been the remission of outstanding debts of taxes (Herodotus 6.59): alongside the stressed continuity, the king's accession also marked a new beginning for his subjects.

The king, the court and the Persian nobility

How did the king maintain his position of pre-eminence? How did he manage to assure himself of the support of the Persian aristocracy? The question arises in particularly stark form, when we think of Darius' seizure of the throne (see pp. 664–667): Herodotus knew stories according to which any one of his fellow conspirators might have become king, i.e. Darius' claim was no stronger than that of his peers. Further, Darius in his own account of his accession (Kent 1953 DB) names the people who helped him in the struggle, and commends their families for all time to future Persian kings. So there can be no doubt that they were prominent individuals. In addition, one of them, Gobryas, is depicted and named, standing behind Darius, on the façade of the king's tomb at Naqsh-i Rustam. Another Persian noble, Aspathines, not mentioned in the Behistun inscription, also appears with his name on Darius I's tomb. Everything suggests that there was a powerful established group of hereditary Persian nobles, whose support the king needed to harness and whose political influence he had to control: they had, after all, with his personal assistance, assassinated the accepted, reigning king – if they were antagonised they might do so again and Darius would be their victim.

Herodotus (3.84) tells us that after the murder of Bardiya the seven conspirators agreed among themselves certain privileges which the one who ultimately became king was bound to grant. They were to be allowed free access to the the king, without going through the formal court-ceremonial (unless the king was with a woman), and the king agreed to take his wives exclusively from their families. It is possible that they were also granted tax exemptions on their estates (Herodotus 3.97). In effect, then, the Persian king was compelled to accede to pressure from his nobles as a price for their support and loyalty. That is the story. Did it work like this in practice?

The first thing to note is that, as discussed above (pp. 682–683), the Persian kings managed to keep the nobility at a healthy distance from royal power. Darius excluded the grandson of Gobryas from the kingship, promoting instead Xerxes, whose maternal family was extinct. Darius II, perhaps to gain support in his bid for the throne, married two of his children to members of the family of the Persian noble Hydarnes. When his oldest son, Artaxerxes (II), acceded to the throne, his mother, Parysatis, worked to remove his Hydarnid wife and persuaded him to marry one of his daughters instead. The motive behind this was probably to ensure that the throne stayed firmly within the inner Achaemenid family. So the king did not openly backtrack on his agreement to intermarry only with the families of the six noble helpers – he subverted it, by marrying members of his own family, and giving those offspring preference, where possible, in selection for the throne.

The free access granted to the nobles was also a privilege rapidly curtailed. Herodotus (3.118–119) tells the story of Intaphernes, one of the conspirators, who insisted on seeing Darius although he was told that the king had withdrawn with one of his wives. Suspecting that Darius was not honouring the agreement, Intaphernes mutilated the guards. When they reported to Darius, he suspected a plot to topple him and had Intaphernes together with his family imprisoned and sentenced to death; virtually the entire clan was wiped out. Darius' rapid action served as a warning to the remaining five nobles not to presume on their privileges; it effectively robbed them of any real advantage.

The result of Darius' handling of the nobility was to demote them from a peer-group to servants, dependent for their status and position on the king, like others. Their names were famous, their past deeds celebrated, their families remained highly honoured among the Persians – to be descended from the family of one of Darius' helpers continued to carry great prestige with it – but, in relation to the king, they had no special rights, no greater claim on his person than anyone else. They were all the king's *bandaka*, an Old Persian word which means, literally, 'bondsman', 'servant'. This, significantly, is the word Darius uses to describe them, again and again, in the Behistun inscription. It expresses their dependence and the personal bond of loyalty which tied them to the king.

While all were the king's subjects, what mattered within Persian society was an individual's relative position in the social scale. There was considerable ranking according to birth and privilege within the Persian élite. It was only the élite who underwent the Persian education system, part of which consisted in replicating the social *status quo* and Persian aristocratic ideals, so that all knew their place in the system and how to behave to those above and below them. According to Herodotus (1.134), ranking was signalled by the way in which people greeted each other: equals kissed each other on the mouth; if one was slightly inferior to the other they kissed on the cheek; in the case of great social difference the inferior prostrated himself before his superior. What precisely determined position is not easy to make out. Family descent clearly played an important role, and provided access to high office: the key positions in the imperial government and army were held by Persians from the nobility, with members of the Achaemenid royal family pre-dominating.

But noble birth was not the only factor. Crucial was royal favour. Those whom the king publicly honoured, whom he kept close to him, turned to for advice, entrusted with special missions, were the most eminent (Xenophon *Anabasis* 1.9). Their status is expressed by the Aramaic term *br byt'* (cf. Akk. *mār bīti*), which means literally 'son of the [royal] house' and renders the Old Iranian term **vith(a)puça* = 'prince'.[5] Although the apparent meaning is that they were royal offspring, it is clear from its usage that it was a title reserved for highly honoured members of the Persian aristocracy and does not necessarily indicate a blood relationship to the king. It was the title held, for example, by Arsames the governor of Egypt in the second half of the fifth century. Although it indicates a rank, not royal blood, the high position of such 'princes' also made them eligible husbands for the king's daughters and other female relatives, so that they could become, literally, 'royal sons' by marrying into the royal family.

Subtle distinctions in rank were marked in various ways: we hear of distinguished Persians 'who had special chairs' (Herodotus 3.144); the soldiers close to the king carried spears decorated with golden apples (Herodotus 7.41); the Persian governor of Armenia, Tiribazus, is described as 'a personal friend of the king, and when he was present no one else had the right to assist the king in mounting his horse' (Xenophon *Anabasis* 4.4). Physical proximity to the king was a highly sought favour, hence to become one of the king's table companions (*suntrapezos*; *sundeipnos*; *sumpotos*) was a great honour. The king normally ate in a room separated by a curtain from his fellow-banqueters, and invited individual guests to drink with him afterwards. The opportunity this offered for personal advancement and for one's standing *vis-à-vis* lesser folk was highly valued and eagerly sought.

The king's favour was expressed through the bestowal of gifts: all privileges enjoyed emanated from the throne. They were rewards for loyal service, such as conspicuous acts of bravery in war. When Xerxes sat above the straits of Salamis to watch the battle, he was not settling back to enjoy a spectacle, he was observing the performance of his soldiers for future reward:

> During the whole of the battle Xerxes sat at the base of the hill called Aegaleos, over against Salamis; and whenever he saw any of his own captains perform a worthy exploit he enquired concerning him; and the man's name was taken down by his scribes, together with the names of his father and his city.

> (Herodotus 8.90)

In addition to giving a royal daughter in marriage (an exceptionally high honour), the gifts shared out by the king could be appointment to high office, the grant of a landed estate (or its revenues) and (most commonly) items for use and wear, which the honorand displayed daily on his person. They included a horse with a gold bit, gold necklaces, bracelets, a Persian robe, a gold dagger (*akinakes*), a gold bowl (sometimes inscribed with the king's name; Sancisi-Weerdenburg 1989). Several of the stunning items in the 'Oxus treasure' (originating in Tadjikistan, now in the British Museum) show in detail the elaborate workmanship and precious materials that went into these objects (Dalton 1964; Pitschikijan 1992); the reliefs at Persepolis, the brightly coloured, glazed brick reliefs from Susa, and sculptures show us honoured individuals displaying these public marks of royal esteem. The persons wearing such items were publicly recognised as belonging to the highest ranks of the court, close to the king and hence worth cultivating.

Given the politically symbolic role the royal gifts fulfilled, we may assume that the presentation ceremony was public, although our evidence is slight (Sancisi-Weerdenburg 1989). Public distribution of gifts by the king guaranteed their source; public acceptance served to stress the loyalty of the recipient and his dependence for all social advancement on the king. The system of royal rewards thus worked to strengthen the king's pre-eminence in the political system and place the recipients under continuing obligation to the donor. Conversely, rebellion, betrayal of trust, corrupt practice led to the public withdrawal of royal favour, signalled by the offender being stripped of his court ornaments (see Grelot 1972 no. 102, for a possible reference) – in very serious cases, followed by public and horrific executions or slow death by torture.

Satrapies and subjects

Provinces and central control

The entire territory of the Persian empire was divided into provinces, usually called 'satrapies' (from OP *khshaçapavan-* = 'protecting the kingdom'); the governors in control of satrapies were 'satraps'. But the terminology is not always precise: the word can be used of less powerful governors, and Greek writers even apply it on occasion to any officers surrounding the king. But the general pattern of satrapies is fairly clear, although there are uncertainties about their exact boundaries (Petit 1990; for Central Asia, see Briant 1984a).

All the different areas of the empire were thus united in a single political structure, and the satrapal pattern created an administrative uniformity. Alongside this, there were considerable regional diversities in government and variations in the degree and nature of dependence. The pastoralists of the great Zagros mountain chain, for example, were never fully integrated into the central government system by being turned into a Persian province. The productive capacities of the region were limited and it was difficult to conduct military campaigns in the mountainous terrain. Further, it was hard to pin down the local population, because they had refuges and hiding-places on inaccessible peaks and in caves. The Persians therefore set up a *modus vivendi* for handling the scattered mountain dwellers. The Persian king regularly presented local leaders with gifts, which placed the recipients under an obligation to help him. The king was thus able to use their resources of manpower when necessary, the tribes helped to secure routes for him through the mountains, and their good-will meant that tribal raids on adjacent settled communities was reduced (Briant 1982a, ch. 2). The Arab tribes enjoyed another kind of relationship with the central authority. The Arabs helped the Persians find safe routes through the desert (as in Cambyses' invasion of Egypt, p. 662), and organised the lucrative caravan trade between the southern tip of Arabia and the Persian-controlled Palestinian ports, such as Gaza. In return, they did not pay the normal tax, but presented the king with a regular 'gift' of incense (Briant 1982a, ch. 3). Another important frontier-group were the Scythians, who lived in the area of the lower Oxus. Their traditional life-style was nomadic: horse-borne warrior-élites maintained their social position through the rich booty acquired on raids. The precise manner in which the Persian authorities managed relations with the Scythians is unclear; but the extensive use of Scythians in the Persian army suggests the Persians were able to set up a mutually profitable arrangement (Briant 1982a, ch. 4). Links with the Scythian tribes would have given the Persians indirect access to northern Central Asia and Siberia: a carpet found in one of the Scythian 'frozen tombs' in the Altai mountains (near China) is decorated in Achaemenid style, as is a saddle-cloth (Rolle 1989: 95–98; Barber 1991 [OF]: 199–203). Had they accompanied a Persian noble lady married to a Scythian leader? Were they gifts bestowed on a Scythian warrior by the king? In these three instances, the physical environment meant that direct rule by a Persian satrap was inappropriate, and so the inhabitants were granted a measure of regulated independence, which worked to the mutual benefit of king and 'subjects'.

Each satrapy was fairly extensive, each satrapal governor was, to judge by the names, virtually always a Persian (or at least Iranian) noble. The satrap conducted affairs from the provincial capital, often identical with the old capitals of the states which had been conquered. In Egypt, for example, the satrapal centre was at Memphis, in Lydia at Sardis, in Media at Ecbatana, in Babylonia at Babylon. Some new governmental centres were also created following subdivision of very large provinces: Damascus was (probably) the administrative centre of the new province 'Beyond the River'; Daskyleion became the satrapal seat of Hellespontine Phrygia.

The satrapal capital was a microcosm of the royal centres. The provincial taxes were collected and stored here (some were sent on to the centre) to provide resources for the satrap and his staff. Some taxes were in kind and could be used directly to feed and maintain local garrisons: the soldiers at

Elephantine (p. 651), for example, were entitled, together with their families, to draw rations for their sustenance from the provincial storehouse. The workmen in the Persepolis region, too, were generally supplied with rations in kind from royal storehouses. Taxes paid in precious metals, usually silver, were kept in reserve for exceptional expenditure (Descat 1989). The Alexander historians provide some idea of the enormous surpluses garnered in Persian government centres. Harpalus, for example, who was put in charge of the treasury of Babylon in 331, was still able, after five years of riotous living, to take 5,000 talents of silver away with him (D.S. 17.108.4–6). The treasuries were well protected in the citadel of the satrapal centre; other fortified centres, too, served as additional treasuries, under the control of treasurers (*gazophylakes*, a Greek word linked to OP **ganzabara*-'treasurer'). The satrap himself could probably only use this stored wealth with royal authorisation (Briant 1982b: 29 n. 3). Other storehouses, in which materials were gathered and processed, were carefully overseen by the satrap and his staff. A striking example is a document from Elephantine (Cowley 1923 no. 26; Grelot 1972 no. 61) concerning a boat used by two Egyptians for government purposes. They ask that it be repaired, and the request is passed up the administrative ladder to Arsames, satrap of Egypt, who orders his subordinates to have the boat brought into dry dock; the storehouse accountants (in Elephantine) and chief carpenter are to see whether the repair is indeed necessary and provide a detailed inventory of the materials needed. The report is made out, together with a recommendation that the old materials from the boat should go back to the storehouse. Once Arsames has approved the report, he orders a storehouse official to issue the chief carpenter with the necessary materials for repairs. The Persepolis tablets, too, reveal the existence of centres, staffed by workers (men, women and children) involved in the manufacture of a range of goods (Hinz 1971).

The satrap's residence was palatial. The provincial capitals had palaces, often taken over from the earlier kings. They were also maintained for use by the kings when travelling through the empire. The Persian-style building in the citadel of Babylon (probably built by Artaxerxes II, see p. 674) provides us with physical evidence of how part of one of these official buildings looked. Xenophon paints a vivid picture of the residence and park at Daskyleion, belonging to Pharnabazus, satrap of Hellespontine Phrygia:

> It was in Daskyleion that Pharnabazus had his palace. All around the place were numbers of large villages, very well stocked with provisions, and also some very beautiful wild animals, kept either in enclosed parks or the open country. A river full of all kinds of fish ran past the palace and there were also plenty of birds to be caught by those who knew how to do so.
>
> (Xenophon *Hellenica* 4.1.16)

In the provincial palaces were archives where royal orders received by the satrap were kept. The regional bureaucracy operated from here: petitions to the satrap were sent here and copies of satrapal resolutions, endorsing local decisions which affected city-land and income, were stored for future reference (Briant 1986: 434–437). We hear a little of these archives when the Jerusalem community appealed, through the satrap, to the king to uphold the edict granting them the right to rebuild their temple:

'Your Majesty, let search be made in the royal archives in Babylon, to discover whether a decree was issued by King Cyrus for the rebuilding of this house of God in Jerusalem . . .'
Then King Darius issued an order, and search was made in the archives where the treasures were deposited in Babylon. But it was in Ecbatana, in the royal residence in the province of Media, that a scroll was found on which was written the following memorandum (Cyrus' edict follows).

(*Ezra* 5.17–6.2)

In the excavations of Old Kandahar (satrapal centre of Arachosia) in Afghanistan, archaeologists found fragments of an Elamite tablet. The find implies that the bureaucratic practices attested at Persepolis were replicated in the eastern part of the empire (Helms 1982).[6] A palace is attested in Samarkand (Arrian *Anabasis* 3.30.6), across the Oxus in Uzbekistan (part of the satrapy of Bactria–Sogdiana): it is described as a royal residence, but could have been used on occasion by the satrap, too. Although our evidence is fullest for the government of the western empire, because of the nature of the surviving sources, there is every reason to suppose that the eastern regions were governed in broadly similar fashion (Briant 1984a).

Roads

The Persepolis tablets support this conclusion. They record the movement of groups or individuals travelling to Persia, and we can see that India, Arachosia, Carmania, Bactria were all linked into the extensive road system for which the Achaemenids are famous through Herodotus' description (5.52–54; 8.98). He provides valuable information on the road linking Sardis to Susa: there were way-stations set along the route at one-day intervals, where a courier on urgent state business could get food and new mounts and so continue at top speed. At strategic points, such as river crossings and mountain passes, the road was heavily guarded by soldiers to monitor travellers. Maintenance of the supply and guard posts was probably one of the duties of the relevant satrap, since communication was crucial for efficient government.[7] The Persepolis texts allow us to see that the network of roads criss-crossed the immense territory of the Persian empire, so the system of guards, supply points and the necessary governmental control operated in all the provinces, from east to west (Graf 1994).

Use of the way-stations along the highways was limited to individuals bearing a sealed authorisation (El. *halmi*) from the king or recognised official. We have reports from way-stations monitoring the passage of travellers and their permits, but only one example of such a 'passport' has been preserved. It was issued (in Aramaic) by Arsames, satrap of Egypt, to his estate manager and companions for a journey from northern Babylonia:

> From Arsames to Marduk, superintendent (*pqyd'*) in [. . .]; Nabudalani, superintendent in Lair; Zatuvahya, superintendent in Arzuhin; Upastabara, superintendent in Arbela, [. . .], and Matalubash; Bagafarna, superintendent in Salam; and Fradafarna and Gauzana, superintendents in Damascus.
>
> [Now then,] my superintendent, named Nehtihor, is going to Egypt. You are to give him rations charged to my estate in your provinces daily: 'White' flour, two quarts; 'Rami' flour, three quarts; wine or beer, two quarts; [sheep], one. Also to his ten servants, each per day: flour, one quart; fodder for his horses. Give rations to the two Cilicians and one artisan – all three are servants of mine who are going to Egypt with him – each man per day: flour, one quart. Each superintendent in turn, according to the route from province to province until it reaches Egypt, is to give them these rations. If he should be more than one day in a place, then for these days do not give them any more rations.
>
> Knows about this order: Bagasrava
> Scribe: Rashta
> (Driver 1957/1965 no. 6; Grelot 1972 no. 67; Whitehead 1974: 64–66)

The document allowed Nehtihor, and his companions, to obtain daily food and fodder by presenting it along their route at the way-stations. The relevant official furnished the stipulated amount and reported it to the central accounting office, where the authoriser's (in this case, Arsames') account was debited. Access to supplies was carefully regulated – if the party dragged its feet, the officials were forbidden to give out more provisions. If we remember that this is the only surviving note authorising food-supplies for a journey among the thousands that were issued (as shown by the Fortification archive, Hallock 1969: Q texts), we begin to get some idea of the enormous complexity of the imperial administration.

Land, labour and manpower

Arsames refers to his estates in the document, which was made out in favour of the manager of his estates in Egypt. The collection of letters making up the Arsames correspondence (Driver 1957/1965) gives us a valuable insight into estates held by members of the Persian nobility here. The Murashu archives from Babylonia (Stolper 1985) show that many Persians, including members of the Persian royal house, held substantial estates there as well. The

Persepolis texts, too, refer to estates in Persia belonging to royal women. Several Greek writers mention Persian land owners and other recipients of revenue from land in western Asia Minor. The king himself owned estates the length and breadth of his kingdom. The ownership of estates by members of the king, his family, the high nobility and favoured subjects spread the Persian presence throughout the empire, and helped to strengthen control. This is well illustrated by a passage in Xenophon's *Anabasis*:

> Here (sc. Pergamum in Mysia) Xenophon was given a good reception by Hellas, the wife of Gongylos of Eretria, and mother of Gorgion and Gongylos. She told him there was a Persian called Asidates, living in the plain, and that if he went by night with three hundred men he could capture this Persian together with his wife and children and property, which was considerable . . .
>
> They arrived at the place about midnight, and the slaves outside the castle together with most of the cattle there, got away safely from them, since they were leaving all this aside in order to capture Asidates himself and his own personal belongings. They failed in their attempt to storm the tower, which was high and strong, with battlements and manned by large numbers of good soldiers, and so they attempted to make a breach in it. The wall was eight earthen bricks thick, but by daybreak a breach was made. The moment it appeared, someone from inside with a large spear for roasting oxen ran it right through the thigh of the man nearest to the opening. Then, by letting off volleys of arrows, they made it unsafe even to get near. The defenders shouted out too, and made signals by waving torches, and so Itamenes with his force came out to their relief, and from Comania there came some Assyrian hoplites and about eighty Hyrcanian cavalrymen, also in the king's pay, and then about eight hundred peltasts, with cavalry as well, some from Parthenium, and some from Apollonia and the country nearby.
>
> (Xenophon *Anabasis* 7.8)

This is a fine vignette of a Persian-owned estate on the north-western frontier: well fortified with a tower to serve as a lookout, heavily manned by well-equipped soldiers; beyond the fortifications were fields with herds tended by slaves. Moreover, it was not an isolated outpost: another Persian landowner with troops was near enough to respond to torch signals and rush to aid his neighbour; a substantial force of cavalry, heavy- and light-armed soldiers were also alerted and approached swiftly to beat off the Greek raid. Further, unlike royal estates and those belonging to the highest echelons of the aristocracy, whose owners were not permanent residents on their land, this estate appears to have belonged to a middle-ranking Persian who had settled here, since the Greeks expected to be able to capture him and his family. Even in the case of absentee landlords, the Egyptian material and the Babylonian

Murashu archives show that the basic structure of landed estates was similar. On Arsames' estate in Egypt, for example, there was an estate supervisor who held a grant of land (on which he owed tax) with servants, an Aramaean sculptor with a household staff, a groom(?) also with his own staff, a garrison commander and the soldiers under him, and further servants and labourers (Ar. *grd'*).

In Babylonia we gain some information about the organisation of modest land-parcels granted to individuals in return for military service; some, but not all, were attached to large estates (Stolper 1985). The military grants were of three different types, according to the type of service and equipment expected: horse-land, bow-land, chariot-land reflecting the basic fighting units of the Achaemenid army (Sekunda and Chew 1992). The grantees and their obligation were registered in a royal census, kept by army scribes at the main mustering points in the satrapy (Ebeling 1952; Stolper 1985: 29–30). As the empire stabilised and territorial expansion ceased, the necessity for constant empire-wide call-ups receded. The descendants of the grantees were, therefore, expected to pay a silver tax when their personal service was not required. Many met this need by leasing their land to the Babylonian entrepreneurial family of Murashu, who sublet it to tenants. The tenants paid the Murashu their dues in agricultural products, which the firm transformed into silver by marketing it; some of the silver was then paid back to the original grantees' families so that they could pay their state taxes. But the basic obligation to supply a soldier never lapsed: the census ensured that grantees could not escape service, when needed, in some form – they may not necessarily have discharged their military duties in person, but the census officers made sure that *a* soldier matching the obligation of each land grant appeared at the call-up (*RLA* 8: 205–207).

The system explains the ability of Darius III in 333 and 331 to field large armies made up of all the peoples of the empire against Alexander (cf. also Artaxerxes II's army at Cunaxa in 401). It is wrong to think of the Persian fighting machine as depending totally on Greek mercenary forces: there were garrisons stationed throughout the empire made up of many different ethnic groups (Tuplin 1987a; 1987b), and military colonists, ready at a moment's notice to take up arms in defence of the state, as shown by the Xenophon passage above for one. From Egypt we know of Elamite, Cilician, Syrian, Jewish, Median, Arab and Babylonian soldiers; Greek material reveals the presence of Persian, Assyrian, Hyrcanian (south-east Caspian) troops in western Asia Minor; Scythian soldiers were stationed near Carchemish. How exactly the members of the different population groups arrived in the places where they appear as soldiers or military settlers is not always clear. The Jewish soldiers at Elephantine had already served the Saite kings (see chapter 12b), and were taken into Persian service subsequently. Some of the many ethnic groups living in Babylonia could also have been descendants from people settled in the Neo-Babylonian period (see chapter 11e). The Persians certainly used mass deportation at times to weaken centres of resistance, and that may explain the presence of some people settled far from home.

It is likely that the 'colonists' were not only obliged to fight for the king: general government needs for labour (transport and construction-work are the most obvious) were probably also met through the system, at least in part. But that was not the only way in which the kings had access to manpower. People called *kurtaš* (in the Elamite of the Persepolis texts) figure prominently as workers in the Persepolis archives. Similar groups also appear in Aramaic and Babylonian documents (Ar. *grd'*; Akk. *gardu*). Who they were is debated. Opinions differ as to whether the term defines slaves, free workers, some kind of dependent element in the population, or whether it is simply a way in which the administration defined the available labour force recruited from a range of sources (Dandamaev 1975; Stolper 1985: 56–59; Zaccagnini 1983: 262–264; Uchitel 1991; Briant in press, ch. 11/9).

Persian government, local autonomy and local traditions

The impression we have of the government of the Achaemenid empire is that the top posts were in the hands of a tiny group, drawn exclusively from the highest levels of the Persian aristocracy. Is it right to see it as an impermeable stratum of powerholders defined by their ethnicity? Probably not (Sancisi-Weerdenburg 1990). First, there is evidence of at least one non-Persian rising to the coveted position of satrap, as a result of his loyal support during Darius II's struggle for the throne (the Babylonian, Belesys; Stolper 1987). Second, we have the example of Metiochus, the son of the Athenian general Miltiades, about whom Herodotus says:

> Darius, however, when the Phoenicians brought Metiochus into his presence, far from doing him any harm, loaded him with favours. He gave him a house and estate, and also a Persian wife, who bore him children who were counted Persians.
>
> (Herodotus 6.41)

In other words, the king could bestow the rank of 'Persian' on people not of pure Persian descent. Also not to be underestimated is the interaction at a regional level between Persians and local élites. We mostly do not know who the wives of the satraps were, for example, never mind the wives of slightly lesser-ranking Persian commanders and officials. Who was the wife of Asidates in the Pergamum region, for example? It is quite possible that she was a local woman. There were certainly marriages between local nobles and Persian women, like the marriage of the Paphlagonian prince, Otys, and the daughter of the Persian noble, Spithridates (Xenophon *Hellenica* 4.1.6–7). Such alliances gave the local élite a potential foothold in the Persian system of honours, as shown by the Herodotus passage quoted above. Most interesting is the fact that the king himself took women from among the subject peoples into his household as 'concubines'. The only instance we know of is Artaxerxes I, but there is no reason to think he was unusual: three Babylonian women bore him children – two sons and a daughter; the two sons struggled for the throne and the victor became Darius II, who was married to the daughter, Parysatis. As it was possible for bastard sons to accede to the throne, it thus lay within the grasp of the local nobility to gain access to the highest office in the empire through their daughters.

At the level below governor of a satrapy, the Persian system can be seen to depend very much on co-operation with local power-holders. Within each satrapy were subdivisions (not very well known), which could be governed by locals (cf. the family of Mausolus; Hornblower 1982). Further, satrapies such as 'Beyond the River', Lydia, Hellespontine Phrygia and Bactria–Sogdiana included a multiplicity of different political entities usually run along traditional lines by their own authorities. In 'Beyond the River', for example, were the following administrative districts: Jerusalem and the sub-province of Yehud retained its sacred laws, its priests and was administered by Jews (Avigad 1976: 30–36); neighbouring Samaria was governed by the local family of Sanballat (Cross 1963); the Phoenician cities continued to be ruled by their traditional dynasts (Betlyon 1980); recently evidence has come to light showing that Ammon, east of the Jordan, also formed a provincial sub-division, probably under a local governor (Shuba': Herr 1992). This mosaic of different socio-political units all came under the authority of the satrap in Damascus.

The evidence for the existence of very disparate political structures inside the Persian provinces has sometimes produced the impression that the Persians were content to sit in their satrapal capitals, receive tribute and let the locals get on with governing themselves with little interference. As a result, local potentates ran matters to suit themselves with little reference to the Persian authorities, and central control grew steadily weaker. The reality is rather different, with the Persians *using* the local institutions to work in their interests, and keeping a very tight watch on their internal machinations. A good example is the case of Pharnabazus, satrap of Hellespontine Phrygia and the local dynasts of Dardanus:

> This Aeolis was indeed part of Pharnabazus' province, but Zenis of Dardanus had, while he was alive, governed it for him as satrap. After he fell ill and died, Pharnabazus had planned to give the satrapy to someone else, but Mania, the wife of Zenis, who was also from Dardanus, set out to visit him with a great company of attendants and with gifts for Pharnabazus himself and for use in winning the favour of his concubines and of the most influential people at his court. She was granted an interview with him and spoke as follows:
> 'Pharnabazus, my husband was always a good friend to you and used to pay you all the tribute due. For this you praised and honoured him.

Now if I serve you just as loyally as he did, what need is there to appoint someone else as governor? And if I fail to please you, surely it is in your power to take the satrapy away from me and give it to someone else.' After hearing this, Pharnabazus decided that the woman should be satrap. She, when she had taken over her province, paid the tribute just as regularly as her husband had done and, in addition, never visited Pharnabazus without bringing gifts for him. And whenever he came down to her country, she gave him a far more splendid and enjoyable reception than did any of his other governors. She not only kept loyal to him all the cities which she had taken over but gained control over other cities on the coast which had not been subject to him before – Larissa, Hamaxitus and Colonae. She used a Greek mercenary force for these operations and, while they were attacking the walls, used to look on from a carriage. Anyone who won her approval would be rewarded with the most splendid gifts, so that this force of hers was magnificently equipped. She also used to join forces with Pharnabazus even when, in retaliation for raids on the king's territory, he invaded the land of the Mysians and the Pisidians. In return for all this, Pharnabazus gave her special honours and privileges and sometimes called her in as a counsellor. When she was more than 40 years old, her daughter's husband, Meidias, found it intolerable to hear people saying that it was a disgrace for the country to be ruled by a woman and for him to be merely an ordinary individual. Against other people Mania always took the precautions that are normal for an absolute ruler, but she trusted Meidias and was fond of him, as a woman naturally would be of her son-in-law. He was therefore able, so it is said, to make his way into her presence and to strangle her. He also killed her son, who was a remarkable good-looking boy of about 17. Next he seized the fortresses of Scepsis and Gergis, where Mania had kept most of her treasure; but the other cities refused him entry and were held for Pharnabazus by their garrisons. Meidias then sent gifts to Pharnabazus and claimed that he should be appointed ruler of the province just as Mania had been. But Pharnabazus told him to keep his gifts and look after them well. 'I shall come soon,' he said, 'to take them and you too. For, if I fail to avenge Mania, I would rather not live.'

(Xenophon Hellenica 3.1.10ff.)

The passage illustrates beautifully the advantage of using a local person to defend Persian interests, continuing the arrangement in the same family once it has been proved to work well, the dependence of the local dynasts on the Persian satrap, and his power to strip the family of its position if the arrangement breaks down and threatens Persian control.

The government of the empire has often been described as a *laissez-faire* régime in other respects, too. The Persians 'allow' regional cultures, artistic, linguistic and religious, to flourish; local people carry on holding positions of authority; local patterns of production continue with no discernible Persian impact. This view of the Achaemenid empire overemphasises one aspect of Persian control and gives it a negative slant. It ignores the fact that the Persians harnessed diverse local traditions to exercise power flexibly and that they interacted closely with their subjects. Although the Achaemenid kings used local languages for their decrees, they also employed Aramaic as a kind of *lingua franca*, and spread its use throughout the imperial territories (see p. 650). Moreover, the form Aramaic developed in the Achaemenid period reflects an underlying Persian bureaucratic usage. So, at the regional level people did *not* simply continue to use their own languages as though nothing had changed – Aramaic was employed alongside them regularly and predominated in royal and satrapal directives (Metzger *et al.* 1979; Briant 1986).

In the realm of religion, too, the Persian kings did *not* simply let everyone do what they wished. In Egypt and Babylonia, they were careful to appear as active upholders of local cults in order to ensure control of the wealthy sanctuaries and the adherence of their staff. In smaller centres, such as Jerusalem and Magnesia-on-the-Maeander, they granted some privileges to the temples, because they acknowledged the support their gods had given the Persians, as shown by this Greek translation of a letter from Darius I:

> The king of kings, Darius, son of Hystaspes, to his servant (*doulos*) Gadatas speaks thus:
>   I hear that you are not carrying out my instructions in all respects: that you are cultivating my land by planting fruits from the other side of the Euphrates in the region of Lower Asia, this decision of yours I praise and for this reason great favour will continue to exist for you in the house of the king. But that you are ignoring my instruction about the gods I shall give you, if you do not change, proof of my annoyance. Because you have demanded a tax (*phoros*) from the sacred gardeners of Apollo and ordered them to cultivate unconsecrated land, misunderstanding the intention of my ancestors towards the god, who announced the precise truth (*atrekeia*) to the Persians and . . .
> (F. Lochner-Hüttenbach in Brandenstein and Mayrhofer 1964: 91–98;
> Boffo 1978)

Conversely, the shrines of people who had rebelled could be, and were, destroyed (the Apollo sanctuary at Didyma, Herodotus 6.19; the Athena temple in Athens, Herodotus 8.53). We also have the statement by Berossus that Artaxerxes II introduced a statue-cult of Anahita in the imperial centres (see p. 674). The aim was probably to reinforce the cohesion of the Persian communities living far from the imperial heartland, a way of strengthening their sense of identity as members of the governing élite. One effect was to distinguish the Persians of the diaspora through their cult and it introduced Iranian shrines into the provincial capitals.

Persian court art and practices also had an impact on the conquered lands: local seal-types adopt Persian motifs (Collon 1987 [OM]: 90–93); local coins show Persian scenes (Betlyon 1980 pls. 1–4); precious metal drinking sets reflect the widepread adoption of Persian styles of banqueting by local élites (*CHI* II ch. 21). The small palace in the citadel at Babylon was typically Persian in layout and decoration (Haerinck 1973), and the seat of a local dynast in the mountains of Cilicia had carved reliefs imitating scenes from Persepolis (Davesnes *et al.* 1987). Egyptian private sculpture shows dignitaries in standard Egyptian pose, but wearing typical Persian court jewellery (Bothmer 1960 figs. 151–152).

Individuals who had held power under former régimes and moved to support the Persian conquerors were recruited into the new king's entourage, with their authority definitively diminished. Udjahorresnet, for example (see pp. 662–663), had been a naval commander under the Saite rulers; following Cambyses' conquest, he was stripped of his military post, granted the rank of royal 'friend', and assigned a prominent position in the Neith temple at Sais. In other words, he retained an honoured social position within Egyptian society, but forfeited effective political power (Briant 1988).

Local modes of agricultural production continued in their basic form – they had to. But the imperial grip on productive resources was tight: the king, royal family, Persian nobles and courtiers held extensive tracts of land the length and breadth of the realm (see pp. 693–695). Villagers within satrapies were assigned duties, in addition to the regular burden of tax and services, which affected the amount they were obliged to produce from their fields: they had to supply the satrapal court with food (*Nehemiah* 5.14–15; Herodotus 1.192), as well as the soldiers manning local garrison posts (Segal 1983 no. 24; cf. Hoglund 1992: 213). Perhaps most significant was the Persian king's control of access to water: royal officials managed the crucial canal system in Babylonia, which was crown property (Stolper 1985, ch. 2). The kings are also known to have constructed an extensive underground irrigation system (*qanat*) in northern Iran (Polybius 10.28). Herodotus describes Darius blocking off a river, on which the surrounding people depended for water, and only allowing channels to be opened in response to petitioning and payment (Herodotus 3.117). The imperial heartland, Persia, experienced the most striking transformation in the Achaemenid period. First, the two magnificent royal cities, Pasargadae and Persepolis, were founded. Second, in the four to five hundred years preceding the development of the Persian state, it was a sparsely settled region, with virtually no urban centres; subsistence was based on herding animals, rather than farming land (see p. 653). Archaeological surveys show that this pattern of life changed radically in the sixth to fourth centuries, when settlements increased enormously in number (Sumner 1986). In the late fourth century, the Greek historian Hieronymus of Cardia (used by Diodorus) described Persia as a veritable Garden of Eden:

... high land, blessed with a healthy climate and full of the fruits appropriate to the season. There were glens heavily wooded and shady cultivated trees of various kinds in parks, and also naturally converging glades full of trees of every sort and streams of water, so that travellers lingered with delight in places pleasantly inviting repose. Also there was an abundance of cattle of every kind ... those who inhabited the country were the most warlike of the Persians, every man being a bowman and a slinger, and in density of population, too, this country far surpassed the other satrapies.

(D.S. 19.21.2–4)

* * *

The great socio-cultural diversity of the Persian empire should not mislead us into dismissing it as a weak and ramshackle structure. The very length of time it survived, and the fact that Alexander's successors, the Seleucids (311–146), were able to build on Achaemenid institutions to hold their own substantial dominions together (Sherwin-White and Kuhrt 1993) are measures of the success of the imperial system evolved by the Persian kings.

Notes

1 The courtiers on the Persepolis reliefs wear different garments, conventionally called 'Persian' and 'Median' dress respectively. The style of dress does not indicate ethnicity (Calmeyer 1987).
2 H. Sancisi-Weerdenburg is preparing a study of Old Persian *arta*; I would like to acknowledge my debt to her on this question.
3 As elsewhere, the king seems, normally, to have chosen his eldest son to succeed. This norm is perhaps implicitly acknowledged in Xerxes' inscription.
4 For a full study of women in the Persian empire, particularly the activities of royal women as illustrated by the Persepolis tablets, see Brosius, in press.
5 The term has now also been identified in a demotic Egyptian document (G. Vittmann, *AfO* 38–39 (1991–2): 159–160).
6 Three Elamite tablets found at Armavir Blur (former Soviet Armenia) may also be administrative documents akin to the Persepolis texts, concerning tax and grain (H. Koch *ZA* 83 (1993): 219–236; but see Vallat *NABU* 1995 note 46). Together with an important article by G. Summers on Achaemenid material from eastern Turkey (especially Altin Tepe, *AnSt* 43 (1993): 85–108), we are finally getting a clearer impression of the Achaemenid province of Armenia, showing that its administration was (broadly) similar to better-documented regions.
7 There is no evidence that the roads were used by merchants. Trade in the Persian empire is very poorly documented (see Wiesehöfer 1982 for a conspectus). The general impression is that commerce was conducted independently by individuals using the trade circuits, which had evolved in the Neo-Assyrian period (Salles 1991; 1994). The government levied traditional tolls and dues at the regional level, but beyond that we know of no real royal involvement or promotion of trade (Briant in press, ch. 9/3).

BIBLIOGRAPHY

Introduction: select bibliography and references

A General

Arnaud D. 1970 *Le Proche-Orient Ancien de l'invention de l'écriture à l'hellénisation* Paris

Baines J., Málek J. 1980 *Cultural Atlas of Ancient Egypt* Oxford

Burney C. 1977 *From Village to Empire: an introduction to Near Eastern archaeology* Oxford

David A.R. 1975 *The Egyptian Kingdoms* Oxford

Hrouda B. (Hsg.) 1991 *Der Alte Orient* Munich (French trans.: Paris 1991)

Moorey P.R.S. 1975 *Biblical Lands* Oxford

Postgate J.N. 1977 *The First Empires* Oxford

Roaf M. 1990 *Cultural Atlas of Mesopotamia and the Ancient Near East* Oxford

Sasson J.M. (ed.) 1995 *Civilizations of the Ancient Near East* New York

Schmökel H. 1961 *Kulturgeschichte des Alten Orients* Stuttgart

von Soden W. 1993 *The Ancient Orient: an introduction to the study of the ancient Near East* (trans. of German pub. 1985) Leominster

Wiseman D.J. (ed.) 1973 *Peoples of Old Testament Times* Oxford

B Textbooks with contributions by different specialists

Bottéro J., Cassin E., Vercoutter J. (eds) 1967a *The Near East: the early civilizations* (trans. of Fischer Weltgeschichte Band 2) London

—— 1966 *Die Altorientalischen Reiche* II (Fischer Weltgeschichte Band 3) Frankfurt-am-Main

—— 1967b *Die Altorientalischen Reiche* III: *die erst Hälfte des 1. Jahrtausends* (Fischer Weltgeschichte Band 4) Frankfurt-am-Main (the three volumes cover history down to the Persian conquest)

Cambridge Ancient History I; II; III/1; III/2; IV; VI (rev. edn); 1972–94 Cambridge

C Textbooks covering most of the region

Garelli P. 1969 *Le Proche-Orient Asiatique* I (Nouvelle Clio) Paris (detailed study from *c.* 3000 to *c.* 1200, excluding Egypt)

Garelli P., Nikiprowetzky W. 1974 *Le Proche-Orient Asiatique: Israël* II (Nouvelle Clio) Paris (detailed study from *c.* 1200 to 539, excluding Egypt)

Hallo W.W., Simpson W.K. 1971 *The Ancient Near East: a history* New York (from *c.* 3000 to the Persian conquest)

Klengel H. *et al.* 1989 *Kulturgeschichte des Alten Vorderasien* (Veröffentlichungen des Zentralinstituts für Alte Geschichte und Archäologie der Akademie der Wissenschaften der DDR 18) Berlin (from the Neolithic to Alexander, excluding Egypt)

Knapp B. 1988 *The Ancient History of Western Asia and Egypt* Chicago (from the Neolithic to Alexander, including the Aegean)

Liverani M. 1988 *Antico Oriente: storia, società, economia* Rome (detailed study from *c.* 3000 to Alexander, excluding Egypt)

Schmökel H. 1957 *Geschichte des alten Vorderasien* (HdO) Leiden (*c.* 3000 to 539, excluding Egypt)

D Textbooks on Egyptian history

Drioton E., Vandier J. 1984 *L'Egypte: des origines à la conquête d'Alexandre* (6th edn) Paris

Gardiner A. 1961 *Egypt of the Pharaohs* Oxford

Grimal N. 1992 *A History of Ancient Egypt* (trans.) Oxford

Helck W. 1968 *Geschichte des alten Ägypten* (HdO) Leiden

Trigger B., Kemp B., O'Connor D., Lloyd A. 1983 *Ancient Egypt: a social history* Cambridge (the first three essays appeared originally as chapters of the *Cambridge History of Africa* I (1982))

E Collected essays, symposia, Festschriften: a selection of important and recent ones

Alster B. (ed.) 1980 *Death in Mesopotamia* Copenhagen (includes studies of Hittite, Ugaritic and Arab-Persian Gulf material)

Archi A. (ed.) 1984 *Circulation of Goods in Non-Palatial Contexts in the Ancient Near East* (Incunabula Graeca 82) Rome

Bounni 1990 = *Resurrecting the Past: a joint tribute to Adnan Bounni* (eds P. Matthiae, M. van Loon, H. Weiss) Leiden 1990

Cameron A., Kuhrt A. (eds) 1983 *Images of Women in Antiquity* (rev. edn 1993) London

Campbell E.F., Freedman D.N. (eds) 1983 *Biblical Archaeologist Reader* IV Sheffield

Cassin E. 1987 *Le Semblable et le Différent: symbolismes du pouvoir dans le proche-orient ancien* Paris

Diakonoff I.M. (ed.) 1969 *Ancient Mesopotamia: socio-economic history* (trans. of articles by Soviet scholars) Moscow

Diakonoff Studies = *Societies and Languages of the Ancient Near East: studies in honour of I.M. Diakonoff* (ed. M. Dandamaev *et al.*) Warminster 1982

Durand J.-M. (ed.) 1987 *La Femme dans le Proche-Orient Antique* Paris

Finkelstein Essays = *Essays on the Ancient Near East in Memory of J.J. Finkelstein* (ed. M. deJong Ellis) Hamden, Conn. 1977

Garelli P. (ed.) 1974 *Le Palais et la Royauté* Paris

Garelli Études = *Marchands, Diplomates et Empereurs: études sur la civilisation mésopotamienne offerts à Paul Garelli* (eds D. Charpin *et al.*) Paris 1991

Gibson McG., Biggs R.D. (eds) 1987 *The Organization of Power: aspects of bureaucracy in the ancient Near East* Chicago

Goedicke H., Roberts J.M. (eds) 1975 *Unity and Diversity: essays in the history, literature, and religion of the ancient Near East* (Johns Hopkins Near Eastern Studies) Baltimore, MD

Hallo 1993 = *The Tablet and the Scroll: Near Eastern studies in honor of William W. Hallo* Bethesda, MD

Jacobsen T. 1970 *Toward the Image of Tammuz and Other Essays on Mesopotamian History and Culture* (ed. W. Moran; Harvard Semitic Series 21) Cambridge, Mass.

Kraeling C.H., Adams, R.McC. (eds) 1960 *City Invincible* Chicago

Kramer Studies = *Studies in the Literature of the Ancient Near East dedicated to S.N. Kramer* (ed. J.M. Sasson = *JAOS* 103 (1983): 1–353)

Kraus Festschrift = *Zikir šumim: Assyriological studies presented to F.R. Kraus* (ed. G. van Driel *et al.*) Leiden 1982

Landsberger Studies = *Studies in Honor of Benno Landsberger* (AS 16) Chicago 1965

Larsen M.T. (ed.) 1979 *Power and Propaganda: a symposium on ancient empires* Copenhagen

Lesko B.S. (ed.) 1989 *Women's Earliest Records from Ancient Egypt and Western Asia* (Brown Judaic Studies 166) Atlanta, Ga.

Lipiński E. (ed.) 1979 *State and Temple Economy in the Ancient Near East* (2 vols) Louvain

Moran Studies = *Lingering over Words: studies in ancient Near Eastern literature in honor of William L. Moran* (eds T. Abusch *et al.*) Atlanta, Ga. 1990

Nissen H., Renger J. (eds) 1982 *Mesopotamien und seine Nachbarn* (2 vols) Berlin

Powell M.A. (ed.) 1987 *Labor in the Ancient Near East* (AOS 68) New Haven, Conn.

Rowlands M., Larsen M., Kristiansen K. (eds) 1987 *Centre and Periphery in the Ancient World* (New Directions in Archaeology) Cambridge

Stato Economia Lavoro nel Vicino Oriente Antico (Istituto Gramsci Toscano: Seminario di Orientalistica Antica) Milan 1988

Ucko P.J., Tringham R., Dimbleby G.W. (eds) 1972 *Man, Settlement and Urbanism* London

Veenhof K. (ed.) 1986 *Cuneiform Archives and Libraries* Leiden

F Basic technology

Barber E.J.W. 1991 *Prehistoric Textiles: the development of cloth in the Neolithic and Bronze Ages with special reference to the Aegean* Princeton NJ.

Hodges H. 1970 *Technology in the Ancient World* Harmondsworth

—— 1976 *Artifacts: an introduction to early materials and technologies* (rev. edn) London

Lucas A. 1962 *Ancient Egyptian Materials and Industries* (rev. J. R. Harris) London

Moorey P.R.S. 1985 *Materials and Manufacture in Ancient Mesopotamia: the evidence of art and archaeology* Oxford

G Regional historical–cultural background

a) Egypt

Harris J.R. (ed.) 1971 *The Legacy of Egypt* (2nd edn) Oxford

James T.G.H. 1979 *An Introduction to Ancient Egypt* London

Kees H. 1961 *Ancient Egypt: a cultural topography* (trans.) Chicago

Kemp B. 1989 *Ancient Egypt: anatomy of a civilization* London

Robins G. 1993 *Women in Ancient Egypt* London

Smith H.S., Hall R. 1983 *Ancient Centres of Egyptian Civilization* London
Spencer A.J. 1982 *Death in Ancient Egypt* Harmondsworth
Strouhal E. 1992 *Life in Ancient Egypt* (trans.) Cambridge
Watterson B. 1991 *Women in Ancient Egypt* Stroud

b) Mesopotamia

Bottéro J. 1992 *Mesopotamia: writing, reasoning and the gods* (trans.) Chicago
Bottéro J. et al. 1992 *Initiation à l'Orient Ancien: de Sumer à la Bible* Paris
Bottéro J., Stève M.-J. 1993 *Il était une fois la Mésopotamie* Paris
Curtis J. (ed.) 1982 *Fifty Years of Mesopotamian Discovery: the work of the British School of Archaeology in Iraq, 1932–1982* London
Oates J. 1986 *Babylon* (rev. edn) London
Oppenheim A.L. 1974 *Ancient Mesopotamia: portrait of a dead civilization* (rev. edn) Chicago
Roux G. 1980 *Ancient Iraq* (2nd edn) Harmondsworth
Saggs H.W.F. 1963 *The Greatness That Was Babylon* London

c) Syria

Chavalas M.W., Hayes J.L. (eds) 1992 *New Horizons in the Study of Ancient Syria* (Bibliotheca Mesopotamica 25) Malibu, Cal.
Klengel H. 1992 *Syria 3000 to 300* BC: *a handbook of political history* Berlin
Land des Baal: Syrien – Forum der Völker und Kulturen (exhibn cat., Museum für Vor- und Frühgeschichte, Berlin) Munich 1982
Weiss H. (ed.) 1985 *Ebla to Damascus: art and archaeology of ancient Syria* Washington

d) Palestine

Aharoni Y. 1979 *The Land of the Bible: a historical geography* (rev. edn) London
—— 1982 *The Archaeology of the Land of Israel: from the prehistoric beginnings to the end of the first temple period* (trans.) London
Bienkowski P. (ed.) *The Art of Ancient Jordan* Liverpool
Kenyon K 1979 *Archaeology in the Holy Land* (4th edn; pbk repr. 1985) London
Mazar A. 1990 *Archaeology of the Land of the Bible: 10,000–586 BCE* (The Anchor Bible Reference Library; rev.edn 1992) New York
Moorey P.R.S. 1981 *Excavation in Palestine* Farnham
Tubb J., Chapman R. (eds) 1990 *Archaeology and the Bible* London
Weippert H. 1988 *Palästina in vorhellenistischer Zeit* (Handbuch der Archäologie) Munich

e) Anatolia

McQueen J.G. 1986 *The Hittites and Their Contemporaries in Asia Minor* (rev. edn) London
Schatten uit Turkije (Treasures from Turkey) (Dutch and Turkish text, some English: lavishly illustrated exhibn cat.) Leiden 1986

706

BIBLIOGRAPHY

f) Arab-Persian Gulf

al-Khalifa S.H.A., Rice M. (eds) 1986 *Bahrain through the Ages: the archaeology* London
Potts D.T. 1990 *The Arabian Gulf in Antiquity* (2 vols) Oxford

g) Nubia

Adams W.Y. 1975 *Nubia: Corridor to Africa* London
Africa in Antiquity: the arts of ancient Nubia and Sudan (Brooklyn Museum Exhibition Catalogue) New York 1978
Davies W.V. (ed.) 1991 *Egypt and Africa: Nubia from prehistory to Islam* London

h) Central Asia

Kohl P.L. (ed.) 1981 *The Bronze Age Civilizations of Central Asia: recent Soviet discoveries* New York
Masson V.M., Sarianidi V.I. 1972 *Central Asia: Turkmenia before the Achaemenids* London

i) Iran

Frye R.N. 1964 *The Heritage of Iran* London
Huot J.-L. 1970 *Persia* I: *From the Origins to the Achaemenids* (trans.) London
Matheson S. 1972 *Persia: an archaeological guide* London
Tucci G. (ed.) 1978 *La Città Brucciata nel deserto salato* Venice

j) India

Allchin B., Allchin R. 1982 *The Rise of Civilization in India and Pakistan* Cambridge
Fairservis W.A. 1975 *The Roots of Ancient India: the archaeology of early Indian civilization* (2nd edn) Chicago
Ratnagar S. 1991 *Enquiries into the Political Organization of Harappan Society* Pune
Thapar R. 1966 *A History of India* I Harmondsworth

k) Early contacts and trade between Western Asia and the East

Curtis J. (ed.) 1993 *Early Mesopotamia and Iran: contact and conflict c. 3500–1600* BC (proceedings of a seminar in memory of V.G. Lukonin) London
Herrmann G. 1968 'Lapis-lazuli: the early phases of its trade' *Iraq* 30: 21–57
Kohl P. 1975 'Carved chloride vessels: a trade in finished commodities in the mid-third millennium' *Expedition* 18/1: 18–31
Lamberg-Karlovsky C.C. 1972 'Trade mechanisms in Indus–Mesopotamian inter-relations' *JAOS* 92: 222–9

H Writing systems

André B., Ziegler C. 1982 *Naissance de l'écriture: cunéiformes et hiéroglyphes* Paris
Diringer D. 1948 *The Alphabet: a key to the history of mankind* London

Driver G.R. 1976 *Semitic Writing from Pictograph to Alphabet* (3rd rev. edn) London
Gelb I.J. 1963 *A Study of Writing* (rev. edn) Chicago
Hooker J.T. (ed.) 1991 *Reading the Past: ancient writings from cuneiform to the alphabet* London
Naveh J. 1982 *The Early History of the Alphabet* Jerusalem
Powell M.A. (ed.) 1981 *Aspects of Cuneiform Writing* (= *Visible Language* 15/4)
World Archaeology 17/3 (1986): Early Writing Systems

I Literature and texts in translation

Breasted J.H. 1906 *Ancient Records of Egypt* (5 vols) Chicago
Dalley S. 1989 *Myths from Mesopotamia: creation, the flood, Gilgamesh and others* Oxford
Erman A. 1927 *The Literature of the Ancient Egyptians* (trans.) rep. as: *The Ancient Egyptians: a sourcebook of their writings* New York 1966
Foster B.R. 1993 *Before the Muses: an anthology of Akkadian literature* (2 vols) Bethesda, MD
Kaiser O. *et al.* (Hsg.) *Texte aus der Umwelt des Alten Testaments* Gütersloh 1982– (in progress)
Kovacs M.G. 1989 *The Epic of Gilgamesh* Stanford, Cal.
Lichtheim M. 1973–80 *Ancient Egyptian Literature: a book of readings* (3 vols) Berkeley, Cal.
Oppenheim A.L. 1967 *Letters from Mesopotamia* Chicago
Pritchard J.B. (ed.) 1969 *Ancient Near Eastern Texts Relating to the Old Testament* Princeton, NJ
Simpson W.K. (ed.) 1972 *The Literature of Ancient Egypt: an anthology of stories, instructions and poetry* New Haven, Conn.
Veenhof K. (ed.) 1983 *Schrijvend Verleden* Leiden

J Studies of literary texts

Brunner H. 1966 *Grundzüge einer Geschichte der altägyptischen Literatur* Darmstadt
Farber W. 1989 *Schlaf, Kindchen, Schlaf! Mesopotamische Baby-Beschwörungen und -Rituale* (Mesopotamian Civilization 2) Winona Lake, IN
Hecker K., Sommerfeld W. (Hsg.) 1986 *Keilschriftliche Literaturen* (Berliner Beiträge zum Vorderen Orient 6) Berlin
Mindlin M., Geller M.J., Wansbrough J.E. (eds) 1987 *Figurative Language in the Ancient Near East* London
Reiner E. 1985 '*Your thwarts in pieces, your mooring rope cut': poetry from Babylonia and Assyria* Ann Arbor, Mich.
Röllig W. (Hsg.) 1978 *Altorientalische Literaturen* (Neues Handbuch der Literaturwissenschaft 1) Wiesbaden
Vogelzang M.E., Vanstiphout H.L.J. (eds) 1992 *Mesopotamian Epic Literature: oral or aural?* Queenston, Ontario

K Historiography

Albrektson B. 1967 *History and the Gods: an essay on the idea of historical events as divine manifestations in the ancient Near East* Lund

Cancik H. 1976 *Grundzüge der hethitischen und alttestamentlichen Geschichts-schreibung* Wiesbaden

Dentan R.C. (ed.) 1954 *The Idea of History in the Ancient Near East* (repr. 1983) New Haven, Conn.

Glassner J.-J. 1993 *Chroniques Mésopotamiennes* (La roue à livres) Paris

Grayson A.K. 1975 *Assyrian and Babylonian Chronicles* (TCS 5) Locust Valley, NY

Orientalia 49/2 (1980): Historiography in the Ancient Near East

Redford D.B. 1986 *Pharaonic King-lists, Annals and Day-books: a contribution to the study of the Egyptian sense of history* (SSEA Publications IV) Mississauga, Ontario

Tadmor H., Weinfeld M. (eds) 1983 *History, Historiography and Interpretation: studies in biblical and cuneiform literatures* Jerusalem

van Seters J. 1983 *In Search of History* New Haven, Conn.

L Religion and mythology

Black J., Green A. 1992 *Gods, Demons and Symbols of Ancient Mesopotamia: an illustrated dictionary* London

Bottéro J., Kramer S.N. 1989 *Lorsque les dieux faisaient l'homme: mythologie mésopotamienne* Paris

Clark R.T. Rundle 1959 *Myth and Symbol in Ancient Egypt* (repr. 1978) London

Frankfort H. 1948 *Kingship and the Gods: a study of ancient Near Eastern religion as the integration of society and nature* (repr. 1978) Chicago

Frymer-Kensky T. 1992 *In the Wake of the Goddesses: women, culture and the biblical transformation of pagan myth* New York

Hornung E. 1983 *Conceptions of God in Ancient Egypt* (trans.) London

Jacobsen T. 1976 *The Treasures of Darkness: a history of Mesopotamian religion* New Haven, Conn.

Leick G. 1991 *A Dictionary of Ancient Near Eastern Mythology* London

Lurker M. 1980 *The Gods and Symbols of Ancient Egypt* London

McCall H. 1990 *Mesopotamian Myths* London

Thomas A.P. 1986 *Egyptian Gods and Myths* (Shire Egyptology) Aylesbury

M Art

Amiet P. 1980 *Art of the Ancient Near East* New York

Collon D. 1987 *First Impressions: cylinder seals in the ancient Near East* London

Frankfort H. 1954 *The Art and Architecture of the Ancient Orient* (rev. edn 1975) Harmondsworth

Gunter A. (ed.) 1990 *Investigating Artistic Environments in the Ancient Near East* Washington DC

Leick G. 1988 *A Dictionary of Ancient Near Eastern Architecture* London

Moortgat A. 1984 *Die Kunst des alten Mesopotamien* (rev. edn, 2 vols) Cologne

Muscarella O. 1988 *Bronze and Iron: ancient Near Eastern artefacts in the Metropolitan Museum of Art* New York

Orthmann W. 1975 *Der Alte Orient* (Propyläen Kunstgeschichte 14; repr. 1988) Berlin

Robins G. 1986 *Egyptian Painting and Relief* (Shire Egyptology) Aylesbury

Seton-Williams V. 1981 *Babylonia: treasures from Mesopotamia* Luxembourg

Stevenson Smith W. 1958 *The Art and Architecture of Ancient Egypt* (rev. edn 1965) Harmondsworth

Strommenger E., Hirmer M. 1965 *The Art of Ancient Mesopotamia* (trans.) London

N Geography and economy

Beaumont P., Blake G.H., Wagstaff J.M. 1976 *The Middle East: a geographical study* Chichester
Bulletin on Sumerian Agriculture Cambridge (1986-)
Bulliet R. 1990 *The Camel and the Wheel* (rev. edn) New York
Oates J. (ed.) 1993 *Ancient Trade: New Perspectives* (= *World Archaeology* 24/3)
Silver M. 1985 *Economic Structures of the Ancient Near East* London

O Some chronological debates

Aström P. (ed.) 1987–9 *High, Middle or Low? Acts of an International Colloquium on Absolute Chronology Held at the University of Gothenburg, 20th-22nd August, 1987* Gothenburg
Bietak M. (ed.) 1992 *High, Middle or Low? Acts of the Second International Colloquium on Absolute Chronology: the Bronze Age in the Eastern Mediterranean* Vienna
Ehrich R.W. (ed.) 1992 *Chronologies in Old World Archaeology* (3rd rev. edn, 2 vols) Chicago
Gates M.-H.C. 1981 *Alalakh Levels VI and V: a chronological reassessment* (Syro-Mesopotamian Studies 4/2) Malibu, Cal.
Huber P.J. 1982 'Astronomical dating of Babylon I and Ur III' *Occasional Papers on the Near East* 1/4 Malibu, Cal.: 107–199
Na'aman N. 1984 'Statements of time-spans by Babylonian and Assyrian kings and Mesopotamian chronology' *Iraq* 46: 115–124

P The Neolithic background

Dixon J.E., Cann J.R., Renfrew C. 1972 'Obsidian and the origins of trade' *Old World Archaeology: foundations of civilization* (Readings from the *Scientific American*) San Francisco: 80–88
Kenyon K. 1972 'Ancient Jericho' *Old World Archaeology: foundations of civilization* (Readings from the *Scientific American*) San Francisco: 89–94
Mellaart J. 1967 *Çatal Hüyük: a neolithic town in Anatolia* (New Aspects of Antiquity) London
—— 1975 *The Neolithic of the Near East* London
McNairn B. 1980 *The Method and Theory of V. Gordon Childe: economic, social, and cultural interpretations of prehistory* Edinburgh
Oates D. and J. 1976 *The Rise of Civilization* Oxford
Unger-Hamilton R.J.S. 1985 *Method in Micro-ware Analysis: sickles and other tools from Arjoune, Syria* (London, diss.)

Q Specialist encyclopaedias

Encyclopedia of Archaeological Excavations in the Holy Land (eds M. Avi-Yonah and E. Stern; 4 vols) Oxford 1975–8
Lexikon der Ägyptologie (Hsg. W. Helck *et al.*; 6 vols) Wiesbaden 1975–86
The New Encyclopedia of Archaeological Excavations in the Holy Land (ed. E. Stern) New York 1993
Reallexikon der Assyriologie (Hsg. D.O. Edzard *et al.*) Berlin 1928- (in progress)

For complete lists of standard abbreviations and conventions see Borger R. 1968–75
  Handbuch der Keilschriftliteratur Berlin
Chicago Assyrian Dictionary Chicago 1964– (in progress)
Hornung E. 1967 *Einführung in die Ägyptologie* Darmstadt
Lexikon der Ägyptologie Wiesbaden 1975–1986

Chapter 1

General

Liverani 1988 [OC], chs 4–9; *CAH* I, chs 12, 13, 16, 17, 19, 22; Bottéro *et al.* 1967a
  [OB], chs 1–4; Oates and Oates 1976 [OP]); Oates 1986 [OGb], chs 1–2; Klengel *et
  al.* 1989 [OC]: 36–143
and (details below)
Crawford 1991; Hauptman and Waetzoldt 1988; Kramer 1956; Liverani 1993;
  Matthiae 1989; Nissen 1988; Postgate 1992; Schmandt-Besserat 1976

References

Adams R.McC. 1966 *The Evolution of Urban Society: early Mesopotamia and
  prehispanic Mexico* Chicago
—— 1981 *Heartland of Cities: surveys of ancient settlement and landuse in the central
  floodplain of the Euphrates* Chicago
Alberti A., Pomponio F. 1986 *Pre-Sargonic and Sargonic Texts from Ur edited in
  UET 2, Supplement* (Studia Pohl, Series Maior 13) Rome
Al-Fouadi A.H. 1976 'Bassetki statue with an Old Akkadian royal inscription of
  Naram-Sîn of Agade' *Sumer* 32: 63–75
Algaze G. 1993 *The Uruk World System: the dynamics of expansion of early
  Mesopotamian civilization* Chicago
Alster B. 1974 *The Instructions of Shuruppak to his son Ziusudra* (Mesopotamia 2)
  Copenhagen
Amiet P. 1976 *Art d'Agadé au Musée du Louvre* Paris
—— 1980 'The mythological repertoire in cylinder seals of the Agade period' in
  Porada E. (ed.) *Ancient Art in Seals* Princeton, NJ: 35–53
Asher-Grève J. 1985 *Frauen in altsumerischer Zeit* Malibu, Cal.
Becker A. 1985 'Neusumerische Renaissance? Wissenschaftsgeschichtliche Unter-
  suchungen zur Philologie und Archäologie' *BaM* 16: 30–316
Berlin A. 1983 'Ethnopoetry and epics of the Enmerkar cycle' in Kramer Studies [OE]:
  17–24
Biggs R.D. 1974 *Inscriptions from Tell Abu Salabikh* (OIP 99) Chicago
Buccellati G.G. 1966 *The Amorites of the Ur III Period* Naples
Carter and Stolper 1984 [chapter 7]
Charvát P. 1978 'The growth of Lugalzagesi's empire' in Hruška B., Komoróczy G.
  (eds) *Festschrift für L. Matouš* Budapest: 43–49
Civil M. 1987 'Ur III bureaucracy: quantitative aspects' in Gibson and Biggs [OE]:
  35–44
Cohen S. 1973 *Enmerkar and the Lord of Aratta* (Univ. of Penn. diss.)
Cooper J.S. 1973 'Sumerian and Akkadian in Sumer and Akkad' *Or.* 42: 239–246
—— 1980 'Apodotic Death and the historicity of "historical" omens' in Alster [OE]:
  99–105
—— 1983a *The Curse of Agade* Baltimore

—— 1983b *Reconstructing History from Ancient Inscriptions: the Lagash-Umma border conflict* (Sources from the Ancient Near East 2/1) Malibu, Cal.

—— 1986 *Sumerian and Akkadian Royal Inscriptions* vol. 1: *Pre-Sargonic Inscriptions* (AOS Translation Series I) Winona Lake, IN

Cooper J., Heimpel W. 1983 'The Sumerian Sargon Legend' *JAOS* 103: 67–82

Crawford H.E.W. 1977 *The Architecture of Iraq in the Third Millennium* BC Copenhagen

—— 1991 *Sumer and the Sumerians* Cambridge

Deimel A. 1931 *Sumerische Tempelwirtschaft zur Zeit Urukaginas und seiner Vorgänger* Rome

Diakonoff I.M. 1959 *Structure of Society and State in Early Dynastic Sumer* (trans.; Monographs on the Ancient Near East I/3, 1974) Malibu, Cal.

—— 1971 'On the structure of Old Babylonian society' in Klengel H. (Hsg.) *Beiträge zur sozialen Struktur des alten Vorderasien* Berlin: 15–31

—— 1974 'Slaves, helots and serfs in early antiquity' *AAASH* 22: 45–78

Edzard D.O. 1968 *Sumerische Rechtsurkunden des III Jahrtausends aus der Zeit vor der III Dynastie von Ur* Munich

—— 1968–9 'Die Inschriften der altakkadischen Rollsiegel' *AfO* 22: 12–20

—— 1974 'Zum sumerischen Eid' *Sumerological Studies in Honor of Thorkild Jacobsen (AS 20) Chicago: 63–98*

Falkenstein A. 1936 *Archaische Texte aus Uruk* 1: *Archaische Texte aus Uruk* (ADFU 2) Berlin

—— 1954 'La cité-temple sumérienne' *Cahiers d'histoire mondiale* 1: 748–814 (= trans. *The Sumerian Temple City*; Monographs on the Ancient Near East I/1, Malibu, Cal.)

—— 1956–7 *Die neusumerischen Gerichtsurkunden* (Abhandlungen der Bayerischen Akademie der Wissenschaften 39, 40, 44) Munich

—— 1966 *Die Inschriften Gudeas von Lagash* (AnOr 30) Rome

Farber W. 1983 'Die Vergöttlichung Naram-Sins' *Or.* 62: 67–72

Finkelstein J.J. 1963 'Mesopotamian Historiography' *PAPHS* 107: 461–472

—— 1968–9 'The laws of Ur-Nammu' *JCS* 22: 66–82

Forest D. 1983 *Les pratiques funéraires en Mésopotamie du cinquième millénaire au début du troisième millénaire* Paris

Foster B. 1980 'Notes on Sargonic royal progress' *JANES* 12: 29–42

—— 1981 'A new look at the Sumerian temple state' *JESHO* 24: 225–234

—— 1982a *Administration and Use of Institutional Land in Sargonic Sumer* (Mesopotamia 9) Copenhagen

—— 1982b *Umma in the Sargonic Period* Hamden

—— 1985 'The Sargonic victory stele from Telloh' *Iraq* 47: 15–30

—— 1986 'Archives and empire in Sargonic Mesopotamia' in Veenhof [OE]: 46–52

Foxvog D. 1980 'Funerary furnishings in an early Sumerian text from Adab' in Alster [OE]: 67–75

Galter H. 1986 'Probleme historisch-lehrhafter Dichtung in Mesopotamien' in Hecker and Sommerfeld [OJ]: 71–80

Gelb I.J. 1961 *Old Akkadian Writing and Grammar* (MAD 2) Chicago

—— 1965 'The ancient Mesopotamian ration system' *JNES* 24: 230–243

—— 1969 'On the alleged temple and state economies in ancient Mesopotamia' *Studi in Onore di Edoardo Volterra* vol. 6, Rome: 137–154

—— 1977 *Thoughts about Ibla* (Syro-Mesopotamian Studies I/1) Malibu, Cal.

—— 1979a 'Definition and discussion of slavery and serfdom' *UF* 11: 283–297

—— 1979b 'Household and family in early Mesopotamia' in Lipiński [OE] I: 1–97

Gelb I.J., Kienast B. 1990 *Die altakkadischen Königsinschriften des dritten Jahrtausends v.Chr.* (FAOS 7) Freiburg-im-Breisgau

Glassner J.-J. 1985 'Aspects du don de l'échange et formes d'appropriation du sol dans la Mésopotamie du IIIe millénaire avant la fondation de l'empire d'Ur' *JA* 173: 11–59

—— 1986 *La chute d'Akkadé: l'événement et sa mémoire* (Beiträge zum Vorderen Orient 5) Berlin

—— 1988 'Le récit autobiographique de Sargon' *RA*: 1–11

Goodnick-Westenholz J. 1983 'Heroes of Akkad' *JAOS* 103: 327–336

Green M.W. 1980 'Animal husbandry at Uruk in the archaic period' *JNES* 39: 1–35

Green M.W., Nissen H.J. 1987 *Archaische Texte aus Uruk 2: Zeichenliste der archaischen Texte aus Uruk* (ADFU 11) Berlin

Güterbock H.G. 1934/1938 'Die historische Tradition und ihre literarische Gestaltung bei Babyloniern und Hethitern' *ZA* 42: 1–91; 44: 45–119

Hallo W.W. 1960 'A Sumerian amphictyony' *JCS* 14: 88–114

—— 1963 'Royal hymns and Mesopotamian unity' *JCS* 17: 112–118

—— 1966 'The coronation of Ur-Nammu' *JCS* 20: 133–141

—— 1971 'Gutium' *RLA* 3: 708–720

—— 1974 'Toward a history of Sumerian literature' *Sumerological Studies in Honor of Thorkild Jacobsen* (AS 20) Chicago: 181–203

—— 1976 'Women of Sumer' in Schmandt-Besserat 1976: 23–40

—— 1983 'Sumerian historiography' in Tadmor and Weinfeld [OK]: 9–20

Hallo W.W., van Dijk J.J. 1968 *The Exaltation of Inanna* (YNER 3) New Haven, Conn.

Hansen D.P. 1963 'New votive plaques from Nippur' *JNES* 22: 145–166

—— 1992 'Royal building activity at Sumerian Lagash in the Early Dynastic period' *BibArch* 55: 206–211

Hauptman H., Waetzoldt H. (Hsg.) 1988 *Wirtschaft und Gesellschaft von Ebla* Heidelberg

Helbaek H. 1972 'Samarran irrigation agriculture at Choga Mami in Iraq' *Iraq* 34: 35–48

Hirsch H. 1963 'Die Inschriften der Könige von Agade' *AfO* 20: 1–82

Huot J.-L. 1991 *'Oueili: travaux de 1985* Paris

—— 1992 'The first farmers at 'Oueili' *BibArch* 55: 188–195

Jacobsen T. 1939a 'The assumed conflict between Semites and Sumerians' *JAOS* 59: 485–495 (repr. in Jacobsen 1970 [OE]: 187–192)

—— 1939b *The Sumerian King List* (AS 11) Chicago

—— 1943 'Primitive democracy in ancient Mesopotamia' *JNES* 2: 159–172 (repr. in Jacobsen 1970 [OE]: 157–172)

—— 1953 'The reign of Ibbi-Suen' *JCS* 7: 36–47 (repr. in Jacobsen 1970 [OE]: 173–186)

—— 1957 'Early political development in Mesopotamia' *ZA* 52: 91–140 (repr. in Jacobsen 1970 [OE]: 132–156)

—— 1982 *Salinity and Irrigation Agriculture in Antiquity* (Bibliotheca Mesopotamica 14) Malibu, Cal.

Johansen F. 1978 *Statues of Gudea, Ancient and Modern* (Mesopotamia 6) Copenhagen

Jones T.B. (ed.) 1969 *The Sumerian Problem* New York

—— 1974 'Sumerian administrative documents: an essay' *Sumerological Studies in Honor of Thorkild Jacobsen* (AS 20) Chicago: 41–61

Kang S. 1972 *Sumerian Economic Texts from the Drehem Archive* Urbana, Ill.

—— 1973 *Sumerian Economic Texts from the Umma Archive* Urbana, Ill.

Kärki I. 1986 *Die Königsinschriften der dritten Dynastie von Ur* Helsinki

Katz D. 1987 'Gilgamesh and Akka: was Uruk ruled by two assemblies?' *RA* 81: 105–114

Keiser C.E. 1971 *Neo-Sumerian Account Texts from Drehem* New Haven, Conn.

King L.W. 1907 *Chronicles Concerning Early Babylonian Kings* London

Klein J. 1981a *The Royal Hymns of Shulgi, King of Ur* (= *TAPhA* 71/VII)

—— 1981b *Three Shulgi Hymns: Sumerian royal hymns glorifying King Shulgi of Ur* Ramat Gan

Kramer S.N. 1940 *Lamentation over the Destruction of Ur* Chicago

—— 1956 *From the Tablets of Sumer* (= *History Begins at Sumer*) (new edn) Philadelphia, Penn.

—— 1967 'The death of Ur-Nammu' *JCS* 21: 104–122

—— 1983a *Le Mariage Sacré* (trans. with additions) Paris

—— 1983b 'The Ur-Nammu Law Code: who was its author?' *Or.* 52: 453–456

Kutscher R. 1989 *The Brockman Tablets: royal inscriptions* Haifa

Lambert M. 1953 'Textes commerciaux de Lagash (époque présargonique)' *RA* 47: 57–69

Lees G.M., Falcon N.L. 1952 'The geographical history of the Mesopotamian plain' *Geographical Journal* 118: 24–39

Lewis B. 1980 *The Sargon Legend: a study of the Akkadian text and the tale of the hero who was exposed at birth* Cambridge, Mass.

Limet H. 1960 *Le travail du métal au pays de Sumer* Paris

Liverani M. (ed.) 1993 *Akkad, the First World Empire: structure, ideology, traditions* (History of the Ancient Near East/Studies 5) Padua

Maisels C. 1990 *The Emergence of Civilization: from hunting and gathering to agriculture, cities and the state in the Near East* London

Mallowan M.E.L. 1946 'Excavations in the Balikh Valley' *Iraq* 8: 111–159

Malul M. 1985 'The *bukannum*–clause – relinquishment of rights by previous right holder' *ZA* 75: 66–77

—— 1987 'To drive in the nail' *OA* 26: 17–35

Martin H.P. 1988 *Fara: a reconstruction of the ancient Mesopotamian city of Shurruppak* Birmingham

Matthiae P. 1989 *Ebla: un impero ritrovato dai primi scavi alle ultime scoperte* (rev. edn) Turin

Michalowski P. 1975 'The bride of Simanum' *JAOS* 95: 716–719

—— 1980a 'Königsbriefe' *RLA* 6: 57–59

—— 1980b 'New sources concerning the reign of Naram-Sin' *JCS* 32: 233–246

—— 1983 'History as charter: more observations on the Sumerian King List' *JAOS* 103: 237–248

—— 1985 'Third millennium contacts: observations on the relationships between Mari and Ebla' *JAOS* 105: 293–302

—— 1987 'Charisma and control: on continuity and change in early Mesopotamian bureaucratic systems' in Gibson and Biggs [OE]: 45–57

—— 1989 *The Lamentation over the Destruction of Sumer and Ur* (Mesopotamian Civilization 1) Winona Lake, IN.

Moorey P.R.S. 1977 'What do we know about the people buried in the Royal Cemetery?' *Expedition* 20/1: 24–40

—— 1984 'Where did they bury the kings of the Third Dynasty of Ur?' *Iraq* 46: 1–18

Muhly 1983 [chapter 2]

Nissen H.J. 1988 *The Early History of the Ancient Near East 9000–2000* BC (trans; rev. edn) Chicago

Oates J. 1960 'Ur and Eridu, the prehistory' in Mallowan M.E.L., Wiseman D.J. (eds) *Ur in Retrospect* (= *Iraq* 22) London: 32–50

Pollock S. 1991 'Of priestesses, princes and poor relations: the dead in the royal cemetery of Ur' *Cambridge Archaeological Journal* 1/2: 171–189

Pomponio F. 1983 'Archives and the prosopography of Fara' *ActSum* 5: 127–145
—— 1984 'Urukagina 4 VII 11 and an administrative term from the Ebla texts' *JCS* 36: 96–100
Postgate J.N. 1992 *Early Mesopotamia* London
Powell M.A. 1977 'Sumerian merchants and the problem of profit' *Iraq* 39: 23–29
—— 1978 'A contribution to the history of money in Mesopotamia prior to the invention of coinage' in Hruška B., Komoróczy G. (eds) *Festschrift für L. Matouš* Budapest, II: 211–243
—— 1985 'Salt, seed and yields in Sumerian agriculture: a critique of the theory of progressive salinisation' *ZA* 75: 7–38
Redman C. 1978 *The Rise of Civilization: from early farmers to urban society in the ancient Near East* San Francisco
Römer W.H.Ph. 1980 *Das sumerische Kurzepos 'Bilgamesh und Akka'* Neukirchen-Vluyn
Sanlaville P. 1989 'Considerations sur l'évolution de la basse Mésopotamie au cours des derniers millénaires' *Paléorient* 15/2: 5–27
Schmandt-Besserat D. (ed.) 1976 *The Legacy of Sumer* (Bibliotheca Mesopotamica 4) Malibu, Cal.
—— 1977 'An archaic recording system and the origins of writing' *Syro-Mesopotamian Studies* I/2: 1–32
—— 1983 'Tokens and Counting' *BibArch* 46: 117–120
—— 1992 *Before Writing* I: *from counting to cuneiform* Austin, Texas
Sigrist M. 1993 *Drehem* Bethesda, MD
Sjöberg A. 1974 'The Old Babylonian Eduba' in *Sumerological Studies in Honor of Thorkild Jacobsen* (AS 20) Chicago: 159–179
Sjöberg A., Bergman E. 1969 *The Collection of Sumerian Temple Hymns* and Gragg G. *The Keš Temple Hymn* (both in TCS 3) Locust Valley, NY
Sollberger E. 1954–6 'Sur la chronologie des rois d'Ur et quelques problèmes connexes' *AfO* 17: 10–48
Sollberger E., Grayson A.K. 1976 'L'insurrection générale contre Naram-Suen' *RA* 70: 103–128
Sollberger E., Kupper J.R. 1971 *Inscriptions royales sumériennes et akkadiennes* (LAPO 3) Paris
Steible H. 1991 *Die Neusumerischen Bau- und Weihinschriften* (Teil 2, FAOS 9/2) Stuttgart
Steible H., Behrens H. 1982 *Die altsumerischen Bau- und Weihinschriften* (2 Teile; FAOS 5) Wiesbaden
Steinkeller P. 1987a 'The administrative and economic organisation of the Ur III state: the core and the periphery' in Gibson and Biggs [0E]: 19–42
—— 1987b 'The foresters of Umma: toward a definition of Ur III labor' in Powell [0E]: 73–115
—— 1988 'On the identity of the toponym LÚ.SU(A)' *JAOS* 108: 197–202
—— 1989 *Sale Documents of the Ur III Period* (FAOS 17) Stuttgart
Strommenger E. 1960 'Das Menschenbild in der altmesopotamischen Rundplastik von Mesilim bis Hammurapi' *BaM* 1: 1–103
—— 1980 *Habuba Kabira: eine Stadt vor 5000 Jahren* Mainz
Tunca Ö. 1986 'Le problème des archives dans l'architecture religieuse proto-dynastique' in Veenhof [0E]: 37–45
Uchitel A. 1984 'Daily work at Sagdana millhouse' *ActSum* 6: 75–98
van de Mierop M. 1989 'Women in the economy of Sumer' in Lesko [0E]: 53–66
Waetzold H. 1972 *Untersuchungen zur neusumerischen Textilienindustrie* Rome
—— 1987 'Compensation of craft workers and officials in the Ur III period' in Powell [0E]: 117–142

Weiss H., Young T.C. 1975 'The merchants of Susa: plateau-lowland relations in the late fourth millennium BC' *Iran* 13: 1–18

Westenholz A. 1979 'The Old Akkadian empire in contemporary opinion' in Larsen [OE]: 107–123

Winter I.J. 1985 'After the battle is over: the stele of the vultures and the beginning of pictorial narrative in the art of the ancient Near East' in Kessler H.L., Simpson M.S. (eds) *Pictorial Narrative in Antiquity and the Middle Ages* (Studies in the History of Art 16) Washington: 11–32

—— 1986 'The king and the cup: iconography of the royal presentation scene on Ur III seals' in *Insight through Images: studies in honor of Edith Porada* (Bibliotheca Mesopotamica 21) Malibu, Cal.: 253–268

—— 1987a 'Legitimation and authority through image and legend: seals belonging to officials in the administrative bureaucracy of the Ur III state' in Gibson and Biggs [OE]: 69–116

—— 1987b 'Women in public: the disc of Enheduanna, the beginning of the office of *EN*-priestess and the weight of visual evidence' in Durand [OE]: 189–201

Woolley C.L. 1934 *Ur Excavations 2: The Royal Cemetery* (2 vols) London

—— 1954 *Excavations at Ur* (2nd edn) London

—— 1982 *Ur of the Chaldees: the final account* (ed. P.R.S. Moorey) London

Yıldız F. 1981 'A tablet of Codex Ur-Nammu from Sippar' *Or.* 50: 87–97

Zettler R. 1984 'The genealogy of the House of Ur-me-me: a second look' (app. by M.T. Roth) *AfO* 31: 1–14

Chapter 2

General

CAH I, ch. 22; II, chs 1, 2, 5, 7; Bottéro *et al.* 1967a [OB], ch. 5; Liverani 1988 [OC], chs 10–14; Oates 1986 [OGb], chs 2–3; Klengel *et al.* 1989 [OC]: 163–218; Klengel 1992 [OGc], ch. 2.
and (details below)
Charpin 1992; Dalley 1984; Edzard 1957; Larsen 1976; Malamat 1992; Postgate 1992.
(The Mari texts are published (in transliteration, translation and with extensive commentary) in the series ARM (= Archives Royales de Mari), in progress. The main results of current research on Mari are published in the journal *MARI* (= *Mari: Annales de Recherches Interdisciplinaires*). For more details, see J.-G. Hintz 1990 *Bibliographie de Mari: archéologie et textes (1933–1988)* Wiesbaden; Klengel 1992 [OGc]: 46–47.)

References

Abdallah F. 1985 *Les relations internationales entre le royaume d'Alep/Yamhad et les villes de Syrie du Nord, 1800 à 1594 av. J.-C.* Paris

Alp S. 1968 *Zylinder- und Stempelsiegel aus Karahüyük-Konya* Ankara

Anbar M. 1991 *Les Tribus Ammorites de Mari* (OBO 108) Freiburg, Göttingen

Andrae W. 1938 *Das wiedererstandene Assur* Leipzig (rev. enlarged edn by B. Hrouda, Munich 1977)

Aynard J., Spycket A. 1989 'Mari B. Archäologisch' *RLA* 7: 390–418

Baqir T. 1959 *Tell Harmal* Baghdad

Batto, B.F. 1974 *Studies on Women at Mari* Baltimore, MD

Belli O. 1991 'The problem of tin deposits in Anatolia and its needs for tin according to the written sources' in Çilingiroğlu A., French D.H. (eds) *Anatolian Iron Ages*

(Proceedings of the Second Anatolian Iron Age Colloquium held Izmir, 4–8 May 1987: British School of Archaeology at Ankara Monographs 13) Oxford: 1–9

Bittel 1970 [chapter 5]

Bottéro J. 1981 'L'ordalie en Mésopotamie ancienne' *ASNP* III/11: 1005–1067

Charpin D. 1986 *Le clergé d'Ur au temps d'Hammurabi XIXe–XVIIIe siècle av. J.-C.* Geneva

—— 1987 'Le rôle économique du palais en Babylonie sous Hammurabi et ses successeurs' in Lévy E. (ed) *Le système palatial en Orient, en Grèce et à Rome* Strasbourg: 111–126

—— 1992 'Mari entre l'est et l'ouest: politique, culture, religion' *Akkadica* 78: 1–10

Charpin D., Durand J.-M. 1984 'La prise du pouvoir par Zimri-Lim' *MARI* 4: 293–343

Charpin D., Joannès F., Lackenbacher S., Lafont B. 1988 *Archives épistolaires de Mari* I/2 (ARM XXVI) Paris

Dalley S. 1984 *Mari and Karana: two Old Babylonian cities* London

Dalley S., Hawkins J.D., Walker C. 1976 *The Old Babylonian Tablets from Tell al-Rimah* London

Diakonoff 1971 [chapter 1]

Dossin G. 1938 'Les archives épistolaires du palais de Mari' *Syria* 19: 105–126

—— 1970 'La route de l'étain en Mésopotamie au temps de Zimrilim' *RA* 64: 97–106

Durand J.-M. 1987 'L'organisation de l'espace dans le palais de Mari: le témoignage des textes' in Lévy E. (ed) *Le système palatial en Orient, en Grèce et à Rome* Strasbourg: 39–110

—— 1988 *Archives épistolaires de Mari* I/1 (ARM XXVI) Paris

Edzard D.O. 1957 *Die Zweite Zwischenzeit Babyloniens* Wiesbaden

Eidem J. 1985 'News from the eastern front: the evidence from Tell Shemshara' *Iraq* 47: 83–107

—— 1992 *The Shemshara Archives* 2: *The Administrative Texts* Copenhagen

Finkelstein J. 1961 'Ammisaduqa's Edict and the Babylonian "Law Codes"' *JCS* 15: 91–104

—— 1965 'Some new *misharum* material and its implications' *Landsberger Studies* [OE]: 223–246

—— 1966 'The geneaology of the Hammurapi dynasty' *JCS* 20: 95–118

Frayne D.R. 1990 *Old Babylonian Period (2003–1595* BC*)* (RIM, Early Periods 4) Toronto

Garelli P. 1963 *Les Assyriens en Cappadoce* Paris

Gates M.-H. 1984 'The Palace of Zimrilim at Mari' *BibArch* 47: 70–87

Gelb I.J. 1935 *Inscriptions from Alishar and Vicinity* Chicago

—— 1977 [chapter 1]

Grayson A.K. 1971 'The early development of the Assyrian monarchy' *UF* 3: 311–319

—— 1972 *Assyrian Royal Inscriptions* vol. I Wiesbaden

—— 1976 [chapter 7]

—— 1987 *Assyrian Rulers of the Third and Second Millennia BC* (RIM, Assyrian Periods 1) Toronto

Greengus A. 1966 'Old Babylonian marriage ceremonies and rites' *JCS* 20: 55–72

—— 1988 Review of Kraus 1984, *JAOS* 108: 153–157

Hallo W.W. 1964 'The road to Emar' *JCS* 18: 57–88

Harris R. 1975 *Ancient Sippar* Leiden

—— 1989 'Independent women in ancient Mesopotamia?' in Lesko 1989 [OE]: 145–156

Hecker K. 1980 'Der Weg nach Kaniš' *ZA* 70: 185–197

Hrouda B. 1977–87 *Isin-Išan Bahriyat* I-III *(Ergebnisse der Ausgrabungen 1973–1978; 1983–4)* (Bayerische Akademie der Wissenschaften, phil.-hist. Kl. Abh. (NF) Heft 79; 87; 94) Munich

Jeyes U. 1980 'The act of extispicy in ancient Mesopotamia: an outline' *Assyriological Miscellanies* I: 13–32
—— 1983 'The *nadītu* women of Sippar' in Cameron and Kuhrt [OE]: 260–272
—— 1989 *Old Babylonian Extispicy: omen texts in the British Museum* Istanbul
Kärki I. 1984 'Die sumerischen und akkadischen Königsinschriften der altbaby-lonischen Zeit, II. Babylon' *Studia Orientalia* 55: 37–94
al-Khalesi Y.M. 1978 *The Court of the Palms: a functional interpretation of the Mari palace* (Bibliotheca Mesopotamica 8) Malibu, Cal.
Klengel H. 1965–70 *Geschichte Syriens im 2. Jahrtausend v.u.Z.* (3 vols) Berlin
Kramer 1940 [chapter 1]
—— 1969 'Lamentation over the destruction of Nippur: a preliminary report' *EI* 9: 89–93
Kraus F.R. 1951 *Nippur und Isin nach altbabylonischen Rechtsurkunden* (= *JCS* 3)
—— 1958 *Ein Edikt des Königs Ammisaduqa von Babylon* Leiden
—— 1979 '"Der Palast", Produzent und Unternehmer im Königreiche Babylon nach Hammurabi (ca. 1750–1600 v. Chr.)' in Lipiński [OE]: 423–434
—— 1984 *Königliche Verfügungen in altbabylonischer Zeit* Leiden
Kupper J.R. (ed.) 1967 *La Civilisation de Mari* Liège
—— 1989 'Mari A. Philologisch' *RLA* 7: 382–390
Laessøe J. 1959 *The Shemshara Tablets: a preliminary report* Copenhagen
—— 1965 'IM 62100: a letter from Tell Shemshara' *Landsberger Studies* [OE]: 189–196
Landsberger B. 1940 'Vier Urkunden von Kültepe' *TTAED* 4: 7ff.
—— 1954 'Assyrische Königsliste und "dunkles Zeitalter"' *JCS* 8: 31–45; 47–73; 106–133
—— 1965 'Tin and lead: the adventures of two vocables' *JNES* 24: 285–296
Landsberger B., Balkan K. 1950 'Die Inschriften des altassyrischen Königs Irishum, gefunden in Kültepe 1948' *Belleten* 14: 219–268
Larsen M.T. 1967 *Old Assyrian Caravan Procedures* Istanbul
—— 1976 *The Old Assyrian City-State and Its Colonies* (Mesopotamia 4) Copenhagen
—— 1987 'Commercial networks in the ancient Near East' in Rowlands *et al.* [OE]: 47–56
Leemans W.F. 1950 *The Old Babylonian Merchant: his business and social position* Leiden
—— 1960 *Foreign Trade in the Old Babylonian Period* Leiden
—— 1968 'Old Babylonian letters and economic history' *JESHO* 11: 171–226
Luke J.T. 1965 *Pastoralism and Pastoralists in the Mari Period: re-examination of the character and political significance of the major West-Semitic groups on the Middle Euphrates c.1828–1758* (Chicago, diss.)
Malamat A. 1983 'Silver, gold and precious stones from Hazor in a new Mari document' *BibArch* 46: 169–174
—— 1992 *Mari and the Early Israelite Experience* (Schweich Lectures 1984) Oxford
Malul M. 1989 '*Susapinnu*: the Mesopotamian paranymph and his role' *JESHO* 32: 241–278
Margueron J.L. 1982 *Recherches sur les Palais Mésopotamiens de l'Age du Bronze* Paris
Matthews V.H. 1978 *Pastoral Nomadism in the Mari Kingdom* Philadelphia, Penn.
Matthiae P. 1984 'New discoveries at Ebla: the excavations of the western palace and the royal necropoleis of the Amorite period' *BibArch* 47: 18–32
Mellaart J. 1957 'Anatolian chronology: the Early and Middle Bronze Age' *AnSt* 7: 55–88
Michalowski 1983 [chapter 1]
—— 1989 [chapter 1]
Moorey P.R.S. 1986 'The emergence of the light, horse-drawn chariot in the Near

East *c.* 2000–1500 BC' *World Archaeology* 18/2 (Weaponry and Warfare): 196–215

Morris 1992 [chapter 8]

Muhly J.D. 1973 *Copper and Tin* New Haven, Conn.

—— 1983 'Kupfer. Archäologisch' *RLA* 6: 348–364

—— 1985 'Sources of tin and the beginning of bronze metallurgy' *AJA* 89: 275–291

—— 1993 'Early Bronze Age tin and the Taurus' *AJA* 97: 239–253

Muhly J.D., Wertime T. 1973 'Evidence for the sources and use of tin during the Bronze Age of the Near East: a reply to J.E. Dayton' *World Archaeology* 5: 111–122

Munn-Rankin M. 1956 'Diplomacy in western Asia in the early second millennium BC' *Iraq* 18: 68–110

Oppenheim A.L. 1954 'The sea-faring merchants of Ur' *JAOS* 74: 6–17

Orlin L.L. 1970 *Assyrian Colonies in Cappadocia* The Hague

Özgüç N. 1968 *Seals and Seal Impressions of Level Ib from Karum Kanish* Ankara

—— 1980 'Seal impressions from the palace at Acemhöyük' in Porada E. (ed.) *Ancient Art in Seals* Princeton, N.J.: 61–100

Özgüç T. 1959 *Kültepe-Kaniš I: new researches at the center of the Assyrian trade colonies* Ankara

—— 1963 'An Assyrian trading outpost' *Scientific American* (February; reprinted in *Old World Archaeology: Readings from Scientific American*, San Francisco: 243–249)

—— 1986 *Kültepe-Kaniš II: new researches at the trading center of the ancient Near East* Ankara

Petschow H. 1984 'Die §§45 und 46 des Codex Hammurapi' *ZA* 74:181–212

Postgate 1992 [chapter 1]

Powell M. 1977 [chapter 1]

Ries G. 1989 'Altbabylonische Beweisurteile' *ZSS* 106: 56–80

Römer W. 1965 *Sumerische 'Königshymnen' der Isin-Zeit* Leiden

Rouault O. 1984 *Terqa Final Reports no. 1 – L'archive de Puzurum* (Bibliotheca Mesopotamica 16) Malibu, Cal.

Sasson J.M. 1969 *The Military Establishments at Mari* Rome

Sjöberg 1974 [chapter 1]

Stech T., Pigot V.C. 1986 'The metals trade in southwest Asia in the third millennium BC' *Iraq* 48: 39–64

Steele F.R. 1948 *The Code of Lipit-Ishtar* Philadelphia, Penn.

Steible H. 1975 *Rimsîn, mein König: drei kultische Texte aus Ur mit der Schlussdoxologie ᵈri-im-ᵈSîn lugal-mu* (FAOS 1) Wiesbaden

Stol M. 1976 *Studies in Old Babylonian History* Leiden

Stone E. 1977 'Economic crisis and social upheaval in Old Babylonian Nippur' in Young T.C., Levine L.D. (eds) *Mountains and Lowlands: essays in the archaeology of Greater Mesopotamia* (Bibliotheca Mesopotamica 7) Malibu, Cal.: 267–289

—— 1982 'The social role of the *nadītu* woman in Old Babylonian Nippur' *JESHO* 25: 50–70

—— 1987 *Nippur Neighborhoods* (SAOC 44) Chicago

Stone E., Zimansky P. 1992 'Mashkan-shapir and the anatomy of an Old Babylonian city' *BibArch* 55: 212–218

van de Mierop M. 1987 *Crafts in the Early Isin Period: a study of the Isin craft archive from the reign of Išbi-Erra and Šu-Ilišu* Leuven

van Dijk J. 1965 'Une insurrection générale au pays de Larsa avant l'avènement de Nuradad' *JCS* 19: 1–25

Vanstiphout H.L.J. 1983 'Een sumerische Stadsklacht uit de oudbabylonische periode: Turmenuna, of de Nippurklacht' in Veenhof [OI]: 330–341 (trans. based on unpublished text edn)

Veenhof K.R. 1972 *Aspects of Old Assyrian Trade and Its Terminology* Leiden
—— 1985 'Limu of the later Old Assyrian period and Mari chronology' *MARI* 4: 191–218
—— 1987 '"Dying tablets" and "hungry silver": elements of figurative language in Akkadian commercial terminology' in Mindlin M. *et al.* [OE]: 41–75
Walters S.D. 1970 *Water for Larsa: an Old Babylonian archive dealing with irrigation* (YNER 4) New Haven, Conn.
—— 1970/1 'The sorceress and her apprentice' *JCS* 23: 27–38
Weadock P.N. 1975 'The *giparu* at Ur' *Iraq* 37: 101–128
Weiss H. 1985 'Tell Leilan on the Habur Plain of Syria' *BibArch* 48: 5–34
Westbrook R. 1989 'Cuneiform law codes and the origins of legislation' *ZA* 79: 201–222
Woolley L. 1953 *A Forgotten Kingdom* London
Yaron R. 1969 *The Laws of Eshnunna* Jerusalem
Yoffee N. 1977 *The Economic Role of the Crown in the Old Babylonian Period* (Bibliotheca Mesopotamica 5) Malibu, Cal.
Yuhong W., Dalley S. 1990 'The origins of the Manana dynasty at Kish, and the Assyrian king list' *Iraq* 16: 159–165
Zaccagnini C. 1983 'On gift exchange in the Old Babylonian Period' in Carruba O., Liverani M., Zaccagnini C. (eds) *Studi Orientalistici in Ricordo di Franco Pintore* (Studia Mediterranea 4) Pavia: 189–253

Chapter 3

General

Trigger in Trigger *et al.* 1983 [OD]: 1–70; Kemp in Trigger *et al.* 1983 [OD]: 71–182; Kemp 1989 [0Ga], parts I and II; *CAH* I, chs 9a, 11, 14, 20; II, chs. 2, 3; Gardiner 1961 [OD], chs 5–7, 14–15; Helck 1968 [OD], chs 1–11; Drioton and Vandier 1984 [OD], chs 1–8; Bottéro *et al.* 1967a [OB], chs 6–11; Grimal 1992 [OD], parts 1–2 *and (details below)*
Aldred 1965; Bourriau 1988; Hayes 1953; Málek 1986; Quirke 1991; Redford 1992, part 1; Rice 1990; Spencer 1993; Trigger 1976; Winlock 1947

References

Adams B. 1988 *Predynastic Egypt* (Shire Egyptology) Aylesbury
Aldred C. 1950 *Middle Kingdom Art in Egypt 2300–1590* BC London
—— 1965 *Egypt to the end of the Old Kingdom* London
Arnold D. 1974 *Der Tempel des Königs Mentuhotep II von Deir el-Bahari* (2 vols) Mainz (trans. New York, 1979)
Baer K. 1960 *Rank and Title in the Old Kingdom* Chicago
Baines J. 1982 'Interpreting *Sinuhe*' *JEA* 68: 31–44
—— 1989 'Communication and display: the integration of early Egyptian art and writing' *Antiquity* 63: 471–482
Barta W. 1970 *Das Selbstzeugnins eines ägyptischen Künstlers (Stèle Louvre C14)* (Münchener Ägyptologische Studien 22) Berlin
—— 1981 'Chronologie der 1. bis 5. Dynastie' *ZÄS* 108: 11–23
Baumgartel E. 1955/1960 *The Cultures of Predynastic Egypt* Oxford
—— 1970 *Petrie's Naqada Excavations: a supplement* London
Beckerath J. von 1962 'The date of the end of the Old Kingdom' *JNES* 21 :140–147
—— 1966 'Die Dynastie der Herakleopoliten (9/10 Dynastie)' *ZÄS* 93: 13–20

—— 1984 *Untersuchungen zur politischen Geschichte der Zweiten Zwischenzeit in Ägypten* (2nd edn) Glückstadt

Bell B. 1971 'The Dark Ages in ancient history: 1. The first dark age in Egypt' *AJA* 75: 1–26

Ben-Tor A. 1992 'The Early Bronze Age' in *id.* (ed.) *The Archaeology of Ancient Israel* (trans.) New Haven, Conn.: 81–125

Bietak M. 1975 *Tell el-Daba* II Vienna

—— 1981 *Avaris and Piramesse: archaeological exploration in the eastern Nile Delta* London (= *Proceedings of the British Academy* 65 (1979): 225–290; rev. edn 1986)

—— 1987 'Canaanites in the Nile Delta' in Rainey A.F. (ed.) *Egypt, Israel, Sinai: archaeological and historical relationships in the biblical period* Tel Aviv: 41–56

—— 1992 'Minoan wall-paintings unearthed at ancient Avaris' *Egyptian Archaeology* 2: 26–28

Blackman A.M. 1932 *The Story of Sinuhe* (Bibliotheca Aegyptiaca II) Brussels

Bourriau J. 1988 *Pharaohs and Mortals: Egyptian art in the Middle Kingdom* Cambridge

—— in press 'Beyond Avaris: the Second Intermediate Period in Egypt outside the Delta' (paper given at a seminar in the University Museum, Philadelphia, Penn., on the theme '*The Culture of the Hyksos Period*', org. and ed. E. Oren)

Brunner H. 1937 *Die Texte aus den Gräbern der Herakleopolitenzeit von Siut* (Ägyptologische Forschungen 5) Glückstadt

Brunner-Traut E. 1940 'Die Lehre des Djedefre' *ZÄS* 76: 3–9

Butzer K.W. 1976 *Early Hydraulic Civilization in Egypt: a study in cultural ecology* (Prehistoric Archaeology and Ecology Series) Chicago

Dévaud E. 1916 *Les Maxims de Ptahhotep* Fribourg

Dever W. 1985 'Relations between Syria and Egypt: redating the Hyksos at ed-Daba' in Tubb J. (ed.) *Palestine in the Bronze and Iron Ages* London: 69–87

Dreyer G. 1993 'A hundred years at Abydos' *Egyptian Archaeology* 3: 10–12

Emery W.B. 1961 *Archaic Egypt* Harmondsworth

—— 1965 *Egypt in Nubia* London

Erman A. 1890 *Die Märchen des Papyrus Westcar* (Mitteilungen aus den Orientalischen Sammlungen 5–6) Berlin

Eyre C. 1987 'Work and organisation of work in the Old Kingdom' in Powell [0E]: 5–47

Fakhry A. 1972 'The search for texts in the western desert' *Textes et langages de l'Égypte pharaonique* II Cairo: 207–222

Faulkner R.O. 1972 *The Ancient Egyptian Pyramid Texts* Oxford

Franke D. 1985 'An important family from Abydos of the seventeenth dynasty' *JEA* 71: 175–176

—— 1991 'The career of Khnumhotpe III of Beni Hasan and the so-called "Decline of the Nomarchs"' in Quirke 1991: 51–67

Gardiner A.H. 1909 *The Admonitions of an Egyptian Sage* Leipzig

—— 1932 *Late Egyptian Stories* (Bibliotheca Aegyptiaca I) Brussels

—— 1946a 'Davies' copy of the great Speos Artemidos inscription' *JEA* 32: 43–56

—— 1946b 'The instructions addressed to Kagemni and his brethren' *JEA* 32: 71–74

—— 1957 *Egyptian Grammar* (3rd rev. edn) Oxford

—— 1959 *The Royal Canon of Turin* Oxford

Gardiner A.H., Peet T.E. 1952–5 *The Inscriptions of Sinai* (2 parts, rev. J. Černy) London

Gestermann L. 1987 *Kontinuität und Wandel in Politik und Verwaltung des frühen Mittleren Reiches* (Göttinger Orientforschung IV Reihe: Ägypten) Wiesbaden

Giddy L.L. 1987 *Egyptian Oases: Bahariya, Dakhla, Farafra and Kharga during pharaonic times* Warminster

Gödecken K. 1976 *Eine Betrachtung der Inschriften des Meten im Rahmen der sozialen und rechtlichen Stellung von Privatleuten im ägyptischen Alten Reich* (ÄgAbh 29) Wiesbaden

Goedicke H. 1960 *Die Stellung des Königs im Alten Reich* (ÄgAbh 2) Wiesbaden

—— 1967 *Königliche Dokumente aus dem Alten Reich* Wiesbaden

—— 1977 *The Prophecy of Neferty* Baltimore, MD

—— 1979 'Cult temple and "state" in Old Kingdom Egypt' in Lipiński [OE] I: 113–131

Grapow H. 1953 'Liederkranz' *MIO* 1: 189–209

Griffith F. Ll. 1896 'The Millingen papyrus' *ZÄS* 34: 35–51

—— 1898 *The Petrie Papyri: hieratic papyri from Kahun and Gurob* London

Habachi L. 1972 *The Second Stela of Kamose and His Struggle against the Hyksos Ruler and His Capital* Glückstadt

Hankey V. 1993 'Egypt, the Aegean and the Levant' *Egyptian Archaeology* 3: 27–29

Hayes W.C. 1947 'Horemkha'uef of Nekhen and his trip to It-towe' *JEA* 33: 3–11

—— 1953 *The Scepter of Egypt* vol. 1 New York

—— 1955 *A Papyrus of the Late Middle Kingdom in the Brooklyn Museum (Papyrus Brooklyn 35.1446)* Brooklyn, NY

Helck W. 1977 *Die Lehre für König Merikare* (Kleine Ägyptische Texte) Wiesbaden

Hintze F. 1964 'Das Kerma Problem' *ZÄS* 91: 79–86

Hoffman M. 1980 *Egypt before the Pharaohs: the prehistoric foundations of Egyptian civilization* London

James T.G.H. 1962 *The Hekanakhte Papers and Other Early Middle Kingdom Documents* New York

Janssen J.J. 1978 'The early state in Egypt' in Claessen H.J.M., Skalník P. (eds) *The Early State* The Hague: 213–234

Junge F. 1973 'Zur Fehldatierung des sogenannten Denkmals memphitischer Theologie oder: Der Beitrag der ägyptischen Theologie zur Geistesgeschichte der Spätzeit' *MDAIK* 29: 195–204

Junker H. 1941 *Die politische Lehre von Memphis* (APAW Phil.-hist. Kl. 6) Berlin

Kanawati N. 1977 *Egyptian Administration in the Old Kingdom* Warminster

—— 1980 *Governmental Reforms in Old Kingdom Egypt* Warminster

Kemp B. 1966 'Abydos and the royal tombs of the first dynasty' *JEA* 52: 13–22

Krauss R. 1985 *Sothis- und Monddaten: Studien zur astronomischen und technischen Chronologie Altägyptens* (Hildesheimer Ägyptologische Beiträge 20) Hildesheim

Lacovara P. 1990 *Deir el-Ballas: preliminary report on the Deir el-Ballas expedition 1980–1986* Winona Lake, IN

Lichtheim M. 1988 *Ancient Egyptian Autobiographies Chiefly of the Middle Kingdom: a study and an anthology* (OBO 84) Freiburg

Lloyd A.B. 1992 'The great inscription of Khnumhotpe II at Beni Hasan' in *id.* (ed.) *Studies in Pharaonic Religion and Society in Honour of J. Gwyn Griffiths* London: 21–36

Luft U. 1992 *Das Archiv von Illahun, Briefe 1* (Hieratische Papyri aus den Staatlichen Museen zu Berlin, Preussischer Kulturbesitz Lfg. 1) Berlin

Luria S. 1929 'Die Ersten werden die Letzten sein' *Klio* 22: 405–431

Málek J. 1982 'The original version of the royal canon of Turin' *JEA* 68: 93–106

—— 1986 *In the Shadow of the Pyramids: Egypt during the Old Kingdom* London

—— 1992 'The annals of Amenemhet II' *Egyptian Archaeology* 2: 18

Millet N.B. 1990 'The Narmer macehead and related objects' *JARCE* 27: 53–59

Mills A.J. 1980 'Dakhleh Oasis Project: report on the second season of survey, September–December 1979' *SSEA Journal* 10: 251–282

Montet P. 1933 'La stèle de l'an 400 retrouvée' *Kêmi* 4: 191–215

Moorey P.R.S. 1987 'On tracking cultural transfers in prehistory: the case of Egypt and lower Mesopotamia in the fourth millennium BC' in Rowlands *et al.* [OE]: 36–46

Newberry P.E. 1893 *Beni Hasan* I London

Niemeier W.D. 1991 'Minoan artisans travelling overseas: the Alalakh frescoes and the painted plaster floor at Tell Kabri (W. Galilee)' in Laffineur R., Basch L. (eds) *Thalassa: L'Égéé préhistorique et la mer* Liège: 189–202

Pardey E. Martin 1976 *Untersuchungen zur ägyptischen Provinzialverwaltung bis zum Ende des Alten Reiches* Hildesheim

—— 1989 'Die Verwaltung im Alten Reich' *BiOr* 46: 533–552

Parker R.A. 1950 *The Calendars of Ancient Egypt* Chicago

Parkinson R.B. 1991 *Voices from Ancient Egypt: an anthology of Middle Kingdom writings* London

Petrie W.M.F. 1901 *Diospolis Parva: the cemeteries of Abadiyeh and Hu: 1898–9* (Egypt Exploration Fund Memoirs 21) London (repr. 1973)

—— 1920/1921 *Predynastic Egypt* and *Corpus of Prehistoric Pottery and Palettes* (British School of Archaeology in Egypt) London (repr. as one vol. 1974)

Porada E. 1982 'Remarks on the Tôd treasure from Egypt' in *Diakonoff Studies* [OE]: 285–303

Posener G. 1940 *Princes et pays d'Asie et de Nubie* Brussels

—— 1956 *Littérature et politique dans l'Égypte de la XIIe dynastie* (Bibliothèque de l'École des Hautes Études 307) Paris

—— 1971 'Literature' in Harris [OGa]: 220–256

Posener-Kriéger P. 1976 *Les Archives du temple funéraire de Néferirkare-Kakaï (les Papyrus d'Abousir)* Cairo

—— 1983 'Les nouveaux papyrus d'Abousir' *SSEA Journal* 13: 51–57

Quark J.F. 1989 'Die Datierungen der Siegelabdrücke von Tel "En Basor"' *ZDPV* 105: 18–26

Quirke S. (ed) 1991 *Middle Kingdom Studies* New Malden

Redford D.B. 1970 'The Hyksos invasion in history and tradition' *Or.* 39: 1–51

—— 1992 *Egypt, Canaan, and Israel in Ancient Times* Princeton, NJ

Reisner G. 1923 *Excavations at Kerma* Boston

—— 1936 'The dog which was honored by the King of Upper and Lower Egypt' *BMFA* 34: 96–99

Rice M. 1990 *Egypt's Making: the origins of ancient Egypt 5000–2000* BC London

Robins G. 1983 [chapter 4]

Robins G., Shute C. 1990 *The Rhind Mathematical Papyrus* London

Roccati A. 1968 'Una lettera inedita dell'Antico Regno' *JEA* 54: 14–22

—— 1982 *La littérature historique sous l'ancien empire égyptien* (LAPO 11) Paris

Roth A.M. 1987 'The organisation and functioning of the royal mortuary cults of the Old Kingdom in Egypt' in Gibson and Biggs [OE]: 133–140

Rothenberg 1972 [chapter 6]

Säve-Söderbergh T. 1941 *Ägypten und Nubien* Lund

Scandone-Matthiae G. 1979–80 'Ebla et l'Égypte à l'ancien et au moyen empire' *AAAS* 29/30: 189–199

—— 1982 'Inscriptions royales égyptiennes de l'ancien empire à Ebla' in Nissen and Renger [OE]: 125–130

Scharff A. 1920 'Ein Rechnungsbuch des königlichen Hofes aus der 13. Dynastie (Papyrus Boulaq Nr. 18)' *ZÄS* 56: 51–68

Scharff A., Moortgat A. 1950 *Aegypten und Vorderasien* Munich

Schenkel W. 1964 'Zum Feudalismus in der ersten Zwischenzeit Ägyptens' *Or.* 33: 263–266

—— 1965 *Memphis, Herakleopolis, Theben: Die ägyptischen Zeugnisse der 7–11 Dynastie* Wiesbaden

Sethe K. 1907 *Die altägyptischen Pyramidentexte* Leipzig

Simpson W.K. 1956 'The single-dated monuments of Sesostris I: an aspect of the institution of co-regency in the twelfth dynasty' *JNES* 15: 214–219

—— 1963 'Studies in the twelfth Egyptian dynasty I: the residence of Itj-towe' *JARCE* 2: 53–59

Smith H.S., Smith A. 1976 'A reconsideration of the Kamose text' *ZÄS* 103: 48–76

Smithers P.C. 1942 'An Old Kingdom letter concerning the crimes of Count Sabni' *JEA* 28: 16–19

Spencer A.J. 1993 *Early Egypt: the rise of civilisation in the Nile Valley* London

Stern L. 1874 'Urkunde über den Bau des Sonnentempels zu On' *ZÄS* 12: 85–96

Stock H. 1949 *Die erste Zwischenzeit Ägyptens* (Studia Aegyptiaca II) Rome

Strudwick N. 1985 *Administration in Egypt during the Old Kingdom* London

Théodoridés A. 1971 'Les contrats d'Hâpidjefa' *RIDA* 18: 109–251

Trigger B. 1976 *Nubia under the Pharaohs* London

Valbelle D. 1990 *Les Neufs Arcs: l'égyptien et les étrangers de la préhistoire à la conquête d'Alexandre* Paris

Vandersleyen C. 1971 *Les Guerres d'Amosis* Brussels

Vandier J.1950 *Mo'alla: la tombe d'Ankhtify et la tombe de Sebekhotep* (Bib. d'Études 18) Cairo

Van Seters J. 1966 *The Hyksos: a new investigation* New Haven, Conn.

Volten A. 1945 *Zwei altägyptische politische Schriften* (Analecta Aegyptiaca 4) Copenhagen

Ward W. 1983 'Reflections on some Egyptian terms presumed to mean "harem", "harem-woman", "concubine"' *Berytus* 31: 67–74

Weill R. 1912 *Les décrets royaux de l'ancien empire égyptien* Paris

Weinstein 1981 [chapter 6]

Wildung D. 1969 *Die Rolle ägyptischer Könige im Bewusstsein ihrer Nachwelt* (Münchner Ägypologische Studien 17) Munich, Berlin

Wilson J.A. 1951/1956 *The Culture of Ancient Egypt* Chicago (orig. pub. as *The Burden of Egypt*)

Winlock H. 1924 'The tombs of the kings of the seventeenth dynasty at Thebes' *JEA* 10: 217–277

—— 1943 'The eleventh Egyptian dynasty' *JNES* 2: 249–283

—— 1947 *The Rise and Fall of the Middle Kingdom at Thebes* New York

Wright M. 1988 'Contacts between Egypt and Syro-Palestine during the Old Kingdom' *BibArch* 51: 143–161

Chapter 4

General

Gardiner 1961 [OD], chs 8–11; Helck 1968 [OD], chs 12–14; O'Connor in Trigger *et al.* 1983 [OD], ch. 3; *CAH* II, chs 8–10, 19, 23, 35; Bottéro *et al.* 1966 [OB], ch. 4; Drioton and Vandier 1984 [OD], chs 9–11; Kemp 1989 [OGa], part III; Grimal 1992 [OD], part 3

and (details below)

Aldred 1968; 1973; *Aménophis III* 1993; James 1984; Kitchen 1982; Redford 1984; 1992 [chapter 3], part 2; Steindorff and Seele 1955

References

Aldred C. 1968 *Akhenaten Pharaoh of Egypt* (New Directions in Archaeology; rev. edn with title: *Akhenaten King of Egypt*, 1988) London

—— 1973 *Akhenaten and Nefertity* Brooklyn, NY

Aménophis III: le Pharaon-Soleil 1993 (exhibn cat. by A.P. Kozloff, B.M. Bryan, E. Delange) Paris

Baines J. 1986 'The stela of Emhab' *JEA* 72: 41–53

Beckerath J. von 1951 *Tanis und Theben* (Ägyptologische Forschungen 16) Glückstadt

—— 1984 [chapter 3]

Bell L. 1985 'Luxor temple and the cult of the royal KA' *JNES* 44: 251–294

Bennett J. 1939 'The restoration inscription of Tut'ankhamun' *JEA* 25: 8–15

Bierbrier M. 1982 *The Tomb Builders of the Pharaohs* London

Bietak 1975 [chapter 3]

—— 1981/1986 [chapter 3]

Blankenberg-van Delden C. 1969 *The Large Commemorative Scarabs of Ameno-phis III* (Documenta et Monumenta Oriens Antiqui 15) Leiden

Brissaud P., Bulté J., von Känel F., Thirion M., Yoyotte J. 1987 *Cahiers de Tanis* I Paris

Bryan B. 1991 *The Reign of Thutmose IV* Baltimore, MD

Butzer 1976 [chapter 3]

Caminos R. 1954 *Late Egyptian Miscellanies* (Brown Egyptological Studies 1) London

Cooney J.D. 1965 *Amarna Reliefs from Hermopolis* Brooklyn, NY

Cumming B. 1982–4 *Egyptian Historical Records of the Later Eighteenth Dynasty* (fascicles I-III) Warminster

Davies N. de G. 1903–8 *The Rock Tombs of El Amarna* London

—— 1943 *The Tomb of Rekhmire* London

Davies V. 1982 'The origin of the blue crown' *JEA* 68: 69–76

de Buck A. 1927 'The judicial papyrus of Turin' *JEA* 23: 152–164

Desroches-Noblecourt C. 1963 *Tutankhamen: life and death of a pharaoh* (trans.) London

Edgerton W.F. 1947 'The government and the governed in Egypt' *JNES* 6: 152–160

—— 1951 'The strikes in Ramses III's twenty-ninth year' *JNES* 10: 137–145

Edgerton W.F., Wilson J.A. 1936 *Historical Records of Ramesses III: the texts of Medinet Habu* (2 vols) Chicago

Gardiner A.H. 1937 *Late Egyptian Miscellanies* (Bibliotheca Aegyptiaca VII) Brussels

Gardiner A.H., Faulkner R.O. 1941–52 *The Wilbour Papyrus* Brooklyn, NY

Gentet D., Maucourant J. 1991 'Une étude critique de la hausse des prix à l'ère ramesside' *DHA* 17/1: 13–31

Gohary J. 1992 *Akhenaten's Sed Festival at Karnak* London

Gonen R. 1984 [chapter 6]

—— 1992 [chapter 6]

Griffith F. Ll. 1927 'The Abydos decree of Seti I at Nauri' *JEA* 13: 193–206

Hachmann R. 1983 (Hsg.) *Frühe Phöniker im Libanon: 20 Jahre deutsche Ausgrabungen in Kāmid el-Lōz* Mainz am Rhein

Helck H.W. 1939 *Der Einfluss der Militärführer in der 18. ägyptischen Dynastie* (Untersuchungen zur Geschichte und Altertumskunde Ägyptens 14) Leipzig

—— 1961–70 *Materialien zur Wirtschaftgeschichte des Neuen Reiches* (6 parts) Wiesbaden

—— 1971 *Die Beziehungen Ägyptens zu Vorderasien im 3. und 2. Jt. v. Chr.* (2nd edn) Wiesbaden

James T.G.H. 1984 *Pharaoh's People: scenes from life in imperial Egypt* London

Janssen J. 1975 *Commodity Prices of the Ramesside Period* Leiden

Katawy S.L.D. 1989 *Land Tenure in the Ramesside Period* London

Kemp B.J. 1976 'The window of appearances at El-Amarna and the basic structure of the city' *JEA* 62: 81–99

—— 1977 'The city of el-Amarna as a source for the study of urban society in ancient Egypt' *World Archaeology* 9: 123–139

—— 1978 'The harîm-palace at Medinet el-Ghurab' *ZÄS* 105: 122–133

Kitchen K.A. 1968– *Ramesside Inscriptions, Historical and Biographical* Oxford (I–VI)

—— 1973 *The Third Intermediate Period in Egypt* Warminster (2nd edn 1986)

—— 1982 *Pharaoh Triumphant: the life and times of Ramesses II* Warminster

Krauss 1985 [chapter 3]

Kruchten J.-M. 1981 *Le Décret d'Horemheb* Brussels

Liverani 1979 [chapter 6]

—— 1987 [chapter 8]

—— 1990 'A seasonal pattern for the Amarna letters' in Moran Studies [0E]: 337–348

Meyer C. 1982 *Senenmut: eine prosopographische Untersuchung* Hamburg

Montet P. 1952 *Les Énigmes de Tanis* Paris

Moran 1987/1992 [chapter 6]

Morkot R. 1986 'Violent images of queenship' *Wepwawet* 2: 1–9

Murnane W.J., van Siclen III C.C. 1993 *The Boundary Stelae of Akhenaten* London

Peet T.E. 1924 'A historical document of the Ramesside age' *JEA* 10: 116–127

—— 1930 *The Great Tomb Robberies of the 20th Egyptian Dynasty* London

Peet T.E., Woolley C.L., Frankfort H., Pendlebury J.D.S. *et al.* 1923–51 *The City of Akhenaten* (3 parts) London

Petrie W.M.F. 1894 *Tell el-Amarna* London

Redford D.B. 1967 *History and Chronology of the Eighteenth Dynasty of Egypt: seven studies* (Near and Middle East Series 3) Toronto

—— 1984 *Akhenaten the Heretic King* Princeton, NJ.

—— (ed.) 1988 *The Akhenaten Temple Project*, vol. II: *Rwd-mnw, foreigners and inscriptions* Toronto

—— 1992 [chapter 3]

Reeves N. (ed.) 1992a *After Tut'ankhamun: research and excavation in the royal necropolis at Thebes* London

—— 1992b *The Complete Tutankhamun: the king, the tomb, the royal treasure* London

Robins G. 1983 'The God's Wife of Amun in the 18th dynasty in Egypt' in Cameron and Kuhrt [0E]: 65–78

Samson J. 1977 'Nefertiti's regality' *JEA* 63: 88–97

Säve-Söderbergh T. 1946 *The Navy of the Eighteenth Egyptian Dynasty* Uppsala

Schulman A.R. 1964 *Military Rank, Title and Organisation in the Egyptian New Kingdom* Berlin

—— 1979 'Diplomatic marriage in the Egyptian New Kingdom' *JNES* 38: 177–193

—— 1988 *Ceremonial Executions and Public Rewards* (OBO 75) Freiburg

Smith R.W., Redford D.B. 1977 *The Akhenaten Temple Project*, vol. I: *the initial discoveries* Warminster

Spencer A.J., Bailey D.M. 1983–92 *Excavations at El-Ashmunein* London

Steindorff G., Seele K. 1955 *When Egypt Ruled the East* Chicago

Tanis 1987 = *Tanis: l'Or des Pharaons* Paris 1987

Trigger 1976 [chapter 3]

Troy L. 1986 *Patterns of Queenship in Ancient Egyptian Myth and History* (Boreas: Uppsala Studies in Ancient Mediterranean and Eastern Civilisations 14) Uppsala

Uphill E. 1968/1969 'Pithom and Raamses: their location and significance' *JNES* 27: 291–316; 28: 15–39

—— 1984 *The Temples of Per-Ramesses* Warminster

Valbelle 1990 [chapter 3]

von Känel F. 1984 'Les courtisanes de Psousennes et leurs tombes à Tanis' *BSFE* 100: 31–43

Weinstein 1981 [chapter 6]

Chapter 5

General

Liverani 1988 [0C], chs 15 and 18; *CAH* II, chs 6, 15, 17, 21a, 24; Bottéro *et al.* 1966 [0B], ch. 2; *RLA* 4: 162–172; 371–389; Otten in Schmökel 1961 [0A]: 313–416; McQueen 1986 [0Ge]; Gurney in Larsen 1979 [0E]: 151–166; Klengel *et al.* 1989 [0C]: 234–267.

and (details below)

Akurgal and Hirmer 1962; Bittel 1970; 1976; Cavaignac 1950; Cornelius 1973; Goetze 1957; Gonnet 1975; Gurney 1990; Klengel and Klengel 1970; Laroche 1971; Lehmann 1986; Neve 1992; Walser 1964

References

Akurgal E., Hirmer M. 1962 *The Art of the Hittites* (trans.) London

Alkım U.B., Bilgi Ö., Alkım H. 1988 *Ikiztepe* I: *the first and second season (1974–1975)* Ankara

Alp S. 1980 'Die hethitischen Tontafelentdeckungen auf dem Maşat-Höyük: vorläufiger Bericht' *Belleten* 44: 25–59

Archi A. 1971 'The propaganda of Hattusili III' *Studi Micenei ed Egeo-Anatolici* 14: 185–215

Balkan K. 1957 *Letter of King Anum-hirbi of Mama to King Warshama of Kanish* (Türk Tarih Kurumu Yayinlarindan 31a) Ankara

—— 1973 *Eine Schenkungsurkunde aus Inandık* Ankara

Beal R.H. 1986 'The history of Kizzuwatna and the date of the Sunassura treaty' *Or.* 55: 424–445

—— 1992 'The location of Cilician Ura' *AnSt* 42: 65–73

Beckman G. 1982 'The Hittite assembly' *JAOS* 102: 435–442

Bin-Nun S.R. 1975 *The Tawananna in the Hittite Kingdom* Heidelberg

Bittel K. 1970 *Hattusha: the capital of the Hittites* Oxford

—— 1975 *Das hethitische Felsenheiligtum von Yazilikaya* Berlin

—— 1976 *Die Hethiter: die Kunst Anatoliens vom Ende des 3. bis zum Anfang des 1. Jt.* Munich

Blegen C.W. *et al.* 1953/1958 *Troy* III and IV Princeton, NJ

Bryce T.R. 1974 'Some geographical and political aspects of Mursilis' Arzawan campaign' *AnSt* 24: 103–116

—— 1989 'The nature of Mycenean involvement in western Anatolia' *Historia* 38: 1–21

—— 1990 'The death of Niphururiya and its aftermath' *JEA* 76: 97–105

Carruba O. 1974 'Tahurwaili von Hatti' in Bittel K. *et al.* (eds) *Anatolian Studies presented to H.G. Güterbock* Istanbul: 73–93

Cavaignac E. 1950 *Les Hittites* (L'Orient Ancien Illustré) Paris

Cornelius F. 1973 *Geschichte der Hethiter* Darmstadt

Daddi F. Pecchioli 1975 'Il *hazan(n)u* nei testi di Hattusa' *OA* 14: 93–136

Easton D.F. 1981 'Hittite land donations and tabarna seals' *JCS* 33: 3–43

Forrer E. 1924a 'Die Griechen in den Boghaz-köi Texten' *OLZ*: 113–118

—— 1924b 'Vorhomerische Griechen in den Keilschrifttexten aus Boghaz-köi' *MDOG* 63: 1–22

Friedrich J. 1926/1930 *Staatsverträge des Hatti-Reiches in hethitischer Sprache* (MVAeG 31; 34) Leipzig

—— 1959 *Die hethitischen Gesetze* (repr. 1971) Leiden

Garelli 1963 [chapter 2]

Garstang J., Gurney O.R. 1959 *The Geography of the Hittite Empire* (British Institute of Archaeology at Ankara, Occasional Publications 5) London

Goetze A. 1925 *Hattušiliš. Der Bericht über seine Thronbesteigung nebst den Paralleltexten* (MVAeG 29/3) Leipzig (cf. MVAeG 34/2 (1930)

—— 1933 *Die Annalen des Muršiliš* (MVAeG 38/Hethitische Texte 6) Leipzig (repr. Darmstadt 1967)

—— 1957 *Kulturgeschichte Kleinasiens* (Handbuch der Altertumswissenschaft III/1 iii; 2nd edn) Munich

Goldman H. 1956 *Excavations at Gözlü Kule, Tarsus* II Princeton, NJ.

Gonnet H. 1975 *Catalogue des documents royaux hittites du IIe millénaire avant J-C* Paris

Gunter A. 1990 *Gordion Final Reports* III Philadelphia, Penn.

Gurney O. 1974 'The Hittite line of kings and chronology' in Bittel K. *et al.* (eds) *Anatolian Studies Presented to H.G. Güterbock* Leiden: 105–111

—— 1977 *Some Aspects of Hittite Religion* (Schweich Lectures 1976) London

—— 1979 'The anointing of Tudhaliya' in Carruba O. (ed.) *Studia Mediterranea Piero Merriggi Dicata* Pavia, I: 213–223

—— 1990 *The Hittites* (rev. edn) Harmondsworth

Güterbock H.G. 1938 [chapter 1]

—— 1954 'Authority and Law in the Hittite Kingdom' *JAOS* 74 (Supp. 17): 16–24

—— 1956 'The Deeds of Suppiluliuma as told by his son Mursili II' *JCS* 10: 41–68; 75–98; 107–130

—— 1960 'An outline of the Hittite AN.TAH.ŠUM festival' *JNES* 19: 80–89

—— 1961 'The north central area of Hittite Anatolia' *JNES* 20: 85–97

—— 1964 'Religion und Kultus der Hethiter' in Walser 1964: 54–73

—— 1975 'Yazılıkaya: à propos a new interpretation' *JNES* 34: 273–277

—— 1982 *Les Hièroglyphes de Yazilikaya (à propos d'un travail récent)* Paris

—— 1983 'The Hittites and the Aegean World: Part 1. The Ahhiyawa Problem Reconsidered' (see also: 'Part 2. Archaeological Comments on Ahhiyawa-Achaians in Western Anatolia' (by M. Mellink); 'Part 3. Response to Hans Güterbock' (by E.T. Vermeule)) *AJA* 87: 133–143

Güterbock H.G., van den Hout T.P.J. 1991 *The Hittite Instructions for the Royal Bodyguard* (AS 24) Chicago

Haas V. 1970 *Der Kult von Nerik* (Studia Pohl 4) Rome

Haas V., Wäfler M. 1974 'Yazılıkaya und der Grosse Tempel' *OA* 13: 211–226

Haase R. 1979 *Die keilschriftlichen Rechtssammlungen in deutscher Fassung* (2nd edn) Wiesbaden

—— 1984 *Texte zum hethitischen Recht: Eine Auswahl* Wiesbaden

Hawkins J.D. 1987 [chapter 8]

Heinhold-Krahmer S. 1977 *Arzawa: Untersuchungen zu seiner Geschichte nach den hethitischen Quellen* Heidelberg

Hoffmann I. 1984 *Der Erlass Telepinus* (Texte der Hethiter Heft 11) Heidelberg

Hoffner H.A. 1965 *The Hittite Laws* (Brandeis Univ., diss.)

—— 1974 *Alimenta Hethaeorum* New Haven, Conn.

—— 1975 'Propaganda and political justification in Hittite historiography', in Goedicke and Roberts [0E]: 49–62

Houwink ten Cate P. 1970 *The Records of the Early Hittite Empire (c. 1430–1370BC)* Leiden

—— 1983/4 'The history of warfare according to Hittite sources: the Annals of Hattusili I' *Anatolica* 10: 91–109; 11: 47–83

—— 1992 'The bronze tablet of Tudhaliya IV and its geographical and historical relations' *ZA* 82: 233–270

BIBLIOGRAPHY

Imparati F., Saporetti C. 1965 'L'autobiografia di Hattusili I' *SCO* 14: 40–85

Jakob-Rost L. 1966 'Beiträge zum hethitischen Festzeremoniell (IBoT I 36)' *MIO* 11: 165–225

Klengel E. and H. 1970 *Die Hethiter: Geschichte und Umwelt: eine Kulturgeschichte Kleinasiens von Çatal Hüyük bis zu Alexander dem Grossen* Vienna

Košak S. 1982 *Hittite Inventories* Heidelberg

Koşay H.Z., Akok M. 1966 *Ausgrabungen von Alaca Hüyük 1940–1948* Ankara

Kümmel H. M. 1967 *Ersatzrituale für den hethitischen König* (StBoT 3) Wiesbaden

Laroche E. 1971 *Catalogue des textes hittites* Paris

—— 1982 'Documents hittites et hourrites' in Beyer 1982 [chapter 6]: 53–60

Lebrun R. 1976 *Šamuha – foyer réligieux de l'empire hittite* Paris

—— 1992 'Traité de Tudhaliya IV avec Kurunta de Tarhuntassa' in Briend J., Lebrun R., Puéch E. *Traités et serments dans le proche-orient ancien* (Suppl. au Cahier Évangile 81/Septembre 1992), no. 8

Lehmann J. 1986 *Die Hethiter: Volk der tausend Götter* Munich

Liverani 1987 [chapter 8]

Lloyd S., Mellaart J. 1955 'Beycesultan Excavations: first preliminary report' *AnSt* 5: 39–93

—— 1956 'Beycesultan Excavations: second preliminary report' *AnSt* 6: 101–135

McQueen J.G. 1968 'Geography and history in western Asia Minor in the second millennium' *AnSt* 18: 169–185

Mellaart J. 1968 'Anatolian trade with Europe and Anatolian geography and culture provinces in the Late Bronze Age' *AnSt* 18: 187–202

Moran 1987/1992 [chapter 6]

Muhly J.D. *et al.* 1985 'Iron in Anatolia and the nature of the Hittite iron industry' *AnSt* 35: 67–84

Murnane W.W. 1985 *The Road to Kadesh* Chicago

Neu E. 1974 *Der Anitta-Text* (StBoT 18) Wiesbaden

Neve P. 1992 *Hattuša – Stadt der Götter und Tempel: Neue Ausgrabungen in der Hauptstadt der Hethiter* (Antike Welt/Sondernummer) Munich

Oettinger N. 1976 *Die militärischen Eide der Hethiter* (StBoT 22) Wiesbaden

Orlin 1970 [chapter 2]

Otten H. 1958 *Hethitische Totenrituale* (Deutsche Akademie der Wissenschaften zu Berlin: Institut für Orientforschung Veröffentlichungen Nr. 37) Berlin

—— 1964 'Aufgaben eines Bürgermeisters in Hattusa' *BaM* 3: 91–95

—— 1973 *Eine althethitische Erzählung um die Stadt Zalpa* (StBoT 17) Wiesbaden

—— 1981 *Die Apologie Hattusilis III: Das Bild der Überlieferung* (StBoT 24) Wiesbaden

—— 1983 'Der Anfang der *HAZANNU*-Instruktion' *Or.* 62: 133–142

—— 1986 'Das hethitische Königshaus im 15. Jahrhundert v. Chr.' *Anzeiger der Österreichischen Akademie der Wissenschaften* 123: 21 ff.

—— 1988 *Die Bronzetafel aus Boğazköy: ein Staatsvertrag Tudhaliyas IV* (StBoT Beiheft) Wiesbaden

Otten H., Souček V. 1965 *Das Gelübde der Königin Puduhepa an die Göttin Lelwani* (StBoT 1) Wiesbaden

Özgüç T. 1957 'The Bitik vase' *Anatolica* 2: 57–78

—— 1978 *Maşat Hüyük I: excavations at Maşat Hüyük and investigations in its vicinity* Ankara

—— 1982 *Maşat Hüyük II: a Hittite centre north-east of Boğazköy* Ankara

—— 1988 *Inandık: an important cult centre of the Old Hittite period* Ankara

Riemschneider K.K. 1958 'Die hethitischen Landschenkungsurkunden' *MIO* 6: 321–381

Sandars 1978 [chapter 8]

Singer I. 1983 'Western Anatolia in the thirteenth century BC according to Hittite sources' *AnSt* 33: 205–218

—— 1983–4 *The Hittite KI.LAM festival* (StBoT 27–8) Wiesbaden

—— 1985 'The battle of Nihriya and the end of the Hittite empire' *ZA* 75: 100–123

Sturtevant E.H., Bechtel G. 1935 *A Hittite Chrestomathy* (William Dwight Whitney Linguistic Series) Philadelphia, Penn.

Süel A. 1992 'Ortaköy: eine hethitische Stadt mit hethitischen und hurritischen Tontafelentdeckungen' in Otten H., Ertem H., Süel A. (eds) *Hittite and Other Anatolian and Near Eastern Studies in Honour of Sedat Alp* Ankara: 487–492

Ünal A. 1974 *Hattusili III* Teil I: *Hattusili bis zu seiner Thronbesteigung* Bd. 1: *Historischer Abriss* (Texte der Hethiter 3) Heidelberg

—— 1978 *Ein Orakeltext über die Intrigen am hethitischen Hof (KUB XXII 70 = Bo2011)* (Texte der Hethiter 6) Heidelberg

von Schuler E. 1957 *Hethitische Dienstanweisungen für höhere Hof- und Staatsbeamte* (AfO Beiheft 10) Graz

—— 1959 'Hethitische Königserlässe als Quellen der Rechtsfindung und ihr Verhältnis zum kodifizierten Recht' in Kienle R. *et al.* (eds) *Festschrift Friedrich* Heidelberg: 435–472

—— 1965 *Die Kaškäer* Berlin

Walser G. (ed.) 1964 *Neuere Hethiterforschung* (Historia Einzelschriften 7) Wiesbaden

Weidner E. 1923 *Politische Dokumente aus Kleinasien: die Staatsverträge in akkadischer Sprache aus dem Archiv von Boghazköi* (Boghazköi-Studien 8 und 9) Leipzig

Werner R. 1967 *Hethitische Gerichtsprotokolle* Wiesbaden

Wilhelm 1982 [chapter 6]

Chapter 6

General

Liverani 1988 [0C], chs 17 and 19; *CAH* II, chs 1, 10, 11, 20, 21b; Bottéro *et al.* 1966 [0B], chs 2 and 3; Klengel *et al.* 1989 [0C]: 267–295; Klengel 1992 [0Gc], ch. 3 *and (details below)*

Actes de la 24e Rencontre Assyriologique Internationale 1977; Beyer 1982; Curtis 1985; Haas 1988; Imparati 1964; Klengel 1965–70; Liverani 1962; O'Callaghan 1948; Redford 1992 [chapter 3], part 2; Saadé 1977; Schaeffer 1939–70; *SDB* s.v. 'Ras Shamra'; Wilhelm 1982; Young 1981

References

Actes de la 24e Rencontre Assyriologique Internationale, Paris 1977: *Les Hourrites* (= *Revue hittite et asianique* 36)

Albright W.F. 1944 'A prince of Taanach in the fifteenth century BC' *BASOR* 94: 12–27

Arnaud D. 1982 'Les textes suméro-accadiens: un florilège' in Beyer 1982: 43–51

—— 1986 *Recherches au Pays d'Ashtata, Emar VI/4: textes de la bibliothèque: transcriptions et traductions* Paris

—— 1991 *Textes Syriens de l'Age du Bronze Récent* (Aula Orientalia Supp. 1) Barcelona

Barrelet M.-T. 1977 'Le "cas" hourrite et la pratique archéologique' in *id.* (ed.)

Problèmes concernant les Hourrites I: *méthodologie et critique* Paris: 1–20

Beal 1992 [chapter 5]

Beyer D. (ed.) 1982 *Méskéne-Emar: dix ans de travaux, 1972–1982* Paris

Bordreuil P. 1981 'Les récentes découvertes épigraphiques à Ras Shamra et à Ras Ibn Hani' in Young 1981: 43–48

Bottéro J. 1949 'Les inventaires de Qatna' *RA* 43: 1–40; 137–215

Buccellati G., Kelly M. 1988 *Mozan* I: *the soundings of the first two seasons* (Bibiotheca Mesopotamica 20) Malibu, Cal.

Caquot A. *et al.* 1974 *Textes ougaritiques* vol. 1: *Mythes et légendes* (LAPO 7) Paris

—— 1989 *Textes ougaritiques* vol. 2: *Textes religieux-rituels; correspondance* (LAPO 14) Paris

Cassin E. 1938 *L'Adoption à Nuzi* Paris

—— 1969 'Pouvoirs de la femme et structures familiales' *RA* 3: 121–148

—— 1974 'Le palais de Nuzi et la royauté d'Arrapha' in Garelli [OE]: 373–392

Cumming 1982 [chapter 4]

Curtis A. 1985 *Ugarit (Ras Shamra)* (Cities of the Biblical World) Cambridge

Diakonoff I.M. 1972 'Die Arier im Vorderen Orient: Ende eines Mythos' *Or.* 41: 91–120 (review of Kammenhuber 1968)

Dietrich M., Loretz O. 1969/70, 1970 'Die soziale Struktur von Alalakh und Ugarit' *UF* 1: 37–64; *WO* 5: 57–93; *ZA* 60: 88–123

—— 1978 'Das "seefahrende Volk" von Šikila (RS 34.129)' *UF* 10: 53–56

Dobel A., Asara F., Michel H.V. 1977 'Neutron activation analysis and the location of Waššukanni' *Or.* 46: 375–382

Dosch G. 1987 'Non-slave labor in Nuzi' in Powell [OE]: 223–235

—— 1993 *Zur Struktur der Gesellschaft des Königreichs Arraphe* (Heidelberger Studien zum Alten Orient 5) Heidelberg

Edzard D.O. 1970 'Die Tonafeln aus Kamid el-Loz' in Edzard and Hachmann 1970: 50–62

Edzard D.O., Hachmann R. *et al.* 1970 *Kamid el-Loz – Kumidi* (Saarbrücker Beiträge zur Altertumskunde 7) Bonn

Eichler B. 1973 *Indenture at Nuzi: the personal tidennutu contract and its Mesopotamian analogues* (YNER 5) New Haven, Conn.

Fleming D. 1992 *The Installation of Baal's High Priestess at Emar: a window on ancient Syrian religion* Atlanta, Ga.

Frandsen P.J. 1979 'Egyptian Imperialism' in Larsen [OE]: 167–190

Fritz-Münche S. 1984 'Steinzeug von Tell Huera: das früheste Beispiel für die Herstellung dichtgebrannter Keramik' *ZA* 74: 123–132

Garelli 1963 [chapter 2]

Gelb I.J. 1944 *Hurrians and Subarians* (SAOC 22) Chicago

Giles F.J. 1970 *Ikhnaton: legend and history* London

Giveon R. 1971 *Les Bédouins Shosu des documents égyptiens* Leiden

Goetze 1957 [chapter 5]

Golénischeff W. (ed.) 1913 *Les Papyrus hiératiques no. 1115, 1116A et 1116B de l'Ermitage Impériale à St. Petersbourg* St Petersburg

Gonen R. 1984 'Urban Canaan in the Late Bronze period' *BASOR* 253: 61–74

—— 1992 'The Late Bronze Age' in Ben-Tor A. (ed.) *The Archaeology of Ancient Israel* (trans.) New Haven, Conn.: 211–257

Gordon C.H. 1971 *Forgotten Scripts: the story of decipherment* (rev. edn) Harmondsworth

Grosz K. 1983 'Bridewealth and dowry in Nuzi' in Cameron and Kuhrt [OE]: 193–206

—— 1987 'Daughters adopted as sons at Nuzi and Emar' in Durand [OE]: 81–86

—— 1989 'Some aspects of the position of women in Nuzi' in Lesko [OE]: 167–180

Güterbock H. 1946 *Kumarbi, Mythen vom churritischen Kronos* (Istanbuler Schriften 16) Zürich

—— 1948 'The Hittite version of the Hurrian Kumarbi myths: oriental forerunners of Hesiod' *AJA* 52: 123–134

—— 1951/1952 'The Song of Ullikummi' *JCS* 5: 135–161; 6: 8–42

—— 1954 'The Hurrian element in the Hittite empire' *Cahiers d'histoire mondiale* 2: 383–394

Haas V. 1988 (Hrsg) *Hurriter und Hurritisch* (Konstanzer Altorientalisches Symposium v 2) Konstanz

Haas V., Thiel J.P. 1978 *Die Beschwörungsrituale der Allaiturah(h)i und verwandte Texte* (Hurritologische Studien 2, AOAT 31) Kevelaer, Neukirchen-Vluyn

Haas V., Wegner I. 1988 *Die Rituale der Beschwörerinnen* ^SAL^*ŠU.GI* (2 vols) (Corpus der Hurritischen Sprachdenkmäler I Abt./Die Texte aus Boğazköy 5) Rome

Haas V., Wilhelm G. 1974 *Hurritische und luwische Riten aus Kizzuwatna* (Hurritologische Studien 1, AOAT Sonderreihe 3) Kevelaer, Neukirchen-Vluyn

Hachmann R. 1970 'Kamid el-Loz – Kumidi' in Edzard and Hachmann 1970: 63–94

Hallo 1964 [chapter 2]

Healey J. 1990 *The Early Alphabet* London (repr. in Hooker 1991 [OH])

Helck H.W. 1971 *Die Beziehungen Ägyptens zu Vorderasien im 3. und 2. Jahrtausend v.u.Z.* (2nd edn; ÄgAbh 5) Wiesbaden

Heltzer M. 1976 *The Rural Community in Ugarit* Wiesbaden

—— 1978 *Goods, Prices and the Organization of Trade in Ugarit* Wiesbaden

—— 1982 *The Internal Organization of the Kingdom of Ugarit* Wiesbaden

Hrouda B. 1985 'Zum Problem der Hurriter' *MARI* 4: 595–613

Imparati F. 1964 *I Hurriti* Florence

Kammenhuber A. 1961 *Hippologia Hethitica* Wiesbaden

—— 1968 *Die Arier im Vorderen Orient* Heidelberg

Kempinski A. 1974 'Tell el-'Ajjûl – Beth-Aglayim or Sharuhen?' *IEJ* 24: 145–152

Kitchen K. 1977 'The king list of Ugarit' *UF* 9: 131–142

Klengel H. 1965–70 *Geschichte Syriens* (3 vols) Berlin

Kramer C. 1977 'Pots and People' in Young, T.C., Levine L.D. (eds) *Mountains and Lowlands: essays in the archaeology of greater Mesopotamia* (Bibliotheca Mesopotamica 7) Malibu, Cal.: 91–112

Kühne H. 1973a *Die Chronologie der internationalen Korrespondenz von el-Amarna* (AOAT 17) Kevelaer, Neukirchen-Vluyn.

—— 1973b 'Ammištamru und die Tochter der "Grossen Dame"' *UF* 5: 175–184

Kupper 1957 [chapter 2]

Laessøe 1959 [chapter 2]

Laroche E. 1979 'Le problème des Indo-Aryens occidentaux' *CRAIBL*: 677–685

—— 1982 [chapter 5]

Liverani M. 1962 *Storia di Ugarit nell'età degli archivi politici* Rome

—— 1979 *Three Amarna Essays* (Monographs on the Ancient Near East I/5) Malibu, Cal.

Loretz O. 1984 *Habiru-Hebräer: eine sozio-linguistische Studie über die Herkunft des Gentiliziums 'ibrî vom Apellativum* habiru (Beiheft ZAW 160) Berlin

Maidman M.P. 1976 *A Socio-Economic Analysis of a Nuzi Family Archive* (Univ. of Penn., diss.)

Malamat A. 1961 'Campaigns of Amenhotep II and Tuthmosis IV to Canaan' *Scripta Hierosolymitana* 8: 218–231

Matthews D., Eidem J. 1993 'Tell Brak and Nagar' *Iraq* 55: 201–207

Merillees R.S. 1968 *The Cypriot Bronze Age Pottery Found in Egypt* (Studies in Mediterranean Archaeology 18) Lund

Millard A.R. 1973 'The Canaanites' in Wiseman 1973 [OA]: 29–52

Moorey 1986 [chapter 2]

Moran W. 1987/1992 *Les Lettres d'el Amarna* (LAPO 13) Paris (English updated edn 1992, Baltimore, MD)

Morkot R. 1988 'Studies in New Kingdom Nubia 1. Politics, economics and ideology: Egyptian imperialism in Nubia' *Wepwawet* 3: 29–49

Morris 1992 [chapter 8]

Morrison M.A. 1983 'The Jacob and Laban narratives in the light of Near Eastern Sources' *BibArch* 46: 155–164

Morrison M.A., Owen D.I. (eds) 1981 *Studies in the Civilization and Culture of Nuzi and the Hurrians* Winona Lake, IN

Oates D. 1985 'Excavations at Tell Brak, 1983–84' *Iraq* 47: 159–173

O'Callaghan R.T. 1948 *Aram Naharaim* Rome

Pardee D. 1988 *Les textes paramythologiques de la 24e campagne (1961)* (Ras Shamra-Ougarit 4) Paris

Parrot A., Nougayrol J. 1948 'Une document de fondation hourrite' *RA* 42: 1–20

Pfeiffer R.H. 1932 *Excavations at Nuzi*, II: *The Archives of Shilwateshub, Son of the King* Cambridge, Mass.

Pitard W.T. 1987 *Ancient Damascus: a historical study of the Syrian city-state from earliest times until its fall to the Assyrians in 732 BCE* Winona Lake, IN

Pope M. 1981 'The cult of the dead at Ugarit' in Young 1981: 159–179

Redford 1967 [chapter 4]

—— 1992 [chapter 3]

Rothenberg B. 1972 *Timna: valley of the biblical copper mines* (New Aspects of Antiquity) London

Saadé G. 1977 *Ougarit* Damascus

Sasson J.M. 1974 'Hurrians and Hurrian names in the Mari texts' *UF* 6: 353–400

—— 1981 'On Idrimi and Šarruwa, the scribe' in Morrison and Owen 1981: 309–324

Schaeffer H. 1939–70 *Ugaritica* (6 vols) Paris

Schulman A. 1978 ''Ankhosenamun, Nofretity and the Amka affair' *JARCE* 15: 43–48

—— 1988 'Hittites, helmets and Amarna: Akhenaten's first Hittite war' in Redford 1988 [chapter 4]: 53–79

Several M. 1972 'Reconsidering the Egyptian empire in Palestine during the Amarna period' *PEQ* 104: 123–133

Singer I. 1988 'Merneptah's campaign to Canaan and the Egyptian occupation of the southern coastal plain of Palestine in the Ramesside period' *BASOR* 269: 1–10

Smith S. 1949 *The Statue of Idrimi* London

Speiser E.A. 1929 'A letter of Saushshatar and the date of the Kirkuk tablets' *JAOS* 49: 269ff.

Stein D. 1984 *Khabur ware and Nuzi ware* (Assur 4.1) Malibu, Cal.

—— 1989 'A Reappraisal of the 'Sauštatar Letter from Nuzi' *ZA* 79: 36–60

Stucky R. 1983 *Ras Shamra-Leukos Limen: die nach-Ugaritische Besiedlung von Ras Shamra* (Mission Archéologique de Ras Shamra 1) Paris

Thureau-Dangin F. 1939 'Tablettes hourrites provenant de Mari' *RA* 36: 1–28

Trigger 1976 [chapter 3]

van Soldt W. H. 1983 'Een koniklijke Echtscheiding te Ugarit' in Veenhof [OI]: 150–159

—— 1991 *Studies in the Akkadian of Ugarit: Dating and Grammar* (AOAT 40) Neukirchen-Vluyn

Vargyas P. 1988 'Stratification sociale à Ugarit' in Heltzer M., Lipiński E. (eds) *Society and Economy in the Eastern Mediterranean (c. 1500–1000* BC) (OLA 23) Leuven: 111–123

Wegner I. 1981 *Gestalt und Kult der Ištar-šawuška in Kleinasien* (Hurritologische Studien 3, AOAT 36) Kevelaer, Neukirchen-Vluyn

Weidner 1923 [chapter 5]

Weinstein J. 1981 'The Egyptian empire in Palestine: a reconsideration' *BASOR* 241: 1–28

Weippert 1971 [chapter 8]

Wilhelm G. 1982 *Grundzüge der Geschichte und Kultur der Hurriter* Darmstadt (trans. with updating and additions: *The Hurrians* Warminster 1989)

—— 1983 'Die Keilschrifttexte aus Kamid el-Loz' in Hachmann 1983 [chapter 4]: 40–42

—— 1991 'A Hurrian letter from Tell Brak' *Iraq* 53: 159–169

Wiseman D.J. 1953 *The Alalakh Tablets* (British Institute of Archaeology in Ankara, Occasional Publications 2) London

Woolley 1953 [chapter 2]

Yon M. 1990 'Ougarit et ses dieux (travaux 1978–1988)' in Bounni 1990 [OE]: 325–343

Young G.D. (ed.) 1981 *Ugarit in Retrospect: 50 years of Ugarit and Ugaritic* Winona Lake, IN

Zaccagnini C. 1977 'The merchant at Nuzi' *Iraq* 39: 171–189

—— 1979 *The Rural Landscape of the Land Arraphe* (Quaderni di Geografia Storica 1) Rome

Chapter 7

General

Liverani 1988 [OC], chs 20, 21, 27; Oates 1986 [OGb]: 83–107; Bottéro *et al.* 1966 [OB], ch. 1; *CAH* II, chs 18, 25, 29, 31, 32; Garelli and Nikiprowetzky 1971 [OC], ch. 1; Klengel *et al.* [OC]: 295–334.

and (details below)

Brinkman 1968 [chapter 11]; 1980; Carter and Stolper 1984; Diakonoff 1985; Harper, Aruz, Tallon 1992; Hinz 1972; Saggs 1984 [chapter 9], ch. 5.

References

Adams 1981 [chapter 1]

Adams R.McC., Nissen H.J. 1972 *The Uruk Countryside: the natural setting of urban societies* Chicago

Akkermans, P.M.M.G., Rossmeisl I. 1990 'Excavations at Tell Sabi-Abyad, northern Syria: a regional centre on the Assyrian frontier' *Akkadica* 66: 13–60

Amiet P. 1966 *Elam* Paris

—— 1988 *Suse: 6000 ans d'histoire* (Musée du Louvre) Paris

Artzi P. 1982 '"The king and the evil portending, ominous sign in his house" (EA 358)' in Nissen and Renger [OE]: 317–320

Astour M. 1986 'The name of the 9. Kassite ruler' *JAOS* 106: 327–331

Aynard M.-J., Durand J.-M., Amiet P. 1980 'Documents d'époque médio-assyrienne' *Assur* 3/1: 1–54

Balkan K. 1954 *Kassitenstudien I: Die Sprache der Kassiten* New Haven, Conn.

Baqir T. 1942–6 'Iraq Government excavations at Aqar Quf' *Iraq Suppl.* 1942–3; 1943–4; *Iraq* 8: 73–93

Black 1981 [chapter 11]

Borger R. 1971 'Gott Marduk und Gott-König Šulgi als Propheten: zwei prophetische Texte' *BiOr* 28: 3–24

Brinkman 1968 [chapter 11]

—— 1974 'The monarchy of the Kassite dynasty' in Garelli [OE]: 409–415

—— 1976 *Materials and Studies for Kassite History* vol. I: *A Catalogue of Cuneiform Sources Pertaining to Specific Monarchs of the Kassite Dynasty* Chicago

—— 1980 'Die Kassiten' *RLA* 5: 464–473

—— 1993 'A Kassite seal mentioning a Babylonian governor of Dilmun' *NABU* note 106

Brinkman J.A., Matthews D. 1990 'A grandson of Kurigalzu' *NABU* note 103

Cameron 1948 [chapter 13]

Cagni L. 1977 *The Poem of Erra* (Sources for the Ancient Near East) Malibu, Cal.

Canby J.V. 1976 'The Stelenreihe in Assur, Tell Halaf, and Massebôt' *Iraq* 38: 113–128

Cardascia G. 1969 *Les Lois Assyriennes* (LAPO 2) Paris

Carter E., Stolper M.W. 1976 'Middle Elamite Malyan' *Expedition* 18/2: 33–42

—— 1984 *Elam: surveys of political history and archaeology* (University of California Near Eastern Studies 25) Berkeley, Cal.

de Waele E. 1989 'Musicians and musical instruments on the rock reliefs in the Elamite sanctuary of Kul-e Farah (Izeh)' *Iran* 27: 29–37

Diakonoff I.M. 1985 'Elam' *CHI* II: 1–24

Dougherty R.P. 1932 *The Sealand of Ancient Arabia* (YOSR 19) New Haven, Conn.

Driver G.R., Miles J.C. 1935 *The Assyrian Laws* Oxford

Edzard D.O. 1960 'Die Beziehungen Babyloniens und Ägyptens in der neubabylonischen Zeit und das Gold' *JESHO* 3: 38–55

Ghirshman R. 1963 *Persia from the Origins to Alexander the Great* (trans.) London

—— 1966–70 *Tchoga Zanbil* (4 vols) Paris

Goody J. 1990 *The Oriental, the Ancient and the Primitive: systems of marriage and the family in the pre-industrial societies of Eurasia* (Studies in Literacy, Family, Culture and the State) Cambridge

Grayson A.K. 1972/1976 *Assyrian Royal Inscriptions* (2 vols) Wiesbaden

—— 1975 *Babylonian Historical-literary Texts* (Toronto Semitic Texts and Studies 3) Toronto

—— 1987 [chapter 2]

—— 1991 *Assyrian Rulers of the Early First Millennium BC (1114–859 BC)* (RIM Assyrian Periods 2) Toronto

Grillot F. 1988 'A propos d'un cas de "levirat" élamite' *JA* 276: 61–70

Grillot-Susini F. (avec coll. de C. Roche) 1987 *Éléments de grammaire élamite* Paris

Gurney O.R. 1983 *The Middle Babylonian Legal and Economic Texts from Ur* London

Hallock 1969 [chapter 13]

—— 1971 [chapter 13]

Hansman J. 1972 'Elamites, Achaemenians and Anshan' *Iran* 10: 101–125

Harper P., Aruz J., Tallon F. (eds) 1992 *The Royal City of Susa: ancient Near Eastern treasures in the Louvre* New York (rev. French edn, Paris, 1994)

Henrickson R.C. 1984 'Šimaški and central western Iran: the archaeological evidence' *ZA* 74: 98–122

Herrero P. 1976 'Tablettes administratives de Haft Tépé' *CDAFI* 6: 93–116

Herrero P., Glassner J.J. 1990 'Haft-Tépé: choix de textes I' *IrAnt* 25: 1–45

—— 1991 'Haft-Tépé: choix de textes II' *IrAnt* 26: 39–80

Hinz W. 1967 'Elams Vertrag mit Naram-Sîn von Akkade' *ZA* 58: 66–96

—— 1968 'Zu den Zeughaustäfelchen aus Susa' in *Festschrift für W. Eilers* Wiesbaden: 35–42

—— 1972 *The Lost World of Elam* (trans.) London

Jas R. 1990 'Two Middle-Assyrian lists of personal names from Sabi Abyad' *Akkadica* 67: 33–39

Kammenhuber 1968 [chapter 6]

König W. 1926 *Mutterrecht und Thronfolge im alten Elam* Vienna

—— 1965 *Die elamischen Königsinschriften* (AfO Beiheft 16) Graz

Kühne H. 1990 'Gedanken zur historischen und städtebaulichen Entwicklung der assyrischen Stadt Dur-Katlimmu' in Bounni 1990 [OE]: 153–169

Kuhrt 1987 [chapter 11]

Lackenbacher S. 1982 'Nouveaux documents d'Ugarit I: une lettre royal' *RA* 76: 141–156

Lambert M. 1972 'Hutéludush-Inshushinak et le pays d'Anzan' *RA* 66: 61–76

Lambert W.G. 1957 'Ancestors, authors and canonicity' *JCS* 11: 1–14; 112

—— 1960 *Babylonian Wisdom Literature* Oxford

—— 1963 'The reign of Nebuchadnezzar I: a turning point in the history of ancient Mesopotamian religion' in MacCullough W.S. (ed.) *The Seed of Wisdom: essays in honor of T.G. Meek* Toronto: 3–13

—— 1965 'A new look at the Babylonian background of Genesis' *JTS* 16: 287–300

—— 1976 'Tukulti-Ninurta I and the Assyrian king list' *Iraq* 38: 85–94

Liverani 1979 [chapter 6]

Machinist P. 1976 'Literature as politics: the Tukulti-Ninurta epic and the bible' *CBQ* 38: 460–482

Mayer W. 1988 'Der babylonische Feldzug Tukulti-Ninurtas I von Assyrien' *Cananea Selecta: Festschrift Oswald Loretz* Rome: 143–161

Mayrhofer M. 1966 *Die Indo-Arier im Vorderen Orient* Wiesbaden

Miglus P.A. 1984 'Another look at the "Stelenreihen" in Assur' *ZA* 74: 133–140

Miroschedji P. de 1982 'Notes sur la glyptique de la fin de l'Elam' *RA* 76: 51–63

—— 1985 [chapter 13]

Moorey 1986 [chapter 2]

Moran 1987 [chapter 6]

Morris 1992 [chapter 8]

Müller K.F. 1937 *Das assyrische Ritual* Teil I: *Texte zum assyrischen Königsritual* (MVAeG 41/3) Leipzig

Negahban E. 1990 *Excavations at Haft Tepe, Iran* (University Museum Monographs 70) Philadelphia, Penn.

Nissen H.J. 1993 'The context of the emergence of writing in Mesopotamia and Iran' in Curtis [OGk]: 54–76

Oppenheim A.L. 1970 *Glass and Glassmaking in Ancient Mesopotamia (An edition of the cuneiform texts which contain instructions for glassmakers. With a catalogue of surviving objects)* Corning Museum, New York

Paper H.H. 1955 'Elamite Texts from Tchogha-Zambil' *JNES* 14: 42–48

Pedersen O. 1985 *Archives and Libraries in the City of Assur: a survey of the material from the German excavations* part I Uppsala

Porada E. 1965 *Ancient Iran: the art of pre-Islamic times* London

—— 1981–2 'The cylinder seals found at Thebes in Boeotia' *AfO* 28: 1–70

Postgate J.N. 1979 'On some Assyrian ladies' *Iraq* 41: 89–103

—— 1986 'Administrative archives from the city of Assur in the Middle Assyrian period' in Veenhof [OE]: 168–183

Reiner E. 1969 'Das Elamische' *Die altkleinasiatischen Sprachen* (HdO) Leiden

—— 1973 'The location of Anshan' *RA* 67: 57–62

Roberts J.J.M. 1976 'Nebuchadnezzar I's Elamite crisis in theological perspective' Finkelstein Essays [OE]: 183–187

Roth (1987) [chapter 9].

Saggs 1984 [chapter 9]

Saggs H.W.F., Wiseman D.J. 1968 'The Tell al Rimah tablets, 1965 and 1966' *Iraq* 30: 154–205

Saporetti C. 1979 *The Status of Women in the Middle Assyrian Period* (Sources and Monographs on the Ancient Near East 2/1) Malibu, Cal.

Seidl U. 1968 'Die babylonischen Kudurru-reliefs: Symbole mesopotamischer Gottheiten' *BaM* 4: 7–220 (rev. edn 1989 Freiburg)
—— 1986 *Die elamischen Felsreliefs von Kurangun und Naqš-e Rustam* Berlin
Steinkeller 1988 [chapter 1]
—— 1990 'More on LÚ.SU.(A) = Šimaški' *NABU* note 13
Steinmetzer F.X. 1922 *Die babylonischen Kudurru (Grenzsteine) als Urkundenform untersucht* (Studien zur Geschichte und Kultur des Altertums 11/IV-V) Paderborn
Stève M.-J. 1967 *Tchoga Zanbil (Dur Untash)* vol. III: *Textes élamites et accadiens de Tchoga Zanbil* (Mémoires de la Mission Archéologique en Iran 41) Paris
Stolper M.W. 1982 'On the dynasty of Šimaški and the early sukkalmahs' *ZA* 72: 42–67
—— 1984 *Texts from Tall-i Malyan* vol. 1: *Elamite administrative texts (1972–4)* Philadelphia, Penn.
Stolper M.W., Wright H.T. 1990 'Elamite brick fragments fron Chogha Pahn East and related fragments' *Mélanges J. Perrot* Paris: 151–163
Sumner W. 1994 'Archaeological measures of cultural continuity and the arrival of the Persians in Fars' *AchHist* 8: 97–105
Tadmor H. 1958 'Historical implications of the correct rendering of Akkadian *dakû*' *JNES* 17: 129–141
Thomas R. 1992 *Literacy and Orality in Ancient Greece* (Key Themes in Ancient History) Cambridge
Thureau-Dangin F. 1935 'Une lettre assyrienne à Ras Shamra' *Syria* 16: 188–193
Tomabechi Y. 1983 'Wall paintings from Dur Kurigalzu' *JNES* 42: 123–131
Vallat F. 1980 *Suse et l'Elam* Paris
van Dijk J. 1986 'Die dynastischen Heiraten zwischen Kassiten und Elamern: eine verhängnisvolle Politik' *Or.* 55: 159–170
van Praag A. 1945 *Droit matrimonial Assyro-Babylonien* Amsterdam
Walker C.B.F 1982 'Babylonian Chronicle 25: a chronicle of the Kassite and Isin II dynasties' Kraus Festschrift [OE]: 398–417
Weadock 1975 [chapter 2]
Weidner E.F. 1928–9 'Historisches Material in der babylonischen Omina-Literatur' *MAOG* 4: 226ff.
—— 1956 'Hof- und Haremserlasse assyrischer Könige aus dem 2. Jt. v. Chr.' *AfO* 17: 257ff.
—— 1959 *Die Inschriften Tukuti-Ninurtas I und seiner Nachfolger* (AfO Beiheft 12) Graz
Zaccagnini C. 1983 'Patterns of mobility among Near Eastern craftsmen' *JNES* 42: 245–264
Zeder M.A. 1991 *Feeding Cities: specialised animal economy in the ancient Near East* (Smithsonian Series in Archaeological Inquiry) Washington DC.

Chapter 8

General

Liverani 1988 [OC], chs 22–26; *CAH* II, chs 26a and b, 28, 33, 34; III, chs 9–12, 29, 32; Bottéro *et al.* 1966 [OB]: 200–221; 1967b [OB], ch. 3; Garelli and Nikiprowetzky 1974 [OC], chs 1; 4/2 Klengel *et al.* 1989 [OC]: 413–459; Klengel 1992 [OGc], ch. 4; Aharoni 1979 [OGd]; Weippert 1988 [OGd]; Mazar 1990 [OGd]
and (details below)
Archaeology 43/5 (1990); *BASOR* 279 (1990): 1–64; Clements 1989; de Vaux 1961; *Dictionnaire de la civilisation phénicienne et punique*; Dupont-Sommer 1949; Gras, Rouillard, Teixidor 1989; Hawkins in press; Hayes and Maxwell Miller 1977;

Knight and Tucker 1985; Lemche 1988; Malamat 1979; Maxwell Miller and Hayes 1987; Moscati 1988; Redford 1992 [chapter 3], parts 3 and 4; Sader 1987; Sandars 1978; *Studia Phoenicia*

References

Abou Assaf A. 1985 "Ain Dara' in Weiss 1985 [0Gc]: 347–350

Abou Assaf A., Bordreuil P., Millard A.R. 1982 *La Statue de Tell Fekherye et sa bilingue assyro-araméenne* Paris

Ackroyd P. 1983 'Goddesses, women and Jezebel' in Cameron and Kuhrt [0E]: 245–259

Aharoni Y. 1974 'The building activities of David and Solomon' *IEJ* 24: 13–16

Ahlström G.W. 1984 'An archaeological picture of Iron Age religions in ancient Palestine' *StOr* 55: 117–145

—— 1986 *Who Were the Israelites?* Winona Lake, IN.

Ahlström G.W., Edelman D. 1985 'Merneptah's Israel' *JNES* 44: 59–61

Akurgal E. 1961 *Die Kunst Anatoliens von Homer bis Alexander* Berlin

—— 1962 *The Art of the Hittites* London

—— 1966 *The Birth of Greek Art: the Mediterranean and the Near East* London

Albright W.F. 1939 'The Israelite Conquest of Canaan' *BASOR* 74: 11–23

Alt A. 1925/1966 'The Settlement of the Israelites in Palestine' *Essays on Old Testament History and Religion* (trans.) New York: 133–169

—— 1930/1966 'The formation of the Israelite state in Palestine' *Essays*: 171–237

Anderson W.P. 1988 *Sarepta I: the Late Bronze and Iron Age strata of area II, Y* Beirut

Archaeology 43/5 (Mar.–Apr. 1990 'Special Section: the Phoenicians' (pp. 22–35))

Astour M. 1965 'The last days of Ugarit' *AJA* 69: 253–258

Attridge H.W., Oden R. 1981 *Philo of Byblos: the Phoenician history* (CBQ Monographs 9) Washington, DC.

Aubet M.-E. 1993 *The Phoenicians and the West: politics, colonies and trade* (trans.) Cambridge

Barkay G. 1992 'Iron II-III' in Ben-Tor A. (ed.) *The Archaelogy of Ancient Israel* (trans.) New Haven, Conn.: 302–373

Barr J. 1974 'Philo of Byblos and his "Phoenician History"' *Bulletin of the John Rylands Library* 57: 17–68

Bartlett J. 1982 *Jericho* (Cities of the Biblical World) Guildford

BASOR 279 (August 1990: articles on Phoenician culture by Bikai, Stieglitz, Clifford, Markoe (pp. 1–64))

Bass G.F. 1973 'Cape Gelidonya and Bronze Age maritime trade' in Hoffner H.(ed.) *Occident and Orient: studies presented to Cyrus H. Gordon* (AOAT 22) Neukirchen-Vluyn: 29–57

Bass G.F. *et al.* 1989 'The Bronze Age shipwreck at Ulu Burun: 1986 campaign' *AJA* 93: 1–29 (contains refs to reports of earlier campaigns)

Baumgarten A.J. 1981 *The Phoenician History of Philo of Byblos: a commentary* Leiden

Becking B. 1992 *The Fall of Samaria: an historical and archaeological study* (Studies in the History of the Ancient Near East 2) Leiden

Bienkowski P. 1986 *Jericho in the Late Bronze Age* Warminster

Bikai P.M. 1978 *The Pottery of Tyre*, Warminster

Bimson J. 1981 *Redating the Exodus and Conquest* (2nd edn) Sheffield

Bing J.D. 1991 'Alexander's sacrifice *dies praesidibus loci* before the battle of Issus' *JHS* 111: 161–165

Biran A., Naveh J. 1993 'An Aramaic stele fragment from Tel Dan' *IEJ* 43: 81–98

Borger R. 1956 [chapter 9]

Bright J 1959 *A History of Israel* (2nd rev. edn 1972) London

Brinkman J.A. 1968 [chapter 11]

—— 1977 'Notes on Aramaeans and Chaldaeans in southern Babylonia in the early seventh century BC' *Or.* 46: 304–325

—— 1984 [chapter 11]

Bron F. 1979 *Recherches sur les Inscriptions Phéniciennes de Karatepe* (Centre de Recherches d'Histoire et de Philologie II; Hautes Études Orientales 11) Paris

Bryce 1986 [chapter 10]

Bunnens G. 1979 *L'Expansion phénicienne en Mediterranée* Brussels

Cazelles H. 1973 'The Hebrews' in Wiseman 1973 [0A]: 1–28

Chaney M.L. 1983 'Ancient Palestinian peasant movements and the formation of premonarchic Israel' in Freedman and Graf 1983: 39–90

Claessen H.J.M., Skalník P. (eds) 1981 *The Study of the State* The Hague

Clements R.E. (eds) 1989 *The World of Ancient Israel: sociological, anthropological and political perspectives* Cambridge

Clifford R.J. 1990 'Phoenician religion' *BASOR* 279: 55–64

Courbin P. 1990 'Fragments d'amphores protogéometriques grecques à Bassit' in Bounni 1990 [0E]: 49–58

Culican W. 1968 'The iconography of some Phoenician seals and seal impressions' *Australian Journal of Biblical Archaeology* 1: 50–103

Dalley S. 1985 'Foreign chariotry and cavalry in the armies of Tiglath-pileser III and Sargon II' *Iraq* 47: 31–48

Delaporte L. 1940 *Malatya-Arslantepe* Paris

de Vaux R. 1961 *Ancient Israel: its life and institutions* (trans.) London

—— 1972 'The king of Israel, vassal of Yahweh' *The Bible and the Ancient Near East* (trans.) London: 152–180

—— 1978 *The Early History of Israel* (2 vols; trans) London

Dever W.G. 1969–70 'Iron Age epigraphic material from the area of Khirbet el-Kôm' *HUCA* 40/41: 139–204

Dictionnaire de la Civilisation Phénicienne et Punique (sous la direction de E. Lipiński) Turnhout 1992

Dietrich M. 1970 *Die Aramäer Südbabyloniens in der Sargonidenzeit (700–648)* (AOAT 7) Kevelaer, Neukirchen-Vluyn

Dietrich and Loretz 1978 [chapter 6]

Donbaz V. 1990 'Two Neo-Assyrian stelae in the Antakya and Kahamanmaraş Museum' *RIM Annual Review* 8: 5–24

Donner H., Röllig W. 1973–9 *Kanaanäische und Aramäische Inschriften* (3 vols) Wiesbaden

Dothan T. 1982 *The Philistines and Their Material Culture* New Haven, Conn.

Drews R. 1992 'Herodotus 1.94, the drought of ca.1200 BC, and the origin of the Etruscans' *Historia* 41: 14–39

Dupont-Sommer A. 1949 *Les Araméens* Paris

Edelman D. 1987 'Biblical *molek* reassessed' *JAOS* 107: 727–731

Edgerton and Wilson 1936 [chapter 4]

Eissfeldt O. 1965 *The Old Testament: an introduction* (trans.) Oxford

Emerton J.A. 1982 'New light on Israelite religion: the implications of the inscriptions from Kuntillet 'Ajrud' *ZAW* 94: 2–20

Eph'al I. 1982 *The Ancient Arabs: nomads on the borders of the fertile crescent 9th-5th centuries BC* Jerusalem

Finkelstein I. 1988 *The Archaeology of the Israelite Settlement* Jerusalem

Frankenstein S. 1979 'The Phoenicians in the far west: a function of Neo-Assyrian imperialism' in Larsen [OE]: 263–294

Freedman D.N., Graf D. (eds) 1983 *Palestine in Transition: the emergence of ancient Israel* (The Social World of Biblical Antiquity Series 2) Sheffield

Fried M.H. 1975 *The Notion of Tribe* (Cummings Modular Program in Anthropology) Menlo Park, Cal.

Fritz V. 1987 'Conquest or settlement? The early Iron Age in Palestine' *BibArch* 50: 84–100

Frost H. 1972 'Ancient harbours and anchorages in the eastern Mediterranean' in *Underwater Archaeology: a nascent discipline* Paris: 95–114

Garbini G. 1986 *History and Ideology in Ancient Israel* (trans.) London

Garelli P. 1982 'Importance et rôle des Araméens dans l'administration de l'empire assyrien' in Nissen and Renger [OE]: 437–447

Garstang J. and J.B.E. 1948 *The Story of Jericho* (2nd edn) London

Genge H. 1979 *Nordsyrisch-südanatolische Reliefs: Datierung und Bestimmung* (2 Teile) Copenhagen

Geva S. 1982 'Archaeological evidence for the trade between Israel and Tyre?' *BASOR* 248: 69–72

Gibson J.C.L. 1971–82 *Textbook of Syrian Semitic Inscriptions*; vol. 1: *Hebrew and Moabite Inscriptions*; vol. 2: *Aramaic Inscriptions*; vol. 3: *Phoenician Inscriptions* Oxford

Gonen R. 1984 [chapter 6]

—— 1992 [chapter 6]

Gottwald N.K. 1979 *The Tribes of Yahweh: a sociology of the religion of liberated Israel 1250–1050 BCE* Mayknoll, NY

Graf K.H. 1866 *Die geschichtlichen Bücher des Alten Testaments* Leipzig

Graham A.J. 1986 'The historical interpretation of Al-Mina' *DHA* 12: 51–65

Gras M., Rouillard J., Teixidor J. 1989 *L'Univers Phénicien* Paris

Grayson A.K. 1976 *Assyrian Royal Inscriptions* 2 Wiesbaden

—— 1991 [chapter 7]

Haines R.C. 1971 *Excavations in the Plains of Antioch* vol. 2 Chicago

Hawkins J.D. 1972 'Building inscriptions of Carchemish' *AnSt* 22: 87–114

—— 1975 'The negatives in hieroglyphic Luwian' *AnSt* 25: 119–156

—— 1979 'Some historical problems of the hieroglyphic Luwian inscriptions' *AnSt* 29: 153–168

—— 1980 'Karkamiš' *RLA* 5: 426–446

—— 1986 'Royal statements of ideal prices: Assyrian, Babylonian, and Hittite' in Canby J.V., Porada E., Ridgway B.S., Stech T. (eds) *Ancient Anatolia: aspects of change and cultural development (Essays in honor of Machteld J. Mellink)* Madison, Wis.: 93–102

—— 1987 'The Kululu lead strips: economic documents in hieroglyphic Luwian' *AnSt* 37: 135–162

—— 1988 'Kuzi-Tešub and the "Great Kings" of Karkamiš' *AnSt* 38: 99–108

—— in press *The Hieroglyphic Luwian Inscriptions of the Iron Age* (3 vols) Berlin

Hawkins J.D., Morpurgo Davies A. 1978 'On the problems of Karatepe: the hieroglyphic text' *AnSt* 28: 103–120

Hayes J.H., Maxwell Miller J. (eds) 1977 *Israelite and Judaean History* London

Heaton E.W. 1974 *Solomon's New Men* London

Helm P. 1980 *'Greeks' in the Neo-Assyrian Levant and 'Assyria' in Early Greek Writers* (Univ. of Penn., diss)

Hestrin R. 1991 'Understanding Asherah: exploring Semitic iconography' *BAR* 17 (Sep.-Oct.): 50–59

Hogarth D.G., Woolley C.L., Barnett R.D. 1914–52 *Carchemish* (3 vols) London

Hooftijzer J., van der Kooij G. 1976 *Aramaic Texts from Deir 'Alla* Leiden

Isserlin B.S.J., du Plat Taylor J. 1974 *Motya: a Phoenician and Carthaginian city of Sicily* I Leiden

Kalaç M., Hawkins J.D. 1989 'The hieroglyphic Luwian rock inscription at Malpınar' *AnSt* 39: 105–112

Kenyon K. 1987 *The Bible and Recent Archaeology* (rev. edn by P.R.S. Moorey) London

Kestemont G. 1972 'Le commerce phénicien et l'expansion assyrien du XIe–VIIe siècle' *OA* 11: 137–144

Khalifeh I.A. 1988 *Sarepta II: the Late Bronze and Iron Age periods of area II, X* Beirut

Knight D., Tucker G. (eds) 1985 *The Hebrew Bible and Its Modern Interpreters* Philadelphia, Penn.

Koch K. 1969 *The Growth of the Biblical Tradition: the form-critical method* (trans.) London

Lapp N. (ed.) 1981 *The Third Campaign at Tell el-Ful: the excavations of 1964* (AASOR 45) Philadelphia, Penn.

Layton S.C. 1988 'Old Aramaic inscriptions' *BibArch* 51: 172–189

Lemaire A. 1977 *Inscriptions Hébraïques* vol. I: *Les Ostraca* (LAPO 9) Paris

—— 1991 'Hazaël de Damas, roi d'Aram' in Garelli Études [0E]: 91–108

Lemche N.P. 1985 *Early Israel: anthropological and historical studies on the Israelite society before the monarchy* Leiden

—— 1988 *Ancient Israel: a new history of Israelite society* Sheffield

Liverani M. 1987 'The collapse of the Near Eastern regional system at the end of the Bronze Age: the case of Syria' in Rowlands *et al.* [0E]: 66–73

Loretz 1984 [chapter 6]

Malamat A. 1963 'Aspects of the foreign policies of David and Solomon' *JNES* 22: 1–17

—— 1982 'How inferior Israelite forces conquered fortified Canaanite cities' *BAR* 8/2 (Mar.–Apr.): 25–35

Malamat A. (ed. with I. Eph'al) 1979 *World History of the Jewish People*, 1st series, vol. 4, 1–2: *The Age of the Monarchies: Political History; Culture and Society* Jerusalem

Mallowan M.E.L. 1972 'Carchemish' *AnSt* 22: 63–85

Martin J.D. 1975 *The Book of Judges* (Cambridge Bible Commentary on the New English Bible) Cambridge

Maxwell Miller J. 1976 *The Old Testament and the Historian* London

Maxwell Miller J., Hayes J.H. 1987 *A History of Israel and Judah* London

Mazar A. 1992 'The Iron Age I' in Ben-Tor A. (ed) *The Archaeology of Ancient Israel* (trans) New Haven, Conn.: 258–301

Mendenhall G.E. 1962 'The Hebrew Conquest of Palestine' *BibArch* 25: 66–87

Meriggi P. 1966–1975 *Manuale di Eteo Geroglifico* (Incunabula Graeca 13–14; 3 vols) Rome

Meyer E. 1884–1902 *Geschichte des Altertums* (5 vols) Stuttgart

Meyers C. 1988 *Discovering Eve: ancient Israelite women in context* Oxford

Millard A.R. 1990 'Israelite and Aramaean history in the light of inscriptions' *Tyndale Bulletin* 41/2: 261–275

Millard A.R., Bordreuil P. 1982 'A statue from Syria with Assyrian and Aramaic inscriptions' *BibArch* 45: 135–141

Mittman S. 1981 'Die Grabinschrift des Sängers Uriahu' *ZDPV* 97: 139–152

Moran W.L. 1987 'Join the *'apiru* or become one?' in Gallant D.M. (ed., with S.T. Hollis) *'Working with No Data': Semitic and Egyptological studies presented to Thomas O. Lambdin* Winona Lake, IN.: 209–212

Morris S.P. 1992 *Daidalos and the Origins of Greek Civilization* Princeton, NJ.

Moscati S. 1968 *The World of the Phoenicians* (trans. pbk edn 1973) London

—— (ed.) 1988 *The Phoenicians* London

Muhly J. 1985 'End of the Bronze Age' in Weiss 1985 [0Gc]: 261–270

Na'aman N. 1991 'The kingdom of Judah under Josiah' *Tel Aviv* 18: 1–69

Noth M. 1930 *Das System der zwölf Stämme Israels* (Beiträge zur Wissenschaft vom Alten und Neuen Testament IV/1) Stuttgart

—— 1958 *The History of Israel* (trans.) London

Oded 1978 [chapter 9]

Oden R. 1978 'Philo of Byblos and Hellenistic historiography' *PEQ* 110: 115–126

Oren E.D. 1982 'Ziklag – a biblical city on the edge of the Negev' *BibArch* 45: 155–166

Orthmann W. 1971 *Untersuchungen zur späthethitischen Kunst* (Saarbrücker Beiträge zur Altertumskunde 8) Bonn

Otzen B. 1979 'Israel under the Assyrians' in Larsen [0E]: 251–261

Payton R. 1991 'The Ulu Burun writing board set' *AnSt* 41: 99–106

Pitard 1987 [chapter 6]

Postgate J.N. 1974 'Remarks on the Assyrian countryside' *JESHO* 17: 225–243

Pritchard J.B. (ed.) 1974 *Solomon and Sheba* London

—— 1978 *Recovering Sarepta, a Phoenician city*, Princeton, NJ.

—— 1988 *Sarepta IV: the objects from area II, X* Beirut

Rainey A. 1987 review of Gottwald 1979 and Loretz 1984 in *JAOS* 107: 541–543

—— 1991 'Scholars disagree: Can you name the panel with the Israelites? Rainey's challenge' *BAR* 17/6 (Nov.–Dec.): 54–60; 93

Rendtorff R. 1983 *The Old Testament: an introduction* (trans.) London

Redford 1992 [chapter 3]

Riis P.J., Buhl M.L. 1990 *Hama 2/II: les objets de la période dite syro-hittite (âge du fer)* (Nationalmuseets Skrifter, Støwe Beretninger 12) Copenhagen

Rowley H.H. 1967 *The Growth of the Old Testament* (3rd edn) London

Sader H.S. 1987 *Les États Araméens de Syrie depuis leur fondation jusqu'à leur transformation en provinces assyriennes* (Beiruter Texte und Studien 36) Beirut

Salles J.-F. 1991a 'Du bon et du mauvais usages des Phéniciens' *Topoi: Orient-Occident* 1: 48–70

—— 1991b 'Du blé, de l'huile et du vin . . . (Notes sur les échanges commmerciaux en Mediterranée orientale vers le milieu du 1er millénaire av. J.-C.)' (parts 1 and 2) *AchHist* 6: 207–236

—— 1994 'Du blé, de l'huile et du vin . . .' (part 3) *AchHist* 8: 191–215

Sandars N. K. 1978 *The Sea Peoples: warriors of the ancient Mediterranean* London (rev. edn 1985)

Scnyzer M. (ed) 1988 *Les Phéniciens à la conquête de la Méditerranée* (= *Dossiers histoire et archéologie* 132/Nov.)

Shaw J.W. 1989 'Phoenicians in southern Crete' *AJA* 93: 165–183

Shiloh Y. 1984 *Excavations at the City of David* I (Qedem 19) Jerusalem

Smelik K.A.D. 1985 *Historische Dokumente aus dem alten Israel* (trans.) Göttingen (English trans. 1991)

Soggin J.A. 1984 *A History of Israel: from the beginnings to the Bar Kochba revolt, AD 135* (trans.) London

Stager L.E. 1985 'The archaeology of the family in ancient Israel' *BASOR* 260: 1–36

—— 1991 'When Canaanites and Philistines ruled Ashkelon' *BAR* 17/2: 24–43

Stager L.E., Wolff S.R. 1984 'Child sacrifice at Carthage: religious rite or population control?' *BAR* 10: 30–51

Stiebing W.H. 1989 *Out of the Desert? Archaeology and the exodus/conquest narratives* Buffalo, NY.

Strobel A. 1976 *Der spätbronzezeitliche Seevölkersturm* Berlin

Studia Phoenicia (sous la direction de E. Lipiński) I– Leuven 1983–

Symington D. 1991 'Late Bronze Age writing boards and their uses: textual evidence from Anatolia and Syria' *AnSt* 41: 111–123

Tadmor H. 1958a [chapter 7]

—— 1958b [chapter 9]

—— 1982 'The Aramaization of Assyria: aspects of western impacts' in Nissen and Renger [OE]: 449–470

Talmon S. 1987 'Har and midbar: an antithetical pair of biblical motifs' in Mindlin *et al* [OJ]: 117–142

Tappy R.E. 1992 *The Archaeology of Israelite Samaria* vol. 1: *Early Iron Age through the Ninth Century BCE* (Harvard Semitic Studies 44) Atlanta, Ga.

Tritsch F.J. 1973 'Sackers of Cities and the movement of populations' in Crossland R.A., Birchell A. (eds) *Bronze Age Migrations in the Agean* London: 233–238

Tubb J.N. 1988 'Tell es-Sa'idiyeh: preliminary report on the first three seasons of renewed excavation' *Levant* 20: 23–88

Ussishkin D. 1973 'King Solomon's palaces' *BibArch* 36: 78–105 (repr. in Campbell and Freedman [OE]: 227–248)

van Loon M. 1977 'The place of Urartu in 1. millennium BC trade' *Iraq* 39: 229–231

van Seters J. 1975 *Abraham in History and Tradition* New Haven, Conn.

Vattioni F. 1969–78 'I sigilli ebraici' I: *Biblica* 50 (1969): 357–388; II: *Augustinum* 11 (1971): 447–454; III *AION* 38 (1978): 227–254.

von Rad G. 1975 *Old Testament Theology* (2 vols; trans.) London

Ward W.A., Joukowsky M.S. (eds) 1992 *The Crisis Years: the twelfth century BC from beyond the Danube to the Tigris* Dubuque

Warnock P., Pendleton M. 1991 'The wood of the Ulu Burun diptych' *AnSt* 41: 107–110

Weber M. 1947 *The Theory of Social and Economic Organization* (trans. and ed. by Talcott Parsons) New York

Weinstein 1981 [chapter 6]

Weippert M. 1971 *The Settlement of the Israelite Tribes in Palestine* (trans.) London

Weitzman M. 1978 'The things you are liable to read . . .' in Bermant C., Weitzman M. 1979 *Ebla: an archaelogical enigma* London: 44–69

Wellhausen J. 1883 *Prolegomena zur Gechichte des Alten Israel* Berlin (trans., Edinburgh 1885; repr. 1957)

Whitelam K.W. 1986 'The symbols of power: aspects of royal propaganda in the United Monarchy' *BibArch* 49: 166–173

Willi T. 1972 *Die Chronik als Auslegung: Untersuchungen zur literarischen Gestaltung der historischen Überlieferung Israels* (Forschungen zur Religion und Literatur des Alten und Neuen Testaments 106) Göttingen

Winter I. 1976 'Phoenician and North Syrian ivory carving in historical context: questions of style and distribution' *Iraq* 38: 1–22

—— 1979 'On the problems of Karatepe: the reliefs and their context' *AnSt* 29: 153–168

—— 1983 'Carchemish *ša kišad puratti*' *AnSt* 33: 177–198

Wood B.G. 1991 'The Philistines enter Canaan: were they Egyptian lackeys or invading conquerors?' *BAR* 17/6 (Nov.–Dec.): 44–52

Wright G.E. 1962 *Biblical Archaeology* (2nd edn) Philadelphia, Penn.

Yadin Y. 1968 'And Dan, why did he abide by the ships?' *Australian Journal of Biblical Archaeology* 1: 9–23

—— 1970 'Megiddo of the Kings of Israel' *BibArch* 33: 66–96

—— 1972 *Hazor: the rediscovery of a great citadel of the Bible* (Schweich Lectures 1970) London

—— 1982 'Is the biblical account of the Israelite conquest historically reliable?' *BAR* 8/2 (Mar.–Apr.): 16–23

Yurco F.J. 1991 'Yurco's response to Rainey' *BAR* 17/6 (Nov.–Dec.): 61

Chapter 9

General

Liverani 1988 [OC], chs 28–29, and pp. 880–884; Garelli and Nikiprowetztry 1974 [OC], chs 2; 3/1; *CAH* III chs 6, 22–26; Bottéro *et al.* 1967b [OB], ch. 1; Klengel *et al.* 1989 [OC]: 339–388.
and (details below)
Contenau 1954; Fales 1981b; Grayson 1976; Luckenbill 1926; Postgate 1992; Reade 1983; Saggs 1984; Schramm 1973; van der Spek 1993.

References

Albenda P. 1983 'Western Asiatic women in the Iron Age: their image revealed' *BibArch* 46: 82–88.
—— 1986 *The Palace of Sargon King of Assyria* Paris
Barkay 1992 [chapter 8]
Barnett R.D. 1957 *The Nimrud Ivories in the British Museum* London
—— 1976 *The Sculptures of Ashurbanipal* London
Barnett R.D., Falkner M. 1962 *The Sculptures of Assur-nasir-pal II, Tiglath-Pileser III, Esarhaddon from the Central and South-West Palace at Nimrud* London
Becking 1992 [chapter 8]
Berger 1975 [chapter 11]
Borger R. 1956 *Die Inschriften Asarhaddons, Königs von Assyrien* (AfO Beiheft 9) Graz
—— 1965 'Der Aufstieg des neubabylonichen Reiches' *JCS* 19: 59–78
Börker-Klähn J. 1982 *Vorderasiatische Bildstelen und vergleichbare Bildreliefs* (2 vols; BaF 4) Mainz
Briant P. in press [chapter 13]
Brinkman J.A. 1984 [chapter 11, Brinkman 1984a]
—— 1990 'The Babylonian chronicle revisited' in Moran Studies [OE]: 73–104
Brown 1986 [chapter 13]
Canby J.V. 1971 'Decorated garments in Ashurnasirpal's sculpture' *Iraq* 33: 31–53
Carter, Stolper 1984 [chapter 7]
Cassin E. 1968 *La splendeur divine: introduction à l'étude de la mentalité méso-potamienne* (Civilisation et Société 8) Paris
Claessen, Skalník 1981 [chapter 8]
Cogan M. 1974 *Imperialism and Religion: Assyria, Judah and Israel in the eighth and seventh centuries BCE* Missoula
Contenau G. 1954 *Everyday Life in Babylonia and Assyria* (trans.) London
Dalley S. 1985 [chapter 8]
Dalley S., Postgate J.N. 1984 *The Tablets from Fort Shalmaneser* (CTN 3) London
Deller K.-H. 1987 '*Tamkaru*-Kredite in neuassyrischer Zeit' *JESHO* 30: 1–29
Diakonoff 1974 [chapter 1]
Donbaz 1990 [chapter 8]
Elat M. 1982 'Mesopotamische Kriegsrituale' *BiOr* 39: 5–25
—— 1987 'Der *tamkaru* im neuassyrischen Reich' *JESHO* 30: 233–254
Eph'al I. 1982 [chapter 8]
Fadhil A. 1990a 'Die in Nimrud/Kalhu aufgefundene Grabinschrift der Jabâ' *BaM* 20: 461–470
—— 1990b 'Die Grabinschrift der Mulissu-mukannišat-Ninua aus Nimrud/Kalhu und andere in ihrem Grab' *BaM* 20: 471–482
Fales F.M. 1973 *Censimenti e Catasti di Epoca Neo-Assira* Rome

—— 1981a 'A literary code in Assyrian royal inscriptions: the case of Ashurbanipal's Egyptian campaign' in Fales 1981b: 169–202

—— (ed.) 1981b *Assyrian Royal Inscriptions: new horizons in literary, ideological and historical analysis* Rome

Fales F.M., Jakob-Rost L. 1991 *Neo-Assyrian Texts from Assur: private archives in the Vorderasiatische Museum of Berlin (Part 1)* (*SAAB* 5/I-II) Padua

Fales F.M., Postgate J.N. 1992 *Imperial Administrative Records* Part I: *Palace and Temple Administration* (SAA 7) Helsinki

Frame G. 1992 [chapter 11]

George A. 1990 'Royal tombs at Nimrud' *Minerva* I/1: 29–31

Gerardi P. 1987 *Assurbanipal's Elamite Campaigns: a literary and political study* (Univ. of Penn., diss.)

Gibson 1971–82 [chapter 8]

Glassner J.-J. 1991 'A propos des jardins mésopotamiens' *Jardins d'Orient* (Res Orientales III) Paris: 9–17

Goody J. (ed.) 1966 *Succession to High Office* (Cambridge Papers in Social Anthropology 4) Cambridge

Grayson A.K. 1970 'Chronicles and the Akitu festival' *Actes de la 17. Rencontre Assyriologique* Ham-sur-Heure: 160–170

—— 1976 *Assyrian Royal Inscriptions* vol. 2 Wiesbaden

—— 1980–3 'Königslisten' *RLA* 6: 86–135

—— 1991 [chapter 7]

Grelot 1972 [chapter 13]

Gurney O.R. 1956 'The Assyrian tablets from Sultantepe' *Proceedings of the British Academy* 41: 21–41

Gurney O.R., Finkelstein J.J. 1957 *The Sultantepe Tablets* I London

Gurney O.R., Hulin P. 1964 *The Sultantepe Tablets* II London

Haller A. 1953 *Die Gräber und Grüfte von Assur* (WVDOG 65) Berlin

Harper R.F. 1892–1914 *Assyrian and Babylonian Letters Belonging to the Kouyounjik Collection of the British Museum* I-XIV London, Chicago

Hawkins 1972 [chapter 8]

—— in press [chapter 8]

Helm 1980 [chapter 8]

Herrmann G. 1986 *Ivories from Nimrud* IV: *Ivories from Room SW37, Fort Shalmaneser* London

—— 1992 *Ivories from Nimrud* V: *The Small Collections from Fort Shalmaneser* London

Hrouda B. 1965 *Die Kulturgeschichte des assyrischen Flachbildes* (Saarbrücker Beiträge zur Altertumskunde 2) Bonn

Hunger H. 1992 *Astrological Reports to Assyrian Kings* (SAA 8) Helsinki

Ismail B.K., Roaf M., Black J. 1983 ''Ana in the cuneiform sources' *Sumer* 39: 191–194

Jacobsen T., Lloyd S. 1935 *Sennacherib's Aqueduct at Jerwan* (OIP 24) Chicago

Johns C.H.W. 1898–1923 *Assyrian Deeds and Documents Recording the Transfer of Property Including the So-called Private Contracts, Legal Decisions and Proclamations, Preserved in the Kouyounjik Collections of the British Museum, Chiefly of the 7th Century BC* (4 vols) Cambridge

—— 1901 *An Assyrian Doomsday Book or Liber Censualis of the District Round Harran, in the Seventh Century BC* Leipzig

Katja L. 1987 'A Neo-Assyrian document on two cases of river ordeal' *SAAB* I/2: 65–68

King L.W. 1915 *Bronze Reliefs from the Gates of Shalmaneser, King of Assyria BC 860–825* London

Kinnier Wilson J.V. 1972 *The Nimrud Wine Lists* (CTN 1) London

Kitchen 1986 [chapter 12]

Klauber E.G. 1913 *Politisch-religiöse Texte aus der Sargonidenzeit* Leipzig

Knudtzon J.A. 1893 *Assyrische Gebete an den Sonnengott für Staat und königliches Haus aus der Zeit Asarhaddons und Asurbanipals* (2 vols) Leipzig

Kohler J., Ungnad A. 1913 *Assyrische Rechtsurkunden* Leipzig

Kuhrt A. 1982 'Assyrian and Babylonian traditions in classical authors: a critical synthesis' in Nissen and Renger [OE]: 539–553

—— 1987 'Berossus' *Babyloniaca* and Seleucid rule in Babylonia' in Kuhrt A., Sherwin-White S. (eds) 1987 *Hellenism in the East: the interaction of Greek and non-Greek civilizations from Syria to Central Asia after Alexander* London, Berkeley, Cal.: 32–56

Kwasman T. 1988 *Neo-Assyrian Legal Documents in the Kouyounjik Collection of the British Museum* (Studia Pohl, Series Maior 14) Rome

Kwasman T., Parpola S. 1991 *Legal Transactions of the Royal Court of Nineveh*, Part I: *Tiglath-pileser III through Esarhaddon* (SAA 6) Helsinki

Landsberger B. 1965 *Brief eines Bischofs von Esagila an König Asarhaddon* (Mededelingen der Koninklijke Akademie van Wetenschapen, Nieuwe reeks 28/VI) Amsterdam

Landsberger B., Parpola S., Tadmor H. 1989 'The sin of Sargon and Sennacherib's last will' *SAAB* 3: 1–51

Lanfranchi 1990 [chapter 10]

Lanfranchi G.B., Parpola S. 1990 *The Correspondence of Sargon* part II: *Letters from the Northern and Northeastern Provinces* (SAA 5) Helsinki

Lemaire A., Durand J.-M. 1984 *Les inscriptions araméennes de Sfiré et l'Assyrie de Shamshi-ilu* Geneva, Paris

Levine L.D. 1974 *Geographical Studies in the Neo-Assyrian Zagros* Toronto (also pub. in *Iran* 11 (1973): 1–27; 12 (1974): 99–124)

—— 1977 'Sargon's eighth campaign' in Levine L.D., Young T.C. (eds) *Mountains and Lowlands* (Bibliotheca Mesopotamica 7) Malibu, Cal.: 135–151

Lie A.G. 1929 *The Inscriptions of Sargon II, King of Assyria* part I: *The Annals* Paris

Liverani M. 1979 'The ideology of the Assyrian empire' in Larsen [OE]: 297–317

—— 1981 'Critique of variants and the titulary of Sennacherib' in Fales 1981b: 225–258

—— 1988 'The growth of the Assyrian empire' *SAAB* II/2: 81–98

Livingstone A. 1989 *Court Poetry and Literary Miscellenea* (SAA 3) Helsinki

Luckenbill D.D. 1924 *The Annals of Sennacherib* (OIP 2) Chicago

—— 1926 *Ancient Records of Assyria and Babylonia* (2 vols) Chicago

Lyon D.G. 1883 *Keilschrifttexte Sargons, Königs von Assyrien (722–705 v. Chr.)* Leipzig

Madhloom T.A. 1970 *The Chronology of Neo-Assyrian Art* London

Malbran-Labat F. 1982 *L'Armée et l'Organisation Militaire de l'Assyrie* Paris

Mallowan M.E.L. 1966 *Nimrud and Its Remains* (2 vols) London

Mallowan M.E.L., Herrmann G. 1974 *Ivories from Nimrud III: Furniture from SW7, Fort Shalmaneser* London

Marcus M.I. 1987 'Geography as an organizing principle in the imperial art of Shalmaneser III' *Iraq* 49: 77–90

Mayer W.R. 1988 'Ein neues Köngisritual gegen feindliche Bedrohung' *Or.* 57: 145–164

McKay J. 1973 *Religion in Judah under the Assyrians* (SBT 26) London

Millard A. 1965 'The Assyrian royal seal type again' *Iraq* 27: 12–16

—— 1983 'Assyrians and Aramaeans' *Iraq* 45: 101–108

—— 1990 [chapter 8]

—— 1994 *The Eponyms of the Assyrian Empire 910–612 BC* (SAA Studies 2) Helsinki

Millard, Bordreuil 1982 [chapter 8]

Miroschedji 1985 [chapter 13]

Na'aman N. 1974 'Sennacherib's "Letter to God" on his campaign to Judah' *BASOR* 214: 25–39

—— 1991a 'Chronology and history in the Late Assyrian empire (631–619 BC)' *ZA* 81: 243–267

—— 1991b [chapter 8]

Oates J. 1965 'Assyrian Chronology 631–612 BC' *Iraq* 27: 135–159

Oded B. 1979 *Mass Deportations and Deportees in the Neo-Assyrian Empire* Wiesbaden

—— 1992 *War, Peace and Empire: justifications for war in Assyrian royal inscriptions* Wiesbaden

Olmstead A.T. 1916 *Assyrian Historiography: a source study* Missouri

Oppenheim A.L. 1955 'Siege documents from Nippur' *Iraq* 17: 69–89

—— 1960 'The City of Assur in 714 BC' *JNES* 19: 133–147

Paley S.M. 1976 *King of the World: Ashurnasirpal II of Assyria 883–859 BC* Brooklyn, NY

Parpola S. 1970/1983 *Letters from Assyrian Scholars to Kings Esarhaddon and Assurbanipal* (2 parts; AOAT 5/1 and 2) Kevelaer, Neukirchen-Vluyn

—— 1971 *Letters from Assyrian Scholars to Kings Esarhaddon and Assurbanipal* Part IIA: *Introduction and Appendixes* (diss., Helsinki) Neukirchen-Vluyn

—— 1972 'A letter from Šamaš-šumu-ukin to Esarhaddon' *Iraq* 34: 21–34

—— 1980 'The murderer of Sennacherib' in Alster [OE]: 171–182

—— 1987 'Neo-Assyrian treaties from the royal archives of Nineveh' *JCS* 39: 161–187

—— 1988 'The Neo-Assyrian word for "queen"' *SAAB* II/2: 73–76

Parpola S., Watanabe K. 1988 *Neo-Assyrian Treaties and Loyalty Oaths* (SAA 2) Helsinki

Pečírková J. 1977 'The administrative organization of the Neo-Assyrian empire' *ArOr* 45: 211–228

Pedersen 1985 [chapter 7]

Piepkorn A. 1933 *Historical Prism Inscriptions of Ashurbanipal* (AS 5) Chicago

Place V. 1867–70 *Ninive et l'Assyrie* (3 vols) Paris

Pongratz-Leisten B., Deller K., Bleibtreu E. 1992 'Götterstreitwagen und Götterstandarten: Götter auf dem Feldzug und ihr Kult im Feldlager' *BaM* 23: 291–356

Porter B. 1987 *Symbols of Power: figurative aspects of Esarhaddon's Babylonian policy (681–669 BC)* (Univ. of Penn., diss; pub. as *Images, Power and Politics* (Mem. Am. Phil. Soc. 208) 1993)

Postgate J.N. 1969 *Neo-Assyrian Royal Grants and Decrees* (Studia Pohl, Series Maior 1) Rome

—— 1973 *The Governor's Palace Archive* (CTN 2) London

—— 1974a *Taxation and Conscription in the Assyrian Empire* (Studia Pohl, Series Maior 3) Rome

—— 1974b 'Royal exercise of justice under the Assyrian empire' in Garelli [OE]: 417–426

—— 1976 *Fifty Neo-Assyrian Legal Documents* Warminster

—— 1979 'The economic structure of the Assyrian empire' in Larsen [OE]: 193–221

—— 1980 '"Princeps Iudex" in Assyria' *RA* 74: 180–182

—— 1987 'Employer, employee and employment in the Neo-Assyrian period' in Powell [OE]: 257–270

—— 1992 'The land of Assur and the yoke of Assur' *World Archaeology* 23: 247–263

Reade J. 1970 'The Accession of Sinsharishkun' *JCS* 23: 1–9

—— 1972 'The Neo-Assyrian court and army: evidence from the sculptures' *Iraq* 34: 87–112

—— 1979 'Ideology and propaganda in Assyrian art' in Larsen [OE]: 329–343

—— 1983 *Assyrian Sculpture* London

—— 1987 'Was Sennacherib a feminist?' in Durand [OE]: 139–146

Roth M.T. 1987 'Age at marriage and the household: a study of Neo-Assyrian and Neo-Babylonian forms' *Comparative Studies in Society and History* 29: 715–747

Russell J. 1991 *Sennacherib's Palace without a Rival at Nineveh* Chicago

Sachs A.J. 1953 'The late Neo-Assyrian royal seal type' *Iraq* 15: 167–170

Saggs H.W.F. 1955a/1955b/1956/1958/1959/1963/1965/1966 'The Nimrud Letters 1952 – Parts I–VIII' *Iraq* 17: 21–56, 126–160; 18: 40–56; 20: 182–212; 21: 158–179; 25: 70–80; 27: 17–32; 28: 177–191

—— 1975 'Historical texts and fragments of Sargon II of Assyria: 1. The "Assur Charter"' *Iraq* 37: 11–20

—— 1984 *The Might That Was Assyria* London

Salles J.-F. 1989 'Les échanges commerciaux dans le golfe arabo-persique dans le courant du 1er millénaire av. J.-C.: réflexions sur Makkan et Meluhha' in Fahd T. (ed.) *L'Arabie préislamique et son environnement* (Colloque de Strasbourg 1987) Strasbourg: 67–96

Sancisi-Weerdenburg 1988 [chapter 13]

Schramm W. 1972 'War Semiramis assyrische Regentin?' *Historia* 21: 513–521

—— 1973 *Einleitung in die assyrischen Königsinschriften* 2. Teil: *934–722* (HdO) Leiden

Seux M.-J. 1980–3 'Königtum' *RLA* 6: 140–173

Starr I. 1990 *Queries to the Sungod: divination and politics in Sargonid Assyria* (SAA 4) Helsinki

Stearns J.B. 1961 *Reliefs from the Palace of Assurnasirpal II* (AfO Beiheft 15) Graz

Streck M. 1916 *Assurbanipal* Bd. 1–3 (VAB 7) Leipzig

Stronach D. 1989 'When Assyria fell: new light on the last days of Nineveh' *Mar Šipri* 2/2: 1–2

Stronach D., Lumsden S. 1992 'UC Berkeley's excavations at Nineveh' *BibArch* 55: 227–233

Tadmor H. 1958 'The Campaigns of Sargon II of Assyria' *JCS* 12: 22–40; 77–100

—— 1975 'Assyria and the West: the ninth century and its aftermath' in Goedicke and Roberts [OE]: 36–48

—— 1977 'Observations on Assyrian historiography' in Finkelstein Essays [OE]: 209–213

—— 1981 'History and ideology in the Assyrian royal inscriptions' in Fales 1981b: 13–34

—— 1983 'Autobiographical apology in the royal Assyrian literature' in Tadmor and Weinfeld [OK]: 36–57

Tadmor H., Millard A.R. 1973 'Adad-Nirari III in Syria' *Iraq* 35: 57–64

Thomas 1992 [chapter 7]

Thomas F. 1993 'Sargon II, der Sohn Tiglat-pilesers III' in Dietrich M., Loretz O. (Hsg.) *Mesopotamica – Ugaritica – Biblica: Festschrift für Kurt Bergerhof zur Vollendung seines 70. Lebensjahres am 7. Mai 1992* (AOAT) Kevelaer, Neukirchen-Vluyn: 465–470

Thureau-Dangin F. 1912 *Une relation de la huitième campagne de Sargon* (TCL 3) Paris

Thureau-Dangin F., Dunand M. 1936 *Til Barsib* Paris

Turner G. 1970 'Tell Nebi Yunus: the *ekal mašarti* of Nineveh' *Iraq* 32: 68–85

Ungnad A. 1938 'Eponymen' *RLA* 2: 412–457 (for new edn cf. A. Millard 1994)

van der Spek R.J. 1993 'Assyriology and history: a comparative study of war and empire in Assyria, Athens and Rome' in Hallo 1993 [OE]: 262–270

van Dijk J. 1962 'Die Tontafeln aus dem reš-Heiligtum' *UVB* 18: 43–61

van Driel G. 1969 *The Cult of Assur* Leiden

—— 1970 'Land and people in Assyria' *BiOr* 27: 168–175

von Voigtlander 1963 [chapter 11]

Wäfler M. 1975 *Nicht-Assyrer neuassyrischer Darstellungen* (AOAT 26) Kevelaer, Neukirchen-Vluyn

Watanabe K. 1987 *Die adê-Vereidigungen anlässlich der Thronfolgeregelung Asarhaddons* (BaM Beiheft 3) Berlin

Waterman L. 1930–36 *Royal Correspondence of the Assyrian Empire* (4 vols) Ann Arbor, Mich.

Weidner E. 1926 'Die grosse Königsliste aus Assur' *AfO* 3: 66ff.

—— 1932–3 'Assyrische Beschreibungen der Kriegs-Reliefs Aššurbânaplis' *AfO* 8: 175–203

Weidner 1940 = J. Friedrich, G.R. Meyer, A. Ungnad, E. Weidner *Die Inschriften vom Tell Halaf: Keilschrifttexte und aramäische Urkunden aus einer assyrischen Provinzhauptstadt* (AfO Beiheft 6) Berlin 1940

Weippert M. 1973–4 'Die Kämpfe des assyrischen Königs Assurbanipal gegen die Araber. Redaktionskritische Untersuchung des Berichtes in Prisma A' *WO* 7/I: 39–85

—— 1981 'Assyrische Prophetien der Zeit Asarhaddons und Assurbanipals' in Fales 1981b: 71–116

Winter 1983 [chapter 8]

Wiseman D.J. 1952 'A new stele of Assurnasirpal II' *Iraq* 14: 24–44

—— 1958 *The Vassal Treaties of Esarhaddon* London (= *Iraq* 20: 1–100)

Zablocka J. 1971 *Stosunki agrarna w panstwie Sargonidow* (with German summary) Poznań

Zawadski S. 1988 *The Fall of Assyria and Median-Babylonian Relations in Light of the Nabopolassar Chronicle* Poznań, Delft

Chapter 10

General

CAH III, chs 8 and 34; Liverani 1988 [OC]: 852–864; 871–879; Bottéro *et al.* 1967b [OB]: 44–51; Schmökel 1961 [OA], section 4; Klengel *et al.* 1989 [OC]: 474–482 *and (details below)*

Bryce 1986; Burney and Lang 1971, ch. 5; Diakonoff 1984; Frankel 1979; Haas 1986b; Hanfman 1983b; Pedley 1972; Zimansky 1985

References

Badaljan R.S. *et al.* 1992 'Archaelogical investigations at Horom in the Shirak Plain of North-West Armenia, 1990' *Iran* 30: 31–48

—— 1993 'Preliminary report on the 1992 excavations at Horom, Armenia' *Iran* 31: 1–24

Benedict W.C. 1961 'The Urartian-Assyrian inscription of Kelishin' *JAOS* 81: 359–385

Boehmer R. 1973 'Phrygische Prunkgewänder des 8. Jahrhunderts v. Chr.' *AA* 88: 149–172

Brinkman J.A. 1989 'The Akkadian words for "Ionia" and "Ionian"' in *Daidalikon: Studies in honor of Raymond V. Schoder, S.J.* Waucoda, Ill.: 53–71

Brische C., Lejeune M. 1984 *Corpus des inscriptions paléo-phrygiennes* I: *Textes*; II: *Planches* Paris

Bryce T.R. 1986 *The Lycians in Literary and Epigraphic Sources* (The Lycians 1) Copenhagen

Burney C.A. 1969–70/1972–6 Haftavan excavations and preliminary reports in *Iran* 7: 177–179; 8: 157–171; 182–183; 10: 127–142; 169–170; 11: 153–172; 12: 213–214; 13: 149–164; 14: 157–158

Burney C.A., Lang M.D. 1971 *The Peoples of the Hills* London

Cogan M., Tadmor H. 1977 'Gyges and Ashurbanipal: a study in literary transmission' *Or.* 46: 65–85

Diakonoff I.M. 1963 *Urartskie pis'ma i dokumenty* Moscow, Leningrad

—— 1984 *The Prehistory of the Armenian People* (trans.) Delmar, NY

Dyson R.H. 1964 'In the city of the golden bowl' *Illustrated London News* (12 Sept.): 372–374

—— 1965 [chapter 13]

Dyson R.H., Muscarella O. 1989 'Constructing the chronology and historical implications of Hasanlu IV' *Iran* 27: 1–27

Forbes T.B. 1983 *Urartian Architecture* (BAR International Series 170) Oxford

Frankel D. 1979 *The Ancient Kingdom of Urartu* London

Greenewalt C.H., Jr. 1976 *Ritual Dinners in Early Historic Sardis* (University of California Classical Studies 17) Berkeley, Cal.

Haas V. 1986a 'Die ältesten Nachrichten zur Geschichte des armenischen Hochlands' in Haas 1986b: 21–30

—— 1986b *Das Reich Urartu: ein altorientalischer Staat im 1. Jahrtausend v. Chr* (Xenia: Konstanzer Althistorische Vorträge und Forschungen 17) Konstanz

Hanfman G.M.A. 1983a 'Lydian society and culture' in Hanfman 1983b: 67–99

—— 1983b *Sardis from Prehistoric to Roman Times: results of the archaeological exploration of Sardis 1958–1975* Cambridge, Mass.

Hartog F. 1988 *The Mirror of Herodotus: the representation of the other in the writing of history* (trans.; The New Historicism: Studies in Cultural Poetics 5) Berkeley, Cal.

Işik F. 1987 'Zur Enstehung der phrygischen Felsdenkmäler' *AnSt* 37: 163–178

Kessler K.-H. 1986 'Die Beziehungen zwischen Urartu und Mesopotamien' in Haas 1986b: 59–86

König F.W. 1965–7 *Handbuch der Chaldischen Inscriften* (2 vols) Graz

Kristensen A.K.G. 1988 *Who Were the Cimmerians, and Where Did They Come From? Sargon II, the Cimmerians, and Rusa I* (trans.) Copenhagen

Kroll S. 1972 'Excavations at Bastam, Iran, the first Urartian site uncovered in Iran' *Archaeology* 25 (Oct.): 292–297

—— 1976 *Keramik urartäischer Festungen in Iran* Berlin

Lanfranchi G.B. 1983 'Some new texts about a revolt against the Urartian king Rusa I' *OA* 22: 123–35

—— 1990 *I Cimmeri: emergenza delle militari iraniche nel Vicino Oriente (VIII-VII sec. AC)* (History of Ancient Near East/Studies II bis) Padua

Lanfranchi, Parpola 1990 [chapter 9]

Melikishvili G.A. 1971 *Die Urartäische Sprache* Munich

Merhav R. (ed.) 1991 *Urartu: a metalworking centre in the first millennium BCE* Jerusalem

Özgüç T. 1966 *Altintepe: architectural monuments and wall paintings* Ankara

—— 1967 'Ancient Ararat' *Scientific American* 216/3: 38–46

Pedley J.G. 1972 *Ancient Literary Sources on Sardis* (Archaeological Exploration of Sardis) Cambridge, Mass.

Piotrovsky B. 1967 *Urartu: the kingdom of Van and its art* London

Prag A.J.N.W. 1989 'Reconstructing King Midas: a first report' *AnSt* 39: 159–165

Porada 1965 [chapter 7]

Ramage A. 1987 'Lydian Sardis' in Guralnick E. (ed.) *Sardis: twenty-seven years of discovery* Chicago: 6–15

Rolle R. 1989 *The World of the Scythians* (trans.) London

Salvini M. 1979 'Zu den beschrifteten Tonbullen' in Kleiss W. *Bastam* I: *Ausgrabungen in den urartäischen Anlagen 1972–1975* (Teheraner Forschungen 4) Berlin: 133–136

—— 1986 'Tušpa, die Hauptstadt von Urartu' in Haas 1986b: 31–44

Schaus G.P. 1992 'Imported West Anatolian pottery at Gordion' *AnSt* 42: 151–177

Seidl U. 1979 'Die Siegelbilder' in Kleiss W. *Bastam* I: *Ausgrabungen in den urartäischen Anlagen 1972–1975* (Teheraner Forshungen 4) Berlin: 137–149

Sevin V. 1991 'The early Iron age in the Elazığ region and the problem of the Muškians' *AnSt* 41: 87–97

Thureau-Dangin 1912 [chapter 9]

van Loon M. 1966 *Urartian Art: its distinctive traits in the light of new excavations* Leiden

—— 1974 'The Euphrates mentioned by Sarduri II of Urartu' in Bittel K. (ed.) *Anatolian Studies Presented to Hans Gustav Güterbock on the Occasion of His 65th Birthday* Istanbul: 189–194

Wallace R. 1988 'WALWE. and .KALI.' *JHS* 108: 203–207

Wartke R.-B. 1990 *Toprakkale: Untersuchungen zu den Metallobjekten im Vorderasiatischen Museum zu Berlin* (Schriften zur Geschichte und Kultur des Alten Orients, Bd. 22) Berlin

Wilhelm 1982 [chapter 6]

Young R.S. 1981 *Three Great Early Tumuli* (University Museum Monograph 43: the Gordion Excavations Final Reports 1) Philadelphia, Penn.

Zimansky P.E. 1985 *Ecology and Empire: the structure of the Urartian state* (SAOC 41) Chicago

Chapter 11

General

CAH III, chs 7, 21, 27–28; Oates 1986 [OGb]: 107–135; Bottéro *et al.* 1967b [OB]: 99–110; Liverani 1988 [OC], ch. 21; Garelli and Nikiprowetzky 1974 [OC], ch. 3/2; Klengel *et al.* 1989 [OC]: 388–413
and (details below)
Brinkman 1968; 1984a; Frame 1992; von Voigtlander 1963; Wiseman 1956

References

Adams 1981 [chapter 1]

Beaulieu P.-A. 1987 *The Reign of Nabonidus, King of Babylon 556–539 BC* (YNER 10) New Haven, Conn.

Berger, P.R. 1970 'Das Neujahrsfest nach den Königsinschriften des ausgehenden babylonischen Reiches' in Finet A. (ed.) *Actes dela XVIIe Rencontre Assyriologique Internationale: Université Libre de Bruxelles, 30 juin–4 juillet, 1969* Ham-sur-Heure: 155–159

—— 1973 *Die neubabylonischen Königsinschriften* (AOAT 4/1) Neukirchen-Vluyn

—— 1975 'Der Kyros-Zylinder mit dem Zusatzfragment BIN II Nr. 32 und die akkadischen Personennamen im Danielbuch' *ZA* 64: 192–234

Black J. 1981 'The New Year ceremonies in ancient Babylon: "taking Bel by the hand" and a cultic picnic' *Religion* 11: 39–59

Böhl M.T. de Liagre 1937–8 'De dochter van Koning Nabonidus' *JEOL* 5: 357–360

Borger 1956 [chapter 9]

BIBLIOGRAPHY

Brinkman J.A. 1965 'Ur: 721–605' *Or.* 34: 241–258

— 1968 *A History of Postkassite Babylonia (1158–722)* (AnOr 43) Rome

— 1969 'The akitu inscription of Bēl-ibni and Nabû-zēra-ušabši' *WO* 5/1: 39–50

— 1979 'Babylonia under the Assyrian Empire 745–c. 627' in Larsen [OE]: 223–250

— 1984a *Prelude to Empire: Babylonian society and politics, 747–626 BC* Philadelphia, Penn.

— 1984b 'Settlement surveys and documentary evidence: regional variation and secular trend in Mesopotamian demography' *JNES* 43: 169–180

— 1986 'The Elamite–Babylonian frontier in the Neo-Elamite period, 750–625 BC' *Fragmenta Historiae Elamicae: Mélanges offerts à M.J. Stève* Paris: 199–207

Brinkman J.A., Dalley S. 1988 'A royal kudurru from the reign of Aššur-nādin-šumi' *ZA* 78: 76–98

Brinkman J.A., Kennedy D.A. 1983 'Documentary evidence for the economic base of early Neo-Babylonian society' *JCS* 35: 1–90

— 1986 'Supplement to the survey of dated Neo-Babylonian economic texts, 721–626 BC' *JCS* 38: 99–106

Carter, Stolper 1984 [chapter 7]

Cavigneaux A., Ismail B.Kh. 1990 'Die Stadthalter von Suhu und Mari im 8. Jh. v. Chr. anhand neuer Texte aus den irakischen Grabungen im Staugebiet des Qadissiya-Damms' *BaM* 20: 321–456

Charpin D. 1986 [chapter 2]

Dalley, Postgate 1984 [chapter 9]

Dandamaev M.A. 1982 'The Neo-Babylonian elders' Diakonoff Studies [OE]: 38–41

— 1984 *Slavery in Babylonia* (rev. edn; trans.) De Kalb, Ill.

— 1990 [chapter 13]

Doty L.T. 1977 *Cuneiform Archives from Hellenistic Uruk* (Yale, diss.)

Dupont-Sommer A. 1948 'Un papyrus araméen d'époque saïte découverte à Saqqara' *Semitica* 1: 43–68

Durand J.-M. 1979 'Les "slave documents" de Merodach Baladan' *JA* 267: 245–260

Edel E. 1978 [chapter 12]

Eph'al I. 1983 'On warfare and military control in the ancient Near Eastern empires: a research outline' in Tadmor and Weinfeld [OK]: 88–106

Frame G. 1984 'The "First Families" of Borsippa during the early Neo-Babylonian period' *JCS* 36: 67–80

— 1992 *Babylonia 689–627 BC: a political history* Leiden

Gadd C.J. 1958 'The Harran inscriptions of Nabonidus' *AnSt* 8: 35–92

Galter H. 1984 'Die Zerstörung Babylons durch Sanherib' *StOr* 55: 161–173

Garelli P. n.d. 'Les sujets du roi d'Assyrie ' in Finet A. (ed.) *La voix de l'opposition en Mesopotamie* Brussels: 189–213

Gasche H. *et al.* 1987 'Habl aṣ-Ṣahr 1983–85: Nebuchadnezzar II's cross-country wall north of Sippar' *NAPR* 1: 3–46

— 1989 'Habl aṣ-Ṣahr, nouvelles fouilles. L'ouvrage defensif de Nabuchodonosor au nord de Sippar' *NAPR* 2: 23–70

George A. 1992 *Babylonian Topographical Texts* (OLA 40) Leuven

— 1993 'Babylon revisited: archaeology and philology in harness' *Antiquity* 67: 734–746

Gerardi 1987 [chapter 9]

Gibson 1971–82 [chapter 8]

Graham J.N. 1984 'Vineyards and plowmen: 2 *Kings* 25:12 and *Jeremiah* 52:16' *BibArch* 47: 55–58

Grayson 1975 [chapter 7]

Helm 1980 [chapter 8]

Ismail, Roaf, Black 1983 [chapter 9]

Joannès F. 1980 'Kaššaia, fille de Nabuchodonosor II' *RA* 74: 183–4

—— 1982 'La location de Surru à l'époque néo-babylonienne' *Semitica* 32: 35–42

—— 1987 'Un cas de remarriage d'époque néo-babylonienne' in Durand [OE]: 91–96

—— 1989 *Archives de Borsippa: la famille Ea-ilûta-bâni* Geneva

Killick R. 1984 'Northern Akkad Project: excavations at Ḥabl aṣ-Ṣaḥr' *Iraq* 46: 125–130

King L.W. 1912 *Babylonian Boundary Stones and Memorial Tablets in the British Museum* London

Koldewey R. 1913 *Das wiedererstehende Babylon* Leipzig

Kuhrt A. 1987 'Usurpation, conquest and ceremonial: from Babylon to Persia' in Cannadine D., Price S. (eds) *Rituals of Royalty: power and ceremonial in traditional societies* (Past and Present Publications) Cambridge: 20–55

—— 1988 'The Achaemenid empire: a Babylonian perspective' *PCPS* 214 (n.s.) 34: 60–76

—— 1990a 'Alexander and Babylon' in *AchHist* 5: 121–130

—— 1990b 'Nabonidus and the Babylonian priesthood' in Beard M., North J. (eds) *Pagan Priests* London: 119–155

Kümmel H.M. 1979 *Familie, Beruf und Amt im spätbabylonischen Uruk: prosopographische Untersuchungen zu Berufsgruppen des 6. Jahrhunderts v. Chr. in Uruk* (ADOG 20) Berlin

Lambert W.G. 1960 [chapter 7]

—— 1968–9 'A new source for the reign of Nabonidus' *AfO* 22: 1–8

Landsberger 1965 [chapter 9]

Landsberger B., Bauer T. 1927 'Zu neuveröffentlichten Geschichtsquellen aus der Zeit von Asarhaddon bis Nabonid' *ZA* 37: 61–98; 215–222

Landsberger, Parpola, Tadmor 1989 [chapter 9]

Langdon S.H. 1912 *Die neubabylonischen Königsinschriften* (VAB 4) Leipzig

Leemans W. 1944–8 'Marduk-apal-iddina II, zijn tijd en zijn geslacht' *JEOL* 3/9–10: 432–455

—— 1946 '*Kidinnu*: un symbole de droit divin babylonien' in David M., van Groningen B.A., Meijers E.M. (eds) *Symbolae ad Jus et Historiam Antiquitatis Pertinentes Julio Christiano van Oven dedicatae* Leiden: 36–61

Levine L.D. 1982 'Sennacherib's southern front: 704–689 BC' *JCS* 34: 28–58

Luckenbill 1924 [chapter 9]

McEwan G.J.P. 1982 *The Late Babylonian Tablets in the Royal Ontario Museum* (Royal Ontario Museum Cuneiform Texts 2) Toronto

MacGinnis J.D. 1991 *Letter Orders from Sippar and the Administration of the Ebabbara in the Late Babylonian Period* (Cambridge, diss.; pub. Poznań 1995)

Miroschedji 1985 [chapter 13]

—— 1990 'La fin de l'Elam: essai d'analyse et d'interprétation' *IrAnt* 25: 47–96

Oelsner J. 1976 'Erwägungen zum Gesellschaftsaufbau Babyloniens von der neubabylonischen bis zur achämenidischen Zeit (7.-4. Jh. v.u.Z.)' *AOF* 4: 131–149

—— 1981 'Gesellschaft und Wirtschaft des seleukidischen Babyloniens: einige Beobachtungen in den Keilschrifttexten aus Uruk' *Klio* 63: 39–44

—— 1986 *Materialien zur babylonischen Gesellschaft und Kultur in hellenistischer Zeit* Budapest

Oppenheim 1955 [chapter 9]

—— 1967 'An essay on overland trade in the first millennium BC' *JCS* 21: 236–254

Parpola 1970/1983 [chapter 9]

—— 1972 [chapter 9]

Pinches T.G. 1917 'From world-dominion to subjection: the story of the fall of Nineveh and Babylon' *JTVI* 49: 107ff.

Porter 1987 [chapter 9]

Powell M.A. 1985 [chapter 1]

Reiner E. 1982 'The Babylonian Fürstenspiegel in practice' in Diakonoff Studies [OE]: 320–326

Rollinger R. 1993 *Herodots Babylonischer Logos: eine kritische Untersuchung der Glaubwürdigkeitsdiskussion* (Innsbrucker Beiträge zur Kulturwissenschaft, Sonderheft 84) Innsbruck

Roth 1987 [chapter 9]

—— 1988 'Women in transition and the *bīt mār banî*' *RA* 82: 131–138

—— 1989 *Babylonian Marriage Agreements, 7th to 3rd Centuries BC* (AOAT 222) Kevelaer, Neukirchen-Vluyn

Sack R. 1972 *Amēl-Marduk 562–560 BC: a study based on cuneiform, Old Testament, Greek, Latin and rabbinical sources* (AOAT 4) Kevelaer, Neukirchen-Vluyn

—— 1992 *Images of Nebuchadnezzar: the emergence of a legend* Selinsgrove, Penn.

Saggs H.W.F. 1955 'The Nimrud Letters 1952-I: the Ukin-zer rebellion and related texts', *Iraq* 17: 21–50

Salles J.-F. 1987 'The Arab-Persian Gulf under the Seleucids' in Kuhrt A., Sherwin-White S. (eds) 1987 *Hellenism in the East: the interaction of Greek and non-Greek civilizations from Syria to Central Asia after Alexander* London: 75–109

San Nicoló M. 1941 *Beiträge zu einer Prosopographie neubabylonischer Beamten der Zivil- und Tempelverwaltung* (SBAW II.2) Munich

Shiff L.B. 1987 *The Nur-Sin Archive: private entrepreneurship in Babylon (603–507 BC)* (Univ. of Penn. diss.)

Streck 1916 [chapter 9]

Tadmor H. 1958 'The "Sin of Sargon"' (in Hebrew with English summary) *EI* 5: 150–163; 93*

Unger E. 1931/1970 *Babylon die heilige Stadt nach der Beschreibung der Babylonier* Berlin (repr. 1970)

Ungnad A. 1941–4 'Das Haus Egibi' *AfO* 14: 57–64

van der Spek R.J. 1987 'The Babylonian city' in Kuhrt A., Sherwin-White S. (eds) 1987 *Hellenism in the East: the interaction of Greek and non-Greek civilizations from Syria to Central Asia after Alexander* London: 57–74

Vleeming S.P., Weselius J.W. 1985 *Studies in Papyrus Amherst 63: essays on the Aramaic texts in Aramaic/demotic Papyrus Amherst 63* vol. I Amsterdam

von Voigtlander E.N. 1963 *A Survey of Neobabylonian History* (Univ. of Michigan, diss.)

Weidner E. 1939 'Jojachin, König von Juda, in babylonischen Keilschrifttexten' *Mélanges syriens offerts à Monsieur René Dussaud* Paris, II: 923–935

—— 1954–6 'Hochverrat gegen Nebuchadnezar II' *AfO* 17: 1–9

Weingort S. 1939 *Das Haus Egibi in neubabylonischen Rechtsurkunden* (Berlin, diss.)

Weisberg D. 1974 'Royal women of the Neo-Babylonian period' in Garelli [OE]: 447–454

Wilhelm G. 1973 'La première tablette cunéiforme trouvée à Tyr' *Bulletin du Musée de Beyrouth* 26: 35–39

Wiseman D.J. 1956 *Chronicles of Chaldaean Kings* London

—— 1985 *Nebuchadrezzar and Babylon* (Schweich Lectures 1983) Oxford

Wunsch C. 1993 *Die Urkunden des babylonischen Geschäftsmannes Iddin-Marduk: zum Handel mit Naturalien im 6. Jahrhundert v. Chr.* (Cuneiform Monographs 3a and 3b) Groningen

Zadok R. 1976 'On the connections between Iran and Babylon in the sixth century BC' *Iran* 14: 67–77

Zawadski 1988 [chapter 9]

Chapter 12

General

Trigger *et al.* 1983 [OD]: 232–278 and ch. 4; Bottéro *et al.* 1967b [OB], chs 5 and 6; *CAH* III/1, ch. 13; *CAH* III/2, ch. 35; Drioton and Vandier 1984 [OD], chs 12–13; Grimal 1992 [OD], chs 13–14
and (details below)
Kienitz 1953; Kitchen 1986; Leahy 1990; Redford 1992 [chapter 3], part 4; Yoyotte *et al.*1990

References

Austin M. M. 1970 *Greece and Egypt in the Archaic Age* (PCPS Suppl. 2) Cambridge
Blackman A.M. 1941 'The Stela of Shoshenk, great chieftain of the Mšwš' *JEA* 27: 83–95
Boardman J. 1980 *The Greeks Overseas* (rev. edn) London
Borger 1956 [chapter 9]
Bothmer B.V. 1960 *Egyptian Sculpture of the Late Period, 700* BC–100 AD Brooklyn, NY.
Caminos R.A. 1958 *The Chronicle of Prince Osorkon* Rome
—— 1964 'The Nitokris adoption stele' *JEA* 50: 71–101
Coulson W.D.E., Leonard Jr. A. 1981 *Cities of the Delta, Part I: Naukratis. Preliminary Report on the 1977–78 and 1980 Seasons* (ARCE Reports 4) Malibu, Cal.
Cruz-Urribe E. 1988 *Hibis Temple Project* I: *Translations, Commentary, Discussions and Sign List* San Antonio, Tex.
de Meulenaere 1968 'La famille du roi Amasis' *JEA* 54: 183–187
Edel E. 1978 'Amasis und Nebukadrezar II' *GM* 29: 13–20
Graefe E. 1981 *Untersuchungen zur Verwaltung und Geschichte der Institution der Gottesgemahlin des Amun vom Beginn des Neuen Reiches bis zur Spätzeit* (2 vols) Wiesbaden
Griffith F. Ll. 1909 *Catalogue of the Demotic Papyri in the John Rylands Library Manchester* Manchester
Kemp B. 1977 'The palace of Apries at Memphis' *MDAIK* 33: 101–108
Kienitz F.K. 1953 *Die politische Geschichte Ägyptens vom 7. bis zum 4. Jahrhundert vor der Zeitwende* Berlin
Kitchen K. 1986 *The Third Intermediate Period in Egypt* (2nd rev. edn) Warminster
Leahy A. 1988 'The earliest dated monument of Amasis and the end of the reign of Apries' *JEA* 74: 183–200
—— (ed.) 1990 *Libya and Egypt: c. 1300–750* BC London
Lloyd A.B. 1975–88 *Herodotus II* (3 vols) Leiden
—— 1982 [chapter 13]
—— 1988 [chapter 13]
Mariette A. 1882 *Le Sérapéum de Memphis* Paris
Masson O. 1978 *Carian Inscriptions from North Saqqara and Buhen* (EES Texts from Excavations: Fifth Memoir) London
Menu B 1988 'Les actes de vente en Égypte ancienne particulièrement sous les rois kouchites et saïtes' *JEA* 74: 165–182
Murray O. 1970 'Hecataeus of Abdera and pharaonic kingship' *JEA* 56: 141–171
Na'aman 1991 [chapter 8]

Otto E. 1954 *Die biographischen Inschrifen der ägyptischen Spätzeit* (Probleme der Ägyptologie 2) Leiden

Petrie W.M.F. 1886 *Naukratis I (1884–5)* London

Petrie W.M.F., Walker J.H. 1909a *Memphis I* London

—— 1909b *The Palace of Apries (Memphis II)* London

Porten 1968 [chapter 13]

Priese K.-H. 1978 'The kingdom of Kush: the Napatan period' *Africa in Antiquity* [OGg]: 74–88

Redford 1992 [chapter 3]

Rougé J. 1988 'La navigation en Mer Erythrée dans l'antiquité' in Salles J.-F. (ed.) *L'Arabie et ses mers bordières* I: *itinéraires et voisinages* (TMO 16) Lyon

Russman E.R. 1974 *The Representation of the King in the 25th Dynasty* Brussels

Smith H.S. 1974 *A Visit to Ancient Egypt: life at Memphis and Saqqara c. 500–30 BC* Warminster

—— 1992 'The death and life of the mother of Apis' in Lloyd A.B. (ed.) *Studies in Pharaonic Religion and Society in Honour of J. Gwyn Griffiths* London: 201–225

Spiegelberg W. 1914 *Die sogenannte demotische Chronik des Papyrus 215 der Bibliothèque Nationale zu Paris* (Demotische Studien 7) Leipzig

Streck 1916 [chapter 9]

Tait J. 1992 'Demotic literature and Egyptian society' in Johnson J.H. (ed.) *Life in a Multi-cultural Society: Egypt from Cambyses to Constantine and Beyond* (SAOC 51) Chicago: 303–310

Tanis 1987 [chapter 4]

Thompson D.J. 1988 *Memphis under the Ptolemies* Princeton, NJ.

Trigger 1976 [chapter 3]

Vercoutter J. 1962 *Textes biographiques du Sérapéum de Memphis* Paris

Wallinga 1987 [chapter 13]

—— 1991 'Polycrates and Egypt: the testimony of the *samaina*' *AchHist* 6: 179–197

Wessetzky W. 1963 'Die Familiengeschichte des Peteêse als historische Quelle für die Innenpolitik Psametiks I' *ZÄS* 88: 69–73

Yoyotte J. 1960 'Néchao II' *SDB* 6: 363–393

—— 1961 'Les principautés du Delta au temps de l'anarchie libyenne' *Mélanges Maspéro* 1/4 Cairo: 121–181

—— 1972 'Les adoratrices de la troisième période intermédiaire' *BSFE* 57: 19–30

Yoyotte J. *et al.* 1990 *L'Égypte des millénaires obscurs* Paris

Chapter 13

General

CAH IV, sections I and II; V; VI
and (details below)
AchHist 1–8 (see List of Abbreviations for details); Bengtson 1968; Briant 1992a; in press; Briant and Herrenschmidt 1989; Burn 1984; *Cambridge History of Iran* II; *Cambridge History of Judaism* I; Cook 1983; Dandamaev 1990; Dandamaev and Lukonin 1989; Frye 1984; Sancisi-Weerdenburg 1982; *Transeuphratène*; Walser 1972; Walser 1984; Wiesehöfer 1994; Yamauchi 1990

References

Amiet P. 1992 'Sur l'histoire élamite' *IrAnt* 27: 75–94

Avigad N. 1976 *Bullae and Seals from a Post-Exilic Judaean Archive* (Qedem 4) Jerusalem

Badian E. 1987 'The peace of Callias' *JHS* 107: 1–39

Balcer J. 1987 *Herodotus and Bisitun* (Historia Einzelschriften 49) Wiesbaden

Bengtson H. (ed.) 1968 *Greeks and Persians* (trans.) London

Betlyon J.W. 1980 *The Coinage and Mints of Phoenicia: the pre-Alexandrine period* (Harvard Semitic Monographs 26) Chico, Cal.

Bickerman E.J. 1967 *Four Strange Books of the Bible* New York

Bickerman E.J., Tadmor H. 1978 'Darius I, pseudo-Smerdis, and the magi' *Athenaeum* 56: 239–261

Boffo L. 1978 'La lettera di Dario I a Gadata: i privilegi del tempio di Apollo a Magnesia sul Meandro' *Bulletino dell'Istituto di Diritto Romano 'Vittorio Scialoja'* 81: 267–303

Bothmer 1960 [chapter 12]

Boucharlat R. 1990 'Suse et la Susiane à l'époque achéménide: données archéologiques' *AchHist* 4: 149–175

Boyce M. 1975– *A History of Zoroastrianism* vol. 1- (HdO) Leiden

—— (ed. and trans.) 1984 *Zoroastrianism* (Texts and Sources for the Study of Religion) Manchester

Brandenstein W., Mayrhofer M. 1964 *Handbuch des Altpersischen* Wiesbaden

Bresciani E., Kamil M. 1966 *Le Lettere Aramaiche di Hermopoli* (Atti della Accademia Nazionale dei Lincei Memorie, ser. VIII.12.5) Rome

Briant P. 1982a *États et pasteurs au Moyen-Orient ancien* (Coll. Production Pastoral et Société) Cambridge

—— 1982b *Rois, tributs et paysans: études sur les formations tributaires au Moyen-Orient ancien* Paris

—— 1984a *L'Asie Centrale et les royaumes proche-orientaux du premier millénaire* Paris

—— 1984b 'La Perse avant l'empire (Un état de la question)' *IrAnt* 19: 71–118

—— 1985 'Dons de terres et de villes: l'Asie Mineure dans le contexte achéménide' *REA* 87/1–2: 53–71

—— 1986 'Polythéisme et empire unitaire (Remarques sur la politique religieuse des Achéménides)' *Les Grandes Figures Religieuses: fonctionnement pratique et symbolique dans l'antiquité (Besançon 25–26 avril 1984)* (Centre de Recherches d'Histoire Ancienne, vol. 68) Paris: 425–443

—— 1987 'Pouvoir central et polycentrisme culturel dans l'empire achéménide: quelques réflexions et suggestions' *AchHist* 1: 1–31

—— 1988 'Ethno-classe dominante et populations soumises dans l'empire achéménide: le cas d'Egypte' *AchHist* 3: 137–173

—— 1990 'Hérodote et la société perse' *Hérodote et les peuples non-grecs* (Entretiens sur l'Antiquité Classique 35) Vandoeuvres–Geneva: 69–104

—— 1991 'Le roi est mort: vive le roi! Remarques sur les rites et rituels de succession chez les achéménides' in Kellens J. (ed.) *La Religion Iranienne à l'Époque Achéménide* (IrAnt Suppl. 5) Gent: 2–11

—— 1992a *Darius, les perses et l'empire* Paris

—— 1992b 'La date des revoltes babyloniennes contre Xerxès' *StIr* 21: 7–20

—— 1994a *Alexandre le Grand* (4th edn; Que sais-je?) Paris

—— 1994b 'L'eau du grand roi' in Milano L. (ed.) *Drinking in Ancient Societies: History and Culture of Drinks in the Ancient Near East* (History of the Ancient Near East/Studies VI) Padua: 45–65

—— in press *De Cyrus à Alexandre: histoire de l'empire achéménide* (AchHist 9 & 10) Leiden

Briant P., Herrenschmidt C. (eds) 1989 *Le tribut dans l'empire achéménide* (Travaux de l'Institut d'Etudes Iraniennes de l'Université de la Sorbonne Nouvelle 13) Paris

Brosius M. in press *Royal and Non-royal Women in Achaemenid Persia (559–331 BC)* (Oxford Classical Monographs) Oxford

Brown S.C. 1986 'Media and secondary state formation in the Neo-Assyrian Zagros: an anthropological approach to an Assyriological problem' *JCS* 38: 107–119

—— 1988 'The *Medikos Logos* of Herodotus and the evolution of the Median state' *AchHist* 3: 71–86

Burn A. R. 1984 *Persia and the Greeks: the defence of the West, c. 546–478* BC (2nd edn with postscript by D.M. Lewis) London

Calmeyer P. 1979 'Fortuna-Tyche-Khvarnah' *Jahrbuch des Deutschen Archäologischen Instituts* 94: 347–365

—— 1987 'Greek historiography and Achaemenid reliefs' *AchHist* 2: 11–26

—— 1992 'Zwei mit historischen Szenen bemalte Balken der Achaimenidenzeit' *Münchener Jahrbuch der Bildenden Kunst* 43: 7–18

Cambridge History of Iran II: *The Median and Achaemenian Periods* Cambridge 1985

Cambridge History of Judaism I: *Introduction; The Persian Period* Cambridge 1984

Cameron G.G. 1948 *The Persepolis Treasury Tablets* (OIP 65) Chicago

Cardascia G. 1952 *Les Archives des Murašû: une famille d'hommes d'affaires babyloniennes à l'époque perse (455–403 av. J.-C.)* Paris

Cargill J. 1977 'The Nabonidus chronicle and the fall of Lydia: consensus with feet of clay' *AJAH* 2: 97–116

Carter E. 1994 'Bridging the gap between the Elamites and Persians in southwestern Khuzistan' *AchHist* 8: 65–95

Carter, Stolper 1984 [chapter 7]

Cook J.M. 1983 *The Persian Empire* London

Cowley A.E. 1923 *Aramaic Papyri of the Fifth Century* BC Oxford

Cross F.M. 1963 'The discovery of the Samaria papyri' *BibArch* 26: 110–124

Cruz-Urribe E. 1980 'On the existence of Psammetichus IV' *Serapis* 5/2: 35–39

—— 1988 [chapter 12]

Dalton O.M. 1964 *The Treasure of the Oxus with Other Examples of Early Oriental Metal-work* (2nd edn) London

Dandamaev M. 1975 'Forced labour in the palace economy in Achaemenid Iran' *AOF* 2: 71–78

—— 1976 *Persien unter den ersten Achämeniden (6. Jahrhundert v. Chr.)* (trans.; Beiträge zur Iranistik 8) Wiesbaden

—— 1990 *Political History of the Achaemenids* (trans.) Leiden

Dandamaev M., Lukonin V. 1989 *Economic and Social History of Ancient Iran* (trans.) Cambridge

Davesnes A., Lemaire A., Lozachmeur H. 1987 'Le site archéologique de Meydancikkale (Turquie): du royaume Pirindu à la garnison ptolémaïque' *CRAIBL*: 365–377

Descat R. 1985 'Mnésimachos, Hérodote et le système tributaire achéménide' *REA* 87: 97–112

—— 1989 'Notes sur la politique tributaire de Darius Ier' in Briant and Herrenschmidt 1989: 77–93

Drews R. 1973 *Greek Accounts of Near Eastern History* Cambridge, Mass.

Driver G.R. 1957/1965 *Aramaic Documents of the Fifth Century* BC (abridged and rev. edn) Oxford

Dyson R.H. 1965 'Problems of proto-historic Iran as seen from Hasanlu' *JNES* 24: 193–217

Ebeling E. 1952 'Die Rüstung eines babylonischen Panzerreiters nach einem Vertrag aus der Zeit Dareios II' *ZA* 50 (n.f.16): 203–214

Frye R.N. 1984 *The History of Ancient Iran* (Handbuch der Altertumswissenschaft III.7) Munich

Genito B. 1986 'The Medes: a reassessment of the archaeological evidence' *East and West* 36: 11–81

Gharib B. 1968 'A newly found inscription of Xerxes' *IrAnt* 8: 54–69

Grabbe L. 1992 *Judaism from Cyrus to Hadrian* vol. 1: *The Persian and Greek Periods* Minneapolis, Minn.

—— 1994 'What was Ezra's mission?' in Eskenazi T.C., Richards K.H. (eds) *Second Temple Studies 2: Temple Community in the Persian Period* (JSOT Supplementary Series 173) Sheffield: 286–299

Graf D.F. 1985 'Greek tyrants and Achaemenid politics' in Eadie J.W., Ober J. (eds) *The Craft of the Ancient Historian: essays in honor of Chester G. Starr* Lanham, Maryland: 79–123

—— 1994 'The Persian royal road system' *AchHist* 8: 167–189

Grayson 1975 [chapter 7]

Greenfield J., Porten B. 1982 *The Bisitun Inscription of Darius the Great, Aramaic version* (Corpus Inscriptionum Iranicarum Part I: Inscriptions of Ancient Iran, vol. V: The Aramaic Versions of the Achaemenian Inscriptions, Texts I) London

Grelot P. 1972 *Documents Araméens d'Égypte* (LAPO 5) Paris

Gropp D.M. 1986 *The Samaria Papyri from Wadi ed-Daliyeh* (Harvard, diss.)

Haerinck E. 1973 'Le palais achéménide de Babylone' *IrAnt* 10: 108–132

Hall E. 1989 *Inventing the Barbarian: Greek self-definition through tragedy* (Oxford Classical Monographs) Oxford

—— 1993 'Asia unmanned: images of victory in classical Athens' in Rich J., Shipley G. (eds) *War and Society in the Greek World* London: 108–133

Hallock R.T. 1969 *The Persepolis Fortification Tablets* (OIP 92) Chicago

—— 1971 *The Evidence of the Persepolis Tablets (being one chapter of CHI II)* Cambridge

—— 1977 'The use of seals on the Persepolis Fortification Tablets' in Gibson McG., Biggs R.D. (eds) *Seals and Sealing in the Ancient Near East* (Bibliotheca Mesopotamica 6) Malibu, Cal.: 127–133

—— 1978 'Selected Fortification texts' *CDAFI* 8: 109–136

Helms S.W. 1982 'Excavations at the "the city and the famous fortress of Kandahar"' *Afghan Studies* 3/4: 1–24

Herr L.G. 1992 'Two stamped jar impressions from the Persian province of Ammon from Tell el-'Umeiri' *Annals of the Department of Antiquities, Jordan* 36: 163–166

Herrenschmidt C. 1977 'Les créations d'Ahuramazda' *StIr* 6: 17–58

—— 1990 'Nugae Antico-Persianae' *AchHist* 4: 37–61

Hinz W. 1971 'Achämenidische Hofverwaltung' *ZA* 61: 260–311

Hoglund K.G. 1992 *Achaemenid Imperial Administration in Syria-Palestine and the Missions of Ezra and Nehemiah* (Society of Biblical Literature Dissertation Series 125) Atlanta, Ga.

Hornblower S. 1982 *Mausolus* Oxford

Jacobs B. 1987 *Griechische und persische Elemente in der Grabkunst Lykiens z. Zt. der Achämenidenherrschaft* (Studies in Mediterranean Archaeology 78) Jonsered

Kaptan-Bayburtluoğlu D. 1990 'A group of seal impressions on the *bullae* from Ergili/Daskyleion' *EpAn* 16: 15–26

Kent R. 1953 *Old Persian. Grammar, Texts, Lexicon* New Haven, Conn.

Kuhrt A. 1983 'The Cyrus Cylinder and Achaemenid imperial policy' *JSOT* 25: 83–97

—— 1988 'Earth and water' *AchHist* 3: 87–99

—— 1990a [chapter 11]

—— 1990b [chapter 11]

Kuhrt A., Sherwin-White S. 1987 'Xerxes' destruction of Babylonian temples' *AchHist* 2: 69–78

Lewis D.M. 1977 *Sparta and Persia* (Cincinnati Classical Studies n.s. 1) Leiden

—— 1990 'The Persepolis Fortification texts' *AchHist* 4: 1–6

Lloyd A.B. 1982 'The inscription of Udjahorresnet: a collaborator's testament' *JEA* 68: 166–180

—— 1988 'Herodotus on Cambyses: some thoughts on recent work' *AchHist* 3: 55–66

Machinist P., Tadmor H. 1993 'Heavenly wisdom' in Hallo 1993 [OE]: 146–152

Malandra W.W. 1983 *An Introduction to Ancient Iranian Religion: readings from the Avesta and the Achaemenid inscriptions* Minneapolis, Minn.

Metzger H., Dupont-Sommer A., Laroche E., Mayrhofer M. 1979 *Fouilles de Xanthos*: vol. VI: *La stèle trilingue du Letôon* (Institut Français d'Études Anatoliennes) Paris

Mierse W.E. 1983 'The Persian period' in Hanfman 1983b [chapter 10]: 100–108

Miroschedji P. de 1985 'La fin du royaume d'Anshan et de Suse et la naissance de l'empire perse' *ZA* 75: 265–306

Momigliano A.D. 1977 'Eastern elements in postexilic Jewish and Greek historiography' in *Essays in Ancient and Modern Historiography* Oxford: 25–35

Moorey P.R.S. 1975 'Iranian troops at Deve Hüyük in the early 5th century BC' *Levant* 7: 108–117

—— 1980 *Cemeteries of the 1st millennium BC at Deve Hüyük near Carchemish, salvaged by T.E. Lawrence and C.L. Woolley in 1913* (BAR Monographs 87) Oxford

Morkot R. 1991 'Nubia and Achaemenid Persia: sources and problems' *AchHist* 6: 321–336

Muscarella O. 1987 'Median art and medizing scholarship' *JNES* 46: 109–127

Nollé M. 1992 *Denkmäler vom Satrapensitz Daskyleion (Die Daskyleionstele): Studien zur graeco-persischen Kunst* (Antike in der Moderne) Berlin

Nylander C. 1970 *Ionians at Pasargadae: studies in Old Persian architecture* Uppsala

Petit T. 1990 *Satrapes et satrapies dans l'empire achéménide de Cyrus le Grand à Xerxès Ier* (Bibliothèque de la Faculté de Philosophie et Lettres de l'Université de Liège, fasc. 254) Paris

Petschow H. 1988 'Das Unterkönigtum Cambyses, "König von Babylon"' *RA* 82: 781–82.

Pitschikijan I.R. 1992 *Oxos-Schatx und Oxos-Tempel: Achämenidische Kunst in Mittelasien* (Antike in der Moderne) Berlin

Porten B. 1968 *Archives from Elephantine: the life of an ancient Jewish military colony* Berkeley, Cal.

Posener G. 1936 *La Première Domination Perse en Égypte: recueil d'inscriptions hiéroglyphiques* Cairo

Rolle R. 1989 [chapter 10]

Root M.C. 1979 *The King and Kingship in Achaemenid Art: essays on the creation of an iconography of empire* (Acta Iranica 3/9) Leiden

—— 1991 'From the heart: powerful Persianisms in the art of the western empire' *AchHist* 6: 1–29

Sachs A.J., Hunger H. 1988 *Astronomical Diaries and Related Texts from Babylonia* vol. I: *Diaries from 652 BC to 262 BC* (Österreichische Akademie der Wissenschaften, Phil.-hist. Kl., Denkschr., 195. Bd.) Vienna

Said E. 1978 *Orientalism* New York

Salles J.-F. 1988 'La circumnavigation de l'Arabie dans l'antiquité classique' in Salles, J.F. (ed.) *L'Arabie et ses mers bordières* I: *Itinéraires et voisinages* (TMO 16) Lyon

—— 1990 'Les Achéménides dans le golfe arabo-persique' *AchHist* 4: 111–130

—— 1991 [chapter 8]

—— 1994 [chapter 8]

Sancisi-Weerdenburg H. 1980 *Yaunā en Persai: Grieken en Perzen in een ander perspectief* (Univ. of Leiden, diss.)

—— 1982 *Geschiedenis van het Perzische Rijk* Huizen

—— 1983a 'Exit Atossa: images of women in Greek historiography on Persia' in Cameron and Kuhrt [OE]: 20–33

—— 1983b 'Zendan and Ka'bah' in Koch H., Mackenzie D.N. (Hsg.) *Kunst, Kultur und Geschichte der Achämenidenzeit* (AMI Ergänzungsband 10) Berlin: 88–92

—— 1987a 'Decadence in the empire or decadence in the sources? From source to synthesis: Ctesias' *AchHist* 1: 33–45

—— 1987b 'The fifth oriental monarchy and hellenocentrism' *AchHist* 2: 117–131

—— 1988 'Was there ever a Median empire?' *AchHist* 3: 197–212

—— 1989 'Gifts in the Persian empire' in Briant and Herrenschmidt 1989: 129–146

—— 1990 'The quest for an elusive empire' *AchHist* 4: 263–274

—— 1993 'Political concepts in Old Persian royal inscriptions' in Raaflaub K. (Hsg.) *Anfänge politischen Denkens in der Antike* (Schriften des Historischen Kollegs Kolloquien 24) Oldenburg

—— 1994 'The orality of Herodotus' *Medikos Logos' AchHist* 8: 39–55

Schlumberger D. *et al.* 1958 'Une bilingue gréco-araméenne d'Asoka' *JA* 246: 1–48

Schmidt E.F. 1953–7 *Persepolis* (2 vols) Chicago

Segal J.B. 1983 *Aramaic Texts from North Saqqara with Some Fragments in Phoenician* (EES Texts from Excavations: 6. Memoir) London

Seidl U. 1976 'Ein Relief Dareios' I. in Babylon' *AMI* 9: 125–130

Sekunda N., Chew S. 1992 *The Persian Army 560–330* BC (Osprey Military Elite Series 42) London

Shahbazi A.S. 1980 'An Achaemenid symbol II: farnah (godgiven) fortune "symbolised"' *AMI* 13: 119–147

Sherwin-White S., Kuhrt A. 1993 *From Samarkhand to Sardis: a new approach to the Seleucid empire* London

Sims-Williams N. 1981 'The final paragraph of the tomb-inscription of Darius I (DNb, 50–60): the Old Persian text in the light of an Aramaic version' *BSOAS* 44: 1–7

Spiegelberg 1914 [chapter 12]

Stern E. 1982 *The Material Culture of the Land of the Bible in the Persian Period* (trans.) Warminster

Stolper M.W. 1983 'The death of Artaxerxes I' *AMI* 16: 223–236

—— 1985 *Entrepreneurs and Empire: the Murašû archive, the Murašû firm, and Persian rule in Babylonia* Leiden

—— 1987 'Belshunu the satrap' in Rochberg-Halton F. (ed.) *Language, Literature and History: philological and historical studies presented to Erica Reiner* (AOS series 67) New Haven, Conn.: 389–402

—— 1989 'The governor of Babylon and Across-the-River in 486 BC' *JNES* 48: 283–305

Stronach D. 1978 *Pasargadae* Oxford

—— 1994 'Parterres and stone watercourses at Pasargadae: notes on the Achaemenid contribution to garden design' *Journal of Garden History* 14: 3–12

Sumner W. 1986 'Achaemenid settlement in the Persepolis plain' *AJA* 90: 3–31

Tilia A.B. 1972–8 *Studies and Restorations at Persepolis and Other Sites of Fars* (IsMEO Reports and Memoirs 16 and 18) Rome

Transeuphratène: études sur la Syrie-Palestine et Chypre à l'époque perse I– Paris 1989–

Trümpelmann L. 1967 'Zur Enstehungsgeschichte des Monumentes Dareios I. von Bisutun und zur Datierung der Einführung der altpersischen Schrift' *AA* : 281–298

Tuplin C. 1987a 'The administration of the Achaemenid empire' in Carradice I (ed.) *Coinage and Administration in the Athenian and Persian Empires: the ninth Oxford symposium on coinage and monetary history* (BAR International Series 143) Oxford: 109–158

—— 1987b 'Xenophon and the garrisons of the Achaemenid empire' *AMI* 20: 167–245

—— 1991 'Darius' Suez canal and Persian imperialism' *AchHist* 6: 237–283

Uchitel A. 1991 'Foreign workers in the Fortification archive' in de Meyer L. (ed.) *Mésopotamie et Élam (Actes de la XXXVe Rencontre Assyriologique Internationale)* Gent: 127–135

Vallat F. 1989 'Le palais d'Artaxerxès II à Babylone' *NAPR* 2: 3–6

van der Spek R.J. 1993 'The Astronomical Diaries as a source for Achaemenid and Seleucid history' *BiOr* 50: 91–101

van Driel G. 1989 'The Murašûs in context' *JESHO* 32: 203–229

von Voigtlander 1963 [chapter 11]

—— 1978 *The Bisitun Inscription of Darius the Great, Babylonian Version* (Corpus Inscriptionum Iranicarum I: Inscriptions of Ancient Iran vol. II, Texts i) London

Wallinga H. 1987 'The ancient Persian navy and its predecessors' *AchHist* 1: 47–78

—— 1993 *Ships and Sea-power before the Great Persian Wars: the ancestry of the ancient trireme* Leiden

Walser G. (ed.) 1972 *Beiträge zur Achämenidengeschichte* (Historia Einzelschriften 18) Wiesbaden

—— 1984 *Hellas und Iran: Studien zu den griechisch-persischen Beziehungen* (Erträge der Forschung 209) Darmstadt

—— 1987 'Persischer Imperialismus und griechische Freiheit (Zum Verhältnis zwischen Griechen und Persern in frühklassischer Zeit)' *AchHist* 2: 155–165

Weisskopf M. 1989 *The So-called 'Great Satraps' Revolt', 366–360 BC: concerning local instability in the Achaemenid far west* (Historia Einzelschriften 63) Wiesbaden

Whitehead J.D. 1974 *Early Aramaic Epistolography: the Arsames correspondence* (Univ. of Chicago, unpub. diss.)

Wiesehöfer J. 1978 *Der Aufstand Gaumatas und die Anfänge Dareios' I.* (Habelts Dissertationsdrucke: Reihe Alte Geschichte 13) Bonn

—— 1982 'Beobachtungen zum Handel des Achämenidenreiches' *Münstersche Beiträge zur Antiken Handelsgeschichte* 1: 5–15

—— 1994 *Das antike Persien: von 550 v. Chr. bis 650 n. Chr.* Munich

Yamauchi E. 1990 *Persia and the Bible* Grand Rapids, MI.

Zaccagnini 1983 [chapter 7]

INDEX